Vietnam,
Laos & Cambodia
a travel survival kit

Daniel Robinson
Joe Cummings

Vietnam, Laos & Cambodia – a travel survival kit

1st edition

Published by

Lonely Planet Publications Pty Ltd (ACN 005 607 983)
PO Box 617, Hawthorn, Vic 3122, Australia
Lonely Planet Publications, Inc
PO Box 2001A, Berkeley, CA 94702, USA

Printed by

Colorcraft Ltd, Hong Kong

Photographs by

Terry Anderson (TA), Joe Cummings (JC), Luke Golobitsh (LG),
Robert Mülder (RM), Karin Oosterhuis (KO), Orbitours (OT),
Richard Ringold (RR), Daniel Robinson (DR), Paul Stebbings (PS)
Black & White photographs by Luke Golobitsh

Front cover: Women sorting freshly caught fish, Vung Tau (DR)
Back cover: Perfume River, Hué (DR)

Published
February 1991

Although the authors and publisher have tried to make the information as
accurate as possible, they accept no responsibility for any loss, injury or
inconvenience sustained by any person using this book.

National Library of Australia Cataloguing in Publication Data

Robinson, Daniel
Vietnam, Laos & Cambodia – a travel survival kit.

1st ed.
Includes index.
ISBN 0 86442 098 6.

1. Vietnam – Description and travel – 1975–   – Guide-books.
2. Laos – Description and travel – 1976–   –Guide-books.
3. Cambodia – Description and travel – 1975–   –Guide-books.
I. Cummings, Joe. II. Title.

919.590453

Daniel Robinson

Daniel, researcher and writer of the Vietnam and Cambodia sections, was raised in the San Francisco Bay Area and Glen Ellyn, Illinois. He has travelled extensively in the Middle East and South, South-East and East Asia. Daniel holds a BA in Near Eastern Studies from Princeton University; his major languages of study and research were Arabic and Hebrew. He is now pursuing a master's degree in modern European history.

Joe Cummings

Joe, researcher and writer of the Laos section, has been a student of South-East Asian affairs since the '60s when he organised student moratoriums in Washington, DC against US involvement in Indochina. He also served as a Peace Corps volunteer in the late '70s and since then has been a translator/interpreter of Thai language in San Francisco, a graduate student in South-East Asian Studies at the University of California at Berkeley (MA 1981), a university lecturer in Malaysia and a Lao bilingual consultant for public schools in California. He is the author of LP's *Thailand – a travel survival kit* and *Thai Phrasebook* and has been a researcher or co-author for LP's guides to Burma, China, Malaysia/Singapore and Indonesia.

From the Authors

From Daniel The Vietnam section would be much the poorer had it not been for the friendship and assistance of Tran Hung, who did most of the legwork in the Mekong Delta, his wife Suzie and their children; and Dang Hoang Long of VAP, with whom I travelled by motorcycle to the Dalat area.

In Vietnam, I am also deeply appreciative of the assistance of Nguyen Nhiep Nhi, Dang Van Tin, Vo Dai Bo and Tran Lan Hinh of Vietnam Tourism's Saigon office; Duong Van Day, director of Saigon Tourist; Pham Truong Son of Saigon Tourist; Cherie and Beth Clark of the International Mission of Hope/Friends of Children of Viet Nam (IMH/FCVN), which is based in Denver; Nguyen Thanh Long of the Protocol Section of the Foreign Ministry; the ever-effervescent Khuong Binh Tay of Saigon; Le Hoa of Khanh Hoa Tourism; Bonze Le Trung Nashio of Linh Son Pagoda, Dalat; Nguyen Dinh An, vice-president of the People's Committee of Quang Nam-Danang Province; Truong Hao and Lam Quang Minh of the Foreign Economic Relations Department of Quang Nam-Danang Province; Mr Hai of Danang Tourism; Tran Ky Phuong, director of the Cham Museum in Danang; Tran Van Nhan of the Hoi An Monuments Management Authority; Cao Huu Dien of the Foreign Language Teachers Club of Hué; Le Hung Vong of *Song Huong Magazine* in Hué; Tran Dinh Quy of Hué Tourism; Diem of Thua Thien-Hué Tourism; Tran M' Ngoi, keeper of the tunnels of Vinh N

Dang Sung of Vietnam Tourism in Hanoi; and Vern Weitzel of the Department of Prehistory & Anthropology of the Australian National University.

In Cambodia, I am greatly indebted to Mme Tan Sotho of the General Directorate of Tourism in Phnom Penh, who went well beyond the call of duty to make researching the Cambodia section possible despite very difficult conditions. I wish her and her daughter well. I would also like to thank So Hoan, his intrepid guide from Angkor Conservation; Gail Morrison of Australia, who is putting Cambodia's National Library back together; Claire Bel of Operation Handicap International; Mme Pan Chamnan of the General Directorate of Tourism; Chum Bun Rong, head of the Foreign Ministry's Press Department; Maya Krell of the Ecumenical Coalition on Third World Tourism; and his Phnom Penh cyclo driver, Sok San.

I would also like to acknowledge the assistance of Gloria Emerson of Princeton; Kevin Bowen, co-director of the William Joiner Center at U-Mass Boston; Judy Henchy, archivist of the Joiner Center; John McAuliffe of the US-Indochina Reconciliation Project in Philadelphia; Sarinah Kalb of Cambridge, Masachusetts; the Interlibrary Loan Department and the Rare Books Collection staff of Firestone Library, Princeton University; Ross Meador and Carol Davis of Berkeley, CA; Jim Satterly of Atlanta; Drs Paul and Susan Balter of River Forest, IL; Alphonse Durieux of Guerneville, CA; Lisa Hsu of Princeton University; Son Nguyen & Tiffany Ho of New York; Thierry Di Costanzo of Avignon, France; Nevada Weir of Santa Fe, NM; Jill Kast Reuhrdanz of Broomfield, CO; Joe Cummings, author of the Laos section; LP's Eric Kettunen, Caroline Miller, Katie Cody and Richard Everist; and, for their patience and encouragement, Professors Sadiq al-Azm, Charles Issawi, Mark Cohen and Andras Hamori and Dean Richard Williams of Princeton University.

Researching and writing this book would have been impossible without the encouragement and support of my parents - and their letting me take over half the house while writing the Cambodia section. Thanks Mom. Thanks Dad.

For letters, thanks to: Patrick Field, Lorne Goldman (Canada), Paul Greening Jane Hinds (NZ), Brendon Hyde (Aust), Andy McNeilly (Aust) and Paul Stebbings (UK).

From Joe Thanks to the following people for assisting in the Laos research in one way or another: Michael Clark, Claude Vincent, Karin Oosterhuis and Paul Anspach, Linda D'Ari, Ann Goldman, Jan Weisman, Kampha and Khitkham.

Dedication Daniel would like to dedicate this book to the memory of Ori Maoz (1966-88), who never had a chance to travel.

From the Publisher
This first edition of Vietnam, Laos & Cambodia was edited at the Lonely Planet office in Australia by Katie Cody, and Glenn Beanland was responsible for design, cover design, title pages and maps.

Thanks must also go to Tom Smallman, Michelle de Kretser, and Helen Dormer for proofreading; Tamsin Wilson and Chris Lee Ack for map drawing and corrections; Vicki Beale for invaluable help with Ventura and corrections, Margaret Jung for script paste-up; Sharon Wertheim for keying in additional text and index; Graham Imeson and Greg Herriman for mapping; and Kathy Yates for illustrations and bromiding.

Warning & Request
Things change, prices go up, schedules change, good places go bad and bad ones go bankrupt – nothing stays the same. So if you find things better or worse, recently opened or long since closed, please write and tell us and help make the next edition better!

Your letters will be used to help update future editions and, where possible, important changes will also be included as a Stop Press section in reprints.

All information is greatly appreciated, and the best letters will receive a free copy of the next edition, or any other Lonely Planet book of your choice.

Contents

CAMBODIA

MAP LEGEND

BOUNDARIES

—·—·—· ....International Boundaries
—··—··—·· ....Internal Boundaries
—·—··—· ......National Parks, Reserves
—————— ....The Equator
············· ....The Tropics

SYMBOLS

◉ NEW DELHI ....National Capital
● BOMBAY ......Provincial or State Capital
● Pune ....Major Town
● Barsi ....Minor Town
🖃 ....Post Office
✈ ....Airport
ℹ ....Tourist Information
◉ ....Bus Station, Terminal
66 ....Highway Route Number
☾ † ‡ ....Mosque, Church, Cathedral
∴ ......Temple, Ruin or Archaeological Site
▲ ....Hostel
✚ ....Hospital
☀ ....Lookout
⋏ ....Camping Areas
⊓ ....Picnic Areas
⌂ ....Hut or Chalet
▲ ....Mountain
++‖++ ....Railway Station
⧶ ....Road Bridge
⧶ ....Road Rail Bridge
⇗ ⤾ ....Road Tunnel
⤸ ⇖ ....Railway Tunnel
⊓⊓⊓⊓ ....Escarpment or Cliff
⟋ ....Pass
〜 ....Ancient or Historic Wall

ROUTES

——————— ....Major Roads and Highways
– – – – – – – ....Unsealed Major Roads
——————— ....Sealed Roads
–·–·–·–· ......Unsealed Roads, Tracks
——————— ....City Streets
+++++++++++++ ....Railways
━━◉━━ ....Subways
················ ....Walking Tracks
– – – – – – – ....Ferry Routes
‖‖–‖‖–‖‖–‖‖ ......Cable Car or Chair Lift

HYDROGRAPHIC FEATURES

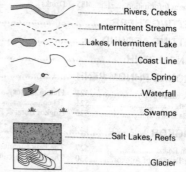

............Rivers, Creeks
............Intermittent Streams
......Lakes, Intermittent Lake
............Coast Line
............Spring
............Waterfall
............Swamps
......Salt Lakes, Reefs
............Glacier

OTHER FEATURES

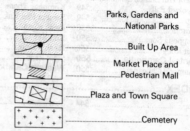

Parks, Gardens and National Parks
............Built Up Area
Market Place and Pedestrian Mall
............Plaza and Town Square
............Cemetery

Note: Not all the symbols displayed above will necessarily appear in this book

Vietnam

Introduction

In the decades following WWII the name 'Vietnam' came to signify to many Westerners either a brutal jungle war or a spectacular failure of American power - or both. Bumper stickers in the United States demanded that there be 'No more Vietnams in Central America'. Half-a-dozen major motion pictures, several television drama series, countless university courses and hundreds of books about Vietnam captivated audiences around the globe, but virtually all were about the American war in Indochina, not Vietnam the country. The real Vietnam, with its unique and rich civilisation, highly cultured people and hauntingly beautiful mountains, plains and coastline, was almost entirely ignored.

After the fall of South Vietnam to Communist North Vietnamese forces in 1975, xenophobia on the part of the leadership in Hanoi and a US-led campaign to isolate Vietnam internationally resulted in a sharp reduction in the quality and quantity of information available in Vietnam, especially that which transcended the narrowly political. But towards the end of the 1980s the Hanoi government began trying to reduce Vietnam's international isolation, in part by opening the country's doors to foreign visitors. Around the same time, the new spirit of cooperation that has come to characterise superpower relations started having an impact on Indochina, resulting in a perceptible shift in US policy towards Vietnam in 1990. The reasons for this are for the most part political and economic, but the results have given travellers the first opportunity in over a generation to visit a Vietnam at peace with itself and its neighbours.

Most visitors to Vietnam are overwhelmed by the sublime beauty of the country's natural setting. The Red River Delta in the north, the Mekong Delta in the south and almost the entire coastal strip are a patchwork of brilliant green rice paddies tended from dawn to dusk by peasant women in conical hats. Vietnam's 3260 km of coastline - considerably longer than the West Coast of the USA - include countless km of pristine beaches and a number of stunning lagoons; some sections are shaded by coconut palms and casuarinas, others bounded by seemingly endless expanses of sand dunes or rugged spurs of the Truong Son Mountains. Between the two deltas, the coastal paddies lining the South China Sea give way to soaring mountains, some of whose slopes are cloaked with the richest of rainforests. A bit further from the littoral are the refreshingly cool plateaus of the Central Highlands, which are dotted with waterfalls. The area is home to dozens of distinct ethnolinguistic groups (hill tribes), more than almost any other country in Asia.

Visitors to Vietnam have their senses thrilled by all the sights, sounds, tastes and smells of a society born of over a century of contact between an ancient civilisation and the ways of the West. There's nothing quite like grabbing a delicious lunch of local delicacies at a food stall deep inside a marketplace, surrounded by tropical fruit vendors and legions of curious youngsters. Or sitting by a waterfall in the Central Highlands, sipping soda water with lemon juice and watching newlywed couples on their honeymoons tiptoe up to the streambank in their 'Sunday finest'. Or being invited by a *bonze* (Buddhist monk) to attend prayers at his pagoda conducted, according to ancient Mahayana rites, with chanting, drums and gongs.

Fiercely protective of their independence and sovereignity for 2000 years, the Vietnamese are also graciously welcoming of foreigners who come as their guests (rather than as conquerors or suzerains). No matter what side they (or their parents) were on during the war, the Vietnamese are, almost without exception, friendly to Western visitors (including Americans) and supportive of more contact with the outside world. People who visit Vietnam during the first years of the country's renewed interaction within the West will play an important role in conveying to the Vietnamese the potentialities of such contact. They will also have the opportunity to experience the energetic and purposeful hustle and bustle of Saigon, Cholon and Danang and other cities whose resurgent dynamism is reviving the moribund Vietnamese economy.

Travel to Vietnam requires a bit more creativity and perseverance than does visiting other countries in the region, but things should get easier if present liberalising trends continue, and in any case you can usually work around most of the bureaucratic and political hurdles.

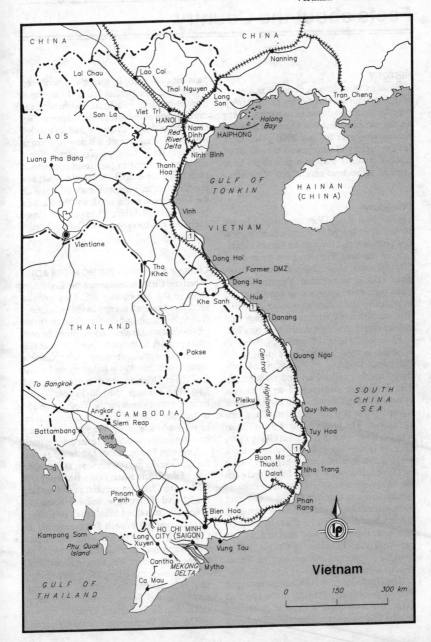

Vietnam

Facts about the Country

Visitors to Vietnam will notice that, invariably, the major streets of every city and town bear the same two dozen or so names. These are the names of Vietnam's greatest national heroes who, over the last 2000 years, have led the country in its repeated expulsions of foreign invaders and whose exploits have inspired subsequent generations of patriots.

Prehistory

The origins of the Vietnamese people are shrouded in legend. Recent archaeological finds indicate that the earliest human habitation of northern Vietnam goes back about 500,000 years. Mesolithic and Neolithic cultures existed in northern Vietnam 10,000 years ago; these groups may have engaged in primitive agriculture as early as 7000 BC. The sophisticated Bronze Age Dong Son culture emerged around the 13th century BC.

From the 1st to the 6th centuries, the south of what is now Vietnam was part of the Indianised kingdom of Funan, which produced notably refined art and architecture. The Funanese constructed an elaborate system of canals which were used for both transportation and the irrigation of wet rice agriculture. The principal port city of Funan was Oc-Eo in what is now Kien Giang Province. Archaeological excavations have yielded evidence of contact between Funan and China, Indonesia, India, Persia and even the Mediterranean. One of the most extraordinary artefacts found at Oc-Eo was a gold Roman medallion dated 152 AD and bearing the likeness of Antoninus Pius. In the mid-6th century, Funan was attacked by the pre-Angkorian kingdom of Chenla, which gradually absorbed the territory of Funan into its own.

The Hindu kingdom of Champa appeared around present-day Danang in the late 2nd century. Like Funan, it became Indianised (eg the Chams adopted Hinduism, employed Sanskrit as a sacred language and borrowed a great deal from Indian art) by lively commercial relations with India and through the immigration of Indian literati and priests. By the 8th century, Champa had expanded southward to include what is now Nha Trang and Phan Rang. Champa was a semi-piratic country that lived in part from conducting raids along the entire Indochinese coast; as a result, it was in a constant state of war with the Vietnamese to the north and the Khmers to the west. Brilliant examples of Cham sculpture can be seen in the Cham Museum in Danang.

Chinese Rule (circa 200 BC to 938 AD)

When the Chinese conquered the Red River Delta in the 2nd century BC, they found a feudally organised society based on hunting, fishing and slash-and-burn agriculture; these proto-Vietnamese also carried on trade with other peoples in the area. Over the next few centuries, significant numbers of Chinese settlers, officials and scholars moved to the Red Delta, taking over large tracts of land. The Chinese tried to impose a centralised state system on the Vietnamese and to forcibly Sinicise their culture, but local rulers made use of the benefits of Chinese civilisation to tenaciously resist these efforts.

The most famous act of resistance against the Chinese during this period was the rebellion of the Trung Sisters (Hai Ba Trung). In 40 AD, the Chinese executed a high-ranking feudal lord. His widow and her sister, the Trung Sisters, rallied tribal chieftains, raised an army and led a revolt that compelled the Chinese governor to flee. The sisters then had themselves proclaimed queens of the newly independent Vietnamese entity. In 43 AD, however, the Chinese counterattacked and defeated the Vietnamese; rather than surrender, the Trung Sisters threw themselves into the Hat Giang River.

The early Vietnamese learned a great deal

from the Chinese, including the use of the metal plough and domesticated beasts of burden and the construction of dikes and irrigation works. These innovations made possible the establishment of a culture based on rice-growing, which remains the basis of the Vietnamese way of life to this day. As food became more plentiful, the population grew, forcing the Vietnamese to seek new lands on which to grow rice.

During this era, Vietnam was a key port of call on the sea route between China and India. The Vietnamese were introduced to Confucianism and Taoism by Chinese scholars who came to Vietnam as administrators and refugees. Indians sailing eastward brought Theravada (Hinayana) Buddhism to the Red River Delta while simultaneously, Chinese travellers introduced Mahayana Buddhism. Buddhist monks carried with them the scientific and medical knowledge of the civilisations of India and China; as a result, Vietnamese Buddhists soon counted among their own great doctors, botanists and scholars.

There were major rebellions against Chinese rule – which was characterised by tyranny, *corvée* (forced labour) and insatiable demands for tribute – in the 3rd and 6th centuries, but all (along with numerous minor revolts) were crushed. In 679, the Chinese named the country 'Annam', which means the 'pacified sóuth'. But ever since this era, the collective memory of those early attempts to throw off the Chinese yoke has played an important role in shaping Vietnamese identity.

Independence from China (10th C)
The dynasties of independent Vietnam:

Ngo Dynasty	939-965
Dinh Dynasty	968-980
Early Le Dynasty	980-1009
Ly Dynasty	1010-1225
Tran Dynasty	1225-1400
Ho Dynasty	1400-1407
Post-Tran Dynasty	1407-1413
Chinese Rule	1414-1427
Later Le Dynasty	1428-1524
	(nominally until 1788)

Mac Dynasty	1527-1592
Trinh Lords of the North	1539-1787
Nguyen Lords of the South	1558-1778
Tay Son Dynasty	1788-1802
Nguyen Dynasty	1802-1945

In the aftermath of the collapse of the T'ang Dynasty in China in the early 10th century, the Vietnamese revolted against Chinese rule. In 938 AD, Ngo Quyen vanquished the Chinese armies at a battle on the Bach Dang River, ending 1000 years of Chinese rule. Ngo Quyen established an independent Vietnamese state, but it was not until 968 that Dinh Bo Linh ended the anarchy that followed Ngo Quyen's death and, following the custom of the times, reached an agreement with China: in return for recognition of their de facto independence, the Vietnamese accepted Chinese sovereignty and agreed to pay triennial tribute.

The dynasty founded by Dinh Bo Linh survived only until 980, when Le Dai Hanh overthrew it, beginning what is known as the Early Le Dynasty (980-1009).

Ly Dynasty (1010-1225)
From the 11th to the 13th centuries, the independence of the Vietnamese Kingdom (Dai Viet) was consolidated under the emperors of the Ly Dynasty (1010-1225), founded by Ly Thai To. They reorganised the administrative system, founded the nation's first university (the Temple of Literature in Hanoi), promoted agriculture and built the first embankments for flood control along the Red River. Confucian scholars fell out of official favour because of their close cultural links to China; at the same time, the early Ly monarchs, whose dynasty had come to power with Buddhist support, promoted Buddhism.

The Confucian philosophy of government and society, emphasising educational attainment, ritual performance and government authority, reasserted itself with the graduation of the first class from the Temple of Literature in 1075. Following years of study which emphasised classical education, these scholars went into government service, becoming what the West came to call mandarins. The outlines of the Vietnamese mandarinal system of government – according to which the state was run by a scholar-class recruited in civil service examinations – date from this era.

During the Ly Dynasty, the Chinese, Khmers and Chams repeatedly attacked Vietnam but were repelled, most notably under the renowned strategist and tactician Ly Thuong Kiet (1030-1105), a military mandarin of royal blood who is still revered as a national hero.

Vietnamese conquests of Cham territory, which greatly increased the acreage under rice cultivation, were accompanied by an aggressive policy of colonisation that reproduced social structures dominant in the north in the newly settled territories. This process did not make allowances for the potential technological and cultural contributions of the Chams (and indeed destroyed Cham civilisation), but it did result in a chain of homogeneous villages that eventually stretched from the Chinese border to the Gulf of Thailand.

Tran Dynasty (1225-1400)

After years of civil strife, the Tran Dynasty (1225-1400) overthrew the Ly Dynasty. The Tran increased the land under cultivation to feed the growing population and improved the dikes on the Red River.

After the dreaded Mongol warrior Kublai Khan completed his conquest of China in the mid-13th century, he demanded the right to cross Vietnamese territory on his way to attack Champa. The Vietnamese refused this demand but the Mongols – 500,000 of them – came anyway. The outnumbered Vietnamese under Tran Hung Dao attacked the invaders and forced them back to China; but the Mongols returned, this time with 300,000 men. Tran Hung Dao then lured them deep into Vietnamese territory; at high tide he attacked the Mongol fleet as it sailed on the Bach Dang River, ordering a tactical retreat of his forces to lure the Mongols into staying and fighting. The battle continued for many hours until low tide when a sudden Vietnamese counteroffensive forced the Mongol boats back, impaling them on steel-tipped bamboo stakes set in the river bed the night before. The entire fleet was captured or sunk.

When the Tran Dynasty was overthrown in 1400 by Ho Qui Ly both the Tran loyalists and the Chams (who had sacked Hanoi in 1371) encouraged Chinese intervention. The Chinese readily complied with the request and took control of Vietnam in 1407, imposing a regime characterised by heavy taxation and slave labour; Chinese culture and ways of doing things were forced on the population. The Chinese also took the national archives – and some of the country's intellectuals as well – to China, an irreparable loss to Vietnamese civilisation. Of this period, the great poet Nguyen Trai (1380-1442) would write:

Were the water of the Eastern Sea to be exhausted, the stain of their ignominy could not be washed away; all the bamboo of the Southern Mountains would not suffice to provide the paper for recording all their crimes.

Later Le Dynasty (1428-1524)

Le Loi was born into a large and prosperous family in the village of Lam Son in Thanh Hoa Province and earned a reputation for using his wealth to aid the poor. The ruling Chinese invited him to join the mandarinate but he refused. In 1418, Le Loi began to organise what came to be known as the Lam Son Uprising, travelling around the countryside to rally the people against the Chinese. Despite several defeats, he persisted in his efforts, earning the respect of the peasantry by ensuring that even when facing starvation his guerrilla troops did not pillage the land. After his victory in 1428, Le Loi declared himself Emperor Ly Thai To, thus beginning the Later Le Dynasty. To this day, Le Loi is revered as one of Vietnam's greatest national heroes.

After Le Loi's victory over the Chinese, Nguyen Trai, a scholar and Le Loi's companion in arms, wrote his famous *Great Proclamation* (*Binh Ngo Dai Cao*), extraordinary for the compelling voice it gave to Vietnam's fierce spirit of independence:

Our people long ago established Vietnam as an independent nation with its own civilisation. We have our own mountains and our own rivers, our own customs and traditions, and these are different from those of the foreign country to the north... We have sometimes been weak and sometime powerful, but at no time have we suffered from a lack of heroes.

The Later Le Dynasty ruled until 1524 and, nominally, up to 1788. Le Loi and his successors instituted a vast programme of agrarian reform and land redistribution. They also launched a campaign to take over Cham lands to the south. In the 15th century Laos was forced to recognise Vietnamese suzerainty.

Under the Le Dynasty, an attempt was made to break free of the cultural and intellectual domination of Chinese civilisation. In the realms of law, religion and literature, indigenous traditions were brought to the fore. The Vietnamese language gained favour among scholars – who had previously disdained it, preferring Chinese – and a number of outstanding works of literature were produced. Legal reforms gave women almost-equal rights in the domestic sphere, but two groups were excluded from full civil rights: slaves (many of them prisoners of war) and, oddly, actors. In the culture of the elite, however, Chinese traditions and language continued to hold sway, and neo-Confucianism remained dominant in the areas of social and political morality.

The Trinh & Nguyen Lords
Throughout the 17th and 18th centuries, Vietnam was divided between the Trinh Lords, who ruled in the north under the titular kingship of the Later Le monarchs, and the Nguyen Lords, who controlled the south and also nominally recognised the Later Le Dynasty. The Trinh Lords repeatedly failed in attempts to take over areas under Nguyen control, in part because the Portuguese weaponry used by the Nguyen was far superior to the Dutch armaments

supplied to the Trinh. During this period the Nguyen extended Vietnamese control into the Khmer territories of the Mekong Delta, populating the area with Vietnamese settlers. Cambodia was forced to accept Vietnamese suzerainty in the mid-17th century.

Buddhism enjoyed the patronage and support of both the Trinh and the Nguyen, and pagodas were built over the country. But by this time Vietnamese Buddhism was no longer doctrinally pure, having become intermingled with animism, ancestor worship and popularised Taoism.

Early Contact with the West
According to Chinese records, the first Vietnamese contact with Europeans took place in 166 AD when travellers from the Rome of Marcus Aurelius arrived in the Red River Delta.

The first Portuguese sailors landed in Danang in 1516; they were followed by Dominican missionaries 11 years later. During the next few decades the Portuguese began to trade with Vietnam, setting up a commercial colony alongside those of the Japanese and Chinese at Faifo (present-day Hoi An, which is near Danang).

Franciscan missionaries from the Philippines settled in central Vietnam in 1580, followed in 1615 by the Jesuits, who had just been expelled from Japan. In 1637, the Dutch were authorised to set up trading posts in the north, and one of the Le kings even took a Dutch woman as one of his six wives. The first English attempt to break into the Vietnamese market ended with the murder of an agent of the East India Company in Hanoi in 1613.

One of the most illustrious of the early missionaries was the brilliant French Jesuit Alexandre de Rhodes (1591-1660). He is most recognised for work in devising *quoc ngu*, the Latin-based phonetic alphabet in which Vietnamese is written to this day. Over the course of his long career, de Rhodes flitted back and forth between Hanoi, Macao, Rome and Paris, seeking support and funding for his missionary activities and battling both Portuguese colonial opposition and the intractable Vatican bureaucracy. In 1645, he was sentenced to death for illegally entering Vietnam to proselytise but was expelled instead; two of the priests with him were beheaded.

By the late 17th century most of the European merchants were gone; trade with Vietnam had not proved particularly profitable. But the missionaries remained, and the Catholic Church eventually had a greater impact on Vietnam than on any country in Asia except the Philippines, which were ruled by the Spanish for 400 years. The Vietnamese – especially in the north – proved highly receptive to Catholicism, but mass conversions were hindered by the Catholic stand against polygamy and by the opposition of the Vatican to ancestor worship. The Catholic emphasis on individual salvation undermined the established Confucian order, and wary officials of the mandarinate often restricted the activities of missionaries and persecuted their followers. But despite this friction, the imperial court retained a contingent of Jesuit scholars, astronomers, mathematicians and physicians.

The European missionaries did not hesitate to use secular means to help them achieve their goal: the conversion to Catholicism of all of Asia. Towards this end, French missionaries, who had supplanted the Portuguese by the 18th century, actively campaigned for a greater French political and military role in Vietnam.

Tay Son Rebellion (1771-1802)

In 1765, a rebellion against misgovernment broke out in the town of Tay Son near Qui Nhon. It was led by three brothers from a wealthy merchant family: Nguyen Nhac, Nguyen Hue and Nguyen Lu. By 1773, the Tay Son Rebels (as they came to be known) controlled the whole of central Vietnam, and in 1783 they captured Saigon and the rest of the south, killing the reigning prince and his family (as well as 10,000 Chinese residents of Cholon). Nguyen Lu became king of the south, and Nguyen Nhac became king of central Vietnam.

Prince Nguyen Anh, the only survivor of the defeated Nguyen clan, fled to Thailand and requested military assistance from the Thais. He also met the French Jesuit missionary Pigneau de Behaine (the Bishop of Adran), whom he eventually authorised to act as his intermediary in seeking assistance from the French. As a sign of good faith, Nguyen Anh sent his 4 year old son Canh with Pigneau de Behaine to France. The exotic entourage created quite a sensation when it arrived at Versailles in 1787, and Louis XVI authorised a military expedition. Louis XVI later changed his mind, but the bishop managed to convince French merchants in India to buy him two ships, weapons and supplies. With a force of 400 French deserters he had recruited, de Behaine set sail from Pondicherry, India, in June 1789.

Meanwhile, the Tay Son overthrew the Trinh Lords in the north and proclaimed allegiance to the Later Le Dynasty. The weak Le emperor, however, proved unable to retain his control of the country, but rather than calling on the Tay Son, he asked the Chinese for help. Taking advantage of the unstable situation, the Chinese sent 200,000 troops to Vietnam under the pretext of helping the emperor. In 1788, with popular sentiment on his side, one of the Tay Son brothers, Nguyen Hue, proclaimed himself Emperor Quang Trung and set out with his army to expel the Chinese. In 1789, Nguyen Hue's forces overwhelmingly defeated the Chinese army at Dong Da (near Hanoi) in one of the most celebrated military achievements in Vietnamese history.

In the south, Nguyen Anh, whose forces were trained by Pigneau de Behaine's young French adventurers, gradually pushed back the Tay Son. In 1802, Nguyen Anh proclaimed himself Emperor Gia Long, thus beginning the Nguyen Dynasty. When he captured Hanoi, his victory was complete, and for the first time in 2 centuries, Vietnam was united. Hué became the new national capital.

Nguyen Dynasty (1802-1945)
Emperors of the Nguyen Dynasty:

Gia Long	1802-1819
Minh Mang	1820-1840
Thieu Tri	1841-1847
Tu Duc	1848-1883
Duc Duc	1883
Hiep Hoa	1883
Kien Phuc	1883-1884
Ham Nghi	1884-1885
Dong Khanh	1885-1889
Thanh Thai	1889-1907
Duy Tan	1907-1916
Khai Dinh	1916-1925
Bao Dai	1925-1945

Emperor Gia Long (reigned 1802-19) initiated what historian David Marr has called 'a policy of massive reassertion of Confucian values and institutions' in order to consolidate the dynasty's shaky position by appealing to the conservative tendencies of the elite, who had felt threatened by the atmosphere of reform stirred up by the Tay Son Rebels.

Gia Long also began a large-scale programme of public works (dikes, canals, roads, ports, bridges, land reclamation) to rehabilitate the country, which had been devastated by almost 3 decades of warfare. The Mandarin Rd linking the national capital, Hué, to both Hanoi and Saigon was constructed during this period, as was a string of star-shaped citadels – built according to the principles of the French military architect Vauban – in provincial capitals. All these projects imposed a heavy burden on the population in the forms of taxation, military conscription and *corvée* (forced labour).

Gia Long's son, Emperor Minh Mang (reigned 1820-41), worked to consolidate the state and establish a strong central government. Because of his background as a Confucian scholar, he emphasised the importance of traditional Confucian education, which consisted of the memorisation and orthodox interpretation of the Confucian classics and texts of ancient Chinese history. As a result, education and spheres of activity dependent on it stagnated.

Minh Mang was profoundly hostile to Catholicism, which he saw as a threat to the Confucian state, and he extended this antipathy to all Western influences. Seven missionaries and an unknown number of Vietnamese Catholics were executed in the 1830s, inflaming passions among French Catholics who demanded that their government intervene in Vietnam.

Serious uprisings broke out in both the north and the south during this period, growing progressively more serious in the 1840s and 1850s. To make matters worse, the civil unrest in the deltas was accompanied by smallpox epidemics, tribal uprisings, drought, locusts and – most serious of all – repeated breaches in the Red River dikes, the result of government neglect.

The early Nguyen emperors continued the expansionist policies followed by preceding dynasties, pushing into Cambodia and westward into the mountains along a wide front. They seized huge areas of Lao territory and clashed with Thailand over control of the lands of the weak Khmer Empire.

The first half of the 19th century was marked by a great deal of literary activity. It was during this period that Nguyen Du (1765-1820), a poet, scholar, mandarin and diplomat, wrote one of Vietnam's literary masterpieces, *Kim Van Kieu (The Tale of Kieu)*.

Minh Mang was succeeded by Emperor Thieu Tri (reigned 1841-47), who expelled most of the foreign missionaries. He was followed by Emperor Tu Duc (reigned 1848-83), who continued to rule according to conservative Confucian precepts and in imitation of Ch'ing practices in China. Both responded to rural unrest with repression.

French Rule (1859-1954)
Ever since Pigneau de Behaine's patronage of Nguyen Anh in the late 18th century and his son Canh's appearance at Versailles in 1787, certain segments of French society had retained an active interest in Indochina. But it was not until the Revolution of 1848 and the advent of the Second Empire that there arose a coalition of interests – Catholic, com-

mercial, patriotic, strategic and idealistic (fans of the *mission civilisatrice*) – with sufficient influence to initiate large-scale, long-term colonial efforts. However, for the next 4 decades, the French colonial venture in Indochina was carried out haphazardly and without any preconceived plan. In fact, it was repeatedly on the verge of being discontinued altogether, and at times only the insubordinate and reckless actions of a few adventurers kept it going.

France's military activity in Vietnam began in 1847, when the French Navy attacked Danang harbour in response to Thieu Tri's actions against Catholic missionaries. In 1858 a joint military force of 14 ships from France and the Spanish colony of the Philippines stormed Danang after the killing of several missionaries. As disease began to take a heavy toll and the expected support from Catholic Vietnamese failed to materialise, the force left a small garrison in Danang and followed the monsoon winds southward, seizing Saigon in early 1859. Huge quantities of Vietnamese cannon, firearms, swords, saltpetre, sulphur, shot and copper coins were seized; a fire set in rice storage granaries is said to have smouldered for 3 years.

The French victory in the 1861 Battle of Ky Hoa (Chi Hoa) marked the beginning of the end of formal, organised Vietnamese military action against the French in the south and the rise of popular guerrilla resistance led by the local scholar-gentry, who had refused en masse to collaborate with the French administration. This resistance took the form of ambushing French rivercraft, denying food supplies to French bases and assassinating collaborators.

In 1862, Tu Duc signed a treaty that gave the French the three eastern provinces of Cochinchina. In addition, missionaries were promised the freedom to proselytise everywhere in the country, several ports were opened to French and Spanish commerce, and Tu Duc undertook to pay a large indemnity. To raise the necessary cash he authorised the sale of opium in the north and sold the monopoly to the Chinese. In addi-

tion, he debased the meritocratic mandarinate by putting low-ranking mandarinal posts up for sale.

The French offensive of 1867 broke the morale of the resistance, causing the scholar-gentry who had not been killed to flee the delta. Cochinchina became a French colony, and the peasantry assumed a position of non-violent resignation. At the same time, voices among the more educated classes of Vietnamese began to advocate cooperation with and subordination to the French in the interest of technical and economic development.

During this era, the Vietnamese might have been able to reduce the impact of the arrival of the European maritime powers and to retain their independence, but this would have required a degree of imagination and dynamism lacking in Hué. Indeed, until the mid-19th century, the imperial court at Hué, which was dominated by extreme Confucian conservatism, behaved almost as if Europe did not exist, though events such as the Opium War of 1839 in China should have served as a warning. In addition, resistance to colonialism was severely handicapped by an almost total lack of political and economic intelligence about France and the French.

The next major French action came in the years 1872 to 1874, when Jean Dupuis, a merchant seeking to supply salt and weapons to a Yunnanese general by sailing up the Red River, seized the Hanoi Citadel. Captain Francis Garnier, ostensibly dispatched to reign in Dupuis, instead took over where Dupuis left off. After capturing Hanoi Garnier's gunboats proceeded to sail around the Red River Delta demanding tribute from provincial fortresses, an activity that ended only when Garnier was killed by the Black Flags (Co Den), a semi-autonomous army of Chinese, Vietnamese and hilltribes troops who fought mostly for booty but resisted the French in part because of a strong antipathy toward Westerners.

These events threw the north into chaos: the Black Flags continued their piratic activities; local bands were organised to take vengeance on the Vietnamese – especially

Catholics – who had helped the French; Chinese militias in the pay of both the French and the Nguyen emperors sprung up; Le Dynasty pretenders began asserting their claims; and the hilltribes revolted. As central government authority collapsed and all established order broke down, Tu Duc went so far as to petition for help from the Chinese and to ask for support from the British and even the Americans.

In 1882, a French force under Captain Henri Rivière seized Hanoi, but further conquests were stubbornly resisted by both Chinese regulars and the Black Flags, especially the latter. The following year, Black Flags units ambushed Rivière at Cau Giay, killing him and 32 other Frenchmen, and triumphally paraded his severed head from hamlet to hamlet.

Meanwhile, only a few weeks after the death of Tu Duc in 1883, the French attacked Hué and imposed a Treaty of Protectorate on the imperial court. There then began a tragicomic struggle for royal succession notable for its palace coups, mysteriously-dead emperors and heavy-handed French diplomacy. Emperors Duc Duc and Hiep Hoa were succeeded by Kien Phuc (reigned 1883-84), who was followed by 14 year old Emperor Ham Nghi (reigned 1884-85). By the time Ham Nghi and his advisors decided to relocate the court to the mountains and to lead resistance activities from there, the French had rounded up enough mandarin collaborators to give his French-picked successor, Emperor Dong Khanh (reigned 1885-89), sufficient legitimacy to survive.

Ham Nghi held out against the French until 1888 when he was betrayed, captured by the French and exiled to Algeria. Although the Indochinese Union (consisting of Cochinchina, Annam, Tonkin, Cambodia, Laos and the port of Kwangchowan in China), proclaimed by the French in 1887, effectively ended the existence of an independent Vietnamese state, active resistance to colonialism continued in various parts of the country for the duration of French rule. The establishment of the Indochinese Union ended Vietnamese expansionism, and the Vietnamese were forced to give back lands taken from Cambodia and Laos.

Continuing in the tradition of centuries of Vietnamese dynasties, the French colonial authorities carried out ambitious public works, constructing the Saigon-Hanoi rail line as well as ports, extensive irrigation and drainage systems, improved dikes, various public services and research institutes. To fund these activities, the government heavily taxed the peasants, devastating the traditional rural economy. The colonial administration also ran alcohol, salt and opium monopolies for the purpose of raising revenues. In Saigon, they produced a quick-burning type of opium which helped increase addiction and thus revenues.

And since colonialism was supposed to be a profitable proposition, French capital was invested for quick returns in anthracite coal, tin, tungsten and zinc mines and tea, coffee and rubber plantations, all of which became notorious for the abysmal wages they paid and the sub-human treatment to which their Vietnamese workers were subjected. Out of the 45,000 indentured workers at one Michelin rubber plantation, 12,000 died of disease and malnutrition between 1917 and 1944.

As land, like capital, became concentrated in the hands of a tiny percentage of the population (in Cochinchina, 2.5% of the population came to own 45% of the land), a sub-proletariat of landless and uprooted peasants was formed. In the countryside these people were reduced to sharecropping, paying up to 60% of their crop in rents. Whereas the majority of Vietnamese peasants had owned their own land before the arrival of the French, by the 1930s about 70% of them were landless. Because French policies impoverished the people of Indochina, the area never became an important market for French industry.

Vietnamese Anti-Colonialism

Throughout the colonial period, the vast majority of Vietnamese retained a strong desire to have their national independence restored. Seething nationalist aspirations often broke out into open defiance of the French, which took forms ranging from the publishing of patriotic periodicals and books to an attempt to poison the French garrison in Hanoi.

The imperial court in Hué, corrupt though it was, was a centre of nationalist feeling, a fact most evident in the game of musical thrones orchestrated by the French. Upon his death the subservient Dong Khanh was replaced by 10 year old Emperor Thanh Thai (reigned 1889-1907), whose rule the French ended when he was discovered to have been plotting against them. He was deported to the Indian Ocean island of Réunion, where he remained until 1947.

His son and successor, Emperor Duy Tan (reigned 1907-16), was only in his teens in 1916 when he and the poet Tran Cao Van planned a general uprising in Hué that was discovered the day before it was scheduled to begin; Tran Cao Van was beheaded and Duy Tan was exiled to Réunion. Duy Tan was succeeded by the docile Emperor Khai Dinh (reigned 1916-25). On his death he was followed by his son Emperor Bao Dai (reigned 1926-45), who at the time of his accession was 12 years old and in school in France.

Some Vietnamese nationalists (such as the scholar and patriot Phan Boi Chau, who rejected French rule but not Western ideas and technology) looked to Japan and China for support and political inspiration, especially after Japan's victory in the Russo-Japanese war of 1905 showed all of Asia that Western powers could be defeated. Sun Yat-Sen's 1912 revolution in China was also closely followed in Vietnamese nationalist circles.

The Viet Nam Quoc Dan Dang (VNQDD), a largely middle class nationalist party modelled after the Chinese Kuomintang, was founded in 1927 by nationalist leaders including Nguyen Thai Hoc, who was guillotined along with 12 comrades in the savage French retribution for the abortive 1930 Yen Bai uprising.

Another source of nationalist agitation was among those Vietnamese who had spent time in France, where they were not hampered by the restrictions on political activity in force in the colonies. In addition, over 100,000 Vietnamese were sent to Europe as soldiers during WW I.

Ultimately, the most successful anti-colonialists proved to be the Communists, who were uniquely able to relate to the frustrations and aspirations of the population – especially the peasants – and to effectively channel and organise their demands for more equitable land distribution.

The institutional history of Vietnamese Communism – which in many ways is the political biography of Ho Chi Minh – is rather complicated. In brief, the first Marxist grouping in Indochina was the Vietnam Revolutionary Youth League (Viet Nam Cach Menh Thanh Nien Dong Chi Hoi), founded by Ho Chi Minh in Canton, China in 1925. The Revolutionary Youth League was succeeded in February 1930 by the Vietnamese Communist Party (Dang Cong San Viet Nam), a union of three groups effected by Ho which was renamed the Indochinese Communist Party (Dang Cong San Dong Duong) in October 1930. In 1941, Ho Chi Minh formed the League for the Independence of Vietnam (Viet Nam Doc Lap Dong Minh Hoi), better known as the Viet Minh, which resisted the Japanese occupation (and thus received Chinese and American aid) and carried out extensive political organising during WW II. Despite its broad nationalist programme and claims to the contrary, the Viet Minh was, from its inception, dominated by Ho's Communists.

Communist successes in the late 1920s included major strikes by urban workers. During the Nghe Tinh Uprising (1930-31), revolutionary committees (or soviets) took control of parts of Nghe Tinh Province (thus all the streets named 'Xo Viet Nghe Tinh'), but after an unprecedented wave of terror, the French managed to re-establish control. A 1940 uprising in the south was also brutally suppressed, seriously damaging the Party's infrastructure. French prisons, filled with arrested cadre, were turned by the captives into revolutionary 'universities' in which Marxist-Leninist theory was taught.

WW II

When France fell to Nazi Germany in 1940, the Indochinese government of Vichy-appointed Admiral Jean Decoux concluded an agreement to accept the presence of Japanese troops in Vietnam. For their own convenience, the Japanese, who sought to exploit the area's strategic location and its natural resources, left the French administration in charge of the day-to-day running of the country. The only group that did anything significant to resist the Japanese occupation was the Communist-dominated Viet Minh, which from 1944 received funding and arms from the American Office of Strategic Services (OSS), predecessor of the CIA. This affiliation offered the Viet Minh the hope of eventual US recognition of their demands for independence; it also proved useful to Ho in that it implied that he had the support of the Americans.

In March 1945, as a Viet Minh offensive was getting under way and Decoux's government was plotting to resist the Japanese – something they hadn't tried in the preceding 4½ years – the Japanese overthrew Decoux, imprisoning both his troops and his administrators. Decoux's administration was replaced with a puppet regime – nominally independent within Japan's Greater East-Asian Co-Prosperity Sphere – led by Emperor Bao Dai, who abrogated the 1883 treaty that made Annam and Tonkin French protectorates. During the same period, Japanese rice requisitions and the Japanese policy of forcing farmers to plant industrial crops – combined with floods and breaches in the dikes – caused a horrific famine in which 2 million of northern Vietnam's 10 million people starved to death.

By the spring of 1945 the Viet Minh controlled large parts of the country, especially in the north. In mid-August – after the atomic bombing of Japan – Ho Chi Minh formed the National Liberation Committee and called for a general uprising, later known as the August Revolution (Cach Mang Thang Tam), to take advantage of the power vacuum. Almost immediately, Viet Minh assumed complete control of the north. In central Vietnam, Emperor Bao Dai abdicated in favour of the new government (which later appointed him as its 'Supreme Advisor', whatever that means). In the south, the Viet Minh soon held power in a shaky coalition with non-Communist groups. On 2 September 1945, Ho Chi Minh – with American OSS agents at his side and borrowing liberally from the stirring prose of the American Declaration of Independence – declared the Democratic Republic of Vietnam independent at a rally in Hanoi's Ba Dinh Square. During this period, Ho wrote no fewer than eight letters to President Truman and the US State Department asking for US aid but did not receive replies.

A minor item on the agenda of the Potsdam Conference of 1945 was the procedure for disarming the Japanese occupation forces in Vietnam. It was decided that the Chinese Kuomintang would accept the Japanese surrender north of the 16th parallel and the British would do the same south of that line.

When the British arrived in Saigon chaos reigned, with enraged French settlers beginning to take matters into their own hands and competing Vietnamese groups on the verge of civil war. With only 1800 British, Indian and Ghurka troops at his disposal, British General Gracey ordered the defeated Japanese troops (!) to help him restore order. He also released and armed 1400 imprisoned French paratroopers who immediately went on a rampage around the city, overthrowing the Committee of the South government, breaking into Vietnamese homes and shops and indiscriminately clubbing men, women and children. The Viet Minh and allied groups responded by calling a general strike and by beginning a guerrilla campaign against the French. On 24 September, French General Jacques Philippe Leclerc arrived in Saigon, declaring, 'We have come to reclaim our inheritance'.

Meanwhile, in Hué, the imperial library was demolished (priceless documents were being used in the marketplace to wrap fish), and in the north 180,000 Kuomintang troops were pillaging their way southward towards Hanoi. Ho tried to placate them, but as the months of Chinese occupation dragged on, he decided to accept a temporary return of the French in order to get rid of the Chinese, who, in addition to everything else, were supporting the Viet Minh's nationalist rivals. The French were to stay for 5 years in return for recognising Vietnam as a free state within the French Union. As Ho put it at the time:

The last time the Chinese came, they stayed a thousand years. The French are foreigners. They are weak. Colonialism is dying. The white man is finished in Asia. As for me, I prefer to sniff French shit for 5 years than eat Chinese shit for the rest of my life.

The British wanted out, the French wanted in, Ho Chi Minh wanted the Chinese to go and the Americans under President Truman were not as actively opposed to colonialism as they had been under President Roosevelt. So the French, employing their usual duplicitous methods (such as ignoring the provisions of solemnly signed agreements), managed to regain control of Vietnam, at least in name. But when the French shelled Haiphong in November 1946 after an obscure customs dispute, killing hundreds of civilians, the patience of the Vietnamese people ended. A few weeks later fighting broke out in Hanoi, marking the start of the Franco-Viet Minh War. Ho and his forces fled to the mountains, where they would remain for 8 years.

Franco-Viet Minh War (1946-54)
In the face of Vietnamese determination that their country regain its independence, the French proved unable to reassert their control. Despite massive American aid and the existence of significant indigenous anti-Communist elements – who in 1949 rallied to support Bao Dai's 'Associated State' within the French Union – it was an unwinnable war. As Ho said to the French at the time: 'You can kill 10 of my men for every one I kill of yours, but even at those odds, you will lose and I will win'.

After 8 years of fighting, the Viet Minh controlled much of Vietnam and neighbouring Laos. On 7 May 1954, after a 57-day siege, over 10,000 starving French troops surrendered to the Viet Minh at Dien Bien Phu; a catastrophic defeat that shattered the remaining public support for the war in France. The next day, the Geneva Conference opened to negotiate an end to the conflict; 2½ months later, the Geneva Accords were signed. The Geneva Accords provided for an exchange of prisoners, the temporary division of Vietnam into two zones at the Ben Hai River (near the 17th parallel), the free passage oDien Bien Phuf people across the 17th parallel for a period of 300 days, and the holding of nationwide elections on 20 July 1956. In the course of the Franco-Viet Minh War, more than 35,000 men were killed and 48,000 wounded on the French side, but Vietnamese casualties were much greater.

South Vietnam
After the signing of the Geneva Accords, the south was ruled by a government led by Ngo Dinh Diem (pronounced 'zee-EM'), a fiercely anti-Communist Catholic whose brother had been killed by the Viet Minh in 1945. His power base was significantly strengthened by some 900,000 refugees –* many of them Catholics – who fled the Communist north during the 300 day free-passage period.

In 1955, Diem, convinced that if elections were held Ho Chi Minh would win, refused – with US encouragement – to implement the Geneva Accords; instead he held a referendum on his continued rule. Diem claimed to have won 98.2% of the vote in an election that was by all accounts rigged (in Saigon, he received a third more votes than there were registered voters!). After Diem declared himself president of the Republic of Vietnam, the new regime was recognised by France, the US, Great Britain, Australia, New Zealand, Italy, Japan, Thailand and South Korea.

During the first few years of his rule, Diem consolidated power fairly effectively, defeating the Binh Xuyen crime syndicate and the private armies of the Hoa Hao and Cao Dai sects. During a 1957 official visit to the US President Eisenhower called Diem the 'miracle man' of Asia. But as time went on he became increasingly nepotistic in making high government appointments and arbitrarily tyrannical in dealing with dissent. His land-reform programme ended up reversing land redistribution effected by the Viet Minh in the '40s. The favouritism he showed to Catholics alienated many Buddhists. In the early 1960s, the South was rocked by anti-Diem unrest led by university students and Buddhist clergy, including several self-immolations by bonzes that shocked the world. When Diem used French contacts to explore negotiations with Hanoi, the US threw its support behind a military coup; in November 1963 he was overthrown and killed. Diem was succeeded by a succession of military rulers who continued his repressive policies.

North Vietnam

The Geneva Accords allowed the leadership of the Democratic Republic of Vietnam to return to Hanoi and to assert control of all territory north of the 17th parallel. The new government immediately set out to eliminate elements of the population that threatened its power. A radical land reform programme was implemented, providing about half a hectare of land to some 1.5 million peasants. Tens of thousands of 'landlords', some with only tiny holdings – and many of whom had been denounced to 'security committees' by envious neighbours – were arrested; hasty 'trials' resulted in 10,000 to 15,000 executions and the imprisonment of 50,000 to 100,000 people. In 1956, the Party, faced with serious rural unrest caused by the programme, recognised that the People's Agricultural Reform Tribunals had gotten out of hand and began a 'Campaign for the Rectification of Errors'.

On 12 December 1955 – shortly after Diem had declared the South a republic – the US closed its consulate in Hanoi. Since then there has been no American diplomatic representation in the north.

The Beginning of the Vietnam War

Though there were Communist-led guerrilla attacks on Diem's government during the mid-1950s, the real campaign to 'liberate' the South began in 1959, when Hanoi, responding to the demands of southern cadre that they be allowed to resist the Diem regime, changed from a strategy of 'political struggle' to one of 'armed struggle'. Shortly thereafter, the Ho Chi Minh Trail, which had been in existence for several years, was expanded. In April 1960, universal military conscription was implemented in the north, and 8 months later the formation of the National Liberation Front (NLF) – whose platform called for a neutralisation of Vietnam, the withdrawal of all foreign troops and gradual reunification – was announced in Hanoi. In the South, the NLF came to be known derogatorily as the 'Viet Cong' or just the 'VC'; both are abbreviations for *Viet Nam Cong San*, which means 'Vietnamese Communist' (today, the words 'Viet Cong' and 'VC' are no longer considered pejoratives).

When the NLF campaign got under way, the military situation of the Diem government rapidly deteriorated. To turn things around, the Strategic Hamlet Programme (Ap Chien Luoc) was begun in 1962. Following tactics employed successfully by the British in Malaya during the '50s, peasants were forcibly moved into fortified 'strategic hamlets' in order to deny the Viet Cong bases of support. The sheer incompetence and brutality with which the programme was carried out created countless new enemies for the Saigon government, and many of the 'strategic hamlets' were soon under firm VC control.

In 1964, Hanoi began infiltrating regular North Vietnamese Army units into the South. By early 1965, the Saigon government was in desperate straits; desertions from the South Vietnamese army, whose command was notorious for corruption on a massive scale, had reached 2000 per month. It was losing 500 men and a district capital each week, yet since 1954, only one senior South Vietnamese Army officer had been wounded. The army was getting ready to evacuate Hué and Danang and the Central Highlands seemed about to fall. The South Vietnamese general staff even prepared a plan to move its headquarters from Saigon to the Vung Tau peninsula, which was easy to defend and was only minutes from ships that could spirit them out of the country. It was at this point that the US committed its first combat troops.

American Involvement

The first Americans to set foot in Vietnam were the crew of the clipper ship *Franklin* under the command of Captain John White of Salem, Massachusetts, which docked at Saigon in 1820. Edmund Roberts, a New Englander selected by President Andrew Jackson, led the first official American mission to Vietnam in 1832. In 1845, the USS *Constitution* under Captain 'Mad Jack' Percival sent an armed party ashore at Hué to rescue a French bishop who was under sentence of death, taking several Vietnamese officials hostage. When this failed to convince Emperor Thieu Tri to free the bishop, Percival's men opened fire on a crowd of civilians. In the 1870s, Emperor Tu Duc sent a respected scholar, Bui Vien, to Washington in an attempt to garner international support to counter the French. Bui Vien met President Ulysses S Grant but, lacking the proper documents of accreditation, was sent back to Vietnam empty-handed.

During the early 1950s – and especially after the start of the Korean War – the Americans saw France's colonial war in Indochina as an important part of the worldwide struggle against Communist expansionism. By 1954, US military aid to the French war effort topped 2 billion dollars (and that's 1950s dollars). In 1950, 35 US soldiers arrived in Vietnam as part of the US Military Assistance Advisory Group, ostensibly to instruct troops receiving US weapons how to

use them; there would be American soldiers on Vietnamese soil for the next 25 years.

The People's Republic of China established diplomatic relations with the Democratic Republic of Vietnam in 1950; shortly thereafter, the Soviet Union did the same. Only then did Washington recognise Bao Dai's French-backed government. The circumstances of this event are instructive: though Ho's government had been around since 1945, the USSR didn't get around to recognising it until the Communist Chinese did so, and the US State Department – which at the time was reverberating with recriminations over who was to blame for 'losing China' to Communism – recognised Bao Dai's government as a *reaction* to these events. From that point until the present day, US policy in Indochina has been a reaction against whatever the Communists do.

When the last French troops left Vietnam in April 1956, the US Military Advisory Group (MAAG), now numbering several hundred men, assumed responsibility for training the South Vietnamese military; the transition couldn't have been neater. The first American troops to die in the Vietnam War were killed at Bien Hoa in 1959 at a time when about 700 US military personnel were in Vietnam.

As the military position of the South Vietnamese government continued to deteriorate, the Kennedy Administration (1961-63) sent more and more military advisors to Vietnam. By the end of 1963, there were 16,300 American military personnel in the country.

A major turning-point in American strategy was precipitated by the 1964 Gulf of Tonkin Incidents in which two American destroyers, the *Maddox* and the *Turner Joy*, claimed to have come under 'unprovoked' attack while sailing off the North Vietnamese coast. Subsequent research indicates that the first attack took place while the *Maddox* was in North Vietnamese territorial waters assisting a secret South Vietnamese commando raid and that the second attack simply never took place.

But on President Johnson's orders, carrier-based jets flew 64 sorties against the North, the first of thousands of such missions that would hit every single road and rail bridge in the country as well as 4000 of North Vietnam's 5788 villages. Two American aircraft were lost, and the pilot of one, Lieutenant Everett Alvarez, became the first American POW of the conflict; he would remain in captivity for 8 years.

A few days later, an indignant (and misled) Congress almost-unanimously (only two Senators dissented) passed the Gulf of Tonkin Resolution, which gave the President the power to 'take all necessary measures' to 'prevent further aggression'. Until its repeal in 1970, the resolution was treated by US presidents as a blank cheque to do whatever they chose in Vietnam – without congressional oversight.

As the military situation of the Saigon government reached a new nadir, the first US combat troops splashed ashore at Danang in March 1965, ostensibly to defend Danang air base. But once you had 'American boys' fighting and dying, you had to do everything necessary to protect and support them, including sending over more American boys. By December 1965, 184,300 American military personnel were in Vietnam, and American dead numbered 636. Twelve months later, the totals were 385,300 American troops in Vietnam and 6644 dead. By December 1967, 485,600 American soldiers were in-country and 16,021 had died. With South Vietnamese and 'Free World Forces' counted in, in 1967 there were 1.3 million men – one for every 15 people in South Vietnam – under arms for the Saigon government.

The Tet Offensive of early 1968 marked a crucial turning point in the war. On the evening of 31 January, as the country celebrated the New Year, the Viet Cong launched a stunning offensive in over 100 cities and towns, including Saigon. As the TV cameras rolled, a VC commando team took over the courtyard of the downtown-Saigon US Embassy building.

The South Vietnamese and Americans counterattacked with utter ruthlessness, bombing and shelling heavily populated cities as they had the open jungle. In Ben Tre, an American officer explained that 'we had to destroy the town in order to save it'. In mid-February, the US casualty rate reached an all-time high: 543 killed and 2547 wounded in action in a single week. According to American estimates, 165,000 civilians died in the 3 weeks following the start of the Tet Offensive; 2 million more became refugees.

General Westmoreland, commander of US forces in Vietnam, insisted that the uprising had been a decisive blow to the Communists (and he was right – by their own admission, the VC never recovered from their incredibly high casualties) and asked for an additional 206,000 troops. But after years of hearing that they were winning, many Americans – having watched the chaos in Saigon on their nightly TV newscasts – stopped believing what they were being told by their government. And American leaders, lulled into a sense of confidence by years of self-servingly optimistic assessments by the Pentagon, were taken completely by surprise.

Despite growing opposition in the US, President Johnson and his successor, President Nixon, continued to pour American troops into Vietnam, at the same time beginning negotiations with Hanoi. Massive defoliation and the use of virtually indiscriminate firepower in many areas continued to devastate the countryside. Millions of refugees poured into coastal cities, creating enormous slums (between 1965 and 1974, 57% of the population of the South was made homeless). In April 1969, the number of US soldiers in Vietnam reached an all-time high: 543,400. By the end of 1969, American troop levels were down to 475,200; 40,024 Americans had been killed in action as had 110,176 South Vietnamese.

In 1969, the US began secretly bombing Cambodia. The following year, American ground forces were sent into Cambodia to extricate units of the South Vietnamese Army, whose weaknesses became more and more apparent as Nixon's policy of

'Vietnamisation' – making the South Vietnamese fight the war – was implemented. This new escalation infuriated previously quiescent elements of the American public, leading to bitter anti-war protests, including the demonstrations at Kent State University in Ohio in which four protesters were shot dead by National Guard troops.

In the spring of 1972, the North Vietnamese launched an offensive across the 17th parallel; during the same period, the US increased its bombing of the North and mined North Vietnamese harbours. After the 'Christmas Bombing' of Hanoi and Haiphong at the end of 1972, which was meant to wrest concessions from North Vietnam at the negotiating table but instead further outraged many Americans, Henry Kissinger and Le Duc Tho reached agreement. The Paris Agreements, signed by the USA, North Vietnam, South Vietnam and the Viet Cong, provided for a cease fire, the establishment of a National Council of Reconciliation and Concord, the total withdrawal of US combat forces and the release of 590 American prisoners-of-war. The agreement made no mention of approximately 200,000 North Vietnamese troops then in South Vietnam.

In total, 3.14 million Americans (including 7200 women) served in the US armed forces in Vietnam during the war. Nearly 58,000 Americans (including eight women) were killed in action or are listed as missing-in-action. Pentagon figures indicate that by 1972, 3689 fixed-wing aircraft and 4857 helicopters had been lost and 15 million tonnes of ammunition had been expended.

By the end of 1973, 223,748 South Vietnamese soldiers had been killed in action; North Vietnamese and Viet Cong casualties were in the hundreds of thousands. About 4 million civilians – 10% of the population of Vietnam, North and South – were killed or injured during the war. Approximately 1800 Americans and 300,000 Vietnamese are still listed as missing-in-action.

Other Foreign Involvement

Australia, New Zealand, South Korea, Thailand and the Philippines sent military personnel to South Vietnam as part of what the Americans called the 'Free World Military Forces', whose purpose was to internationalise the American war effort and thus confer upon it legitimacy. The Koreans (who numbered nearly 50,000), Thais and Filipino forces were heavily subsidised by the Americans.

Australia's participation in the Vietnam War constituted the most significant commitment of Australian military forces overseas since the 1940s. At its peak strength, the Australian forces in Vietnam – which included army, navy and air force units – numbered 8300, two-thirds larger than the size of the Australian contingent in the Korean War. Overall, 46,852 Australian military personnel served in Vietnam, including 17,424 draftees; Australian casualties totalled 496 killed and 2398 wounded.

Most of New Zealand's contingent, which numbered 548 at its high point in 1968, operated as an integral part of the Australian Task Force, which was stationed near Baria (just north of Vung Tau).

The Australian foreign affairs establishment decided to commit Australian troops to the Vietnam War in order to encourage US military involvement in South-East Asia, thus, they argued, furthering Australia's defence interests by having the Americans play an active role in an area of great importance to Australia's long-term security. The first Australian troops in Vietnam were 30 guerrilla warfare specialists with experience in Malaya and Borneo sent to Vietnam in May 1962. Australia announced the commitment of combat units in April 1965, only a few weeks after the first American combat troops arrived in Danang. The last Australian combat troops withdrew in December 1971; the last advisors returned home a year later. The Australian and New Zealand forces preferred to operate independently of US units in part because they felt that the Americans took unnecessary risks and were willing to sustain unacceptably high numbers of casualties.

Royal Thai army troops were stationed in Vietnam from 1967-73; Thailand also allowed the US air force to base B-52's and fighter aircraft on its territory. The Philippines sent units for non-combat 'civic action' work. South Korea's soldiers, who operated in the South between 1965 and 1971, acquired a reputation for extreme brutality.

The Fall of the South (1975)

A massive North Vietnamese ground attack across the 17th parallel in January 1975 – a blatant violation of the Paris Agreements – panicked the South Vietnamese army and government, which had been severely weakened by years of dependency on the Americans. A tactical withdrawal to more defensible positions deteriorated into a chaotic rout as soldiers deserted in order to try to save their families. Whole brigades disintegrated and fled southward, joining the hundreds of thousands of civilians clogging National Highway 1. City after city – Buon Ma Thuot, Quang Tri, Hué, Danang, Qui Nhon, Tuy Hoa, Nha Trang – fell or were abandoned. There were scenes of pillage, rape and murder in Danang and elsewhere as panicked soldiers and civilians tried to escape the Communist offensive by air and sea. The US Congress, fed up with the war and its drain on the treasury, refused to send emergency aid that President Nixon (who had resigned the previous year because of Watergate) had promised would be forthcoming in the event of such a invasion.

President Nguyen Van Thieu, in power since 1967, resigned on 21 April 1975 and fled the country. He was replaced by Vice President Tran Van Huong, who quit a week later, turning the presidency over to General Duong Van Minh, who surrendered on the morning of 30 April 1975 in Saigon's Independence Hall (now Reunification Hall) after only 43 hours in office. (The last Americans had been evacuated by helicopter from the US Embassy roof a few hours before.) As the South collapsed, 135,000 Vietnamese fled the country; in the next 5 years, at least 545,000 of their compatriots would do the same. Those who left by sea would become known to the world as 'boat people'.

Since Reunification

The success of the 1975 North Vietnamese offensive surprised the North almost as much as it did the South. As a result, Hanoi had not prepared specific plans to deal with integrating the two parts of the country, whose social and economic systems could hardly have been more different. Until the formal reunification of Vietnam in July 1976, the South was nominally ruled by a Provisional Revolutionary Government.

Because the Communist Party did not really trust the southern urban intelligentsia – even those of its members who had supported the Viet Cong – large numbers of northern cadres were sent southward to manage the transition. This created enormous resentment among southerners who had worked against the Thieu government and then, after its overthrow, found themselves frozen out of positions of responsibility.

After months of debates, those in Hanoi who wanted to implement a rapid transition to socialism (including the collectivisation of agriculture) in the south gained the upper hand. Great efforts were made to deal with the south's social problems: millions of illiterates and unemployed, several hundred thousand prostitutes and drug addicts, and tens of thousands of people who made their livings by criminal activities. But the results of the transition to socialism were disastrous to the southern economy.

The takeover of the south was accompanied by large-scale political repression. Despite repeated promises to the contrary, hundreds of thousands of people who had ties to the previous regime were rounded up and imprisoned without trial in forced-labour camps euphemistically known as 're-education camps'. Tens of thousands of intellectuals, artists, journalists, writers and trade union leaders – many of whom had opposed both Thieu and the war – as well as Buddhist monks, Catholic priests and Protestant clergy were also detained; many were tortured. While the majority of the detainees were released within a few years, some (declared to be 'obstinate and counter-revolutionary elements') were to spend the next decade or more in what has been called the 'Vietnamese gulag'. The purge prompted hundreds of thousands of southerners to flee their homeland by sea and overland through Cambodia.

In May 1977, Vietnam and the US opened negotiations in Paris to normalise relations. US opposition to Vietnamese membership in the United Nations was dropped, and Vietnam became the UN's 149th member-state. However, the talks failed to solve other outstanding difference between the two countries, including the search for 2500 Americans listed as 'missing in action' in Indochina and the Vietnamese demand for billions of dollars in reparations.

In 1978, a campaign against 'commercial opportunists' hit the ethnic-Chinese particularly hard, and there is evidence that behind the Marxist-Leninist rhetoric was the ancient Vietnamese antipathy towards the Chinese. In response, China cut off all aid to Vietnam, cancelled dozens of development projects, withdrew 800 technicians and, in February 1979, invaded northern Vietnam 'to teach the Vietnamese a lesson'. During this period, as many as 500,000 of Vietnam's 1.8 million ethnic-Chinese are believed to have fled the country, those in the north to China, those in the south by sea.

After attacks on Vietnamese border villages, Vietnam invaded Cambodia at the end of 1978, driving the murderous Khmer Rouge from power in early 1979 and setting up a pro-Hanoi regime in Phnom Penh. The last Vietnamese forces are supposed to have left Cambodia in September 1989, but there is evidence that Vietnamese troops wearing Cambodian uniforms were still involved in the fighting in 1990.

Vietnam Today

The recent liberalisation of foreign investment laws and the relaxation of visa regulations for tourists seem to be part of a general Vietnamese opening-up to the world.

In the past few years, Vietnam's Foreign Ministry has launched a concerted campaign to improve the country's international standing. Sweden, the first Western country to establish diplomatic relations with Hanoi, did so in 1969; since that time, most Western nations have followed suit. The major holdout is the USA, which still rigorously enforces the Trading with the Enemy Act, a law prohibiting Americans from engaging in commercial contacts with Vietnam.

In response to American conditions for the normalisation of relations, Vietnam has allowed American MIA teams to search for the 1800 US soldiers still listed as missing-in-action in Vietnam. The Vietnamese withdrawal from Cambodia in September 1989 was another step toward fulfilling Western conditions for improved relations. But American antipathy – both official and popular – to its victorious enemy as well as concern over Vietnam's dismal human rights record has so far prevented an improvement in relations.

However, Washington's decision in July 1990 to begin discussions with Hanoi on the Cambodian civil war may herald more dramatic changes in the US position towards Vietnam.

The recent dramatic changes in Eastern Europe have not been viewed with favour in Hanoi. The Vietnamese have denounced the participation of non-Communists in Eastern European governments as 'bourgeois liberalisation', calling the democratic revolutions 'a counterattack from imperialist circles' against socialism.

Nguyen Van Linh, speaking for the Vietnamese Communist Party of which he is General Secretary, declared at the end of 1989 that 'we resolutely reject pluralism, a multi-party system and opposition parties'. As turmoil in Eastern Europe spread, official control over literature, the arts and the media were tightened in a campaign against 'deviant ideological viewpoints'. The Party is concerned that the Vietnamese students and workers in the USSR and East European countries (estimated to number somewhere between 60,000 and several hundred thousand) will return home with politically unacceptable ideas. There is at least one group that Hanoi needn't worry about – when the Berlin Wall was breached at the end of 1989, about 500 Vietnamese crossed into West Berlin and asked for asylum.

The Orderly Departure Programme (ODP), which is carried out under the auspices of the UN, was designed to allow orderly resettlement in the West (mostly in the USA) of Vietnamese political refugees who otherwise might have tried to flee the country by land or sea. After years of stalling by Hanoi, the programme finally began functioning properly at the end of the 1980s, and thousands of Amerasians and their families were flown via Bangkok to the Philippines, where they underwent 6 months of English instruction before proceeding to the US.

In 1990, an agreement was signed that will allow hundreds of thousands of former officials of the South Vietnamese government and their families to resettle in the US.

The ODP has been of little help in stemming the flow of boat people from the north. Many sail to Hong Kong, where all but a handful are declared to be economic migrants rather than political refugees. In 1990, the Hong Kong government began the forcible repatriation of Vietnamese refugees, prompting an international outcry. Both the US and Vietnam oppose sending the refugees back against their will.

GEOGRAPHY

Vietnam stretches over 1600 km along the eastern coast of the Indochinese Peninsula (from 8°34' N to 23°22' N). The country's land area is 329,566 sq km, making it slightly larger than Italy and a bit smaller than Japan. Vietnam has 3260 km of coastline and land borders of 1650 km with Laos, 1150 km with China and 950 km with Cambodia.

Vietnamese often describe their country as resembling a bamboo pole supporting a basket of rice on each end. The country is S-shaped, broad in the north and south and very narrow in the centre, where at one point it is only 50 km wide.

The country's two main cultivated areas are the Red River Delta (15,000 sq km) in the north and the Mekong Delta (60,000 sq km) in the south. Silt carried by the Red River and its tributaries, which are confined to their paths by 3000 km of dikes, has raised the level of the riverbeds above that of the surrounding plains. Breaches in the levees result in disastrous flooding. The Mekong Delta is very fertile where drainage is adequate. It was created by silt deposited by the Mekong River.

Three-quarters of the country consists of mountains and hills, the highest of which is 3143 metre high Phan Si Pan Mountain (also spelled Fan Si Pan) in the Hoang Lien Mountains in the far north-west of northern Vietnam. The Truong Son Mountains (Annamite Cordillera), which form the Central Highlands, run almost the full length of the country, along Vietnam's borders with Laos and Cambodia. Spurs of the Truong Son Mountains stretch eastward to the South China Sea, segmenting the fertile coastal plain.

The Vietnamese speak of their country as having three distinct geographical areas: Bac Bo (the north), Trung Bo (the central region) and Nam Bo (the south), which correspond to the French administrative divisions of Tonkin (Nam Ky), Annam (Trung Ky) and Cochinchina (Bac Ky). Between 1954 and 1975, the country was divided at the Ben Hai River (the 17th parallel) into the Republic of Vietnam, with its capital at Saigon, and the Democratic Republic of Vietnam, which was governed from Hanoi.

Offshore Islands

Vietnam claims assorted offshore islands in the Gulf of Thailand and the South China Sea, including Phu Quoc Island off the Cambodian coast, the Tho Chu Islands south-west of Phu Quoc, the Con Dau Islands south-east of the Mekong Delta, the Paracel Islands (Quan Dao Hoang Xa) 300 km east of Danang and the Spratly Islands

(Quan Dao Thruong Xa) 475 km south-east of Nha Trang.

Several of the Paracel Islands, which historically have been occupied only sporadically, were seized by the People's Republic of China in 1951. In the 1960s a few of the islands were occupied by the South Vietnamese, who were driven out by Chinese forces in 1964, an action protested by both the Saigon and Hanoi governments.

The Spratlys, which consist of hundreds of tiny islets, are closer to Borneo than to Vietnam. They are claimed by virtually every country in the vicinity, including the Philippines, Malaysia, Indonesia, China, Taiwan and Vietnam. In 1988, Vietnam lost two ships and 70 sailors in a clash with China over the Spratlys. Both archipelagos have little intrinsic value but the country that has sovereignty over them can claim huge areas of the South China Sea – reported to hold vast oil reserves – as its territorial waters.

CLIMATE

There are no good or bad seasons for visiting Vietnam. When one region is wet or cold or steamy hot, there is always somewhere else that is sunny and pleasantly warm.

Vietnam has a remarkably diverse climate because of its wide range of latitudes and altitudes. Although the entire country lies in the inter-tropical zone, local conditions vary from frosty winters in the far northern hills to the year-round sub-equatorial warmth of the Mekong Delta. At sea level, the mean annual temperature is about 27°C in the south, falling to about 21°C in the extreme north. There is a drop in mean annual temperature of about half a degree for each increase of 100 metres in elevation. Because about one-third of Vietnam is more than 500 metres above sea level, much of the country enjoys a sub-tropical or – above 2000 metres – even a temperate climate.

Vietnam lies in the South-East Asian inter-tropical monsoon zone. Its weather is determined by two monsoons, which set the rhythm of rural life. The relatively dry winter monsoon, which mainly affects the part of Vietnam north of Danang, comes from the

north-east between October or November and March. From April or May to October, the south-western monsoon blows, its winds laden with moisture picked up while crossing the Indian Ocean and the Gulf of Thailand. The south-western monsoon brings warm, damp weather to the whole country except those areas sheltered by mountains (such as the central coastal lowlands and the Red River Delta).

Between July and November, violent and unpredictable typhoons often develop over the ocean east of Vietnam, hitting central and northern Vietnam with devastating results. The frequency of such storms has increased in recent years, possibly because of changes in local climatic conditions resulting from the massive deforestation of Vietnam during the last 3 decades.

Most of Vietnam receives about 2000 mm of rain annually, though parts of the Central Highlands get approximately 3300 mm of precipitation per annum.

The South

The south, whose climate is sub-equatorial, has two main seasons: the wet and the dry. The wet season, brought by the south-west monsoon, lasts from May to November. During this period, there are short downpours almost every day. The dry season runs from December to April. February, March and April are hot and very humid.

In Saigon, the average annual temperature is 27°C. In April, daily highs are usually in the low 30s. In January, the daily lows average 21°C. Average humidity is 80% and annual rainfall averages 1979 mm. The coldest temperature ever recorded in Saigon is 14°C.

Central Vietnam

The coastal lowlands are denied significant rainfall from the south-west monsoon (April or May to October) by the Truong Son Mountains (Annamite Cordillera), which are very wet during this period. Much of the coastal strip's precipitation is brought between December and February by the north-east monsoon, the southern part of which picks up moisture over the South China Sea. Thus, Nha Trang's dry season lasts from June to October while Dalat's dry season goes from December to March.

Dalat, like the rest of the Central Highlands, is much cooler than the Mekong Delta and the coastal strip. From November to March, Dalat's daily highs are usually in the low to mid-20s.

The cold and dry winter weather of the north-central coastal lowlands is accompanied by fog and fine drizzle (*crachin*). Because typhoons account for a significant part of the area's precipitation annual rainfall totals are erratic (at Hué they average 2890 mm).

The North

Areas north of the 18th parallel (southern Nghe Tinh Province) have two seasons: winter and summer. Winter, which is quite cool (and even cold), is brought by the irregular north-eastern monsoon and usually lasts from about November to April. During January (the coldest month of the year), the mean temperature in Hanoi is 17°C. February and March are marked by a persistent drizzling rain the Vietnamese call 'rain dust'. The hot summers run from May to October. Precipitation, which falls erratically, averages 1678 mm per year in Hanoi. The north is subject to occasional devastating typhoons during the summer months.

FLORA & FAUNA
Flora

Originally, almost the whole of Vietnam was covered with dense forests. Since the arrival of the first human beings many millennia ago, Vietnam has been progressively denuded of forest cover. The first to lose their trees were coastal and low-lying areas, which were ideal for rice-growing. Over the centuries, human exploitation has spread higher and higher into the hills and mountains, a process accelerated by the wars and population growth. While in 1943 44% of the original forest cover was extant, by 1976 only 29% remained and by 1983 only 24% was left.

The forests of Vietnam are estimated to contain 12,000 plant species, only 7000 of which have been identified and 2300 of which are known to be useful to humans for food, medicines, animal fodder, wood products and other purposes.

Currently, an estimated 2000 sq km are deforested every year because of slash-and-burn agriculture by montagnards, forest fires (made all the fiercer by the dead wood of trees killed by Agent Orange), relentless firewood collection and the massive harvesting of exportable hardwood (one of the country's few sources of desperately needed hard currency). Along the forest periphery, firewood gathering greatly exceeds regeneration capacity, causing the forest edge to recede. Environmentalists warn that unless these patterns of use are changed, Vietnam's forests will almost completely disappear by the year 2000. At present only 21% of the country is forested and just 8% to 9% of Vietnam's land area retains its primary forest cover.

Each hectare of land denuded of vegetation contributes to the flooding of areas downstream from water catchment areas, irreversible soil erosion (upland soils are especially fragile), the silting up of rivers, streams, lakes and reservoirs, and unpredictable climatic changes. In an attempt to prevent an ecological and hydrological catastrophe, the government has plans to set aside tens of thousands of square km of forest land and to create 87 national parks and nature reserves. Fourteen reserves (including Cuc Phuong and Cat Ba national parks) totalling 1600 sq km have already received government approval. Ecologists hope that because tropical ecosystems have a high species diversity but low densities of individual species, reserve areas will be large enough to contain viable populations of each species.

For many years, Vietnam has had an active reafforestation programme in which Ho Chi Minh himself is said to have taken a keen interest. However, only 36% of the 8720 sq km of trees planted between 1955 and 1979 were still forested at the end of the period.

Currently, about 1600 sq km are planted with some 500 million trees each year. The Ministry of Education has made the planting and taking care of trees by pupils part of the curriculum. However, even at this rate, reafforestation is not keeping up with forest losses. There are plans to try to reafforest the bald midland hills, which have little or no agricultural value.

Some observers have found it suspicious that Australian aid in the field of forestry has been accompanied by the sudden appearance of large tracts of young eucalyptus trees. Are we witnessing a form of ecological imperialism?!

Fauna

Because Vietnam includes a wide range of habitats – ranging from equatorial lowlands to high temperate plateaus and even alpine

Deer

peaks – the country's wild fauna is enormously diverse. Vietnam is home to 273 species of mammals, 773 species of birds, 180 species of reptiles, 80 species of amphibians, hundreds of species of fish and thousands of kinds of invertebrates. Larger animals of special importance in conservation efforts include the elephant, rhinoceros, tiger, leopard, black bear, honey bear, snub-nosed monkey, douc langur (remarkable for its variegated colours), concolour gibbon, macaque, rhesus monkey, serow (a kind of mountain goat), flying squirrel, kouprey (a blackish-brown forest ox), banteng (a kind of wild ox), deer, peacock, pheasant, crocodile, python, cobra and turtle.

Tragically, Vietnam's wildlife is in a precipitous decline as forest habitats are destroyed and waterways become polluted. In addition, uncontrolled illegal hunting – many people in remote areas have access to weapons left over from the war – has exterminated the local populations of various animals, in some cases eliminating entire species from the country. Officially, the government has recognised 54 species of mammals and 60 species of birds as endangered. The tapir (a large perissodactyl ungulate) and Sumatran rhinoceros are already extinct in Vietnam, and there are thought to be less than 20 koupreys and 20 to 30 Javan rhinoceros left in the country. It is encouraging that some wildlife seems to be returning to reafforested areas. For example, birds, fish and crustaceans have reappeared in replanted mangrove swamps. But unless the government takes immediate remedial measures – including banning the sale and export of tiger skins and ivory – hundreds of species of mammals, birds and plants will become extinct within the next decade.

The Ecological Impact of the War

During the Vietnam War, the USA employed deliberate destruction of the environment (ecocide) as a military tactic on a scale unprecedented in the history of warfare. In an effort to deny bases of operation to the

VC, 72 million litres of the herbicides known as Agent Orange, Agent White and Agent Blue were sprayed on 16% of South Vietnam's land area (including 10% of the inland forests and 36% of the mangrove forests). The most seriously affected regions were the provinces of Dong Nai, Song Be and Tay Ninh. The 40 million litres of Agent Orange used contained 170 kg of dioxin (2,3,7,8-TCDD), the most toxic substance known to humankind. Today, almost 20 years after the spraying, dioxin is still present in the food chain. Researchers report elevated levels of dioxin in samples of human breast milk collected in affected areas, where about 7.5% of the population of the south now lives.

In addition to the spraying, large tracts of forests, agricultural land, villages and even cemeteries were bulldozed, removing both the vegetation and topsoil. Flammable melaleuka forests were ignited with napalm. In mountain areas, landslides were deliberately created by bombing and by spraying acid on limestone hillsides. Elephants, useful for transport, were attacked from the air with bombs and napalm. By war's end, extensive areas had been taken over by tough weeds (known locally as 'American grass') that prevent young trees from receiving enough light to survive. The government estimates that 20,000 sq km of forest and farmland were lost as a direct result of the American war effort.

Overall, some 13,000,000,000 kg (13 million tonnes) of bombs – equivalent to 450 times the energy of the atomic bomb used on Hiroshima – were dropped on the region. This comes to 265 kg for every man, woman and child in Indochina. If the Americans had showered the people of Indochina with the money all those bombs cost (the war cost US$2000 per resident of Indochina) they might have won.

The long-term results of this onslaught have been devastating. The lush tropical forests have not grown back, fisheries (even those in coastal waters) remain depleted in both variety and productivity, wildlife populations have not recovered, cropland productivity is still below its pre-war levels, and among the human population the incidence of various cancers and toxin-related diseases has greatly increased. The land is scarred by 25 million bomb craters up to 30 metres in diameter, many of which have filled up with water and become breeding grounds for malarial mosquitoes (though some of the craters are said to have been converted into ponds for raising fish). In any case, the deep craters – from which tonnes of earth were blown – make significant parts of many rice paddies unplantable.

GOVERNMENT

The Socialist Republic of Vietnam (SRV; Cong Hoa Xa Hoi Chu Nghia Viet Nam) came into existence in July 1976 as a unitary state comprising the Democratic Republic of Vietnam (North Vietnam) and the defeated Republic of Vietnam (South Vietnam). From April 1975 until the declaration of the SRV, the South had been ruled – at least in name – by a Provisional Revolutionary Government.

The SRV espouses a Marxist-Leninist political philosophy. Its political institutions have borrowed a great deal from the Soviet and Chinese models, but in many respects have developed to meet Vietnam's particular circumstances.

Flag & National Anthem

The flag of the Socialist Republic of Vietnam consists of a yellow star in the middle of a red field. Until 1976 this was the flag of the Hanoi-based Democratic Republic of Vietnam. The significance of the yellow star and red field are explained in the national anthem, 'Marching to the Front' (Tien Quan Ca), which reflects the martial history and outlook of the present government. The words are as follows:

Soldiers of Vietnam, we go forward
With the one will to save our Fatherland.
Our hurried steps are sounding on the long and arduous road.
Our flag, red with the blood of victory, bears the spirit of our country.

The distant rumbling of the guns mingles with our
marching song.
The path to glory passes over the bodies of our foes.
Overcoming all hardships, together we build our
resistance bases.
Ceaselessly for the people's cause we struggle,
Hastening to the battlefield!
Forward! All together advancing!
Our Vietnam is strong eternal.

Soldiers of Vietnam, we go forward,
The gold star of our flag in the wind
Leading our people, our native land, out of misery and
suffering.
Let us join our efforts in the fight for the building of
a new life.
Let us stand up and break our chains.
For too long we have swallowed our hatred.
Let us keep ready for all sacrifices and our life will be
radiant.
Ceaselessly for the people's cause we struggle,
Hastening to the battlefield!
Forward! All together advancing!
Our Vietnam is strong eternal.

From 1973 to 1975, virtually every house in
the South had either a South Vietnamese flag
(three horizontal red stripes on a yellow
field) or a National Liberation Front flag (a
yellow star in the centre of a red and blue
field split horizontally) painted near the door.
The Paris Agreements of 1973 gave equal
status in the South to the South Vietnamese
government and the Provisional Revolutionary Government (a group set up in 1969 by
the Viet Cong). Because the areas under the
control of each were non-contiguous and had
no clear boundaries between them, the
control of each village and neighbourhood
was indicated by flags painted on roofs and
near the doorways of every building. When
the international observer force investigated
alleged cease fire violations the flags provided instant publicly acknowledged
information on who was supposed to control
the area.

When the Communists took over the
South they painted over the old flags with
flags of their own – first that of the National
Liberation Front and then the SRV flag. Over
the years, the flags of the SRV faded away or
chipped off, revealing the NLF flags (which
remind southerners of their forcible incorpo-

ration into a unitary state) and, underneath,
the flags of the old Saigon regime. To this
day, if you look carefully, you will see South
Vietnamese flags painted on many buildings,
bridges and other structures in south and
central Vietnam. Is the government too poor
to afford a new coat of paint, or is it that no
one really cares about the old flags any
more?

The Orwellian national slogan, which
appears at the top of every official document,
is *Doc Lap, Tu Do, Hanh Phuc*, which means
'Independence, Freedom, Happiness'. It is
based on one of Ho Chi Minh's sayings.

The Party

Vietnam's political system is dominated by
the 1.8 million member Communist Party
(Dang Cong San Viet Nam), whose influence
is felt at every level of the country's social
and political life. The leadership of the Party
has been collective in style and structure ever
since its founding by Ho Chi Minh in 1930.
The Party's decentralised structure, though
originally necessitated by the difficulty of
communications between Party headquarters and its branches, has allowed local
leaders considerable leeway for initiative.

Relatively speaking, the policies of the
Vietnamese Communist Party have been
characterised by a flexible and non-doctri-
naire approach. For the most part, the Party
has tried to take into account prevailing
material and political limitations when carrying out its revolutionary programmes.

The most powerful institution in the Party
is the Political Bureau (Politburo), which has
about a dozen members. It oversees the
Party's day-to-day functioning and has the
power to issue directives to the government.
The Politburo is formally elected by the
Central Committee, whose 125 or so full
members and about 50 alternate members
meet only once or twice a year. Party Congresses, at which major policy changes are
ratified after a long process of behind-the-
scenes discussions and consultations, were
held in 1935, 1951, 1960, 1976, 1982 and
1986. The last few Party Congresses have
reflected intense intra-Party disagreements

over the path Vietnamese Communism should take, with changing coalitions of conservatives and dogmatists squaring off against more pragmatic elements. The position of Chairman of the Party has been left vacant since Ho Chi Minh's death.

During the 1980s thousands of Party members were expelled, in part to reduce corruption (seen by a fed-up public as endemic) and in part to make room for more young people and workers. A major Party Congress is scheduled for the end of 1990 to set policy in this era of perestroika (*doi moi*) and glasnost.

Women are under-represented in the Party, especially at the highest levels (there have been no female members of the Politburo since 1945).

Constitutions

The Socialist Republic of Vietnam and its Hanoi-based predecessor have had three constitutions. The 1946 Constitution, drafted by a committee headed by Ho Chi Minh, was designed to appeal to a broad spectrum of Vietnamese society while at the same time pre-empting criticism from abroad, especially from France and the USA (with this goal in mind, it contained material taken from the American Declaration of Independence).

The 1959 Constitution was drawn up after it became clear that the 1956 national elections, called for in the Geneva Agreement of 1954, were not going to take place as scheduled. Three years of intense debate over the question of armed struggle in the South produced the 1959 Constitution, which made the goal of creating a Communist society, characterised by central planning and collective property ownership, explicit. Following the Chinese example on ethnic minorities policy, two 'autonomous regions', complete with their own zonal assemblies, administrations and militia forces, were created in northern and north-western North Vietnam.

After reunification in 1975, it was decided that the country again needed a new Constitution. The 1980 Constitution was the result of 4 years of debate on how the south, with its radically different social and economic structure, should be absorbed. It reflects the victory of those who favoured rapid collectivisation. The 1980 Constitution, which borrows heavily from the 1977 Soviet Constitution, declared the Party to be 'the only force leading the State and society, and the main factor in determining all successes of the Vietnamese revolution'. Fearing the implications of creating a third minority autonomous region in the Central Highlands (where the government feared unrest by montagnard insurgents backed, over the years, by France, the US, China and Thailand), the two autonomous regions in the north were abolished.

Administration

The Vietnamese governmental structure administers the country but the main decision-making bodies are those of the Party, especially the Politburo, which can, independently of the government, issue decrees with the force of law. Party cadres dominate the higher echelons of government, and at all levels, promotion in the bureaucracy often depends more on party affiliation than on strict criteria of competence.

The unicameral National Assembly (Quoc Hoi) is Vietnam's highest legislative authority. Its 500 or so deputies, whose terms last 5 years, each represent 100,000 voters. The National Assembly's role is to rubber-stamp – usually unanimously – Politburo decisions and party-initiated legislation during its biannual sessions, which last about a week. During elections, the number of National Assembly candidates (all Party-approved) running in a given constituency usually exceeds the number of contested seats by 20% to 30%. Relative to the population, white-collar workers are over-represented in the National Assembly while peasants and women are greatly under-represented.

The Council of State functions as the country's collective presidency. Its members, who currently number 15, are elected by the National Assembly. The Council of State carries out the duties of the National Assembly when the latter is not in session. The Council of Ministers, is also elected by the National Assembly. It functions as does a Western-style cabinet. Among its current members are the Prime Minister, nine deputy premiers, a secretary-general, 22 ministers with portfolio (Construction, Culture, Education, Finance, Information, Justice, Supply, Transport, etc), the heads of seven State Commissions (Planning, External Economic Relations, etc) and the directors of the State Bank and the Government Inspectorate. During the economic crises and reforms of the last 15 years, cabinet shuffles have been frequent.

Though Hanoi has been promoting the idea that local governments play a greater role in planning, most such administrative units have been unable to come up with the requisite funds to make this possible. Indeed, even agricultural cooperatives, the regime's ideological backbone, have been unable to make ends meet without resorting to corruption and the black market. In the early 1980s, the provinces were allowed to establish their own import-export concerns, but when provisional governments showed a propensity to hoard foreign currency in order to buy goods from abroad, regulations allowing them to keep only part of their hard currency were implemented.

Political Divisions

Vietnam is divided into 40 provinces (*tinh*) which have a significant degree of autonomy. Thus, provinces vary widely in their approach to foreign investment, economic development, economic liberalisation, political reform, tourism, etc. Listed from north to south, Vietnam's provinces are:

Far North: Ha Tuyen, Cao Bang, Hoang Lien Son, Lai Chau, Lang Son, Bac Thai, Son La, Vinh Phu, Ha Bac and Quang Ninh.

Red River Delta Area: Ha Son Binh, Hai Hung, Thai Binh and Ha Nam Ninh.

North-Central Vietnam: Thanh Hoa, Nghe Tinh, Quang Binh, Quang Tri and Thua Thien-Hué.

South-Central Coast: Quang Nam-Danang, Quang Nghi, Binh Dinh, Phu Yen, Khanh Hoa and Thuan Hai.

Central Highlands: Gia Lai-Kontum, Dak Lak (Dac Lac) and Lam Dong.

South: Song Be, Tay Ninh, Dong Nai, Long An, Dong Thap, An Giang, Tien Giang, Ben Tre, Cuu Long, Hau Giang, Kien Giang and Minh Hai.

In addition, there are three independent municipalities: Greater Hanoi, Greater Ho Chi Minh City (which includes Saigon) and Greater Haiphong. Vung Tau-Con Dao Special Economic Zone is under central administration.

The provinces and municipalities are divided into rural and urban districts. Rural districts are subdivided into village-level communes made up of hamlets while urban districts are divided into wards.

After reunification, the provincial structure of the south was completely reorganised. On 1 July 1989, several provinces joined after 1975 were split apart. Maps published before that date show Binh Tri Thien, which has been divided into Quang Binh, Quang Tri and Thua Thien-Hué; Nghia Binh, which has become Quang Ngai and Binh Dinh; and Phu Khanh, which is now Phu Yen and Khanh Hoa.

ECONOMY

Vietnam is one of the poorest countries in the world, with an estimated per capita income of US$130 per year and US$1.4 billion in hard currency debts (owed mainly to the International Monetary Fund and Japan) it is unable to repay. Despite its hard-working, educated workforce, the country's economy is beset by weak exports, a lack of raw materials for industry, chronic shortages of spare parts, a limited supply of consumer goods, unemployment and under-employment rates that defy statistics and, until recently, runaway inflation. The people are so poor that it is said that many able-bodied men and women have become weak and lost the desire to work solely as a result of long-term malnutrition. The economy was hurt by wartime infrastructure damage (not a single bridge in the North survived American air-raids while in the South, many bridges were blown up by the VC) but by the government's own admission, the present economic fiasco is the result of ideologically driven policies followed after reunification and the fact that half the government's budget goes to the military.

I have never been able to figure out how the average Vietnamese manages to survive economically. For example, Vietnam Tourism guides are paid about 60,000d (US$15) per month. Teachers get half that or less. You simply can't survive on 1000d to 2000d (US$0.25 to US$0.50) per day, much less feed a family. So people scrounge on the side, finding some odd job they can do to help them get by. The situation is even more difficult in the north than in the south.

Vietnam's major trading partners are the USSR, Japan, Singapore and Eastern Europe. In recent years, one of Vietnam's most valuable exports has been its people. Desperate for foreign currency, Vietnamese are given jobs that not even Soviets will take – in Siberia, for instance. USSR-bound flights leaving Hanoi are often full of excited young people, many of them young women, off to places like Novosibirsk, where they earn US$500 per month, US$400 of which is paid to the Vietnamese government.

Vietnamese from all parts of the country see a direct correlation between their impoverishment and their country's close relations with the USSR. Indeed, much of their unreserved hostility to resident Russian experts is an outgrowth of the popular feeling that the Soviets are to blame for the pathetic state of the Vietnamese economy. Every poster of those two white guys, Marx and Lenin, emphasises the foreign origin of much of the Party's ideology, including collectivisation and centralised planning.

In addition, the Vietnamese know that much of the best of Vietnam's agricultural produce is sold to the Soviets to pay off the huge national debt. And they can read the abbreviations 'USSR' or 'CCCP' that are conspicuously stamped on the third-rate imported vehicles, tires and machinery that keep breaking down (they much prefer East German goods). As the USA has learned in Central America, the Philippines and elsewhere, dependency breeds hostility.

Economic Reforms
The Vietnamese are keenly aware that while their centralised economy has been stagnating (despite billions of roubles in Soviet aid), the economies of their capitalist neighbours (Thailand, Singapore, Malaysia) have been flourishing. And whereas 25 years ago, Bangkok and Saigon were economically comparable, today the former is one of Asia's boom towns while the latter has hardly changed (except that it has become run-down). The Vietnamese also realise that the South-East Asian technological revolution is passing them by.

Vietnam's efforts to restructure the economy really got under way with the Sixth Party Congress held in December 1986. Recent reforms have cut state subsidies, allowed limited private enterprise, reduced centralised planning, rationalised exchange rates and liberalised foreign investment, permitting foreigners to own property and engage in joint ventures. It is rumoured that major Japanese and Korean conglomerates as well as multinational oil companies are looking into investment in Vietnam. Unfortunately, every level of the bureaucracy is plagued by functionaries who would like to see the reforms fail.

Immediately upon the legalisation of limited private enterprise, family businesses began popping up all over the country. But it is in the south, with its recent experience with capitalism, where the entrepreneurial skills and managerial dynamism needed to effect the reforms are to be found. With 'new thinking' in Hanoi now remaking the economic life of the whole country in the mould of the pre-reunification south, people have been remarking that in the end, the South won the war. The southern economy is improving much faster than that of the north, widening the already-significant gap in standards of living.

The opinions of the country's economic potential held by Westerners working in Vietnam tend to depend on where they are stationed. Hanoi-based diplomats and businesspeople (there are very few of the latter) are gloomy. On the other hand, every major hotel in Saigon seems filled with optimistic, enthusiastic importers, investors, international lawyers and specialists of all stripes. This divergence of opinions reflects the facts on the ground: businesspeople in the north face titanic bureaucratic and infrastructure impediments while the south has a pool of dynamic people who know how business is conducted and are able to make transactions work. Saigon ain't Singapore (not yet, at least), but it's said to be much easier to do business there than in Beijing.

Hanoi is intent on limiting Vietnam's version of perestroika to the economic sphere, keeping ideas such as pluralism and democracy from undermining the present power structure. Whether it is possible to have economic liberalisation without a concurrent liberalisation in the political sphere remains to be seen.

Vietnam's revolutionary leaders generally have a good record in eschewing luxurious living, but economic liberalisation has led to an increase in corruption and access to luxuries big and small on the part of high-ranking cadre. Ironically, it is the children of this class of nouveaux riches cadres whom you see – dressed in jeans and miniskirts – enjoying the discos that have sprung up in the last few years.

Agriculture & Forestry

About 70% of Vietnam's people earn their living from agriculture. Vietnam's most important crop is rice, which is cultivated using both irrigated paddy and dry field culture on 75% of cropped land. Two main types of rice are grown, glutinous and dry. Other important food crops include sugar cane, maize, manioc, potatoes and sweet potatoes. Among Vietnam's cash crops are peanuts, soy beans, pepper, tobacco, coffee, tea, rubber, coconuts and mulberry leaves (to feed silkworms). About 21% of Vietnam's land area is used for agriculture.

Very little agricultural machinery (such as tractors) is in use. Because threshing equipment is in short supply, you often see piles of rice stalks placed in the middle of the highway. As passing vehicles drive over them, the rice is separated from the stalks. Rice and other crops are often dried in the sun at the side of the road.

The country's food production is hindered by floods, droughts and typhoons, all of which have become increasingly frequent in recent years. The progressive devegetation of water catchment areas is causing ever greater flooding problems in the lowlands. The greater frequency of droughts and typhoons is thought to be the result of climatic changes caused by deforestation.

In 1978, collectivisation and natural disasters reduced food production to a low of 12.9 million tonnes, necessitating a cut in the food ration from 18 to 13 kg per person per month, a level 2 kg below the minimum subsistence level set by the UN. Since then, reforms allowing peasants to acquire small land holdings and more market-oriented policies have increased food production, which reached 18 million tonnes in 1985.

Because Vietnam's population is growing at the rate of 2.6% per year, the land available for agricultural use per capita continues to fall. At present, Vietnam has only 1300 sq metres of agricultural land per person. Given adequate capital, irrigation projects could improve yields on the 75% of cultivated land that at present is not irrigated. Better agricultural techniques would increase the productivity of marginal soils. The semi-forced resettlement of hundreds of thousands of people in agriculture-based New Economic Zones has not proved particularly successful.

Diplomatic sources report that while the best-quality rice is exported in order to get desperately needed foreign exchange, inferior rice is imported to feed the population. In recent years, poor food distribution and localised crop failures (resulting from floods, typhoons, etc) have created pockets of near-starvation. There are rumours that in the spring of 1989 trains transporting rice in north-central Vietnam were attacked and looted by hungry peasants whose own rice crops had failed.

The main source of energy in Vietnam is wood harvested from the country's shrinking natural forests. Vietnam also earns foreign currency by exporting rare hardwoods. Particles of shrapnel embedded in many of the trees make the wood less valuable. In recent years, Vietnam has begun cutting hardwood trees in the highland forests of Cambodia and Laos.

Minerals

Vietnam has an unusually wide range of mostly untapped mineral resources, including antimony, asbestos, bauxite, bitumen, calcium phosphate (apatite), chromium, coal, copper, ferro-manganese, gold, graphite, iron, kaolin, lead, limestone, manganese, magnetite, mercury, molybdenum, nickel, pyrite, silver, tin (cassiterite), titanium, wolfram and zinc. Coal deposits are being exploited in the northern provinces of Quang Ninh, Nghe Tinh and Quang Ninh. Oil and gas deposits thought to lie under the Mekong Delta and in the South China Sea are being explored by Vietsovpetro and Western multinationals.

An unexpected source of mineral wealth has been created by the war. Vietnam is now the world's largest supplier of scrap metal, much of which is sold to Japan. Local industries use some of the aluminium, brass and steel as well. The aluminium in that spoon you ate lunch with was almost certainly once part of an American helicopter (or aeroplane or armoured vehicle), and the bronze from which newly cast Buddhas are fashioned most likely came to Vietnam in the form of American artillery shell casings.

Fishing

Fish, which constitutes the main source of protein in the diets of many Vietnamese, is the most important staple food after rice. Fishing employs 550,000 people.

About 2000 species of fish, 100 of which are of economic value, have been identified in Vietnam's extensive network of rivers, streams and lakes and in the country's coastal waters. Whereas central reef and deep sea fishing areas are under-exploited relative to sustainable catch levels, inshore fisheries are over-fished, resulting in decreasing yields over the past few years. Efforts to expand deep-sea fishing have been hampered by the loss of thousands of boats taken by refugees fleeing the country by sea.

Some freshwater fisheries have been polluted by agricultural chemicals and the by-products of herbicides used by the Americans during the war. Coral reefs are being destroyed for the production of quicklime despite the fact that Vietnam has extensive onshore limestone deposits.

In recent years, the Australians have begun investing in the production of seafood (prawns and the like) for export.

Manufacturing

Great emphasis was placed on heavy industry in the 5 year plans of 1976-80 and 1981-85, but shortages of fuel and capital, under-utilisation of industrial capacity, insufficient maintenance and inadequate standards have almost crippled industrial development. Major products include processed foods, textiles, cement, chemical fertilisers, glass and tires. Since the war, a metal casting industry based on melting down old war materiel has developed. Fireworks are produced using the gunpowder from left-over American munitions.

Vietnam's main imports are petroleum, steel products, railroad equipment, chemicals, medicines, raw cotton, fertiliser and grain.

POPULATION

In mid-1989, Vietnam's population was estimated at 66.8 million, making it the 12th most populous country in the world. Eighty-four percent of the population is ethnic-Vietnamese, 2% ethnic-Chinese and the rest Khmers, Chams and members of some 60 ethno-linguistic groups.

Vietnam has an overall population density of 200 persons per sq km, one of the world's highest for an agricultural country. Much of the Red River Delta has a population density of 1000 people per sq km. The rate of population growth is 2.6% per year. Life expectancy at birth is 57.7 for males and 62.1 for females. Infant mortality is 59 per 1000.

PEOPLE
Ethnic-Vietnamese

The Vietnamese people (called 'Annamites' by the French) developed as a distinct ethnic group between 200 BC and 200 AD through the fusion of a people of Indonesian stock with Viet and Tai immigrants from the north and Chinese who arrived, along with Chinese rule, starting from the 2nd century AD. Vietnamese civilisation was profoundly influenced by China and, via Champa and the Khmers, India, but the fact that the Vietnamese were never absorbed by China indicates that a strong local culture existed prior to the 1000 years of Chinese rule, which ended in 938 AD.

The Vietnamese have lived for thousands of years by growing rice and, as a result, have historically preferred to live in lowland areas suitable for rice growing. Over the past 2 millennia, they have slowly pushed southward along the narrow coastal strip, defeating the Chams in the 15th century and taking over the Mekong Delta from the Khmers in the 18th century. The Vietnamese have tended to view highland areas (and their inhabitants) with suspicion.

Vietnamese who have emigrated are known as *Viet Kieu* (Overseas Vietnamese).

Ethnic-Chinese

The ethnic-Chinese (*Hoa*) constitute the largest single minority group in Vietnam. Today, most of them live in the south, especially in Saigon's sister-city Cholon. Though the families of most of Vietnam's ethnic-Chinese have lived in Vietnam for generations, they have historically tried to maintain their separate Chinese identities, languages, school systems and even citizenships. The Chinese have organised themselves into communities, known as 'congregations' (*bang*), according to their ancestors' province of origin and dialect. During the 1950s, President Diem tried, without much success, to forcibly assimilate South Vietnam's ethnic-Chinese population. In the North, too, the ethnic-Chinese have resisted Vietnamisation.

Historical antipathies between China and Vietnam and the prominence of ethnic-Chinese in commerce have generated a great deal of animosity towards them. During the late 1970s, about one-third of the country's ethnic-Chinese fled to China and the West after a campaign against 'bourgeois elements' (considered a euphemism for the ethnic-Chinese) turned into open persecution.

Ethno-Linguistic Minorities

Vietnam has one of the most complex ethno-linguistic mixes in all of Asia. The country's 60 minority groups, many of whom are related to Thailand's hilltribes, live mostly in the Central Highlands and the mountainous regions of the north. The French called them 'montagnards' (which means 'highlanders'), a term they themselves still use when speaking English or French. The Vietnamese often refer to the hill-tribe people as *Moi*, a derogatory word meaning 'savages' that unfortunately reflects all-too-common popular attitudes. The present government, which prefers the term 'national minorities', is trying to 'integrate' the montagnards, which means that it is attempting to Vietnamise them culturally, linguistically, socially and ideologically.

Linguistically, the montagnards can be divided into three main groups: those whose languages are of the Austro-Asian family (the Bru, Pacoh, Katu, Cua, Hre, Rengao, Sedang, Bahnar, M'nong, Maa and Stieng who speak Mon-Khmer languages, and the Tai (Thai or Thay) groups), the Malayo-Polynesian family (the Jarai, Hroi, Raday, Raglai, Chru, Chams) and the Sino-Tibetan family (the Hmong and Mien). Religiously, the minority groups are very diverse, practising ancestor worship, animism and – as a result of proselytising in recent decades – Protestantism and Catholicism.

Some of the national minorities have lived in Vietnam for thousands of years while others have migrated into the region in the last few centuries. The areas inhabited by each group are often delimited by altitude, with later arrivals settling at higher elevations. Many of the groups have little in common with each other except a history of inter-tribal warfare.

Historically, the highland areas were allowed to remain virtually independent as long as their leaders recognised Vietnamese sovereignty and paid tribute and taxes. The 1980 Constitution abolished two vast autonomous regions established for the ethnic minorities in the northern mountains in 1959. During the Vietnam War, both the Communists and the USA actively recruited fighters among the montagnards of the Central Highlands.

Many of the hilltribes are semi-nomadic, living by slash-and-burn agriculture. Because such practices destroy the ever-dwindling forests, the government is trying to turn them to settled agriculture.

Chams

Vietnam's 60,000 Chams are the remnant of the once-vigorous Indianised kingdom of Champa which flourished from the 2nd to the 15th centuries and was destroyed as the Vietnamese expanded southward. Most of them live along the coast between Nha Trang and Phan Thiet and in the Mekong Delta province of An Giang.

Today, the Chams are best known for the many brick sanctuaries (known as 'Cham towers') they constructed all over the southern half of the country. The Cham language is of the Malayo-Polynesian (Austronesian) group. It can be written either in a traditional script of Indian origin or in a Latin-based script created by the French. Most of the Chams, who were profoundly influenced by both Hinduism and Buddhism, are now Muslims. There is a superb collection of Cham statues at the Cham Museum in Danang.

Khmers

The Khmers (ethnic-Cambodians) number about 700,000 and are concentrated in the south-western Mekong Delta. They practise Hinayana (Theravada) Buddhism.

Indians

Almost all of South Vietnam's population of Indians, most of whose roots were in southern India, left in 1975. The remaining community in Saigon worship at the Mariamman Hindu temple and the Central Mosque.

Amerasians

One of the most tragic legacies of the Vietnam War is the plight of thousands of Amerasians, most of whom are now in their late teens. Marriages and other less formal unions between American soldiers and Vietnamese women – as well as prostitution – were common during the war. But when the Americans were rotated home, all too often they abandoned their 'wives' and mistresses, leaving them to raise children who were half-white or half-black in a society not particularly tolerant of such racial mixing.

After 1975, the Amerasians – living reminders of the American presence – were often mistreated by Vietnamese society and even abandoned by their mothers and other relatives. Many were forced to live on the street. When, in the early 1980s, it became known that the American government would resettle the Amerasians in the USA, Amerasian children were adopted by people eager to emigrate. At the end of the '80s, the Orderly Departure Programme finally began to function as planned and the crowds of Amerasian street kids began to disappear from downtown Saigon.

Older Vietnamese who are of mixed race are most likely the offspring of unions between French soldiers – some of whom came from France's African colonies – and local women.

Europeans

There are almost no ethnic-European citizens of Vietnam, but Vietnam does have a considerable colony of European expatriates, most of whom are either diplomats or experts from the USSR and Eastern Europe.

The only Caucasians most younger Vietnamese have ever seen are Russians. Unfortunately, the Soviets have earned a reputation for being unfriendly and cheap. I say 'unfortunately' not because of the breach in socialist solidarity this situation has produced but because in many parts of the country, all Westerners are assumed to be Russians and are treated accordingly.

EDUCATION

Compared to other desperately poor countries, Vietnam's population is very well educated. Vietnam's literacy rate is estimated at 78%, though official figures put it even higher (95%). Before the colonial period, the majority of the population possessed some degree of literacy, but by 1939 only 15% of school-age children were receiving any kind of instruction and 80% of the population was illiterate.

Today, almost all children receive primary education and 30% to 40% go on to secondary school, though a significant number of children are barred from enrolling in school because of their parents' political background. The country's 94 universities, technical colleges and other institutes enrol 30,000 students each year. Approximately 500 students per year go abroad for advanced training, mostly to the USSR and East Germany.

During the late 19th century, one of the few things that French colonial officials and Vietnamese nationalists agreed on was that the traditional Confucian educational system, on which the mandarinal civil service was based, was in desperate need of reform. Mandarinal examinations were held in Tonkin until WW I and in Annam until the war's end.

Many of Indochina's independence leaders were educated in elite French-language secondary schools such as the Lycée

Albert Sarraut in Hanoi and the Lycée Chasseloup Laubat in Saigon.

CULTURE

Architecture

The Vietnamese have not been great builders like their neighbours the Khmers, who erected the monuments of Angkor in Cambodia, and the Cham, whose graceful brick towers, constructed using sophisticated masonry technology, grace many parts of southern half of the country. For more information on Cham architecture, see Po Klong Garai under Phan Rang-Thap Cham, Po Nagar in the section on Nha Trang and My Son in the Danang chapter

Most of what the Vietnamese have built has been made of wood and other materials that proved highly vulnerable in the tropical climate. Because almost all of the stone structures erected by the Vietnamese have been destroyed in countless feudal wars and invasions, very little pre-modern Vietnamese architecture is extant. The orientation of houses, communal meeting halls (dinh), tombs and pagodas is determined by geomancers, which is why cemeteries have tombstones turned every which way.

Plenty of pagodas and temples founded hundreds of years ago are still functioning but their physical plan has usually been rebuilt many times with little concern for making the upgraded structure an exact copy of the original. As a result, modern elements have been casually introduced into pagoda architecture, with neon haloes for statues of the Buddha only the most glaring example of this.

Because of the Vietnamese custom of ancestor worship – and despite the massive dislocations of populations during the Vietnam War – many graves from previous centuries are still extant. These include temples erected in memory of high-ranking mandarins, members of the royal family and emperors.

Memorials for Vietnamese who died in the wars against the French, Americans and Chinese are usually marked by cement obelisks inscribed with the words *To Quoc Ghi*

Cong (The country will remember their exploits). Many of the tombstones were erected over empty graves; most Viet Minh and Viet Cong dead were buried where they fell.

Sculpture

Vietnamese sculpture has traditionally centred on religious themes and functioned as an adjunct to architecture, especially that of pagodas, temples and tombs. Many inscribed stelae, erected hundreds of years ago to commemorate the founding of a pagoda or important national events, can still be seen (eg at Thien Mu Pagoda in Hué and the Temple of Literature in Hanoi).

The Cham civilisation produced spectacular carved sandstone figures for its Hindu and Buddhist sanctuaries. Cham sculpture was profoundly influenced by Indian art but, over the centuries, also incorporated Indonesian and Vietnamese elements. The largest single collection of Cham sculpture in the world is at the Cham Museum in Danang. For more information on Cham sculpture, see Cham Museum in the Danang chapter.

Ceramic Elephant

Dress

The graceful national dress of Vietnamese women is known as the *ao dai* (pronounced 'ow-zai' in the north and 'ow-yai' in the south). It consists of a close-fitting blouse with long panels in the front and back that is worn over loose black or white trousers. One sees fewer and fewer women wearing *ao dais* these days, though they are still popular for formal occasions.

Traditionally, men have also worn *ao dais*. The male version is shorter and looser fitting. Before the end of dynastic rule, the colours of the brocade and embroidery indicated the rank of the wearer. Gold brocade accompanied by embroidered dragons was reserved for the emperor. High ranking mandarins wore purple while lower ranking mandarins had to settle for blue.

Mourners usually wear either white or black *ao dais* (white is the traditional colour of mourning).

Folk Crafts

The art of making lacquerware was brought to Vietnam from China in the mid-15th century. Before that time, the Vietnamese used lacquer solely for practical purposes (such as making things watertight). During the 1930s, the Fine Arts School in Hanoi employed several Japanese teachers who introduced new styles and production methods. Their influence can still be seen in the noticeable Japanese elements in some Vietnamese lacquerware, especially that made in the north. Although a 1985 government publication declares that 'at present, lacquer painting deals boldly with realistic and revolutionary themes and forges unceasingly ahead', most of the lacquerware I saw was inlaid with mother-of-pearl and was of traditional design.

Lacquer is a resin extracted from the *son* tree (*cay son*). It is creamy white in raw form but is made black (*son then*) or brown (*canh dan*, 'cockroach wing') by mixing it with rosin in an iron container for 40 hours. After the object to be lacquered (traditionally made of teak) has been treated with a fixative, 10 coats of lacquer are applied. Each coat must be dried for a week and then thoroughly sanded with pumice and cuttlebone before the next layer can be applied. A specially refined lacquer is used for the 11th and final coat, which is sanded with a fine coal powder and lime wash before the object is decorated. Designs may be added by engraving in low relief, by painting, or by inlaying mother-of-pearl, egg shell, silver or even gold.

The production of ceramics *(gom)* has a long history in Vietnam. In ancient times, ceramic objects were made by coating a wicker mould with clay and baking it. Later, ceramics production became very refined, and each dynastic period is known for its particular techniques and motifs.

For more information on Vietnamese folk art, see *Handicrafts* (Xunhasaba, Hanoi), number 62 in the English and French-language *Vietnamese Studies* series.

Literature

Vietnamese literature can be divided into three types:

1) Traditional oral literature *(Truyen Khau)* which was begun long before recorded history and includes legends, folk songs and proverbs.
2) Sino-Vietnamese literature *(Han Viet)*, which was written in Chinese characters *(chu nho)*. It dates from 939 AD, when the first independent Vietnamese kingdom was established. Sino-Vietnamese literature was dominated by Confucian and Buddhist texts and was governed by strict rules of metre and verse.
3) Modern Vietnamese literature *(Quoc Am)* includes anything recorded in *nom* characters or the Romanised *quoc ngu* script. The earliest extant text written in *nom* is the late 13th century *Van Te Ca Sau (Ode to an Alligator)*. Literature written in *quoc ngu* has played an important role in Vietnamese nationalism.

Painting

Painting done on frame-mounted silk dates from the 13th century. Silk-painting was at one time the preserve of scholar-calligraphers, who also painted scenes from nature. Before the advent of photography, realistic portraits for use in ancestor worship were produced. Some of these – usually of former head monks – can still be seen in Buddhist pagodas.

During this century, Vietnamese painting has been influenced by Western trends. Much of the recent work done in Vietnam has had political rather than aesthetic or artistic motives. According to an official account, the fighting of the Vietnam War provided painters with 'rich human material: People's Army combatants facing the jets, peasant and factory women in the militia who handled guns as well as they did their production work, young volunteers who repaired roads in record time..., old mothers offering tea to anti-aircraft gunners...' There's lots of this stuff at the Fine Arts Museum in Hanoi.

Music

Though heavily influenced by the Chinese and, in the south, the Indianised Cham and Khmer musical traditions, Vietnamese music has a high degree of originality in style and instrumentation. The traditional system of writing down music and the five note (pentatonic) scale are of Chinese origin. Vietnamese choral music is unique in that the melody must correspond to the tones; it cannot be rising during a word that has a falling tone.

There are three broad categories of Vietnamese music:

1) Folk music, which includes children's songs, love songs, work songs, festival songs, lullabies, lamentations and funeral songs. It is usually sung without instrumental accompaniment.
2) Classical music (or 'learned music'), which is rather rigid and formal. It was performed at the imperial court and for the entertainment of the mandarin elite. A traditional orchestra consists of 40 musicians. There are two main types of classical

chamber music: Hat A Dao (from the north) and Ca Hué (from central Vietnam).

3) Theatre music, which includes singing, dancing and instrumentation (see the Theatre sub-section for more information).

Each of Vietnam's ethno-linguistic minorities has its own musical and dance traditions which often include colourful costumes and instruments such as reed flutes, lithophones (similar to xylophones), bamboo whistles, gongs and stringed instruments made from gourds. While in most hilltribes the majority of the dancers are women, a few montagnard groups allow only the men to dance. A great deal of anthropological research has been carried out in recent years in order to preserve and revive minority traditions.

At present, there are music conservatories teaching both traditional Vietnamese and Western classical musics in Hanoi, Hué and Saigon.

Theatre & Puppetry

Vietnamese theatre integrates music, singing, recitation, declamation, dance and mime into a single artistic whole. There are five basic forms:

1) Classical theatre is known as *Hat Tuong* in the north and *Hat Boi* ('songs with show dress') in the south. It is based on Chinese opera and was probably brought to Vietnam by the 13th century Mongol invaders chased out by Tran Hung Dao. *Hat Tuong* is very formalistic, employing gestures and scenery similar to Chinese theatre. The accompanying orchestra, which is dominated by the drum, usually has six musicians. Often, the audience also has a drum so it too can comment on the on-stage action.

Hat Tuong has a limited cast of typical characters who establish their identities using combinations of makeup and dress that the audience can readily recognise. For instance, red face-paint represents courage, loyalty and faithfulness. Traitors and cruel people have white faces. Lowlanders are given green faces; highlanders have black ones. Horizontal eyebrows represent honesty, erect eyebrows symbolise cruelty and lowered eyebrows belong to characters with a cowardly nature. A male character can express emotions (pensiveness, worry, anger, etc) by fingering his beard in various ways.

2) Popular theatre (*Hat Cheo*) often engages in social protest through the medium of satire. The singing and declamation are in everyday language and include many proverbs and sayings. Many of the melodies are of peasant origin.

3) Modern theatre (*Cai Luong*) originated in the south in the early 20th century and shows strong Western influences.

4) Spoken drama (*Kich Noi* or *Kich*), whose roots are Western, appeared in the 1920s. It is popular among intellectuals and students.

5) Conventional puppetry (*Roi Can*) and that uniquely Vietnamese art form, water puppetry (*Roi Nuoc*), draw their plots from the same legendary and historical sources as other forms of traditional theatre. It is thought that water puppetry developed when determined puppeteers in the Red River Delta managed to carry on with the show despite flooding.

These days, the various forms of Vietnamese theatre are performed by dozens of state-funded troupes and companies around the country. Water puppetry can be seen at the Saigon Zoo, in Hanoi and at Thay Pagoda (near Hanoi).

Film

One of Vietnam's first cinematographic efforts was a newsreel of Ho Chi Minh's 1945 proclamation of independence. After Dien Bien Phu, parts of the battle were restaged for the benefit of movie cameras.

Prior to reunification the South Vietnamese movie industry concentrated on producing sensational, low-budget flicks. Until recently, most North Vietnamese film-making efforts have been dedicated to 'the mobilisation of the masses for economic reconstruction, the building of socialism and the struggle for national reunification'. Predictable themes include 'workers devoted to socialist industrialisation', 'old mothers who continuously risk their lives to help the people's army' and 'children who are ready to face any danger'.

The relaxation of ideological censorship of the arts has proceeded in fits and starts, but in the last few years, the gradual increase in artistic freedoms has affected film-making as well as other genres. In late 1989, there was a return to greater government control of the arts.

RELIGION

Four great philosophies and religions have shaped the spiritual life of the Vietnamese people: Confucianism, Taoism, Buddhism and Christianity. Over the centuries, Confucianism, Taoism and Buddhism have fused with popular Chinese beliefs and ancient Vietnamese animism to form what is known collectively as the 'Triple Religion', or *Tam Giao*. Confucianism, more a system of social and political morality than a religion, took on many religious aspects. Taoism, which began as an esoteric philosophy for scholars, mixed with Buddhism among the peasants, and many Taoist elements became an intrinsic part of popular religion. If asked their religion a Vietnamese is likely to say that they are a Buddhist, but when it comes to family or civic duties they are likely to follow Confucianism while turning to Taoist conceptions in understanding the nature of the cosmos.

Mahayana Buddhism

Mahayana Buddhism (*Dai Thua* or *Bac Tong*, which means 'from the north', ie China; also known as the Greater Wheel school, Greater Vehicle school and Northern Buddhism) is the predominant religion in Vietnam. The largest Mahayana sect in the country is Zen (Dhyana; in Vietnamese: *Thien*), also known as the school of meditation. *Dao Trang* ('the pure land school'), the second-largest Mahayana sect in Vietnam, is practised mainly in the south.

Mahayana Buddhism differs from Theravada Buddhism in several important ways. Whereas the Theravadin strives to become a perfected saint (Arhat) ready for Nirvana, the Mahayanist ideal is that of the Bodhisattva, one who strives to perfect himself or herself in the necessary virtues (generosity, morality, patience, vigour, concentration and wisdom) but even after attaining perfection chooses to remain in the world in order to save others.

Mahayanists consider Gautama Buddha to be only one of the innumerable manifestations of the one ultimate Buddha. These countless Buddhas and Bodhisattvas, who are as numberless as the universes to which they minister, gave rise in popular Vietnamese religion – with its innumerable Taoist divinities and spirits – to a pantheon of deities and helpers whose aid can be sought through invocations and offerings.

Mahayana Buddhist pagodas in Vietnam usually include a number of elements. In front of the pagoda is a white statue of a standing Quan The Am Bo Tat (Avaloketeçvara Bodhisattva, the Goddess of Mercy). Inside the main sanctuary are representations of the three Buddhas: A Di Da (pronounced 'AH-zee-dah'; Amitabha), the Buddha of the Past; Thich Ca Mau Ni (Sakyamuni, or Siddhartha Gautama), the Historical Buddha; and Di Lac (pronounced 'zee-lock'; Maitreya), the Buddha of the Future. Nearby are often statues of the eight Kim Cang (Genies of the Cardinal Directions), the La Han (Arhats) and various *Bo Tat* (bodhisattvas) such as Van Thu (Manjusri), Quan The Am Bo Tat (Avaloketeçvara) and Dia Tang (Ksitigartha). Sometimes, an altar is set aside for Taoist divinities such as Ngoc Hoang (the Emperor of Jade) and Thien Hau Thanh Mau (the Queen of Heaven), who is also known as Tuc Goi La Ba (the Goddess of the Sea and Protectress of Fishermen and Sailors). Every pagoda has an altar for funerary tablets memorialising deceased *bonzes* (who are often buried in stupas near the pagoda) and lay-people.

The function of the Vietnamese *bonze* is to minister to the spiritual and superstitious needs of the peasantry, but it is largely up to him whether he invokes the lore of Taoism or the philosophy of Buddhism. A *bonze* may live reclusively on a remote hilltop or he may manage a pagoda on a busy city street. And he may choose to fulfil any number of functions: telling fortunes, making and selling talismans (*fu*), advising where a house should be constructed, reciting incantations at funerals or even performing acupuncture.

History Theravada Buddhism was brought to Vietnam from India by pilgrims at the end of the 2nd century AD. Simultaneously, Chinese monks introduced Mahayana Buddhism. Buddhism did not become popular with the masses until many centuries later.

Buddhism received royal patronage during the 10th to 13th centuries. This backing included recognition of the Buddhist hierarchy, financial support for the construction of pagodas and other projects, and the active participation of the clergy in ruling the country. By the 11th century, Buddhism had filtered down to the villages. Buddhism was proclaimed the official state religion in the mid-12th century.

During the 13th and 14th centuries, Confucian scholars gradually replaced Buddhist monks as advisors to the Tran Dynasty. The Confucians accused the Buddhists of shirking their responsibilities to family and country because of the Buddhist doctrine of withdrawal from worldly matters. The Chinese invasion of 1414 reinvigorated Confucianism while at the same time resulting in the destruction of many Buddhist pagodas and manuscripts. The Nguyen Lords (1558-1778), who ruled the southern part of the country, reversed this trend.

A revival of Vietnamese Buddhism began throughout the country in the 1920s, and Buddhist organisations were begun in various parts of the country. In the 1950s and '60s, attempts were made to unite the various streams of Buddhism in Vietnam. During the early 1960s, South Vietnamese Buddhist *bonzes* and laypeople played an active role in opposing the regime of Ngo Dinh Diem.

Over the centuries, the Buddhist ideals and beliefs held by the educated elite touched only superficially the rural masses (90% of the population), whose traditions were transmitted orally and put to the test by daily observance. The common people were far less concerned with the philosophy of good government than they were with seeking aid from supernatural beings for problems of the here and now. Gradually, the various Mahayana Buddhas and Bodhisattvas became mixed up with mysticism, animism, polytheism and Hindu tantrism as well as the multiple divinities and ranks of deities of the Taoist pantheon.

Over the centuries, the Triple Religion flourished despite clerical attempts to maintain some semblance of Buddhist orthodoxy and doctrinal purity. Although most of the population has only a vague notion of Buddhist doctrines they invite bonzes to participate in such life-cycle ceremonies as funerals. And Buddhist pagodas have come to be seen by many Vietnamese as a physical and spiritual refuge from an uncertain world.

After 1975, many monks, including some who actively opposed the South Vietnamese government and the war, were rounded up and sent to re-education camps. In the last few years, restrictions on the training of young monks seem to have been relaxed a bit.

Theravada Buddhism
Theravada Buddhism (*Tieu Thua* or *Nam Tong*, which means 'from the south,' ie India and Sri Lanka); also known as Hinayana, the Lesser Wheel school, the Lesser Vehicle school and Southern Buddhism) came to Vietnam directly from India. It is practised mainly in the Mekong Delta region, mostly by ethnic-Khmers. The most important Theravada sect in Vietnam is the disciplinary school, Luat Tong. For more information, see 'Facts About the Country' in the Laos section.

Confucianism
While it is more a religious philosophy than an organised religion, Confucianism (*Nho Giao* or *Khong Giao*) has been an important

force in shaping Vietnam's social system and the everyday lives and beliefs of its people.

Confucius (in Vietnamese: *Khong Tu)* was born in China around 550 BC. He saw people as social beings formed by society yet capable of shaping their society. He believed that the individual exists in and for society and drew up a code of ethics to guide the individual in social interaction. This code laid down a person's specific obligations to family, society and the state. Central to Confucianism are an emphasis on duty and hierarchy.

According to Confucian philosophy, which was brought to Vietnam by the Chinese during their 1000-year rule (111 BC to 938 AD), the emperor alone, governing under the mandate of heaven, can intercede on behalf of the nation with the powers of heaven and earth. Only virtue, as acquired through education, gave one the right (the mandate of heaven) to wield political power. From this it followed that an absence of virtue would result in the withdrawal of this mandate, sanctioning rebellion against an unjust ruler. Natural disasters or defeat on the battlefield were often interpreted as a sign that the mandate of heaven had been withdrawn.

Confucian philosophy was in some senses democratic: because virtue could be acquired only through learning, education rather than birth made a person virtuous. Therefore, education had to be widespread. Until the beginning of this century, Confucian philosophy and texts formed the basis of Vietnam's educational system. Generation after generation of young people – in the villages as well as the cities – were taught their duties to family (including ancestor worship) and community and that each person had to know their place in the social hierarchy and behave accordingly.

A system of government-run civil service examinations selected from among the country's best students those who would join the non-hereditary ruling class, the mandarins. As a result, education was prized not only as the path to virtue but as a means to social and political advancement. This system helped create the respect for intellectual and literary accomplishment for which the Vietnamese are famous to this day.

The political institutions based on Confucianism finally degenerated and became discredited, as they did elsewhere in the Chinese-influenced world. Over the centuries, the philosophy became conservative and backward-looking. This reactionary trend became dominant in Vietnam in the 15th century, suiting despotic rulers who emphasised the divine right of kings rather than their responsibilities under the doctrine of the mandate of heaven.

Taoism

Taoism *(Lao Giao* or *Dao Giao)* is based on the philosophy of Lao Tse *(Thai Thuong Lao Quan)*, which emphasises contemplation and simplicity of life. Its ideal is returning to the Tao, the essence of which all things are made. Only a small elite in China and Vietnam has ever been familiar with Taoist philosophy, which is based on various correspondences (eg the human body, the microcosmic replica of the macrocosm) and complimentary contradictions *(am* and *duong,* the Vietnamese equivalents of *yin* and *yang).* As a result, there are very few Taoist pagodas and clergy in Vietnam.

According to the Taoist cosmology, Ngoc Hoang, the Emperor of Jade (in Chinese: *Yu-huang),* whose abode is in heaven, rules over a world of divinities, genies, spirits and demons in which the forces of nature are incarnated as supernatural beings and great historical personages have become gods. It is this aspect of Taoism that has become assimilated into the daily lives of most Vietnamese as a collection of superstitions and mystical and animistic beliefs. Much of the sorcery and magic that are now part of popular Vietnamese religion have their origins in Taoism.

Ancestor Worship

Vietnamese ancestor worship, which is the ritual expression of filial piety *(hieu),* dates from long before the arrival of Confucianism or Buddhism. Some people consider it to be a religion unto itself.

The cult of the ancestors is based on the belief that the soul lives on after death and becomes the protector of its descendants. Because of the influence the spirits of one's ancestors exert on the living, it is considered not only shameful for them to be upset or restless but downright dangerous. A soul with no descendants is doomed to eternal wandering because it will not receive homage.

Traditionally, the Vietnamese venerate and honour the spirits of their ancestors regularly, especially on the anniversary of the ancestor's death when sacrifices are offered to both the god of the household and the spirit of the ancestors. To request intercession for success in business or on behalf of a sick child, sacrifices and prayers are offered to the ancestral spirits. The ancestors are informed on occasions of family joy or sorrow, such as weddings, success in an examination, or death. Important elements in the cult of the ancestor are the family altar, a plot of land whose income is set aside for the support of the ancestors, and the designation of a direct male descendent of the deceased to assume the obligation to carry on the cult.

Many pagodas have altars on which memorial tablets and photographs of the deceased are displayed. One may look at the young faces in the photographs and ponder the tragedy of so many people having had their lives cut short. Some visitors wonder if they died as a result of the wars. The real explanation is less tragic: most of the dead had passed on decades after the photos were taken, but rather than use a picture of an aged, infirm parent, survivors chose a more flattering (though slightly outdated) picture of the deceased in their prime.

Caodaism

Caodaism is an indigenous Vietnamese sect that seeks to create the ideal religion by fusing the secular and religious philosophies of both East and West. It was founded in the early 1920s based on messages revealed in seances to Ngo Minh Chieu, the group's founder. The sect's colourful headquarters is in Tay Ninh, 96 km north-west of Saigon. There are currently about 2 million followers of Caodaism in Vietnam. For more information about Caodaism, see 'Tay Ninh' in the 'Around Saigon' chapter.

Hoa Hao Buddhist Sect

The Hoa Hao Buddhist sect (*Phat Giao Hoa Hao*) was founded in the Mekong Delta in 1939 by Huynh Phu So, a young man who had studied with the most famous of the region's occultists. After he was miraculously cured of sickliness, So began preaching a reformed Buddhism based on the common people and embodied in personal faith rather than elaborate rituals. His philosophy emphasised simplicity in worship and denied the necessity for intermediaries between human beings and the Supreme Being.

In 1940, the French, who called Huynh Phu So the 'mad *bonze*', tried to silence him. When arresting him failed, they committed him to an insane asylum, where he soon converted the Vietnamese psychiatrist assigned to his case. During WW II, the Hoa Hao Sect continued to grow and to build up a militia with weapons supplied by the Japanese. In 1947, after clashes between Hoa Hao forces and the Viet Minh, Huynh Phu So was assassinated by the Viet Minh, who thereby earned the animosity of what had by then become a powerful political and military force in the Mekong Delta, especially around Chau Doc. The military power of the Hoa Hao was broken in 1956 when one of its guerrilla commanders was captured by the Diem government and publicly guillotined. Subsequently, elements of the Hoa Hao army joined the Viet Cong.

There presently are thought to be about 1½ million followers of the Hoa Hao sect.

Catholicism

Catholicism was introduced into Vietnam in the 16th century by missionaries from Portugal, Spain and France. Particularly active during the 16th and 17th centuries were the French Jesuits and Portuguese Dominicans.

Pope Alexander VII assigned the first bishops to Vietnam in 1659, and the first Vietnamese priests were ordained 9 years later. According to some estimates, there were 800,000 Catholics in Vietnam by 1685. Over the next 3 centuries, Catholicism was discouraged and at times outlawed. The first known edict forbidding missionary activity was promulgated in 1533. Foreign missionaries and their followers were severely persecuted during the 17th and 18th centuries.

When the French began their efforts to turn Vietnam into a part of their empire, the treatment of Catholics was one of their most important pretexts for intervention. Under French rule the Catholic church was given preferential status and Catholicism flourished. Though it incorporated certain limited aspects of Vietnamese culture, Catholicism (unlike Buddhism, for instance) succeeded in retaining its doctrinal purity.

Today, Vietnam has the highest percentage of Catholics (8% to 10% of the population) in Asia outside of the Philippines. Many of the 900,000 refugees who fled North Vietnam to the South in 1954 were Catholics, as was South Vietnamese President Ngo Dinh Diem. Since 1954 in the North and 1975 in the South, Catholics have faced restrictions on their religious activities, including strict limits on the ordination of priests and religious education.

Protestantism

Protestantism was introduced to Vietnam in 1911. The majority of Vietnam's Protestants, who number about 200,000, are montagnards living in the Central Highlands. Until 1975, the most active Protestant group in South Vietnam was the Christian and Missionary Alliance. After reunification, many Protestant clergymen – especially those trained by American missionaries – were imprisoned. The religious activities of Protestant churches are still restricted by the government.

Islam

Muslims – mostly ethnic-Khmers and Chams – constitute about 0.5% of Vietnam's population. There were small communities of Malaysian, Indonesian and south Indian Muslims in Saigon until 1975, when almost all of them fled. Today, Saigon's 5000 Muslims (including a handful of south Indians) congregate in about a dozen mosques, including the large Central Mosque in the city centre.

Arab traders reached China in the 7th century and may have stopped in Vietnam on the way, but the earliest evidence of an Islamic presence in Vietnam is a 10th century pillar inscribed in Arabic which was found near the coastal town of Phan Rang. It appears that Islam spread among Cham refugees who fled to Cambodia after the destruction of their kingdom in 1471 but that these converts had little success in propagating Islam among their fellow Chams still in Vietnam.

The Vietnamese Chams consider themselves Muslims despite the fact that they have only a vague notion of Islamic theology and laws. Their communities have very few copies of the Koran and even their religious dignitaries can hardly read Arabic. Though Muslims the world over pray five times a day, the Chams pray only on Fridays and celebrate Ramadan (a month of dawn to dusk fasting) for only 3 days. Their worship services consist of the recitation of a few Arabic verses from the Koran in a corrupted form. Instead of performing ritual ablutions, they make motions as if they were drawing water from a well. Circumcision is symbolically performed on boys at age 15; the ceremony consists of a religious leader making the gestures of circumcision with a wooden knife. The Chams of Vietnam do not make the pilgrimage to Mecca and though they do not eat pork, they do drink alcohol. In addition, their Islam-based religious rituals exist side-by-side with animism and the worship of Hindu deities. The Chams have even taken the Arabic words of common Koranic expressions and made them into the names of deities.

Cham religious leaders wear a white robe and an elaborate turban with gold, red or brown tassels. Their ranks are indicated by the length of the tassels.

Hinduism

Champa was profoundly influenced by Hinduism and many of the Cham towers, built as Hindu sanctuaries, contain lingams (phallic symbols of Shiva) that are still worshipped by ethnic-Vietnamese and ethnic-Chinese alike. After the fall of Champa in the 15th century, most Chams who remained in Vietnam became Muslims but continued to practise various Brahmanic (high-cast Hindu) rituals and customs.

HOLIDAYS & FESTIVALS

Year 1 of the Vietnamese lunar calendar corresponds to 2637 BC. Each lunar month has 29 or 30 days, resulting in years with 355 days. Approximately every 3rd year, an extra month is added between the 3rd and 4th months to keep the lunar year in sync with the solar year (if this weren't done, you'd end up having the seasons gradually rotate around the lunar year, playing havoc with all elements of life linked to the agricultural year). To find out the Gregorian date corresponding to a lunar date, check any Vietnamese calendar.

Instead of dividing time into centuries, the Vietnamese calendar uses units of 60 years called *hoi*. Each *hoi* consists of six 10-year cycles (*can*) and five 12-year cycles (*ky*). The name of each year in the cycle consists of the *can* name followed by the *ky* name, a system which never produces the same combination twice.

The 10 heavenly stems of the *can* cycle are as follows:

Giap	water in nature
At	water in the home
Binh	lighted fire
Dinh	latent fire
Mau	wood
Ky	wood prepared to burn
Canh	metal
Tan	wrought metal
Nham	virgin land
Quy	cultivated land

The 12 zodiacal stems of the *ky* are as follows:

Ty	rat
Suu	buffalo
Dan	tiger
Meo	cat
Thin	dragon
Ty	snake
Ngo	horse
Mui	goat
Than	monkey
Dau	cock (chicken)
Tuat	dog
Hoi	pig

Religious Festivals

The following major religious festivals are listed by lunar date:

1st to 7th days of the 1st month

Tet (Tet Nguyen Dan), the Vietnamese New Year, is the most important festival of the year. Marking the new lunar year as well as the advent of spring, the week-long holiday usually falls in late January or early February. Tet is a time for family reunions, the payment of debts, the avoidance of arguments, special foods, new clothes, flowers and new beginnings. Great importance is attached to starting the year properly because it is believed that the 1st day and 1st week of the new year will determine one's fortunes for the rest of the year. Homes are decorated with sprigs of plum tree blossoms (*cay mai*).

The first pre-Tet ceremony, *Le Tao Quan*, is designed to send the Spirit of the Hearth (Tao Quan) off to report to the Emperor of Jade (Ngoc Hoang) in a positive frame of mind. A New Year's Tree (Cay Neu) is constructed to ward off evil spirits. Later, a sacrifice (Tat Nien) is offered to deceased family members. Finally, at midnight, the old year is ushered out and the new welcomed in with the ritual of *Giao Thua*, which is celebrated both in homes and in pagodas. Firecrackers, gongs and drums commemorate the new year and welcome back the Spirit of the Hearth. The first visitor of New Year's Day is considered very important and great care is taken to ensure that they be happy, wealthy and of high status.

The Tet festival continues for 7 days, with special events and commemorations for each day. A seasonal favourite is *banh chung*, which is sticky rice, yellow beans, pig fat and spices wrapped in leaves and boiled for half a day.

Visitors to Vietnam around Tet should take into account that flights into, out of and around the country are likely to be booked solid and accommodation impossible to find.

5th day of the 3rd month

Holiday of the Dead (Thanh Minh) People pay solemn visits to graves of deceased relatives – specially tidied up a few days before – and make offerings of food, flowers, joss sticks and votive papers.

8th day of the 4th month

Buddha's Birth, Enlightenment & Death This day is celebrated at pagodas and temples which, like many private homes, are festooned with lanterns. Processions are held in the evening.

5th day of the 5th month

Summer Solstice Day (Doan Ngu) Offerings are made to spirits, ghosts and the God of Death to ward off epidemics. Human effigies are burned to satisfy the requirements of the God of Death for souls to staff his army.

15th day of the 7th month

Wandering Souls Day (Trung Nguyen) This is the second largest festival of the year. Offerings of food and gifts are made in homes and pagodas for the wandering souls of the forgotten dead.

15th day of the 8th month

Mid-Autumn Festival (Trung Thu) This festival is celebrated with moon cakes of sticky rice filled with such things as lotus seeds, watermelon seeds, peanuts, the yolks of duck eggs, raisins and sugar. Colourful lanterns in the form of boats, unicorns, dragons, lobsters, carp, hares, toads, etc are carried by children in an evening procession accompanied by drums and cymbals.

28th day of the 9th month

Confucius' Birthday

December

Christmas (25th)This is celebrated in festively decorated Catholic and Protestant churches with special masses and services.

Secular Holidays

The following secular holidays are listed according to the Western solar calendar:

February

Anniversary of the Founding of the Vietnamese Communist Party (3rd) The Vietnamese Communist Party was founded on this date in 1930.

April

Liberation Day (3rd) The date on which Saigon surrendered is commemorated nationwide as Liberation Day. Many cities and provinces also commemorate the anniversary of the date in March or April of 1975 on which they were 'liberated' by the North Vietnamese Army.

May

International Workers' Day (May Day) (1st)

This falls back to back with Liberation Day giving everyone a 2 day holiday.

Ho Chi Minh's Birthday (19th) Ho Chi Minh is said to have been born on this date in 1890 near Vinh, Nghe Tinh Province.

September

National Day This commemorates the promulgation in Hanoi of the Declaration of Independence of the Democratic Republic of Vietnam by Ho Chi Minh on 2 September 1945.

Anniversary of Ho Chi Minh's Death (3rd) Ho Chi Minh actually died on 2 September 1969, but officials recently admitted that they reported his date of death as 3 September so it would not coincide with National Day.

LANGUAGE

The Vietnamese language (*kinh*) is a fusion of Mon-Khmer, Tai and Chinese elements. From the monotonic Mon-Khmer languages, Vietnamese derived a significant percentage of its basic words. From the Tai languages, it adopted certain grammatical elements and tonality. Chinese gave Vietnamese most of its philosophical, literary, technical and governmental vocabulary as well as its traditional writing system.

The most widely spoken Western languages in Vietnam are French, English and Russian. To a large extent, the divisions between who speaks each is generational. People in their 50s and older (who grew up during the colonial period) are much more likely to understand some French than southerners of the following generation, for whom English was indispensable for professional and commercial contacts with the Americans. Some southern men – former combat interpreters – speak a peculiar form of English peppered with all sorts of Texasisms and pronounced with a perceptible drawl. Apparently, they mistook the twangy tones of some American officer from El Paso or Dallas as standard English and diligently learned every nuance.

Since reunification, the teaching of Russian has been stressed all over the country.

Writing

For centuries, the Vietnamese language was written in standard Chinese characters (*chu nho*). Around the 13th century, the Vietnamese devised their own system of writing (*chu nom* or just *nom*), which was derived by combining Chinese characters or using them for their phonetic significance only. Both writing systems were used simultaneously until the 20th century: official business and scholarship was conducted in *chu nho* while *chu nom* was used for popular literature.

The Latin-based *quoc ngu* script, in wide use since WW I, was developed in the 17th century by Alexandre de Rhodes, a brilliant French Jesuit scholar who first preached in Vietnamese only 6 months after arriving in the country in 1627. By replacing *nom* characters with *quoc ngu*, Rhodes facilitated the propagation of the gospel to a wide audience. The use of *quoc ngu* served to undermine the position of mandarin officials, whose power was based on traditional scholarship written in *chu nho* and *chu nom* and largely inaccessible to the masses.

Pronunciation & Tones

Most of the names of the letters of the *quoc ngu* alphabet are pronounced as are the letters of the French alphabet. Dictionaries are alphabetised as in English except that each vowel/tone combination is treated as a different letter. The consonants of the Romanised Vietnamese alphabet are pronounced more-or-less as they are in English with a few exceptions.

c	Like a 'K' but with no aspiration.
đ	With a crossbar; like a hard 'D'.
d	Without a crossbar; like a 'Z' in the north and a 'Y' in the south.
gi-	Like a 'Z' in the north and a 'Y' in the south.
kh-	Like '-ch' in the German *buch*.
ng-	Like the '-ng a-' in 'long ago'.
nh-.	Like the Spanish 'Ñ' (as in *mañana*)
ph-	Like an 'F'.
r	Like 'Z' in the north and 'R' in the south.
s	Like an 'S' in the north and 'Sh' in the south.
tr-	Like 'Ch-' in the north and 'Tr-' in the south.
th-	Like a strongly aspirated 'T'.
x	Like an 'S'.
-ch	Like a 'K'.
-ng	Like '-ng' in 'long' but with the lips closed.
-nh	Like '-ng' in 'sing'.

The hardest part of studying Vietnamese for Westerners is learning to differentiate between the tones. Each of the six tones in Vietnamese is represented by a different diacritical mark. Thus, every syllable in Vietnamese can be pronounced six different ways. Depending on the tones, the word *ma* can be read to mean phantom, but, mother, rice seedling, tomb or horse. *Ga* can mean railroad station and chicken as well several other things.

Grammar

Vietnamese grammar is fairly straightforward, with a wide variety of sentence structures possible. The numbers and genders of nouns are generally not explicit nor are the tenses and moods of verbs. Instead, tool words (such as *cua*, which means 'belong to') and classifiers are used to show a word's relationship to its neighbours. Verbs are turned into nouns by adding *su*.

Questions are asked in the negative, as with *n'est-ce pas?* in French. When the Vietnamese ask 'Is it OK?' they say 'It is OK, is it not?' The answer 'no' means 'Not OK it is not,' which is the double-negative form of 'Yes, it is OK'. The answer 'yes', on the other hand, means 'Yes, it is not OK' or as we would say in English 'No, it is not OK.' The result is that when negative questions ('It's not OK, is it?') are posed to Vietnamese, great confusion often results.

Pronouns

he
  cậu ấy or *anh ấy*
I
  tôi
she
  cô ấy

they
họ

we
chúng tôi

you (to an older man/men)
(các) ông

you (to an older woman/women)
(các) bà

you (to a man/men) of your own age
(các) anh

you (to a woman (women) of your own age)
(các) cô

Some Useful Words & Phrases

Do you understand?
(Insert appropriate form of you) *có hiểu không?*

I like...
Tôi thích...

I don't like...
Tôi không thích...

I don't understand.
Tôi không hiểu.

I want (+ verb or noun)...
Tôi muốn ...

I don't want...
Tôi không muốn....

I need (+ verb or noun)...
Tôi cần ...

boulevard
đại lộ (precedes the name)

change money
đổi tiền

come
tới

fast
nhanh (in the north), *mau* (in the south)

give
cho

hotel
khách sạn

man
nam

office
văn phòng

Overseas Vietnamese
Việt Kiều

post office
bưu điện

restaurant
nhà hàng

slow
chậm

street
đường, phố (precedes the name)

telephone
điện thoại (abbreviated *DT*)

tourism
du lịch (pronounced 'zoo lick'/'you lick')

understand
hiểu

water
nước

woman
nữ

Greetings & Civilities

Can you speak...?
(Insert appropriate form of you) *có nói tiếng...được không?*

Don't worry, it doesn't matter.
Không sao đâo,đừng.

I am not a Russian.
Tôi không phải là người Liên Xô. or Không phải Liên Xô.

I can't.
Tôi không thể.

I can speak a little Vietnamese.
Tôi có thể nói một ít tiếng Việt.

I come from...
Tôi đến từ...

My name is...
Tên tôi là...

Thank you very much.
Cám ởn rất nhiều.

What country do you come from?
(Insert appropriate form of you) *là người gì*

I am an American.
Tôi là người Mỹ. (*Mỹ* (American) is pronounced as if followed by a question mark).

I am an Australian.
Tôi là người Úc.

I am a(n)...
Tôi là người (plus the name of a country).

Australia
Úc Đại Lợi, or *Oxtorelia* or *O Xtray Li A*

Austria
Áo

Belgium
Bỉ

Brazil
Ba Tây, Bra Din or Bra Xin

California
Ca Li

Cambodia
Cam Pu Chia or Cam Bốt

Canada
Canada or Gia Ná Đại

China
Trung Hoa or Trung Quốc

Denmark
Đan Mạch

Egypt
Ai Cập

England
Anh

Finland
Phần Lan

France
Pháp

Germany
Đức

Greece
Hi Lạp or Hy Lạp

Hong Kong
Hương Cảng or Hồng Công

India
Ấn-Độ

Indonesia
Indonexia

Ireland
Aĭ Nhĭ Lan, Airo Lan Ai Len

Israel
Do Thái or Ixraen

Italy
Ý Đại Lợi or Italia

Japan
Nhật Bản

Korea
Triều Tiên or Đại Hàn

Laos
Lào

Malaysia
Malayxia or Mả Lai Á

Myanmar (Burma)
Miến Điện

Netherlands
Hòa Lan or Mà Lan

New Zealand
Tân Tây Lan or Niu Dilan

Nigeria
Nigieria

Norway
Nauy

Philippines
Phi Luật Tân or Philippin

Portugal
Bồ Đào Nha

Singapore
Tân Gia Ba, Xingapua or Xin Ga Po

South Africa
Nam Phi

Soviet Union
Liên Xô

Spain
Tây Ban Nha

Sri Lanka
Sri Lan Ca

Sweden
Thụy Điền

Switzerland
Thụy Sỹ

Thailand
Thái Lan

United States
Hoa Kỳ

What is your name?
Tên (insert appropriate form of you) là gì?

Where (in Vietnam) do you come from?
(Insert appropriate form of you) từ đâu đến?

excuse me (often used before questions)
xin lỗi.

no
không

thank you
cám ơn (ask someone to help you get the tones right)

yes
phải

Accommodation

Where is there a (cheap) hotel?
Xin lỗi, ở đâu có khách sạn (rẻtiền)?

How much does a room cost?
Giá một phòng bao nhiêu?

I would like an inexpensive room.
Tôi thích một phòng loại rẻ.
I would like a single/double/triple room.
Tôi muốn một phòng chiếc/đôi/ba giường.
Please change the sheets.
Xin lỗi, làm ón thay ra trải giường.
What is the price of your cheapest room?
Xin lỗi, phòng rẻ nhất ở đây tốn bao nhiêu?
air-conditioning
máy lạnh
bathroom
nhà tắm
bed
giường
blanket
chăn in the north and *mền* in the south
cold water
nước lạnh
dormitory accommodation
nhà trọ
fan
quạt máy
hotel
khách sạn (Chinese construct)
hotel or guest house
nhà khách (Vietnamese construct)
hot water
nước lạnh
laundry
giặt quần áo
reception
riếp tân
room
phòng
1st class room
phòng hang nhất
2nd class room
phòng hang nhì
mattress
nệm
mosquito net
mùng
sheet
ra trãi giường
shower
bông sen
sleeping mat
chiếu

toilet
nhà vệ sinh
towel
khăn tắm

Getting Around

What time does the first bus depart?
Chuyến xe buýt sớm nhất sẽ chạy lúc mấy giờ?
What time does the last bus depart?
Xin lỗi mấy giờ chuyến xe buýt cuối cùng sẽ rời bến?
How many km is it to...
...cách xa đây bao nhiêu kilomet?
How many hours does the journey take?
Chuyến viễn du nầy sẽ kéo dài bao nhiêu giờ?
How much does it cost to go to...
Tốn bao nhiêu tiền để đi....
I need to leave at (5) o'clock tomorrow morning.
Tôi phải đi lúc (năm) giờ sáng mai.
I want to pay in dong.
Tôi muốn trả bằng tiền Việt Nam.
I would like to go to...
Tôi muốn đi.....
What time does it arrive?
Xe sẽ đến lúc mấy giờ?
What time does it depart?
Xe sẽ chạy lúc mấy giờ?
bus
xe buýt
bus station
bến xe
cyclo (pedicab)
xe xích lô
hire an automobile
mướn xe hói
go
đi
railroad station
ga xa lứa
receipt
biên lai
sleeping berth
giường ngủ
ticket counter
quày bán vé
timetable
bảng giờ giấc

train
xe lửa

went or has gone
đã đi

will go
sẽ đi

In the Country

bridge
cầu

east
đông

highway
xa lộ

island
hòn đảo

mountain
núi

National Highway 1
Quốc Lộ 1

north
bắc

river
sông

south
nam

square (in a city)
công trường

west
tây

Shopping

Do you have...?
(Insert appropriate form of you) *có.....?*

Don't have.
không có

How much is this?
Xin lỗi, cái nầy bao nhiêu tiền?

What do you call this in Vietnamese?
Xin lỗi, cái nầy tiếng Việt kêu là gì?

What is this?
Xin lỗi, cái nầy bảo là gì?

buy
mua

expensive
đắt tiền

inexpensive, cheap
rẻ tiền

market
chợ

really expensive
rất đắt tiền

sell
bán

Colours

black
đen

blue
xanh da trời

brown
nâu

a little
một ít

green
xanh lá cây

red
đỏ

white
trắng

yellow
vàng

Medical Emergencies

hospital
bệnh viện

pharmacy
nhà thuốc

doctor
bác sĩ

dentist
nha sĩ

I need a doctor.
Tôi cần gặp bác sĩ.

Time & Dates

Monday
thứ hai

Tuesday
thứ ba

Wednesday
thứ tư

Thursday
thứ năm

Friday
thú sáu

Saturday
thứ bảy

Sunday		6	sáu
chủ nhật		7	bảy
January		8	tám
tháng giêng		9	chín
February		10	mười or chục
tháng hai		11	mười một
March		19	mười chín
tháng ba		20	hai mươi
April		21	hai mươi mốt
tháng tư		30	ba mươi
May		90	chín mươi
tháng năm		100	một trăm
June		200	hai trăm
tháng sáu		900	chín trăm
July		1000	một nghìn
tháng bảy		10,000	mười nghìn
August		100,000	trăm nghìn
tháng tám		1 million	một triệu
September			
tháng chín			
October			

From three upwards, the cardinal and ordinal numbers are the same.

October
tháng mười
November
tháng mười một
December
tháng mười hai
evening
chiều
month
tháng (as in 30 Thang 4 St, which means 30 April St)
morning
sáng
now
bây giờ
today
hôm nay
tomorrow
ngày mai
yesterday
hôm qua

Numbers

first	nhất
second	nhì
1	một
2	hai
3	ba
4	bốn
5	năm

Books for Language Study

A number of pocket English-Vietnamese (Anh-Viet) and Vietnamese-English (Viet-Anh) dictionaries (tu dien) have been published in Vietnam over the years. Used copies may be available in the book shops listed in the text. Among the best scholarly dictionaries are the 992 page Tu Dien Viet-Anh (Vietnamese-English Dictionary) (Hanoi University Press (Truong Dai Hoc Tong Hop Ha Noi Xuat Ban), Hanoi, 1986), which costs only 8000d; and the massive 1960 page English-Vietnamese Tu Dien Anh-Viet (Nha Xuat Ban Khoa Hoc Xa Hoi, Hanoi, 1975), which sells for 28,000d. It is worth taking a look at Nguyen Dinh Hoa's Essential English-Vietnamese Dictionary (Charles E Tuttle Co, Rutland, Vermont, and Tokyo, Japan, 1983) and Essential Vietnamese-English Dictionary (Charles E Tuttle Co, Rutland, Vermont, and Tokyo, Japan, 1966) before you go.

There are several fairly useful phrase books around which you may be able to pick up at Asia Books in Bangkok or in Vietnam. Speak Vietnamese (Hay Noi Tieng Viet; Foreign Languages Publishing House, Hanoi, 1982) gives phrases in Vietnamese,

English, French and Russian and might prove useful in dealing with Soviets and French people as well as the locals. *Say it in Vietnamese* (Charles E Tuttle Co, Rutland, Vermont, and Tokyo, Japan, 1966) by Nguyen Dinh Hoa includes such phrases – sure to generate goodwill – as 'Raise your hands!' and 'Obey or I'll fire!' But aside from such signs of the times during which it was published, it has solid information on pronunciation as well as useful word lists. A larger, updated version is *Hoa's Vietnamese Phrase Book* by Nguyen Dinh Hoa (Charles E Tuttle Co, Rutland, Vermont, and Tokyo, Japan).

A two volume set for serious students of Vietnamese, there's *Introductory Vietnamese* and *An Intermediate Vietnamese Reader* (South-East Asia Program, Cornell University, Ithaca, New York, 1972) by Robert M Quinn. Two other works still available are *Speak Vietnamese* and *Read Vietnamese* by Nguyen Dinh Hoa (Charles E Tuttle Co, Rutland, Vermont, and Tokyo, Japan, 1966). All four books are available in the USA through Schoenhof's Foreign Books (tel (617) 547-8855) at 76A Mount Auburn St in Cambridge, Massachusetts 02138.

Facts for the Visitor

VISAS & TRAVEL RESTRICTIONS

While more creativity and perseverance are necessary to travel to Vietnam than to non-socialist countries in the region, arranging the necessary paperwork is not all that daunting. And as Vietnamese officialdom gets more used to 'capitalist tourists' exploring the country on their own – and leaving behind their hard currency – getting into Vietnam will probably become easier.

These days, by far the best place to get Vietnamese visas is Bangkok. Several types of visas are available: tourist, business, long-term multiple-entry business, journalist, official and family-visit. Single-entry visas cost 350B, multiple-entry visas 700B. Vietnamese embassies around the world may issue visas if you give them enough lead time, but often they'll simply have you pick up your visa in Bangkok.

Tourist Visas

Officially, tourist visas are available only to participants in organised tour groups, which are sold by various travel agents in Thailand and elsewhere but actually run by Vietnam Tourism (the state tourism authority) or Saigon Tourist (Ho Chi Minh City's tourism authority). Tourist visas are stamped 'tourist' in big red letters, and the Immigration Police seem to have orders to treat bearers of such visas more restrictively than other foreigners.

If you book a tour in Bangkok, agents with good connections can procure a tourist visa – issued on a separate piece of paper so they don't even need to take your passport – within 24 hours if necessary. Apparently you can request that your tourist visa be stamped right in your passport, but rumour has it that the presence of a Vietnamese visa in your passport might cause hassles with US consular authorities when you go to request permission to visit the USA.

It may also be possible to procure a tourist visa in Bangkok without actually booking a tour. The going rate for a 7-day tourist visa is about US$100. Outrageous, yes, but even with the plane ticket added in, it comes out quite a bit less than the cheapest package tour. Tourist visas are usually good for 3 days to 1 week, though the word on the streets has it that a 1-month visa is available to anyone willing to pay the right people for it.

For a while, the Vietnamese Embassy in Vientiane was giving out tourist visas with no hassles, but this policy may change.

For more information on tours to Vietnam, see the Tours section in this chapter.

Other Visas

Business visas are a bit more complicated. But first the good news: such visas are usually valid for longer periods of time than tourist visas and allow greater freedom of movement inside Vietnam. The lucky few get multiple-entry visas good for 3 or even 6 months. Once all the necessary documents are in order, actually stamping the visa in your passport is very quick – you bring it to the embassy in Bangkok in the morning and get it back at about 3 pm.

Before issuing a business visa, the embassy must have a letter, fax, telex or telegram of invitation from some official body in Vietnam. Because communications with Vietnam are often difficult, letting your contacts know that you are waiting for an invitation can be a hit-or-miss proposition. And once the right people know of your situation, it can take even more time for the invitation to arrive in Bangkok. Many busy businesspeople end up spending frustrating days or even weeks stranded in Thailand because of foul-ups with their documents. Complaining to consular officials is of limited efficacy because they see their role as issuing visas, not helping you procure official invitations.

Sometimes, official invitations from Vietnamese companies or ministries telexed to the Bangkok Embassy are mislaid. You might do better to have your invitation sent to you by fax or telex somewhere else in the city (such as your hotel or office).

If you need to get in touch with your contacts in Vietnam and can't find someone to hand-carry a letter in, it is possible to telephone or fax Vietnam from Bangkok for 195B per 3 minutes. Sending a telex costs 65B per minute. It is not possible to place person-to-person calls to Vietnam, but phone calls from abroad are treated with sufficient seriousness that chances are messages will be passed on – just make sure they know where you're calling from. In any case, after a few calls you should be able to track down your contact, and nothing beats actually talking to someone to get the ball rolling. Mail service between Thailand and Vietnam is slow and unreliable.

If you can't seem to confirm that things are moving on your visa, it might be worthwhile to consider going in on a tourist visa and working things out from Saigon or Hanoi. However, there may later be a problem changing your visa status without leaving the country and re-entering.

The procedure for getting journalist, official and family-visit visas is similar to that for business visas except that the embassy may also need ministerial authorisation from Hanoi. Journalists are often hosted by either the Ministry of Information or the Foreign Ministry. To a certain degree, these ministries compete with each other for guests because of the tidy profit – in US dollars, of course – they make from charging you for a car, driver, guide, etc.

Family-visit visas have been taking longer recently, and some Overseas Vietnamese have had to wait in Bangkok a full month for their request to be approved.

Other Restrictions

Registration For people on organised tours, the paperwork is all taken care of. That's part of what they pay for. But foreigners travelling independently must take care of registration with the police and internal travel permits themselves. They neglect to do so at their peril, despite the fact that no one is likely to explain what needs to be done or how to go about it.

All foreigners must register with the Immigration Police within 2 days of their arrival in Vietnam. Whereas visas (issued by the Foreign Ministry) get you into Vietnam, registration means that you have the permission of the Immigration Police (an arm of the powerful Interior Ministry) to stay wherever you are. For tourists, this is usually taken care of through Vietnam Tourism or, in Hanoi, TOSERCO. You must re-register each time you enter the country (such as after a visit to Phnom Penh).

When individual travellers arrive somewhere they intend to stay for more than 48 hours, they are officially required to register with the local police. Hotels are required to register their guests – foreign and domestic – with the police, which is why they collect tourists' passports and locals' identity papers. Travellers not staying at a hotel might consider registering themselves, especially since it is unlikely that they have escaped police notice.

For travellers who have booked a tour with Vietnam Tourism and are travelling around independently before it begins, having a written itinerary from Vietnam Tourism with you may prove helpful in convincing provincial police officials that the proper people know about you and what you are doing.

Internal Travel Permits Foreigners must also have internal travel permits (*giay phep di lai*) to go anywhere outside the city in which they registered with the Immigration Police. Internal travel permits are issued by the Immigration Police in Saigon and Hanoi and through TOSERCO in Hanoi. In general, permits are not required for day trips but are necessary if you want to spend the night somewhere. When you get where you are going you may also need to register with the police authorities, though this is usually taken care of by the hotel.

The Interior Ministry in Hanoi keeps changing its policies on issuing travel permits to individual travellers, but they seem to prefer to try out more liberal guidelines in Hanoi, where they can keep an eye on things. Bearers of visas stamped 'tourist' seem to have a much harder time getting permission to go where they want than, say, businesspeople.

Internal travel permits are issued (or often refused) by the Immigration Police in Saigon and Hanoi and TOSERCO in Hanoi for travel to certain destinations during a specific period of time. It is difficult to predict which applications will be approved, but in Saigon reasonable requests include permits to Cantho, Dalat, Danang, Hué, Mytho, Nha Trang, Phan Rang-Thap Cham, Tay Ninh and Vung Tau.

In Hanoi, permits might be issued for Do Son, Dien Bien Phu, Haiphong (at least for transit), Halong Bay, Hoa Binh, Kim Son (Phat Diem), Mai Chau, Sam Son, Tam Dao and Viet Tri. Lang Son and Cao Bang are closed at present. As provinces clamour for tourist dollars, more parts of the country may be opened up to tourism.

Visitors caught violating the internal travel permit regulations have been fined US$50 to US$120 and sent back to Hanoi or Saigon. One fellow was asked to pay US$280 for a government car to drive him from Nha Trang back to Saigon, a demand he managed to negotiate his way out of.

Port of Departure Be aware that Vietnamese visas specify from which point(s) – usually Ho Chi Minh City's Tan Son Nhut Airport or Hanoi's Noi Bai Airport – you are permitted to leave the country. If you intend to exit from someplace not listed on your visa (such as to Cambodia via Moc Bai), make sure to have the Saigon or Hanoi office of the Foreign Ministry add the additional border crossing to your visa.

Lost Passport If you are a national of a country without diplomatic relations with Vietnam and lose your passport while in the country the situation is not hopeless. If the Immigration Police are unable to locate the passport, you will be issued documents allowing you to leave the country. You may be allowed to stay in Vietnam until your visa (the validity of which is on record with the police) expires.

Trading with the Enemy Act The war has been over for more than 15 years, but the US Treasury Department still vigorously enforces the provisions of the Foreign Assets Control Regulations, better known as the Trading with the Enemy Act. According to the Treasury Department, the Act:

prohibits persons subject to US jurisdiction from performing any unlicensed transaction in which Vietnam, Cambodia, North Korea or nationals thereof have an interest.

However, section 500.563 of the regulations contains a general licence...

for individuals to travel to and from Vietnam and to pay for living expenses and purchase goods for personal consumption while there. The general licence does *not* permit purchases of goods or services unrelated to travel, such as non-emergency medical treatment.

The general licence is, 'in purpose and effect, an authorisation directed to individuals, authorising their individual travel-related transactions'. It...

does not extend to the arrangement, promotion or facilitation of group travel to Vietnam by US travel service providers nor does it extend to the use of credit cards in Vietnam or other extensions of credit to Vietnam. In addition, the general license authorises the purchase and importation into the US as accompanied baggage of merchandise in non-commercial quantities valued at up to US$100 for personal use only. This authorisation can be used once every 6 months. Please note that the regulations prohibit business dealings with Vietnam and Vietnamese nationals. Therefore, business dealings with Vietnam Airlines are prohibited.

For more information, contact the Office of Foreign Assets Control, Treasury Department, Washington, DC 20220 (tel (202) 376-0392).

A (DR)
B (LG)
C (DR)
D (LG)
E (LG)
F (LG)

Visa Extensions

Getting your tourist visa extended is not necessarily a difficult process, but success depends in part on knowing how the system works. Like everything else in Vietnam these days, visa regulations are in a state of flux and may change overnight.

Vietnam Tourism representatives will tell you that visa extensions are given only to people who book another tour with them. Officials of the Immigration Police will say that they need a letter of recommendation from Vietnam Tourism in order to issue a visa extension. Back at Vietnam Tourism, the officials will tell you that they cannot write such a letter for you if you do not book a tour. Catch 22.

One way to get a bit of leverage with the immigration authorities is to check with Vietnam Airlines about available flights out of the country before trying to extend your visa. Often, international flights from Saigon and Hanoi are booked out many days in advance. If you can't get a flight out of the country when your visa expires, they won't have much choice but to let you stay until the next available flight. If you are in Hanoi, it might help to get a recommendation letter from your embassy – if you have one.

Rumour has it that bureaucratic miracles can be performed with a bit of palm-greasing, but such manoeuvres can be risky indeed for amateurs.

For visa extensions of more than a few days, you may have no choice but to book another tour with Vietnam Tourism. One option is to arrange for a tour beginning a week or 10 days after the expiration of your visa, time you can use to travel on your own.

Don't count on being able to extend your visa anywhere other than in Saigon and Hanoi. Immigration officials in the provinces are much less likely to risk their jobs by trying something new than are officials in the big cities, who have a better sense of which way the wind is blowing.

Overseas Embassies

Vietnamese embassies around the world include the following:

Afghanistan
Number 27 Peace St, Shar-i-Nua, Kabul (tel (93) 23671)

Albania
Rruga Lek Dukagjini, Tirana (tel 25-56)

Algeria
30 Rue de Chenoua, Hydra, Algiers (telex 52147)

Australia
6 Timbarra Crescent, O'Malley, ACT 2603 (tel (062) 866059; telex 62756)

Bulgaria
Ilia Petrov St 1, Sofia (tel 72.08.79)

Burma (Myanmar)
Komin Kochin Rd, Rangoon (tel (01) 50631)

Cambodia
The consular section is opposite 749 Achar Mean Boulevard, Phnom Penh (tel 2.3142). It is open from 7.30 to 11 am and 2 to 5 pm except Saturday afternoon, Sundays and Vietnamese and Cambodian holidays. Visas usually take 2 days.

China
32 Guang Hua Lu St, Jian Guo Men Wai, Beijing

Congo
BP 988, Brazzaville (tel 81-2621)

Cuba
Avenida 5a, Numero 1802, Miramar, Havana (tel 29-6262)

Czechoslovakia
Holeçvkova 6, 125 55 Prague (tel (2) 536127)

Egypt
27 Sharia Ahmad Hishmat, Zamalek, Cairo (tel (02) 340-2401)

Federal Rebublic of Germany
Konstantinstr. 37, 5300 Bonn 2 (tel (0228) 357022; telex 8861122)

France
62 Rue de Boileau, 75016 Paris (tel 45.24.50.63)

Guinea
BP 551, Conakry

Hungary
Benczúru 18, Budapest VI (tel 429-943)

India
35 Prithviraj Rd, New Delhi 110011 (tel (11) 619200)

Indonesia
Jalan Teuku Umiar 25, Jakarta (tel (021) 347325)

Iraq
29/611 Hay al-Andalus, Baghdad (tel 551-1388)

Italy
Piazza Barberini 12, 00187 Rome (tel (06) 475-4098; telex 610121)

Japan
50-11 Moto Yoyogi-Cho, Shibuya-ku, Tokyo 151 (tel (3) 466-3311)

Laos
  Thanon That Luang (tel 5578)
Libya
  Sharia Talha Ben Abdullah, PO Box 587, Tripoli
  (tel 45753)
Madagascar
  Antananarivo (tel 27651)
Malaysia
  4 Pesiaran Stonor, Kuala Lumpur (tel (03) 248-
  4036)
Mexico
  Sierra Ventana 255, 11000 Mexico, DF (tel 540-
  1612/32)
Mongolia
  Ulan Bator (tel 249)
Mozambique
  Avenida Julius Nyerere 1555, CP 1150, Maputo
  (tel 741948)
Nicaragua
  Zona Residencial Planetarium, Paseo Saturno,
  Casa CS 10, esq Via Láctea, Managua, JR
Pakistan
  60 Embassy Rd, Ramna 6/3, Islamabad
Philippines
  554 Vito Cruz, Malate, Metro Manila (tel (02)
  500364)
Poland
  Kawalerii 5, 00-488 Warsaw (tel 413369)
Romania
  Str Gr Alexandrescu 86, Bucharest
Sweden
  Örby Slottsväg 26, 125 36 Älvsjö (tel (8) 86-12-
  18; telex 10332)
Syria
  9 Avenue Malki, Damascus (tel 335008)
Tanzania
  9 Ocean Rd, PO Box 2194, Dar-es-Salaam
Thailand
  83/1 Wireless Rd, Bangkok (tel (02) 251-
  7201/2/3, 251-5836). The visa section is open
  weekdays 8.30 to 11.30 am and 1 to 4 pm.
UK
  12-14 Victoria Rd, London W8 5RD (tel 937-
  1912, 937-8564, 937-1912; telex 887361).
USA
  Vietnamese Mission to the United Nations, 20
  Waterside Plaza (lobby), New York, NY 10010
  (tel (212) 685-8001, 679-3779). For non-tourist
  visas, they can sometimes cable ahead to
  Bangkok so your visa will be ready when you get
  there.
USSR
  Bolshaya Pirogovskaya ul 13, Moscow (tel (095)
  247-02-12)
Yugoslavia
  Topcviderski Venac 4, Belgrade (tel 661466;
  telex 11292)

TOURS

The simplest way to get into Vietnam is to purchase a package tour in Bangkok. The visa issued along with your tour will be good for exactly the number of days your tour lasts, but once in Vietnam it is usually possible to get an extension.

Before booking a tour with the intention of extending your visa once you get there, try to find out from other travellers whether visa extensions have recently been easier in Hanoi or Saigon. The tourism policies of the Interior and Foreign Ministries keep changing, but arriving in either city during a period of restriction could make for a very short visit indeed. In general, bureaucrats in Hanoi are temperamentally more rigid, but they are also closer to the corridors of power and feel more comfortable implementing new (and hopefully more liberal) government policies.

Package tours are sold by a variety of agencies in Bangkok and elsewhere, but in Vietnam all the tours, which usually follow one of a dozen or so set itineraries, are run by the omnipresent government tourism authorities, Vietnam Tourism and Saigon Tourist. The tours, which include round-trip airfare, are not a total rip-off given what you get (tourist-class accommodation, food, transport, a guide, etc) but then again they're not inexpensive: they range in price from about US$480 for a 3-day Saigon 'shopping tour' to over US$1000 for a week-long trip that includes flying all around the country. Doing the same things on your own can cost as little as US$7 a day (not including airfare).

Most agencies impose a surcharge for tours run for less than *two* people. In other words, a small group can purchase a virtually private tour. If you deal with a travel agent who deals directly with Vietnam, it should be possible to arrange for your itinerary to deviate significantly from the usual packages, but make sure to get any special arrangements *in writing* and to confirm them as soon as you arrive in Vietnam.

Companies in Bangkok selling their own versions of the standard tours often farm out the sale of their offerings to other travel agencies. The price may be pretty much the same if you purchase a tour on Khao San Rd rather than at one of the places listed in this section (most of which are in the vicinity of the Vietnamese Embassy), but you'll be dealing with people less knowledgeable about the ins and outs of travel to Vietnam. And arranging the tour and visa may take much longer – up to a week rather than a day or two.

As of early 1989, tours to Vietnam are no longer available in the USA because of renewed US Treasury Department enforcement of the Trading with the Enemy Act. As a result of the Trading with the Enemy Act, Orbitours (Australia) conducts a lot of US business.

Agencies in Bangkok offering tours to Vietnam include:

Air People Tour & Travel Co Ltd
2nd Floor, Regent House Bldg, 183 Rajdamri Rd, Bangkok 10500 (tel 254-3921/2/3/4/5; telex 82419 APT TH; fax (662) 255-3750)

Diethelm Travel
Kian Gwan Building II, 140/1 Wireless Rd, Bangkok 10500 (tel 255-9150/60/70; telex 81183, 21763, 22700, 22701 DIETRAV TH; fax (662) 256-0248/9). Diethelm tends to be much more expensive than other agencies.

Exotissimo Travel (Bolsa Travelmart)
21/17 Sukhumvit Soi 4, Bangkok 10110 (tel 253-5240/1, 255-2747; telex 20479 ASIAN TH; fax 254-7683)

Lam Son International Ltd
23/1 Sukhumvit Soi 4 (Soi Nana Tai), Bangkok 10110 (tel 255-6692/3/4/5, 252-2340; fax 255-8859)

Namthai Travel
Bangkok (tel 215-9003/10, 215-7339; telex 22663 NAMTHAI TH; fax (662) 215-6240)

Red Carpet Service & Tour
459 New Rama 6 Rd, Phayathai, Bangkok 10400 (tel 215-9951, 215-3331; fax (662) 215-3331)

Thaninee Trading Company
1131/343 Terddumri Rd, Dusit, Bangkok 10300 (tel 243-1794, 243-2601, 243-3245; telex 87411 TANINEE TH; fax (662) 243-0676)

Viet Tour Holidays (The Crescendo Co Ltd)
1717 Lard-Prao Rd, Samsennok, Huay-Kwang, Bangkok 10310 (tel 511-3272; telex ALLENTR 84561 TH; fax 511-3357)

Vikamla Tours (same office as Lam Son International)

Room 401, Nana Condo, 23/11 Sukhumvit Soi 4 (Soi Nana Tai), Bangkok 10110 (tel 252-2340, 255-8859; telex 22586 VIKAMLA TH

Agencies in Australia and New Zealand offering tours to Vietnam include:

Australia
Orbitours, Suite 7, 7th Floor, Dymock's Bldg, 428 George St, Sydney, 2000 (tel (02) 221-7322, fax (02) 221-745) From the USA (tel 1-800-235-5895); from Canada (tel 1-800-665-0809); and from the UK (tel 0800-89-2006).

New Zealand
Destinations, 2nd Floor, Premier Bldg, 4 Durham St, Auckland (tel(09) 390-464)

In North America you might try contacting:

California
Budgetours International, 8907 Westminster Ave, Garden Grove, CA 92644 (tel (714) 221-6539, 637-8229, 895-2528)
Tour Connections, 8907 Westminster Ave, Garden Grove, CA 92644 (tel (213) 465-7315, (714) 895-2839)

New York
Mekong Travel, 151 First Ave, Suite 172, New York, NY 10003 (tel (212) 420-1586)

Pennsylvania
US-Indochina Reconciliation Project, 5808 Green St, Philadelphia, PA 19144 (tel (215) 848-4200)

Quebec
Club Voyages Berri, 1650 Berri, Suite 8, Montreal, Quebec H2L 4E6 (tel (514) 982-6168/9; telex 05561074; fax (514) 982-0820)

New Asia Tours (Tour Nouvelle Asie), 1063 Blvd St Laurent, Montreal, Quebec H2Z 1J6 (tel (514) 874-0266; telex 3959341 (Asia); fax (514) 874-0251)
Que Viet Tours, 1063 Blvd St Laurent, Montreal, Quebec H2Z 1J6; tel (514) 393-3211; telex 4959321 (Asia); fax (514) 874-0251)

In Europe agencies booking tours to Vietnam include:

Austria
View Travel, Sankt Voitgasse 9, A-1130 Vienna (tel (222) 821-8532)

France
Hit Voyages, 21 Rue des Bernardins, 75005 Paris (tel 43 54 17 17)
Pacific Holidays, 34 Ave de General Leclerc,

75014 Paris (tel 45 41 52 58)
International Tourisme, 26 Blvd St Marcel,
75005 Paris (tel 45 87 07 70)

Germany
Indoculture Tours (Indoculture Reisedienst
GmbH), Bismarckplatz 1 D-7000 Stuttgart 1 (tel
0711/61 7057-58)
Saratours, Sallstr 21 D-3000, Hannover 1 (tel
0511-282353)

Switzerland
Exotissimo, 8 Ave du Mail, 1205 Geneva (tel
022-81.21.66; telex 421358 EXOT CH; fax 022-
81 21 71)
Artou, 8 Rue de Rive, 1204 Geneva
Nayak, Steinengrabes 42, CH-4001 Basel (tel
061-224343)

UK
Regent Holidays (UK) Ltd, 13 Small St, Bristol
BS 1 1DE (tel (0272) 211711, fax (0272) 254866,
telex 444606 REGENTG)

In East Asia companies offering tours to
Vietnam include:

Hong Kong
Chu & Associates, Unit E, 5/F, 8 Thomson Rd,
Hong Kong (tel 5-278828/41)
VietnamTours & Trading Company, Room 302,
Loader Commercial Bldg, 54 Hillwood Rd, TST
(tel 3-682493, 3-676663)
Travel Services (HK) Ltd, Metropole Bldg, 57
Peking Rd, Tsim Tsa Tsui, Kowloon (tel 674127)
Phoenix Services Agency, Room B, 6/F, Milton
Mansion, 96 Nathan Rd, Kowloon (tel 7-227378,
telex 3167 PHNXHK)

Japan
Japan-Soviet Travel Service, 5th Floor,
Daihachi-Tanaka Bldg 5-1, Gobancho Chiyoda-
Ku, Tokyo (tel (03) 238-4101)
Sai Travel Service, 2F Suzuki Daini Bldg 4-12-4,
Shinbashi Minato-Ku, Tokyo

Philippines
Impex International, Suite 201, Centrum Bldg,
104 Perea St, Lagaspi Village, Makati (tel 813-
4865/66/67)

Tours Purchased in Vietnam

If you decide to book a tour while in Vietnam
(perhaps in order to get a visa extension),
you'll have the opportunity to design your
own itinerary for what may amount to a
private tour for you and your companions.
Seeing the country this way is almost like
individual travel except that you'll have to
decide where to go in advance and you'll be
accompanied by one or more guides and a

driver. Their presence may cause local
people to be reluctant to have contact with
you.

The cost of a tour booked with Vietnam
Tourism in Vietnam is about US$50 to
US$60 a day for one person (and less each
for two or more people because transport and
lodging costs can be shared). Students
receive a 15% student discount, which they
are more likely to get if they have an official-
looking letter from their university registrar
to show.

The price includes accommodation at a
tourist-class hotel (which costs at least
US$25 per night for a single anyway, though
hotels for domestic tourists cost a tenth of
that), a guide who will accompany you
everywhere, a local guide in each province
you visit, a driver and a car. Insist that your
guides are fluent in a language you know
well. The cost of the car is computed on a
per-km basis. At present, Vietnam Tourism
cars, usually new imports from Japan, are
billed at US$0.33 per km.

When you settle on your itinerary, make
sure to get a written copy from Vietnam
Tourism. If you later find that your guide
feels like deviating from what you paid for,

that piece of paper is your most effective leverage. If your guide asks for the itinerary, keep the original and give him or her a photocopy, as there have been reports of guides taking tourists' itineraries and then running the tour their way.

Visits by US Vietnam Veterans

A growing number of US veterans of the Vietnam War are deciding to visit Vietnam. Many psychologists who deal with the long-term effects of the war believe that 'going back' to Vietnam can help groups of veterans confront the root causes of post-traumatic stress disorder (PTSD). For more information on group trips to Vietnam by veterans (and other veterans' issues), contact:

The William Joiner Center
University of Massachusetts at Boston, Boston, MA 02125 (tel (617) 929-7865)
US-Indochina Reconciliation Project
5808 Greene St, Philadelphia, PA 19144 (tel (215) 848-4200; telex 254830 USIN UR; compuserve: 71001,714)

CUSTOMS

Until very recently, the Vietnamese customs service was run by mid-level bureaucrats who had received their managerial training in China. Their bureaucratic spirit lives on in the form of unpredictable hassles.

Tourists can bring an unlimited amount of foreign currency into Vietnam but they are required to declare it on their customs form upon arrival. Theoretically, when you leave the country you should have exchange receipts for all the foreign currency you have spent. In practice, though, the authorities rarely check.

When entering Vietnam, visitors must also declare all precious metals, jewellery, cameras, radios, tape players, blank video cassettes and unexposed film in their possession. When you leave the country, you may be asked to prove that you are taking these items out with you.

The import and export of dong and live animals is forbidden.

MONEY

US$1	=	6000d
UK£1	=	11,500d
A$1	=	5000d
Thai B1	=	235d

Currency

The currency of Vietnam is the dong (abbreviated by a 'd' following the amount), which is sometimes still called the piastre by old-timers. Banknotes in denominations of 20d, 50d, 100d, 200d, 500d, 1000d, 2000d, and 5000d are presently in circulation. There are no coins currently in use in Vietnam, though the dong used to be subdivided into 10 *hao* and 100 *xu*. All dong-denominated prices in this book are from a time when US$1 was worth about 4000d.

The foreign currency of choice in Vietnam is the US dollar. Gold is also used extensively, especially for major transactions such as the sale of homes. Travellers' cheques denominated in US dollars can be exchanged at a limited number of banks (and then only for dong) and are not accepted by hotels, restaurants, airlines, etc. Not even the Billabong Club at the Australian Embassy in Hanoi takes Australian dollars! Needless to say, the black market is interested only in US dollars cash.

Large-denomination bills are preferred on the black market, but an ample supply of ones, fives and tens is indispensable for tips, small expenses and to make change in dollar-denominated transactions (such as hotel bills). It is a good idea to check that the US dollar bills you bring to Vietnam do not have anything scribbled on them or they may be summarily rejected by uptight clerks.

Be sure to bring enough US dollars cash for your whole visit and to keep it safe (preferably in a money belt). Unless you borrow from a Westerner or get someone to carry it into the country for you, it is almost impossible to get money into Vietnam quickly.

Bangkok Bangkok is a good place to pick up money cabled from overseas, but remember that on top of the fee to send the money,

Thai banks charge a US$10 handling fee and 2½% commission if you want US dollars cash. It ends up being cheaper using the cash-advance services offered by many credit cards.

Because American Express (whose Bangkok office is in Siam Centre on Rama I Rd) is not recognised as a bank in Thailand, it cannot handle money cabled from abroad. As a result, funds cabled to Thailand via American Express get sent to one of half-a-dozen major banks around Bangkok. Unless you want to wait around until a little notice is eventually sent to Amex's poste restante window (which charges each time you have them check if there is any mail for you), you'll have to track down your money by phone. I have found it much easier to have a major international bank wire the money to its Bangkok branch.

Inflation & Deflation

Until the spring of 1989, the inflation rate in Vietnam was astronomical, and the black market rate dropped to 6000d per US dollar. Then something peculiar happened: people realised that the dong was actually undervalued. By the summer, US$1 was only worth about 3800d. The dong turned out to be one of the best currency investments of 1989: relative to the US dollar, it appreciated by 58% in 6 months! It is said that not even the Vietnamese government has any idea how many dong are in circulation.

Changing Money

Exchange Rates Foreign currency can be exchanged for dong in one of four ways: at the bank, through authorised exchange bureaus, at hotel reception desks and on the black market.

The best legal rate is offered by banks, many of which accept US dollars as well as other hard major currencies and dollar-denominated travellers' cheques. The catch is that to squeeze those extra few percent out of your money, you may have to spend 30 to 60 minutes in line sometime during business hours. Authorised exchange bureaus (in jewellery shops, etc, especially in Saigon) offer a rate about 5% below that offered by the banks but can usually execute a transaction in under 5 minutes. Hotel reception counters are also quick but they tend to offer a rate up to 10% lower than the banks. It is always best to get a receipt for exchange transactions – sometimes they do check your currency declaration when you leave the country. For details on exchange options around the country, look under 'Information' in each chapter.

The relatively low values of Vietnamese banknotes mean that almost any currency exchange will leave you with hundreds of banknotes to count and cart around. Notes are usually presented in piles of nine with the tenth wrapped around the others, but even so, counting them is a slow but necessary process.

Black Market There is a thriving black market in Vietnam for gold and US dollars cash. US$50 and US$100 notes are preferred and get a slightly higher rate. If you choose to squeeze that last few percent out of your dollars, be aware that black market transactions are illegal. The manifold rip-off techniques (bait-and-switch, etc) perfected years ago to separate American soldiers from their pay are still being used, especially in Saigon. Many travellers who have changed money on the street (rather than in a shop) have fared poorly. Offers that are way out of line with the going rate are a sure sign of trouble.

Travellers' Cheques At present, travellers' cheques are not very practical in Vietnam. If they get lost or stolen, you won't be able to have them replaced until you leave the country. There are only a handful of banks that accept travellers' cheques (and since the clerks see very few of them, the transaction may prove painfully slow). You cannot get US dollars cash for travellers' cheques, only dong. And there is a 2% commission for exchange transactions involving travellers' cheques.

Travellers' cheques can be used for the purchase of airline tickets, but you must exchange the cheques at a bank for a special receipt in the proper amount before going to pay for your ticket. I'd hate to try to get a refund for an airline ticket bought with travellers' cheques.

Among the travellers' cheques acceptable at least somewhere in Vietnam (that is, in Saigon and Hanoi) are those issued by American Express, Bank of America, Citicorp, First National City Bank, Thomas Cook and Visa. Don't even think of bringing travellers' cheques denominated in anything other than US dollars.

Credit Cards Until recently, credit cards were completely unknown in Vietnam; upon arriving in the country, they reverted back to their natural state of being mere pieces of worthless plastic. That may change soon: Cosevina has plans to provide cash advances to VISA cardholders, and VISA cards may also be accepted by some stores in Ho Chi Minh City. For more information, contact Cosevina (tel 92391, 96648, 91506; telex 18255 COSEVIN) at 102 Nguyen Hue St in Saigon.

Under the Trading with the Enemy Act, the US Treasury Department forbids individuals under its jurisdiction to use credit cards in Vietnam. It is also illegal for American credit card companies to enter into business agreements with Vietnam.

Money Transfers
Money can be cabled into Vietnam via Cosevina, the Overseas Vietnamese Export Services Company, but this takes 3 weeks and funds can only be collected in dong. To provide this service, which is primarily intended to allow Overseas Vietnamese send money to relatives, Cosevina has agreements with companies abroad. For more information in Vietnam, contact the head office of Cosevina (tel 92391, 96648, 91506; telex 18255 COSEVIN), which is in Saigon diagonally across from the Rex Hotel at 102 Nguyen Hue Blvd. Abroad, contact:

Australia
    South-East Asia Cargo Company (SEACO), 505 Bourke St, Surry Hills, NSW 2010
    South-East Asia Cargo Company (SEACO), PO Box 175, Beaconsfield, NSW 2015
Canada
    QTK Express, 1700 Berri, Suite 29, Montreal, Quebec H2L 4E4

Laser Express, 1444A Beaudry, Montreal, Quebec H2L 3E5

Vinamedic, 1446 Beaudry, Montreal, Quebec H2L 3E5

Federal Republic of Germany

ASICO, Eichenstr. 59, 6230 Frankfurt/M 80

VIBA, Hedemannstrabe 14, 1000 Berlin 61

France

Vietnam Diffusion,146 Blvd Vincent Auriol, 75013 Paris

VINA-Paris,142 Blvd Vincent Auriol, 75013 Paris

Singapore

Wanjamil Enterprises (Pte) Ltd, 5001 Beach Rd, Golden Mile Complex, Singapore 0719

USA

VINAMEX, 40 Wall St, suite 2124, New York, NY 10005

VINEXCO, 82 Wall St, suite 1105, New York, NY 10005

COSTS

A survey taken in the early 1970s found that Saigon was the most expensive city in the world for travellers. Back then, it cost 63% more to visit Saigon than it did New York! Today, Vietnam is one of the best travel bargains in the world, with decent hotels, excellent food and serviceable transport all available at very reasonable rates.

Your best bet is to pay for things in dong whenever possible. Dollar-denominated tariffs (such as at tourist-class hotels) are set for wealthy Westerners (and if you can afford to come to Vietnam, you are rich by Vietnamese standards). But dong-denominated prices are almost always intended primarily for locals (though some small hotels unabashedly charge 'capitalist' tourists twice their regular dong rates). Always bargain in dong – then it is clear to everyone involved in the transaction what you are paying relative to what everything else in the country costs.

It is a good idea to save receipts for hotels, transport, etc. Later on, such a paper trail of precedents may prove handy if someone tries to overcharge you or insists that something (such as staying at a cheap hotel) can't be done.

The cost of travelling in Vietnam depends on your tastes and susceptibility to luxuries. Ascetics can get by on US$7 a day, and for US$10 to US$15 a backpacker can live fairly well. Buses are the cheapest form of transportation (and if you can get the dong prices, most trains are even cheaper).

Foreigners are sometimes overcharged in restaurants – especially when unaccompanied by a Vietnamese – on the assumption that they cannot read either the menu or the bill. Such incidents are especially frequent in heavily-touristed areas, such as downtown Saigon.

TIPPING

Tipping according to a percentage of the bill is not expected in Vietnam but it is enormously appreciated. For someone making US$10 per month, 5% or 10% of the cost of your meal can easily equal a day's wages. Government-run hotels and restaurants that specifically cater to tourists usually have an automatic 10% service charge.

People who work with you will also greatly appreciate small gifts such as a pack of cigarettes.

It is considered proper to make a small donation at the end of a visit to a pagoda, especially if the monk has shown you around; most pagodas have contribution boxes for this purpose.

TOURIST INFORMATION
Tourism Authorities

Vietnam Tourism (Du Lich Viet Nam) and Ho Chi Minh City's Saigon Tourist (which runs tours to Cambodia) are state-run organisations that are responsible for all aspects of a tourist's stay in Vietnam – everything from visas to accommodation and transport. When you enter Vietnam on a tourist visa (which you got by booking one of their tours, at least theoretically), you technically become their responsibility.

Vietnam Tourism and Saigon Tourist have neither the inclination nor indeed the staff to keep tabs on you (though the police often seem to have both), but you may have to work through them to get visa extensions and internal travel permits. The local low-down on both bodies and their functioning is listed in the Saigon & Cholon and Hanoi chapters.

Every province has some sort of provincial tourism authority with which Vietnam Tourism coordinates its activities. As a result, if you book a tour to Danang with Vietnam Tourism, you'll have a Vietnam Tourism guide as well as a Quang Nam-Danang Province Tourism guide (in addition to a driver) – quite an entourage! Because every organisation in Vietnam – from the Foreign Ministry on down to the smallest industrial concern – desperately want US dollars, it is often possible to bypass Vietnam Tourism by working directly with provincial tourism authorities, whose addresses are listed under Information in the capital city of each province.

Chamber of Commerce

Vietcochamber, the Chamber of Commerce and Industry, is supposed to initiate and facilitate contacts between foreign businesspeople and Vietnamese companies. They may also be able to help with receiving and extending business visas. Vietcochamber publishes *Vietnam Foreign Trade* magazine and the *Trade Directory*, a listing of government companies and how to contact them.

In Saigon, the Vietcochamber office (tel 25604, 90301; telex 8215 CHAMMER HCM; cable address: CHAMMERCE HCM) is at 69 Dong Khoi St. In Hanoi, the Vietcochamber office (tel 25961/2, 53023, 56446; telex 4257 VIETCO VN) is at 33 Ba Trieu St. In Danang, contact the Foreign Economic Relations Department of Quang Nam-Danang Province (tel 21092) at 136 Ong Ich Khiem St.

Non-Governmental Organisations

Among the non-governmental humanitarian aid organisations working in Vietnam are: American Friends Service Committee, Catholic Charities, Committee Twee (Netherlands), Church World Services, Enfance Espoir, the International Mission of Hope (Denver, USA), Kinderhilf EV (West Germany), the Mennonites, Need International, Terre des Hommes, World Rehabilitation Fund and World Vision. Other foreign organisations active in Vietnam include the US-Indochina Reconciliation Project, based in Philadelphia, and the Veterans' Vietnam Restoration Project of Garberville, California.

Orderly Departure Programme

The Saigon offices of the Orderly Departure Programme (ODP) are at 184 BIS Nguyen Thi Minh Khai St, across Le Duan Blvd from Notre Dame Cathedral. This is a United Nations programme through which Vietnamese seeking to emigrate can do so without floating around the South China Sea in small boats.

Processing of emigration requests made via the ODP is a two-stage process. First, prospective emigrants submit request papers to the Vietnamese government. Periodically, the Vietnamese government turns over lists of people whose applications have been approved to the ODP office in Bangkok. ODP then reviews the files and invites the prospective departees to interviews, which are held in Vietnam.

Tourists are often asked to help expedite the processing of ODP cases, many of which have been pending since the early 1980s. Vietnamese law prohibits tourists from taking ODP documents out of the country. Overseas Vietnamese are sometimes thoroughly searched as they leave the country to make sure that they are not carrying such documents.

GENERAL INFORMATION
Post

Every city, town, village and rural sub-district in Vietnam has some sort of post office, but international mail is accepted only at the larger urban post offices and at some tourist hotels. All post offices are marked with the words *Buu Dien*.

The rates for international mail charged by the Vietnamese post office are among the highest in the world. A postcard to 'capitalist' countries costs about 2500d; a 10-gram (!) letter will set you back 4000d. 'International

nation is now 3000d) do not have gum on them; use the paste provided in little pots at post offices. And make sure that the clerk cancels them *while you watch* so that someone for whom the stamps are worth half-a-week's salary does not soak them off and throw your letters away.

Items mailed from anywhere other than Saigon and Hanoi are likely to take over a month to arrive at their destinations. In addition, postal authorities in the provinces may enforce censorship rules more strictly. The fastest way to get correspondence to friends outside the country is to ask another foreigner to mail it for you in Bangkok. The second fastest way is to use the Saigon GPO, which takes about 2 weeks to most Western countries. The 'express' service available in Saigon is said to be even quicker.

If international postal rates in Vietnam seem expensive to you, just think about how the Vietnamese feel. The tariffs are so out of line with most salaries that locals *literally* cannot afford to send letters to their friends and relatives abroad. If you would like to correspond with Vietnamese whom you meet during your visit, try leaving them enough stamps to cover postage for several letters, explaining that the stamps were extras you didn't use and would be of no value to you at home.

Everybody calls Saigon 'Saigon' except when addressing letters – then they write 'Ho Chi Minh City, South Vietnam' or 'Ho Chi Minh City, Socialist Republic of Vietnam'.

Express Mail', which is said to take only 7 to 10 days to anywhere, is available in Saigon for 9070d per item. For a domestic letter you will be charged only 100d (150d for airmail service to the north). Oddly, postal rates vary slightly from place to place, perhaps because postal bureaucrats in Hanoi send their pricing directives to the provinces using their own postal system.

Stamp values have not kept pace with inflation: until recently, 50d stamps were the highest denomination available. Since there is no space on a 10 gram letter for many dozens of stamps (and all those stamps might weigh several tens of grams, necessitating additional postage, which would make the letter yet heavier, requiring more stamps, and so on), the post office began using postal meters, which were issued only to major post offices. Postal branches without metering devices may not be able to send international letters.

Vietnamese stamps (the highest denomi-

Parcels Foreigners sending parcels out of Vietnam have reported having to deal with time-consuming inspections of the contents. Mailing anything larger than an envelope into Vietnam is a dicey proposition, especially if the destination is outside of Saigon or Hanoi.

Telephone

International telephone service from Vietnam is extremely expensive and, outside of Saigon, Danang and Hanoi, unreliable. Vietnam's four new earth stations, which link the country to the International Telecommunications Satellite Organization (INTELSAT) system, should improve service.

For the first 3 minutes, pre-paid calls from Vietnam cost US$23 to the USA; US$18 to Canada and Western Europe; US$15 to Australia, New Zealand, South Korea, the Philippines, Singapore and Taiwan; and US$12 to Hong Kong, Malaysia and Thailand. Each additional minute costs one-third of the 3-minute rates. In some places, there is a 10% service charge on top of this. Collect calls can be made to a number of countries (including Australia, Canada, Finland, France and Japan) but at present this service is not available to foreigners. In Saigon, collect calls to the USA can be made by both locals and foreigners but must be booked several days in advance. Collect calls may carry a 5000d service charge if you get through, 7500d if you don't.

Domestic long-distance telephone calls can be booked at most larger post offices. A 3-minute call from Saigon to Hanoi costs 2550d; 3 minutes between Saigon and Danang costs 1390d. Vietnam does not have long-distance direct-dialling – you must go through a switchboard. Local telephone books, available at most hotel reception desks, are listed by subject (like the yellow pages). For example, to find the phone numbers of hotels look under *khach san*.

Because of US Treasury Department restrictions, AT&T will not place calls from the USA to Vietnam.

Telegraph, Telex & Fax
Most GPOs and many tourist hotels in Vietnam offer domestic and international telegraph and telex services. The minimum (3-minute) charge for telexes is US$22 to the USA, US$18 to Canada and Western Europe, US$14 to Australia, New Zealand and Singapore and US$12 to Hong Kong and Thailand.

The telegraph windows of major GPOs are open 24 hours a day 7 days a week. Telegrams to 'capitalist' countries cost about 3000d *per word* (including each word of the address).

Fax machines are rapidly proliferating in Vietnam. Major Saigon hotels and many companies doing international business already have them. It may be a while, however, until post offices outside of Saigon, Danang and Hanoi offer fax services. Fax charges from the Saigon GPO are: to the USA US$23 for the first page and US$18.50 for subsequent pages; to Western Europe, US$21 for the first page and US$17 for additional pages; and to Australia, US$18 for the first page and US$16 for subsequent pages. In Hanoi, the rates vary slightly.

Express Document Delivery
DHL Worldwide Express offers express document delivery from the Saigon GPO (tel 96203, 90446; telex 8270 or 8271) and the Hanoi GPO (tel 57124; telex 4324 HN). The first 500 grams cost US$70 to North America, US$60 to Europe, US$55 to East Asia and the South Pacific, US$50 to Southeast Asia and US$65 to Africa and the Middle East. Each additional ½ kg costs US$5 to South-East Asia, US$10 to East Asia and the South Pacific and US$15 to other places. Delivery to Australia or Europe takes 3 or 4 days; delivery to North America takes 4 or 5 days. For more information, contact: DHL International (S) Pte Ltd/232 Tanjong Rhu Rd 06-00, Auram House, Singapore 1543 (tel 344-2200; telex RS 367 DHLSRO; fax 344-2703).

Electricity
Electric current in Vietnam is a mixture of 110 volts and 220 volts, both at 50 Hertz (cycles). Often, you'll find two-pin US-type outlets carrying 220 volts and round-prong outlets with just 110 volts. If the voltage is not marked on the socket try finding a light-bulb or appliance with the voltage written on it.

Much of the electrical wiring in Vietnam is improvised. It is not uncommon to find, in place of a wall switch, two exposed wires you are supposed to connect together when you want the fan to work. If you get up in the middle of the night to go to the bathroom and accidentally touch the bare ends of the wires you could easily electrocute yourself.

There are frequent electricity outages, with means that there are probably frequent surges in the current. Sensitive electronic equipment should be shielded with a surge suppressor.

Time

Vietnam, like Thailand, is 7 hours ahead of Greenwich Mean Time (Coordinated Universal Time). Because it is so close to the equator, Vietnam does not have daylight saving time (summer time). Thus 12 noon in Hanoi or Saigon is 10 pm the previous day in San Francisco, 1 am in New York, 5 am in London, 1 pm in Perth and 3 pm in Sydney. When the above-listed cities are on daylight saving time, these times are 1 hour off.

Business Hours

Vietnamese rise early (and consider sleeping in to be a sure indication of illness), in part because Vietnam's location within its time zone causes the sun to rise early and set early. Offices, museums and many shops open between 7 and 8 am (depending on the season – things open a bit earlier in the summer) and close between 4 and 5 pm. They shut down for a 1 or 2-hour lunch break sometime between 11 or 11.30 am and 1 or 2 pm. Almost all government offices and enterprises are closed on Sundays. Most museums are closed on Mondays. Pagodas are open all day every day, but it is considered rude to show up at mealtimes.

Special prayers are held at Vietnamese and Chinese pagodas on days when the moon is either full or just the thinnest sliver. Many Buddhists eat only vegetarian food on these days, which, according to the Chinese lunar calendar, fall on the 14th and 15th days of the month and on the last (29th or 30th) day of the month just ending and the 1st day of the new month.

Weights & Measures

Vietnam uses the metric system. For a metric conversion table, see the back of the book.

Laundry

It is usually easy to find a hotel attendant who will get your laundry spotlessly clean (and perceptibly thinner) for the equivalent of a US dollar or two. Unless you supply laundry soap, the laundry will probably do without it, using friction alone to separate the dirt from the cloth (and often part of the cloth from the rest of the cloth). Allow at least a day and a half for washing and drying, especially in the wet season.

MEDIA
Newspapers & Magazines

There are now about 135 periodicals published in Vietnam, all but 35 of them in Hanoi. Daily newspaper circulation is eight per 1000 people. *Nhan Dan* (The People), published in Hanoi, is the daily newspaper of the Communist Party of Vietnam. *Quan Doi Nhan Dan* (The People's Army), also published in Hanoi, is the daily paper of the army. Saigon's *Saigon Giai Phong* is the daily of the Ho Chi Minh City section of the Vietnamese Communist Party. *Giai Phong Nhat Bao* is published daily in Chinese by the Fatherland Front. The recent liberalisation has yet to significantly reduce party and government control of the press.

The English-language *Vietnam Weekly* is published in Hanoi. Other English periodicals include the *Vietnam Courier*, *Vietnam Foreign Trade*, *Women of Vietnam*, *Vietnamese Trade Unions* and *Vietnam Youth*.

Vietnamese Radio

The Voice of Vietnam broadcasts in 11 foreign languages: Cantonese, English, French, Indonesian, Japanese, Khmer, Lao, Mandarin, Russian, Spanish and Thai. In Hanoi, the daily English broadcast can be picked up from 6 to 6.30 pm on 1010 kHz in the medium-wave (AM) band. Elsewhere in the country, only short-wave reception of foreign-language broadcasts may be available. The Voice of Vietnam can be picked up around the world when short wave propagation is good.

The first broadcast of the Voice of Vietnam took place in 1945. During the

Vietnam War, the Voice of Vietnam broadcast a great deal of propaganda programming to the South, including special English programmes for American GIs. From 1968 to 1976, the Voice of Vietnam used the transmitters of Radio Havana-Cuba to deliver its message direct to the American people. In 1984, there were 6 million radio sets in Vietnam.

Vietnamese domestic national radio broadcasts news and music programmes in the early morning, around noon, and from the late afternoon until midnight. In Saigon, frequencies to try include 610 kHz and 870 kHz in the AM band and 78.5 MHz, 99.9 MHz and 103.3 MHz in the FM band.

The address of the Voice of Vietnam is 58 Quan Su St, Hanoi.

Short-wave Radio
Because up-to-date Western magazines and newspapers are virtually unavailable in Vietnam except from other travellers or embassies, visitors interested in keeping up on events in the rest of the world – and in Vietnam itself – may want to bring along a small short-wave receiver. News, music and features programmes in a multitude of languages can easily be picked up, especially at night. Reception of any given broadcast depends on a variety of variable factors, including ionospheric conditions and sunspot activity. Frequencies you might try for English-language broadcasts include:

Radio Australia
    17,750 kHz, 15,415 kHz, 15,395 kHz, 15,240 kHz, 15,140 kHz, 11,705 kHz, 9770 kHz 9645 kHz and 7205 kHz
BBC World Service
    15,360 (in the early morning); 15,280 kHz (during the day); and 15,310 kHz, 11,750 kHz, 9740 kHz and 6195 kHz (at night). Other frequencies to try include 11,955 kHz, 7145 kHz, 5975 kHz and 3915 kHz.
Voice of America
    17,730 kHz and 15,215 kHz (in the morning); 11,755 kHz (in the evening); 6110 kHz, 9760 kHz and 15,760 kHz (at night)
Christian Science Monitor Radio
    17,780 kHz (around noon).

Television
Vietnamese TV, which began broadcasting in 1970, consists of news and propaganda programming as well as sports and music. In 1984, there were 2.2 million TV sets in the country.

HEALTH
Vaccinations
Recommended vaccinations include tetanus and diphtheria, meningitis, a polio booster and gamma globulin (against hepatitis A).

Travel Insurance
As when travelling anywhere in the world a good travel insurance policy is a very wise idea. If you undergo medical treatment, be sure to collect all receipts and copies of your medical report, in English if possible, for your insurance company.

Medical Kit
A small, straightforward medical kit is a sensible thing to carry. A possible kit list includes:

1. Aspirin or Panadol - for pain or fever.
2. Antihistamine (such as Benadryl) - useful as a decongestant for colds, allergies, to ease the itch from insect bites or stings or to help prevent motion sickness.
3. Antibiotics - useful if you're travelling well off the beaten track, but they must be prescribed and you should carry the prescription with you.
4. Kaolin preparation (Pepto-Bismol), Imodium or Lomotil - for stomach upsets.
5. Rehydration mixture - for treatment of severe diarrhoea, this is particularly important if travelling with children.
6. Antiseptic, mercurochrome and antibiotic powder or similar 'dry' spray - for cuts and grazes.
7. Calamine lotion - to ease irritation from bites or stings.
8. Bandages and Band-aids - for minor injuries.
9. Scissors, tweezers and a thermometer (note that mercury thermometers are prohibited by airlines).
10. Insect repellent, sunscreen, suntan lotion, chap stick and water purification tablets.

Ideally antibiotics should be administered only under medical supervision and should never be taken indiscriminately. Overuse of antibiotics can weaken your body's ability to deal with infections naturally and can reduce the drug's efficacy on a future occasion. Take only the recommended dose as prescribed and continue using the antibiotic for the prescribed period, even if the illness seems to be cured earlier. Antibiotics are quite specific to the infections they can treat; stop immediately if there are any serious reactions and don't use it at all if you are unsure if you have the correct one.

In many countries if a medicine is available at all it will generally be available over the counter and the price will be much cheaper than in the West. However, check the expiry date. It's possible that drugs which are no longer recommended, or have even been banned, in the West are still be being dispensed.

Food & Water

Care in what you eat and drink is the most important health rule; stomach upsets are the most likely travel health problem but the majority of these upsets will be relatively minor. Don't become paranoid, trying the local food is part of the experience of travel, after all.

Water The number one rule is don't drink the water and that includes ice. Since most small eateries in Vietnam lack refrigeration equipment, factory-frozen ice is delivered daily. Not only is the water used to make the ice of questionable potability, but it makes its way to its destination in a filthy sack carried on the bare backs of delivery men. And it is often cracked into manageable pieces on the sidewalk. The filthy outer layer may melt off, but then again, it may not. To be careful, don't drink the water (or drinks containing ice) unless you're sure it has been boiled first. Reputable brands of bottled water or soft drinks are generally fine, although in some places bottles refilled with tap water are not unknown. Take care with fruit juice, particularly if water may have been added. Milk should be treated with suspicion, as it is often unpasteurised. Boiled milk is fine if it is kept hygienically and yoghurt is always

good. Tea or coffee should also be OK, since the water should have been boiled.

Water Purification The simplest way of purifying water is to boil it thoroughly. Technically this means boiling for 10 minutes, something which happens very rarely! Simple filtering will not remove all dangerous organisms, so if you cannot boil water it should be treated chemically. Chlorine tablets (Puritabs, Steritabs or other brand names) will kill many but not all pathogens. Iodine is very effective in purifying water and is available in tablet form (such as Potable Aqua), but follow the directions carefully and remember that too much iodine can be harmful.

If you can't find tablets, tincture of iodine (2%) or iodine crystals can be used. Two drops of tincture of iodine per litre or quart of clear water is the recommended dosage; the treated water should be left to stand for 30 minutes before drinking. Iodine crystals can also be used to purify water but this is a more complicated process, as you have to first prepare a saturated iodine solution. Iodine loses its effectiveness if exposed to air or damp so keep it in a tightly sealed container. Flavoured powder will disguise the taste of treated water and is a good idea if you are travelling with children.

Food Salads and fruit should be washed with purified water or peeled where possible. Ice cream is usually OK if it is a reputable brand name, but beware of ice cream that has melted and been refrozen. Thoroughly cooked food is safest but not if it has been left to cool or if it has been reheated. Take great care with shellfish or fish and avoid undercooked meat. In general, places that are packed with travellers or locals will be fine, while empty restaurants are questionable.

Common Ailments

If you've heard of it, chances are someone in Vietnam's got it. Common diseases, victims of which you'll find in virtually every provincial hospital, include diarrhoeal diseases, pneumonia, malaria, measles, diphtheria, hepatitis, tetanus, plague, tuberculosis, rabies, polio and leprosy. It is important to note, however, that the local population's susceptibility to most of these diseases is the result of endemic deficiencies in immunisation, nutrition, sanitation and medical treatment, factors that are unlikely to affect travellers if they are careful.

Even the most basic nutritional supplements, antibiotics and other medicines, antitoxins, vaccines and medical equipment (everything from scalpels on up to diagnostic gadgets) are either in chronic short supply or totally lacking. Many of the medicines that are available in pharmacies were sent by Overseas Vietnamese to their relatives for resale – check expiry dates. Though foreigners with hard currency will receive the best treatment available, even US dollars will not make what doesn't exist magically appear. If you become seriously ill while in Vietnam, get to Bangkok (or somewhere else convenient) as soon as possible.

Vietnam's children are the most seriously affected by this situation, and routinely die from eminently curable infectious diseases. It is estimated that 50% are malnourished. Protein and vitamin deficiencies often cause blindness, dermatitis, rickets and slowed physical and mental development. When contracted by children under 4, malaria is either fatal or stunts physical and intellectual development.

For information on helping Vietnam's hospitals and orphanages, contact the International Mission of Hope at PO Box 38909, Denver, CO 80238, USA (tel (303) 466-2448 or care of FCVN, 1818 Gaylord St, Denver, CO 80218, USA (tel (303) 321-4224)

Tuberculosis Cases of active tuberculosis are on the increase.

Hepatitis More than 10% of the population suffers from hepatitis B, resulting in a high incidence of liver cancer.

Rabies It is a good idea to steer clear of dogs because few of them are inoculated for rabies.

Malaria There are swarms of potentially malarial mosquitoes in many areas of Vietnam, including parts of even the largest cities. Although mosquito nets are almost always provided by hotels, travellers should consider bringing their own.

Sexually Transmitted Diseases During the war, prostitutes often tried to cure themselves of sexually transmitted diseases (STDs), but by under-medicating themselves with antibiotics, penicillin-resistant strains of gonorrhoea and other diseases – that are probably still around – were created. Very little attention is being paid to AIDS in Vietnam.

Sexual contact with an infected sexual partner spreads these diseases. While abstinence is the only 100% preventative, using condoms is also effective. Gonorrhoea and syphilis are the most common of these diseases; sores, blisters or rashes around the genitals, discharges or pain when urinating are common symptoms. Symptoms may be less marked or not observed at all in women. Syphilis symptoms eventually disappear completely but the disease continues and can cause severe problems in later years. The treatment of gonorrhoea and syphilis is by antibiotics.

There are numerous other sexually transmitted diseases, for most of which effective treatment is available. However, there is no cure for herpes and there is also currently no cure for AIDS. Using condoms is the most effective preventative.

AIDS can be spread through infected blood transfusions; most developing countries cannot afford to screen blood for transfusions. It can also be spread by dirty needles – vaccinations, acupuncture and tattooing can potentially be as dangerous as intravenous drug use if the equipment is not clean. If you do need an injection it may be a good idea to provide the doctor with a new syringe.

Agent Orange
Scientists have yet to assemble conclusive evidence of a link between the residues of

chemicals used by the USA during the war and spontaneous abortions, stillbirths, birth defects and other human health problems. But almost all health professionals in Vietnam, faced with an abnormally high incidence of diseases known to be caused by dioxin and other chemicals found in the defoliant Agent Orange, are absolutely certain that such a link exists. Tests have determined that the soil of southern Vietnam has one of the highest levels of dioxin in the world whereas northern Vietnam, which was not defoliated, has one of the lowest levels of dioxin in the world. And statistics show that the rate of abnormal births is about four times as high in the south as in the north.

It is not clear what level of risk a visitor to Vietnam – especially a woman who is pregnant or soon-to-be-so – may face from these chemicals as a result of exposure to the air, water and food of the south. The risks of short-term exposure are probably minimal. But because the effects are potentially devastating, women – especially those in the early months of pregnancy – may want to consider either postponing their visit or travelling only in the north. Or they may want to try to limit their intake of food and liquid to things unlikely to contain chemical residues, such as food grown in the north, imported tinned food, canned drinks, granola bars, etc. Bread made with Soviet grain would be ideal if you could be sure it wasn't grown near Chernobyl...

WOMEN TRAVELLERS

Like Thailand and other predominantly Buddhist countries, Vietnam is, in general, relatively free of serious hassles for women travellers. An important exception seems to be in or around cheap hotels where prostitution is a major part of the business.

DANGERS & ANNOYANCES
Undetonated Mines, Mortars, & Bombs

Four armies expended untold energy and resources for over 3 decades mining, booby-trapping, rocketing, strafing, mortaring, bombing and bombarding wide areas of Vietnam. When the fighting stopped most of this ordnance remained exactly where it had landed or been laid; American estimates at the time placed the quantity of unexploded ordnance at 150,000 tonnes. After the war only small areas were effectively cleared of mines and other explosives.

Since 1975, many thousands of Vietnamese have been maimed or killed by this leftover ordnance while clearing land for cultivation or ploughing their fields. While cities, cultivated areas and well-travelled rural roads and paths are safe for travel, straying away from these areas could land you in the middle of a minefield which, though known to the locals, may be completely unmarked.

Never touch any rockets, artillery shells, mortars, mines or other relics of the war you may come across. Such objects can remain lethal for decades. In Europe, people are still sometimes injured by ordnance left over from WW II and even WW I, and every few years you read about city blocks in London or Rotterdam being evacuated after an old bomb is discovered in someone's backyard.

Especially dangerous are white phosphorus artillery shells (known to the Americans as 'Willy Peter'), whose active ingredient does not deteriorate as quickly as do explosives. Upon contact with the air the white phosphorus contained in the shells ignites and burns intensely; if any of it gets on your body it will eat all the way through your hand, leg or torso unless scooped out with a razor blade. This stuff terrifies even scrap-metal scavengers. If you want to find out more about it, just ask the doctors at any provincial hospital in an area that saw heavy fighting.

And don't climb inside bomb craters – you never know what undetonated explosive device is at the bottom.

Theft & Street Crime

Vietnamese are convinced that their cities are very dangerous and full of criminals. Before reunification street crime was rampant in the South, especially in Saigon. Motorbike-borne thieves would speed down major thoroughfares, ripping pedestrians' watches off their wrists. Pickpocketing and confidence tricks were also common. After the fall of Saigon, a few bold criminals even swindled the newly arrived North Vietnamese troops. When a few such outlaws were summarily shot street crime almost disappeared overnight.

When the Vietnamese withdrawal from Cambodia was completed in 1989, the government accelerated its programme to cut military expenditures by discharging tens of thousands of soldiers from the army. Most of them are joining an already oversaturated job market without marketable skills and without government assistance in finding employment. Unable to earn a living and angry that while they were in Cambodia most Vietnamese their age were building their lives, some turned to crime. Crime rates – especially for break-ins and robberies – have risen precipitously all over the country in the past couple of years. The criminals have not overlooked the lucrative tourism sector.

The street crime for which Saigon and Cholon were infamous before 1975 has recently been making a comeback. Foreigners have reported having their eyeglasses snatched from their heads and expensive pens plucked from their pockets by drive-by thieves. Pickpocketing, sometimes involving groups of kids who divert your attention while one of their number snags your money, is also becoming more of a problem. While changing money is usually safe in shops it is extremely inadvisable to change money on the street, especially in Ho Chi Minh City.

There have been recurrent reports, especially from Saigon, of baggage handlers slitting open the luggage of airline passengers on outward bound flights and pilfering the contents.

Security

Though someone apparently took a pot shot at an obnoxious American journalist at Cu Chi a few years ago, the only other cases I know of physical attacks on foreigners have been against Americans who were mistaken for Russians! One fellow I know was assaulted twice in Haiphong by Vietnamese toughs shouting angrily *Lien Xo! Lien Xo!* (Soviet! Soviet!).

Your personal safety cannot be guaranteed in remote parts of the Central Highlands (where army deserters are said to hide out) and if you travel between towns alone at night by bicycle or motorbike. There are rumours that in areas with localised food shortages hungry people sometimes take to stopping and robbing vehicles, even tourist cars.

FILM & PHOTOGRAPHY

Film

Fresh Kodacolor print film, imported in bulk, is widely available, as are 35 mm colour print films made by Konica, Fuji and Agfa. Western-made slide films, which cannot be developed in Vietnam, are hard to find. Impoverished photographers may want to experiment with inexpensive Soviet products, sold under the 'Foto' label, and 'ORWO' print and slide films from the old East Germany. Whereas a 36-exposure roll of Kodak Gold 100 colour print film sells for 10,000d, a 36 exposure roll of black-and-white ORWO costs only 1800d.

If you buy film in Vietnam, be sure to check the expiry date. This is especially important if the film has been stored in a warm environment, which is very likely. A tattered and scuffed film box is a sign that the product was resold by a tourist who may have inadvertantly allowed it to be exposed to airport x-rays.

If you have a particular fondness for the 35 mm SLRs of the 1970s, Vietnam is the place to shop. Some newer models, sent by Overseas Vietnamese to their families in Vietnam, are also available. If you buy a new or used camera professionals suggest that you shoot a roll of black-and-white film immediately to make sure it is working properly.

Developing

Several photo shops in Saigon are equipped with the latest Japanese 1-hour colour-printing equipment. For addresses of photo shops, see the Things to Buy sections in Saigon & Cholon and Hanoi chapters.

Airport X-Ray Machines

Vietnamese airports are equipped with ancient x-ray machines that will severely damage or destroy *any* film, whether it is exposed or unexposed and no matter how low the ASA or Din rating is. Prints made from irradiated negatives will come out all reddish; slides get washed out.

No matter what the customs people tell you, do *not* let them x-ray your film as you leave the country. And remember that baggage is x-rayed when it *arrives* in Vietnam (to check for contraband, especially electronic equipment). Do not put your film in your checked luggage! Your best bet, even on domestic flights, is to keep all film on your person.

Customs regulations require that all film be declared upon arrival in the country. When you leave Vietnam, they may want you to produce the exact number of rolls of film you had when you came in, as indicated on your customs form. Films in excess of the declared number might be confiscated. I'm not sure what happens if you bought film in Vietnam – it might be wise to keep receipts for all film purchases and developing.

The Vietnamese are not overly uptight about what you photograph so long as its not obviously of great military importance (such as airports, Vung Tau port, the Soviet base at Cam Ranh Bay, Haiphong harbour and the Chinese border area). Photography from aircraft is also prohibited – if you're going to try it, do it on a foreign carrier or wait until your flight out. Don't even think of trying to get a snapshot of Ho Chi Minh in his glass sarcophagus! Taking pictures inside pagodas and temples is usually all right, but as always it is better to ask permission from the monks.

ACCOMMODATION
Hotels

Until 1989 'capitalist' tourists were allowed to stay in only a few large tourist-class hotels that required payment in US dollars cash. These days, all sorts of options are available, ranging from almost-international-standard hotels in Saigon to district-level official guest houses without electricity. The particulars of what is available are listed under each city and town in the 'Places to Stay' section.

At present, hotel tariffs in Vietnam are in a state of flux, and many prices quoted in this book (based on an exchange rate of 4000d to the US dollar) will have changed for reasons other than inflation by the time you use it.

The best hotels in Saigon and Hanoi are often booked out weeks in advance. The need for more world-class hotel rooms has not been lost on hawk-eyed investors, and Saigon and Hanoi are continually abuzz with rumours of new hotel deals. The story that the bankrupt floating hotel from Australia's Great Barrier Reef would come to the Saigon River turned out to be true. Will Saigon's Holiday Inn be finished on schedule (or ever)? Will Club Med's much-heralded beach resort actually be built? Stay tuned...

During the festival of Tet (New Year), which usually falls in late January or early February, Vietnam's hotels are packed with domestic tourists and overseas Vietnamese visiting relatives. Tet is a wonderful time to see Vietnam at its most festive, but before, during and after the week-long festivities it is extremely difficult to find accommodation at any price.

Vietnam Tourism may tell you that you can only stay in their dollar-priced hotels – don't listen to them. Smaller hotels (most run by the various echelons of provincial and municipal government, large state companies and central government ministries) are becoming aware of the benefits of admitting foreign guests, and unless there is a serious crackdown on individual travel very few are likely to refuse a request for a room. Many such places have yet to set their prices for 'capitalist' tourists. Some of those that have have unwittingly priced themselves out of the market, and others will take their sudden popularity with Western travellers as a cue to raise their rates. As market forces become a major factor in pricing (with different sectors of the centralised economy competing for tourist dong) hotel managers will learn, by trial and error, what the market will bear and tariffs will stabilise.

In hotels for domestic travellers Westerners are often steered towards the most expensive room available. If you prefer something simpler, quickly look around for a posted price list and point good-naturedly to the prices. At this point, younger travellers might try producing documentation of their status as a student – the more impressively official-looking the better – which can also serve to establish that you are younger than they think. Explain that you are not rich and a cheaper room may suddenly become available.

It is a good idea to keep all hotel receipts, especially if you are staying for more than a few days. Confusion, sometimes intentional, often arises over how many days you have paid for and how much you still owe. This is especially true of cheaper places with chaotic bookkeeping, since one shift at the front desk has no clue about what people from other shifts have and have not done.

Regulations require hotels to hold the identity cards of domestic guests for the duration of their stay. All hotel guests, including foreigners, must be registered with the police, for which your passport will probably be required. It is at this point that most travellers encounter problems with the police if their papers are not in order: for a brief period, a specific individual (a hotel clerk, a police official) has personal responsibility to make sure that you are supposed to be there. If you prefer to have your passport with you rather than sitting in some unlocked drawer behind the counter, you can ask to have it returned when the formalities are done.

The following are some of the more common hotel names and their translations:

Bong Sen	lotus
Cuu Long	nine dragons
Doc Lap	independence
Ha Long	descending dragon
Hoa Binh	peace
Huong Sen	lotus fragrance
Huu Nghi	friendship
Thang Long	ascending dragon
Thong Nhat	reunification
Tu Do	freedom

Note: Vietnam, once famous for its legions of wartime prostitutes, will once again be famous for prostitution if present trends continue. Despite repeated declarations by the government that Communism has eliminated such vices, prostitution is flourishing in Vietnam. The largest hotels in Ho Chi Minh City have massage services that can provide more than just relief from aching muscles. Some cheaper hotels have turned into veritable brothels and don't even offer a good night's sleep. The policies of the ever-greedy Vung Tau local government have allowed and even encouraged the proliferation of 'massage parlours' so that parts of the town are beginning to resemble the seedy sections of Thailand's provincial capitals. Nha Trang is moving in the same direction.

Camping

Perhaps because so many millions of Vietnamese spent much of the war years living in tents (either as soldiers or refugees), camping is not the popular pastime it is in the West. Even in Dalat, where youth groups often come for out-of-doors holidays, very little proper equipment can be hired. For more information on camping in the Dalat area, see the Central Highlands chapter.

Home Stays

It may be possible to arrange to stay in the homes of local people, but remember that regulations require Vietnamese to report all overnight visitors to their homes – even relatives – to the police.

FOOD

One of the delights of visiting Vietnam is the amazing cuisine – there are said to be nearly 500 different traditional Vietnamese dishes – which is, in general, superbly prepared and very reasonably priced. Regional specialties are mentioned at the beginning of the Places to Eat listing in each section.

The proper way to eat Vietnamese food is to take rice from the large shared dish and put it in your rice bowl. Using your chop sticks, take meat, fish or vegetables from the serving dishes and add them to your rice. Then, holding the rice bowl near your mouth, use your chop sticks to eat. Leaving the rice bowl on the table and conveying your food, precariously perched between chop sticks, all the way from the table to your mouth strikes Vietnamese as very odd. When not eating, it is acceptable to set your chop sticks on top of your rice bowl. Do not place your chopsticks in the food and leave them there.

The meat of some snakes and forest animals, is considered a delicacy by those who can afford it. Special restaurants around the country cater to this market, offering the fresh meat of such animals as cobras, deer, porcupines, bats, turtles, wild pigs and pangolins (scaly animals similar to anteaters). Often, the animals to be eaten are kept alive in cages inside the restaurant until ordered by a customer. A 1-metre cobra weighing about 1 kg costs 80,000d. Whole cobras pickled in large glass jars with special Chinese spices are another favourite.

Vegetarian Food

Because Buddhist monks of the Mahayana tradition are strict vegetarians, Vietnamese vegetarian cooking (an chay) has a long history and is an integral part of Vietnamese cuisine. In general, the focus of vegetarian cuisine in Vietnam has been on reproducing traditional dishes prepared with meat, chicken, seafood or egg without including these ingredients. Instead, tofu, mushrooms and raw, dried, cooked and fermented vegetables are used. Because it does not include many expensive ingredients, vegetarian food is unbelievably inexpensive.

On days when there is a full or sliver moon (the beginning and middle days of the lunar month), many Vietnamese and Chinese do not eat meat, chicken, seafood or eggs – or even nuoc mam (fermented fish sauce). On such days, some food stalls, especially in the marketplaces, serve vegetarian meals. To find out when the next sliver or full moon will be, consult any Vietnamese calendar.

Vegetables are rau. A vegetarian person is a nguoi an chay. Tiem com chay means 'vegetarian rice shop'. When looking for a vegetarian restaurant try showing these words to local people.

Where to Eat

There are a wide variety of places to eat, including curb-side food stands, road-side food stalls, high-volume government-run eateries catering to locals, Chinese restaurants, Western-style cafes, hotel restaurants (which are usually quite good), pastry shops, restaurants serving traditional (rather than everyday) Vietnamese dishes, and restaurants that specialise in the exotic (cobra, etc). Most places can rustle up something Western (such as a steak with chips) if you're desperate. For some inexplicable reason, tour groups are often served Western food unless the participants specifically request a Vietnamese menu.

Rice and soup stalls along highways can be identified by signs reading Com Pho.

Your best bet for a late meal (after 8.30 pm) is usually a hotel restaurant.

To get the bill (cheque), politely catch the attention of the waiter or waitress and write in the air as if with a pen on an imaginary piece of paper.

How to Read a Menu

On menus, dishes are usually listed according to their main ingredient. For instance, all the chicken dishes appear together, as do all the beef dishes, and so on. Usual headings for menu categories are:

beef	bo
fish	ca
crab	cua
frog	ech
chicken	ga
eel	uon
oyster	so
shrimp	tom

Restaurants specialising in exotic fare may also offer:

goat	de
bat	doi qua
gecko	dong
wild pig	heo rung
small homless deer	men
venison	nai
porcupine	nhim
cobra	ran ho
turtle	rua
pangolin	truc
python	tran

Condiments

Nuoc mam (pronounced something like 'nuke mom') is a type of fermented fish sauce – instantly identifiable by its distinctive smell – without which no Vietnamese meal is complete. Though nuoc mam is to Vietnamese cuisine what soy sauce is to Japanese food, many hotel restaurants do not automatically serve it to foreigners, fearing, perhaps, that they will find the odour offensive. Nuoc mam is made by fermenting highly salted fish in large ceramic vats for 4 to 12 months. It is is rich in phosphorus, minerals and amino acids.

Mam tom is a strong shrimp sauce.

Salt with chilli and lemon juice is often served as a condiment.

Soups & Noodles

Pho is the Vietnamese name for the noodle soup that is eaten at all hours of the day but is a special favourite for breakfast. It is prepared by quickly boiling noodles and placing them into a bowl along with greens (shallots, parsley) and shredded beef, chicken or pork. A broth made with boiled bones, prawns, ginger and nuoc mam is then poured into the bowl. Some people take their pho with chilli sauce or lemon.

Lau is fish and vegetable soup served in a bowl resembling a samovar with the top cut off. Live coals in the centre keep it hot.

Mien luon is vermicelli soup with eel seasoned with mushrooms, shallots, fried eggs and chicken.

Bun thang is rice noodles and shredded chicken with fried egg and prawns on top. It is served with broth made by boiling chicken, dried prawns and pig bones.

Xup rau is vegetable soup.

Canh kho hoa is a bitter soup said to be especially good for the health of people who have spent a lot of time in the sun.

The noodles served with Vietnamese soups are of three types: white, rice noodles (banh pho), clear noodles made from rice mixed with manioc powder (mien), and yellow, wheat noodles (mi). Many noodle soups are available either with broth (nuoc leo) or without (kho, literally 'dry').

Side Dishes

Vietnamese spring rolls are called cha gio (pronounced 'chow yau') in the south and nem Sai Gon or nem ran in the north. They are made of rice paper filled with minced pork, crab, vermicelli, moc nhi (a kind of edible fungus), onion, mushroom and eggs and then fried until the rice paper turns a crispy brown. Nem rau are vegetable spring rolls.

Banh cuon is a steamed rice pancake into which minced pork and moc nhi is rolled. It is served with a special sauce made from watered-down nuoc mam, vinegar, sugar, pepper, clove and garlic.

Oc nhoi is snail meat, pork, chopped green onion, nuoc mam and pepper rolled up in ginger leaves and cooked in snail shells.

Gio is lean pork seasoned and then pounded into paste before being packed into banana leaves and boiled.

Cha is pork paste fried in fat or broiled over hot coals. Cha que is cha prepared with cinnamon.

Chao tom is grilled sugar cane rolled in spiced shrimp paste.

Dua chua is bean sprout salad that tastes vaguely like Korean kimchi.

Western-style side-dishes include:

bread	banh my
butter	bo
boiled egg	trung luoc
fried egg	trung chien
omelette	trung op la
cheese	pho mat

Main Dishes

The basis of Vietnamese cuisine is the plain rice (*com trang*) with which most meals are eaten. Common dishes include the following:

Cha ca is filleted fish slices broiled over charcoal. It is often served with noodles, green salad, roasted peanuts and a sauce made from *nuoc mam*, lemon and a special volatile oil.

Ech tam bot ran is frog meat soaked in a thin batter and fried in oil. It is usually served with a sauce made of watered-down *nuoc mam*, vinegar and pepper.

Rau xao hon hop is fried vegetables.

Bo bay mon are sugar-beef dishes.

Com tay cam is rice with mushrooms, chicken and finely sliced pork flavoured with ginger.

Types of food preparation include the following:

boiled	*luoc* (as in *ga luoc*, which means 'boiled chicken')
broiled	*nuong*
fried	*chien* (as in *com chien*, which means 'fried rice')
steamed	*chung* or *hap*

Fruits

Fruit (*qua* or *trai*) is available in Vietnam all year round, but many of the country's most interesting specialties have short seasons. Vietnam's fruits include the following:

avocado	*bo* (the same word means butter)
banana	*chuoi*
cinnamon apple (*pomme canelle*)	*mang cau* (in the south), *na* (in the north)
coconut	*dua*
grapes	*nho*
green dragon fruit (see 'Nha Trang')	*thanh long*
longan	*han*
lychee	*chom chom*
mandarin orange	*quit*
melon	*dua*
orange	*cam*
papaya	*du du*
pineapple	*thom*
pomelo	*qua buoi*
rambutan	*xam bu che*
starfruit	*khe*
a lumpy fruit with three seeds similar in size, shape, and colour to a cherry	*sori*

Avocado is often eaten in a glass with ice and sweetened with either sugar or condensed milk.

Cinnamon apple is also known in English as custard apple, sugar apple and sweetsop. It is ripe when very soft and the area around the stem turns blackish.

Mature coconuts are eaten only by children or as jam. For snacking, Vietnamese prefer the soft jelly-like meat and fresher milk of young coconuts.

Sweets & Deserts

Sweets (*do ngot*) and deserts (*do trang mieng*) you are likely to have an opportunity to sample include the following:

Banh chung, a traditional Tet favourite, is a square cake made from sticky rice and filled with beans, onion and pork and boiled in leaves for 10 hours.

Banh deo is a cake made of dried sticky rice flour mixed with a boiled sugar solution. It is filled with candied fruit, sesame seeds, fat, etc.

Banh dau xanh is mung bean cake served with hot tea. It is said to melt on your tongue.

Mut (candied fruit or vegetables) is made with carrot, coconut, cumquat, gourd, ginger root, lotus seeds, tomato, etc.

Banh bao is a filled Chinese pastry that can most easily be described as looking like a woman's breast, complete with a reddish dot on top. Inside the sweet, doughy exterior is meat, onions and vegetables. *Banh bao* is often eaten dunked in soy sauce.

Banh it nhan dau, a traditional Vietnamese

treat, is a gooey pastry made of pulverised sticky rice, beans and sugar. It is steamed (and sold) in a banana leaf folded into a triangular pyramid. You often see *banh it nhan dau* on sale at Mekong Delta ferry crossings. *Banh it nhan dua* is a variation made with coconut instead of beans.

Ice cream (*kem*) was introduced to Vietnam on a large scale by the Americans, who made ensuring a reliable supply of the stuff a top wartime priority. The US Army hired two American companies, Foremost Dairy and Meadowgold Dairies, to build dozens of ice cream factories all around the country. Inevitably, local people developed a taste for their product. Even 15 years after bona fide Foremost products ceased to be available in the Socialist Republic, the company's orange-and-white logo is – in Saigon at least – still synonymous with ice cream.

Ice cream served in a baby coconut (*kem dua* or *kem trai dua*) deliciously mixes ice cream, candied fruit and the jelly-like meat of young coconut.

Ice cream stalls usually sell little jars or plastic cups of sweetened frozen yoghurt (*yaourt*).

A number of sweet soups and local pastries are listed under Places to Eat in the Hué chapter.

DRINKS
Cold Beverages

ice	*nuoc da*
drinking water	*nuoc vong*
boiled water	*nuoc dun soi*
cold water	*nuoc lanh*
mineral water	*nuoc suoi*
soda water	*nuoc ngot ,nuoc xo da*
lemon soda	*soda chanh*
orange soda	*soda cam*
coconut milk	*nuoc dua*
yoghurt	*yaourt*
iced coffee	*café da*
iced coffee & milk	*café sua da*
beer	*bia*
glass	*ly*
bottle	*chai*

Mineral Water The selection of mineral water (*nuoc suoi*) is still very limited, but when the Vietnamese realise that foreigners are willing to pay good money for water sealed in bottles there is sure to be an adequate supply. Domestic Vinh Hao brand is carbonated and a bit salty but is a clear choice over the world's nastiest mineral water, a salty Soviet brand with Cyrillic and Armenian characters on the red, black and white label.

Coconut Milk There is nothing more refreshing on a hot day than fresh coconut milk (*nuoc dua*), perhaps sweetened with a bit of sugar. Coconut milk is as hygienic and safe to drink as the vessel it is served in is clean. The Vietnamese believe that coconut milk, like hot milk in Western culture, makes you tired. Athletes, for instance, never drink it before a competition.

Soft Drinks The products of BGI, the nationalised successor to Brasseries et Glacières de l'Indochine, vie with Burma's Vimto and company for the title of 'The World's Most Vile Soft Drinks'. Mercifully, lemon soda (*soda chanh*), made of soda water, fresh lemon juice, sugar and ice, is a cheap and refreshing alternative if you are willing to risk the ice. Coca-Cola in cans is widely available.

Beer Vietnam has some of the world's cheapest prices for imported beers. Cans of Heineken, San Miguel, Old Milwaukee, etc are available in hotels for 3500d to 4000d and in the marketplaces for even less (the best deal I've seen is 2000d, about US$0.50). The pick of the native brews, Saigon Export (do they really export it?), costs about the same as imported brands in cans and half that (2000d to 2500d) in bottles. Bottles of inferior Hanoi Beer are available in the north for about the same price. 'Thirty-Three' (pronounced 'ba-me-ba') is a decent southern brand sold only in bottles. Nameless regional beers, though watery and often flat, are available in bottles for a bit less than the name brands. On tap, they go for as little as 400d per glass. One traveller described such 'no-label beers' as being a cross between light beer and iced tea.

Wine

Vietnam produces over 50 varieties of wine (*ruou*), many of them made from rice.

Hard Liquor Eastern European brandy, vodka and other alcoholic beverages (*ruou manh*) are very cheap in Vietnam thanks to the favourable exchange rate of dongs to roubles, zlotys, leus, forints, levs and korunas. A bottle of Romanian cherry brandy, for instance, costs only 6000d. Locally produced Hanoi Vodka is also available.

Cobra blood is used to make a special alcoholic cocktail.

Hot Beverages

boiling water	*nuoc soi*
tea	*cha*(north), *tra*(south)
coffee	*café* or *ca phe*
coffee with milk	*café sua*
sugar	*duong*
condensed milk (sweetened)	*sua dac*

BOOKS & BOOKSHOPS

A large number of English-language books about Vietnam have been published in the last 3 decades. They range from popular paperbacks to outstanding works of scholarship. Most focus on American involvement in Indochina (rather than on Vietnam itself) but quite a few also cover various aspects of Vietnamese culture, history, political development, etc. A sampling of the best are listed here.

Asia Books, which carries a good selection of English-language books, has three locations in Bangkok:

221 Sukhumvit, between Soi 15 and Soi 17 (tel 252-7277, 250-1822, 252-4373, 251-6042)

2nd Floor, Peninsula Plaza, Rajdamri Rd between the Erawan and Regent hotels (tel 253-9786/7/8)

3rd Floor, Landmark Plaza, Sukhumvit Rd between Soi 4 and Soi 6; open 10 am to 8 pm (tel 252-5654/5)

General

An excellent little book by Ellen Hammer, *Vietnam: Yesterday & Today* (Holt, Rinehart & Winston, New York, 1966) is one of the few American works on Vietnam from the mid-60s to have retained its usefulness. For a very readable account of Vietnamese history from prehistoric times until the fall of Saigon (with a focus on the American war) try Stanley Karnow's *Vietnam: A History* (Viking Press, New York, 1983), which was published as a companion volume to the American Public Broadcasting System series 'Vietnam: A Television History'. *The Socialist Republic of Vietnam* (Foreign Languages Publishing House, Hanoi, 1980) gives the pre-perestroika Party line on Vietnam's history, economy, etc.

If you're having trouble keeping your dynasties, emperors and revolutionary patriots straight, Danny J Whitfield's solid *Historical & Cultural Dictionary of Vietnam* (Scarecrow Press, Metuchen, NJ, 1976) and William J Duiker's *Historical Dictionary of Vietnam* (Scarecrow Press, Metuchen, NJ & London, 1989) will be of great help. Duiker's book has a comprehensive bibliography in the back.

Vietnam: Opening Doors to the World by Rick Graetz (Graetz Publications, 1989) is a full-colour coffee table book on Vietnam and its people today.

Vietnamese Studies is a series of books published quarterly in both English and French by Xunhasaba (Hanoi). Each issue has a number of in-depth articles dealing with a particular subject, ranging from recent history to archaeology and ethnography. Histories and essays on political topics tend to be polemical.

Archaeology, Culture & Religion

During the colonial period, French researchers wrote quite a number of works on Vietnam's cultural history and archaeology that remain unsurpassed. Several good ones on the Chams are *Les États Hinduisés d'Indochine et d'Indonésie* by Georges Coedes (Paris, 1928), *L'Art du Champa et Son Evolution* by Philippe Stern (Toulouse,

1942), and *Le Royaume du Champa* by Georges Maspero (Paris & Brussels, 1928). *Les Arts du Champa: Architecture et Sculpture* by Tran Ky Phuong, curator of the Cham Museum in Danang and Vietnam's foremost scholar of the Chams, will be published in Paris in 1990.

Two collections of Vietnamese legends are *Land of Seagull & Fox* by Ruth Q Sun (Charles E Tuttle, Rutland, VT & Tokyo, 1967) and *Vietnamese Legends* by George F Schultz (Charles E Tuttle, Rutland, Vermont & Tokyo, 1965).

One of the most scholarly works on Caodaism is *Caodai Spiritism: A Study of Religion in Vietnamese Society* by Victor L Oliver (E J Brill, Leiden, 1976).

History

The Birth of Vietnam by Keith Weller Taylor (University of California Press, Berkeley, 1983) covers the country's early history.

Vietnamese Nationalism *Vietnamese Anticolonialism 1885-1925* by David G Marr (University of California, Berkeley, Los Angeles & London, 1971) has become a classic in its field. *Tradition on Trial 1920-1945* (University of California Press, Berkeley, 1981) is another work by Marr, who is one of the most outstanding Western scholars of Vietnam (he is now at the Australian National University).

William J Duiker's *The Communist Road to Power in Vietnam* (Westview Press, Boulder, Colorado, 1981) and *The Rise of Nationalism in Vietnam 1900-1941* (Cornell University Press, Ithaca, New York & London, 1976) trace the development of Vietnam's 20th century anti-colonialist and nationalist movements.

A number of biographies of Ho Chi Minh have been written, including *Ho Chi Minh: A Political Biography* by Jean Lacouture (Random House, New York, 1968) and *Ho* by David Halberstam (Random House, New York, 1971).

The Franco-Viet Minh War On this topic I suggest taking a look at Peter M Dunn's *The*

First Vietnam War (C Hurst & Company, London, 1985) or two works by Bernard B Fall, *Street Without Joy: Indochina at War 1946-54* (Stackpole Company, Harrisburg, Pennsylvania, 1961) and *Hell in a Very Small Place: The Siege of Dien Bien Phu* (Lippincott, Philadelphia, 1967).

The American War The earliest days of US involvement in Indochina – when the US Office of Strategic Services (OSS), predecessor of the CIA, was providing funding and weapons to Ho Chi Minh at the end of WW II – are recounted in *Why Vietnam?*, a riveting work by Archimedes L Patti (University of California Press, Berkeley, Los Angeles & London, 1980). Patti was the head of the OSS team in Vietnam and was at Ho Chi Minh's side when he declared Vietnam independent in 1945.

Three of the finest essays on the Vietnam War are collected in *The Real War* by Jonathan Schell (Pantheon Books, New York, 1987). An overview of the conflict is provided by George C Herring's *America's Longest War*, 2nd edition (Alfred A Knopf, New York, 1979 & 1986). *Fire in the Lake* by Francis Fitzgerald (Vintage Books, New York, 1972) is a superb history of American involvement in Vietnam; it received the Pulitzer Prize, the National Book Award and the Bancroft Prize for History. A highly acclaimed biographical account of the US war effort is *A Bright Shining Lie: John Paul Vann & America in Vietnam* by Neil Sheehan (Random House, New York, 1988); it won both the Pulitzer Prize and the National Book Award.

Ellen J Hammer's *A Death in November* (E P Dutton, New York, 1987) tells of the US role in Diem's overthrow in 1963. *The Politics of Heroin in South-East Asia* by Alfred W McCoy (Harper & Row, 1972; recently reprinted in Singapore) traces how the CIA used drug-smuggling to finance its operations in Indochina. Much of the heroin was eventually sold to US soldiers.

Two accounts of the fall of South Vietnam are *The Fall of Saigon* by David Butler (Simon & Schuster, New York, 1985) and *55*

Days: The Fall of South Vietnam by Alan Dawson (Prentice Hall, Englewood Cliffs, New Jersey, 1977).

An oft-cited analysis of where US military strategy in Vietnam went wrong is *On Strategy* by Colonel Harry G Summers Jr (Presidio Press, Novato, California, 1982 & Dell Publishing, New York, 1984). *The Pentagon Papers* (paperback version by Bantam Books, Toronto, New York & London, 1971), a massive top-secret history of the US role in Indochina, were commissioned by Defence Secretary Robert McNamara in 1967 and published amidst a great furore by the *New York Times* in 1971.

Readers of Hebrew may want to take a look at Moshe Dayan's account of his 1966 visit to South Vietnam, *Yoman Vietnam (Vietnam Diary)* (Devir, Tel Aviv, 1977).

Australia Australia's involvement in the Vietnam War is covered in *Australia's Vietnam* (Allen & Unwin, Sydney, London & Boston, 1983), a collection of essays edited by Peter King; *Australia's War in Vietnam* by Frank Frost (Allen & Unwin, Sydney, London & Boston, 1987); Gregory Pemberton's *All the Way: Australia's Road to Vietnam* (Allen & Unwin, Sydney & Boston, 1987); *Desperate Praise: The Australians in Vietnam* by John J Coe (Artlook Books, Perth, 1982); and *Vietnam: The Australian Experience* (Time-Life Books of Australia, Sydney, 1987).

Soldiers' Experiences Some of the better books about what it was like to be an American soldier in Vietnam include: *Born on the Fourth of July* by Ron Kovic (Pocket Books, New York, 1976), which has recently been made into a powerful movie; the journalist Michael Herr's superb *Dispatches* (Avon Books, New York, 1978); *Chickenhawk* by Robert Mason (Viking Press, New York, 1983 & Penguin Books, Middlesex, UK, 1984), a stunning autobiographical account of the helicopter war; *A Rumor of War* by Philip Caputo (Ballantine Books, New York, 1977); and *Nam* by Mark Baker (Berkley Books, New York, 1981). *A Piece of My*

Heart by Keith Walker (Ballantine Books, New York, 1985) tells the stories of American women who served in Vietnam.

Two oral histories are: *Everything We Had*, by Al Santoli (Ballantine Books, New York, 1981) and *Bloods: An Oral History of the Vietnam War by Black Veterans* by Wallace Terry (Ballantine Books, New York, 1984).

Some of the horror of the My Lai massacre of 1968 comes through in Lieutenant General W R Peers' *My Lai Inquiry* (W W Norton & Company, New York & London, 1979).

Brothers in Arms by William Broyles Jr (Avon Books, New York, 1986) is the story of the 1984 visit to Vietnam by an American journalist who served as an infantry lieutenant during the war.

Viet Cong Memoir by Truong Nhu Tang (Harcourt Brace Javanovich, San Diego, 1985) is the autobiography of a VC cadre who later became disenchanted with post-1975 Vietnam. *Portrait of a Vietnamese Soldier* (Red River Press, Hanoi) was written from the perspective of North Vietnamese who fought against the Americans.

National Geographic Since its first article on Indochina in 1912, *National Geographic* has kept up a lively interest in the region. Listed chronologically, articles on Vietnam include:

The French Period: 'Glimpses of Asia' (May 1921, pp 553-68); 'Along the Old Mandarin Road of Old Indochina' (Aug 1931, pp 157-99); 'Under the French Tricolor in Indochina' (Aug 1931, pp 166-99); 'By Motor Trail Across French Indochina' (Oct 1935, pp 487-534); 'Tricolor Rules the Rainbow in French Indochina' (Oct 1935, pp 495-518); 'Portrait of Indochina' (April 1951) and 'Indochina Faces the Dragon' (Sept 1952, pp 287-328).

During the Vietnam War: 'South Vietnam Fights the Red Tide' (Oct 1961, pp 445-89); 'Helicopter War in South Vietnam' (Nov1962, pp 723-54); 'Slow Train Through Vietnam's War' (Sept 1964, pp 412-44), 'American Special Forces in Action'

(January 1965, pp 38-65); 'Saigon, Eye of the Storm' (June 1965, pp 834-72); 'Of Planes & Men' (Sept 1965, pp 298-349); 'Water War in Vietnam' (Feb 1966, pp272-96); 'Behind the Headlines in Vietnam' (Feb 1967, pp 149-89); 'Vietnam's Montagnards' (April 1968, pp 443-87) and 'The Mekong River of Terror & Hope' (Dec 1968, pp737-87).

Since reunification: 'Hong Kong's Refugee Dilemma' (Nov 1979, pp 709-32); 'Thailand: Refuge From Terror' (May 1980, pp 633-42); 'Troubled Odyssey of Vietnamese Fishermen' (Sept 1981, pp 378-95); and 'Vietnam: Hard Road to Peace' (Nov 1989, pp 561-621).

Politics & Society

Vietnam: Politics, Economics and Society by Melanie Beresford (Pinter Publishers, London & New York, 1988) gives a good overview of the aspects of post-reunification Vietnam mentioned in its title. You'll find out more than you ever wanted about life in the Red River Delta in *Hai Van: Life in a Vietnamese Commune* by François Houtard and Geneviève Lamercinier (Zed Books, London, 1984).

The Vietnamese Gulag by Doan Van Toai (Simon & Schuster, New York, 1986) tells of one man's experiences in the post-reunification 're-education camps'.

Travel Guides

This volume is by far the most comprehensive travel guidebook to Vietnam on the market. Barbara Cohen's *The Vietnam Guidebook* (Harper & Row, New York & Eurasia Press, Teaneck, New Jersey, 1990) does a better job conveying how things used to be during the Vietnam War than it does in giving hands-on, how-to-travel information. Other efforts in this direction are *Guide to Vietnam* by John R Jones (Bradt Publications, UK, 1989 & Hunter Publishing, Edison, New Jersey, 1989) and a forthcoming book from Insight guides.

In French, you might take a look at *Vietnam: Guide de Voyage*, by Jean Michel Strobino, Marc Diasparra, Valerie Daniel and Helene Laffargue (Alticoop Édition, Nice, 1989) and a short work, *Cambodge, Laos, Vietnam*, by Michel Blanchard (Guide Arthaud, Paris, 1989). In German, Hans Illner has written *Reiseland Vietnam* (Edition Aragan, Moers, 1989). Anelise Wulff, a specialist on the Chams, is writing a German-language guidebook scheduled to be published by Dumont of Cologne in 1990.

In 1974, Jeanne M Sales of the American Women's Association of Saigon wrote *Guide to Vietnam* without once mentioning the war! *Customs & Culture of Vietnam* by Ann Caddell Crawford (Charles E Tuttle, Rutland, Vermont & Tokyo, 1966) is a bit dated.

The classic guidebooks to Indochina were published by Claudius Madrolle before WW II. The English edition, *Indochina* (Société d'Éditions Géographiques, Maritimes et Coloniales, Paris, 1939) is a much condensed version of the outstanding two-volume set in French, *Indochine du Sud* and *Indochine du Nord*. The 2nd augmented edition of *Indochine du Sud* and the 3rd augmented edition of *Indochine du Nord* were published in 1939 by the Société d'Éditions Géographiques, Maritimes et Coloniales in Paris. Earlier editions of both books were published by Librarie Hachette, Paris in the 1920s. The only place to find the Madrolle guides these days is in major university libraries and antiquarian book shops.

Fiction

Graham Greene's 1954 novel *The Quiet American*, which is set during the last days of French rule, is probably the most famous Western work of fiction on Vietnam. Much of the action takes place at Saigon's Continental Hotel and at the Caodai complex in Tay Ninh.

MAPS

Urban orienteering is very easy in Vietnam. Like Indonesian, Vietnamese is written with a Latin-based alphabet. You can read the street signs and maps! In addition, finding out where you are is easy: street signs are plentiful, and almost every shop and restaurant has the street name and number right on its sign. Street names are sometimes abbreviated on street signs with just the initials ('DBP' for 'Dien Bien Phu St,' etc). Most street numbering is sequential with odd and even numbers on opposite sides of the street (although there are important exceptions in Saigon, Cholon and Danang – see Orientation in those sections for details), but unfortunately, number 75 is often three blocks down the street from number 76.

A few tips: many restaurants are named after their street addresses. For instance, 'Nha Hang 51 Nguyen Hue' (*nha hang* means restaurant) is at number 51 Nguyen Hue St. If you are travelling by bus or car, a good way to find out where you are is to look for the post office – the words following *Buu Dien* (post office) on the sign are the name of the district, town or village you're in.

Excellent maps of Saigon, Hanoi, Danang, Hué and a few other places are issued in slightly different forms every few years. If you will be travelling by road outside of the main cities and towns, it is worthwhile purchasing a map of the whole country in booklet form entitled *Tap Ban Do Viet Nam Hanh Chinh Va Hinh The* (Cuc Do Dac Va Ban Do Nha Nuoc, Hanoi, 1986).

The best place in the country to get all the maps you'll need during your stay is Saigon, where entrepreneurs selling virtually every map on the market can be found behind little stands on the sidewalks along Nguyen Hue Blvd and on Le Loi Boulevard between the Municipal Theatre and the Rex Hotel. In the finest capitalist tradition these map-mongers offer their wares at vastly inflated prices, but for the tourist the cost – especially after a bit of bargaining – is still reasonable. Other places to look for maps include central post offices and hotel gift shops.

The War of the Names

One of the primary battlegrounds for the hearts and minds of the Vietnamese people during the last 4 decades has been the naming of Vietnam's provinces, districts, cities, towns, streets and institutions. Some places have been known by three or more names

since WW II, and in many cases more than one name is still used.

Urban locations have borne: 1) French names (often of the generals, administrators and martyrs who made French colonialism possible); 2) names commemorating the historical personages chosen for veneration by the Saigon government; and 3) the alternative set of heroes selected by the Hanoi government. Buddhist pagodas have formal names as well as one or more popular monikers. Chinese pagodas bear various Chinese appellations – most of which also have Vietnamese equivalents – based on the titles and celestial ranks of those to whom they are consecrated. In the highlands, both montagnard and Vietnamese names for mountains, villages, etc are in use. The slight differences in vocabulary and pronunciation between the north, centre and south sometimes result in the use of different words and spellings (such as 'Pleiku' and 'Playcu').

When French control of Vietnam ended in 1954, almost all French names were replaced in both the North and the South. For example, Cap St Jacques became Vung Tau, Tourane was rechristened Danang and Rue Catinat in Saigon was renamed Tu Do (Freedom) St (since reunification it has been known as Dong Khoi (Uprising) St). In 1956, the names of some of the provinces and towns in the South were changed as part of an effort to erase from popular memory the Viet Minh's anti-French exploits, which were often known by the places where they took place. The village-based southern Communists, who by this time had gone underground, continued to use the old designations and boundaries in running their regional, district and village organisations. The peasants quickly adapted to this situation, using one set of names for where they lived when dealing with the Communists and a different set of names when talking to representatives of the Saigon government.

Later, the US soldiers in Vietnam gave nicknames (such as China Beach near Danang) to places whose Vietnamese names they found inconvenient or difficult to remember or pronounce. This helped to make a very foreign land seem to them a bit more familiar.

After reunification, the first order of Saigon's provisional municipal Military Management Committee changed the name of the city to 'Ho Chi Minh City', a decision confirmed in Hanoi a year later. The new government immediately began changing street names considered inappropriate – a process which is still continuing – and renamed almost all the city's hotels, dropping English and French names in favour of Vietnamese ones. The only French names still in use are those of Albert Calmette (1893-1934; developer of a tuberculosis vaccine), Marie Curie (1867-1934; she won the Nobel Prize for her research into radio-activity), Louis Pasteur (1822-95; chemist and bacteriologist) and Alexandre Yersin (1863-1943; discoverer of the plague bacillus).

All this renaming has had mixed results. Streets, districts and provinces are usually known by their new names. But Saigon is still Saigon, especially since Ho Chi Minh City is in fact a huge area that stretches from near Cambodia all the way to the South China Sea. And visitors will find that the old names of the city's hotels are making a comeback.

All this makes using anything but the latest street maps a risky proposition, though fortunately most of the important street name changes were made before any of the maps currently on sale were published.

THINGS TO BUY
Handicrafts available for purchase as souvenirs include lacquerware items (see Folk Crafts in the Facts About the Country chapter for details on how they are made), mother-of-pearl inlay, ceramics (including enormous elephants), colourful embroidered items (hangings, tablecloths, pillow cases, pyjamas and robes), custom-tailored women's *ao dais*, greeting cards with silk paintings on the front, wood-block prints, oil paintings, watercolours, blinds made of hanging bamboo beads (my favourite is a replica of the Mona Lisa), reed mats (rushes

are called *coi* in the north, *lac* in the south), Chinese-style carpets, jewellery and leatherwork (available in Saigon on Le Thanh Ton St).

Women all over the country wear conical hats, in part to keep the sun off their faces (though they also function like umbrellas in the rain). The finest conical hats are produced in the Hué area.

Objects made of ivory and tortoiseshell are on sale everywhere. Please remember that purchasing them directly contributes to the extinction of the world's endangered populations of elephants and sea turtles. And if that's not enough of an incentive to buy other souvenirs, maybe this is: ivory purchased in Vietnam might be confiscated by customs officials when you get home anyway.

US Government Restrictions
US citizens and residents should take into account that the Trading With the Enemy Act allows only US$100 worth of Vietnamese goods to be brought into the United States as accompanied baggage. The Treasury Department has had this information printed in every US passport under 'Treasury'. Such goods cannot be sent by mail, must be for personal use only and cannot be resold. It is permitted to take advantage of this allowance once every 6 months. Single copies of Vietnamese publications are not included in the US$100 limit.

WHAT TO BRING
Aside from what is necessary on any trip, travellers to Vietnam may want to consider bringing the following:

a pocket short-wave radio (short-wave broadcasts of the BBC, VOA, Radio Australia, etc are the only source of hard news)
reading material (very little in English is available)
a French-English English-French dictionary (useful for communicating with older Vietnamese who were educated under the French)
a torch (flashlight) for use during frequent power outages and when visiting caves
batteries (rechargeables and chargers can be bought in Saigon)

water purification tablets

a canteen (in which you can treat water with water purification tablets)

a money belt (the best kind is worn inside your pants or skirt)

a small cable lock (for locking up your bicycle or, on the train, your pack)

a transformer (the country has both 110v & 220v current)

official letters of introduction

extra visa photos

small-denomination US dollar bills (for tips, paying hotel bills, etc)

small gifts (Western cigarettes, etc).

Thai postage stamps so foreigners heading to Bangkok can mail your postcards and letters for you

enough film for the whole trip (only ASA 100 colour print film is reliably available in Vietnam)

laundry soap (even if you'll have someone else do your laundry, they may not use detergent unless you provide it)

clogs (thongs) for the shower

tampons & sanitary napkins (if you run out in Vietnam, try Saigon's Minimart in the Saigon Intershop)

contraceptives

a first aid kit

malaria prophylactics (see your physician for details and a prescription)

Pepto Bismol or some similar concoction

medications, including perhaps a general antibiotic

a mosquito net (necessary only if you will be staying somewhere other than hotels – even the cheapest dives have them)

a collapsible umbrella and other rain gear (for the monsoon season only)

Like elsewhere in eastern Asia, exchanging business cards is an important part of even the smallest transaction or business contact. In Bangkok, shops using the latest laser-printing technology to make inexpensive (US$12 for 200) custom-designed business cards in 20 minutes can be found in Sogo Department Store in Amarin Plaza and in the Central Department Store, both of which are on Ploenchit Rd.

Vietnamese who work with you will greatly appreciate small gifts such as packs of Western cigarettes, which can be purchased in any airport duty-free shop. The 555 brand (said to be Ho Chi Minh's favourite) is popular, as are most US brands (especially in the south). If you run out in Vietnam, don't

worry – every street corner seems to have a little stand selling foreign cigarettes, sometimes for less than you paid duty-free!

If you'll be doing any cycling, bring all necessary safety equipment (helmet, reflectors, mirrors, etc) as well as an inner tube repair kit.

If you can prove you are a student (with an ID card or, better yet, an official-looking letter from the registrar), it may be possible to get a 15% student discount for services bought through Vietnam Tourism.

CONDUCT

The following are a few tips to make your visit to Vietnam a bit smoother:

1) When dealing with local people, it is important to be extremely sensitive to indications that they are concerned that contact with you is likely to get them into trouble with the police. Vietnamese are much less afraid of being seen with Westerners than they were a few years ago, but there are still reports – especially in the north – of conversations with Westerners resulting in questioning and harassment by the police.

2) A good way to anger adult Vietnamese is to offer sweets to a group of shy children you come across. You may have to practically force them to take it, but children know a good thing when they see it, and soon they may be tagging along behind tourists demanding gifts. US soldiers used to do this during the war, creating gangs of 6-year-old beggars and causing a great deal of resentment.

3) The traditional Vietnamese form of greeting is to press your hands together in front of your body and to bow slightly. These days, the Western custom of shaking hands has taken over, but the traditional greeting is still sometimes used by Buddhist monks and nuns, to whom it is proper to respond in kind. Shoes must be removed inside Buddhist pagodas. In Chinese pagodas, on the other hand, shoes can usually be left on. Be sure not to let the bottoms of your feet point towards other people or anything sacred, especially figures of Buddhas.

4) Short pants are generally worn only by small children and extremely casually dressed men.

5) On sunny days trendy Vietnamese women can often be seen strolling under the shade of an umbrella in order to keep from tanning (as in 19th century Europe, peasants get tanned and those who can afford it do not).

Proper Names

Most Vietnamese names consist of a family name, a middle name and a given name, in that order. Thus, if Henry David Thoreau had been Vietnamese, he would have been named Thoreau David Henry. He would have been addressed as Mr Henry – people are called by their given name but to do so without the title Mr, Mrs or Miss (I don't know if Ms has arrived in Vietnam yet) is considered as expressing either great intimacy or arrogance of the sort a superior would use with his or her inferior.

In Vietnamese, Mr is *Ong* if the man is of your grandparents' generation, *Bac* if he is of your parents' age, *Chu* if he is younger than your parents and *Anh* if he is in his teens or early 20s. Mrs is *Ba* if the woman is of your grandparents' age and *Bac* if she is of your parents' generation or younger. Miss is *Co* unless the woman is very young, in which case *Chi* might be more appropriate. Other titles of respect are:

Buddhist monk	*Thay*
Buddhist nun	*Ba*
Catholic priest	*Cha*
Catholic nun	*Co*

There are 300 or so family names in use in Vietnam, the most common of which is Nguyen (pronounced something like 'nwyen'). About half of all Vietnamese have the surname Nguyen! When women marry, they usually (but not always) take their husband's family name. The middle name may be purely ornamental, may indicate the sex of its bearer or may be used by all the male members of a given family. A person's given name is carefully chosen so that it forms a harmonious and meaningful ensemble with his or her family and middle names and with the names of other family members.

Former South Vietnamese Soldiers & Officials

Many of the Vietnamese who speak English learned it while working with the Americans during the Vietnam War. After reunification, almost all of them spent periods of time ranging from a few months to 14 years in 're-education camps'. Many such former South Vietnamese soldiers and officials will be delighted to renew contact with Americans, with whose compatriots they spent so much time, often in very difficult circumstances, half-a-lifetime ago. Former long-term prisoners often have friends and acquaintances all over the country (you meet an awful lot of people in 10 or more years), constituting an 'old-boys' network' of sorts.

Staring Squads

If you are doing something interesting (such as just standing there), many curious people – especially children – may gather round you to watch. When you get fed up with being the perennial centre of attention, hotel restaurants are a good place of refuge.

Lien Xo!

The main reason children shout *Lien Xo!* (literally 'Soviet Union') at Caucasians – all of whom are assumed to be Soviets – has something to do with people's motivations for tapping on aquarium fish tanks and catching the attention of primates at the zoo: they want to be recognised by an exotic being and to provoke some kind of reaction. The intent is also to annoy the Russians resident in Vietnam, whose unpopularity is legendary.

It also seems that *Lien Xo* means something like 'Hey, look, a white person!' and is intended to alert other curious youngsters that a strange-looking human is in the vicinity. Often, children will unabashedly come up to you and grab the hair on your arms or legs or dare each other to touch your skin. Some travellers have been pinched or kicked without provocation.

How to Make Friends & Influence People

Vernon Weitzel of the Australian National University sends these 10 tips for successfully dealing with Vietnamese officials, businesspeople, etc:

1) Always smile and be pleasant.
2) Don't run around complaining about everything.
3) If you want to criticise someone, do it in a joking manner to avoid confrontation.
4) Expect delays – build them into your schedule.
5) Never show anger – ever! Getting visibly upset is not only rude – it will cause you to lose face.
6) Don't be competitive. Treating your interaction as a cooperative enterprise works much better.
7) Don't act as though you deserve service from anyone. If you do, chances are you'll be delayed.
8) Don't be too inquisitive about personal matters.
9) Sitting and sipping tea and the exchange of gifts (sharing cigarettes, for instance) are an important prelude to any business interaction.
10) The mentality of officialdom is very Confucian, especially in the north. Expect astounding amounts of red tape.

Top: Overlooking Saigon (OT)
Left: Notre Dame Cathedral, Saigon (DR)
Right: Museum, Saigon (OT)

Top: Inside the tunnels of Cu Chi (DR)
Left: Vegetable vendor in central market, Cantho (DR)
Right: Rice field, Mekong Delta (TA)

Getting There

AIR

The only practicable way into or out of Vietnam for Western travellers (except those coming from Cambodia) is by air. Regularly scheduled air services presently linking Ho Chi Minh City's Tan Son Nhut Airport and Hanoi's Noi Bai Airport with points outside the country are listed in the following paragraphs. In most cases, there is a return flight out of Vietnam on the same day as each flight into the country arrives. It is essential to reconfirm all reservations out of the country.

It is extremely difficult to get reservations for flights to or from Vietnam around Tet (New Year), which usually falls in late-January or early-February. If you will be in Vietnam during this period (which is a favourite time for family visits by Overseas Vietnamese) make reservations well in advance or you may find yourself marooned in Bangkok on the way in or stranded in Saigon on the way out. Travellers have reported that ticket scalpers and corrupt airline officials will come up with a seat (or jump you to the head of the waitlist queue) during Tet for a 'fee' of US$100 or so.

The 20 kg checked-luggage weight limit is strictly enforced, especially on Vietnam Airlines. On flights out of Vietnam, they can prevent you from leaving unless you pay the steep overweight fee.

To/From Bangkok

Bangkok, only 80 minutes flying time from Ho Chi Minh City, has emerged as the most convenient port of embarkation for air travel to Vietnam, in part because the Vietnamese Embassy in Bangkok is the easiest place to get visas to Vietnam.

Thai Airways International (THAI), Air France and Vietnam Airlines (Hang Khong Viet Nam) offer Bangkok-Ho Chi Minh City service for 3310B (US$133 each way). THAI Airbus A300s leave at 10.40 am on Tuesdays, Wednesdays, Fridays and Sundays. Air France 747s depart in the early afternoon on Mondays and Thursdays. Soviet-built Tupolev 134s of Vietnam Airlines – used on all of Vietnam Airlines international routes – depart at 1.30 pm on Tuesdays, Thursdays and Saturdays.

There are five flights a week from Bangkok to Hanoi. THAI 737s leave at 11 am on Wednesday, Saturday and Sunday. Vietnam Airlines Tupolev 134s depart at 1.30 pm on Mondays and Fridays. The one-way fare is 4275B (US$170).

Return tickets issued specifically for Vietnam Airlines are not endorsable in Vietnam for return flights on other carriers. On the other hand, Vietnam Airlines *will* honour tickets for Air France and THAI flights. To facilitate last-minute schedule changes, it is usually better to book the return leg on THAI or Air France.

Refunds for tickets to Vietnam are possible but there is a 500B (US$40) cancellation charge and getting your money back – especially from Vietnam Airlines – could take several months. If you intend to use a 3-day Saigon tour as the basis for a longer stay that may include flying out of Hanoi, you might try to purchase a one-way ticket into Vietnam (though for some reason, the airlines sometimes insist that this is not possible). Ho Chi Minh City-Bangkok tickets *can* be endorsed for Hanoi-Bangkok flights for a US$10 surcharge, but such a ticket will be of no use at all if you choose to stop over in Vientiane.

To/From Manila

Philippine Airlines flies Manila-Ho Chi Minh City at 8.35 am on Tuesdays. Vietnam Airlines flies Manila-Ho Chi Minh City at 3.30 pm on Fridays. The cheapest fare is US$240 each way.

To/From Singapore

Vietnam Airlines flies from Singapore to Ho Chi Minh City at 1 pm every Saturday.

Another good way from Singapore to Ho

Chi Minh City is to pick up the twice weekly Garuda flight that departs at 10 am from Batam, an island only a short hydrofoil ride from Singapore. A round-trip excursion fare (good for 30 days) from Batam to Ho Chi Minh City costs US$403 if purchased in Indonesia and S$1020 if bought in Singapore. The regular one-way fare is US$252.

Cassidy Airlines, a charter company, has weekly flights from Singapore to Ho Chi Minh City. Tickets purchased in Saigon cost US$220 one way and US$370 round trip.

Remember that there is no Vietnamese embassy in Singapore, so unless you pick up a visa somewhere else (the nearest Vietnamese consulate is in Kuala Lumpur), there is no way to get one in Singapore except by mail.

To/From Indonesia
Every Monday and Friday morning, a Garuda flight connects Denpasar, Jakarta and Batam with Ho Chi Minh City. A Denpasar-Ho Chi Minh City ticket is US$497 each way. Flying Jakarta-Ho Chi Minh City costs US$437 each way. From Batam, the fare is US$252 each direction. Round-trip excursion fares to Ho Chi Minh City (good for 30 days) cost US$795 from Denpasar, US$700 from Jakarta and US$403 from Batam.

To/From Kuala Lumpur
The Malaysian Airline System has flights from Kuala Lumpur to Ho Chi Minh City on Wednesday and Saturday mornings.

To/From Laos
Lao Aviation flies Antonov An24 prop-planes from Vientiane to Hanoi every Tuesday. Vietnam Airlines flies its usual Tupolev 134s from Vientiane to Hanoi on Thursdays. The fare is US$80. There are flights from Vientiane and Pakse to Ho Chi Minh City on Thursday mornings.

To/From Cambodia
There is service from Phnom Penh to Saigon (US$46 each way) on either Kampuchean Airlines, Vietnam Airlines or Aeroflot on most Mondays, Tuesdays, Wednesdays and Thursdays. The flight takes 40 minutes by prop-driven Antonov An24 and even less time by Tupolev 134 jet. Kampuchean Airlines and Vietnam Airlines fly Tupolev 134s and Antonov An24s between Phnom Penh and Hanoi (US$175 each way) every Tuesday or Wednesday. There is a US$5 airport tax to fly out of Cambodia.

To/From South Asia
Air France stops in Karachi (Mondays and Thursdays) and New Delhi (Mondays) on the way from Paris to Ho Chi Minh City. Czechoslovak Airlines' weekly Prague-Ho Chi Minh City service has a stopover in either Dubai or Tashkent.

To/From Europe
Air France 747s from Charles de Gaulle Airport in Paris to Ho Chi Minh City (usually via Karachi, New Delhi and Bangkok) depart on Wednesdays and Saturdays. The flight takes 22 to 24 hours. The cheapest regular fare is 8510 francs (US$1470).

Aeroflot flies Ilyushin IL86s and IL62s from Moscow to Ho Chi Minh City on Sundays and Mondays using one of two routes: 1) via Tashkent, Karachi, Calcutta and Hanoi; 2) via Bombay and Phnom Penh. The whole hopscotch across Asia takes 21 to 24 hours. Czechoslovak Airlines (CSA) has service every week or so from Prague (via Dubai or Tashkent) to Ho Chi Minh City.

Aeroflot has Moscow-Hanoi service (via Tashkent, Karachi and Calcutta) on Ilyushin IL86s departing every Monday, Wednesday, Thursday, Friday and Sunday. Czechoslovak Airlines flies from Prague to Hanoi on Tuesdays and Thursdays. Interflug has flights to Hanoi from East Berlin to Hanoi every week or two.

Coming Soon
Word has it that there will soon be direct flights from Vancouver and Tokyo to Saigon. When the USA and Vietnam establish diplomatic relations, there will undoubtedly be flights to Ho Chi Minh City from Hawaii and the US West Coast.

General Agents for Vietnam Airlines

Bangkok

Safe Travel Limited (tel 254-8550/1; fax: 662-255-6800), 15th Floor, Maneeya Centre Bldg, 518/5 Ploenchit Rd, Bangkok 10500

Thai Airways International (THAI) (reservations tel 233-3810; ticketing tel 234-3100, extension 19), 485 Silom Rd, Bangkok 10500

At the Vietnamese Embassy (tel 251-7201/2; fax: (662) 251-7202), 83/1 Wireless Rd

Phnom Penh

Kampuchean Airlines (tel 2.5887), 62 Tou Samouth Blvd. Open 7 to 11 am & 2 to 5 pm

Vientiane

Lao Aviation (tel 2093), 2 Thanon Pang Kham

Fear of Flying

When airline safety is being discussed in the pages of East Asia's English-language periodicals, two carriers inevitably come out on the bottom of the list: Burma Airways Corporation (which has lost half of its fleet to crashes in the last few years) and Vietnam Airlines (Hang Khong Viet Nam). Horror-stories about Vietnam Airlines' Tupolev 134s are legion among Westerners working in Vietnam. There are tales of emergency exits bolted shut (or, alternately, of curious cadres, in a passenger jet for the first time, trying to open the emergency exit during flight), of severe shortages of spare parts and lubricants, of planes making multiple approaches before landing, and of whispered advice from friendly Soviet aircraft mechanics that they themselves wouldn't board the planes they service.

The bottom line is that some Western aid officials, businesspeople and even Lonely Planet authors – people who, by their own admission, will usually fly on any aircraft with both wings visibly intact – refuse to fly with Vietnam Airlines. Those who can afford it travel between Hanoi and Saigon by taking THAI or Air France via Bangkok! This is one of the reasons why it is often difficult to get a seat on THAI and Air France flights to and from Vietnam. The mood of near-hysteria about the safety of Vietnam Airlines can be traced to the late-1988 crash of a Vietnam Airlines Tupolev 134 near Bangkok Airport. All aboard, including 22 UN employees and the Indian ambassador, were killed.

Under the US Trading with the Enemy Act, it is forbidden for persons subject to the jurisdiction of the USA to engage in business with Vietnam Airlines. According to the US Embassy in Bangkok, US citizens are permitted to fly on Vietnam Airlines but they advise against it for safety reasons.

OVERLAND

To/From Cambodia

The major frontier crossings between Cambodia and Vietnam are: between Kep in Kampot Province and Ha Tien in Kien Giang Province; between Svay Rieng Province and Moc Bai in Tay Ninh Province; between Kandal Province and Chau Doc in An Giang Province (by Mekong River ferry); and between Ratanakiri Province and Chu Nghe in Gia Lai-Kon Tum Province, which is 65 km west of Pleiku.

Buses run every day between Phnom Penh and Saigon (via Moc Bai). Officials, especially in Cambodia, take a dim view of foreigners making the crossing by bus. See the Phnom Penh and Saigon & Cholon chapters for details. Vehicles belonging to non-governmental organisations (NGOs) working in Cambodia are always going back and forth between Phnom Penh and Saigon (via Moc Bai). The only land route from Phnom Penh to Cambodia's north-eastern province of Ratanakiri is through Vietnam.

The Cambodian Foreign Ministry is always ready to provide a car and driver for the trip between Phnom Penh and Saigon if you are willing to fork out US$300 each way! Contact the Cambodian Consulate in Saigon for details.

To/From Laos

The land crossings between Laos and Vietnam are presently closed to foreigners. When both Laos and Vietnam open up to tourism, it should be possible to drive between the southern Lao province of Savannakhet and central Vietnam via the border crossing at Lao Bao, which is on National Highway 9, 80 km west of Dong Ha. For more information on Lao Bao and nearby Khe Sanh, see the DMZ & Vicinity chapter.

To/From Thailand

There are ambitious plans to open up the Thai-Cambodian border to tourism as soon as the Cambodian civil war ends. The Bangkok-Phnom Penh railway line and a major road cross the frontier near Poipet. For more information, see the Getting There & Away chapter in the Cambodia section.

When Laos' relations with Thailand get sorted out and the Vietnamese relax their restrictions, is should be possible to go overland from Ubon Ratchathani to central Vietnam via Savannakhet Province and the Lao Bao border crossing. For more information on overland travel between Thailand and Laos, see the Getting There & Away chapter in the Laos section.

To/From China

Vietnam's land borders with China have been closed since the 1979 Chinese invasion. Small-scale trade (peasants carrying Chinese beer and thermos bottles suspended from bamboo poles) across the heavily fortified frontier has resumed at places such as Dong Dang (14 km north of Lang Son).

Before 1979, an 851 km metre-gauge rail line, inaugurated in 1910, linked Hanoi with Kunming in Yunnan Province. A regular-gauge line, built in the early 1960s to carry war materiel and other imports, connects Hanoi with Nanning in Guangxi Province. It may someday be possible (as it was just before WW II) to take trains all the way from Beijing or Hong Kong to Hanoi and Saigon and, after travelling by road to Phnom Penh, from there by rail to Bangkok, Kuala Lumpur and Singapore! The train trip from Beijing to Singapore would take, by my estimate, about 150 hours.

BOAT

Major port facilities at Haiphong, Danang, Vung Tau and Ho Chi Minh City are frequent ports of call for freighters, especially from the Eastern Europe. At present, the only international travellers using these (and other Vietnamese) ports seem to be boat people fleeing to the West.

Yachts and fishing boats that have shown up without authorisation in Vietnamese territorial waters have been seized and their crews imprisoned, sometimes for many months.

ONWARD VISAS

Hanoi is a great place to pick up a 5 day Lao transit visa. For more information, see the list of embassies in the 'Hanoi' chapter.

Vietnam has become the transport and paperwork gateway to Cambodia, mostly because the Phnom Penh government, originally set up by the Vietnamese, has legations in less than a dozen countries, almost all of them in the Eastern Europe. Recently, several travellers have requested Cambodian visas in Hanoi and after a few weeks spent lazily working their way southward to Saigon, have picked up their visas at the Cambodian Consulate in Saigon. For more information on Cambodian consular services in Vietnam, see Information in the Hanoi and Saigon & Cholon chapters.

Hanoi's 36 embassies and Saigon's seven consulates do very little visa business. Depending on the country, that means that it's either a lot easier or a lot harder than elsewhere to get onward visas in Vietnam.

Getting Around

AIR

All air travel within Vietnam is handled by Vietnam Airlines (Hang Khong Viet Nam). Flights fill up fast (some flights are literally standing room only) so reservations should be made at least several days before departure. Many provincial destinations are included as a stopover on Hanoi-Saigon flights; there will be a Ho Chi Minh City-Hué-Hanoi run on 1 day of the week and a Hanoi-Hué-Ho Chi Minh City flight on another. In a given city, reservations can be made only for travel originating in that city. In Saigon, for instance, you can book a flight to Danang but cannot – unless you cable ahead – make reservations from Danang to Hanoi. The baggage weight limit on all domestic flights is 20 kg. Reservations and ticketing are handled by Vietnam Airlines' domestic booking offices, whose addresses are listed under 'Information' in the 'Saigon & Cholon' and 'Hanoi' chapters and under 'Getting There & Away' in other chapters.

'Capitalist tourists' must pay for airline tickets with US dollars. Vietnam Airlines does not accept other hard currencies or travellers' cheques; both must be exchanged at a bank before you can buy a ticket. When changing either for payment to Vietnam Airlines, make sure to specify that you will be buying an airline ticket and to check that the total on the receipt equals or exceeds the price of the ticket. Unused tickets for domestic flights are theoretically refundable, but you may have to wait months to get your money back.

Vietnam Airlines' all-Soviet line-up of aircraft includes the 70 seat Tupolev 134 jet (Tu134), the 45 passenger prop-powered Antonov An24 , the 22 passenger propeller-driven AK40 and assorted helicopters. Don't be alarmed if clouds of vapour pour out of the ventilation system, filling the aircraft cabin with a pea-soup fog so thick that people across the aisle become mere silhouettes. For some reason, this happens all the time on Soviet-built aircraft, especially older models.

From Hanoi, Vietnam Airlines has regular flights to Buon Ma Thuot, Cao Bang, Dalat (Lien Khuong; US$143), Danang, Dien Bien Phu, Ho Chi Minh City (US$150), Hué (Phu Bai; US$67), Na San (in Son La Province near Mai Son), Nha Trang, Pleiku, Qui Nhon (Phu Cat) and Vinh.

From Danang, there are said to be flights to Buon Ma Thuot, Dalat (Lien Khuong), Hanoi, Ho Chi Minh City, Nha Trang, Qui Nhon (Phu Cat) and Pleiku.

From Vung Tau there is helicopter service to Con Dau (Con Son) Island.

For information on hiring a helicopter for a private excursion, contact Vietnam Tourism. The price tag is likely to be in the thousands of US dollars.

Scheduled Vietnam Airlines Domestic Flights out of Ho Chi Minh City

Destination	Cost	Departure	Aircraft
Buon Ma Thuot	US$33	Wedneday	An24
Dalat (Lien Khuong)	US$28	Friday	AK40
Danang	US$28	M, W, Sat	Tu134
Hanoi	US$150	Daily	Tu134
Hué (Phu Bai)	US$90	Wednesday	AK40
Nha Trang	US$39	Sunday	An24
Phu Quoc Island	US$62	Friday	An24
Pleiku	US$54	Friday	An24
Qui Nhon (Phu Cat)	US$55	Friday	AK40
Rach Gia	US$39	Tuesday	An24

BUS

Vietnam's extensive network of buses and other passenger vehicles reaches virtually every corner of the country. Many cities have several bus stations between which responsibilities are divided according to the location of the destination (whether it is north or south of the city) and the type of service being offered (local or inter-city express or non-express). Almost all Vietnamese buses suffer from frequent breakdowns (many have been in service for 2 to 4 decades), tiny seats or benches, almost no legroom and chronic overcrowding (overloaded buses are often pulled over by the police but let go in exchange for a bribe).

The appellation 'express' (*toc hanh*) is applied rather casually in Vietnam. Genuine 'express' buses are considerably faster than local buses, which drop off and pick up peasants and their produce at each cluster of houses along the highway. But many 'express' buses are the same decrepit vehicles used on local runs except that as they limp along the road – kept rolling by the sheer ingenuity and willpower of the driver/mechanic and the assistant – they stop a bit less frequently. A good rule of thumb is that local buses average 15 to 25 km/h over the course of a journey. 'Express' buses rarely exceed an average speed of 35 km/h. Real 'express' runs – the microbus from Saigon to Vung Tau, for instance – can average 50 km/h or more.

However slow they may be, 'express' buses do offer certain advantages. At ferries, they are usually given priority, which can save an hour or more at each crossing. And since they are marginally more expensive than regular buses, people lugging large parcels around the country to make a few dong reselling something are likely to consider their time and comfort less valuable than the cash.

Most inter-city buses depart in the early morning. Often, half-a-dozen vehicles to the same destination will leave at the same time, usually around 5.30 am. A few overnight runs have begun since curfew regulations were relaxed in early 1989 but people are not yet in the habit of travelling all night long. Short-distance buses – which, like service taxis, depart when full (ie jam-packed with people) – often operate throughout the day, but don't count on anything leaving after about 4 pm.

TRAIN

The 2600 km Vietnamese railway system (Duong Sat Viet Nam) runs along the coast between Saigon and Hanoi and links the capital with Haiphong and points north. While usually even slower than buses, the trains offer a more relaxing way to get around. Large-bodied Westerners will find that the trains offer a bit more leg and body room than the jam-packed buses. And dilapidated as the tracks, rolling stock and engines may appear, I have found the trains to be more reliable than the country's ancient bus fleet. One key factor to take into account when deciding whether to go by train or bus should be the hour at which the train gets to where you want to go – trying to find a place to stay at 3 am is likely to be very frustrating.

Even the fastest trains in Vietnam are extremely slow, averaging 30 km/h and slowing to 5 or 10 km/h in some sections. The quickest rail journey between Hanoi and Saigon takes 52 hours at an average speed of 33 km/h. The slowest trains average only 15 km/h over the course of a journey. There are several reasons for the excruciating slowness. First of all, the track network is metre-gauge (except for 300 km in the north). Second, much of the track system is in poor condition, in part because of inadequate post-reunification repair of Viet Cong sabotage in the south and US bombing in the north. And third, there is only one track running between Saigon and Hanoi. Trains can pass each other only at those few points where a siding has been constructed. Each time trains go by each other, one of them has to stop on the prearranged sidetrack and wait for the oncoming train to arrive. If one is late, so is the other, and subsequent trains going in both directions may also be delayed.

Petty crime is a problem on Vietnamese trains. I don't think there are organised packnapping gangs as there are in India, but the Vietnamese seem convinced that the young men and boys you see hanging out in the stations and on trains have only larceny on their minds. To protect your belongings, always keep your backpack or suitcase near you and lock or tie it to something at night. If you must leave your pack for a moment, ask someone who looks responsible to keep an eye on it.

History

Construction of the 1729 km Hanoi-Saigon rail line – the 'Transindochinois' – was begun in 1899 (under Governor-General Paul Doumer) and completed in 1936. In the late-30s, the trip from Hanoi to Saigon took 40 hours and 20 minutes at an average speed of 43 km/h. During WW II, the Japanese made extensive use of the rail system, resulting in Viet Minh sabotage on the ground and US bombing from the air. After the war, efforts were made to repair the Transindochinois, major parts of which were either damaged or overgrown.

During the Franco-Vietminh War, the Viet Minh engaged in massive sabotage against the rail system. Sometimes, they would pry up and carry off several km of track in a single night. In response, the French introduced in 1948 two armoured trains equipped with turret-mounted cannon, anti-aircraft machine guns, grenade launchers and mortars (similar trains are used in Cambodia today on the Phnom Penh-Battambang line). During this period, the Viet Minh managed to put into service 300 km of track in an area wholly under their control (between Ninh Hoa and Danang), a fact to which the French responded with sabotage of their own.

In the late 1950s, the South, with US funding, reconstructed the track between Saigon and Hué, a distance of 1041 km. But between 1961 and 1964 alone, there were 795 VC attacks on the rail system, forcing the abandonment of large sections of track (including the Dalat spur). A major reconstruction effort was carried out between 1967 and 1969 and three sections of track were put back into operation: one in the immediate vicinity of Saigon, another between Nha Trang and Qui Nhon and a third between Danang and Hué.

By 1960, the North had repaired 1000 km of track, mostly between Hanoi and China. During the US air war against the north, the northern rail network was repeatedly bombed. Even now – almost 2 decades since the end of US bombing – clusters of bomb craters can be seen around virtually every rail bridge and train station in the north.

After reunification, the government immediately set about re-establishing the Hanoi-Saigon rail link as a symbol of Vietnamese unity. By the time the Reunification (Thong Nhat) Trains were inaugurated on 31 December 1976, 1334 bridges, 27 tunnels, 158 stations and 1370 shunts (switches) had been repaired.

Today, the Vietnamese railway system still has 106 steam engines in service. Some (models such as the Pacific and Mikado) date from the colonial period while others were purchased over the years from Poland. In 1962, one steam engine was even built in Vietnam. The 129 diesel-powered engines include the French-built Alsthom, the Belgian BN/Cockerill and assorted American military, Czech and Indian equipment. The system's 4000 train wagons include 600 passenger cars from the French period. There is a staff of 70,000. There is a major railway repair yard at Thap Cham (near Phan Rang) which it may be possible to visit.

Recently, Ofermat (the French agency responsible for cooperation in the field of railway transport) began unofficially exploring the possibility of assisting Vietnam upgrade the Hanoi-Saigon line. And rumour has it that the Franco-Belgian group Compagnie Internationale des Wagons-Lits et du Tourisme is considering operating trains in Vietnam as it does in Egypt and elsewhere. Although the project to build a rail link with Laos has been shelved, the possibility of someday reopening the 84 km Thap Cham-Dalat line (44 km of which is cog-wheel crémaillère) is being looked into.

The Network

Odd-numbered trains travel southward; even-numbered trains travel northward. The Reunification (Thong Nhat) Trains go between Saigon and Hanoi. Local rail services connect various cities along the coast. Hanoi is linked with Haiphong and points between the capital and the Chinese border.

Three Reunification Trains, numbered TN2, STN4 and STN6 going north and TN1, STN3 and STN5 going south, connect Saigon and Hanoi. All offer sleeping berths. If TN2 leaves Saigon on a Monday evening (departure time is 7 pm), it is scheduled to arrive in Nha Trang at 8.45 am on Tuesday; in Danang at 12.20 am early on Wednesday morning; in Hué at 5.20 am on Wednesday; in Vinh at 6 pm Wednesday; and in Hanoi at 5 am on Thursday. If TN1 departs from Hanoi on a Monday evening (departure time is 7 pm), it is scheduled to arrive in Vinh at 5.45 am on Tuesday; in Hué at 6.35 pm on Tuesday; in Danang at 10.50 pm on Tuesday; in Nha Trang at 4.05 pm on Wednesday; and in Saigon at 5 am on Thursday. On TN1 and TN2, total travelling time between Saigon and Hanoi is 58 hours.

STN4 and STN3 take 52 hours to go between Saigon to Hanoi and stop at Saigon, Nha Trang, Dieu Tri (near Qui Nhon), Danang, Hué, Vinh and Hanoi. Trains STN6 and STN5 also take 52 hours between Vietnam's two largest cities, stopping at Saigon, Nha Trang, Danang, Hué and Hanoi. Because they are a bit faster, STN trains are

Travel Times (in hours) on Trains TN1 (southbound) & TN2 (northbound)

	Saigon	Nha Trang	Dieu Tri	Danang	Hué	Vinh	Hanoi
Saigon		14	21	29	34	47	58
Nha Trang	14		6	14	19	32	43
Dieu Tri	21	6		8	13	26	37
Danang	29	14	8		3	16	27
Hué	34	19	13	3		12	23
Vinh	47	32	26	16	12		10
Hanoi	58	43	37	27	23	10	

Travel Times (in hours) on Trains STN3 & STN5 (southbound) & STN4 & STN6 (northbound)

	Saigon	Nha Trang	Danang	Hué	Hanoi
Saigon		12	26	30	52
Nha Trang	12		14	18	39
Danang	26	14		3	25
Hué	30	18	3		21
Hanoi	52	39	25	21	

Daily Time Schedule for Reunification Trains Heading North from Saigon

Destination	Train TN2		Day	STN4/STN6		Day
	arrives	departs		arrives	departs	
Saigon		19.00	1		10.00	1
Muong Man (Phan Tiet)	01.40	02.10	2			
Thap Cham (Phan Rang)	06.25	06.30	2			
Nha Trang	08.45	09.45	2	22.02	22.32	1
Tuy Hoa	12.57	13.02	2			
Dieu Tri (near Qui Nhon)	15.35	16.05	2		04.34*	
Quang Ngai	20.55	21.00	2			
Danang	00.20	02.00	3	12.10	12.50	2
Hué	05.20	05.50	3	16.05	16.35	2
Dong Hoi	10.35	11.05	3			
Vinh	18.00	18.40	3		04.14*	
Thanh Hoa	23.05	23.35	3			
Nam Dinh	02.12	02.23	4			
Hanoi	05.00		4	14.00		3

*STN4 only

Daily Time Schedule for Reunification Trains Heading South from Hanoi

Destination	Train TN1		Day	STN3/STN5		Day
	arrives	departs		arrives	departs	
Hanoi		19.00	1		10.00	1
Nam Dinh	21.22	21.42	1			
Thanh Hoa	00.30	01.00	2			
Vinh	05.45	06.25	2	19.15	19.35*	1
Dong Hoi	13.20	13.50	2			
Hué	18.35	19.05	2	07.00	07.20	2
Danang	22.50	00.30	2/3	10.55	11.35	2
Quang Nghai	04.10	04.15	3			
Dieu Tri (near Qui Nhon)	09.25	09.55	3	19.23	19.40*	2
Tuy Hoa	12.16	12.21	3			
Nha Trang	16.05	17.05	3	01.32	02.02	3
Thap Cham (Phan Rang)	19.30	19.53	3			
Muong Man (Phan Tiet)	23.10	23.40	3			
Saigon	05.00		4	14.00		3

*STN3 only

Trains Along the Coast

Train No	Route	Duration
TN1 & TN2	Saigon-Hanoi	58 hrs
STN3 & STN4	Saigon-Hanoi	52 hrs
STN5 & STN6	Saigon-Hanoi	52 hrs
AR1 & AR2	Saigon-Nha Trang 1	12 hrs
DS	Saigon-Qui Nhon 2	24 hrs
	Nha Trang-Qui Nhon	10 hrs
NH1 & NH2	Nha Trang-Hué 3	21 hrs
171 & 172	Qui Nhon-Danang	12-13 hrs
165 & 166	Danang-Hué	6 hrs
DH1 & DH2	Danang-Hué	4 hrs
163 & 164	Hué-Dong Hoi	7 hrs
DH3 & DH4	Hué-Dong Hoi	5 hrs
VD1 & VD2	Dong Hoi-Vinh	
V81 & V82	Vinh-Thuong Tinh 4	16 hrs
T83 & T84	Thanh Hoa-Thuong Tinh 4	8 hrs
ND1 & ND2	Nam Dinh-Thuong Tinh	44 hrs

1 This autorail leaves Saigon for its trip northward on Mondays, Wednesdays & Fridays & leaves Nha Trang for its southward run on Tuesdays, Thursdays and Sundays
2 DS trains run northward on odd days of the month and southward on even days of the month
3 Runs northward from Nha Trang on even days of the month and southward from Hué on odd days of the month
4 Truong Tinh is 17.5 km south of Hanoi Railway Station

Local Trains Between Hanoi & Points in Far Northern Vietnam

Train No	Route	Duration
HP1 & HP2	Hanoi-Haiphong	3 hrs (Exp)
H61 & H62	Hanoi-Haiphong	5 hrs
H63 & H64	Hanoi-Haiphong	5 hrs
91 & 92	Hanoi-Quan Trieu	4 hrs
93 & 94	Hanoi-Quan Trieu	4 hrs
LS1 & LS2	Hanoi-Lang Son	6 hrs
LS3 & LS4	Hanoi-Lang Son	7 hrs
PL1 & PL2	Hanoi-Pho Lu (via Yen Bai)	10 hrs
PL3 & PL4	Hanoi-Pho Lu (via Yen Bai)	11 hrs
Y71 & Y72	Gia Lam-Yen Bai	9 hrs
Y73 & Y74	Gia Lam-Yen Bai	10 hrs

slightly more expensive than TN trains. Depending on what day it is, either STN4 or STN6 departs from Saigon at 10 am and either STN3 or STN5 leaves Hanoi at 10 am. STN4, leaving Saigon at 10 am on Monday, is scheduled to reach Nha Trang at 10.02 pm on Monday, Danang at 12.10 pm on Tuesday, Hué at 4.05 pm on Tuesday and Hanoi at 2 pm on Wednesday. STN3, departing from Hanoi at 10 am on Monday, is scheduled to arrive in Hué at 7 am on Tuesday, Danang at 10.55 pm on Tuesday, Nha Trang at 1.32 am on Wednesday and Saigon at 5 am on Wednesday.

Various local trains run between cities along the coast. They are incredibly slow, partly because other trains are given priority in both equipment and switching and partly because most of them stop at every one-horse town on the way. Most offer only very basic hard-seat cars.

Three rail lines link Hanoi with the other parts of northern Vietnam. One takes you east to the port city of Haiphong. A second heads north-east to Lang Son and Nanning, China. A third goes north-west to Pho Lu (which is 30 km short of Lao Cai) and Kunming, China. Train service to China was discontinued in 1979.

Classes
There are two classes of train travel in Vietnam: hard-seat and hard-sleeper. Since it's the only thing the vast majority of Vietnamese can afford, hard-seat is usually packed. Hard-seat is fine for day travel, but overnight it can be even less comfortable than the bus, where at least you are hemmed in and thus propped upright.

Sleeping cars have three tiers of berths. Because it is hotter and gets less air circulation up there, the upper berth is 8% cheaper than the middle and lower berths. The best bunk is the one in the middle because the bottom berth is invaded by seatless travellers during the day.

Reservations
As with all forms of transport in Vietnam, the supply of train seats is insufficient to meet demand. Reservations for all trips – even short ones – should be made at least 1 day in advance. For sleeping berths, you may have to book passage 3 or more days before the date of travel. Bring your passport and internal travel permits when buying train tickets. Though such documents are rarely checked at bus stations, train personnel may ask to have a look at them.

In any given city, reservations can be made only for travel originating in that city. In Nha Trang, for instance, you can reserve a place to Danang but cannot book passage from Danang to Hué. For this reason – and because train stations are often located far from the part of town with the hotels in it – it is a good idea to make reservations for onward travel as soon as you arrive in a city (provided the ticket office is open). Local information on rail services, train station hours, etc is provided in the 'Getting There & Away' listing under each city

If you are unable to make reservations in advance, try showing up at the station half-an-hour before departure time. Station staff may make some sort of provision for you, but be aware that because you are their guest, that provision may be the conductor's ordering some hapless Vietnamese to give up his or her seat.

If you are travelling with a bicycle (for which there is a small surcharge), it may only be possible to get it out of checked baggage at certain stations.

Costs
The main disadvantage of rail travel is that officially, foreigners and Overseas Vietnamese are supposed to pay a surcharge of between 375% and 480% over and above what Vietnamese pay! I am not averse to paying a bit more for things than do the citizens of impoverished countries, but this is outrageous. Local prices for train tickets are a great deal – a bit cheaper than buses, even. But paying five or six times as much as the locals – in US dollars cash only – makes long-haul rail travel by sleeping berth almost as expensive as flying. Many foreigners have managed to pay local dong prices,

but many others have left Vietnam's train stations disappointed and frustrated.

The price of a train journey is computed by multiplying the length of the trip (in km) by the tariff for the class you are travelling. Whereas domestic travellers pay US$0.04 per km for travel in a hard-seat car, the same seat costs foreigners US$0.02 per km, and sleepers cost US$0.04 to US$0.06 per km. Vietnamese are charged the equivalent of US$9.25 in dong for a sitter from Saigon to Hanoi, but foreigners are supposed to pay US$44. A sleeper berth for the 52-hour trip from Saigon to Hanoi, for which locals pay the equivalent of US$20, costs tourists US$116.50, only US$33.50 less than the 2-hour flight!

By Western standards – and compared to how much you paid to fly into Vietnam – these prices are not, for most people, unaffordable. But they are way out of line with the costs of other goods and services in Vietnam, the cheapness of which may have been one of your reasons for coming here in the first place. As always, there are ways around this pricing system. One is to take the bus, though that's not as much fun. Another option is to insist on paying in dong. A US$50 bill means very little to most Vietnamese, but US$50, when considered as 200,000d stacked in a huge pile, may seem to the ticket clerk an outrageous sum for a train ticket to anywhere. The obvious unfairness of your paying so much may give you a bit of leverage when you ask to pay local prices. Explaining that you are a student – and offering documentation – may also help. A third option is to ask a local person to buy the ticket for you and chances are, the conductor who collects your tickets will not notice that your ticket does not indicate that you paid the foreigners' rate. The only problem with this tactic is that the ticket agent usually writes the name of the traveller on the ticket.

You might also combine train travel with cheaper modes of transport, taking the train only for the most scenic sections of your journey (say, between Danang and Hué), or only when the train schedule fits the times you wish to depart and arrive (you wouldn't want to arrive in Nam Dinh at 2 am no matter how cheap the ticket was).

BOAT

Vietnam has an enormous number of rivers that are at least partly navigable, the most important of which are the multi-branched Mekong River in the south and the Red River and its tributaries in the north. Both deltas are crisscrossed with waterways which can be crossed by boat. Vessels of all sorts can be hired in most riverine and seaside towns. For more information, see the Getting There & Away sections of Saigon & Cholon, the Mekong Delta cities and Hoi An; the Getting Around sections of Nha Trang and Hué; and Halong Bay.

DRIVING

Drive-them-yourself rental cars have yet to make their debut in the Socialist Republic, but cars with drivers can be hired from a variety of sources. For details on exactly what is available in each city, see each city's Getting There & Away and Getting Around sections. Saigon has an especially wide selection of government bodies, state companies and private concerns that hire out vehicles.

Overall, the Vietnamese inter-city road network of two-lane highways is fairly good, especially in the south (thanks to huge US war-time infrastructure investments). Though maintenance has been spotty and potholes are a major problem, highway travel is fast if you have a serviceable vehicle. On inter-city roads, honking at all pedestrians (to warn them of your approach) is considered a basic element of safe driving.

Black market petrol (gasoline; in Vietnamese: *xang*) is sold – along with oil (*dau*) – at little stalls along city streets and intercity highways. The petrol, some of it siphoned from government vehicles, is measured out in glass litre bottles and larger plastic containers.

MOTORBIKE & MOTORCYCLE

Motorbikes and motorcycles are a popular

form of transport among people – mostly in the south – who receive remittances from relatives abroad. As of this writing, no one has begun hiring out motorbikes anywhere in the country. Potholes make inter-city travel – especially at night – a risky proposition. And during the monsoon season, motorbike travel can be rather wet (a waterproof suit is a must). As far as I know, no Westerner has ever purchased a motorbike in Vietnam, so the issue of insurance has yet to be addressed by Vietnam's insurance firms.

Travellers contemplating availing themselves of two-wheeled motorised transport should be aware that Vietnam does not have an emergency rescue system or even a proper ambulance network – if something happens to you out on the road, you could be many hours from even rudimentary medical treatment.

Only the very cheapest motorcycle helmets are sold in Vietnam, and even then only at a handful of sports shops in Saigon (most of which are on Cach Mang Thang Tam St between Ben Thanh Market and the Immigration Police Office).

BICYCLE

Vietnam is a great place for inter-city cycling: much of the country is flat, the roads are of a serviceable standard (especially those built by the Americans in the south, many of which have wide shoulders) and the shortage of vehicles makes for relatively light traffic. Bicycles can be transported around the country on the top of buses or in train baggage compartments.

Groups of Western cyclists have recently begun touring Vietnam. The route of a group I met went from Saigon to Mytho, Vinh Long, Cantho, Soc Trang, Cantho, Long Xuyen, Chau Doc and back to Saigon. And at the end of the '80s, one brave soul cycled southward from Hanoi without any permits and apparently made it quite a way before being turned back! For more information on cycling tours to Vietnam, contact Saigon Tours or Que Viet Tours (tel (514) 393-3211) in Montreal.

By far the best way to get around

Vietnam's towns and cities is to do as the locals do: ride a bicycle. During rush hours, urban thoroughfares approach gridlock as rushing streams of cyclists force their way through intersections without the benefit of traffic lights. Riders are always crashing into each other and getting knocked down, but because bicycle traffic is so heavy, they are rarely going fast enough to be injured. Westerners on bicycles are often greeted enthusiastically by locals, who may never have seen a foreigner pedalling around before.

The major cities have bicycle parking lots – usually just roped-off section of sidewalk – which charge 100d to 200d to guard your bike (bicycle theft is a major problem). When you pull up, a number will be chalked on the seat or stapled to the handlebars and you'll be handed a reclaim chit. Without it, getting your wheels back may be a real hassle, especially if you come back after the workers have changed shifts.

Equipment & Its Repair

No one seems to be in the business of renting out bicycles just yet, so the easiest way to procure a bicycle is either to borrow one or, if you'll be riding for more than a day or two, to purchase one. Be aware that recently, people who have loaned bicycles to foreigners have sometimes gotten in trouble with the police.

Many travellers buy a cheap bicycle, use it during their visit, and at the end either sell it or give it to a Vietnamese friend. Locally produced bicycles are available starting at about US$25 but are of truly inferior quality (in fact, they are absolutely the worst bicycles I have ever seen). A decent three-speed bicycle with imported parts costs about US$100. Basic cycling safety equipment is not available in Vietnam so such items as helmets, front and rear reflectors, leg reflectors and rear-view mirrors should be brought along. Another useful accessory to buy abroad is a pocket-size inner tube repair kit. Information on bicycle stores is listed under Bicycle in the Getting Around sections of Saigon & Cholon, Danang, Hanoi, etc.

All Vietnamese-made bicycles have the same 'mixte' frame, but the various models are equipped with different accessories. The best of the lot is the 'Corporate' (is that an appropriate name for a good socialist bicycle?), which goes for 135,500d. The 'Saigon' costs 90,000d. The bottom-of-the-line 'Huu Nghi' will set you back 85,000d. The Vietnamese-made frame is serviceable but moving parts (including brakes, the crank shaft, pedals and gears as well as tyre inner tubes) that are all locally produced should be avoided unless you want to spend as much time haggling with bicycle mechanic as you would have with cyclo drivers if you hadn't bought the bicycle in the first place. The simplest place to buy a domestic bicycle is at government stores, but watch out for misaligned wheels, improperly assembled brakes, crooked bolts and worn threadings. In general, private shops provide superior assembly work.

My own experience is, I think, illustrative. Two weeks after I bought my shiny new 'Corporate', the bearings on the 'Forever' crankshaft brand began grinding horribly and thereafter required frequent adjustments. Two weeks later, one of the pedals suddenly snapped off. The brakes barely functioned from the first and were only marginally better than having no brakes at all (though it was comforting to think of them as brakes). One of the tyres blew out at least once every 2 days. According to newspaper reports, the state-run bicycle-making company is going broke: under the new economic policies, the company is now responsible for the huge stocks of unsold bicycles that are accumulating in warehouses because no one will buy them.

There are innumerable roadside bicycle repair stands in every city and town in Vietnam. Usually, they consist of no more than a pump, an upturned military helmet and a metal ammunition box filled with oily bolts and a few wrenches. In the south, the men who run these repair stands are mostly South Vietnamese Army veterans who are denied other opportunities to make a living.

Pumping up a tyre costs 100d. Fixing a punctured inner tube should cost between 400d and 1000d depending on the size of the patch, the time of day and the presence of competition. The mechanics employ a brilliant system that allows them to patch inner tubes without removing the wheel from the frame or even taking the tyre off the rim. The tire and inner tube are taken half off the rim and the exposed inner tube is partially pumped up and wetted. As the air drains out of the hole, bubbles, which are easily visible and audible, are formed in the water. After the tyre is dried and sanded, rubber cement is used to glue on a patch.

RUNNING

The conditions that make Vietnam ideal for cycling make it equally suited for long-distance running. At the end of the '80s, someone actually ran from Hanoi to Danang.

HITCHING

Westerners have reported great success at hitching in Vietnam. In fact, the whole system of passenger transport in Vietnam is premised on people standing along the highways and flagging down buses or trucks. To get a bus, truck or other vehicle to stop, stretch out your arm and gesture towards the ground with your whole hand. Drivers will expect to be paid for being picked up. Some Western travellers have had their offers to pay refused, but don't count on this. My experience is that you rarely wait for more than a few passenger vehicles to pass before one stops, but on certain stretches of highway, traffic of passenger vehicles (or trucks with any room left) can be light indeed. Vehicles crossing the old DMZ (ie travelling between Dong Ha and Vinh) are especially infrequent, particularly after the early morning.

The engines of most older trucks are equipped with an ingenious gravity-powered heat-dissipation system. When the vehicle's original cooling system failed, a barrel was attached to the roof of the cab and connected to the engine by a hose routed via the driver's window, where a stopcock was installed to allow him to control the flow. Cold water in the rooftop barrel slowly drains into the engine; hot water squirts out the side of the truck from a little nozzle. When the barrel is empty, the truck stops at any of the numerous water-filling stations that line major highways.

Licence Plates

You can learn a great deal about a vehicle by examining its licence plate. Whether you are in a confusing bus station looking for the right bus or hitchhiking and wish to avoid accidentally flagging down an army truck, the following information should prove useful.

The first two numerals on a number plate are the two digit code assigned to the vehicle's province of origin. Because the vast majority of vehicles in the country are controlled at the provincial level and used to link a given province with other parts of the country, there is usually a 50-50 chance that the vehicle is headed towards its home territory.

First, types of licence plates: Vehicles with white numbers on a green field are owned by the government. Vehicles operated by cooperatives or private concerns have black numbers on white. Diplomatic cars have the letters NG in red over green numbers on a white field. Other cars owned by foreigners begin with the letters NN and are green-on-white. Military plates have white numerals on red.

The two-digit number codes for most provinces (listed more or less north to south) are as follows:

13	Ha Bac
15	Greater Haiphong
17	Thai Binh
18	Ha Nam Ninh
20	Bac Thai
21	Hoang Lien Son
28	Ha Son Binh
29	Greater Hanoi
36	Thanh Hoa
37/38	Nghe Tinh
39/40	Quang Binh, Quang,Tri & Thua Thien-Hué (formerly Binh Tri Thien)
43	Quang Nam-Danang
44	Quang Ngai & Binh Dinh (formerly Nghia Binh)
45	Phu Yen & Khanh Hoa (formerly Phu Khanh)
46	Gia Lai-Kontum
47	Dak Lak
48	Thuan Hai
49	Lam Dong
50	Ho Chi Minh City (government)
51- 55	Ho Chi Minh City (private)
60	Dong Nai
61	Song Be
62	Long An
63	Tien Giang
64	Cuu Long
65	Hau Giang
66	Dong Thap
67	An Giang
69	Minh Hai
70	Tay Ninh
71	Ben Tre
72	Vung Tau-Con Dau SEZ

TAXI

Western-style taxis are just beginning to make their appearance in Saigon. Vietnam Tourism will hire out new Japanese cars with drivers for US$0.33 per km (with a minimum per-day charge). The same service is offered by various competing companies, including many provincial tourism authorities. For details on exactly what is available in each city, see the Getting There & Away and Getting Around sections of each chapter. Saigon is particularly rich in options.

CYCLO

The cyclo (pedicab; in Vietnamese: *xich lo*), short for the French *cyclo-pousse*, is an easy, inexpensive way to get around Vietnam's cities. Groups of cyclo drivers always hang out near major hotels and markets, and quite a number of them speak at least a bit of English (in the south, many of the cyclo drivers are former South Vietnamese Army soldiers).

Fares are very cheap, but only if you bargain: the drivers know that US$1 or its dong equivalent is nothing to most Westerners. If the cyclo drivers waiting outside the hotel want too much, flag down someone else less used to spendthrift tourists. Settle on a fare *before* going anywhere or you're likely to be asked for some outrageous quantity of dong at trip's end.

In Saigon, short hops between any two points in the city centre should cost about 1000d, though some impecunious travellers have paid half that after intensive bargaining. Hanoi fares are cheaper, at about 500d per km. Have your money counted out and ready before getting on a cyclo. It also pays to have the exact money – drivers will sometimes claim they cannot make change for a 5000d note.

LAMBRETTA

Lambrettas are tiny three-wheeled trucks used for short-haul passenger and freight transport.

HONDA ONG

The *Honda ong* is an ordinary motorbike on which you ride seated behind the driver. Getting around this way with luggage is quite a challenge. The fare is a bit more than a cyclo for short trips and about the same as a cyclo for longer distances.

IN THE MEKONG DELTA

Two forms of transport used mostly in the Mekong Delta are the *xe dap loi*, a wagon pulled by a bicycle, and the *xe Honda loi*, a wagon pulled by a motorbike.

Saigon & Cholon

Ho Chi Minh City (population 3.45 million) covers an area of 2056 sq km stretching from the South China Sea almost to the Cambodian border. Its land is overwhelmingly rural (93%), dotted with villages and groups of houses set amidst rice paddies. The downtown section of Ho Chi Minh City is still known as Saigon; the huge Chinese district is called Cholon. Along with surrounding areas, Saigon and Cholon constitute the industrial and commercial heart of Vietnam, accounting for 30% of Vietnam's manufacturing output and 25% of its retail trade. It is to Saigon that the vast majority of foreign businesspeople come to invest and trade. It is to Saigon that ambitious young people and bureaucrats – from the north as well the south – gravitate to make a go of it. And it is here that the economic changes sweeping Vietnam – and their social implications – are most evident.

Saigon and Cholon, with a population of about 3 million people, make up one of the most densely populated urban areas in the world (the average density in the city is 20,000 per sq km). The huge numbers of people and their obvious industriousness give Saigon a bustling, dynamic, vital atmosphere. The streets, where much of the city's life takes place, are lined with stores, shops, stalls, stands-on-wheels and vendors with their wares spread out on the sidewalk selling everything from soup to sophisticated electronics. While their rural compatriots are working from dawn to dusk in the country's rice paddies, the Saigonese are working just as hard at the pursuits of city-people: selling vegetables, buying necessities, cutting business deals, commuting. There is something exhilarating about it all, something reassuring about being surrounded by living evidence of the tenacious will of human beings to survive and improve their lot.

Saigon's neoclassical and international-style buildings (and nearby sidewalk kiosks selling French rolls and croissants) give certain neighbourhoods a vaguely French atmosphere. Other sections of the city are obviously American, at least in architecture. If you've ever wanted to visit (or revisit) a small American city of the 1960s, Saigon's US-era buildings, which have not been completely redecorated every 5 years like those in the USA, may be the closest you'll ever get. There are places in Saigon where miniskirts and bell-bottom polyester leisure suits would blend in perfectly with the rest of the decor.

Saigon was captured by the French in 1859, becoming the capital of the French colony of Cochinchina a few years later. In 1950, Norman Lewis described Saigon as follows: 'its inspiration has been purely commercial and it is therefore without folly, fervour or much ostentation...a pleasant, colourless and characterless French provincial city'. The city served as the capital of the Republic of Vietnam from 1956 until 1975, when it fell to advancing North Vietnamese forces.

Cholon rose to prominence after Chinese merchants began settling there in 1778. Though Cholon still constitutes the largest ethnic-Chinese community in Vietnam, hundreds of thousands of Cholonese have fled the country since reunification because of anti-Chinese persecution by the government, most notably in the late '70s.

Orientation

Ho Chi Minh City is divided into 12 urban districts (*quan*) and six rural districts (*huyen*). Many of the urban districts are numbered. District 1 corresponds to Saigon proper and District 5 is Cholon.

The centre of Saigon is the area around Nguyen Hue Blvd and Le Loi Blvd. The Rex Hotel (Ben Thanh Hotel), which is at the intersection of these two streets, is a convenient landmark. Nearby, at the intersection of Le Loi Blvd and Dong Khoi St, is the Municipal Theatre. Ben Thanh Market, which fronts a traffic roundabout at the southern end of Le Loi Blvd, is also a handy landmark. Dong Khoi St (known as Tu Do St before 1975, and as Rue Catinat under the French) stretches 1.1 km from the waterfront to Notre Dame Cathedral. On maps lacking a scale, you can use the known length of Dong Khoi St to estimate distances elsewhere in the city. Le Duan Blvd runs behind Notre Dame Cathedral between Reunification Hall and the Zoo.

The centre of Cholon is around Hung Vuong Blvd and Chau Van Liem Blvd. The major thoroughfares linking Saigon and Cholon are: Tran Hung Dao Blvd; Xo Viet Nghe Tinh St and Tran Phu Blvd; and Dien Bien Phu St and Ngo Gia Tu Blvd. As you head westward away from Saigon, Tran Hung Dao Blvd becomes Tran Hung Dao B Blvd (and the street numbers restart) at An Binh St. A bus line runs along the Tran Hung Dao boulevards.

The main thoroughfare connecting Tan Son Nhut Airport to Saigon is Nguyen Van Troi St, which becomes Nam Ky Khoi Nghia St. Dien Bien Phu St leads north-westward out of town towards northbound National Highway 1, Bien Hoa, Vung Tau and Dalat. Hau Giang Blvd and Hung Vuong Blvd merge to form National Highway 4, which links up with southbound National Highway 1 and leads to Mytho and the rest of the Mekong Delta. Cach Mang Tang Tam St heads west to Cu Chi, Tay Ninh and Phnom Penh.

Most streets have even numbers on one side and odd numbers on the other, but there are confusing exceptions. In some places, consecutive buildings are numbered 15A, 15B, 15C and so forth, while elsewhere, consecutive addresses read 15D, 17D, 19D, etc. Often, two numbering systems – the old confusing one and the new even-more-confusing one – are in use simultaneously, so that an address may read '1743/697'. In some cases (such as Lac Long Quan St, where Giac Lam Pagoda is located), several streets, numbered separately, have been run together under one name so that as you walk along, the numbers go from one into the

hundreds (or thousands) and then start over again.

For fans of Graham Greene's 1954 novel *The Quiet American*, Rue Catinat is now Dong Khoi St; Blvd Charner has become Nguyen Hue Blvd; Blvd Bonnard is now known as Le Loi Blvd; Place François Garnier is at the intersection of Le Loi and Nguyen Hue boulevards; Blvd de la Somme is now Ham Nghi Blvd; Avenue Galliéni has become Tran Hung Dao Blvd; Quai de la Marne is now called Ben Van Don St; and Rue D'Ormay has become Mac Thi Buoi St.

Information

Tourist Office The main southern office of the state tourism authority, Vietnam Tourism (tel 92442, 90775; telex 295 DULIVINA SGN, 8450 VIETOUR HCM; fax 84-90775), is at 69-71 Nguyen Hue Blvd in downtown Saigon. It is open from 7.30 to 11.30 am and 1 to 4.30 pm Monday to Saturday. The staff of Vietnam Tourism are friendly, but since their job is to provide package tours, they have only a limited interest in individual travellers. However, they are a good source of information about visa extensions and their assistance may be crucial in extending your stay.

Vietnam Tourism is planning to open an office at Tan Son Nhut Airport. As you exit from the customs hall, go up the stairs to the left.

Saigon Tourist is a government-run travel agency commissioned to operate tours in southern Vietnam. Saigon Tourist also has a concession to run tours to Cambodia, for which 'capitalist tourists' are asked to pay US$700 for a 3-day trip!

Saigon Tourist's Tourist Guide Office (tel 24987, 98914) is at 49 Le Thanh Ton St (corner Dong Khoi St). It is supposedly possible for individual foreigners to book tours here. In general, I have found the people in this office to be pleasant but unhelpful; they go by the book and any innovation (including individual travel) seems to appal them.

The administrative offices of Saigon Tourist (tel 95000, 95534) are at 39 Le Thanh Ton St. Saigon Tourist's Tourism Develop-

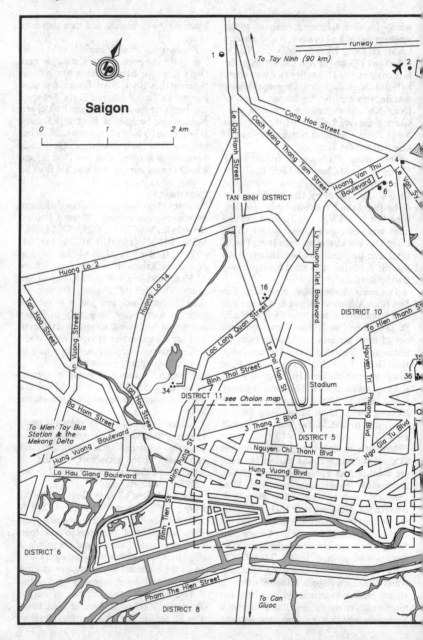

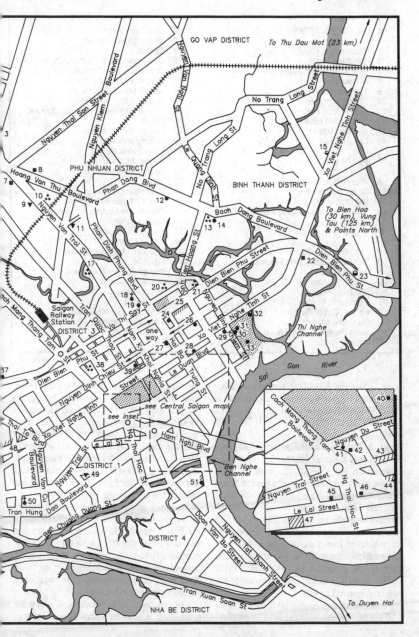

GO VAP DISTRICT   To Thu Dau Mot (23 km)

No Trang Long

PHU NHUAN DISTRICT

BINH THANH DISTRICT

To Bien Hoa
(30 km), Vung
Tau (125 km)
& Points North

Bach Dang Boulevard

Dien Bien Phu Street

Saigon Railway Station

DISTRICT 3

Thi Nghe Channel

one way

Sai   Gon   River

see Central Saigon map

see inset

DISTRICT 1

Ben Nghe Channel

DISTRICT 4

NHA BE DISTRICT   To Duyen Hai

Cach Mang Thang Tam Boulevard

Nguyen Du Street

Nguyen Trai Street

Le Lai Street

■ PLACES TO STAY

4	Thanh Binh Hotel
6	Tan Binh Hotel
7	Nha Khach Viet Kieu (hotel & restaurant)
8	Tan Son Nhat Hotel
22	Thanh Tung Hotel
27	Que Huong Hotel
42	Hoang Gia Hotel
45	Hai Son Hotel
46	Le Lai Hotel

▼ PLACES TO EAT

9	Phu Nhuan Restaurant
11	Tri Ky Restaurant
25	Ice Cream Shop
49	Traditional Vietnamese Restaurants

● OTHER

1	Tay Ninh Bus Station
2	Tan Son Nhut Airport Terminal
3	Airport Gate
5	Public Swimming Pool
10	Dai Giac Pagoda
12	Lambretta Station
13	Le Van Duyet Temple
14	Ba Chieu Market
15	Mien Dong Bus Station

16	Giac Lam Pagoda
17	Vinh Nghiem Pagoda
18	Church
19	Cua Hang Sach Cu (bookshop)
20	Tran Hung Dao Temple
21	Emperor of Jade Pagoda
23	Van Thanh Bus Station
24	Cambodian Consulate
26	Vietnam Airlines Domestic Booking Office
28	Former US Embassy
29	Military Museum
30	Main Zoo Gate
31	History Museum
32	Back Entrance of Zoo
33	Zoo
34	Giac Vien Pagoda
35	Hoa Ky Amusement Park
36	Skeleton of Unfinished Viet Nam Quoc Tu Pagoda
37	Hoa Binh Theatre
38	Xa Loi Pagoda
39	Museum of American War Crimes
40	Stadium
41	Immigration Police Office
43	Motorbike Shops
44	Bicycle Shops
47	Bus Depot
48	Motorbike Repair Shops
50	Cho Quan Church
51	Bicycle Shops

ment Office (tel 93444) is at 55 Dong Khoi St. Saigon Tourist's general telex address is 8275 SAIGON; the fax number is 84-98540 SAIGON TOURIST.

Post & Telecommunications Saigon's French-style General Post Office (Buu Dien Thanh Pho Ho Chi Minh), with its glass canopy and iron frame, is right next to Notre Dame Cathedral. The structure was built between 1886 and 1891 for use as a post office. Under the benevolent gaze of Ho Chi Minh, you will be charged exorbitant rates for whatever international postal and tele-communications services you require. The staff at the information desk (tel 96555, 99615), which is to the left as you enter the building, speak English.

Postal services are available daily from 6.30 am to 7.30 pm. Postcards to 'capitalist' countries cost about 2500d; 10 gram letters cost about 4000d. For domestic letters, the tariff is only 100d (150d for airmail service to the north). International 'express' mail, which supposedly takes 7 to 10 days (rather than the usual 2 weeks), costs 9070d for a 10 gram letter to any destination. Pens, envelopes, aerograms and postcards are on sale at the counter to the right of the entrance and outside the GPO along Nguyen Du St.

Pre-paid international calls, which are excruciatingly expensive (eg US$18.70 for the first 3 minutes to Western Europe), can be made every day from 6.30 am to 10 pm at counter 27. The wait is usually short (5 to 15 minutes) but can sometimes take up to an hour. Pre-paid international calls can also be placed from major hotels.

Collect calls to a number of countries (including Australia, Canada and France) can be made from the GPO, but at present this service is *not* available to foreigners. Collect calls carry a 5000d service charge if you get through and a 7500d charge if you don't. Domestic long-distance calls can be made at windows 37 and 38, which are open 6.30 am to 10 pm daily. Three minutes to Hanoi will cost you 2550d.

Collect calls to the USA, which are not restricted to Vietnamese, must be booked 3 to 5 days in advance at the office (tel 90448) to the right and up a short flight of stairs from the GPO entrance. After you make the booking, the post office will call the USA to see if your friends or relatives will accept the charges. If the answer is no, you will be informed; if the answer is yes, they will set a time for your call. The office is open from 7.30 to 11.45 am and 1 to 4.30 pm daily except Sundays.

Telegrams can be sent 24 hours a day, 7 days a week from counters 31 and 32. Telex services are available at counters 29 and 30 from 6.30 am to 6.30 pm daily. Faxes can be sent at counter 35 from 7.30 am to 12 noon and 1 to 4.30 pm Monday to Saturday.

DHL Worldwide Express (tel 96203, 90446; telex 8270, 8271; fax 84-98540/1), which offers express document and parcel delivery, has a desk to the left and up the short flight of stairs as you enter the GPO. It is open from 7.30 to 11.45 am and 1 to 4.30 pm Monday to Saturday. Parcels cost between US$50 and US$70 for the first 500 grams (each additional 500 grams costs from US$5 to US$15) and take 3 to 4 days to Europe or Australia and 4 to 5 days to North America.

Postal, telex, telegram and fax services are available at counters run by the post office at the hotels Caravelle, Le Lai, Majestic, Palace and Rex.

The District 1 post office (tel 99086), which serves downtown Saigon, is on Le Loi Blvd across Nguyen Thi Minh Khai St from 57 Le Loi Blvd. This is only a block southwest towards Ben Thanh Market from the Rex Hotel.

Money At Tan Son Nhut Airport, US dollars can be changed at the bank rate (the highest legal rate) at the exchange window to the right as you exit the customs hall.

The Bank for Foreign Trade of Vietnam (Ngan Hang Ngoai Thuong Viet Nam; tel 94223), which offers the bank rate, is at 29 Ben Chuong Duong St (corner Nguyen Thi Minh Khai St), two blocks south of Ham Nghi Blvd. It is open from 7 to 11.30 am and 1.30 to 3.30 pm daily except Saturday afternoons and the last day of the month. The foreign exchange section is upstairs.

At present, this is the only place in southern Vietnam where a wide selection of European and other currencies can be exchanged. The bank accepts banknotes (not travellers' cheques) in Australian dollars, Austrian schillings, Belgian francs, British pounds sterling, Canadian dollars, Danish kroners, Deutchmarks, Dutch guilders, Finnish marks, French francs, Hong Kong dollars, Indian rupees, Italian liras, Japanese yen, Norwegian crowns, Singapore dollars, Swedish kronors, Swiss francs and Thai baht. Travellers' cheques in US dollars can only be changed for a 2% commission.

Bring your passport (or a photocopy of it) for identification. Changing money is a slow process; you must wait while your forms wend their way from window 6 through legions of clerks and typists, collecting rubber stamps and signatures, until they arrive, yellowed but fully approved, at window 18. Just be glad you are not one of the Russian experts whom one often sees here in the queue trying to cash a cashier's cheque denominated in Soviet roubles and drawn on a state bank in Novosibirsk! They do not have the option of changing elsewhere.

Fifteen women work at a long table behind window 18. Each is seated behind what looks like brick-work fortifications but are in fact piles of nearly worthless Vietnamese dong notes. These people's full-time job is counting brick after brick of small-denomination bills.

The Banque Française de Commerce Extérieure (BFCE) may soon re-establish a branch in Saigon. Banque Indovina, a joint

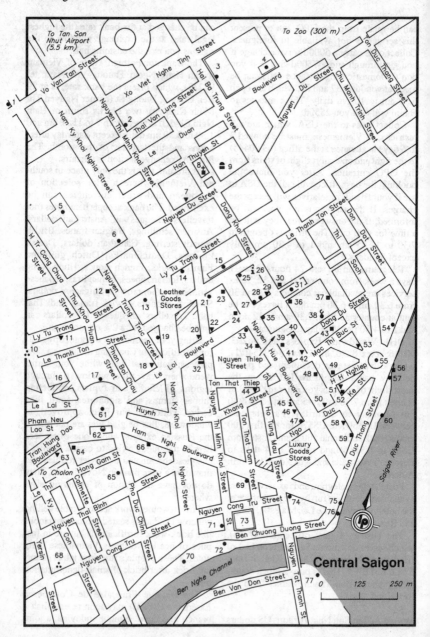

Central Saigon

■ PLACES TO STAY

12	Ben Nghe Hotel
21	Huong Duong Hotel
24	Rex Hotel (Ben Thanh Hotel)
30	Continental Hotel
34	Kim Do Hotel
36	Caravelle Hotel (Doc Lap Hotel) & Air France Reservations Office
37	Khach San 69 Hai Ba Trung (hotel)
39	Oscar Hotel (Thang Long Hotel)
41	Palace Hotel (Huu Nghi Hotel)
43	Saigon Hotel
48	Bong Sen Hotel
49	Huong Sen Hotel
52	Dong Khoi Hotel
56	Saigon Floating Hotel
59	Majestic Hotel (Cuu Long Hotel)
64	Van Canh Hotel
66	Vinh Loi Hotel

▼ PLACES TO EAT

7	Madame Dai's Restaurant
11	Indian Curried Rice Restaurant
16	Food Stalls/Fruit & Vegetable Market
18	Kim Son Restaurant
20	Kem Bach Dang (ice cream parlour)
22	Kem Bach Dang (ice cream parlour)
29	Givral Pâtisserie & Café
40	Brodard Café
42	Nha Hang 95 Dong Khoi (cafe)
44	My Canh 2 Restaurant
46	Nha Hang 51 Nguyen Hue (restaurant)
50	Nha Hang 32 Ngo Duc Ke (restaurant)
51	Pho Hien Hanoi (soup shop)
53	Nha Hang 5 Me Linh (restaurant)
58	Maxim's Restaurant
63	Tin Nghia Vegetarian Restaurant
67	Thang Loi Restaurant

● OTHER

1	Museum of American War Crimes
2	Orderly Departure Program (ODP) Office
3	French Consulate Compound
4	Former United States Embassy
5	Reunification Hall
6	Visitors' Entrance to Reunification Hall
8	Notre Dame Cathedral
9	GPO
10	Mariamman Hindu Temple
13	Municipal Library
14	Museum of the Revolution
15	Hotel de Ville (Town Hall)
17	Ben Thanh Market
19	Saigon Intershop & Minimart
23	Phnom Penh Bus Garage
25	Vietnam Airlines International Booking Office
26	Saigon Tourist 'Tourist Guide Office'
27	Aeroflot Reservations Office
28	Philippine Airlines Reservations Office
31	Municipal Theatre
32	District 1 Post Office
33	Cua Hang Bach Hoa (department store)
35	Cosevina
38	Central Saigon Mosque
45	Vietnam Tourism
47	Microbus Office (Cong Ty Dich Vu Du Lich Quan 1)
54	Ton Duc Thang Museum
55	Me Linh Square & Tran Hung Dao Statue
57	Small Motorised Boats for Rent
60	Dining Cruise
61	Tran Nguyen Hai Statue
62	Ben Thanh Bus Station
65	Art Museum
68	Phung Son Tu Pagoda
69	Vietnam Bank
70	An Duong Vuong Statue
71	Foreign Exchange Bank
72	Wedding Taxis
73	National Bank Building
74	Pre-1967 US Embassy
75	Terminal for Ferries to the Mekong Delta
76	Boats across the Saigon River
77	Ho Chi Minh Museum

Indonesian-Vietnamese venture, is also supposed to get off the ground in the near future.

The Vietnam Bank (Ngan Hang Cong Thuong (Viet Nam) Thanh Pho Ho Chi Minh; tel 90491, 90494, 97266, 97268, 95342, 95343; telex 8266 HCM) does not presently change foreign currencies, but may in the future. The service windows are on the ground floor of a 10-storey building at 79A Ham Nghi Blvd.

The head office of Cosevina (the Overseas Vietnamese Export Services Company; tel 92391, 96648, 91506; telex 18255 COSEVIN) at 102 Nguyen Hue Blvd (corner

Le Loi Blvd) offers speedy currency exchange at the bank rate but it accepts US dollars only. Money can be cabled into Vietnam via Cosevina, but this takes 3 weeks and funds can only be collected in dong (for details, see Money Transfers in the Facts For the Visitor chapter). Cosevina may soon be able to give cash advances to VISA card holders.

You can also get the bank rate at the officially sanctioned exchange windows in the jewellery shops at 71c Dong Khoi St (tel 91522) and 112 Nguyen Hue Blvd (tel 25693). For a rate that is about 5% below the bank rate, try the *bureau de change* at the top of the escalators on the 2nd floor of the Saigon Intershop (101 Nam Ky Khoi Nghia St, just off Le Loi Blvd).

All the major tourist hotels can change money quickly, easily, legally and well after business hours. The catch is that the rate they offer is 5% to 10% lower than the bank rate.

To find a shopkeeper willing to trade dong for dollars on the black market, ask around discreetly. The men who accost you on the street offering great rates are con artists.

Chamber of Commerce The Saigon branch of Vietcochamber (the Chamber of Commerce & Industry of Vietnam; tel 25604, 90301; telex 8215 CHAMMER HCM; cable CHAMMERCE HCM) is at 69 Dong Khoi St. In addition to acting as a liaison between foreign businesspeople and local concerns, Vietcochamber can also help businesspeople with other aspects of their stay in Vietnam, including receiving and extending visas.

Travel Agents Though private travel agencies are not yet permitted to operate except as agents for foreign tour operators, there are a couple of places to keep in mind for when this rule is relaxed: Saigon Tours (tel 25425; telex 8208 HOTHN HCM), the Saigon office of Club Voyages Berri of Montreal, is between the Oscar and Palace hotels at 66 Nguyen Hue Blvd (2nd floor, room 117). Saigon Tours has another office (tel 94253) at 95 Hai Ba Trung St.

Viettour Holidays is at 62 Dong Du St next to the Saigon Mosque. Another place you might contact is Donavik (Dong Nai Viet Kieu; tel 99604) at 14 Vo Van Tan St, room 103A.

Useful Addresses IMC (Investment & Management Consulting Corporation; tel 99062) offers various business services to investors and businesspeople. The External Affairs Office of the Foreign Ministry (tel 23032, 24311) is at 6 Thai Van Lung St. The offices of the Orderly Departure Program (ODP) are at 184 BIS Nguyen Thi Minh Khai St, across Le Duan Blvd from Notre Dame Cathedral.

The Vietnam Youth Travel Centre (Trung Tam Du Lich Viet Nam; tel 94602, 90533) has a branch at 31 Cao Thanh St. To get in touch with students of English, French, Russian, German and Japanese, you might contact the Foreign Language Centre (tel 94585) at 10 3 Thang 2 St. The Franco-Vietnamese Cultural Centre (tel 24577) is at 31 Don Dat St. The address of the Municipal Library is 34 Ly Tu Trong St.

For simple questions about local conditions, ask the well-informed and diligently helpful clerks at the Rex Hotel reception desk.

Registration & Internal Travel Permits If you are not being hosted by an official body that is taking care of your paperwork, do not forget to register at the Immigration Police Office (tel 99398, 97107), 161 Nguyen Du St (corner Cach Mang Thang Tam St). You must re-register each time you enter the country. The Immigration Police Office is open from 8 to 11 am and 1 to 4 pm.

Your registration documents are an internal visa that allow you to stay overnight in Saigon only. In general, permits are not required for day trips (eg to Vung Tau or Tay Ninh) but are necessary if you want to spend the night somewhere outside Saigon.

The Interior Ministry in Hanoi keeps changing its policies on issuing travel permits to individual travellers, and it seems to prefer to try out more liberal guidelines in Hanoi where it can keep an eye on things. It therefore comes as no surprise to find that the Saigon Immigration Police Office has a long record of being politely unhelpful, especially to bearers of visas stamped 'tourist'. Vietnam Tourism officials have no leverage with the Immigration Police on such matters.

Visa Extensions Rules on visa extensions in Saigon are in a state of flux. For up-to-date information, try asking fellow travellers and businesspeople, Vietnam Tourism, Saigon Tourist, private travel agencies, Vietco-Chamber, the Foreign Ministry and the Immigration Police.

Foreign Embassies These are the addresses of Saigon's consulates:

Cambodia
41 Phung Khac Khoan St (tel 92751, 92744, 92752). Open Monday to Saturday from 8 to 11 am and 2 to 5 pm.
Cuba
124-126 Nguyen Dinh Chieu St (tel 95818, 97350, 97351)
Czechoslovakia
176 Tu Duc St (tel 91475, 52512)
France
27 Xo Viet Nghe Tinh St (tel 97231, 97235). The consular services entrance is opposite 62 Xo Viet Nghe Tinh St and is open on business days from 8.15 am to 12 noon and from 2.30 to 5.30 pm by appointment. Other entrances to the compound are at 102 BIS Hai Ba Trung St and 6 Le Duan Blvd.
Hungary
53 Nguyen Dinh Chieu St (tel 99023/7)
Poland
2B Tran Cao Van St (tel 92215)
USSR
40 Ba Huyen Thanh Quan St (tel 92936/7/8)

Airline Offices The Domestic Booking Office of Vietnam Airlines (tel 99910, 99980) is about 2 km from the centre of town at 27B Nguyen Dinh Chieu St. This office can only reserve seats on flights originating from Saigon. Places on flights departing from other cities can be reserved before you get there by cable, something Vietnam Tourism may be able to help with.

The Domestic Booking Office is open from 7 to 10.45 am and from 1 to 3.45 pm daily, except Sunday.

The Vietnam Airlines International Booking Office (tel 92118; telex SGNRRVN) is downtown at 116 Nguyen Hue Blvd, across the street from the Rex Hotel. It is open Monday to Saturday from 7.30 to 11 am and 1 to 4 pm.

This office acts as the general sales agent for Aeroflot, Air France, Czechoslovak Airlines, Garuda, Kampuchean Airlines, Lao Aviation, Philippine Airlines and THAI and is the only place in Ho Chi Minh City where you can actually purchase international airline tickets. Flight reservations can be made either here or at the Aeroflot, Air France and Philippines Airlines offices. The only foreign currency accepted at the International Booking Office is the US dollar.

The Air France reservations office (tel 90981, 90982; telex SGN SSAF) is at 130 Dong Khoi St on the ground floor of the Caravelle Hotel building. Reservations can be made here for all Air France flights around the world and for connecting flights on other airlines. The Air France office is open from 8 am to 12 noon and 2 to 4.30 pm daily except Saturday afternoon and Sunday.

The Philippines Airlines reservations office (tel 25538) is at 4A Le Loi Blvd and is open from 8 am to 5 pm Monday to Friday and 8 am to 12 noon on Saturday. The Aeroflot reservations office (tel 93489) is at 4H Le Loi Blvd, across the street from the Rex Hotel.

Bookshops The Foreign Languages Bookstore (tel 24670) is at 185 Dong Khoi St. It has a limited selection of used books in English and some antiquarian books that might interest the collector. It is open from 7.30 to 11.15 am and 1.30 to 5 pm.

For novels in English, French or German, try Cua Hang Sach Cu in District 3 at 142B Vo Thi Sau St, which is just off of Hai Ba Trung St. It has things you'd never expect to find in Vietnam, such as copies of *Mad* magazine from the 1960s!

Cua Hang Mua Ban Sach Cu is a second-hand bookstore near the Van Canh Hotel at 4-6 Dang Thi Nhu St. Sach Tong Hop (tel 91491) at 40 Ngo Duc Ke St has a few old English and French books along with postage stamps and some Soviet publications.

For dirt-cheap, high-quality art books (which unfortunately weigh a ton) from the USSR, try Xunhasaba (tel 92900), which is an acronym for 'State Enterprise for Export & Import of Books & Periodicals'. The outlet, at 82 Dong Du St (near the Saigon Central Mosque), does not seem to import much from non-Communist countries, but when I was there they were selling several-month-old Paris newspapers, a 2-month old *Herald Tribune* and a 3-month old *Time*! Great stuff if you're desperate!

Maps Maps of Saigon, Cholon and other Vietnamese cities are sold in downtown Saigon at sidewalk stands along Dong Khoi St; along Le Loi Blvd between Dong Khoi St and Nguyen Hue Blvd; and on Nguyen Hue Blvd between Le Loi Blvd and the Palace Hotel. These stalls have the best selection of maps in Vietnam; almost all the maps sold here are impossible to find anywhere else in the country. If you think you will need any maps later in your trip, this is the place to get them. Maps of Saigon and Cholon may also be on sale at the Rex Hotel gift shop.

Overall, the most accurate and up-to-date map of Saigon is dated 9.1988 in the lower right-hand corner. It is printed on cheap paper in pastel colours (yellow, orange, green, pink and grey) and has a useful inset of central Saigon in the upper left-hand corner. Though you'll be asked 5000d for it, the real price is about 1000d.

If you are interested in the pre-1975 names of Ho Chi Minh City's streets, the map with the dark blue border and the inset of Ho Chi Minh City in the lower right-hand corner has an index of old and new names on the back. *Ten Truoc 1975* means 'Name before 1975'.

Emergency Cho Ray Hospital (Benh Vien Cho Ray; tel 55137, 55138; 1000 beds), one of the best medical facilities in Vietnam, is at 201B Nguyen Chi Thanh Blvd in Cholon. There is a section for foreigners on the 10th floor. About a third of the 200 doctors speak

English. You might also try Nhi Dong 2 Hospital (Grall Hospital) on Ly Tu Trong St opposite the Franco-Vietnamese Cultural Centre.

High-ranking cadres enjoy access to Thong Nhat Hospital, a modern five-storey building on the corner of Ly Thuong Kiet Blvd and Cach Mang Thang Tam Blvd.

There are hundreds of pharmacies *(nha thuoc)* around the city. One of the largest is Hieu Thuoc Dong Khoi (tel 90577), conveniently located downtown at 201 Dong Khoi St. The pharmacists speak English and French. It is open from 7.30 to 12 noon and 1.30 to 5 pm. Another pharmacy in Saigon you might try is at 105 Nguyen Hue Blvd; it is open from 8 to 11.30 am and 2 to 6 pm.

Pagodas & Temples – Saigon

Giac Lam Pagoda Giac Lam Pagoda dates from 1744 and is believed to be the oldest pagoda in Ho Chi Minh City. Because the last reconstruction here was in 1900, the architecture, layout and ornamentation remain almost unaltered by the modernist renovations that have transformed so many other religious structures in Vietnam. Ten monks live at this Vietnamese Buddhist pagoda, which also incorporates aspects of Taoism and Confucianism. It is well worth the trip out here from downtown Saigon.

Giac Lam Pagoda is about 3 km from Cholon at 118 Lac Long Quan St in Tan Binh District. Beware: the numbering on Lac Long Quan St is extremely confused, starting over from one several times and at one point jumping to four digits. In many places, odd and even numbers are on the same side of the street.

The best way to get to Giac Lam Pagoda is to take Nguyen Chi Thanh Blvd or 3 Thang 2 Blvd to Le Dai Hanh St. Go north-westward on Le Dai Hanh St and turn right onto Lac Long Quan St. Walk 100 metres; the pagoda gate will be on your left. It is open to visitors from 6 am to 9 pm.

To the right of the gate to the pagoda compound are the ornate tombs of venerated monks. The *bo de* (bodhi, or pipal) tree in the front garden was the gift of a monk from Sri

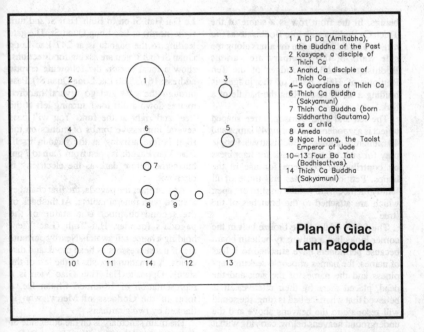

1 A Di Da (Amitabha),
  the Buddha of the Past
2 Kasyape, a disciple of
  Thich Ca
3 Anand, a disciple of
  Thich Ca
4–5 Guardians of Thich Ca
6 Thich Ca Buddha
  (Sakyamuni)
7 Thich Ca Buddha (born
  Siddhartha Gautama)
  as a child
8 Ameda
9 Ngoc Hoang, the Taoist
  Emperor of Jade
10–13 Four Bo Tat
  (Bodhisattvas)
14 Thich Ca Buddha
  (Sakyamuni)

**Plan of Giac
Lam Pagoda**

Lanka. Next to the tree is a regular feature of Vietnamese Buddhist temples, a gleaming white statue of Quan The Am Bo Tat (Avalokiteçvara, the Goddess of Mercy) standing on a lotus blossom, symbol of purity.

The roofline of the main building is decorated both inside and outside with unusual blue and white porcelain plates. Through the main entrance is a reception hall lined with funeral tablets and photos of the deceased. Roughly in the centre of the hall, near an old French chandelier, is a figure of 18-armed Chuan De, another form of the Goddess of Mercy. Note the carved hardwood columns, which bear gilded Vietnamese inscriptions written in *nom* characters, a form of writing in use before the adoption of the Latin-based *quoc ngu* alphabet. The wall to the left is covered with portraits of great monks from previous generations. Monks' names and biographical information about them are recorded on the vertical red tablets in gold

nom characters. A box for donations sits nearby. Shoes should be removed when passing from the rough red floor tiles to the smaller, white-black-grey tiles.

On the other side of the wall from the monks' funeral tablets is the main sanctuary, which is filled with countless gilded figures. On the dais in the centre of the back row sits A Di Da (pronounced 'AH-zee-dah'), the Buddha of the Past (Amitabha). To his right is Kasyape and to his left Anand; both are disciples of the Thich Ca Buddha (the historical Buddha Sakyamuni, whose real name was Siddhartha Gautama). Directly in front of A Di Da is a statue of the Thich Ca Buddha, flanked by two guardians. In front of Thich Ca is the tiny figure of the Thich Ca Buddha as a child. As always, he is clothed in a yellow robe. The fat laughing fellow, seated with five children climbing all over him, is Ameda. To his left is Ngoc Hoang, the Taoist Emperor of Jade who presides over a world of innumerable supernatural beings. In the front row is a statue of the Thich Ca Buddha with four Bodhisattvas (*bo tat*), two on each side. On the altars along the side walls of the sanctuary are various Bodhisattvas and the Judges of the Ten Regions of Hell. Each of the judges is holding a scroll resembling the handle of a fork.

The red and gold Christmas-tree shaped object is a wooden altar bearing 49 lamps and 49 miniature statues of Bodhisattvas. People pray for sick relatives or ask for happiness by contributing kerosene for use in the lamps. Petitioners' names and those of ill family members are written on slips of paper, which are attached to the branches of the 'tree'.

The frame of the large bronze bell in the corner looks like a university bulletin board because petitioners have attached to it lists of names: the names of people seeking happiness and the names of the sick and the dead, placed there by their relatives. It is believed that when the bell is rung, the sound will resonate to the heavens above and the underground heavens below, carrying with it the attached supplications.

Prayers here consist of chanting to the accompaniment of drums, bells and gongs and follow a traditional rite seldom performed these days. Prayers are held daily from 4 to 5 am, 11 am to 12 noon, 4 to 5 pm and 7 to 9 pm.

Giac Vien Pagoda Giac Vien Pagoda and Giac Lam Pagoda are similar architecturally. Both pagodas share the same atmosphere of scholarly serenity, though Giac Vien, which is right next to Dam Sen Lake in District 11, is in a more rural setting. Giac Vien Pagoda was founded by Hai Tinh Giac Vien about 200 years ago. It is said that the Emperor Gia Long, who died in 1819, used to worship at Giac Vien. Today, 10 monks live here.

Because of the impossibly confusing numbering on Lac Long Quan St, the best way to get to Giac Vien Pagoda is to take Nguyen Chi Thanh Blvd or 3 Thang 2 Blvd to Le Dai Han St. Turn left (south-west) off

Le Dai Han St on to Binh Thoi St and turn right (north) at Lac Long Quan St. The gate leading to the pagoda is at 247 Lac Long Quan St (but if you are asking for directions, show a local person the following cryptic address: 161/35/20 Lac Long Quan St). Pass through the gate and go several hundred metres down a dirt road, turning left at the 'tee' and right at the fork. You will pass several impressive tombs of monks on the right before arriving at the pagoda itself. Giac Vien Pagoda is open from 7 am to 7 pm but come before dark as the electricity is often out.

As you enter the pagoda, the first chamber is lined with funeral tablets. At the back of the second chamber is a statue of the pagoda's founder, Hai Tinh Giac Vien, holding a horse-tail swatch. Nearby portraits are of his successors as head monk and disciples. A donation box sits to the left of the statue. Opposite Hai Tinh Giac Vien is a representation of 18-armed Chuan De, a form of the Goddess of Mercy, who is flanked by two guardians.

The main sanctuary is on the other side of the wall behind Hai Tinh Giac Vien. A Di Da, the Buddha of the Past, is at the back of the dais. Directly in front of him is the Thich Ca Buddha (Sakyamuni), flanked by Thich Ca's disciples Anand (on the left) and Kasyape (on the right). To the right of Kasyape is the Ti Lu Buddha; to the left of Anand is the Nhien Dang Buddha. At the foot of the Thich Ca Buddha is a small figure of Thich Ca (Siddhartha Gautama) as a child. Fat, laughing Ameda is seated with children climbing all over him; far on either side of him are guardians, standing. In the front row of the dais is Thich Ca with two Bodhisattvason each side.

In front of the dais is a fantastic brass incense basin with fierce dragon heads emerging from each side. On the altar to the left of the dais is Dai The Chi Bo Tat; on the altar to the right is Quan The Am Bo Tat (Avalokiteçvara), the Goddess of Mercy. The Guardian of the Pagoda is against the wall opposite the dais. Nearby is a 'Christmas tree' similar to the one in Giac Lam Pagoda.

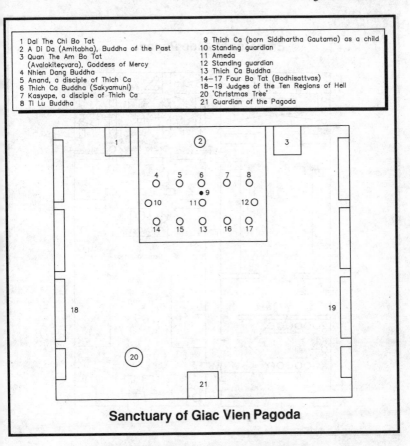

1 Dai The Chi Bo Tat
2 A Di Da (Amitabha), Buddha of the Past
3 Quan The Am Bo Tat
  (Avalokiteçvara), Goddess of Mercy
4 Nhien Dang Buddha
5 Anand, a disciple of Thich Ca
6 Thich Ca Buddha (Sakyamuni)
7 Kasyape, a disciple of Thich Ca
8 Ti Lu Buddha
9 Thich Ca (born Siddhartha Gautama) as a child
10 Standing guardian
11 Ameda
12 Standing guardian
13 Thich Ca Buddha
14—17 Four Bo Tat (Bodhisattvas)
18—19 Judges of the Ten Regions of Hell
20 'Christmas Tree'
21 Guardian of the Pagoda

Sanctuary of Giac Vien Pagoda

Lining the side walls are the Judges of the Ten Regions of Hell (holding scrolls) and 18 Bodhisattvas.

Prayers are held daily from 4 to 5 am, 8 to 10 am, 2 to 3 pm, 4 to 5 pm and 7 to 9 pm.

Emperor of Jade Pagoda The Emperor of Jade Pagoda (known in Vietnamese as Phuoc Hai Tu and Chua Ngoc Hoang), built in 1909 by the Canton Congregation, is truly a gem of a Chinese temple. It is one of the most spectacularly colourful pagodas in Ho Chi Minh City, filled with statues of phantasmal divinities and grotesque heroes. The pungent smoke of burning joss sticks fills the air, obscuring exquisite wood carvings decorated with gilded Chinese characters. The roof is covered with elaborate tilework. The statues, which represent characters from both the Buddhist and Taoist traditions, are made of reinforced papier mâché.

The Emperor of Jade Pagoda is at 73 Mai Thi Luu St in a part of Saigon known as Da Kao (or Da Cao). To get there, go to 20 Dien Bien Phu St and walk half a block north-westward (to the left as you head out of Saigon towards Thi Nghe Channel).

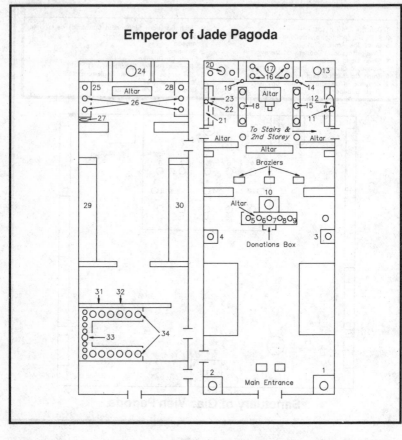

Emperor of Jade Pagoda

As you enter the main doors of the building, Mon Quan, the God of the Gate stands to the right in an elaborately carved wooden case. Opposite him, in a similar case, is Tho Than (Tho Dia), the God of the Land. Straight on is an altar on which are placed, from left to right, figures of: Phat Mau Chuan De, mother of the five Buddhas of the cardinal directions; Dia Tang Vuong Bo Tat (Ksitigartha), the King of Hell; the Di Lac Buddha (Maitreya), the Buddha of the Future; Quan The Am Bo Tat, the Goddess of Mercy; and a bas-relief portrait of the Thich Ca Buddha (Sakyamuni). Behind the

altar, in a glass case, is the Duoc Su Buddha, also known as the Nhu Lai Buddha. The figure is said to be made of sandalwood.

To either side of the altar, against the walls, are two especially fierce and menacing figures. On the right (as you face the altar) is a 4 metre high statue of the general who defeated the Green Dragon. He is stepping on the vanquished dragon. On the left is the general who defeated the White Tiger, which is also getting stepped on.

The Taoist Emperor of Jade, Ngoc Hoang, presides over the main sanctuary, draped in luxurious robes. He is flanked by the 'Four

1	Mon Quan, the God of the Gate	15	Nam Tao, God of the Southern Polar Star and God of Happiness
2	Tho Than (Tho Dia), the God of the Land	16	Tu Dai Kim Cuong, the 'Four Big Diamonds'
3	The general who defeated the Green Dragon	17	Ngoc Hoang, the Emperor of Jade
4	The general who defeated the White Tiger	18	Bac Dau, God of the Northern Polar Star and God of Longevity
5	Phat Mau Chuan De, mother of the five Buddhas of the cardinal directions	19	Goddess of the Moon
6	Dia Tang Vuong Bo Tat, the King of Hell	20	Ong Bac De, a reincarnation of the Emperor of Jade
7	Di Lac Buddha (Maitreya), the Buddha of the future	21	Thien Loi's guards (upper step)
8	Quan The Am Bo Tat (Avalokiteçvara), the Goddess of Mercy	22	Thien Loi, the God of Lightening
		23	Ong Bac De's military commanders (lower step)
9	Thich Ca Buddha (Sakyamuni; in a bas-relief portrait)	24	Thanh Hoang, the Chief of Hell
10	Duoc Su Buddha (Nhu Lai Buddha; in glass case)	25	Am Quan, the God of Yin
		26	Thuong Thien Phat Ac
11	Dai Minh Vuong Quang (on the back of a phoenix)	27	Thanh Hoang's red horse
		28	Duong Quan, the God of Yang
12	The Tien Nhan (God Persons)	29-30	Panels of the Hall of the Ten Hells
13	Phat Mau Chuan De, mother of the five Buddhas of the cardinal directions	31	Dia Tang Vuong Bo Tat, the King of Hell
14	God of the Sun	32	Quan Am Thi Kinh, the Guardian Spirit of Mother and Child
		33	Kim Hoa Thanh Mau, the Chief of all Women
		34	Figurines of 12 Women

Big Diamonds' (Tu Dai Kim Cuong), his four guardians, so named because they are said to be as hard as diamonds. In front of the Emperor of Jade stand six figures, three to each side. On the left is Bac Dau, the Taoist God of the Northern Polar Star and God of Longevity, flanked by his two guardians; and on the right is Nam Tao, the Taoist God of the Southern Polar Star and God of Happiness, also flanked by two guardians.

In the case to the right of the Emperor of Jade is 18-armed Phat Mau Chuan De, mother of the five Buddhas of the north, south, east, west and centre. Two faces, affixed to her head behind each ear, look to either side. On the wall to the right of Phat Mau Chuan De at a height of about 4 metres is Dai Minh Vuong Quang, who was reincarnated as Sakyamuni, riding on the back of a phoenix. Below are the Tien Nhan, literally the 'god-persons'.

In the case to the left of the Emperor of Jade sits Ong Bac De, a reincarnation of the Emperor of Jade, holding a sword. One of his feet is resting on a turtle while the other rests on a snake. On the wall to the left of Ong Bac De, about 4 metres off the ground, is Thien Loi, the God of Lightning, who slays evil people. Below Thien Loi are the military commanders of Ong Bac De (on the lower step) and Thien Loi's guards (on the upper step). At the top of the two carved pillars that separate the three alcoves are the Goddess of the Moon (on the left) and God of the Sun (on the right).

Out the door on the left-hand side of the Emperor of Jade's chamber is another room. The semi-enclosed area to the right (as you enter) is presided over by Thanh Hoang, the Chief of Hell; to the left is his red horse. Of the six figures lining the walls, the two closest to Thanh Hoang are Am Quan, the God of Yin (on the left) and Duong Quan, the God of Yang (on the right). The other four figures, the Thuong Thien Phat Ac, are gods who dispense punishments for evil acts and rewards for good deeds. Thanh Hoang faces in the direction of the famous Hall of the Ten Hells. The carved wooden panels lining the walls graphically depict the varied torments awaiting evil people in each of the 10 regions of hell. At the top of each panel is one of the Ten Judges of Hell examining a book in which the deeds of the deceased are inscribed.

On the wall opposite Thanh Hoang is a bas-relief wood panel depicting Quan Am Thi Kinh, the Guardian Spirit of Mother and Child, standing on a lotus blossom, symbol of purity. Unjustly turned out of her home by her husband, Quan Am Thi Kinh disguised herself as a monk and went to live in a pagoda, where a young woman accused her of fathering her child. She accepted the

Van Long Catholic Church

blame – and the responsibility that went along with it – and again found herself out on the streets, this time with her 'son'. Much later, about to die, she returned to the monastery to confess her secret. When the Emperor of China heard of her story, he declared her the Guardian Spirit of Mother & Child.

It is believed that she has the power to bestow male offspring on those who fervently believe in her. On the panel, Quan Am Thi Kinh is shown holding her 'son'. To her left is Long Nu, a very young Buddha who is her protectress. To Quan Am Thi Kinh's right is Thien Tai, her guardian spirit, who knew the real story all along. Above her left shoulder is a bird bearing prayer beads.

To the right of the panel of Quan Am Thi Kinh is a panel depicting Dia Tang Vuong Bo Tat, the King of Hell.

On the other side of the wall is a fascinating little room in which the ceramic figures of 12 women, overrun with children and wearing colourful clothes, sit in two rows of six. Each of the women exemplifies a human characteristic, either good or bad (as in the case of the woman drinking alcohol from a jug). Each figure represents 1 year in the 12-year Chinese calendar. Presiding over the room is Kim Hoa Thanh Mau, the Chief of Women.

To the right of the main chamber, stairs lead up to a 2nd-floor sanctuary and balcony.

Notre Dame Cathedral Notre Dame Cathedral, built between 1877 and 1883, is set in the heart of Saigon's government quarter. The cathedral faces down Dong Khoi St. Its neo-Romanesque form and two 40 metre high square towers, tipped with iron spires, dominate the city's skyline. In front of the cathedral (in the centre of the square bounded by the GPO) is a statue of the Virgin Mary. If the front gates are locked try the door on the side of the building that faces Reunification Hall.

There are several other interesting French-era churches around Saigon, including one at 289 Hai Ba Trung St.

Xa Loi Pagoda Xa Loi Vietnamese Buddhist Pagoda, built in 1956, is famed as the repository of a sacred relic of the Buddha. In August 1963, truckloads of armed men under the command of President Ngo Dinh Diem's brother, Ngo Dinh Nhu, attacked Xa Loi Pagoda, which had become a centre of opposition to the Diem government. The pagoda was ransacked and 400 monks and nuns, including the country's 80-year-old Buddhist patriarch, were arrested. This raid and others elsewhere helped solidify opposition among Buddhists to the Diem regime, a crucial factor in the US decision to support the coup against Diem. This pagoda was also the site of several self-immolations by bonzes protesting against the Diem regime and the war.

Women enter the main hall of Xa Loi Pagoda by the staircase on the right as you come in the gate; men use the stairs on the left. The walls of the sanctuary are adorned with paintings depicting the Buddha's life.

Xa Loi Pagoda is in District 3 at 89 Ba Huyen Thanh Quan St, near Dien Bien Phu St. It is open daily from 7 to 11 am and from 2 to 5 pm. A bonze preaches every Sunday morning from 8 to 10 am. On days of the full moon and new moon, special prayers are held from 7 to 9 am and from 7 to 8 pm.

Phung Son Tu Pagoda Phung Son Tu Pagoda, built by the Fukien Congregation in the mid-1940s, is more typical of Ho Chi Minh City's Chinese pagodas than is the Emperor of Jade Pagoda. The interior is often hung with huge incense spirals that burn for hours. Worshippers include both ethnic-Chinese and ethnic-Vietnamese. Phung Son Tu Pagoda is dedicated to Ong Bon, Guardian Spirit of Happiness & Virtue, whose statue is behind the main altar in the sanctuary. On the right-hand side of the main hall is the multi-armed Buddhist Goddess of Mercy. This pagoda is only 1 km from downtown Saigon at 338 Nguyen Cong Tru St.

Dai Giac Pagoda This Vietnamese Buddhist pagoda is built in a style characteristic of pagodas constructed during the 1960s. In the courtyard, under the unfinished 10-level red-pink tower inlaid with porcelain chards, is an artificial cave made of volcanic rocks in which there is a gilded statue of the Goddess of Mercy. In the main sanctuary, the 2½-metre gilt Buddha has a green neon halo, while below, a smaller white reclining Buddha (in a glass case) has a blue neon halo. Dai Giac Pagoda is at 112 Nguyen Van Troi St, 1.5 km towards the city centre from the gate to the airport.

Vinh Nghiem Pagoda Vinh Nghiem Pagoda, inaugurated in 1971, is noteworthy for its vast sanctuary and eight-storey tower, each level of which contains a statue of the Buddha. It was built with help from the Japan-Vietnam Friendship Association, which explains the presence of Japanese elements in its architecture. At the base of the tower (which is open only on holidays) is a store selling Buddhist ritual objects. Behind the sanctuary is a three-storey tower which serves as a repository for carefully labelled ceramic urns containing the ashes of people who have been cremated. The pagoda is in District 3 at 339 Nam Ky Khoi Nghia St and is open from 7.30 to 11.30 am and 2 to 6 pm daily.

Le Van Duyet Temple This temple is dedicated to Marshal Le Van Duyet (pronounced 'Lee Van Zyet'), who is buried here with his wife. The Marshal, who lived from 1763 to 1831, was a southern Vietnamese general and viceroy who helped put down the Tay Son Rebellion and reunify Vietnam. When the Nguyen Dynasty came to power in 1802, he was elevated by Emperor Gia Long to the rank of marshal. Le Van Duyet fell into disfavour with Gia Long's successor, Minh Mang, who tried him posthumously and desecrated his grave. Emperor Thieu Tri, who succeeded Minh Mang, restored the tomb, fulfilling a prophesy of its destruction and restoration. Le Van Duyet was considered a great national hero in the South before 1975 but is disliked by the Communists because of his involvement in the expansion of French influence.

Le Van Duyet Temple is 3 km from the centre of Saigon in the Gia Dinh area at 131 Dinh Tien Hoang St (near where Phan Dang Luu Blvd becomes Bach Dang Blvd).

The temple itself was renovated in 1937 and has a distinctly modern feel to it. Since 1975, the government has done little to keep it from becoming dilapidated. Among the items on display are a portrait of Le Van Duyet, some of his personal effects (including European-style crystal goblets) and other antiques. There are two wonderful life-size horses on either side of the entrance to the third and last chamber, which is kept locked.

During celebrations of Tet (Vietnamese New Year) the tomb is thronged with pilgrims. Vietnamese used to come here to take oaths of good faith if they could not afford the services of a court of justice. The tropical fish are on sale to visitors. The caged birds are bought by pilgrims and freed to earn merit. The birds are often recaptured (and liberated again).

Tran Hung Dao Temple This small temple is dedicated to Tran Hung Dao, a Vietnamese national hero who in 1287 vanquished an invasion force, said to have numbered 300,000 men, which had been dispatched by the Mongol emperor Kublai Khan. The temple is at 36 Vo Ti Sau St, a block northeast of the telecommunications dishes that are between Dien Bien Phu St and Vi Thi Su St.

The public park between the antenna dishes and Hai Ba Trung St was built in 1983 on the site of the Massiges Cemetery, burial place of French soldiers and settlers. The remains of French military personnel were exhumed and repatriated to France. Another site no longer in existence is the tomb of the 18th-century French missionary and diplomat, Pigneau de Béhaine, Bishop of Adran, which was completely destroyed after reunification.

Mariamman Hindu Temple Mariamman Hindu Temple, the only Hindu temple still in use in Ho Chi Minh City, is a little piece of southern India in the centre of Saigon.

Though there are only 50 to 60 Hindus in Ho Chi Minh City – all of them Tamils – this temple, known in Vietnamese as Chua Ba Mariamman, is also considered sacred by many ethnic-Vietnamese and ethnic-Chinese. Indeed, it is reputed to have miraculous powers. The temple was built at the end of the 19th century and dedicated to the Hindu goddess Mariamman.

The lion to the left of the entrance used to be carried around Saigon in a street procession every autumn. In the shrine in the middle of the temple are Mariamman flanked by her guardians, Maduraiveeran (to her left) and Pechiamman (to her right). In front of the figure of Mariamman are two lingams. Favourite offerings placed nearby include joss sticks, jasmine flowers, lilies and gladiolus. The wooden stairs, on the left as you enter the building, lead to the roof, where you'll find two colourful towers covered with innumerable figures of lions, goddesses and guardians.

After reunification, the government took over the temple and turned part of it into a factory for joss sticks. A company producing seafood for export was located in another section, and seafood was dried in the sun on the roof. The whole temple will be returned to the local Hindu community in the near future.

Mariamman Temple is only three blocks from Ben Thanh Market at 45 Truong Dinh St. It is open from 7 am to 7 pm daily. Take off your shoes before stepping onto the slightly raised platform.

Saigon Central Mosque Built by South Indian Muslims in 1935 on the site of an earlier mosque, the Saigon Central Mosque is an immaculately clean and well-kept island of calm in the middle of bustling downtown Saigon. In front of the sparkling white and blue structure at 66 Dong Du St, with its four non-functional minarets, is a pool for ritual ablutions (washing), required by Islamic law before prayers. As with any mosque, take off your shoes before entering the sanctuary.

The simplicity of the mosque is in marked

contrast to the exuberance of Chinese temple decorations and the rows of figures, facing elaborate ritual objects, in Buddhist pagodas. Islamic law strictly forbids using human or animal figures for decoration.

Only half-a-dozen Indian Muslims remain in Saigon; most of the community fled in 1975. As a result, prayers – held five times a day – are sparsely attended except on Fridays, when several dozen worshippers (including many non-Indian Muslims) are present. The mass emigration also deprived the local Muslim community of much of its spiritual leadership, and very few Muslims knowledgeable in their tradition and Arabic, language of the Koran, remain.

There are 12 other mosques serving the 5000 or so Muslims in Ho Chi Minh City.

Pagodas & Temples – Cholon

Tam Son Hoi Quan Pagoda Tam Son Hoi Pagoda, known to the Vietnamese as Chua Ba Chua, was built by the Fukien Congregation in the 19th century and retains unmodified most of its original rich ornamentation. The pagoda is dedicated to Me Sanh, the Goddess of Fertility. Both men and women – but more of the latter – come here to pray for children. Tam Son Hoi Pagoda is at 118 Trieu Quang Phuc St, which is very near 370 Tran Hung Dao B Blvd.

To the right of the covered courtyard is the deified general Quan Cong (in Chinese: Kuan Kung) with a long black beard; he is flanked by two guardians, the mandarin general Chau Xuong on the left (holding a weapon) and the administrative mandarin Quan Binh on the right. Next to Chau Xuong is Quan Cong's sacred red horse.

Behind the main altar (directly across the courtyard from the entrance) is the goddess Thien Hau, Goddess of the Sea and Protectress of Fishermen and Sailors. To the right is an ornate case in which Me Sanh (the Goddess of Fertility; in white) sits surrounded by her daughters. In the case to the left of Thien Hau is Ong Bon, Guardian Spirit of Happiness & Virtue. In front of Thien Hau is Quan The Am Bo Tat (also

known as Avolokiteçvara), the Goddess of Mercy, enclosed in glass.

Across the courtyard from Quan Cong is a small room containing ossuary jars (in which the ashes of the deceased are reposited) and memorials in which the dead are represented by their photographs. Next to this chamber is a small room containing the papier mâché head of a dragon of the type used by the Fukien Congregation for dragon dancing. There is a photograph of a dragon dance on the wall between Quan Cong's red horse and Me Sanh.

Thien Hau Pagoda Thien Hau Pagoda (also known as Ba Mieu, Pho Mieu and Chua Ba) was built by the Canton Congregation in the early 19th century. Of late it has become something of a showcase for tours operated by Saigon Tourist and Vietnam Tourism, which may explain the recent extensive renovations. Thien Hau Pagoda is at 710 Nguyen Trai St and is open from 6 am to 5.30 pm.

The pagoda is dedicated to Thien Hau (also known as Tuc Goi La Ba), the Chinese Goddess of the Sea who protects fisherfolk, sailors, merchants and anyone else who travels by sea. It is said that Thien Hau can travel over the oceans on a mat and ride the clouds to wherever she pleases. Her mobility allows her to save people in trouble on the high seas.

Though there are guardians to either side of the entrance, it is said that the real protectors of the pagoda are the two land turtles who live here. There are intricate ceramic friezes above the roofline of the interior courtyard. Near the huge braziers are two miniature wooden structures in which a small figure of Thien Hau is paraded around each year on the 23rd day of the 3rd lunar month. On the main dais are three figures of Thien Hau, one behind the other, each flanked by two servants or guardians. To the left of the dais is a bed for Thien Hau. To the right is a scale-model boat and on the far right is the Goddess Long Mau, Protectress of Mothers & Newborns.

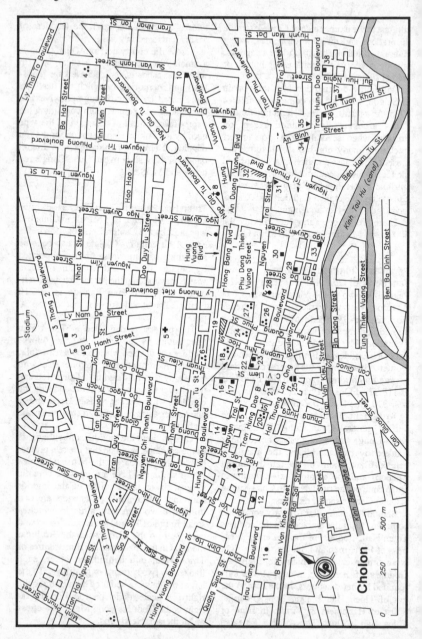

Cholon

Nghia An Hoi Quan Pagoda Nghia An Hoi Quan Pagoda, built by the Trieu Chau Chinese Congregation, is noteworthy for its gilded woodwork. There is a carved wooden boat over the entrance and inside, to the left of the doorway, is an enormous representation of Quan Cong's red horse with its groom. To the right of the entrance is an elaborate altar in which a bearded Ong Bon, Guardian Spirit of Happiness & Virtue, stands holding a stick. Behind the main altar are three glass cases. In the centre is Quan Cong (Chinese: *Kuan Kung);* to either side are his assistants, the general Chau Xuong (on the left) and the administrative mandarin Quan Binh (on the right). To the right of Quan Binh is an especially elaborate case for Thien Hau, Goddess of the Sea & Protectress of Fishermen & Sailors.

Nghia An Hoi Quan Pagoda is at 678 Nguyen Trai St (not far from Thien Hau Pagoda) and is open from 4 am to 6 pm.

Cholon Mosque The clean lines and lack of ornamentation of the Cholon Mosque are in stark contrast to nearby Chinese and Vietnamese pagodas. In the courtyard is a pool for ritual ablutions. Note the tile *mihrab* (the niche in the wall indicating the direction of prayer, which is towards Mecca). The mosque was built by Tamil Muslims in 1932. Since 1975, the mosque has served the Malaysian and Indonesian Muslim communities.

Cholon Mosque is at 641 Nguyen Trai St and is open all day Friday and at prayer times on other days.

Quan Am Pagoda Quan Am Pagoda at 12 Lao Tu St, one block off Chau Van Liem Blvd, was founded in 1816 by the Fukien Congregation. The roof is decorated with fantastic scenes, rendered in ceramic, from traditional Chinese plays and stories. The tableaus include ships, houses, people and several ferocious dragons. The front doors are decorated with very old gold and lacquer panels. On the walls of the porch are murals in slight relief picturing scenes of China from the time of Quan Cong. There are elaborate wooden carvings on roof supports above the porch.

Behind the main altar is A Pho, the Holy Mother Celestial Empress, gilded and in rich raiment. In front of her, in a glass case, are three painted statues of Thich Ca Buddha

(Sakyamuni), a standing gold Quan The Am Bo That (Goddess of Mercy), a seated laughing Ameda, and, to the far left, a gold figure of Dia Tang Vuong Bo Tat (the King of Hell).

In the courtyard behind the main sanctuary, in the pink tile altar, is another figure of A Pho. Quan The Am Bo Tat (Avalokiteçvara, Goddess of Mercy) dressed in white embroidered robes, stands nearby. To the left of the pink altar is her richly ornamented bed. To the right of the pink altar is Quan Cong flanked by his guardians, the general Chau Xuong (on the left) and the administrative mandarin Quan Binh (on the right). To the far right, in front of another pink altar, is the black-faced judge Bao Cong.

Phuoc An Hoi Quan Pagoda Phuoc An Hoi Quan Pagoda, built in 1902 by the Fukien Congregation, is one of the most beautifully ornamented pagodas in Ho Chi Minh City. Of special interest are the many small porcelain figures, the elaborate brass ritual objects, and the fine wood carvings on the altars, walls, columns and hanging lanterns. From outside the building you can see the ceramic scenes, each containing innumerable small figurines, which decorate the roof. Phuoc An Hoi Quan Pagoda is at 184 Hung Vuong Blvd (near the intersection of Chau Van Liem Blvd).

To the left of the entrance is a life-size figure of the sacred horse of Quan Cong. Before leaving on a journey, people make offerings to the horse. They then pet the horse's mane before ringing the bell around its neck. Behind the main altar, with its stone and brass incense braziers, is Quan Cong (Chinese: Kuan Kung), to whom the pagoda is dedicated. Behind the altar to the left is Ong Bon, Guardian Spirit of Happiness and Virtue, and two servants. The altar to the right is occupied by representations of Buddhist (rather than Taoist) personages. In the glass case are a plaster Thich Ca Buddha (Sakyamuni) and two figures of the Goddess of Mercy, one made of porcelain and the other cast in brass.

Ong Bon Pagoda Ong Bon Pagoda (also known as Chua Ong Bon and Nhi Phu Hoi Quan) was built by the Fukien Congregation and is dedicated to Ong Bon, Guardian Spirit of Happiness & Virtue. The wooden altar is intricately carved and gilded. Ong Bon Pagoda is at 264 Hai Thuong Lai Ong Blvd, which runs parallel to Tran Hung Dao B Blvd, and is open from 5 am to 5 pm.

As you enter the pagoda, there is a room to the right of the open-air courtyard. In it, behind the table, is a figure of Quan The Am Bo Tat (Goddess of Mercy) in a glass case. Above the case is the head of a Thich Ca Buddha (Sakyamuni).

Directly across the courtyard from the pagoda entrance, against the wall, is Ong Bon, to whom people come to pray for general happiness and relief from financial difficulties. He faces a fine carved wooden altar. On the walls of this chamber are two rather indistinct murals of five tigers (to the left) and two dragons (to the right).

In the area on the other side of the wall with the mural of the dragons is a furnace for burning paper representations of the wealth people wish to bestow upon deceased family members. Diagonally opposite is Quan Cong flanked by his guardians Chau Xuong (to his right) and Quan Binh (to his left).

Ha Chuong Hoi Quan Pagoda Ha Chuong Hoi Quan Pagoda at 802 Nguyen Trai St is a typical Fukien pagoda. It is dedicated to Thien Hau Thanh Mau, Goddess of the Sea and protectress of all who travel the seas, who was born in Fukien. The four carved stone pillars, wrapped in painted dragons, were made in China and brought to Vietnam by boat. There are interesting murals to either side of the main altar. Note the ceramic relief scenes on the roof.

Cha Tam Church It is in Cha Tam Church that President Ngo Dinh Diem and his brother Nhu took refuge on 2 November 1963 after fleeing the Presidential Palace during a coup attempt. When their efforts to contact loyal military officers failed (of whom there were almost none), Diem and

Nhu agreed to surrender unconditionally and revealed where they were hiding. The coup leaders sent an M-113 armoured personnel carrier to the church to pick them up (Diem seemed disappointed that a limousine befitting his rank had not been dispatched) and the two were taken into custody. But before the vehicle arrived in Saigon, the soldiers in the APC killed Diem and Nhu by shooting them at point blank range and then repeatedly stabbing their bodies.

When news of the death of the brothers was broadcast on the radio, Saigon exploded into rejoicing. Portraits of the two were torn up and political prisoners, many of whom had been tortured, were set free. The city's nightclubs, closed because of the Ngos' conservative Catholic beliefs, reopened.

Cha Tam Church, built around the turn of the century, is an attractive white and pastel-yellow structure. The statue in the tower is of François Xavier Tam Assou (1855-1934), a Chinese-born vicar apostolic of Saigon. (A vicar apostolic is a delegate of the pope who administers an ecclesiastical district in a missionary region.) Today, the church has a very active congregation of 3000 ethnic-Vietnamese and 2000 ethnic-Chinese.

Vietnamese-language masses are held daily from 5.30 to 6 am and on Sundays from 5.30 to 6.30 am, 8.30 to 9.30 am and 3.45 to 4.45 pm. Chinese-language masses are held from 5.30 to 6 pm every day and from 7 to 8 am and 5 to 6 pm on Sundays. Cha Tam Church is at the south-western terminus of Tran Hung Dao B Blvd; the street address is 25 Hoc Lac St.

Khanh Van Nam Vien Pagoda

Built between 1939 and 1942 by the Cantonese, Khanh Van Nam Vien Pagoda is said to be the only Taoist pagoda in all of Vietnam. It serves Ho Chi Minh City's Taoist community, which numbers only 4000. The pagoda is open from 6.30 am to 5.30 pm every day and prayers are held from 8 to 9 am daily. To get there, turn off Nguyen Thi Nho St (which runs perpendicular to Hung Vuong Blvd) between numbers 269B and 271B; the address is 46/5 Lo Sieu St.

A few metres from the door is a statue of Hoang Linh Quan, chief guardian of the pagoda. There is a Yin & Yang symbol on the platform on which the incense braziers sit. Behind the main altar are four figures: Quan Cong (on the right) and Lu Tung Pan (on the left) represent Taoism; between the two of them is Van Xuong representing Confucianism; and behind Van Xuong is Quan The Am Bo Tat (Avalokitecvara), the Buddhist Goddess of Mercy. In front of these figures is a glass case containing seven gods and one goddess, all of which are made of porcelain. In the altars to either side of the four figures are Hoa De (on the left), a famous doctor during the Han Dynasty, and Huynh Dai Tien (on the right), a disciple of the founder of Taoism, Lao Tse.

Upstairs is a 150 cm high statue of the founder of Taoism, Lao Tse (Vietnamese: *Thai Thuong Lao Quan*). Behind his head is a halo consisting of a round mirror with fluorescent lighting around the edge.

To the left of Lao Tse are two stone plaques with instructions for inhalation and exhalation exercises. A schematic drawing represents the human organs as a scene from rural China. The diaphragm, agent of inhalation, is at the bottom. The stomach is represented by a peasant ploughing with a water buffalo. The kidney is marked by four Yin & Yang symbols, the liver is shown as a grove of trees, and the heart is represented by a circle with a peasant standing in it, above which is a constellation. The tall pagoda represents the throat, and the broken rainbow is the mouth. At the top are mountains and a seated figure representing the brain and the imagination, respectively. The 80-year-old chief monk says that he has practised these exercises for the past 17 years and hasn't been sick a day.

The pagoda operates a home at 46/14 Lo Sieu St for 30 elderly people who have no families. Each of the old folk, most of whom are women, have their own wood stove made of brick and can cook for themselves. Next door, also run by the pagoda, is a free medical clinic, which offers Chinese herbal medicines (stored in the wooden drawers) and acupuncture treatments to the community. Before reunification, the pagoda ran (also free of charge) the school across the street from the pagoda.

Phung Son Pagoda Phung Son Pagoda (also known as Phung Son Tu and Chua Go) is extremely rich in statuary made of hammered copper, bronze, wood and ceramic. Some are gilded while others, beautifully carved, are painted. This Vietnamese Buddhist pagoda was built between 1802 and 1820 on the site of structures from the Oc-Eo (Funan) period, which was contemporaneous with the early centuries of Christianity. In 1988, a Soviet archaeological team carried out a preliminary excavation and found the foundations of Funanese buildings, but work

was stopped pending authorisation for a full-scale dig.

Phung Son Pagoda is in District 11 at 1408 3 Thang 2 Blvd, which is a block from Hung Vuong Blvd. Prayers are held three times a day from 4 to 5 am, 4 to 5 pm and 6 to 7 pm. The main entrances are kept locked because of problems with theft but the side entrance (to the left as you approach the building) is open from 5 am to 7 pm.

Once upon a time, it was decided that Phung Son Pagoda should be moved to a different site. The pagoda's ritual objects – bells, drums, statues – were loaded onto the back of a white elephant for transport to the new location, but the elephant slipped because of the great weight and all the precious objects fell into a nearby pond. This

1	Dia Tang Vuong Bo Tat, the Chief of Hell	26-29	Memorial Tablets, portraits of ancestor monks
2	A guardian	30	Memorial Tablets, portraits of ancestor monks
3	Guardian of the Pagoda	31	Thich Ca Buddha (Sakyamuni)
4	Tieu Dien, a guardian	32	Standing Bronze Thich Ca Buddha from Thailand
5	Donations box	33	Thich Ca Buddha
6-7	Judges of the Ten Regions of Hell	34	Ameda, fat and smiling, with six kids
8	Pho Hien Bo Tat	35	Rosewood platform, used as table and for sleeping
9	Dai The Chi Bo Tat		
10	A Di Da Buddha (Amitabha), Buddha of the Past	36	Long Vuong, Dragon King (made of sandalwood)
11	Quan The Am Bo Tat (Aualoketecvara), Goddess of Mercy	37	Statue of Head Monk Hue Thanh, who succeeded Hue Minh
12	Van Thu Bo Tat	38	Rosewood platform, used as table and for sleeping
13	Dai The Che Bo Tat		
14	A Di Da Buddha	39	Statue of Hue Minh, founder of this pagoda
15	Quan The Am Bo Tat		
16-17	Guardians	40	Desk with old photos of monks under glass
18	Thien Tai		
19	Quan The Am Bo Tat	41	Desk with old paper money displayed under glass
20	Lang Nu		
21	Dai The Chi Bo Tat	42	Minature mountain made of volcanic rocks
22	Statuettes of Quan The Am Bo Tat, her guardians and Thich Ca Buddha (born Siddhartha Gautama) as a child	43-44	Rosewood platforms, used as tables and for sleeping
		45	Guardian
23	A Di Da Buddha (Amitabha), Buddha of the Past	46	18-armed Chuan De
		47	Guardian
24	Quan The Am Bo Tat (Aualoketecvara), Goddess of Mercy	48	Dai The Chi Bo Tat
		49	A Di Da Buddha
25	Boddhi Dharma	50	Quan The Am Bo Tat

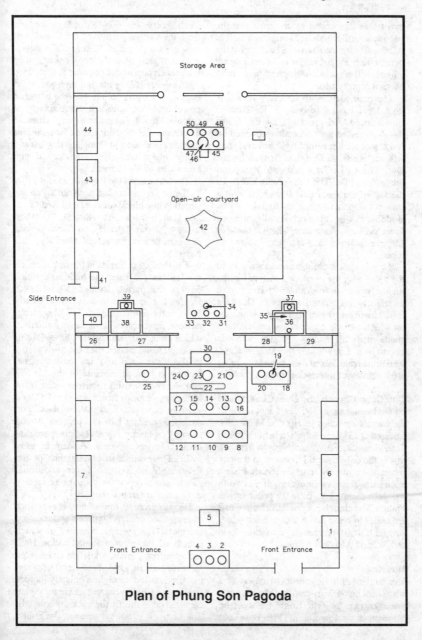

Plan of Phung Son Pagoda

event was interpreted as an omen that the pagoda should remain at its original location. All the articles were retrieved except for the bell, which locals say was heard ringing whenever there was a full or new moon until about a century ago.

The main dais, with its many levels, is dominated by a gilded A Di Da Buddha (pronounced 'AH-zee-dah'), the Buddha of the Past, seated under a canopy flanked by long mobiles resembling human forms without heads. A Di Da is flanked by the Quan The Am Bo Tat, Goddess of Mercy, (on the left) and Dai The Chi (on the right). To the left of the main dais is an altar with a statue of Boddhi Dharma, the founder of Zen Buddhism who brought Buddhism from India to China. The statue, which is made of Chinese ceramic, has a face with Indian features.

As you walk from the main sanctuary to the room with the open-air courtyard in the middle, you come to an altar with five statues on it, including a standing bronze Thich Ca Buddha of Thai origin. To the right is an altar on which there is a glass case containing a statue made of sandalwood. The statue is said to be of Long Vuong, the Dragon King, who brings rain. Around the pagoda building are a number of interesting monks' tombs.

Cho Quan Church Cho Quan Church, built by the French about 100 years ago, is one of the largest churches in Ho Chi Minh City. Located at 133 Tran Binh Trong St (between Tran Hung Dao Blvd and Nguyen Trai St), this is the only church I know of in the city where the figure of Jesus on the altar has a neon halo. The view from the belfry is worth the steep climb. An aide to the priest speaks French. The church is open daily from 4 to 7 am and 3 to 6 pm and Sundays from 4 to 9 am and 1.30 to 6 pm. Sunday masses are held at 5, 6 , and 7 am and 5 pm.

Museums
Museum of the Revolution Housed in a white neoclassical structure built in 1886 and once known as Gia Long Palace, the Museum of the Revolution (Vien Bao Tang Cach Mang; tel 99741) displays artefacts from the various periods of the Communist struggle for power in Vietnam. The photographs of anti-colonial activists executed by the French appear out of place in the gilded 19th-century ballrooms, but then again, the contrast helps you get a feel for the immense power and self-confident complacency of colonial France. The information plaques are in Vietnamese only, but some of the exhibits include documents in French or English and many others are self-explanatory if you know a bit of Vietnamese history.

The Museum of the Revolution is at 27 Ly Tu Trong St (corner Nam Ky Khoi Nghia St), which is one block south-east of Reunification Hall. It is open from 8 to 11.30 am and 2 to 4.30 pm Tuesday to Sunday. The museum offices are at 114 Nam Ky Khoi Nghia St.

The exhibition begins in the first room on the left (as you enter the building), which covers the period from 1859 to 1940. Upstairs, two more rooms are currently open. In the room to the left, is a *ghe* (a long, narrow rowboat) with a false bottom in which arms were smuggled. The weight of the contraband caused the boat to sit as low in the water as would any ordinary *ghe*. Nearby is a small diorama of the Cu Chi tunnels. The adjoining room has examples of infantry weapons used by the VC and various captured South Vietnamese and American medals, hats and plaques. A map shows Communist advances during the dramatic collapse of South Vietnam in early 1975. There are also photographs of the 'liberation' of Saigon. Seven additional rooms are to open as soon as budgetary difficulties are ironed out.

Deep underneath the building is a network of reinforced concrete bunkers and fortified corridors. The system, branches of which stretch all the way to Reunification Hall, included living areas, a kitchen and a large meeting hall. In 1963, President Diem and his brother hid here immediately before fleeing to a Cholon church, where they were captured (and, shortly thereafter, murdered). The network is not yet open to the public because most of the tunnels are flooded, but if you bring a torch, a museum guard may show you around a bit.

In the garden behind the museum is a Soviet tank, an American Huey UH-1 helicopter and an anti-aircraft gun. In the garden fronting Nam Ky Khoi Nghia St is some more military hardware, including the American-built F-5E jet used by a renegade South Vietnamese Air Force pilot to bomb the Presidential Palace (now Reunification Hall) on 8 April 1975.

History Museum The History Museum (Vien Bao Tang Lich Su), built in 1929 by the Société des Études Indochinoises and once the National Museum of the Republic of Vietnam, is situated just inside the main entrance to the Zoo (on Nguyen Binh Khiem St at Le Duan Blvd). The museum has an excellent collection of artefacts illustrating the evolution of the cultures of Vietnam, from the Bronze Age Dong Son civilisation (13th century BC to 1st century AD), through the Oc-Eo (Funan) civilisation (1st to 6th centuries AD), to the Chams, Khmers and Vietnamese. At the back of the building on the 3rd floor is a research library (tel 90268; open Monday to Saturday) with numerous books on Indochina from the French period.

The museum is open from 8 to 11.30 am and 1 to 4 pm, Tuesday to Sunday.

Museum of American War Crimes The Museum of American & Chinese War Crimes, housed in the former US Information Service building, is at the corner of Le Qui Don St and Vo Van Tan St. Many of the atrocities documented in the museum were well-publicised in the West, but it is one thing for US anti-war activists to protest against Pentagon policies and quite another for the victims of US actions to declare, as they do here, *'Nous accusons* – we, the victims, accuse the United States'.

In the yard of the museum, US armoured vehicles, artillery pieces, bombs and infantry weapons are on display. Many of the photographs illustrating US atrocities are from US sources and include a picture of a suspected VC being pushed from a helicopter because he refused to 'cooperate'. In the room on crimes committed by the Chinese during their 1979 invasion, China is portrayed as being allied with US imperialism.

Ho Chi Minh Museum The Ho Chi Minh Museum is in the old customs house on Nguyen Tat Thanh St just across Ben Nghe Channel from the quayside end of Ham Nghi St. The tie between Ho Chi Minh and the museum building is tenuous: 21 year old Ho, having signed on as a stoker and galley-boy on a French freighter, left Vietnam from here in 1911, beginning 30 years of exile in France, the Soviet Union, China and elsewhere. The explanatory signs in the museum are in Vietnamese, but if you know a bit about Uncle Ho, you should be able to follow most of the photographs and exhibits. For a brief biography of Ho (1890-1969), see the entry on his mausoleum in the Hanoi chapter. The museum is open on Tuesday, Wednesday, Thursday and Saturday from 8 to 11.30 am and 2 to 6 pm; on Sundays, it stays open until 8 pm. The museum is closed on Mondays and Fridays.

Military Museum The Military Museum is just across Nguyen Binh Khiem St (corner Le Duan Blvd) from the main gate of the Zoo. US, Chinese and Soviet war materiel is on display, including a Cessna A-37 of the South Vietnamese Air Force and a US-built F-5 Phantom with the 20 mm nose gun still loaded.

Art Museum To see Revolutionary painting and sculpture alongside artefacts from the Oc-Eo (Funan) civilisation, try the Art Museum (Bao Tang My Thuat; tel 97039) at 97A Pho Duc Chinh St. It is open from 7.30 am to 4.30 pm Tuesday to Sunday.

Ton Duc Thang Museum This small, rarely visited museum (tel 94651) is dedicated to Ton Duc Thang, Ho Chi Minh's successor as President of Vietnam, who was born in Long Xuyen, An Giang Province in 1888. He died in office in 1980. Photos illustrate his role in the Vietnamese Revolution, including the time he spent imprisoned on Con Dao Island. The explanations are in Vietnamese only.

The museum is along the waterfront at 5 Ton Duc Thang St, half a block from the Tran Hung Dao statue at the foot of Hai Ba Trung St. It is open Tuesday to Sunday, from 8 to 11 am and 2 to 6 pm.

Markets
Ben Thanh Market Ben Thanh Market (Cho Ben Thanh) and the surrounding streets are one of the city's liveliest, most bustling marketplaces. Everything commonly eaten, worn or used by the average resident of Saigon is available here: vegetables, fruits, meat, spices, biscuits, sweets, tobacco, clothing, hats, household items, hardware and so forth. The legendary slogan of US country stores applies equally well here: 'If we don't have it, you don't need it'. Nearby, food stalls sell inexpensive meals.

Ben Thanh Market is 700 metres southwest of the Rex Hotel at the intersection of Le Loi Blvd, Ham Nghi Blvd, Tran Hung Dao Blvd and Le Lai St. Known to the French as the Halles Centrales, it was built in 1914 of reinforced concrete and covers an area of 11 sq km; the central cupola is 28 metres in diameter. The main entrance, with its belfry and clock, has become a symbol of Saigon.

Opposite the belfry, in the centre of the traffic roundabout, is an equestrian statue of Tran Nguyen Han, the first person in Vietnam to use courier pigeons. At the base, on a pillar, is a small white bust of Quach Thi Trang, a Buddhist woman killed during anti-government protests in 1963.

Binh Tay Market Binh Tay Market (Cho Binh Tay) is Cholon's main marketplace. Much of the business here is wholesale. Binh Tay Market is on Hau Giang Blvd. It is about 1 km south-west of Chau Van Liem Blvd.

Reunification Hall
It was towards this building – then known as Independence Hall or the Presidential Palace – that the first Communist tanks in Saigon rushed on the morning of 30 April 1975. After crashing through the wrought iron gates in a dramatic scene recorded by photojournalists and shown around the world, a soldier ran into the building and up the stairs to unfurl a Viet Cong flag from the 4th-floor balcony. In an ornate 2nd-floor reception chamber, General Minh, who had become head of state only 43 hours before, waited with his improvised cabinet. 'I have been waiting since early this morning to transfer power to you', Minh said to the VC officer who entered the room. 'There is no question of your transferring power', replied the officer, 'you cannot give up what you do not have'.

Reunification Hall (Hoi Truong Thong Nhat) is one of the most fascinating things to see in Saigon, both because of its striking modern architecture and because of the eerie feeling you get, as you walk through the deserted halls, that from here ruled arrogant men wielding immense power who nevertheless became history's losers. The building, once the symbol of the Southern government, is preserved exactly as it was on 30 April 1975, the day that the Republic of Vietnam, which hundreds of thousands of Vietnamese and over 57,000 Americans died trying to save, ceased to exist.

Reunification Hall is open for visitors from 8 to 10 am and 1 to 5 pm daily except Sunday afternoons and when official receptions or meetings are taking place. The visitors' office and entrance is at 106 Nguyen Du St (tel 90629). Individuals or groups are welcome: groups of up to five people pay 10,000d; each additional person is charged 2000d. Reservations can be made in person or by phone and are supposed to be made a day in advance, though if you just show up you may be let in if a guide is available. The guides only speak Vietnamese, and what's worse, they know little about the history of either Reunification Hall or the Republic of Vietnam. If you are on a tour with Vietnam Tourism for part of your visit it is definitely worth seeing Reunification Hall with your Vietnam Tourism guide, who is, hopefully, fluent in English and a bit more knowledgeable.

In 1868 a residence for the French Governor General of Cochinchina was built on this site. The present structure was designed by Paris-trained Vietnamese architect Ngo Viet Thu and completed in 1966. The building, both inside and out, is an outstanding example of 1960s architecture; it is much more interesting up close than you would expect from the street. Reunification Hall has an airy and open atmosphere and its spacious chambers are tastefully decorated with the finest modern Vietnamese art and craft. In its grandeur, the building feels worthy of a head of state.

The ground-floor room with the boat-shaped table was used for conferences. Upstairs, in the Presidential Receiving Room (the one with the red chairs in it, called in Vietnamese *Phu Dau Rong*, or the 'Dragon's Head Room'), South Vietnam's president used to receive foreign delegations. The President sat behind the desk; the chairs with dragons carved into the arms were used by his assistants. The chair facing the desk was reserved for foreign ambassadors. Next door is a meeting room. The room with gold-coloured chairs and curtains was used by the Vice President.

In the back of the structure is the area in which the President lived. Check out the model boats, horse-tails and severed elephants' feet. On the 3rd floor there is a card-playing room with a bar, a movie-screening chamber and a heliport. The 4th floor was used for dancing.

Former US Embassies

There are actually two former US embassies in Saigon: the one from whose roof the famous chaotic helicopter-evacuation took place as the Communists took over the city in April 1975; and the building used before that one was built.

The older former US Embassy is an ugly fortress-like concrete structure at 39 Ham Nghi Blvd (corner Ho Tung Mau St). In 1967, the building was bombed by the VC.

It now serves as a dormitory for young people studying banking.

The newer structure – from which US policy was conducted during the bloody last 8 years of the Republic of Vietnam – is on the corner of Le Duan Blvd and Mac Dinh Chi St in the middle of what was (and still is) a neighbourhood of key government buildings. The main building, once the chancery, is encased in a concrete shield intended to protect it from bomb blastsas well as rocket and shell fire. There are round concrete pillboxes, protected with anti-grenade screens, at each corner of the compound.

The embassy building, which became a symbol of the overwhelming American presence in South Vietnam, was finished just in time to almost get taken over in the 1968 Tet offensive. On TV, 50 million Americans watched chaotic scenes of dazed US soldiers and diplomats firing at the VC commando team which had attacked the embassy, leaving the grounds littered with US and Vietnamese dead. These images were devastating to US home-front support for the war.

The ignominious end of 3 decades of US involvement in Vietnam, also shown around the globe on TV, took place on the roof of the US embassy chancery building. As the last defences of Saigon fell to the North Vietnamese Army and the city's capture became imminent, the Americans, as unprepared for the speed of the collapse of the South as everyone else (including the North Vietnamese), were forced to implement emergency evacuation plans. Thousands of Vietnamese desperate to escape the country (many of them had worked for the Americans and had been promised to be evacuated) congregated around the embassy and tried to get inside; US marine guards forced them back. Overhead, American helicopters (carrying both Americans and Vietnamese) shuttled to aircraft carriers waiting offshore. In the pre-dawn darkness of 30 April 1975, with most of the city already in Communist hands, US Ambassador Graham Martin, carrying the embassy's flag, climbed onto the roof of the building and boarded a helicopter. The end.

The compound is now occupied by the government-owned Oil Exploration Corporation. Present policy is to forbid visitors from entering the grounds. Much of the building, designed for use with powerful air-conditioning equipment, is not in use because the elaborate cooling system is broken.

Hotel de Ville

Saigon's gingerbread Hotel de Ville (City Hall), one of the city's most prominent landmarks, was built between 1901 and 1908 after years of the sort of architectural controversy peculiar to the French. Situated at the north-western end of Nguyen Hue Blvd and facing towards the river, the white-on-pastel-yellow Hotel de Ville, with its ornate façade and elegant interior lit with crystal chandeliers, is now the somewhat incongruous home of the Ho Chi Minh City People's Committee. To visit the interior, ask for permission at the office signposted as Phong Hanh Chanh and Phong So 2 in the wing of the building opposite 77 Le Thanh Ton St (nearest the Huong Duong Hotel). The office and the whole People's Committee Building is closed on Sundays.

For gecko fans: at night, the exterior of the Hotel de Ville is usually covered with thousands of geckos feasting on insects.

Zoo & Botanical Garden

The Zoo and surrounding gardens (entrance fee: 200d) are a delightful place for a relaxing stroll under giant tropical trees, which thrive amidst the lakes, lawns and carefully tended flower beds. The zoo facilities are a bit run-down but they are being repaired, and the animals, which include elephants, crocodiles and big cats, look well fed. Many of the cages are fairly spacious outdoor enclosures. The Botanical Garden, founded in 1864, was one of the first projects undertaken by the French after they established Cochinchina as a colony. It was once one of the finest such gardens in Asia.

The main gate of the Zoo is on Nguyen Binh Khiem St at the intersection of Le Duan Blvd. There is another entrance on Xo Viet Nghe Tinh St near the bridge over Thi Nghe Channel.

The History Museum is next to the main gate. The rickety amusement park rides around the gardens have not worked for years, but children (and adults, of course) are occasionally entertained by water puppet shows performed on a small island in one of the lakes.

There is a basic outdoor restaurant next to the History Museum. Ice cream and fresh French rolls are sold at a few places around the park. Outside the main gate (along Nguyen Binh Khiem St) there are numerous food stalls selling rice dishes, soup and drinks.

French Colonial Architecture

Many of the buildings in Cholon are a distinctive mix of Chinese and French styles. Some of the most interesting structures in Cholon are to be found along Hung Vuong Blvd.

Parks

Cong Vien Van Hoa Park Next to the old Cercle Sportif, an elite sporting club during the French period, the bench-lined walks of Cong Vien Van Hoa Park are shaded with enormous tropical trees. There are entrances across from 115 Nguyen Du St and on Xo Viet Nghe Tinh St.

Ho Ky Hoa Park Ho Ky Hoa Park, whose name means 'Lake and Gardens', is a childrens' amusement park in District 10 just off 3 Thang 2 Blvd. It is near the Hoa Binh Theatre and behind Viet Nam Quoc Tu, the unfinished concrete skeleton of a large pagoda. There are paddleboats, rowboats and sailboats for hire. Fishing is allowed in the lakes and a small swimming pool is open to the public for part of the year. The cafes are open year-round. There are also two arcades of Japanese video games. Ho Ky Hoa Park is open from 7 am to 9.30 pm daily and is crowded on Sundays. The entrance fee is 50d.

Orchid Farm

The Artex Saigon Orchid Farm is the largest in Vietnam, with 50,000 plants representing 1000 varieties. It is primarily a commercial concern but visitors are welcome to stop by to relax in the luxurious garden. This is a great place to sit sipping a cold drink, shaded by coconut palms and bamboo and surrounded by acres of orchids.

The farm, founded in 1970, uses revenues from the sale of orchid flowers for its operating budget but makes its real profit selling orchid plants, which take 6 years to mature and are thus very expensive. In addition to varieties imported from overseas, the farm has a collection of orchids native to Vietnam. Ask to see the orange-yellow Cattleya orchid variety called Richard Nixon; they have another variety named for Joseph Stalin. The best time of year for a visit is the sunny season. The blooms are at their height during January and February.

For reservations, which should be made a day or two in advance, call the English-speaking owner, Tran Kim Khu, at his home (tel 40124) in Saigon. Or you can stop by Kiosk Number 2 on Nguyen Hue Blvd, which is run by the same family.

The Artex Saigon Orchid Farm is 15 km from Saigon in Thu Duc District, a rural part of Ho Chi Minh City, on the way to Bien Hoa. The official address is 5/81 Xa Lo Vong Dai, but this highway is better known as 'Xa Lo Dai Han', the 'Korean Highway', because it was built during the war by Koreans. At 'Km 14' on Xa Lo Dai Han there is a two-storey police post. Turn left (if heading out of Saigon toward Bien Hoa), continue 300 metres, and turn left again.

Places to Stay

Ho Chi Minh City has quite a few large hotels and many more smaller places, ranging from the luxurious Saigon Floating Hotel to truly grungy dives in Cholon available by the hour. As in the rest of Vietnam, all hotels in Ho Chi Minh City are owned and run by various sub-units of the national or municipal governments, ranging from Saigon Tourism to the Vietnamese Army. A

significant number of these places are still known by their pre-1975 or pre-1954 names.

Tourist-class hotels require payment in US dollars. By international standards, the prices set by the government for the best hotels in Ho Chi Minh City are reasonable: US$35 to US$90 per night for a double. Unfortunately, the prices at the city's cheapest tourist-class hotels are not much lower, and the least expensive rooms at such hotels are often mysteriously full. Most hotels corresponding to two stars and above tack on a 10% service charge.

Not all hotels in the city are yet permitted to serve 'capitalist tourists'. Foreigners who inquire into staying at hotels for domestic travellers are sometimes told they are 'full' or offered only the priciest suites. Good-natured persistence (and producing documentation that you are a student) often overcomes front-desk reticence. Many of the smaller hotels are still experimenting with pricing policies and room tariffs, which often change from 1 week to the next. Ask other travellers for the latest low-down on the places currently welcoming foreigners at reasonable rates.

Cholon is a goldmine of cheap hotels and is likely to remain so despite the recent renovations of several places in the area. Cholon is Ho Chi Minh City at its most crowded and bustling, but if you don't mind the congestion staying in this part of the city is certainly worth considering, especially if you enjoy visiting Chinese pagodas. There are half-a-dozen hotels along Chau Van Liem Blvd and quite a few others along Tran Hung Dao B Blvd and Tran Hung Dao Blvd. The powers that be seem to prefer that foreigners stay in central Saigon rather than Cholon; this even goes for businesspeople. While it is not forbidden to stay in Cholon, the police may consider your presence somewhat peculiar and you may be watched or hassled.

The oldest of Ho Chi Minh City's hotels were built early in the century under the French, the newest in the early 1970s to accommodate US military officials, Western businesspeople and war correspondents. Some of the latter seem to have learned most of what they knew about Vietnam over drinks at hotel bars.

When the city surrendered in 1975 North Vietnamese soldiers, fresh from years in the field after having grown up in the spartan North, were billeted in the emptied high-rise hotels. There is an oft-told story about several such soldiers who managed to scrape together enough money to buy fish and produce at the market. To keep their purchases fresh, they put them in the Western-style toilet, an appliance completely foreign to them. Then, out of curiosity, one of the soldiers flushed the toilet and the fish and vegetables disappeared. They were outraged by this perfidious imperialist booby trap and bitterly cursed those responsible. I can't swear that this incident actually took place (or that it happened only once), but I do know that a great deal of damage was done to Saigon's hotels after reunification and that bathroom fixtures were especially targeted. I have stayed in several hotels in which the smashed toilets have yet to be repaired. If only toilets could talk...

Places to Stay – bottom end

The tariffs at bottom-end hotels are meant to be paid by local people and are thus in line with the costs of other goods and services in Vietnam. Of course, the level of service is also in line with what locals will settle for, but overall, these places compare favourably with budget accommodation in Thailand and elsewhere in Asia. Recently, there has been a trend to insist that 'capitalist tourists' pay double what Vietnamese pay, but even so, the prices are still reasonable, ranging from US$2 to US$15 a night.

There has also been a tendency for some hotels serving the domestic market to prepare exorbitant price lists for presentation to the first hapless foreigners to show up at the front desk. Other establishments, however, have realised that reasonable prices bring more tourists, who bring in badly needed cash. The point is, some of the 'bottom end' places may become 'mid-range' and vice versa, so do not pass up a place simply because once-upon-a-time (the day I was there) they were not the best deal around.

Central Saigon The *Kim Do Hotel* (tel 93811; 60 rooms) at 133 Nguyen Hue Blvd affords all of the advantages of the Rex Hotel, which is a mere 100 metres away, at a fraction of the cost. A huge room overlooking Nguyen Hue Blvd with bath and a ceiling fan (and perhaps a few bats) costs 20,000 to 30,000d; an air-con room in the newer section at the back costs about US$15. Registered bicycle parking is available in the lobby for 200d. The food at the ground-floor restaurant is fast, tasty and cheap.

The *69 Hai Ba Trung Hotel* (tel 91513; 18 rooms) is, as its name suggests, at 69 Hai Ba Trung St. This small, pleasant place is very conveniently located just two blocks from the Rex Hotel. Singles or doubles with ceiling fans cost 10,400d for Vietnamese, 14,500d for Overseas Vietnamese and 20,800d for foreigners. Air-con rooms cost 33,000d for Vietnamese, 46,200d for Overseas Vietnamese and 66,000d for foreigners. Triples are also available.

The *Dong Khoi Hotel* (tel 92178; 40 rooms), formerly the *Palace Hotel*, is a grand old French-era building with renovation potential. For foreigners and overseas Vietnamese, spacious air-con suites with 4.5 metre ceilings and French windows overlooking Dong Khoi St cost 55,000d for a double and 80,000d for a triple with a kitchen. The management is friendly and building security is good. The Dong Khoi Hotel is at 8 Dong Khoi St (corner Ngo Duc Ke St).

The seedy *Saigon Hotel* (tel 99734; 100 rooms) is at 47 Dong Du St, across the street from the Saigon Central Mosque. This place is a major centre of prostitution. Male guests have reported repeated propositioning by full-time prostitutes as well as the chambermaids, and some women guests have been hassled by the men such business attracts. Many of the toilets do not flush, especially on the upper floors, and there is a significant population of rats and cockroaches. The only things this sleazy dive has going for it are location and price. For foreigners, doubles cost 24,000d (with a ceiling fan) to 60,000d (with air-con, hot water and a fridge). Locals pay exactly half these prices.

Central Market Area The *Van Canh Hotel* (tel 94963; 12 rooms) is at 184 Calmette St (corner Tran Hung Dao Blvd). For foreigners, a two-room suite for four people costs 55,000d; a double with air-con is 44,000d. These prices are double what locals pay. All rooms have attached bath. Reception is up several flights of stairs and through the large restaurant, which has a live band and dancing every night.

The *Hai Son Hotel* (tel 94170; 39 rooms) is at 12D Le Lai St 50 metres from the fancy Le Lai Hotel. Single rooms, which is all they have, cost 12,000d for locals. Reception is upstairs.

The *Ben Nghe Hotel* (tel 91430, 95019), formerly the Embassy Hotel, is a medium-size place at 35 Nguyen Trung Truc St, not far from Reunification Hall. Singles/doubles begin at US$15.

The *Vinh Loi Hotel* (tel 92672; 30 rooms) occupies the upper floors of a 10-storey building at 129-133 Ham Nghi Blvd. Located in a neighbourhood with a reputation among Saigonese for pickpockets and thieves, locals pay 12,000 to 18,000d for a single and 15,000 to 22,000d for a double. Foreigners are charged 30,800 to 36,300d for a single and 39,600 to 48,400d for a double. The more expensive rooms have air-con. There is a restaurant on the 1st floor.

The *Hoang Gia Hotel* (tel 94846) is at 12D Cach Mang Thang Tam St, around the corner from the Immigration Police Office. This dingy place offers over-priced rooms with air-con for US$20 and with a fan for 60,000d.

Airport Area The *Tan Binh Hotel* (tel 41175/67/99) at 201/3 Hoang Viet St rents out rooms with fans (located in a building across the street from the main part of the hotel) for prices ranging from US$8 for a single to US$15 for four people. To get there, turn off

Hoang Van Thu Blvd opposite number 312 and go south for one block.

Central Cholon The *Phuong Huong Hotel* (tel 51888; 70 rooms) is in an eight-storey building at 411 Tran Hung Dao B Blvd. Also known as the Phenix Hotel, this place is just off Chau Van Liem Blvd in the middle of downtown Cholon. Foreigners are charged 56,000d for a double with air-con; they also have cheaper rooms with fans.

Just up the street is the *Truong Thanh Hotel* (tel 56044; 70 rooms) at 111-117 Chau Van Liem Blvd. Doubles here cost domestic travellers between 11,000 and 13,000d. Half a block away, at 125 Chau Van Liem Blvd, is the *Thu Do Hotel* (tel 59102; 71 rooms). This place, located in a seven storey building, has doubles with fans for 12,000 to 17,000d.

Across the street from the Phuong Huong Hotel, the *Song Kim Hotel* (tel 59773; 33 rooms) is a grungy and somewhat disreputable establishment with doubles for 11,000d (for a single bed) and 13,000d (for two separate beds). Reception is up a flight of stairs. You can do better than this for marginally more money.

The *Truong Mai Hotel* (tel 52101; 50 rooms) is a six storey establishment at 785 Nguyen Trai St, just off Chau Van Liem Blvd. Foreigners pay 34,000d for a double; domestic travellers are charged 17,000d.

The filthy *Quoc Dan Hotel* (no telephone; 9 rooms) is at 843 Nguyen Trai St, a block west of Liem Van Chau Blvd. It has the cheapest single rooms in the city for 4500 to 5500d. The very basic *A Chau Hotel* (tel 53236; 22 rooms) is a block further west at 896 Nguyen Trai St. A single costs 9500d and doubles range from 10,500 to 11,500d.

Along Tran Hung Dao B Blvd The *Bat Dat Hotel* (tel 51662) is a seven-storey building at 238-244 Tran Hung Dao B Blvd (near the pricier Arc En Ciel Hotel). Foreigners are charged 30,800 to 35,800d for a double with a ceiling fan. A double with air-con costs from 40,800 to 50,800d and an air-con room for four costs 60,800d. Single rooms for

Vietnamese start at 15,000d. There is a large restaurant on the ground floor. The *Phu Do 1 Hotel* (tel 56821; 40 rooms) is two blocks from Tran Hung Dao B Blvd on Ngo Quyen St. The official street address is 634-640 Ben Ham Tu St. Doubles here cost from 11,000 to 22,000d.

Further east, the five-storey *Dong Khanh Hotel* (tel 50678; 45 rooms) is at 2 Tran Hung Dao B Blvd; room prices range from 14,300 to 66,000d.

Along Tran Hung Dao Blvd The *Hoa Binh Hotel* (tel 55133; 34 rooms) is in a seven-floor building at 1115 Tran Hung Dao Blvd. Current prices for domestic tourists range from 8800 to 15,400d for a room. The five-storey *Dong Kinh Hotel* (tel 52505; 93 rooms) is two blocks off Tran Hung Dao Blvd at 106-108 Tran Tuan Khai St. Foreigners are charged US$10 to US$18 for a double with air-con. The *Hanh Long Hotel* (tel 50251; 51 rooms) at 1025-1029 Tran Hung Dao Blvd will soon open to foreigners. Vietnamese currently pay from 9900d for a single to 38,500d for the grand suite, with most rooms in the 13,000 to 17,000d price range. Rooms with air-conditioning are available.

One of the best places to stay in Cholon is the *Quoc Thai Hotel* (tel 51657; 21 rooms), which is at 41 Nguyen Duy Duong St, half a km north of the Dong Kinh Hotel between Tran Phu Blvd and Hung Vuong Blvd. This part of Cholon is not so crowded, the hotel is very clean and doubles go for between 15,400 and 25,300d.

Other Areas The *Dong Khanh 5 Hotel* (tel 50632; 16 rooms) is on the edge of Cholon at 1 Nguyen Chi Thanh Blvd. Singles/doubles cost 13,200/15,400d. Reception is upstairs. The ground floor restaurant is one of the city's worst.

The *Thanh Tung Hotel* (tel 91817; 14 rooms) is way out of downtown Saigon but is only about 2 km from Mien Dong Bus Station and a km or so from Van Thanh Bus

Station. The hotel is at 310 Xo Viet Nghe Tinh St on the corner of Dien Bien Phu St. Singles/doubles with ceiling fan cost 6500/8000d.

In the *Mien Tay Bus Station* (tel 55955) in An Lac there are a few rooms for overnighting behind the ticket counters in the building to the left of the station gate as you enter. The cost is 2000d per night. At the *Saigon Railroad Station*, there is dormitory accommodation (*nha tro*) across the parking lot from the station building.

Places to Stay – middle & top end
Central Saigon The classiest hotel in the city is unquestionably the venerable *Hotel Continental* (tel 94456; telex 811344 HOCON VT; fax 84-8-90936; 71 rooms), setting for much of the action in Graham Greene's novel *The Quiet American*. Located across the street from the Municipal Theatre at 132-134 Dong Khoi St, the hotel dates from the turn of the century and recently underwent a US$2.6 million renovation. The Continental, run by the same management as the Rex Hotel, charges US$50 to US$88 for singles and US$66 to US$110 for doubles (including breakfast). Budget travellers may still be able to afford a cold glass of Saigon Export on the terrace by the pool, known as the 'Continental Shelf' to war journalists.

Another preferred hotel in town is the Ben Thanh Hotel (tel 92185, 92186, 93115; telex 811201 HOTBT HCM; fax 84-8-91469), still known as the *Rex Hotel*. Its ambience of mellowed kitsch dates from the time it served as a hotel for US military officers. The Rex is at 141 Nguyen Hue Blvd (corner Le Loi Blvd). Singles cost from US$25 to US$69; doubles are priced between US$30 and US$70. The Rex has, among other amenities, computerised billing, a large gift shop, a tailor, a unisex beauty parlour, photocopy machines, a postal counter with fax and telex services (open from 7.30 am to 8 pm), a massage service, acupuncture, a swimming pool on the 6th floor, an excellent restaurant on the 5th floor, a coffee shop on the ground floor and a beautiful view from the large 5th-floor veranda, which is decorated with caged birds and potted bushes shaped like animals. The Rex is almost always booked up. Reservations should be made several weeks in advance.

The 5-star *Saigon Floating Hotel* (tel 90783; telex VT812614 HOTL VT; fax 84-8-90783/4; 200 rooms) was towed to the Saigon River from Australia's Great Barrier Reef (where it had gone spectacularly bankrupt) in 1989. Amenities offered by the Saigon Floating Hotel, which is moored at 1A Me Linh Square (on Ton Duc Thang St near the Tran Hung Dao Statue), include two restaurants, saunas, a gym, a tennis court, a swimming pool, meeting rooms, audio-visual equipment and a business centre (open 15 hours a day) with international telecommunications links, secretarial services, interpreters and personal computers. The small air-con rooms, which cost between US$150 and US$290, are wired for satellite TV reception. The hotel's mailing address is PO Box 752, Ho Chi Minh City.

Another favourite is the Doc Lap Hotel (tel 93704; telex 811259 HOTDL HCM; fax 84-8-99902; over 100 rooms), still called the *Caravelle Hotel*, at 19-23 Lam Son Square (across the street from the Municipal Theatre). Once owned by the Catholic Diocese of Saigon, the Caravelle is Saigon's most-French hotel, and this heritage is alive and well in the rude reception English-speakers may encounter (and in the form of the Air France office located on the ground floor). Singles/doubles with air-con cost from US$30/35 to US$60/70 (plus 10% service). There are postal, telex, fax and telegraph facilities in the lobby, which are open from 8 am to 7 pm daily, except Sundays. The 9th floor restaurant is open from 6 am to 10 pm. There is dancing nightly on the 10th floor.

The Cuu Long Hotel (tel·95515, 91375; telex 811275 HOTCL HCM; fax 84-8-91470) is still known as the *Majestic Hotel*. Located along the Saigon River at 1 Dong Khoi St, it was once the city's most elegant and prestigious hotel. Singles/doubles with breakfast range from US$27/37 to US$80/90

plus 10%. Postal, telex and fax services are available in the lobby. There are restaurants on the street level and the 5th floor.

The *Huu Nghi Hotel* (tel 97284 , 92860, 22316, 94722; telex 811208 HOTHN HCM; fax 84-8-99872), also known as the *Palace Hotel*, is at 56-64 Nguyen Hue Blvd. This hotel, whose Vietnamese name means 'friendship', occupies the 2nd-tallest building in the city, and the views from the 14th floor restaurant and 15th-floor terrace are superb. Singles/doubles cost from US$30/43 to US$77/93 (plus 10% service). The Palace has telex and fax facilities, a luxury food shop and a small swimming pool on the 16th floor.

The *Thang Long Hotel* (tel 93416), formerly the Oscar (the name 'Oscar' in giant cement letters still overlooks the street from above the 10th floor), is a modest but serviceable place at 68A Nguyen Hue Blvd. Singles/doubles cost between US$11/14 and US$26/32.

The *Huong Sen Hotel* (tel 91415, 90259; 50 rooms) is at 70 Dong Khoi St. Once known as the Astor Hotel, this place charges US$20/26 to US$28/34 (plus 10% service) for singles/doubles with air-con and hot water. The in-house restaurant is on the 6th floor. Nearby, the *Bong Sen Hotel* (tel 99127, 91516, 90545; 85 rooms) at 117-119 Dong Khoi St offers air-con singles/doubles for US$26/32 to US$42/52 (plus 10% service). Formerly called the Miramar Hotel, the Bong Sen is also signposted as the Lotus Hotel, which is a translation of its Vietnamese name. There is a restaurant on the 8th floor.

The *Huong Duong Hotel* (tel 92404, 92805; 75 rooms) is all the way around the block from the Rex Hotel at 150 Nguyen Thi Minh Khai St (corner Le Thanh Ton St). Doubles (which are all they have) cost US$31 to US$44. The hotel has a restaurant on the 6th floor and its own tennis court across the street.

A huge *Holiday Inn Saigon* is supposed to be built next to the Le Lai Hotel. Rumour has it that a *Hilton* and a *Sheraton* are also being planned.

French Consulate Area The *Que Huong Hotel* (tel 94227, 94291, 22188) is two blocks from the French Consulate at 167 Hai Ba Trung St. Singles/doubles are priced from US$20/30 to US$30/40.

Not far away is the *Nha Khach Bo Quoc Phong* (tel 99604, 94989) at 14B Vo Van Tan. This building, which once housed American pilots, is now more of a long-term guest house for foreign experts than it is a hotel, but you might see if they have a vacancy.

Central Market Area Despite its location, the *Le Lai Hotel* (tel 95147/8/9, 91246; telex 8500 HOTLL HCM; fax 84-8-90282; 52 rooms) at 76 Le Lai St is one of Saigon's fanciest. Singles/doubles range from US$37/45 to US$70/80. The telecommunications and postal desk in the lobby, which offers full postal, telex and fax services, is open from 7 to 11 am and 12 noon to 3 pm daily except Sunday. An exchange counter in the lobby offers the bank rate. There are restaurants on the 2nd and 3rd floors.

Airport Area The *Tan Son Nhat Hotel* (tel 41079/39; 25 rooms) at 200 Hoang Van Thu Blvd has some of the nicest rooms in all of Ho Chi Minh City. This place was built as a guest house for top South Vietnamese government officials. In 1975, the North Vietnamese Army inherited it along with the nearby headquarters of the South Vietnamese Army. Recently, the entrepreneurial spirit sweeping the south has infected even the army, which, hoping to earn a bit of extra cash, has renovated this place for use as a hotel. The rooms, which are all doubles and cost US$31 or US$33, have very high ceilings, air-con, refrigerators, hot water and the finest in imported bathroom fixtures, all in vintage early-70s style. A ground-floor room used by South Vietnamese Prime Minister Tran Thien Khiem has been preserved exactly as it was in 1975, plastic fruit and all. There is a small swimming pool out back.

The nearby *Nha Khach Viet Kieu* (the Overseas Vietnamese Guest House; tel 40897) is a brand new hotel and restaurant at 311 Nguyen Van Troi St. Its 31 rooms are open to both foreigners and Overseas Vietnamese.

The *Tan Binh Hotel* (tel 41175, 41167, 41199; telex 8558 HOTTB HCM) at 201/3 Hoang Viet St is a huge place set in a tranquil but remote part of the city about 1 km from the airport. Air-con singles/doubles in the main building go for US$20/24 to US$33/38. A suite for four costs US$55. Rooms with fans in a building across the street from reception cost between US$8 for a single and US$15 for four persons. The hotel has tennis courts, a sauna, massage services and three restaurants; guests have free use of the public swimming pool next door. To get there, turn off Hoang Van Thu Blvd opposite number 312 and go straight (south) for one block.

The *Thanh Binh Hotel* (tel 40984, 40599; 35 rooms) is a mediocre establishment at 315 Hoang Van Thu Blvd. Doubles (which is all they have) cost between US$12 (with fan) to US$22. The ground-floor restaurant is dismal.

Cholon The *Arc En Ciel Hotel* (tel 52550, 56924; 90 rooms) is one of Cholon's few tourist-class hotels; rooms with air-con (and perhaps colour television) cost from US$22 to US$55. The hotel, which is about 1 km from the centre of Cholon at 52-56 Tan Da St (corner Tran Hung Dao B Blvd), also has cheaper rooms with fans.

About 1 km north of Chau Van Liem Blvd is the *Phu Tho Hotel* (tel 51309, 51310) at 527 3 Thang 2 Blvd. The upper floors of this eight-storey structure have remained an unfinished shell for quite some time. Doubles with air-con, a fridge and hot water cost US$20 for foreigners and Overseas Vietnamese; locals pay 25,000d. There is a huge restaurant on the lowest three floors.

Places to Eat – Saigon

There are three categories of restaurants in Ho Chi Minh City: government owned, privately owned and cooperative. They are often hard to tell apart, except by the bill when it comes: the government and cooperative places are cheaper, in part because private businesses are heavily taxed, in part because the prices at the nonprivate places have tended to rise more slowly than inflation. Overall, the food at the private restaurants is better.

Restaurant in Vietnamese is *nha hang*; it usually appears on signs preceding the name of the establishment.

Food Stalls The cheapest food available in Saigon is sold on the streets. In the mornings, *pho*, a tasty soup made of noodles, bean sprouts, scallions and pork, chicken or beef is sold from tiny sidewalk stands that disappear by 11 am. A serving costs about 700d. Late at night, food stands appear on the sidewalk of Nguyen Hue Blvd between the Kim Do Hotel and the Rex Hotel and at other locations downtown.

Pho is available all day long at *Pho Hien Hanoi*, a soup shop in the heart of Saigon at 50 Dong Khoi St. A large bowl of delicious beef *pho* costs 2000d. *Pho Tien* soup shop is on Dong Du St next to the Saigon Hotel. There is another *pho* shop at 99 Nguyen Hue Blvd.

Sandwiches with a French look and a very Vietnamese taste are sold by street vendors. Fresh French *petits pains* (rolls) are stuffed with something resembling luncheon meat (don't ask) and cucumbers and seasoned with soy sauce. A sandwich costs between 500 and 1500d, depending on what is in it and whether you get overcharged. Sandwiches filled with soft cheese, which is imported, cost a bit more.

Just west of the Central Market is a cluster of food stalls. Mobile food stands often set up shop in the vicinity of numbers 178 and 264 Dien Bien Phu St.

Everyday Vietnamese In Saigon, there are a number of government-run restaurants that cater to locals and offer pre-prepared Vietnamese food at very reasonable prices. Most are open at lunch time and dinner time only and are usually crowded. The waiter will assume that everyone in your party will eat some of each of the dishes ordered, so portion size (and price) will be adjusted accordingly. Don't show up just before closing time and expect a complete selection of dishes.

Nha Hang 51 Nguyen Hue at 51 Nguyen Hue Blvd serves superior Vietnamese food at very reasonable prices (about 4000d per person for a meal). It is open from 10.30 am to 2 pm and 4 to 7 pm. *Nha Hang 32 Ngo Duc Ke*, just off Nguyen Hue Blvd at 32 Ngo Duc Ke St, is almost as good. A meal for three, including inferior beer on tap, will cost you about 8000d. It is open from 10.15 am to 2 pm and 4.15 to 8 pm.

The restaurant on the ground floor of the *Kim Do Hotel* at 133 Nguyen Hue Blvd is slightly – but only slightly – upscale from Nha Hang 51 Nguyen Hue. This restaurant offers solid, pre-prepared dishes for reasonable prices (6500d per person for a meal). The kitchen is at the bottom of the shaft of the hotel's inoperable elevator. The stuffed crab here is excellent. This place is open until 10 pm.

Near the Ben Thanh Market, *Nha Hang Kim Son* at 68 Le Loi Blvd (tel 96204) serves excellent Vietnamese food. A meal here costs the equivalent of US$1 to US$3. In this vicinity, you might also try *Nha Hang Thang Loi* (tel 98474), also known as Victory Restaurant, at 55 Ham Nghi Blvd (corner Nam Ky Khoi Nghia St). The fare includes European and Vietnamese dishes.

Traditional Vietnamese *Nha Hang Cay Dua* (tel 98467), also known as *Nha Hang Le Lai*, specialises in traditional (as opposed to common, everyday) Vietnamese cuisine. Located not far from the Le Lai Hotel at 54 Le Lai St, this privately run place is popular with resident foreigners and has an English menu. It is open from 10 am to 9 pm.

Traditional Vietnamese food is the specialty of a cluster of restaurants on Nguyen Cu Trinh St, which is about 1.5 km from Ben Thanh Market towards Cholon along Tran Hung Dao Blvd. The restaurants here include: *Com Viet Nam 85* at 85 Nguyen Cu Trinh; *Com Viet Nam Thanh Son* at 113 Nguyen Cu Trinh; *Tiem Com Phuoc Thanh* at 125 Nguyen Cu Trinh; and *Tiem Com Lam Vien* at 131 Nguyen Cu Trinh.

A number of restaurants in Ho Chi Minh City cater to fans of more exotic traditional Vietnamese specialties such as cobra, python, bat, turtle, porcupine, pangolin, wild pig, turtle dove and venison (deer). Among them are the following:

Nha Hang 5 Me Linh (tel 22623) is two blocks from Nguyen Hue Blvd, near the statue of Tran Hung Dao and the Saigon Floating Hotel. It is open from 10 am to 9 pm. All the traditional specialties, including cobra, are served here in an informal, covered patio. *My Canh 2 Restaurant* is at 125 Ho Tung Mau St (corner Ton That Thiep St) just off of Nguyen Hue Blvd; it is open from 10.30 am to 10 pm.

Tri Ky Restaurant (tel 40968) is about 4 km from central Saigon in a converted villa at 82 Tran Huy Lieu St (just around the corner from the mosque at 5 Nguyen Van Troi St). Most meals at this fancy place (white tablecloths, etc) cost 5000 to 12,000d, but a medium-size cobra may cost 60,000 to 80,000d. It is open from 10 am to 10 pm. About a km north-west of Tri Ky is the huge *Phu Nhuan Restaurant* (tel 40183; 700 seats), built in 1985 in the style of the mid-60s. It is at 8 Truong Quoc Dung St (corner Nguyen Van Troi), opposite the Dai Giac Pagoda.

Out near the airport, you might try the upscale restaurant of *Nha Khach Viet Kieu* (tel 40897), the Overseas Vietnamese Guest House, at 311 Nguyen Van Troi St; it is open from 8 am to 10 pm. This is one of the nicest restaurants in the city, though because it caters to Overseas Vietnamese rather than locals, the prices are a bit high; meals can be ordered in small, medium and large portions and cost from 8000 to 23,000d. A wide selection of imported alcoholic beverages is available. In the evening, there is live Vietnamese and Western music.

Cafes For light Western-style meals or something to drink, there are a number of cafes in central Saigon. *Nha Hang 95 Dong Khoi*, formerly the Imperial Bar, is on the corner of Mac Thi Buoi St at 95 Dong Khoi St; it is open from 5.30 am to 9.30 pm. The old name, worked in wrought metal, is still partly visible above the windows. Nha Hang 95 retains some of its French-era charm and is an ideal place to watch Saigon bustle by while sipping something cold, like soda water with lemon or the weak beer on tap. Both the Vietnamese and European dishes are decent. I am especially fond of their steak & chips. An English menu is available.

The *Hotel Continental* has a coffee shop whose large picture windows overlook Lam Son Square. Government-owned *Givral Pâtisserie & Café* at 169 Dong Khoi St (across the street from the Hotel Continental) has the best selection of cakes and pastries in the city. The cafe section offers home-made ice cream and yoghurt as well as a limited selection of Western food. The house specialty is ice cream served in a baby coconut (*kem trai dua*). Check your bill here carefully! Givral, which is open from 7 am to 11 pm, is the perfect place to grab a snack after an evening at the Municipal Theatre, across the street. A second *Givral Pâtisserie* is at 141 Dien Bien Phu St. Another good source of cakes and the like, including elephant ears and banana cake, is *Cua Hang Ban Banh & Kem* (tel 24673) at 11 Nguyen Thiep St (between Nguyen Hue Blvd and Dong Khoi St near Brodard Café); it is open from 7 am to 9 pm. Out the front, a red neon sign encased in a metal screen reads 'Pâtisserie Glace'.

Brodard Café (tel 25837), also known as *Nha Hang Dong Khoi*, is a favourite with trendy, young, well-off Saigonese who come here in groups to eat to the accompaniment of taped Western pop music. Despite recent renovations, the decor is still vintage 1960s. The food is pretty bad. Brodard is at 131 Dong Khoi St (corner Nguyen Thiep St).

Restaurants Without a doubt, the best restaurant in Saigon (and probably all of Indochina) is *Maxim's* (tel 96676, 25554; telex 8561 FIDIMEX HCM) at 13-17 Dong Khoi St (next to the Majestic Hotel); it is open from 4 to 9.30 pm. This is *the* place for power dining. The French and Chinese menu is truly voluminous, with meals ranging from 6000d (for a simple Chinese dish) to 540,000d (abalone for 12). There is live Western classical music nightly from 7 pm. A number of enthralled backpackers have reported that this place is absolutely not to be missed. The onion soup and filet mignon have received rave reviews. Reservations are necessary for dinners on Saturday and Sunday.

One of my favourite places is *Lam Son Restaurant* (tel 93708), a solid, French-style structure at 19 Cong Truong Lam Son (Lam Son Square), 100 metres from the Caravelle Hotel and across the street from the Municipal Theatre. A house specialty is pork-liver pâté on French bread; a huge portion costs 6000d. Lam Son is open from 7 am to 9 pm.

Hotel Restaurants Many hotel restaurants offer Vietnamese and Western food at very reasonable prices, and a good, solid meal can be had for the equivalent of US$2 to US$5. After 9 pm, very few restaurants other than those in hotels are likely to be open.

One of my favourite places to relax from a day in the noise and bustle of Saigon is the restaurant on the 5th floor of the *Rex Hotel*, presided over by a fine Mona Lisa done in hanging beads. The food is usually excellent, the waiters in black bow ties are highly professional, the place is well-lighted for reading, and meals begin at US$2. During dinner, live Western classical music is performed. The fish Normandie is excellent, as is the *cha gio* (spring rolls). Don't bother coming in shorts, though: such attire is considered inappropriate and the restaurant doorman won't let you past him! The bar out on the veranda is less formal and has a view of the city centre.

The 9th-floor restaurant at the *Caravelle Hotel*, with its white tablecloths and crisp, starched napkins, is open from 6 am to 10 pm and serves one of the best breakfasts in town. There is live music during dinner and lunch.

The 15th-floor restaurant at the *Palace Hotel* affords one of the finest panoramic views in the city. There is also a decent

restaurant at the *Majestic Hotel*. *Nha Hang Hoa Xuan*, which has the usual Vietnamese and Western dishes, is on the ground floor of the Oscar Hotel. It can be reached via the Art Gallery Thang Long at 70 Nguyen Hue Blvd and is open from 2 to 10 pm. The Saigon Floating Hotel has two 'international standard' restaurants, the *Oriental Court* and *The Veranda*.

Madame Dai's *La Bibliothèque de Madame Dai* is a Saigon institution. Run by Madame Nguyen Phuoc Dai, a lawyer and former vice-chairperson of the South Vietnamese National Assembly, Madame Dai's is an intimate little restaurant consisting of half a dozen small tables set in her old law library, which is lined with dusty French legal tomes. The food, French or Vietnamese, is not spectacular, but the real attraction of the place is the cultured ambience. Though she is fluent in English, conversation with Madame Dai is in French, as befits the atmosphere, and unless your French is impeccable (or you switch to English), you won't have much to say. Maybe she prefers it that way.

A good friend of mine, a person not prone to hyperbole or exaggeration, told me that once when she was dining at Madame Dai's a giant rat ran between the tables holding a kitten in its mouth.

A dinner with beer costs 12,000 to 20,000d. Reservations should be made at least a day in advance. Madame Dai's is in an unmarked building not far from Notre Dame Cathedral at 84A Nguyen Du St. If the gate is locked, pull the bell cord. Is this what Princess Di will do after the 'liberation' of London?

Indian *Com Cari An Do* (the name means 'Indian curried rice restaurant') at 169 Ly Tu Trong St may be the only Indian restaurant in the whole country. The specialties at this tiny restaurant, owned by a Muslim Tamil, include excellent curried rice, goat meat (*de*) curry and kebab, soup and sweetened fresh goat's milk. Located around the corner from the Mariamman Hindu Temple, it is open from 7 am to 2 pm only.

Vegetarian The ethnic-Vietnamese owners of *Tin Nghia Vegetarian Restaurant* are strict Buddhists. This small, simple little establishment, which is about 200 metres from Ben Thanh Market at 9 Tran Hung Dao Blvd, serves an assortment of delicious traditional Vietnamese foods prepared without meat, chicken, fish or egg. Instead, tofu, mushrooms and vegetables are used. The prices here are incredibly cheap: meals cost between 1000 and 1700d. It is open from 7 am to 8 pm daily.

On the first and 15th days of the lunar month, food stalls around the city — especially in the markets — serve vegetarian versions of non-vegetarian Vietnamese dishes.

Ice Cream The best ice cream (*kem*) in Ho Chi Minh City is served at *Kem Bach Dang* and *Kem Bach Dang 2* (tel 92707), which are on Le Loi Blvd on either side of Nguyen Thi Minh Khai St. Kem Bach Dang 2 is at 28 Le Loi Blvd. Both are under the same management and serve ice cream, hot and cold drinks and cakes for very reasonable prices. A 2200d specialty is ice cream served in a baby coconut with candied fruit on top (*kem trai dua*).

Dozens of little ice cream and yoghurt (*yaourt*) places line Dien Bien Phu St between numbers 125 and 187. The orange and white Foremost signs out front are the trademark of a US company, still active in Thailand, which sold ice cream and milk products in Vietnam during the war.

Bars Two pokey bars serving hot and cold beverages and ice cream in an ambience of semi-darkness are *Café 46* at 46 Nguyen Hue Blvd and *Café 50* at 50 Nguyen Hue Blvd. The tables in these places have just enough room for 1½ people. There is another quiet, dark place at 8 Nguyen Thiep St (near Brossard Café). If you want to sit at intimate little tables with red lights on them and watch music videos, try the *Hoan Khiem* (tel 25753), also known as the My Man Bar (yes, the name *is* in English), at 27 Ngo Duc Ke St.

Dining Cruise The *Du Lich Tren Song* (Tourist Ferry Boat), which docks on the waterfront near the Majestic Hotel, is Saigon's version of Paris' *bateaux mouches*. Twice a day, this restaurant-on-a-barge is towed along the Saigon River by a tugboat, giving diners a leisurely view of rural Ho Chi Minh City. The lunch cruise (11 am to 2 pm) costs 4000d; the evening cruises (at 6.30 and 9.30 pm) costs 6000d and includes a live band. These prices do not cover the food (which is mediocre) or drink. Tickets are sold at 14 Ton Duc Thang St.

Do-It-Yourself Simple meals can easily be assembled from fruits, vegetables, bread and other basics sold in the city's markets. The widest selection of vegetables in the city is at Ben Thanh Market in Saigon and Binh Tay Market in Cholon. The *Dalat Fruit Kiosk* (kiosk number 13), which is outside the Kim Do Hotel on Nguyen Hue Blvd, has a good selection of seasonal fruits, but make sure you do not get short-weighed or overcharged.

The best bread bakery in town is, according to many Saigonese, *Nhu Lan Bakery* at 66 Ham Nghi Blvd. You can buy oven-fresh bread here from morning till night. Fresh eggs are sold in the pastry shop of *Givral Pâtisserie & Café* at 169 Dong Khoi St. Imported 'luxury' foods – soft cheese, tinned meats, sardines, real chocolate, alcoholic beverages – are available at various shops around the city, including a group of stores and stalls between numbers 48 and 76 Ham Nghi Blvd in Saigon. In Cholon, luxury goods are sold on the odd side of the 100 block of Nguyen Tri Phuong Blvd.

Find yourself daydreaming about Kellogg's Frosties, Pringle's potato chips, Twining's Tea or Campbell's soup? If you have an insatiable craving for Western processed foods, by far the best place to go in Ho Chi Minh City is the *Minimart* (tel 98189, extension 44) on the 2nd floor of the Saigon Intershop, which is at 101 Nam Ky Khoi Nghia St (just off of Le Loi Blvd). If this ultimate symbol of Western capitalism looks like it was transported lock, stock and barrel from Singapore, that's because it was. To enjoy the proffered delights, you must pay in US dollars. The Minimart is open from 9 am to 6 pm daily.

Places to Eat – Cholon
Hotels The *Bat Dat Hotel* at 238-244 Tran Hung Dao B Blvd has a large restaurant on the ground floor. The *Phu Tho Hotel* at 527 3 Thang 2 Blvd has a restaurant occupying the lower three floors of the building.

Vegetarian *Tiem Com Chay Thien Phat Duyen* is a small Chinese vegetarian restaurant about 1 km east of Chau Van Liem Blvd at 509 Nguyen Trai St. *Tiem Com Chay Phat Huu Duyen*, also Chinese, is at 952 Tran Hung Dao Blvd (corner An Binh St, where Tran Hung Dao B Blvd begins); it is open from 7 am to 10 pm. Across An Binh St at 3 Tran Hung Dao B Blvd is another Chinese place, *Tiem Com Chay Van Phat Duyen*, which is open from 7 am to 9 pm.

Entertainment
Sunday Night Live Downtown Saigon is *the* place to be on Sunday and holiday nights. The streets are jam-packed with young Saigonese, in couples and groups, cruising the town on bicycles and motorbikes, out to see and be seen. The mass of slowly moving humanity is so thick on Dong Khoi St that you can hardly get across the street, even on foot. It is utter chaos at intersections, where eight, ten or more lanes of two-wheeled vehicles intersect without the benefit of traffic lights.

Near the Municipal Theatre, fashionably dressed young people take a break from cruising around to watch the endless procession, lining up along the street next to their cycles. The air is electric with the glances of lovers and animated conversations among friends. It is a sight not to be missed.

Municipal Theatre The Municipal Theatre (Nha Hat Thanh Pho; tel 91249, 91584) is on Dong Khoi St between the Caravelle Hotel and the Continental Hotel. It was built in 1899 for use as a theatre but later served as

the heavily fortified home of the South Vietnamese National Assembly.

Each week, the theatre offers a different programme, which may be Eastern European-style gymnastics, nightclub music or traditional Vietnamese theatre. There are performances at 7.30 pm nightly except Mondays. Refreshments are sold during intermission; bathrooms are in the basement.

Hoa Binh Theatre The huge Hoa Binh Theatre complex (Nha Hat Hoa Binh, or the 'Peace Theatre') in District 10 often has several performances taking place simultaneously in its various halls, the largest of which seats 2400 people. The complex is at 14 3 Thang 2 Blvd (next to the white cement skeleton of the unfinished pagoda, Viet Nam Quoc Tu). The ticket office (tel 55199) is open from 7.30 am until the end of the evening show.

Evening performances, which begin at 7.30 pm, are usually held once or twice a week. Shows range from traditional and modern Vietnamese plays to Western pop music, and from circus acts to the occasional band from Eastern Europe. On Sunday mornings, there are marionette shows for children at 9 am in the 400-seat hall, and well-known Vietnamese pop singers begin performances in the large hall at 8.30 and 11 am.

Films are screened all day every day beginning at 8.30 am. Most of the films – from the Socialist countries, France, Hong Kong and the USA (Disney productions are a favourite) – are live-dubbed (someone reads a translation of the script over the PA system), leaving the original soundtrack at least partly audible. A weekly schedule of screenings is posted outside the building next to the ticket counter. Films cost 700d (1200d for a double feature).

The disco on the ground floor is open Tuesday to Sunday from 8 to 11 pm. Admission is 5000d.

Conservatory of Music Both traditional Vietnamese and Western classical music are performed publicly at the Conservatory of

Music (Nhac Vien Thanh Pho Ho Chi Minh; tel 25841, 98646), which is near Reunification Hall at 112 Nguyen Du St. Concerts are held at 7.30 pm each Monday and Friday evening during the two annual concert seasons, from March to May and from October to December. Tickets cost about 1000d.

Students aged 7 to 16 attend the Conservatory, which performs all the functions of a public school in addition to providing instruction in music. The music teachers here were trained in France, Britain and the USA as well as the former Eastern Bloc. The school is free but most of the students come from well-off families because only the well-to-do can afford musical instruments. There are two other conservatories of music in Vietnam, one in Hanoi and the other in Hué.

Dancing & Discos Vietnam is one of the few places left where a major component of the nightlife is still ballroom dancing. Of course, these *soirées dansantes* have become more and more like discos in recent years, and the guests are likely to be wealthy young people dressed in jeans and copies of the latest designer bootlegs from Bangkok, but the principle is the same. A place where dancing takes place is called a *vu truong* in Vietnamese; to dance is *khieu vu*.

There is dancing with a live band at the *Rex Hotel* nightly from 7.30 to 11 pm; admission is 8000d. At the *Caravelle Hotel*, where admission is 10,000d, there is dancing on the 10th floor every night from 8 to 11 pm. At the *Majestic Hotel*, dancing is held every night from 7 to 11 pm; the cover charge is 8000d. The *Palace Hotel* has dancing every night from 8 to 11 pm. You might also try the *Down Under Discotheque* at the Saigon Floating Hotel.

There is said to be a good band at *Saigon Dancing* on the 3rd floor of the Saigon Intershop, which is at 101 Nam Ky Khoi Nghia St; the entrance fee is 7500d. At the *Hoa Binh Theatre* (tel 55199), which is at 14 3 Thang 2 Blvd, the disco on the ground floor is open Tuesday to Sunday from 8 to 11 pm; admission is 5000d. The *Van Canh Res-*taurant (tel 94963), which is at 184 Calmette St on the lower floors of the Van Canh Hotel, has a live band and dancing nightly from 8 pm.

Cinemas Most of the films shown are from the former Eastern Bloc and are either subtitled or dubbed. Many Saigon maps have cinemas (*rap* in Vietnamese) marked with a special symbol. There are several cinemas downtown, including one next door to the Rex Hotel; another on Le Loi Blvd a block towards Ben Thanh Market from the Rex Hotel; and a third, *Rap Mang Non*, on Dong Khoi St 100 metres up from the Municipal Theatre. *Rap Dong Khoi* is at 163 Dong Khoi St.

Things to Buy
Souvenirs Typical souvenir handicrafts are sold at innumerable shops in central Saigon, especially along Dong Khoi St. Many of these places also offer overpriced antiques. Larger stores with this sort of merchandise include Culturimex (tel 92574, 92865) at 94-95 Dong Khoi St, which sells ceramics, wood carvings, hand-painted greeting cards, copies of antiquities and other items you'd expect to find in a shop with a name like the 'Culturimex'. The Saigon Lacquerwares Factory (tel 94183, 92543, 23697) at 139 Hai Ba Trung St (near the French Consulate) is the sort of place to which bus loads of tourists are brought to do their souvenir shopping. The selection of lacquerware, ceramics, etc is large but prices are high. The shop (tel 91623) at 97 Dong Khoi St has some interesting crafts items. The Saigon Intershop at 101 Nam Ky Khoi Nghia St also sells handicrafts.

Oil paintings, watercolours and paintings on silk can be bought at Phuong Tranh Art Arcade, 151 Dong Du St (opposite the Caravelle Hotel). There is another art gallery, Thang Long, at 70 Nguyen Hue Blvd (next to the Oscar Hotel).

Women's *ao dais* (pronounced, in the south, 'ow-yai'), the flowing silk blouse slit up the sides and worn over pantaloons, are tailored at a store on Dong Khoi St one block towards Notre Dame Cathedral from the Municipal Theatre. For embroidered items, try Mai Anh at 91 Mac Thi Buoi St (across from the Palace Hotel).

The Rex Hotel gift shop, like other hotel shops, has souvenirs and other items at reasonable prices set by the government.

Lac Long's, a shop at 143 Le Thanh Ton St (two blocks from the Hotel de Ville), sells fine exotic leathers and much more. This store is run by a gregarious ethnic-Chinese businessman known among socialist and capitalist travellers alike for his interesting connections. Nearby shops (around 121 Le Thanh Ton St) sell high-quality leather boots, sandals and shoes.

War Surplus Market For real and fake US, Chinese and Russian military surplus, the place to go is Dan Sinh Market at 104 Nguyen Cong Tu St (next to Phung Son Tu Pagoda). The front part of the market is filled with stalls selling automobiles and motorbikes, but directly behind the pagoda building you can find out what happened to at least a part of the hundreds of billions of dollars the USA spent losing the Vietnam War. Stall after stall sells everything from gas masks and field stretchers to rain gear and mosquito nets. You can also find canteens, duffel bags, ponchos and boots, a lot of it brand new. Much of the stuff here is newer than you'd guess: enterprising back-alley tailors have made it look just like US government issue. Anyone planning on spending time in Lebanon or the slums of Washington, DC should consider picking up a second-hand flak jacket (demand has slumped since the war, and the prices are very competitive). Exorbitant overcharging of foreigners looking for a poignant souvenir is common.

Photography For film and other photographic needs, there are a number of stores along Nguyen Hue Blvd. There is a large photo shop at 118-120 Dong Khoi St (tel 96614). The latest Japanese-made 1-hour colour developing equipment has been installed in stores at 66A Nguyen Hue Blvd and 110-112 Dong Khoi St (tel 22035) and in the Eden Colour Photo Centre at 4 Le Loi Blvd.

Department Store The biggest department store in Ho Chi Minh City, Cua Hang Bach Hoa, is on the corner of Le Loi Blvd and Nguyen Hue Blvd, across Le Loi from the Rex Hotel. Built as the Grands Magasins Charner 6 decades ago, this three-storey emporium, which for years was run by the government and had a pathetic selection of goods, was recently 'privatised', and floor space is now rented to individual shopowners. Items for sale include consumer electronics, blank and pirated cassette tapes, locally produced bicycles and parts, domestic alcoholic beverages, stationery, little globes of the world labelled in Vietnamese, sports equipment, cheap jewellery and clothing made of synthetic fibres.

Stamps & Coins Many bookshops and antique shops along Dong Khoi St sell overpriced French Indochinese coins and banknotes and packets of Vietnamese stamps. Two stamp stores, selling mostly post-1970 issues, are run by the philatelic department of the post office. One (tel 96230) is at 2C Le Loi Blvd near the Philippine Airlines office and is open from 6.30 am to 7 pm daily. The other, Phong Tem Suu Tap (tel 94509), is at 12 Ton That Dam St (between Ben Chuong Duong St and Ham Nghi Blvd) and is open from 7.30 to 11.30 am and 1 to 4 pm Monday to Saturday.

Electronics Electronics goods of all sorts – from mosquito zappers to video cassette players – are on sale to whoever can afford them on and around Huynh Thuc Khang St between Nguyen Hue Blvd and Ham Nghi Blvd. This whole neighbourhood was known as the Electronics Black Market until early 1989, when it was legalised. Similar items are available in Cholon in the stores around 261 An Duong Vuong Blvd, which is also signposted as Hong Bang Blvd.

Toiletries The best selection of Western shampoos, soaps, diapers, sanitary napkins and the like can be bought at the Minimart (tel 98189, extension 44) on the 2nd floor of the Saigon Intershop, which is at 101 Nam Ky Khoi Nghia St (just off Le Loi Blvd); it is open from 9 am to 6 pm daily. Many hotel gift shops have a limited selection of such items.

Miscellaneous There are numerous tailors' shops in Cholon and several in downtown Saigon; the Rex and Oscar hotels each have in-house tailors.

There are several reliable photocopying places in the centre strip of Nguyen Hue Blvd just outside the Oscar Hotel. A single-side photocopy costs 200d in Saigon, much less than in other parts of Vietnam.

No bureaucracy, Communist or otherwise, can exist without the official stamps and seals that provide the *raison d'être* for legions of clerks. To fill this need, the craftsmen at the shop at 39 Dong Khoi St (tel 92426) make reasonably priced brass and rubber stamps entirely by hand. Letters and numbers – backwards, of course – are carved out of a block of brass (or a chunk of rubber) using a hammer and a tiny chisel. Fascinating to watch.

Stationery is sold next to the GPO and on the even side of Le Loi Blvd between street numbers 30 and 60. There are signmakers' shops on Cach Mang Thang Tam St near the Central Market. For watch repair, try the shop at 133 Nguyen Hue Blvd (next to the Kim Do Hotel).

GETTING THERE & AWAY
Air
Ho Chi Minh City's Tan Son Nhut International Airport is served by Aeroflot, Air France, Cassidy Airlines (a Singaporean charter company), Czechoslovak Airlines, Garuda, Kampuchean Airlines, Lao Aviation, Philippine Airlines, THAI and Vietnam Airlines. There are direct international flights between Ho Chi Minh City and Bangkok, Batam Island (Indonesia), Bombay, Calcutta, Denpasar, Dubai, Jakarta, Karachi, Kuala Lumpur, Manila, New Delhi, Pakse (Laos), Paris, Phnom Penh, Prague,

Singapore, Tashkent and Vientiane. It is essential to reconfirm all reservations for flights out of the country. For more information on international air transport to and from Vietnam, see the Getting There chapter. For details on reservations and ticketing in Saigon, see Airline Offices in the Information section at the start of this chapter.

Domestic flights on Air Vietnam cost US$85 to Danang and US$161 to Hanoi with a stop in Danang. For more information on domestic air transport, see the 'Getting Around' chapter.

All checked baggage coming into Saigon is x-rayed upon arrival for contraband electronic equipment. The primitive x-ray equipment in use will destroy any film in your checked baggage, so keep your film and camera in your carry-on. Visitors have reported pilfering from checked luggage, especially when leaving the country.

Tan Son Nhut Airport (the name is spelled Tan Son Nhat by northerners) was one of the three busiest airports in the world during the late 1960s. The runways are still lined with lichen-covered mortar-proof aircraft revetments and other military structures, some still showing war damage. The sagging aluminium hulks of US-built transport planes sit next to ageing Soviet helicopters and jets of the Vietnamese Air Force. The complex of the US Military Assistance Command (MACV), also known as 'Pentagon East', was blown up by the Americans on 29 April 1975, hours before Saigon surrendered to North Vietnamese troops.

Train
Saigon Railway Station (Ga Sai Gon; tel 45585) is in District 3 at 1 Nguyen Thong St. Trains from here serve cities along the coast north of Saigon. The ticket office is open from 7.15 to 11 am and 1 to 3 pm daily. Payment for tickets at foreigners' prices can be made in dong, US dollars, French francs, and, if you are a 'socialist tourist', in Soviet roubles. Dong prices for foreigners' tickets are computed at a disadvantageous rate. Dormitory accommodation (*nha tro*) is available

across the parking lot from the main terminal building.

To get to the railway station, turn off Cach Mang Thang Tam St next to number 132/9. Go down the alley for about 100 metres and then follow the railway tracks to the left. Or you can go to the roundabout at the intersection of Cach Mang Tang Tam St and 3 Thang 2 Blvd and follow the disused railway tracks a few hundred metres. The tracks run down the middle of the alleyway that begins next to 252/1B Ly Chinh Thang St. A cyclo ride from the city centre to the station should cost 2000d. Ga Sai Gon is marked as 'Ga Hoa Hung' on some older maps; the railroad tracks that once led from Ga Hoa Hung to the square near Ben Thanh Market have been torn up.

The 'Reunification (Thong Nhat) Trains' link Saigon with all the major towns along the coast from Phan Rang-Thap Cham to Hanoi. TN2 leaves Saigon daily at 7 pm and takes 58 hours to get to Hanoi. TN4 and TN6, one of which leaves every day at 10 am, take 52 hours to Hanoi. AR2, which is a two-car autorail, goes from Saigon to Nha Trang. For details on train schedules, see the Getting Around chapter.

Bus

Inter-city buses depart from and arrive at a variety of stations around Ho Chi Minh City. Buses to points south of the city are based at Mien Tay Bus Station in An Lac. Buses to and from places north of Ho Chi Minh City use Mien Dong Bus Station. Van Thanh Bus Station serves destinations in Song Be and Dong Nai provinces. Express (*toc hanh*) buses are not quite as slow as regular buses.

Mien Tay Bus Station Almost all buses to points south of Ho Chi Minh City leave from the enormous Mien Tay Bus Station (Ben Xe Mien Tay; tel 55955), which is about 10 km west of Saigon in An Lac, a part of Binh Chanh District (Huyen Binh Chanh) of Greater Ho Chi Minh City. To get there, take Hau Giang Blvd or Hung Vuong Blvd west from Cholon and then continue past where these thoroughfares merge. As you head out of the city, Mien Tay Bus Station is on the left, opposite 130 Quoc Lo 4. There are buses from central Saigon to Mien Tay Bus Station from the Ben Thanh Bus Station (at the end of Ham Nghi Blvd near Ben Thanh Market).

Mien Tay Bus Station links Ho Chi Minh City with the southern provinces of An Giang, Ben Tre, Cuu Long, Dong Thap, Hau Giang, Kien Giang, Long An, Minh Hai, Tay Ninh and Tien Giang. Express buses and microbuses from Mien Tay Bus Station serve:

Bac Lieu (6 hours)
Camau (8 hours; 11,000d)
Cantho (3½ hours; 5400d)
Chau Doc (6 hours)
Long Xuyen (5 hours)
Rach Gia (6 to 7 hours; 9000d)

These buses, which receive priority treatment at ferry crossings, all depart twice a day: at 4.30 am and at 3 pm. Tickets are sold from 3.30 am for the early buses and from 12 noon for the afternoon runs. Express bus tickets are also on sale at 121 Chau Van Liem Blvd in Cholon; 142 Hung Vuong Blvd west of Cholon; and at 638 Le Hong Phong St in District 10.

The following cities are served by non-express bus service from the Mien Tay Bus Station:

An Phu	Mytho (1700d)
Bac Lieu	Ngoc Hien
Ben Tre	O Mon
Binh Minh Ferry	Phung Hiep
Camau (10 hrs; 7300d)	Rach Gia (6050d)
Cang Long	Sa Dec
Cantho (5 hrs; 3750d)	Soc Trang
Cao Lanh	Tam Binh
Cau Ke	Tam Nong
Cau Ngang	Tan Chau
Chau Doc	Tan Hiep
Chau Phu	Tay Ninh
Cho Moi	Thanh Tri
Duyen Hai	Thoai Son
Ha Tien	Thot Not
Ho Phong	Tieu Can
Hong Ngu	Tinh Bien
Long An	Tra Vinh
Long My	Thu Thua
Long Phu	Vam Cong
Long Xuyen	Vi Thanh
Moc Hoa	Vinh Chau
My Thuan	Vinh Long
My Xuyen	

Tickets for non-express buses are sold from 3.30 am to 4 pm at counters marked according to the province of destination. Non-express buses also leave from platforms arranged by province. At present, buses depart during daylight hours only. To guarantee a seat, you can make reservations a day in advance by asking a Vietnamese-speaker to phone the station office at tel 55955.

There are a few rooms for sleeping behind the sales counters in the building to the left of the main gate as you enter the station. A room costs 2000d per night.

Mien Dong Bus Station Buses to places north of Ho Chi Minh City leave from Mien Dong Bus Station (Ben Xe Mien Dong; tel 94056), which is in Binh Thanh District about 6 km from downtown Saigon on Quoc Lo 13 (National Highway 13). Quoc Lo 13 is the continuation of Xo Viet Nghe Tinh St. The station is about 2 km north of the intersection of Xo Viet Nghe Tinh St and Dien Bien Phu St. The station's main gate is opposite 78 Quoc Lo 13 (according to the new numbering) and next to 229 Quoc Lo 13 (according to the old numbering). To get there, you can take a bus from Ben Thanh Bus Station (at the end of Ham Nghe Blvd near Ben Thanh Market). A cyclo from the city centre should cost about 5000d.

There is express service from Mien Dong Bus Station to:

Buon Ma Thuot (15 hrs)
Dalat (7½ hrs; 9300d)
Danang (26 hrs; 26,000d)
Haiphong (53 hrs)
Hanoi (49 hrs; 46,000d)
Hué (29 hrs; 28,500d)
Nam Dinh (47 hrs)
Nha Trang (11 hrs; 12,800d)
Pleiku (22 hrs)
Quang Ngai (24 hrs)
Qui Nhon (17 hrs)
Tuy Hoa (12 hrs)
Vinh (42 hrs)
Vung Tau (2½ hrs; 4300d)

All the express buses leave daily between 5 and 5.30 am. To Nha Trang, there is also a daily bus at 5 pm. To buy express tickets, turn left as you enter the main gate of the station (which is on Quoc Lo 13) and go all the way to the end to a blue and white one storey building. Tickets are sold between 4 am and 4 pm in the room marked Quay Ban Ve Xe Toc Hanh (Express Bus Ticket Counter). To make express bus reservations by telephone, have a Vietnamese-speaker call tel 94056.

Non-express buses from Mien Dong Bus Station serve:

Bao Loc	Lam Ha
Baria	Long Khanh
Ben Cat	Madagoui
Binh Long	Nha Trang (8960d)
Bu Dang	Phan Rang
Buon Ma Thuot	Phan Ri
Cam Ranh	Phan Thiet
Dai Te	Phu Tuc
Dalat (6160d)	Phuong Lam
Danang (19,460d)	Pleiku
Di Linh	Quang Ngai
Don Duong	Qui Nhon
Dong Xoai	Tan Dinh
Duc Linh	Tan Phu
Duc Trong	Tanh Linh
Gia Nghia	Tay Son
Ham Tan	Thu Dau Mot
Ham Thuan Nam	Tuy Hoa
Hué (21,510d)	Tuy Phong
Kien Duc	Vung Tau (2510d)
Xuyen Moc	

Many of the non-express buses leave around 5.30 am. Tickets for short trips can be bought before departure. For long distance buses, tickets should be purchased a day in advance. The ticket windows, open from 5 am until the last seat on the last bus of the day is sold, and are in a large open shed with a corrugated iron roof across from the express bus ticket counter. Tickets for many buses that leave from the Mien Dong Bus Station can also be purchased at the Mien Tay Bus Station in An Lac.

There are a number of restaurants just outside the station along Quoc Lo 13. The nearest hotel is the Thanh Tung Hotel (tel 91817) at 310 Xo Viet Nghe Tinh St (corner Dien Bien Phu St); singles/doubles with ceiling fan cost 6500/8000d. In the station itself, there are dorm rooms (nha tro) in the long, low building next to the building where express tickets are sold; it is usually full. There are separate rooms for men (*nam*) and women (*nu*). A bed costs 800d for the night and 400d during the day. Watch out for thieves!

Other Bus Stations Buses to Tay Ninh, Cu Chi and points north-east of Saigon depart from the Tay Ninh Bus Station (Ben Xe Tay Ninh), which is in Tan Binh District. To get there, head all the way out Cach Mang Thang Tam St. The station is about 1.5 km past where Cach Mang Thang Tam St merges with Le Dai Hanh St.

Vehicles departing from Van Thanh Bus Station (Ben Xe Van Thanh; tel 94839) serve destinations within a few hours of Saigon, mostly in Song Be and Dong Nai provinces. Van Thanh Bus Station is in Binh Thanh District about 1.5 km east of the intersection of Dien Bien Phu St and Xo Viet Nghe Tinh St at 72 Dien Bien Phu St. As you head out of Saigon, go past where the numbers on Dien Bien Phu St climb up into the 600s. A cyclo ride from central Saigon should cost 3000d.

An assortment of decrepit US vans, Daihatsu Hijets and Citroën Traction 15s leave Van Thanh Bus Station for Baria, Cho Lau, Ham Tan, Long Dien, Long Hai, Phu Cuong, Phu Giao, parts of Song Be Province, Vung Tau (2550d) and Xuan Loc. Lambrettas go to Tay Ninh Bus Station in Tan Binh District. Vehicles leave when full. Van Thanh Bus Station is open from 6 am to about 6 pm.

Microbuses Cong Ty Dich Vu Du Lich Quan 1 (tel 90541) at 39 Nguyen Hue Blvd offers the fastest transport in town to Vung Tau. Express microbuses (tiny Isuzu vans), whose standard compliment is 20 passengers plus the driver, depart from 6 am to 5 pm on the hour. Fifty seat buses leave daily for Dalat (7 hours) at 4.15 am and Nha Trang (10 hours) at 4 am and 4 pm. The office is open from 7 am to 7 pm. Making reservations the

day before you would like to travel is advisable. Tickets for these runs are also sold at 7 Ky Con St in District 1; at Nha Van Hoa Phuong Tan Dinh at 124 Tran Quang Khai St in Da Cao, part of District 1; and at 75 Pham Dinh Ho St in District 6.

To Phnom Penh Daily buses to Phnom Penh, Cambodia, leave from the garage (tel 93754) at 155 Nguyen Hue Blvd, across Le Thanh Ton St from the Hotel de Ville (City Hall). Look for the sign in Khmer and Vietnamese. A one-way ticket costs 10,800d. Vietnamese can book 4-day tours to Cambodia here. If you already have a Cambodian visa, this is by far the cheapest way to get to Phnom Penh. It may be possible to hire a car for the drive to Phnom Penh at the Mien Tay Bus Station in An Lac (tel 55955).

The Cambodian Foreign Ministry will drive you to Phnom Penh in a beautiful new Japanese car for US$300! For more information, inquire at the Cambodian Consulate.

Taxi
If, in this age of compact and sub-compact automobiles, you have ever wondered how it was that US teenagers of the 1950s were supposed to have been sexually initiated in the back seat of a car, experiencing Saigon's boat-like 'marriage taxis' will put to rest forever your logistical confusion. These huge US cars date from the late '50s and early '60s, and many come complete with tail fins and impressive chrome fenders. They are now used mostly to add a touch of class to Vietnamese marriages, but they can also be hired for excursions in and around Ho Chi Minh City. Hop Tac Xa Xe Du-Lich (Tourist Car Corporation; tel 90600), opposite the Foreign Exchange Bank and across the street from 43 Ben Chuong Duong St (corner Nam Ky Khoi Nghia St), is easy to spot: dozens of the old classics are lined up next to the dispatcher's booth. Make reservations the day before your departure. Always specify exactly where you want to go and the times you expect to depart and return *before* you sign anything or hand over any money. The usual deposit is between

one-quarter and one-third of the total; the balance should be paid at the end of the trip.

Vietnam Tourism charges US$0.33 per km for a car. Cong Ty Dich Vu Du Lich Quan 1 (tel 90541) at 39 Nguyen Hue Blvd hires cars for inter-city runs at 700d per km (without air-conditioning) and 1000d per km (with air-con). For a full day within the city, you'll be charged 140,000d; a half-day will cost 70,000d. Trung Tam Du Lich Thanh Nien Viet Nam (the Youth Tourism Centre), which is next door at 44 Ngo Duc Ke St, has competitively priced vehicles as well.

Cars with drivers can also be hired at the Phnom Penh bus garage (155 Nguyen Hue Blvd). Computed on a per-km basis, a 6-day trip from Saigon to Hué costs US$350, including the price of returning the car to Saigon. Cars (and for larger groups, buses) can be arranged through the Mien Tay Bus Station (tel 55955) in An Lac. Reservations should be made 2 to 7 days in advance.

SATAXI (the Saigon Private Taxi Company; tel 97545, 98805, 96624; telex 8480 PRAFIT HCM) is at 27B Nguyen Dinh Chieu in the same building as the Domestic Booking Office of Vietnam Airlines. Major hotels can also arrange for taxis; they charge US$30 to US$35 per day.

Boat

Passenger and goods ferries to the Mekong Delta depart from a dock (tel 97892) at the river end of Ham Nghi Blvd. There is daily service to the provinces of An Giang and Cuu Long and to the towns of Ben Tre (8 hours), Camau (30 hours; once every 4 days), Mytho (6 hours; departs at 11 am) and Tan Chau. Buy your tickets on the boat. Simple food may be available on board. Be aware that these ancient vessels lack the most elementary safety gear, such as life preservers.

GETTING AROUND
Airport Transport

Ho Chi Minh City's Tan Son Nhut International Airport is 7 km from the centre of Saigon. The taxis for hire outside the customs hall will try to grossly overcharge, so bargain hard (a fair price into town is about US$5). Cyclos (pedicabs) can be hailed outside the gate to the airport, which is a few hundred metres from the terminal building. A ride to central Saigon should cost about 5000d. You might also try to flag down a motorbike and hitch a ride seated behind the driver; this should also cost about 5000d to get downtown.

To get to the airport, try hiring a taxi at one of the taxi stands listed in the Taxi section. This will certainly prove cheaper than the US$20 limousine service available at the front desk of the Rex Hotel. If you take a cyclo or motorbike to Tan Son Nhut, you may have to walk from the airport gate to the terminal. There is also a public bus from downtown Saigon.

Bus

There is only limited local public transport. No decent bus map is available and bus stops are mostly unmarked. There is a major depot for local buses on Le Lai St, a few blocks south-west of NguyenThai Hoc Blvd.

There are several bus lines linking Saigon and Cholon. Perhaps the most convenient begins on Nguyen Hue Blvd near the river. The red and white Czech-built Karosa coaches leave from here, turn left onto Le Loi Blvd, pass Ben Thanh Market, continue south-west on Tran Hung Dao Blvd, and turn left on Chau Van Liem Blvd for one block. Then turn right onto Hai Thuong Lan Ong St near the Cholon GPO and continue on to Binh Tay Market.

Ben Thanh Bus Terminal, which is on the other side of the roundabout from Ben Thanh Market, offers transport to other parts of Ho Chi Minh City, including Mien Tay Bus Station in An Lac, Ba Queo, Binh Tay Market in Cholon, Binh Phuoc, Binh Trieu (near the railway station), Nha Be, Phu Lam, Phu Xuan, Quang Trung (the exhibition ground) and Tam Hiep (near Bien Hoa). This part of Saigon is infamous for its many pickpockets, razor artists and lowlifes.

Lambrettas (tiny three-wheeled trucks) to Thu Duc District leave from a parking lot opposite 54 Le Lai St.

Taxi

There are a growing number of places around Ho Chi Minh City where taxis can be hired for short trips in the city. There is a taxi stand on Le Loi Blvd in front of the Rex Hotel and another on the centre strip of Ham Nghi Blvd opposite number 54 (near the luxury goods market). You can also arrange a taxi through the reception desks of the Rex and Caravelle hotels.

In Cholon, there are always a few ancient Renault 4 taxis sitting next to the entrance to the Pham Ngoc Thach Hospital at 120 Hung Vuong Blvd. They are there to transport sick people too ill to walk or ride in a cyclo, but well people who can pay are also welcome to use them. These Renault 4s break down frequently and are not recommended for travel outside the city.

Boat

To see Ho Chi Minh City from the Saigon River, try hiring a motorised 5-metre boat near Me Linh Square (at the foot of Hai Ba Trung St, next to Saigon FloatingHotel). The price should be 8000 to 10,000d per hour. Interesting destinations for short trips include Cholon (along Ben Nghe Channel) and the zoo (along Thi Nghe Channel).

Ferries across the Saigon River leave from a dock at Me Linh Square. They run every half hour or so from 4.30 am to 10.30 pm and cost 50d per person (50d extra for a bicycle). Small boats to the other bank of the Saigon River leave from the end of Ham Nghi Blvd, but to get one you have to brave a gauntlet of greedy boat owners.

Motorbike

There are quite a few motorbike parts shops on Ly Tu Trong St (corner Cach Mang Thang Tam St) and around 77 Ky Con St (corner Nguyen Cong Tru St, near number 304). For motorbike repairs, also try the area around the intersection of Hung Vuong Blvd and Tran Binh Trong St.

Cyclo

Cyclos (pedicabs) can be hailed along major thoroughfares almost any time of the day or night. In Saigon, many of the drivers are former South Vietnamese Army soldiers, and quite a few of them know at least a bit of English. Each of them has a story of war, 're-education' and poverty to tell.

Short hops around the city centre should cost about 1000d. Settle on a price beforehand and have exact change ready.

Honda Ong

A quick (if precarious) way around town is to ride on the back of a motorbike (*Honda ong*). There is no set procedure for finding a driver willing to transport you somewhere. You can either try to flag someone down (most drivers can always use a bit of extra cash) or ask a Vietnamese to find a *Honda ong* for you. The accepted rate is comparable to what cyclos charge.

Bicycle

The best place in Ho Chi Minh City to buy a decent (read 'imported') bicycle is at the shops around 288 Le Thanh Ton St (corner Cach Mang Thang Tam St). Assembled bicycles start at 100,000d. You can also buy bike components: Czech and French frames, Chinese derailleurs, headlamps, etc. A decent bicycle with foreign components costs about US$100. In Cholon, you might try the bicycle shops on Ngo Gia Tu Blvd just south-west of LyThai To Blvd (near An Quang Pagoda). In District 4 there are bicycle parts shops along Nguyen That Thanh St just south of the Ho Chi Minh Museum.

For cheap and poorly assembled domestic bicycles and parts, try the ground floor of Cua Hang Bach Hoa, the department store on the corner of Nguyen Hue Blvd and Le Loi Blvd. Vikotrade Company at 35 Le Loi Blvd (across the street from the Rex Hotel) also has locally made components.

For on-the-spot bicycle repairs, look for an upturned army helmet and a hand pump sitting next to the curb. There is a cluster of bicycle repair shops around 23 Phan Dang Luu Blvd.

Bicycle parking lots in Ho Chi Minh City are usually just roped-off sections of a sidewalk. For 100 to 200d, you can leave your bicycle knowing that it will be there when you get back (bicycle theft is a big problem). When you pull up, your bicycle will have a number written on the seat in chalk or stapled to the handlebars. You will be given a reclaim chit (don't lose it!). If you come back and your bicycle is gone, the parking lot is supposedly required to replace it.

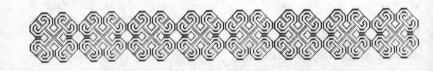

Around Saigon

THE TUNNELS OF CU CHI

The tunnel network of Cu Chi District, now part of Greater Ho Chi Minh City, became legendary during the 1960s for its role in facilitating Viet Cong control of a large rural area only 30 km from Saigon. At its height, the tunnel system stretched from the South Vietnamese capital to the Cambodian border; in the district of Cu Chi alone, there were over 200 km of tunnels. The network, parts of which were several stories deep, included innumerable trap doors, specially constructed living areas, storage facilities, weapons factories, field hospitals, command centres and kitchens.

The tunnels made possible communiction and coordination between VC-controlled enclaves isolated from each other by South Vietnamese and American land and air operations. They also allowed the guerrillas to mount surprise attacks wherever the tunnels went – even within the perimeters of American bases – and to disappear into hidden trapdoors without a trace. After ground operations against the tunnels claimed large numbers of casualties and proved ineffective, the Americans resorted to massive firepower, eventually turning Cu Chi's 420 sq km into what Tom Mangold and John Penycate have called 'the most bombed, shelled, gassed, defoliated and generally devastated area in the history of warfare'.

Today, Cu Chi has become a pilgrimage site for Vietnamese schoolchildren and Party cadres. Parts of this remarkable tunnel network – enlarged and upgraded versions of the real McCoy – are open to the public. The unadulterated tunnels, though not actually closed to tourists, are hard to get to and are rarely visited.

History

The tunnels of Cu Chi were built over a period of 2½ decades beginning in the late 1940s. They were the improvised response of a poorly equipped peasant army to its enemy's high-tech ordnance, helicopters, artillery, bombers and chemical weapons.

The Viet Minh built the first dugouts and tunnels in the hard, red earth of Cu Chi – ideal for the construction of tunnels – during the war against the French. The excavations were used mostly for communication between villages and to evade French army sweeps of the area.

When the Viet Cong insurgency began in earnest around 1960, the old Viet Minh tunnels were repaired and new extensions excavated. Within a few years the system assumed enormous strategic importance, and most of Cu Chi District and nearby areas came under firm Viet Cong control. In addition, Cu Chi was used as a base for infiltrating intelligence agents and sabotage teams into Saigon itself. The stunning attacks in the South Vietnamese capital itself during the 1968 Tet Offensive were planned and launched from Cu Chi.

In early 1963, the Diem government implemented the infamous 'strategic hamlet' programme under which fortified encampments, surrounded by rows of sharp bamboo spikes, were built to house people relocated from Communist-controlled areas. The first 'strategic hamlet' was in Ben Cat District, next door to Cu Chi. Not only was the programme carried out with incredible incompetence and cruelty, alienating the peasantry, but the VC was able to tunnel into the 'strategic hamlets' and control them from within. By the end of 1963, the first showpiece hamlet had been overrun.

The series of setbacks and defeats suffered by the South Vietnamese government forces in the Cu Chi area helped make a complete National Liberation Front (Viet Cong) victory by the end of 1965 seem a distinct possibility. Indeed, in the early months of that year, the guerrillas boldly held a victory parade in the middle of Cu Chi town. VC strength in and around Cu Chi was one of the reasons the Johnson administration decided to involve American combat troops in the war.

To deal with the threat posed by VC control of an area so near the South Vietnamese capital, one of the Americans' first actions was to establish a large base camp in Cu Chi District. Unknowingly, they built it right on top of an existing tunnel network. It took months for the 25th Division to figure out why they kept getting shot at in their tents at night.

The Americans and Australians tried to 'pacify' the area around Cu Chi that came to be known as the 'Iron Triangle' by a variety of methods. They launched large-scale ground operations involving tens of thousands of troops - but failed to locate the tunnels. To deny the VC cover and supplies, rice paddies were defoliated, huge swathes of jungle bulldozed and villages evacuated and razed. The Americans also sprayed chemical defoliants on the area from the air and then, a few months later, ignited the tinder-dry vegetation with gasoline and napalm. But the intense heat interacted with the wet tropical air in such a way as to create cloudbursts that extinguished the fires. The VC remained safe and sound in their tunnels.

When the Americans began using Alsatians trained to use their keen sense of smell to locate trapdoors and guerrillas, the VC put out pepper to distract the dogs. They also began washing with American toilet soap, which gave off a scent the canines identified as friendly. Captured American uniforms, which had the familiar smell of bodies nourished on American-style food, were put out to confuse the dogs further. Most importantly, the dogs were not able to spot booby traps. So many dogs were killed or maimed that their horrified army handlers refused to send them into the tunnels; so the US Army began sending down men instead. These 'tunnel rats', who were often involved in underground fire fights, sustained appallingly high casualty rates.

The Americans declared Cu Chi a free-strike zone: minimal authorisation was needed to shoot at anything in the area, random artillery was fired into the area at night and pilots were told to drop unused bombs and napalm there before returning to base. But the Viet Cong stayed put. Finally, in the late 1960s, the Americans carpet-bombed the whole area with B-52s, destroying most of the tunnels along with everything else around. But it was too late; the United States was already on its way out of the war. The tunnels had served their purpose.

The Viet Cong guerrillas serving in the tunnels lived in extremely difficult conditions and suffered horrific casualties. Only about 6000 of the 16,000 cadres who fought in the tunnels survived the war. In addition, uncounted thousands of civilians in the area, relatives of many of the guerrillas, were killed. Their tenacity despite the bombings, the pressures of living underground for weeks and months at a time and the deaths of countless friends and comrades is difficult to comprehend.

The villages of Cu Chi have been presented with numerous honorific awards, decorations and citations by the government, and many have been declared 'heroic villages'. Since 1975, new hamlets have been established and the population of the area has more than doubled to 200,000, but chemical defoliants remain in the soil and water and crop yields are still poor.

For more details, you might want to take a look at *The Tunnels of Cu Chi* by Tom Mangold and John Penycate (Random House, New York, 1985).

The Tunnels

Over the years, the VC, learning by trial and error, developed simple but effective techniques to make their tunnels difficult to detect or disable. Wooden trapdoors were camouflaged with earth and branches; some were booby-trapped. Hidden underwater entrances from rivers were constructed. To cook, they used 'Dien Bien Phu kitchens', which exhausted the smoke through vents many metres away from the cooking site. Trapdoors were installed throughout the network to prevent tear gas, smoke or water from moving from one part of the system to another. Some sections were even equipped with electric lighting.

The small, renovated section of the tunnel system now open to visitors is near the village of Ben Dinh. In one of the classrooms of the visitors' centre, a large map shows the extent of the network (the area shown is in the north-western corner of Greater Ho Chi Minh City). The tunnels are marked in red. Viet Cong bases are shown in light grey. The light blue lines are rivers (the Saigon River is at the top). Fortified villages held by South Vietnamese and American forces are marked in grey. Blue dots represent the American and South Vietnamese military posts that were supposed to ensure the security of nearby villages. The dark blue area in the centre is the base of the American 25th Infantry Division.

To the right of the large map are two cross-section diagrams of the tunnels. The bottom diagram is a reproduction of one used by General William Westmoreland, the commander of American forces in Vietnam from 1964 to 1968. For once, the Americans seemed to have had their intelligence information right (though the tunnels did not pass under rivers nor did the guerrillas wear headgear underground).

The section of the tunnel system presently open to visitors is a few hundred metres south of the visitors' centre. It snakes up and down through various chambers along its 50 metre length. The unlit tunnels are about 1.2 metres high and 80 cm across. A knocked-out M-48 tank and a bomb crater are near the exit, which is in a reafforested eucalyptus grove.

Getting There & Away

Bus Buses from Ho Chi Minh City to Tay Ninh leave from the Tay Ninh Bus Station (Ben Xe Tay Ninh) in Tan Binh District and Mien Tay Bus Station in An Lac. All buses to Tay Ninh pass though Cu Chi town, but getting from the town of Cu Chi to the tunnels by public transport may prove difficult.

Taxi Hiring a taxi (or 'marriage taxi') in Saigon and just driving out to Cu Chi is not all that expensive, especially if the cost is split by several people. If you want to visit the 'real' tunnels rather than those open to the public, make this clear to your driver before you cut a deal. A non-English speaking guide can be hired at the visitors' centre. For details on hiring vehicles in Saigon, see 'Getting There & Away' and 'Getting Around' in the 'Saigon & Cholon' chapter.

A visit to the Cu Chi tunnel complex can easily be combined with a stop at the headquarters of the Caodai sect in Tay Ninh. A taxi for an all-day excursion to both should cost about US$40.

Tours Organised tours run by Vietnam Tourism often visit Cu Chi. Booking a special 1 day guided tour with Vietnam Tourism is a bit pricey.

TAY NINH

Tay Ninh town (population 26,000), capital of Tay Ninh Province, serves as the headquarters of one of Vietnam's most interesting indigenous religions, Caodaism. The Caodai Great Temple at the sect's Holy See is one of the most striking structures in all of Asia. Built between 1933 and 1955, it is a rococo extravaganza combining the architectural idiosyncrasies of a French church, a Chinese pagoda, the Tiger Balm Gardens and Madame Tussaud's Wax Museum.

Tay Ninh Province, which is north-west of Ho Chi Minh City, is bordered by Cambodia on three sides. The area's dominant geographic feature is Nui Ba Den (Black Lady Mountain), which towers 850 metres above the surrounding plains. Tay Ninh Province's eastern border is formed by the Saigon River. The Vam Co River flows from Cambodia through the western part of the province.

Because of the once-vaunted political and military power of the Caodai, this region was the scene of prolonged heavy fighting during the Franco-Vietminh War. Tay Ninh Province served as a major terminus of the Ho Chi Minh Trail during the Vietnam War. In 1969, the VC captured Tay Ninh town and held it for several days.

During the period of tension between Cambodia and Vietnam in the late-1970s, the Khmer Rouge launched a number of cross-border raids into Tay Ninh Province during which horrific atrocities were committed against the civilian population.

The Religion of Cao Dai

Caodaism (*Dai Dao Tam Ky Pho Do*) is the product of an attempt to create the ideal religion through the fusion of the secular and religious philosophies of East and West. The result is a colourful and eclectic potpourri that includes bits and pieces of most of the religious philosophies known in Vietnam during the early 20th century: Buddhism, Confucianism, Taoism, Hinduism, native Vietnamese spiritism, Christianity and Islam. The term 'Cao Dai', which literally means 'high tower or palace', is used to refer to God. The religion is called 'Caodaism'; its adherents are the 'Caodais'. The hierarchy of the sect, whose priesthood is non-professional, is partly based on the structure of the Roman Catholic Church.

History Caodaism was founded by the mystic Ngo Minh Chieu (also known as Ngo Van Chieu; born 1878), a civil servant who once served as district chief of Phu Quoc Island. He was widely read in Eastern and Western religious works and became active in seances, at which his presence was said to greatly improve the quality of communication with the spirits. Around 1919 he began to receive a series of revelations from Cao Dai in which the tenets of Caodai doctrine were set forth.

Caodaism was officially founded as a religion in a ceremony held in 1926. Within a year, the group had 26,000 followers. Many of the sect's early followers were Vietnamese members of the French colonial administration. By the mid-1950s, one in eight southern Vietnamese was a Caodai, and the sect was famous worldwide for its imaginative garishness. But in 1954, Graham Green, the British author of *The Quiet American* – who himself had once considered converting to Caodaism – wrote in *The Times*

of London: 'What on my first two visits has seemed gay and bizarre (was) now like a game that had gone on too long'.

By the mid-'50s, the Caodai had established a virtually independent feudal state in Tay Ninh Province, and they retained enormous influence in the affairs of Tay Ninh Province for the next 2 decades. They also played a significant political and military role in South Vietnam from 1926 to 1956, when most of the 25,000 strong Caodai army, which had been given support by the Japanese and later the French, was incorporated into the South Vietnamese Army. During the Franco-Vietminh War, Caodai munitions factories specialised in making mortar tubes out of automobile exhaust pipes.

Because they had refused to support the Viet Cong during the Vietnam War – and despite the fact that they had been barely tolerated by the Saigon government – the Caodai feared the worst after reunification. Indeed, all Caodai lands were confiscated by the new Communist government and four members of the sect were executed in 1979, but in 1985, the Holy See and some 400 temples were returned to Caodai control.

Caodaism is strongest in Tay Ninh Province and the Mekong Delta, but Caodai temples can be found throughout southern and central Vietnam. Today, there are an estimated 2 million followers of Caodaism.

Philosophy Much of Caodai doctrine is drawn from Mahayana Buddhism mixed with Taoist and Confucian elements (Vietnam's 'Triple Religion'). Caodai ethics are based on the Buddhist ideal of 'the good person' but incorporate traditional Vietnamese taboos and sanctions as well.

The ultimate goal of the disciple of Caodaism is to escape the cycle of reincarnation. This can be achieved by the performance of certain human duties, including first and foremost following the prohibitions against killing, lying, luxurious living, sensuality and stealing.

The main tenets of Caodaism include believing in one God, the existence of the soul and the use of mediums to communicate with the spiritual world. Caodai practices include priestly celibacy, vegetarianism, communications with spirits through seances, reverence for the dead, maintenance of the cult of ancestors, fervent proselytising and sessions of meditative self-cultivation.

Following the Chinese duality of Yin and Yang, there are two principal deities, the Mother Goddess, who is female, and God, who is male. There is a debate among the Caodai as to which deity was the primary source of creation.

According to Caodaism, history is divided into three major periods of divine revelation. During the first period, God's truth was revealed to humanity through Moses and figures associated with Buddhism, Confucianism and Taoism. The human agents of revelation during the second period were Buddha (Sakyamuni), Lao Tze, Confucius, Jesus and Mohammed. The Caodai believe that their messages were corrupted because of the human frailty of the messengers and their disciples. They also believe that these revelations were limited in scope, intended to be applicable only during a specific age to the people of the area in which the messengers lived.

Caodaism sees itself as the product of the 'Third Alliance Between God and Man', the third and final revelation. Disciples believe that Caodaism avoids the failures of the first two periods because it is based on divine truth as communicated through spirits, which serve as messengers of salvation and instructors of doctrine. Spirits who have been in touch with the Caodai include deceased Caodai leaders, patriots, heroes, philosophers, poets, political leaders and warriors as well as ordinary people. Among the contacted spirits who lived as Westerners are Joan of Arc, René Descartes, William Shakespeare (who hasn't been heard from since 1935), Victor Hugo, Louis Pasteur and Vladimir Ilyich Lenin. Because of his frequent appearances to Caodai mediums at the Phnom Penh mission, Victor Hugo was posthumously named the chief spirit of foreign missionary works.

Communication with the spirits is carried on in Vietnamese, Chinese, French and English. The methods of receiving messages from the spirits illustrate the influence of both East Asian and Western spiritism on Caodai seance rites. Sometimes, a medium holds a pen or Chinese calligraphy brush. In the 1920s, a 66 cm long wooden staff known as a *corbeille à bec* was used. Medium(s) held one end while a crayon attached to the other wrote out the spirits' messages. The Caodai also use what is known as *pneumatographie*, in which a blank slip of paper is sealed in an envelope and hung above the altar. When the envelope is taken down, there is a message on the paper.

Most of the sacred literature of Caodaism consists of messages communicated to Caodai leaders during seances held between 1925 and 1929. Since 1927, only the official seances held at Tay Ninh have been considered reliable and divinely ordained by the Caodai hierarchy, though dissident groups continued to hold seances which produced communications contradicting accepted doctrine.

The Caodai consider vegetarianism to be of service to humankind because it does not involve harming fellow beings during the process of their spiritual evolution. They also see vegetarianism as a form of self-purification. There are several different vegetarian regimens followed by Caodai disciples. The least rigourous involves eating vegetarian food 6 days a month. Priests must be full-time vegetarians.

The clergy (except at the highest levels) is open to both men and women, though when male and female officials of equal rank are serving in the same area, male clergy are in charge. Female officials wear white robes and are addressed with the title *Huong*, which means 'perfume'. Male clergy are addressed as *Thanh*, which means 'pure'. Caodai temples are constructed so that male and female disciples enter on opposite sides; women worship on the left, men on the right.

All Caodai temples observe four daily ceremonies, which are held at 6 am, noon, 6 pm and midnight. These rituals, during which dignitaries wear ceremonial dress and hats, include offerings of incense, tea, alcohol, fruit and flowers. All Caodai altars have above them the 'divine eye', which became the religion's official symbol after Ngo Minh Chieu saw it in a vision he had while on Phu Quoc Island.

Holy See of the Caodai

The Caodao Holy See, founded in 1926, is 4 km east of Tay Ninh in the village of Long Hoa. Guests should wear modest and respectful attire (no shorts or tank tops). The complex includes the Great Temple, administrative offices, residences for officials and adepts, and a hospital of traditional Vietnamese herbal medicine to which people from all over the south travel for treatment. After reunification, the government 'borrowed' parts of the complex for its own use (and perhaps to keep an eye on the sect).

Prayers are conducted in the Great Temple every day at 6 am, noon, 6 pm and midnight. Only a few hundred priests participate in weekday prayers; but on festivals several thousand priests, dressed in special white garments, may attend. The Caodai clergy are pretty mellow about photographing their ceremonies providing you ask permission first.

Above the front portico of the Great Temple is the 'divine eye', the supreme symbol of Caodaism. Americans often comment that it looks as if it were copied from the back of a US$1 bill. Lay women and female guests enter the Great Temple through a door at the base of the tower on the left. Once inside, they walk around the outside of the colonnaded hall in a clockwise direction. Gentlemen (and other males) enter on the right and circumambulate the hall in a counter-clockwise direction. Shoes must be removed upon entering the building. The area in the centre of the sanctuary (between the pillars) is reserved for Caodai priests.

A mural in the front entry hall depicts the three signatories of the 'Third Alliance Between God and Man'. The Chinese statesman and revolutionary leader Dr Sun Yat Sen (1866-1925) holds an inkstone while Vietnamese poet Nguyen Binh Khiem (1492-1587) and Victor Hugo (1802-85), French poet and author, write 'God and Humanity' and 'Love and Justice' in Chinese and French. Victor Hugo uses a quill pen; Nguyen Binh Khiem writes with a brush. Nearby signs in English, French and German each give a slightly different version of the fundamentals of Caodaism.

The Great Temple is built on nine levels, which represent the nine steps to heaven. Each level is marked by a pair of columns. At the far end of the sanctuary, eight plaster columns entwined with multi-coloured dragons support a dome representing – as does the rest of the ceiling – the heavens. Under the dome is a giant star-speckled blue globe with the 'divine eye' on it.

The largest of the seven chairs in front of the globe is reserved for the Caodai pope, a position that has remained unfilled since 1933. The next three chairs are for the three men responsible for the religion's law books. The remaining chairs are for the leaders of the three branches of Caodaism, which are represented by the colours yellow, blue and red.

On both sides of the area between the columns are two pulpits similar in design to the *minbars* found in mosques. During festivals, the pulpits are used by officials to address the assembled worshippers. The upstairs balconies are used if there is an overflow crowd downstairs.

Long Hoa Market

Long Hoa Market is several km south of the Caodai Holy See complex. Open every day from 5 am to about 6 pm, this large market sells meat, food staples, clothing and pretty much everything else you would expect to find in a rural marketplace. Before reunification, the Caodai sect had the right to collect taxes from the merchants here.

Nui Ba Den

Nui Ba Den (Black Lady Mountain), 15 km north-east of Tay Ninh town, rises 850 metres above the rice paddies of the surrounding countryside. Over the centuries, Nui Ba Den has served as a shrine for various peoples of the area, including the Khmer, Chams, Vietnamese and Chinese. There are several cave-temples on the mountain. The summits of Nui Ba Den are much cooler than the rest of Tay Ninh Province, most of which is only a few dozen metres above sea level.

Nui Ba Den was used as a staging ground by both the Viet Minh and the Viet Cong and was the scene of fierce fighting during the French and American wars. At one time, there was a US Army fire base and relay station at the summit of the mountain, which was defoliated and heavily bombed by American aircraft.

The name 'Black Lady Mountain' is derived from the legend of Huong, a young woman who married her true love despite the advances of a wealthy mandarin. While her husband was away doing military service, she would visit a magical statue of Buddha at the summit of the mountain. One day, Huong was attacked by kidnappers but, preferring death to dishonour, threw herself off a cliff. She reappeared in the visions of a monk living on the mountain, who told her story.

Places to Stay

In the town of Tay Ninh, there are a couple of hotels a few hundred metres east and then north of the triple arch bridge.

Places to Eat

Nha Hang So 1 (Restaurant Number 1) is on the western side of the river near the old triple-arch concrete bridge. A full meal costs about 6000d.

Getting There & Away

Bus Buses from Ho Chi Minh City to Tay Ninh leave from the Tay Ninh Bus Station (Ben Xe Tay Ninh) in Tan Binh District and Mien Tay Bus Station in An Lac.

Tay Ninh is 96 km from Ho Chi Minh City on National Highway 22 (Quoc Lo 22). The road passes through Trang Bang, where the famous photo of a young girl, severely burned, screaming and running, was taken during an American napalm attack. There are several Caodai temples along National Route 22 including one, under construction in 1975, that was heavily damaged by the Viet Cong.

Taxi The easiest way to get to Tay Ninh is by taxi or 'marriage taxi', perhaps on a day trip that includes a stop in Cu Chi. An all-day round trip by marriage taxi should cost about US$40. No special permits are required as long as you return to Saigon to sleep.

VUNG TAU

Vung Tau, known under the French as Cap Saint Jacques (it was so named by Portuguese mariners in honour of their patron saint), is a beach resort on the South China Sea, 128 km south-east of Saigon. Vung Tau's beaches are not Vietnam's nicest by any stretch of the imagination, but they are easily reached from Ho Chi Minh City and have thus been a favourite of the Saigonese since French colonists first began coming here around 1890. Seaside areas near Vung Tau are dotted with the villas of the pre-1975 elite, now converted to guest houses and villas for the post-1975 elite.

In addition to sunning on the seashore and sipping sodas in nearby cafes, visitors to this city of 100,000 can cycle around or climb up the Vung Tau Peninsula's two mountains. There are also a number of interesting religious sites around town, including several pagodas and a huge standing figure of Jesus blessing the South China Sea.

Vung Tau serves as the headquarters of Vietsovpetro, a joint Soviet-Vietnamese company that operates oil rigs about 60 km offshore. Soviet expats live together in the most desirable neighbourhood of the city, a compound bordering Front Beach. Perhaps because of the strategic importance of oil exploration (which has recently involved Western multinationals in addition to the Soviets), Vung Tau has a very inquisitive secret police apparatus.

The local fishing fleet is quite active, though many Vietnamese fleeing their homeland by sea set sail from Vung Tau, taking many of the town's fishing trawlers with them. Vietnamese navy boats on patrol

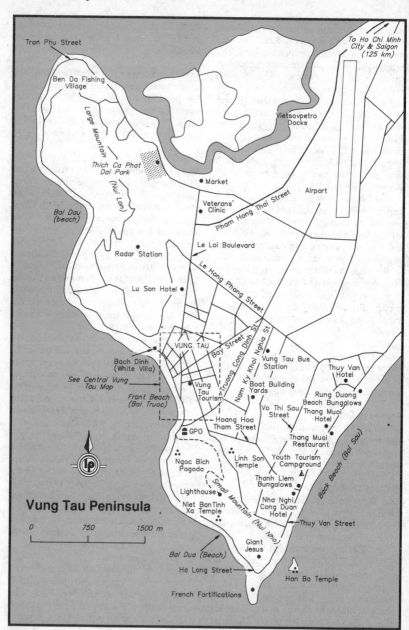

Tran Phu Street

Ben Da Fishing Village

Large Mountain

(Nui Lon)

Thich Ca Phat Dai Park

Bai Dau (beach)

Radar Station

Lu Son Hotel

Vietsovpetro Docks

To Ho Chi Minh City & Saigon (125 km)

Market

Veterans' Clinic

Pham Hong Thai Street

Airport

Le Loi Boulevard

Le Hong Phong Street

VUNG TAU

Bay Street

Truong Cong Dinh St

Nam Ky Khoi Nghia St

Vung Tau Bus Station

Thuy Van Hotel

Bach Dinh (White Villa)

See Central Vung Tau Map

Front Beach (Bai Truoc)

Vung Tau Tourism

Boat Building Yards

Rung Duong Beach Bungalows

Thang Muoi Hotel

Vo Thi Sau Street

Hoang Hoa Tham Street

Thang Muoi Restaurant

GPO

Ngoc Bich Pagoda

Linh Son Temple

Youth Tourism Campground

Back Beach (Bai Sau)

Thanh Liem Bungalows

Lighthouse

Small Mountain

(Nui Nho)

Nha Nghi Cong Duan Hotel

Niet Ban Tinh Xa Temple

Thuy Van Street

Bai Dua (Beach)

Giant Jesus

Ha Long Street

Hon Ba Temple

French Fortifications

Vung Tau Peninsula

0   750   1500 m

offshore ensure that the rest of the fleet comes home each day.

Vung Tau is rapidly becoming the sex capital of Vietnam. 'Massage' parlours are sprouting up everywhere, catering mostly to high-ranking cadres. The entire massage trade in Vung Tau is said to be controlled by the local police and People's Committee. Indeed, the Vung Tau People's Committee is notorious for its avarice and has infuriated countless potential domestic and foreign investors as well as the government in Hanoi, which directly administers Vung Tau (and the Cong Dau Islands) as a Special Economic Zone.

Orientation

The triangular Vung Tau peninsula juts into the South China Sea near the mouth of the Saigon River. The centre of town is on the south-western side of the triangle in a level area with mountains to the north and south. Nui Lon (or the Grand Massif), a 520 metre high hill north of the city with a radar installation on top, is circumnavigated by Tran Phu St. The hill to the south of town, which is circumnavigated by Ha Long St, is called the Nui Nho or the Petit Massif. Back Beach (Bai Sau) stretches along the south-eastern side of the triangle. Thuy Van St runs along Back Beach. Much of Vung Tau's industry, including the Vietsovpetro docks, is located on the northern coast.

Kiosk-lined Quang Trung St curves around Front Beach and is intersected at an oblique angle by Le Loi Blvd, which runs almost exactly north-to-south. Vung Tau's main avenue is Tran Hung Dao St. Bacu St leads from Quang Trung St 2 km out to the Bus Station. The Russian Compound (whose entrances were, until recently, sealed by roadblocks) is the area between Quang Trung St, Hoang Dieu St, Le Loi Blvd and Bacu St. Many of Vung Tau's hotels are found within the compound.

The map issued by the Oil Services Company (dated 1988) is much better than the map produced by Vung Tau Tourism (dated 1984), though both illustrate many of the Vung Tau's beaches and historical sites.

Information

Tourist Office The main office of Vung Tau Tourism (tel 2138, 91961) is at 59 Tran Hung Dao St (corner Ly Tu Trong St). The Oil Service Company (OSC) is based at 2 Le Loi St.

OTAS is a Czech-Vietnamese joint venture company that can provide accommodation, transport, tours and perhaps help with securing internal travel permits. Their address is OTAS (OSC & AKS Tourism and Services), Pacific Hotel, 4 Le Loi St, Vung Tau (tel 2279, 97562, 92239; telex 8549 HCM, OSC HCM 8307; fax Vung Tau 2257; via worldfax 61-2-662-2280)

The company responsible for developing tourism and coordinating the development of the Con Dau Islands is Con Dau Tourism Company (CODATOUR), which has offices at 450 Truong Cong Dinh St, Vung Tau (tel 2580) and 38/3 Nguyen Van Troi St, Phu Nhuan District, Ho Chi Minh City (tel 41481).

Post The GPO (tel 2377, 2689, 2141) is at 4 Ha Long St at the southern end of Front Beach.

Other Addresses The Immigration Police operate out of the police station at 14 Le Loi St, a few doors from the International Hotel.

The Soviet consulate (tel 2474 , 2476) at 54-56 Quang Trung St is the only consular mission in town.

Beaches

Back Beach The main bathing area on the peninsula is Back Beach (Bai Sau, also known as Thuy Van Beach), an 8 km long stretch of sun, sand and Soviets. The southern section of Back Beach is lined with dilapidated but pleasant cafes. The surf here can be dangerous.

Front Beach Front Beach (Bai Truoc, also called Thuy Duong Beach), which is rather dirty, rocky and eroded, borders the centre of town. Shaded Quang Trung St, lined with kiosks, runs along Front Beach. Early in the morning, the local fisherpeople moor here to

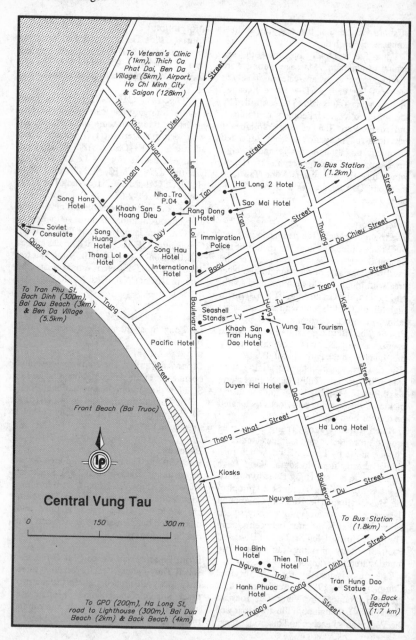

To Veteran's Clinic (1km), Thich Ca Phat Dai, Ben Da Village (5km), Airport, Ho Chi Minh City & Saigon (128km)

To Bus Station (1.2km)

Ha Long 2 Hotel

Sao Mai Hotel

Song Hong Hotel

Nha Tro P.04

Rang Dong Hotel

Khach San 5 Hoang Dieu

Song Huang Hotel

Thang Loi Hotel

Song Hau Hotel

Immigration Police

Soviet Consulate

International Hotel

To Tran Phu St, Bach Dinh (300m), Bai Dau Beach (3km), & Ben Da Village (5.5km)

Do Chieu Street

Seashell Stands

Vung Tau Tourism

Pacific Hotel

Khach San Tran Hung Dao Hotel

Front Beach (Bai Truoc)

Duyen Hai Hotel

Ha Long Hotel

Central Vung Tau

0   150   300 m

Kiosks

Nguyen

To Bus Station (1.8km)

To GPO (200m), Ha Long St, road to Lighthouse (300m), Bai Dua Beach (2km) & Back Beach (4km)

Hoa Binh Hotel

Thien Thai Hotel

Hanh Phuoc Hotel

Tran Hung Dao Statue

To Back Beach (1.7 km)

unload the night's catch and clean their nets. They row themselves between boats or to the beach in *thung chai*, gigantic round wicker baskets sealed with pitch.

Bai Dau Bai Dau, a quiet coconut palm-lined beach, is probably the most relaxing spot in the Vung Tau area. The beach stretches around a small bay nestled beneath the verdant western slopes of the Large Mountain. Bai Dau's many cheap guest houses reflect its popularity with domestic tourists. Bai Dau is 3 km from the city centre along Tran Phu St. The best way to get there is by bicycle.

Bai Dua Bai Dua (Roches Noires Beach) is a small, rocky beach about 2 km south of the town centre on Ha Long St. This is a great place to watch the sun setting over the South China Sea. There are a number of guest houses here.

Pagodas & Temples
Hon Ba Temple Hon Ba Temple (Chua Hon Ba) is on a tiny island just south of Back Beach. It can be reached on foot at low tide.

Niet Ban Tinh Xa Niet Ban Tinh Xa, one of the largest Buddhist temples in Vietnam, is on the western side of the Small Mountain. Built in 1971, it is famous for its 5000 kg bronze bell, a huge reclining Buddha and intricate mosaic work.

Thich Ca Phat Dai Thich Ca Phat Dai, a must-see site for domestic tourists, is a hillside park of monumental Buddhist statuary built in the early 1960s. Inside the main gate and to the right is a row of small souvenir kiosks selling, among other things, inexpensive items made of seashells and coral. Above the kiosks, shaded paths lead to several large white cement Buddhas, a giant lotus blossom and many smaller figures of people and animals. A couple of pathside refreshment stalls sell cold drinks. There are several restaurants near the main gate.

Thich Ca Phat Dai, which is open 6 am to 6 pm, is on the eastern side of the Large Mountain at 25 Tran Phu St. To get there from the town centre, take Le Loi Blvd north almost to the end and turn left onto Tran Phu St.

Lighthouse
The 360° view of the entire hammerhead-shaped peninsula from the lighthouse (*hai dang*) is truly spectacular, especially at sunset. The lighthouse, which is atop the Small Mountain 197 metres above sea level, was built in 1910. The concrete passage from the tower to the building next to it was constructed by the French because of Viet Minh attacks. A 1939 French guidebook warns visitors that photography is not permitted from here, and unfortunately this is still the case half-a-century and four regimes later.

The narrow paved road up the Small Mountain to the lighthouse intersects Ha Long St 150 metres south-west of the GPO. The grade is quite mild and could even by bicycled. There is also a dirt road (which gets muddy during the wet season) to the lighthouse from near Back Beach.

Giant Jesus
An enormous Rio de Janeiro-style figure of Jesus (*Thanh Gioc*) with arms outstretched gazes across the South China Sea from the southern end of the Small Mountain. The figure, 30 metres high, was constructed in 1974 on the site of a lighthouse built by the French a century before. The Giant Jesus can be reached on foot by a path that heads up the hill from a point just south of Back Beach. The path circles around to approach the figure from the back.

Bach Dinh
Bach Dinh, the White Villa (Villa Blanche), is a former royal residence set amidst frangipanis and bougainvilleas on a lushly forested hillside overlooking the sea. It is an ideal place for a picnic. Bach Dinh was built in 1920 and was later used by South Vietnamese President Thieu. The building itself (which is closed to the public) is emphatically French in its ornamentation, which includes colourful mosaics and Roman-style

busts set into the exterior walls. The main entrance to the park surrounding Bach Dinh is just north of Front Beach at 12 Tran Phu St. It is open from 6 am to 9 pm. There are a couple of cafes near the main gate. If you are interested in renting the villa, contact the Song Hong Hotel.

Veterans' Clinic

The Veterans' Clinic (tel 7348, 2573), officially called the Huu Nghi (friendship) Clinic, was built in early 1989 by a group of American veterans of the Vietnam war working alongside war vets from the other side. Its construction marked a milestone in post-1975 cooperation between Americans and Vietnam. Though the California-based Veterans' Vietnam Restoration Project, which initiated and funded the undertaking, was shamelessly overcharged by the local People's Committee, the clinic was completed and is now used for both obstetrics and general medicine. Hundreds of babies are delivered here each year. The clinic also welcomes sick travellers.

The Veterans' Clinic is 1.5 km north of the centre of town. To get there, go 100 metres down an alley across the street from 99 Le Loi Blvd. The clinic entrance, marked by a plaque, is on the right.

Boat-Building Yards

New wooden fishing craft are built at the Boat-Building Yards situated, oddly enough, over a km from the nearest water on Nam Ky Khoi Nghia St, 500 metres south of Vung Tau Bus Station.

Small Mountain Circuit

The 6 km circuit around the Small Mountain (Nui Nho), known to the French as *le tour de la Petite Corniche*, begins at the GPO and continues on Ha Long St along the rocky coastline. A road leads up the hill to the lighthouse (*hai dang*) 150 metres south of the GPO.

Ha Long St passes Ngoc Bich Pagoda (which is built in the style of Hanoi's famous One Pillar Pagoda), Bai Dua Beach and a number of villas before reaching the tip of

the Vung Tau peninsula. The promontory here, reached through a traditional gate, was once guarded by French naval guns whose reinforced concrete emplacements remain, slowly crumbling in the salt air.

Phan Boi Chau St goes from the southern end of Back Beach into town along the eastern base of the Small Mountain, passing century-old Linh Son Temple, which contains a Buddha of pre-Angkorian Khmer origin.

Large Mountain Circuit

Beginning just north of the Soviet consulate, the 10-km circuit around the Large Mountain (Nui Lon) passes seaside villas, Bai Dau Beach, the homes of poor families living in old French fortifications, and a number of quarries where boulders blown out of the hillside by dynamite are made into gravel by workers using sledgehammers. Blasting sometimes closes the road for a few hours. At the northern tip of the Large Mountain is Ben Da fishing village with its large church; from here a road leads up and along the spine of the hill to the old radar installation (*rada*).

On the eastern side of the Large Mountain, which faces tidal marshes and the giant cranes of the Vietsovpetro docks, is Thich Ca Phat Dai statuary park.

Places to Stay

The Vung Tau peninsula has quite a number of hotels and guest houses both in town and at Back Beach, Bai Dau and Bai Dua. Many of the hotels in Vung Tau itself are clustered inside the Russian Compound, an area of the city between Le Loi Blvd and the Soviet consulate where Soviet experts live apart from everyone else. Some of these hotels presently house Russian experts and their dependents and do not accept regular tourists, but this is supposed to change soon. During holidays, Vung Tau's hotels are usually booked out.

Places to Stay – bottom end

The *Duyen Hai Hotel* (tel 2585), whose clientele is almost exclusively Vietnamese, is at 23 Tran Hung Dao Blvd. Nearby, at 37

Tran Hung Dao Blvd, is *Khach San Tran Hung Dao* (tel 2359) which also caters to locals. Prices at both these places are very reasonable.

The *Lu Son Hotel* (tel 2576; 65 rooms) is a bit north of town at 27 Le Loi Blvd according to the new numbering system and at 12 Le Loi Blvd by the old system. The Lu Son Hotel is popular with domestic tourists, who pay between 10,500d (mats only) and 22,500d for rooms. Foreigners are charged 60,000d or US$15 for a 1st class room.

One of the cheapest (and dirtiest) places in town, *Nha Tro P04* (tel 2473 and 2438), which is also known as *Nha Khach P.04*, is next to the Rang Dong Hotel at 1 Thu Khoa Huan St (corner Duy Tan St and Le Loi Blvd). A room for four costs you 8000d.

There are several cheap places to stay along Back Beach. Bai Dau is lined with inexpensive guest houses, as is Bai Dua. See the Back Beach, Bai Dau and Bai Dua listings in this section for details.

Russian Compound The *Thang Loi Hotel* (tel 2135; 80 rooms) is at 1 Duy Tan St (corner Truong Vinh Ky St). Doubles with air-con cost 28,000 to 35,000d for Vietnamese and between US$22 and US$30 for foreigners. The Thang Loi has a decent restaurant.

One of the best deals in town is the *International Hotel* (tel 2571; 22 rooms), also known as the Khach San Quoc Te, at 242 Bacu St (corner Le Loi St). For foreigners, singles cost US$6 to US$18; doubles go for US$8 to US$20. The restaurant is dismal.

The *Song Huong Hotel* (tel 2491; 24 rooms) is next to 56 Truong Vinh Ky St. Its population of Russian experts is scheduled to check out for good in the near future. The *Song Hong Hotel* (tel 2137; 36 rooms) is at 12 Hong Dieu St (corner Truong Vinh Ky St). Doubles with air-conditioning cost 26,400d for locals and US$30.40 for foreigners. *Khach San 5 Hoang Dieu* (tel 2388; 25 rooms) is across the street at 5 Hoang Dieu St. Rooms go for 18,000 to 22,000d for Vietnamese and US$18 to US$$22 for 'capitalist tourists'.

The *Ha Long 2 Hotel* (tel 2462; 18 rooms), which is run by the Oil Service Company, is at 93 Tran Hung Dao Blvd (corner Duy Tan St). Doubles with air-con cost 19,800d for Vietnamese and US$23.40 for foreigners. Next door, the *Sao Mai Hotel* (tel 2462, 2248; 22 rooms), which is also run by the OSC, charges the same prices.

The *Rang Dong Hotel* (tel 2133; 125 rooms) is on Duy Tan St just off Le Loi Blvd. Though it is now filled with Soviet experts and their families, it may open to tourism in the near future. The Rang Dong Hotel owns a tennis court across the street from the main building. Next door is the *Song Hau Hotel* (tel 2589; 23 rooms), which is across from 2 Duy Tan St. It also currently houses only Russian experts.

Central Vung Tau The *Hoa Binh Hotel* (tel 2411), acclaimed as the best in town, is on Nguyen Trai St 100 metres off Quang Trung St. Rooms cost between US$27 and US$43. The *Thien Thai Hotel* is next door. The *Hanh Phuoc Hotel* (tel 2265, 2411), which also serves as an office for express buses to Saigon, is across the street at 11 Nguyen Trai St.

The Czech-run *Pacific Hotel* (tel 2279, 2239; telex OTAS HCM 8549; 35 rooms), also known as the *Thai Binh Duong Hotel*, is at 4 Le Loi St (corner Ly Tu Trong St). Singles/doubles cost US$17/19.

The *Ha Long Hotel* (tel 2175) is on Thong Nhat St across the street from the church; singles cost US$15. Express buses to Saigon leave from here.

Back Beach The Oil Service Company's *Thang Muoi Hotel* (tel 2665, 2674; 93 rooms) is at 4-6 Thuy Van St. The Thanh Muoi's four single-storey buildings are set on spacious grounds across the street from the beach. Air-conditioned doubles cost between US$16 and US$24. Vietnamese pay 22,000 to 33,000d for doubles with air-con and 15,500d for doubles with ceiling fans.

Nha Nghi Cong Duan (tel 2300; 40 rooms), run by the National Bank workers' trade union, is at 15 Hoang Hoa Tham St (corner Thuy Van St). Doubles with air-con, a fridge and hot water cost 40,000 to 70,000d for foreigners. *Nha Nghi* is not far away at 76 Thuy Van St. In this area, you might also try *Phong Tro* at 47 Thuy Van St.

The *Thanh Liem Bungalows* at 46A Thuy Van St (corner Hoang Hoa Tham St) are a collection of 22 red-white-and-blue two person wooden bungalows with steep thatch roofs. Each bungalow has a double bed and costs 8000d per night. The on-site steam bath and massage indicate the sort of business this place does on the side.

The *Youth Tourism Campground* (Khu Du Lich Thanh Nien; tel 2336; 54 rooms) at 46A Thuy Van St (next to the Thanh Liem Bungalows) has rooms for 9000 to 14,000d. Tents for camping under the casuarina trees cost 6000d for a four person tent and 12,000d for a 12 person tent. They charge 500d for you to pitch your own tent.

Rung Duong Beach Bungalows are nestled in a grove of casuarina trees at the northeastern end of Thuy Van St (just past the Giant Prawn Hatchery Project). Each of the 21 steel-roofed bungalows costs 15,000d with a fan and 25,000d with air-con. Camping is permitted here if you have a tent.

The multi-storey *Thuy Van Hotel* is across the street from the Rung Duong Beach Bungalows; it has been under construction for ages.

Bai Dau There are quite a number of guest houses (*nha nghi*) located in former private villas along Bai Dau, a secluded beach 3 km north of downtown Vung Tau. Most of the guest houses have rooms with fans and communal bathrooms. Meals can be taken at the guest houses but must be ordered in advance so the proprietors have time to purchase the ingredients.

Nha Nghi Lien Doanh, with its rooftop terrace overlooking the beach, is at 47 Tran Phu St. A dormitory bed with a soft mattress in a light, airy room will cost you 5000d. *Nha Nghi 120* is across the street at 120 Tran Phu St. Dreary rooms with up to five beds (mats only) cost 10,000d. The office is around the back. *Nha Nghi Tro* is at 128 Tran Phu St.

Rooms for four cost 10,000d. *Nha Nghi 130* at 130 Tran Phu St has a volleyball court and doubles for 10,000d.

Nha Nghi 168 is at 168 Tran Phu St. Rooms are pleasant and clean. Doubles go for 12,000d; triples cost 18,000d. The office is around the back. *Nha Nghi Cuu Long* at 108 Tran Phu St charges 2500d for a bed with a mat. This place is not the cleanest around. *Nha Nghi 118* is nearby at 118 Tran Phu St.

Nha Nghi 96 is an especially large villa at 96 Tran Phu St. Construction Company Number One runs this three storey place, which offer doubles with private bath for 8000d. The management is rather lethargic. Nearby are *Nha Nghi Tay Ninh* at 72 Tran Phu St and *Nha Nghi* at 64 Tran Phu St.

Bai Dua Among the villas-turned-guest houses at Bai Dua are *Nha Nghi 50 Ha Long* at 50 Ha Long St, *Nha Nghi Dro* at 88B Ha Long St and, at 48 Ha Long St, *Nha Nghi 48 Ha Long*, which charges foreigners 30,000d for a triple with air-con. Their cheapest double goes for 15,000d.

Places to Eat

For excellent seafood, try *Huong Bien Restaurant*, which is along Front Beach at 47 Quang Trung St. There are several places to eat nearby and quite a few more along Tran Hung Dao Blvd. Hotels with decent restaurants include the *Hoa Binh* and the *Thang Loi*. There a few small eateries near the gate to Thich Ca Phat Dai.

The largest restaurant along Back Beach is the *Thang Muoi Restaurant* (tel 2515) at 7-9 Thuy Van St. There are several cafes at the southern end of Back Beach.

At Bai Dau, you might try the seaside restaurant run by An Giang Tourism at 41 Tran Phu St, which is across the street from 114 Tran Phu St.

At Bai Dua, there are restaurants at 88 Ha Long St and 126 Ha Long St.

Things to Buy

Colourful seashells and various items made out of shells (purses, plant hangers, necklaces, etc) can be bought for 300d and up at the intersection of Le Loi St and Ly Tu Trong St (across the street from the Pacific Hotel). Other souvenir shops are located along Front Beach and at the Thich Ca Phat Dai statuary park.

The government Tourist Shop at the intersection of Le Loi St and Quang Trung St and other such shops in major hotels carry the sorts of 'luxury goods' likely to interest Russians.

Getting There & Away

Air There are helicopter flights from Vung Tau to the Con Dau Islands.

Bus Buses to Vung Tau from Ho Chi Minh City leave from the Mien Dong Bus Station and the Van Thanh Bus Station. Express microbuses depart from Cong Ty Dich Vu Du Lich Quan 1 (tel 90541) at 39 Nguyen Hue Blvd every hour between 5 am and 6 pm; the 128 km trip takes 2 hours.

Vung Tau Bus Station (Ben Xe Khach Vung Tau) is about 1.5 km from the city centre at 52 Nam Ky Khoi Nghia St. To get there from Front Beach, take either Bacu St or Truong Cong Dinh St to Le Hong Phong St. Turn right and then turn right again onto Nam Ky Khoi Nghia St. There are non-express buses from here to Baria, Bien Hoa, Saigon, Long Khanh, Mytho and Tay Ninh. An express bus to Ho Chi Minh City leaves at 6 am, 9 am and 3 pm.

Express buses and microbuses to Ho Chi Minh City also depart from the Ha Long Hotel (near the church) and the Hanh Phuoc Hotel (across the street from the Hoa Binh Hotel). The last bus of the day from the Hanh Phuoc Hotel departs in the mid-to-late afternoon; tickets should be purchased a day in advance at the reception desk.

Taxi For a day-trip to Vung Tau, you might consider hiring a taxi or 'marriage taxi'. Information on hiring vehicles in Saigon appears in the 'Getting There & Away' section of the 'Saigon & Cholon' chapter.

Boat It may be possible to get from Vung Tau to the Con Dau Archipelago by boat.

Yachters who have shown up in Vung Tau without the necessary authorisations have been imprisoned and had their boats seized.

Getting Around

Bicycle The best way to get around the Vung Tau peninsula is by bicycle. If you can't find anyone renting out bicycles, you might try to borrow or hire one privately.

CON DAU ISLANDS

The Con Dau Archipelago, a group of 14 islands and islets 180 km (97 nautical miles) south of Vung Tau, are administered as part of Vung Tau-Con Dau Special Economic Zone. The largest island in the group, whose total land area is 20 sq km, is partly-forested Con Son Island, which is ringed with bays, bathing beaches and coral reefs. Con Son Island is also known by its Europeanised Malay name, Poulo Condore (Pulau Kundur), which means 'Island of the Squashes'. Local products include teak and pine wood from the islands' forests, fruits (cashews, grapes, coconuts and mangoes), pearls, sea turtles, lobster and coral.

Occupied at various times by the Khmers, Malays and Vietnamese, Con Son also served as an early base for European commercial ventures in the region. The British East India Company maintained a fortified trading post here from 1702 to 1705, an experiment which ended when the English on the island were massacred in a revolt by the Makassar soldiers they had recruited on the Indonesian island of Sulawesi.

Under the French, Con Son was used as a prison for opponents of French colonialism, earning a fearsome reputation for the routine mistreatment and torture of prisoners. In 1954, the prison was taken over by the South Vietnamese Government, which continued to take advantage of its remoteness to hold opponents of the government (including students) in inhuman conditions. The island's Revolutionary Museum has exhibits on Vietnamese resistance to the French, Communist opposition to the Republic of Vietnam, and the treatment of political prisoners held on the island. A ditch in which

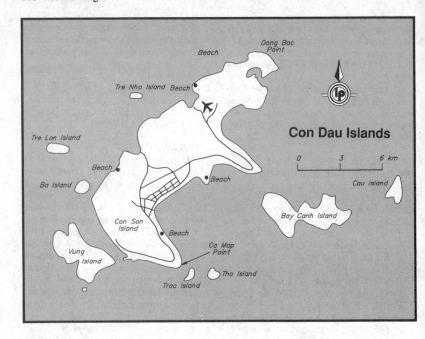

Con Dau Islands

Dong Bac Point

Beach

Tre Nho Island   Beach

Beach

Tre Lon Island

Beach

Ba Island

Cau Island

Con Son Island

Beach

Bay Canh Island

Vung Island

Ca Map Point

Tho Island

Trac Island

0   3   6 km

Communist Party members were dunked in cow's urine is open to the public.

Recently, there has been talk of building a casino and giving Con Dau duty-free status.

Getting There & Away
Air Air Vietnam flies helicopters from Vung Tau to Con Son Island. A one-way ticket costs 108,000d.

Boat The 215 km boat trip from Vung Tau takes 12 hours.

BIEN HOA
Bien Hoa (population 175,000), known as a centre of pottery and porcelain making, is on the east bank of the Dong Hai River 32 km north of Saigon. The city was founded by Chinese refugees and immigrants in the 1680s. During the Vietnam War, Bien Hoa was the site of a huge American airfield and headquarters base.

Pagodas & Temples
Buu Son Temple The most famous religious site in Bien Hoa is Buu Son Temple, which houses a Cham statue of Vishnu dating from the 15th century. The four armed figure, carved in granite, was erected on the orders of a Cham prince who conquered the region. When the area reverted to Khmer control, the statue was hidden in a tree trunk, where it remained until rediscovered in the 18th century by Vietnamese farmers, who built a temple for it. Buu Son Temple is in Binh Thuoc village 1.5 km from town and 150 metres from the river bank.

Thanh Long Pagoda Ornately decorated Thanh Long Pagoda is in Binh Thuoc village about 300 metres from the Bien Hoa Railroad Station.

Dai Giac Pagoda Dai Giac Pagoda is near Bien Hoa on an island not far from the railroad bridge. It is said to be at least 150 years old.

Buu Phong Pagoda Buu Phong Pagoda, with its numerous granite statues, stands on top of a hill of blue granite 7 km from Bien Hoa. The pagoda was built on the site of an earlier Cham or Khmer temple on the orders of Emperor Gia Long.

Tri An Falls
The Tri An Falls are a cascade on the Be River (Song Be) 8 metres high and 30 metres wide. They are especially awesome in the late fall, when the river's flow is at its great-est. Tri An Falls are in Song Be Province 36 km from Bien Hoa and 68 km from Saigon (via Thu Dau Mot).

Getting There & Away
There is a four lane super-highway from Saigon to Bien Hoa (a distance of 32 km) constructed with American aid between 1958 and 1961. Most of the trains heading north from Saigon stop at Bien Hoa.

MYTHO
For information on Mytho, see the 'Mekong Delta' chapter.

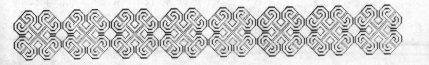

The Mekong Delta

The Mekong Delta is the southernmost region of Vietnam; it was formed by sediment deposited by the Mekong River. Today, the process which created the delta continues, with silt deposits extending the shoreline at the mouths of the river by as much as 79 metres per year.

The land of the Mekong Delta is renowned for its richness; almost half of the region's total land area is under cultivation. The area is known as Vietnam's 'breadbasket', producing enough rice to feed the south and central parts of the country as well as some of the north. Other food products from the delta include coconut, sugar cane, various fruits and fish.

The Mekong River, one of the great rivers of the world, is known to the Vietnamese as Song Cuu Long, 'River of the Nine Dragons'. The Mekong originates high in the Tibetan plateau, flowing 4500 km through China, between Myanmar and Laos, through Laos, along the Lao-Thai border, and through Cambodia and Vietnam on its way to the South China Sea. At Phnom Penh, the Mekong splits into two main branches: the Hau Giang (the Lower River, also called the Bassac River), which flows via Chau Doc, Long Xuyen and Cantho to the sea; and the Tien Giang (Upper River), which splits into several branches at Vinh Long and empties into the sea at six points.

The level of the Mekong begins to rise around the end of May and reaches its highest point in September; its flow ranges from 1900 to 38,000 cubic metres per second depending on the season. A tributary of the river which empties into the Mekong at Phnom Penh drains Cambodia's Tonlé Sap Lake. When the Mekong is at flood stage, this tributary reverses its flow and drains *into* Tonlé Sap, thereby reducing the danger of serious flooding in the Mekong Delta.

The Mekong Delta was once part of the Khmer kingdom and was the last region of modern-day Vietnam to be annexed and settled by the Vietnamese. The Cambodians, mindful that they controlled the area until the 18th century, still call the delta 'Lower Cambodia'. Most of the inhabitants of the Mekong Delta are ethnic-Vietnamese, but there are significant populations of ethnic-Chinese and Khmer as well as a few Chams.

MYTHO

Mytho, capital of Tien Giang Province, is a quiet city of 90,000 easily reached from Saigon yet very near some of the most beautiful rural areas of the Mekong Delta. The city can be visited as a day trip from Saigon; its hotels, restaurants and transport facilities can also be used as a base for exploring Tien Giang Province and the neighbouring island province of Ben Tre.

Mytho was founded in the 1680s by Chinese refugees fleeing Taiwan for political reasons. The economy of the area is based on fishing and the cultivation of rice, coconuts, bananas, mangoes, longans and citrus fruit.

Orientation

Mytho, which is situated along the left bank of the northernmost branch of the Mekong River, is laid out in a fairly regular grid pattern. The bus station, Ben Xe Khach Tien Giang, is several km west of town. Coming from the station, you enter Mytho on Ap Bac

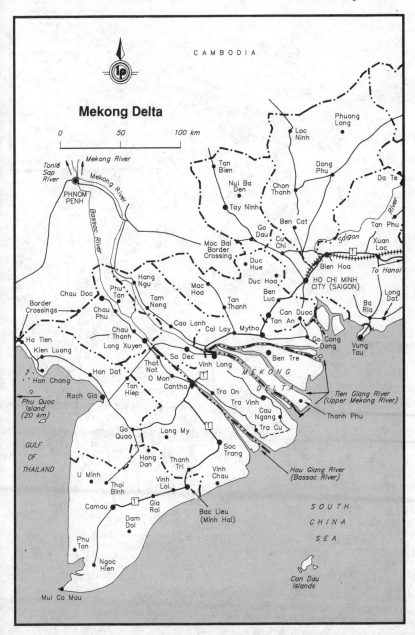

Mekong Delta

0   50   100 km

CAMBODIA

Tonlé Sap River

Mekong River

Mekong River

PHNOM PENH

Bassac River

Phuong Long

Loc Ninh

Dong Phu

Da Te

River

Tan Bien

Nui Ba Den

Chon Thanh

Tay Ninh

Ben Cat

Tan Phu

Go Dau

Cu Chi

Saigon

Xuan Loc

Moc Bai Border Crossing

Duc Hue

Bien Hoa

To Hanoi

Duc Hoa

HO CHI MINH CITY (SAIGON)

Hang Ngu

Mac Hoa

Ben Luc

Ba Ria

Long Dat

Chau Doc

Phu Tan

Tam Nong

Tan Thanh

Can Duoc

Border Crossings

Chau Phu

Cao Lanh

Cai Lay

Tan An

Mytho

Go Cong Dong

Vung Tau

Chau Thanh

Ha Tien

Long Xuyen

Sa Dec

Vinh Long

Ben Tre

Kien Luong

Thot Not

MEKONG

Hon Dat

O Mon

Cantho

DELTA

Hon Chong

Tan Hiep

Tra On

Tien Giang River (Upper Mekong River)

Phu Quoc Island (20 km)

Rach Gia

Tra Vinh

Thanh Phu

Cau Ngang

Tra Cu

GULF OF THAILAND

Go Quao

Long My

Hau Giang River (Bassac River)

Hong Dan

Thanh Tri

Soc Trang

U Minh

Vinh Loi

Vinh Chau

SOUTH

Thoi Binh

Camau

Gia Rai

Bac Lieu (Minh Hai)

CHINA

Dam Doi

SEA

Phu Tan

Ngoc Hien

Con Dau Islands

Mui Ca Mau

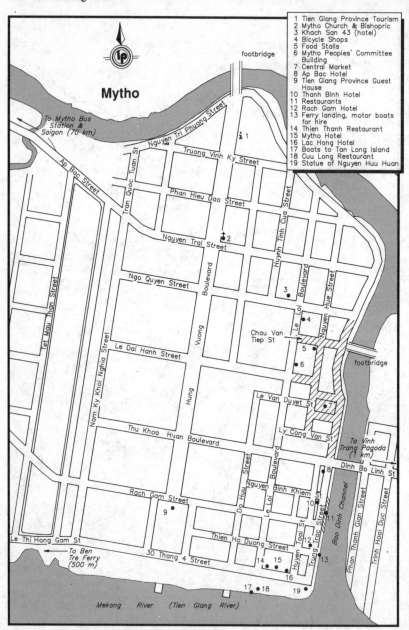

Mytho

To Mytho Bus Station & Saigon (70 km)

footbridge

1 Tien Giang Province Tourism
2 Mytho Church & Bishopric
3 Khach San 43 (hotel)
4 Bicycle Shops
5 Food Stalls
6 Mytho Peoples' Committee Building
7 Central Market
8 Ap Bac Hotel
9 Tien Giang Province Guest House
10 Thanh Binh Hotel
11 Restaurants
12 Rach Gam Hotel
13 Ferry landing, motor boats for hire
14 Thien Thanh Restaurant
15 Mytho Hotel
16 Lac Hong Hotel
17 Boats to Tan Long Island
18 Cuu Long Restaurant
19 Statue of Nguyen Huu Huan

Nguyen Tri Phuong Street
Truong Vinh Ky Street
Phan Hieu Dao Street
Nguyen Trai Street
Ngo Quyen Street
Le Dai Hanh Street
Thu Khoa Huan Boulevard
Rach Gam Street
Le Thi Hong Gam St

Ap Bac Street
Tran Quoc Tuan St
Let Mau Than Street
Nam Ky Khoi Nghia Street

Huynh Tinh Cua Street
Le Loi Boulevard
Hue Street
Nguyen
Chau Van Tiep St
footbridge

Vuong Boulevard
Hung Boulevard

Le Van Duyet St
Ly Cong Van St
To Vinh Trang Pagoda (1 km)

Do Huu Street
Nguyen Binh Khiem St
Le Loi Boulevard
Dinh Bo Linh St

Phan Thanh Gian Street
Trinh Hoai Duc Street

Bao Dinh Channel

Thien Ho Duong Street
30 Thang 4 Street
Huyen Toai St
Trung Trac Street

To Ben Tre Ferry (500 m)

Mekong River (Tien Giang River)

St. Ap Bac St turns into Nguyen Trai St, which is oriented west-east. Other main west-east streets include Thu Khoa Huan Blvd and, along the Mekong River, 30 Thang 4 St.

The main north-south thoroughfare in town (and the widest street in the city) is Hung Vuong Blvd. Other north-south streets are Le Loi Blvd and, along the channel, Trung Trac St, where many of Mytho's hotels and restaurants are located.

Information

Tourist Office Tien Giang Province Tourism (tel 3591, 3154) has an office on the northern edge of the city at 56 Hung Vuong Blvd; it is open Monday to Saturday.

Ben Tre Province Tourism has offices at 65 Dong Khoi St in Ben Tre City and 211 Nam Ky Khoi Nghia St in Saigon (tel 97086).

Island of the Coconut Monk

Until his imprisonment by the Communists for anti-government activities and the consequent dispersion of his flock, the Coconut Monk led a small community a few km from Mytho on Phung Island (Con Phung). In its heyday, the island was dominated by a fantastic open-air sanctuary that looked like a cross between a cheaply built copy of Disneyland and the Tiger Balm Gardens of Singapore. The dragon-enwrapped columns and the multi-platformed tower with its huge metal globe must have once been brightly painted, but these days the whole place is faded, rickety and silent. With a bit of imagination though, you can picture how it all must have appeared as the Coconut Monk presided over his congregation, flanked by elephant tusks and seated on a richly ornamented throne.

The Coconut Monk (Ong Dao Dua), so named because it is said that he once ate only coconuts for 3 years, was born Nguyen Thanh Nam (though he later adopted Western name order, preferring to be called Nam Nguyen Thanh) in 1909 in what is now Ben Tre Province. He studied chemistry and physics in France at Lyons, Caen and Rouen

from 1928 until 1935, when he returned to Vietnam, married and had a daughter.

In 1945 the Coconut Monk left his family to pursue a monastic life. For 3 years, he sat on a stone slab under a flagpole and meditated day and night. He was repeatedly imprisoned by successive South Vietnamese governments, which were infuriated by his philosophy of bringing about the country's reunification through peaceful means.

The Coconut Monk founded a religion, *Tinh Do Cu Si*, which was a mixture of Buddhism and Christianity. Representations of Jesus and the Buddha appeared together, as did the Virgin Mary and eminent Buddhist women. He employed both the cross and Buddhist symbols.

The best way to get from Mytho to Phung Island is to hire a motorised wooden boat, which should cost 10,000d per hour. The trip takes about 20 minutes. The Coconut Monk's complex is visible from the car ferry that runs from near Mytho to Ben Tre Province. The plaques on the 3½ metre high porcelain jar (created in 1972) tell all about the Coconut Monk.

Mytho Church & Bishopric

Mytho Church, a solid pastel-yellow building at 32 Hung Vuong Blvd (corner Nguyen Trai St), was built about a century ago. The stone plaques set in the church walls express *merci* and *cam on* to Fatima and other figures.

Today, the two priests, two sisters and several assistants minister to much of Mytho's Catholic population of 7000. The church is open to visitors every day from 4.30 to 6.30 am and 2.30 to 6.30 pm. Daily masses are held at 5 am and 5 pm. On Sunday, there are masses at 5 am, 7 am and 5 pm and catechism classes in the late afternoon.

Mytho Central Market

Mytho Central Market is an area of town along Trung Trac St and Nguyen Hue St that is closed to traffic. The streets are filled with stalls selling everything from fresh food (along Trung Trac St) and bulk tobacco to boat propellers.

Tan Long Island

The well-known longan (*nhan*) orchards of Tan Long Island are a 5-minute boat trip from the dock at the foot of Le Loi Blvd. The lush, palm-fringed shores of the island are lined with wooden fishing boats similar to those used by the 'boat people' to flee the country. Some of the residents of the island are shipwrights.

Chinese District

The Chinese district is around Phan Thanh Gian St, which is across the Thu Khoa Huan Blvd bridge from Trung Trac St.

Snake Farm

There is a snake farm at Dong Tam, which is about 10 km from Mytho towards Vinh Long.

Vinh Trang Pagoda

Vinh Trang Pagoda, which is often visited by organised tour groups, is an eclectic tourist trap in which sacred Buddhist ritual objects have become one element in a pathetic little amusement park which also includes a repainted US Air Force Cessna and an unhappy zoo. At least the animals, if not healthy, are alive; the sanctuary is spiritless and utterly devoid of life, with unused ritual objects, some holding long-extinguished joss sticks, placed about unlovingly. The only thing worth seeing here is a partly three dimensional portrait of Ho Chi Minh with real hairs making up his beard placed on a altar. Are people supposed to come and worship Ho Chi Minh? Pity the tourist for whom this is the only Buddhist pagoda he or she sees.

Vinh Trang Pagoda is about 1 km from the city centre at 60A Nguyen Trung Truc St. To get there, as you head east out of town turn left off Dinh Bo Linh St at number 43/12 and continue for about a km. The entrance to the sanctuary is on the right-hand side of the building as you approach it from the ornate gate.

Quan Thanh Pagoda

This Chinese pagoda, built by the Fukien and Trieu Chau Congregations, is being repaired for tourists. All the figures, most of which are made of plaster, have been newly repainted. Quan Cong is behind the main altar. Something here rings false. Quan Thanh Pagoda is between Dinh Bo Linh St and Vinh Trang Pagoda at 3/9 Nguyen Trung Truc St.

Places to Stay

The eight storey *Ap Bac Hotel* (tel 3593; 35 rooms), also known as the *Grand Hotel*, is the largest in town. Foreigners are charged US$10 for a double with air-con and US$18 for an air-conditioned suite with hot water. Rooms with fans go for 12,000d. The five storey *Rach Gam Hotel* (20 rooms) at 33 Trung Trac St has doubles with ceiling fans and attached bath for 8000d. The *Thanh Binh Hotel* (4 rooms) at 44 Nguyen Binh Khiem St charges 5000d for doubles without fans or attached bath.

Prices at the *Lac Hong Hotel* (tel 3918; 24 rooms) at 85-87 30 Thang 4 St range from 3000d for a single to 7500d for a large double; toilets are communal. The run-down *My Tho Hotel* (24 rooms) at 67 30 Thang 4 St has singles/doubles without fans for 2500/4000d; a double with a ceiling fan costs 5500d.

Khach San 43 (tel 3126; 24 rooms) is a clean, modern place at 43 Ngo Quyen St with doubles starting at 7000d and a three bed suite with air-con for 15,000d.

The *Tien Giang Province Guest House* is at the southern end of Hung Vuong Blvd (corner Rach Gam St).

Places to Eat

Mytho is known for a special vermicelli soup, *hu tieu My Tho*, which is richly garnished with fresh and dried seafood, pork, chicken and fresh herbs. It is served either with broth or dry (with broth on the side).

Thien Thanh Restaurant is at 65 30 Thang 4 St. Across the street, next to the Tan Long Island ferry dock, is *Cuu Long Restaurant*. There are about half-a-dozen places to eat along Trung Truc St between the statue of

Nguyen Huu Huan (a 19th century anti-colonial fighter) on 30 Thang 4 St and the Thu Khoa Huan Blvd bridge.

Getting There & Away

Road distances from Mytho:

Ben Tre	16 km
Cantho	104 km
Ho Chi Minh City	70 km
Vinh Long	66 km

By car, the drive from Ho Chi Minh City to Mytho on National Highway 1 *(Quoc Lo 1)* takes about 90 minutes.

Bus Mytho is served by non-express buses leaving Ho Chi Minh City from Mien Tay Bus Station in An Lac.

The Mytho Bus Station (Ben Xe Khach Tien Giang; tel 3359) is several km west of town; it is open from 4 am to about 5 pm. To get there from the city centre, take Ap Bac St westward and continue on to National Highway 1.

Buses to Ho Chi Minh City leave when full from the early morning until about 5 pm; the trip takes 1½ hours. There is daily bus service to Cantho (5 hours; departures at 4 am and 9 pm), Chau Doc (leaves at 4 am), Phu Hoa (departs at 6 pm), Tay Ninh (6 hours; departs at 5 am) and Vung Tau (5 hours; leaves at 5 am). There are also buses to Ba Beo, Bac My Thuan, Cai Be, Cai Lay, Go Cong Dong, Go Cong Tay, Hau My Bac, Phu My, Tan An and Vinh Kim. There is no express bus service from Mytho.

Boat A passenger ferry to Mytho leaves Saigon daily at 11 am from the dock at the end of Ham Nghi Blvd; the trip is said to take 6 hours.

The Rach Mieu car ferry to Ben Tre Province leaves from a station (Ben Pha Rach Mieu) about 1 km west of the city centre near 2/10A Le Thi Hong Gam St (Le Thi Hong Gam St is the western continuation of 30 Thang 4 St). The ferry operates from 4 am to 10 pm and runs at least once an hour. Ten

person trucks shuttle between the ferry terminal and the bus station.

Getting Around

Motorised 7 metre boats can be hired at an unmarked ferry landing on Trung Trac St at the foot of Thien Ho Duong St; ferry boats to points across the river also dock here. Wooden rowboats to Tan Long Island leave from the pier at the foot of Le Loi St next to Cuu Long Restaurant; the prices get jacked up for foreigners.

CANTHO

Cantho (population 150,000), capital of Hau Giang Province, is the political, economic, cultural and transportation centre of the Mekong Delta. This friendly, bustling city is connected to most other population centres in the Mekong Delta by a system of rivers and canals. Rice-husking mills are a major local industry.

Orientation

Nguyen Trai St runs from the north-west to the south-east, linking the bus station with Hoa Binh Blvd, a wide avenue with a centre strip. Hoa Binh Blvd becomes 30 Thang 4 Blvd at Nguyen An Ninh St. Hai Ba Trung St runs along the Cantho River waterfront. Phan Dinh Phung St, the main commercial thoroughfare, is two blocks inland from Hai Ba Trung St. Several streets connect Hoa Binh Blvd with Hai Ba Trung St, including Nguyen An Ninh St, Nam Ky Khoi Nghia St, Vo Van Tan St and Nguyen Thai Hoc St.

Information

The office of Hau Giang Province Tourism (tel 20147, 35275) is at 27 Chau Van Liem St. The GPO is a five storey building at the intersection of Hoa Binh Blvd and Ngo Quyen St. The general hospital is on the corner of Nguyen An Ninh St and Hoa Binh Blvd.

Munirangsyaram Pagoda

The ornamentation of Munirangsyaram Pagoda at 36 Hoa Binh Blvd is typical of Khmer Hinayana Buddhist pagodas, lacking

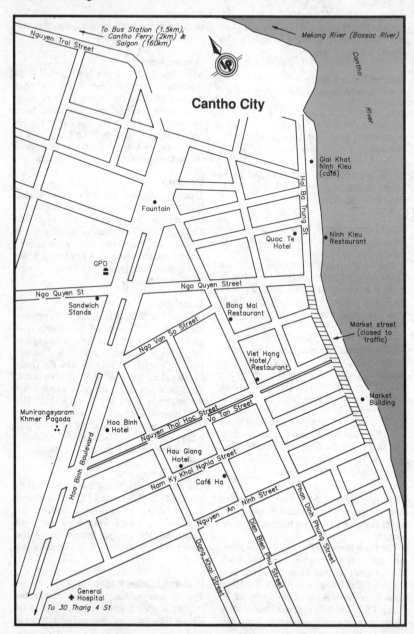

the multiple Bodhisattvas and Taoist spirits common in Vietnamese Mahayana pagodas. In the upstairs sanctuary, a 1½ metre high representation of Siddhartha Gautama, the historical Buddha, sits under a *potthe* (bodhi) tree. Built in 1946, Munirangsyaram Pagoda serves the Khmer community of Cantho, which numbers about 2000. The two Khmer monks, one in his 70s and the other in his 20s, hold prayers at 5 am and 6 pm every day.

Central Market
The Central Market is strung out along Hai Ba Trung St. The main market building is at the intersection of Hai Ba Trung St and Nam Ky Khoi Nghia St.

University of Cantho
Cantho University, founded in 1966, is on 30 Thang 4 Blvd.

Nearby Rural Areas
Rural areas of Hau Giang Province, renowned for their durian, mangosteen and orange orchards, can easily be reached from Cantho by boat or bicycle. There is said to be a bird garden several hours from Cantho by boat.

Places to Stay
Quoc Te Hotel (tel 35793, 35795, 20749; 32 rooms) is along the Cantho River at 12 Hai Ba Trung St; foreigners are charged US$10/14 to US$18/22 for singles/doubles. The six storey *Hau Giang Hotel* (tel 35537, 35581, 20180; 32 rooms) is at 34 Nam Ky Khoi Nghia St; singles/doubles go for US$13/17 to US$18/22 (10% service is extra). The *Hoa Binh Hotel* (tel 20537, 35598) is at 5 Hoa Binh St; a double costs 7000d.

Other hotels in Cantho include, alphabetically: the *Hao Hoa Hotel* (tel 35407) at 6 Lu Gia St; the *Hoang Cung Hotel* (tel 35401) at 55 Phan Dinh Phung St; the *Huy Hoang Hotel* (tel 35403) at 35 Ngo Duc Ke St; the *Khai Hoan Hotel* (tel 35261) at 83 Chau Van Liem St; the *Phong Nha Hotel* (tel 35466) at 79 Chau Van Liem St; the *Phuoc Thanh Hotel* (tel 35406) at 5 Phan Dang Luu St; the

Tay Do Hotel (tel 35265) at 34 Hai Ba Trung St; the *Thuy Tien Hotel* (tel 35412) at 6 Tran Phu St; and the *Tuy Quang Lau Hotel* (tel 35402) at 33 Chau Van Liem St.

Places to Eat
Along the Cantho River waterfront there are several restaurants serving Mekong Delta specialities such as fish, snake, frog and turtle. *Ninh Kieu Restaurant*, run by Hau Giang Tourism, is on a boat across Hai Ba Trung St from the Quoc Te Hotel. There is also a restaurant in the *Quoc Te Hotel*. *Bong Mai Restaurant* is at 19-23 Phan Dinh Phung St.

There are a number of restaurants that cater to a local clientele along Nam Ky Khoi Nghia St, between Phan Dinh Phung St and Dien Bien Phu St. Mobile stands selling soup and French-roll sandwiches are often set up on Hoa Binh Blvd near the GPO.

Kiai Khat Ninh Kieu is a waterside cafe about 50 metres north of the Quoc Te Hotel. *Café Ha*, across the street from 1 Dien Bien Phu St (corner Nam Ky Khoi Nghia St), is a favourite hang-out of young local men. Surrounded by posters of the Bee Gees and Iron Maiden, they listen to country & western music while sipping beers.

Getting There & Away
Road distances from Cantho:

Camau	179 km
Chau Doc	117
Long Xuyen	62 km
Mytho	104 km
Rach Gia	116 km
Sa Dec	51 km
Ho Chi Minh City	168 km
Soc Trang	63 km
Vinh Long	34 km

By car, the ride from Ho Chi Minh City to Cantho along National Highway 1 usually takes about 4 hours. There are two ferry crossings between Ho Chi Minh City and Cantho, the first at Vinh Long and the second at Cantho itself. The Cantho ferry runs from 4 am to 2 am. Fruit, soft drinks and other food are sold where vehicles wait for the ferries.

To get from Hoa Binh Blvd in Cantho to the ferry crossing, take Nguyen Trai St to the bus station and turn right onto Tran Phu St.

Bus Buses to Cantho leave Ho Chi Minh City from Mien Tay Bus Station in An Lac. Non-express buses take 5 hours; the express bus, which has priority at ferry crossings, takes about 3½ hours.

The main bus station in Cantho is several km out of town at the intersection of Nguyen Trai St and Tran Phu St. There is another bus depot near the intersection of 30 Thang 4 Blvd and Mau Than St.

Long Xuyen

Long Xuyen, the capital of An Giang Province, has a population of about 100,000. It was once a stronghold of the Hoa Hao sect, founded in 1939, which emphasises simplicity in worship and does not believe in temples or intermediaries between humans and the Supreme Being. Until 1956, the Hoa Hao had an army and constituted a major military force in this region.

Orientation
Tran Hung Dao St runs north from the bus station and then continues on towards Chau Doc. Nguyen Hue St and Hai Ba Trung St, which are perpendicular to each other, are both wide, divided avenues.

Information
Tourist Office The office of An Giang Tourism (tel 52888, 52086) is at 6 Ngo Gia Tu St, a couple of blocks from the Long Xuyen Bus Station. The Tourism Services Company (Xi Nghiep Dich Vu Du Lich; tel 52277) at 93 Nguyen Trai St runs tours to Cambodia and may be able to provide other services, such as car rental. The GPO is at 11 Ngo Gia Tu St.

Quan Thanh De Pagoda
This small Chinese pagoda, also known as Minh Huong Hoi Quan, was built by the

---

■ PLACES TO STAY

5	An Giang Hotel
6	Long Xuyen Hotel
7	Cuu Long Hotel
12	Thai Binh Hotel
16	Binh Dan Hotel
17	Thien Huong Hotel
18	Phat Thanh Hotel
22	Song Hau Hotel
23	Nha Khach Cong Doan An Giang (hotel)

▼ PLACES TO EAT

10	Small Restaurants
19	Long Xuyen Restaurant

● OTHER

1	Long Xuyen Ferry Terminal
2	GPO
3	Express Bus Office
4	An Giang Tourism
8	Long Xuyen Market
9	Dinh Than Long Xuyen (temple)
11	Cho Moi (An Hoa) Ferry Terminal
13	Luxury Goods Market
14	Long Xuyen Catholic Church
15	Long Xuyen Protestant Church
20	Quan Thanh De Pagoda
21	Express Bus Office
24	Tourism Services Company
25	Long Xuyen Bus Station

Canton Congregation about 70 years ago. It is on Le Minh Ngu On St between Nguyen Hue B St and Nguyen Trai St and is open from 5 am to 8 pm. On the main dais are Quan Cong and his guardians, the general Chau Xuong and the administrative mandarin Quan Binh. To the left of the dais is Ong Bon, Guardian Spirit of Happiness and Virtue. Thien Hau, the Goddess of the Sea, is to the other side of the dais.

Long Xuyen Catholic Church
Long Xuyen Catholic Church, an impressive modern structure with a 50 metre high bell tower, is one of the largest churches in the Mekong Delta. It was constructed between 1966 and 1973 and can seat 1000 worshippers. The church is located on the triangular

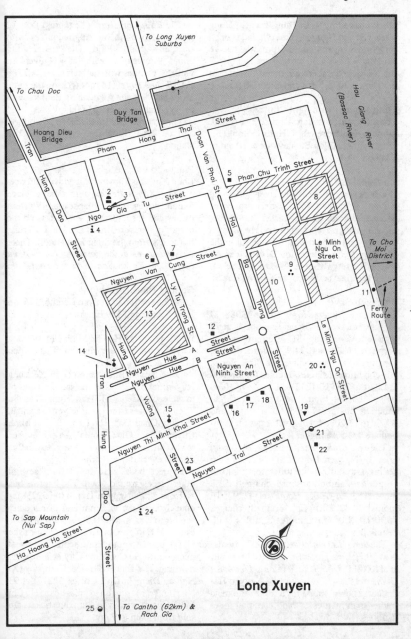

Long Xuyen

block created by Tran Hung Dao St, Hung Vuong St and Nguyen Hue A St and is open for visitors from 4 am to 8 pm. Masses are held daily from 4.30 to 5.30 am and 6 to 7 pm; on Sunday, there are masses from 5 to 6.30 am, 3.30 to 5 pm and 6 to 7.30 pm.

Long Xuyen Protestant Church
Long Xuyen Protestant Church is a small, modern structure at 4 Hung Vuong St. Prayers are held on Sundays from 10 am to 12 noon.

Cho Moi District
Cho Moi District, across the river from Long Xuyen, is known for its rich groves of banana, durian, guava, jackfruit, longan, mango, mangosteen and plum. The women here are said to be the most beautiful in the Mekong Delta. Cho Moi District can be reached by ferry from the Cho Moi (An Hoa) Ferry Terminal at the foot of Nguyen Hue St.

Places to Stay
The *Long Xuyen Hotel* (tel 52308; 37 rooms), run by An Giang Tourism, is at 17 Nguyen Van Cung St. Vietnamese pay between 11,000 and 24,200d for a double; the prices for Cambodians are 50% higher. Air-conditioned singles/doubles for foreigners start at US$10/12. The *Cuu Long Hotel* (tel 52865; 24 rooms) at 15 Nguyen Van Cung St charges 7700d for a single and 9900d to 13,200d for doubles; rates for Cambodians are 50% higher.

The *Thai Binh Hotel* (tel 52184; 24 rooms) is at 12 Nguyen Hue A St. Doubles with ceiling fan and private toilet cost 9900 to 16,500d; Cambodians are charged 50% more. The *An Giang Hotel* (tel 52297; 16 rooms) at 42 Phan Chu Trinh St charges 7500/10,000d for singles/doubles with ceiling fan and attached toilet.

The *Song Hau Hotel* (tel 52979; 26 rooms) is at 10 Hai Ba Trung St; doubles here start at 11,000d. *Nha Khach Cong Doan An Giang* (tel 52041; 39 beds) at 68 Nguyen Trai St charges only 4000d for a triple with mats (rather than mattresses) and common toilet facilities.

The *Binh Dan Hotel* (12 rooms) is at 12 Nguyen An Ninh St; single/doubles with fans cost 7000/8000d. The *Thien Huong Hotel* (9 rooms) is nearby at 4 Nguyen An Ninh St; doubles with fan start at 8000d. The *Phat Thanh Hotel* (14 rooms) is on the same block at 2 Nguyen An Ninh St; doubles with private bath begin at 10,000d.

There are several small, cheap hotels (*nha tro*) on Tran Hung Dao St near the bus station.

Places to Eat
Long Xuyen is known for its flavourful rice.

Long Xuyen Restaurant, a large place which serves both Chinese and Western dishes and specialises in seafood, is on the corner of Nguyen Trai St and Hai Ba Trung St (across from the Song Hau Hotel). There are restaurants in the hotels *An Giang, Cuu Long, Long Xuyen, Song Hau* and *Thai Binh*.

Getting There & Away
Long Xuyen is 62 km from Cantho, 126 km from Mytho and 189 km from Saigon.

Bus Buses from Ho Chi Minh City to Long Xuyen leave from the Mien Tay Bus Station in An Lac.

Long Xuyen Bus Station (Ben Xe Long Xuyen; tel 52125) is at the southern end of town opposite 96/3B Tran Hung Dao St. There are buses from Long Xuyen to Camau, Cantho, Chau Doc, Ha Tien, Ho Chi Minh City and Rach Gia (3 hours). An express bus to Ho Chi Minh City leaves Long Xuyen Bus Station every day at 4 am.

Express buses also leave from several other places around town. The express bus office at 225/4 Nguyen Trai St (tel 52238) is open from 7 am to 5 pm and offers daily service to Ho Chi Minh City at 3 am. The bus office at 11 Ngo Gia Tu St (in front of the GPO), open 8 am to 5 pm, sends an 18 seat microbus to Ho Chi Minh City at 2 am each morning. The Tourist Services Company (Xi Nghiep Dich Vu Du Lich; tel 52277) at 93 Nguyen Trai St runs an express bus to Ho Chi Minh City every day at 4 am; bus tickets are sold from 7 am to 9 pm.

Boat To get to the Long Xuyen Ferry Terminal from Pham Hong Thai St, cross Duy Tan Bridge and turn right. Passenger ferries leave from here to Cho Vam, Dong Tien, Hong Ngu, Kien Luong, Lai Vung, Rach Gia, Sa Dec and Tan Chau.

There may be a ferry service to An Giang Province from Saigon; check at the ferry dock at the river end of Ham Nghi Blvd.

Getting Around

The best way to get around Long Xuyen is to take a *xe dap loi* (a wagon pulled by a bicycle) or a *xe Honda loi* (a wagon pulled by a motorbike).

Car ferries from Long Xuyen to Cho Moi District (across the river) leave from the Cho Moi (An Hoa) Ferry Terminal near 17/4 Nguyen Hue B St every half hour from 4 am to 6.30 pm.

CHAU DOC

Chau Doc (population 40,000) is a riverine commercial centre not far from the Cambodian border. The city was once known for its pirogue (dugout canoe) races. Chau Doc has sizeable Chinese, Cham and Khmer communities.

Orientation

Chau Doc stretches along the right bank of the Hau Giang River. The road closest to the water bears several names and is called (from north to south) Tran Hung Dao St, Gia Long St, Le Loi St and Lien Tinh Lo 10. Lien Tinh Lo 10 leads to Long Xuyen. The centre of town is around Bach Dang St and Chi Lang St, both of which run perpendicular to the river.

Information

The GPO (tel 94550) is on the corner of Bao Ho Thoai St and Gia Long St.

Chau Phu Temple

Chau Phu Temple (Dinh Than Chau Phu) was built in 1926 to worship Thoai Ngoc Hau (1761-1829), who is buried at Sam Mountain. The structure is decorated with both Vietnamese and Chinese motifs. Inside are funeral tablets bearing the names of the deceased and biographical information about them.

Chau Doc Church

This small Catholic church, constructed in 1920, is across the street from 459 Le Loi St and is not far from FB Phu Hiep Ferry Terminal. There are masses every day at 5 am and 5 pm; on Sunday, masses are held at 7 am and 4 pm.

Chau Giang Mosque

Domed and arched Chau Giang Mosque, which serves the local Cham Muslim community, is in Chau Giang District. To get there, take the car ferry from Chau Giang Ferry Terminal in Chau Doc across the Hau Giang River. From the landing, go away from the river for 30 metres, turn left, and walk 50 metres.

Floating Houses

These houses, whose floats consist of empty metal drums, provide both a place to live and a livelihood for their residents. Under each house fish are raised in suspended metal nets: the fish flourish in their natural river habitat, the family can feed them whatever scraps of biological matter it has handy, and catching the fish does not require all the exertions of fishing. Such houses have become all the rage of late and many new ones are being constructed.

Tan Chau District

Tan Chau District is famous all over southern Vietnam for its traditional industry, silk making. The area is also known for its wealth, which is apparent in the proliferation of TV antennas and the widespread ownership of luxury goods (eg electric fans, high-quality cloth) imported from Thailand via Cambodia. The marketplace in Tan Chau has a selection of competitively priced Thai and Cambodian goods.

To get to Tan Chau District from Chau Doc, take a boat across the Hau Giang River from the FB Phu Hiep Ferry Terminal. Then catch a ride on the back of a motorbike

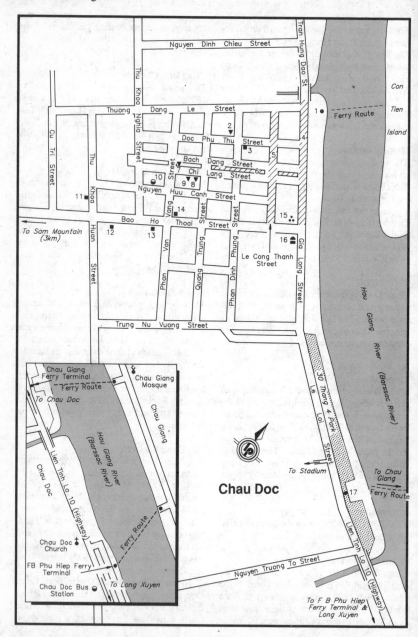

(*Honda ong*) for the 18-km trip from Chau Giang District to Tan Chau District.

Sam Mountain

There are dozens of pagodas and temples, many of them set in caves, around Sam Mountain (Nui Sam), which is about 3 km south-west of Chau Doc out Bao Ho Thoai St.

Tay An Pagoda

Tan An Pagoda (Chua Tay An), on the left as you arrive at Sam Mountain, is renowned for the fine carving of its hundreds of religious figures, most of which are made of wood. Aspects of the building's architecture reflect Hindu and Islamic influences. The first chief *bonze* of Tay An Pagoda, which was founded in 1847, came from Giac Lam Pagoda in Saigon. Tay An Pagoda was last rebuilt in 1958.

The main gate is of traditional Vietnamese design. Above the bi-level roof there are figures of lions and two dragons fighting for possession of pearls, chrysanthemums,

apricot trees and lotus blossoms. Nearby is a statue of Quan Am Thi Kinh, the Guardian Spirit of Mother & Child (for her legend, see the section on the Emperor of Jade Pagoda in the Saigon & Cholon chapter).

In front of the pagoda are statues of a black elephant with two tusks and a white elephant with six tusks. Around the pagoda there are various monks' tombs.

Temple of Lady Chua Xu

The Temple of Lady Chua Xu (Mieu Ba Chua Xu), founded in the 1820s, stands facing Sam Mountain not far from Tay An Pagoda. The first building here was made of bamboo and leaves; the last reconstruction took place in 1972.

According to legend, the statue of Lady Chua Xu used to stand at the summit of Sam Mountain. In the early 19th century, Siamese troops invaded the area and, impressed with the statue, decided to take it back to Thailand with them. But as they carried the statue down the hill, it became heavier and heavier, and they were forced to abandon it by the side of the path.

One day, villagers out cutting wood came upon the statue and decided to bring it back to their village in order to build a temple for it; but it weighed too much for them to budge. Suddenly, there appeared a girl who, possessed by a spirit, declared herself to be Lady Chua Xu. She announced that 40 virgins were to be brought and that they would be able to transport the statue down the mountainside. The 40 virgins were summoned and carried the statue down the slope, but when they reached the plain, it became too heavy and they had to set it down. The people concluded that the site where the virgins halted had been selected by Lady Chua Xu for the construction of a temple, and it is at that place that the Temple of Lady Chua Xu stands to this day.

Another story relates that the wife of Thoai Ngoc Hau, builder of the Vinh Te Canal, swore to erect a temple when the canal, whose construction claimed many lives, was completed. She died before being able to carry through on her oath, but Thoai

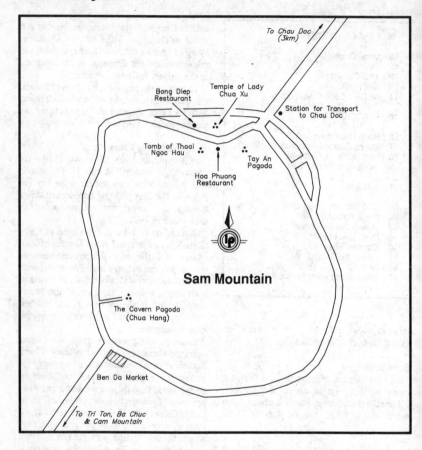

Ngoc Hau implemented her plans by building the Temple of Lady Chua Xu.

The temple's most important festival is held from the 23rd to the 26th of the 4th lunar month. During this time, pilgrims flock here, sleeping on mats in the large rooms of the two storey rest house next to the temple; they are charged only 300d a night.

Tomb of Thoai Ngoc Hau
Thoai Ngoc Hau (1761-1829) was a high-ranking official who served the Nguyen Lords and, later, the Nguyen Dynasty. In early 1829, Thoai Ngoc Hau ordered that a tomb be constructed for himself at the foot of Sam Mountain. The site he chose is not far from Tay An Pagoda.

The steps are made of red 'beehive' (*da ong*) stone brought from the eastern part of southern Vietnam. In the middle of the platform is the tomb of Thoai Ngoc Hau and those of his wives, Chau Thi Te and Truong Thi Miet. Nearby are several dozen other tombs, where officials who served under Thoai Ngoc Hau are buried.

The Cavern Pagoda
The Cavern Pagoda (Chua Hang, also known

as Phuoc Dien Tu) is about halfway up the western side of Sam Mountain. The lower part of the pagoda includes monks' quarters and two hexagonal tombs in which the founder of the pagoda, a female tailor named Le Thi Tho, and a former head *bonze*, Thich Hue Thien, are buried.

The upper section consists of two parts: the main sanctuary, in which there are statues of A Di Da (the Buddha of the Past) and Thich Ca Buddha (Sakyamuni); and the cavern. At the back of the cave, which is behind the sanctuary building, is a shrine dedicated to Quan The Am Bo Tat (the Goddess of Mercy).

According to legend, Le Thi Tho came from Tay An Pagoda to this site half-a-century ago to lead a quiet, meditative life. When she arrived, she found two enormous snakes, one white and the other dark green. Le Thi Tho soon converted the snakes, who thereafter led pious lives. Upon her death, the snakes disappeared.

Places to Stay

The *Chau Doc Hotel* (tel 6484; 42 rooms) is at 17 Doc Phu Thu St. Singles cost 8800 to 11,000d; doubles/triples go for 13,200/16,500d. All rooms have fans and some come with private bath.

The *Tan Tai Hotel* (tel 6563; 11 rooms), also known as the Fuong Chau Phu A Hotel, is at 273 Thu Khoa Huan St. A dormitory bed (with a mat, not a mattress) costs 3000d; doubles are 10,000d. A massage and a steam bath cost 5000d for 45 minutes.

The *Thai Binh Hotel* (tel 6221; 15 rooms) is at 37 Bao Ho Thoai St; doubles cost 7000 to 8000d while a room for four costs 15,000d. The *QDI Hotel* (Khach San QDI; tel 6455; 20 rooms) is at 51 B Bao Ho Thoai St; doubles/triples, some with private toilet, cost 8400/10,500d.

Nha Tro Cong Doan (Union Dormitory; tel 6447; 14 rooms) is on the corner of Bao Ho Thoai St and Phan Van Vang St. A double with common toilet facilities is 7000d; a triple with private bath costs 10,000d.

Next to Chau Doc Bus Station, there is

very basic dormitory accommodation for 2000d per night.

Places to Eat

If you would like to try the specialities of this region, ask for *kho ca loc, mam thai, mam ruot ca, kho ca tra* and *kho ca su.*

Chau Doc *Lam Hung Ky Restaurant* at 71 Chi Lang St serves some of the best Chinese and Vietnamese food in town. Nearby, *Hong Phat Restaurant* at 79 Chi Lang St also has excellent Chinese and Vietnamese dishes. The prices at both places are very reasonable. *Bong Mai Restaurant* is on the corner of Doc Phu Thu St and Phan Dinh Phung St; this place has a limited selection of Western-style dishes.

Cheap Vietnamese food is available in Chau Doc Market, which is spread out along Bach Dang St and nearby streets.

Sam Mountain For tasty Vietnamese specialities (including cobra and turtle) try *Hoa Phuong Restaurant* between Tay An Pagoda and the tomb of Thoai Ngoc Hau. This place has a huge garden. *Bong Diep Restaurant* is across from the Tomb of Thoai Ngoc Hau; the selection here is similar to Hoa Phuong Restaurant but the food is not as good.

Getting There & Away

Chau Doc is 117 km from Cantho, 181 km from Mytho and 245 km from Saigon.

Bus Buses from Ho Chi Minh City to Chau Doc leave from the Mien Tay Bus Station in An Lac; the express bus is said to take 6 hours.

The Chau Doc Bus Station (Ben Xe Chau Doc), which is south-east of town towards Long Xuyen, is opposite 214 Lien Tinh Lo 10 St. There are non-express buses from Chau Doc to Camau (every other day at 8 am), Cantho, Ho Chi Minh City (departing at 3.30 am and in the afternoon), Long Xuyen, Soc Trang (leaving 10 am), Tien Giang (departing every other day at 5 am) and Tra Vinh (leaving daily at 4.30 am).

An express bus to Ho Chi Minh City

leaves from the Chau Doc Hotel (tel 6484) at 17 Doc Phu Thu St. Express buses to Ho Chi Minh City (overnight) and Chau Doc leave from an office on Nguyen Huu Canh St between Thu Khoa Huan St and Phan Van Vang St; it is open from 7.30 am to 5 pm.

Getting Around
Local Transport The main forms of land transport in Chau Doc are the *xe dap loi* (a two wheel trailer towed by a bicycle) and the *xe Honda loi* (a motorbike pulling a two wheel trailer).

Boat Boats to Chau Giang District (across the Hau Giang River) leave from two docks: vehicle ferries depart from Chau Giang Ferry Terminal (Ben Pha Chau Giang), which is opposite 419 Le Loi St; smaller, more frequent boats leave from F B Phu Hiep Ferry Terminal (Ben Pha FB Phu Hiep). To get there from the centre of town, head southeast along Gia Long St (which turns into Le Loi St) and turn left at 349 Le Loi St. Take an immediate right and continue on for 200 metres. The prices of both ferries double at night.

Vehicle ferries to Con Tien Island depart from the Con Tien Ferry Terminal (Ben Pha Con Tien), which is off Gia Long St at the river end of Thuong Dang Le St; prices are double at night.

RACH GIA
Rach Gia, the capital of Kien Giang Province, is a friendly port city on the Gulf of Thailand. The population of about 120,000 includes significant numbers of ethnic-Chinese and Khmers. The economy of the area is based on fishing and agriculture. The Rach Gia area was once famous as the source of large feathers used to make ceremonial fans for the Imperial Court.

Orientation
To get into town from the bus station, head north on Nguyen Trung Truc St, which becomes Le Loi St when you cross the channel. The heart of the city, where most of the hotels and restaurants are located, is

between Le Loi St and Tran Phu St on the island.

Information
Tourist Office The office of Kien Giang Tourism is at 12 Ly Tu Trong St (tel 2081); they may have another office (tel 314) at 38 Nguyen Hung Son St. The Tourism Management Office (Phong Dieu Hanh Du Lich; tel 3669) is at 50 Nguyen Hung Son St.

Post & Money The GPO and the bank are across the channel from the intersection of Tu Duc St and Bach Dang St.

Pagodas & Temples
Nguyen Trung Truc Temple This temple is dedicated to Nguyen Trung Truc, a leader of the Vietnamese resistance campaign of the 1860s against the newly arrived French. Among other exploits, he led the raid that resulted in the burning of the French warship *Esperance*. Despite repeated attempts to capture him, Nguyen Trung Truc continued to fight until 1868, when the French took his mother and a number of civilians hostage and threatened to kill them if he did not surrender. Nguyen Trung Truc turned himself in and was executed by the French in the marketplace of Rach Gia on 27 October 1868.

The first temple structure was a simple building with a thatched roof; over the years it has been enlarged and rebuilt several times. The last reconstruction took place between 1964 and 1970. In the centre of the main hall on an altar is a portrait of Nguyen Trung Truc.

Nguyen Trung Truc Temple is at 18 Nguyen Cong Tru St and is open from 7 am to 6 pm.

Phat Lon Pagoda This large Cambodian Hinayana Buddhist pagoda, whose name means 'big Buddha', was founded about 2 centuries ago. Though all of the 3 dozen monks who live here are ethnic-Khmers, ethnic-Vietnamese also frequent the pagoda. Prayers are held daily from 4 to 6 am and from 5 to 7 pm. The pagoda is open from 4

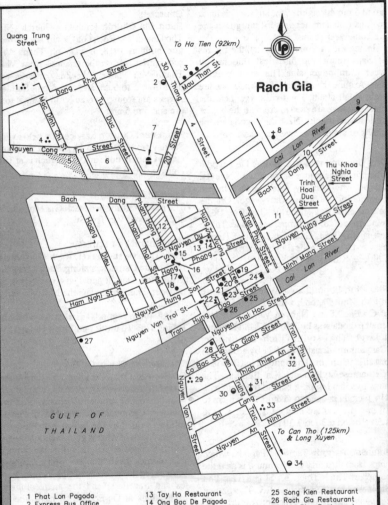

Rach Gia

1 Phat Lon Pagoda
2 Express Bus Office
3 Vietnamese Restaurants
4 Nguyen Trung Truc Temple
5 Rach Gia Park
6 Bank
7 GPO
8 Rach Gia Church
9 Mui Voi Ferry Terminal
10 Vinh Thanh Van Market
11 Kiosks
12 Luxury Goods Market

13 Tay Ho Restaurant
14 Ong Bac De Pagoda
15 Nguyen Trung Truc Statue
16 Binh Minh Hotel
17 To Chau Hotel
18 Nha Khach Uy Ban (hotel)
19 Rach Gia Hotel
20 1 Thang 5 Hotel
21 Rach Gia Museum
22 Kien Giang Tourism
23 Thanh Binh Hotel
24 Dong Ho Restaurant

25 Song Kien Restaurant
26 Rach Gia Restaurant
27 Hoa Bien Restaurant
28 Hai Au Restaurant
29 Pho Minh Pagoda
30 Express Bus Office
31 Protestant Church
32 Tam Bao Pagoda
33 Cao Dai Temple
34 Rach Gia Bus Station

am to 5 pm during the 7th, 8th and 9th lunar months (the summer season) but guests are welcome year-round.

Inside the sanctuary (*vihara*), the figures of Sakyamuni, the historical Buddha, all wear Cambodian and Thai-style pointed hats. Around the exterior of the main hall are eight small altars. The two towers near the main entrance are used to cremate the bodies of deceased monks. Near the pagoda are the tombs of about two dozen monks.

Ong Bac De Pagoda Ong Bac De Pagoda, which is in the centre of town at 14 Nguyen Du St, was built by Rach Gia's Chinese community about a century ago. On the central altar is a statue of Ong Bac De, a reincarnation of the Emperor of Jade. To the left is Ong Bon, Guardian Spirit of Happiness and Virtue; to the right is Quan Cong (in Chinese, Kuan Kung).

Pho Minh Pagoda Two Buddhist nuns live at Pho Minh Pagoda, which is at the corner of Co Bac St and Nguyen Van Cu St. This small pagoda was built in 1967 and contains a large Thai-style Thich Ca Buddha (Sakyamuni) donated in 1971 by a Buddhist organisation in Thailand. Nearby is a Vietnamese-style Thich Ca Buddha. The nuns live in a building behind the main hall. The pagoda is open to visitors from 6 am to 10 pm; prayers are held daily from 3.30 to 4.30 am and 6.30 to 7.30 pm.

Tam Bao Pagoda Tam Bao Pagoda, which dates from the early 19th century, is near the corner of Thich Thien An St and Tran Phu St; it was last rebuilt in 1913. The garden contains numerous trees sculpted as dragons, deer and other animals. The pagoda is open from 6 am to 8 pm; prayers are held from 4.30 to 5.30 am and 5.30 to 6.30 pm.

Cao Dai Temple There is a small Cao Dai Temple, constructed in 1969, at 189 Nguyen Trung Truc St, which is not far from Rach Gia Bus Station.

Churches

Rach Gia Church Rach Gia Church (Nha Tho Chanh Toa Rach Gia), a red brick structure built in 1918, is in Vinh Thanh Van sub-district, across the channel from Vinh Thanh Van Market. Weekday masses are held from 5 to 6 am and 5 to 6 pm; Sunday masses are from 5 to 6 am, 7 to 8 am, 4 to 5 pm and 5 to 6 pm.

Protestant Church Services are held every Sunday from 10 am to 12 noon at the Protestant Church, built in 1972, which is at 133 Nguyen Trung Truc St.

Rach Gia Museum

The newly refurbished Rach Gia Museum is at 21 Nguyen Van Troi St.

Vinh Thanh Van Market

Vinh Thanh Van Market, Rach Gia's main market area, stretches along Bach Dang St, Trinh Hoai Duc St and Thu Khoa Nghia St between Tran Phu St and the Mui Voi Ferry Terminal.

The luxury goods market is between Hoang Hoa Tham St and Pham Hong Thai St.

The Ancient City of Oc-Eo

Oc-Eo was a major trading city during the 1st to 6th centuries AD, when this area (along with the rest of southern Vietnam, much of southern Cambodia and the Malay Peninsula) was ruled by the Indianised empire of Funan. Much of what is known about Funan, which reached its height in the 5th century AD, comes from contemporary Chinese sources (eg the accounts of Chinese emissaries and travellers) and the archaeological excavations at Oc-Eo, which have uncovered evidence of significant contact between Oc-Eo and what is now Thailand, Malaysia, Indonesia, Persia and even the Roman Empire.

An elaborate system of canals around Oc-Eo was used for both irrigation and transportation, prompting Chinese travellers of the time to write about 'sailing across Funan' on their way to the Malay peninsula.

Most of the buildings of Oc-Eo were built on piles, and pieces of these structures indicate the high degree of refinement achieved by Funanese civilisation. Artefacts found at Oc-Eo are on display in Saigon at the History Museum and the Art Museum and in Hanoi at the History Museum.

The remains of Oc-Eo are not far from Rach Gia. The site itself, a hill 11 km inland littered with potsherds and shells, is near Vong The village, which can be reached by jeep from Hue Duc village, a distance of about 8 km. Oc-Eo is most easily accessible during the dry season. Special permission may be required to visit; for more information, contact Kien Giang Tourism.

Places to Stay

The *To Chau Hotel* (tel 3718; 31 rooms), one of the nicest hotels in town, is at 4F Le Loi St (next to the Thang Loi Cinema). For rooms with air-conditioning, Vietnamese are charged 16,500/19,800d for doubles/triples; 'capitalist tourists' pay US$11/15.40 while Overseas Vietnamese pay half these dollar rates. With a ceiling fan, doubles/triples cost 8250/14,300d.

The *Binh Minh Hotel* (tel 016; 15 rooms) is at 48 Pham Hong Thai St; a single costs 5000d, a double 7100d or 8300d and a triple 11,600d; toilets are communal.

Nha Khach Uy Ban (formerly the *Mekong Hotel*; tel 237; 12 rooms) is at 31 Nguyen Hung Son St; singles cost 6000d and doubles begin at 7000d. The *Rach Gia Hotel* is nearby at 46 Nguyen Hung Son St.

The comfortable *1 Thang 5 Hotel* (tel 2103; 26 rooms) is at 39 Nguyen Hung Son St. Double and triple rooms with air-conditioning cost 14,850/16,500d for Vietnamese, US$6.60/8.80 for Overseas Vietnamese and US$11/15.40 for Westerners. Single and double rooms with ceiling fan cost 6600/11,850d.

The *Thanh Binh Hotel* (tel 053; 9 rooms) is at 11 Ly Tu Trong St; singles go for 5000d and 8300d, doubles cost 11,500d.

Places to Eat

Rach Gia is known for its seafood, dried cuttlefish, *ca thieu* (dried fish slices), *nuoc mam* (fish sauce) and black pepper.

For deer, turtle, cobra, eel, frog and cuttlefish (as well as more conventional fare), try *Hoa Binh Restaurant*, which is on the water at the western end of Nguyen Hung Son St. *Tay Ho Restaurant* at 16 Nguyen Du St serves good Chinese and Vietnamese food. *Dong Ho Restaurant* at 124 Tran Phu St has Chinese, Vietnamese and Western dishes. Other places you might try are *Rach Gia Restaurant* on the water at the intersection of Ly Tu Trong St and Tran Hung Dao St and the *Song Kien Restaurant*, which is a block away at the intersection of Tran Hung Dao St and Hung Vuong St. *Hai Au Restaurant* is at the corner of Nguyen Trung Truc St and Nguyen Van Cu St.

Cheap, tasty Vietnamese food is sold along Hung Vuong St between Bach Dang St and Le Hong Phong St. There are several small Vietnamese restaurants on Mau Thanh St near the intersection of 30 Thanh 4 St.

There are restaurants in the *Binh Minh Hotel* and the *1 Thang 5 Hotel*.

Getting There & Away

Rach Gia is 92 km from Ha Tien, 116 km from Cantho and 248 km from Saigon.

Air Air Vietnam flies from Saigon to Rach Gia every Tuesday; the flight costs US$39.

Bus Buses from Ho Chi Minh City to Rach Gia leave from the Mien Tay Bus Station in An Lac; the express bus is said to take 6 to 7 hours. An express mini-bus from Saigon to Rach Gia departs from an office (tel 93318) at 83 Cach Mang Thang Tam St (half a block from the Immigration Police Office) once every 3 days; the trip, which begins at 4 am, costs 9000d.

The Rach Gia Bus Station (Ben Xe Kien Giang; tel 3430, 2185) is south of the city on Nguyen Trung Truc St (towards Long Xuyen and Cantho). Non-express buses link Rach Gia with Cantho, Dong Thap (departs once a day at 7 am), Ha Tien, Ho Chi Minh City and Long Xuyen. There are daily express buses to Ho Chi Minh City (departs 4.30 am) and Ha Tien (leaves 2.30 am). Bus services to rural areas near Rach Gia operate between 3.30 am and 4.30 pm. Destinations include Duong Xuong, Giong Rieng, Go Quao, Hon Chong, Kien Luong, Soc Xoai, Tan Hiep, Tri Ton and Vinh Thuan.

There is an express bus office at 33 30 Thang 4 St offering daily express service to Cantho (departs 5 am), Ha Tien (leaves 4.30 am) and Ho Chi Minh City (departs 3.45 am). Another express bus to Ho Chi Minh City leaves every morning at 4 am from Trung Tam Du Lich Thanh Nien, which is at 78 Nguyen Trung Truc St.

Boat Mui Voi Ferry Terminal (*mui* means 'nose' and *voi* means 'elephant' – so named because of the shape of the island) is at the north-eastern end of Bach Dang St. Boats from here make daily trips to Chau Doc (leaves 5.30 pm), Long Xuyen (departs 12.30 pm) and Tan Chau (departs 4.30 pm).

Getting Around

The main forms of ground transport in Rach Gia are cyclos and *xe dap lois* (wagons pulled by a bicycle).

HA TIEN

Ha Tien (population 80,000) is on the Gulf of Thailand 8 km from the Cambodian border. The area, famous for its nearby white sand beaches and fishing villages, is also known for its production of seafood, black pepper and items made from the shells of sea turtles. Hills near town support plantations of black pepper trees. On a clear day, Phu Quoc Island is visible across the water to the west.

Ha Tien was a province of Cambodia until 1708 when, in the face of attacks by the Thais, the Khmer-appointed governor, a Chinese immigrant named Mac Cuu, turned to the Vietnamese for protection and assistance. Mac Cuu thereafter governed this area as a fiefdom under the protection of the Nguyen Lords. He was succeeded as ruler by his son, Mac Thien Tu. During the 18th century, the area was invaded and pillaged several times by the Thais. Rach Gia and the

southern tip of the Mekong Delta came under direct Nguyen rule in 1798.

During the rule of the genocidal Khmer Rouge regime in Cambodia (1975-79), Khmer Rouge forces repeatedly attacked Vietnamese territory and massacred hundreds of civilians. The entire populations of Ha Tien and nearby villages – tens of thousands of people – fled their homes. During this period, areas north of Ha Tien (along the Cambodian border) were sown with mines and booby-traps which have yet to be cleared.

Orientation

The main drag is Ben Tran Hau St, which runs along the To Chau River; it turns northward just north-east of the floating toll bridge. The city's fresh produce market and general marketplace are between Ben Tran Hau St and the To Chau River. Few of Ha Tien's buildings are numbered.

Pagodas & Temples

Tombs of the Family of Mac Cuu The Tombs of the Family of Mac Cuu (Lang Mac Cuu) are on a low ridge not far from town. They are known locally simply as Nui Lang, the 'hill of the tombs'. Several dozen relatives of Mac Cuu, Chinese émigré and 18th-century ruler of this area, are buried here in traditional Chinese tombs decorated with figures of dragons, phoenixes, lions and guardians.

The largest tomb is that of Mac Cuu himself; it was constructed in 1809 on the orders of Emperor Gia Long and is decorated with finely carved figures of Thanh Long (the Green Dragon) and Bach Ho (the White Tiger). The tomb of Mac Cuu's first wife is flanked by dragons and phoenixes. At the bottom of the ridge is a shrine dedicated to the Mac family.

Tam Bao Pagoda Tam Bao Pagoda, also known as Sac Tu Tam Bao Tu, was founded by Mac Cuu in 1730. It is now home to seven Buddhist nuns. In front of the pagoda is a statue of Quan The Am Bo Tat (the Goddess of Mercy) standing on a lotus blossom in the

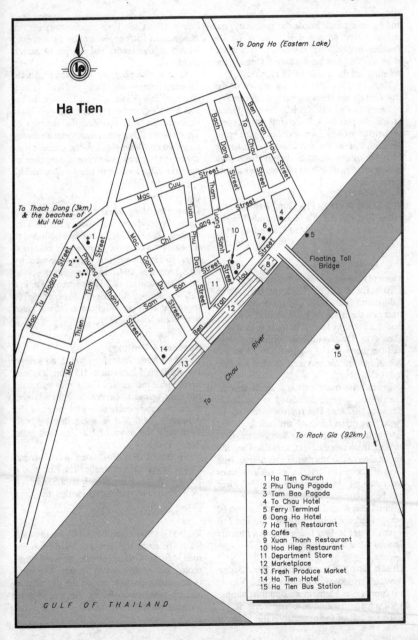

Ha Tien

To Dong Ho (Eastern Lake)

To Thach Dong (3km) & the beaches of Mui Nai

Floating Toll Bridge

To Rach Gia (92km)

Chau River

To

GULF OF THAILAND

1 Ha Tien Church
2 Phu Dung Pagoda
3 Tam Bao Pagoda
4 To Chau Hotel
5 Ferry Terminal
6 Dong Ho Hotel
7 Ha Tien Restaurant
8 Cafés
9 Xuan Thanh Restaurant
10 Hoa Hiep Restaurant
11 Department Store
12 Marketplace
13 Fresh Produce Market
14 Ha Tien Hotel
15 Ha Tien Bus Station

middle of a pond. Inside the sanctuary, the largest statue on the dais is of A Di Da Buddha, the Buddha of the Past. It is made of bronze but has been painted. Outside the building are the tombs of 16 monks.

Near Tam Bao Pagoda is a section of the city wall dating from the early 18th century.

Tam Bao Pagoda is at 328 Phuong Thanh St and is open from 7 am to 9 pm; prayers are held from 8 to 9 am and 2 to 3 pm. From the 15th day of the 4th lunar month to the 15th day of the 7th lunar month (from May to August, more-or-less) prayers are held six times a day.

Phu Dung Pagoda Phu Dung Pagoda, also called Phu Cu Am Tu, was founded in the mid-18th century by Mac Cuu's 2nd wife, Nguyen Thi Xuan. It is now home to one monk.

In the middle of the main hall is a peculiar statue of nine dragons embracing newly born Thich Ca Buddha (Sakyamuni, born Siddhartha Gautama). The most interesting statue on the main dais is a bronze Thich Ca Buddha brought from China; it is kept in a glass case. On the hillside behind the main hall are the tombs of Nguyen Thi Xuan and one of her female servants; nearby are four monks' tombs.

Behind the main hall is a small temple, Dien Ngoc Hoang, dedicated to the Taoist Emperor of Jade. The figures inside are of Ngoc Hoang flanked by Nam Tao, the Taoist God of the Southern Polar Star and the God of Happiness (on the right) and Bac Dao, the Taoist God of the Northern Polar Star and the God of Longevity (on the left). The statues are made of papier mâché moulded over bamboo frames.

Phu Dung Pagoda is open from 6 am to 10 pm; prayers are held from 4 to 5 am and 7 to 8 pm. To get to Phu Dung Pagoda, turn off Phuong Thanh St next to number 374.

Thach Dong Thach Dong, the 'Stone Cavern', also known as Chua Thanh Van, is a subterranean Vietnamese Buddhist temple 3.5 km from town on Mac Tu Hoang St.

To the left of the entrance is the 'stele of hatred' (Bia Cam Thu) commemorating the massacre of 130 people here by the forces of Khmer Rouge leader Pol Pot on 14 March 1979.

Several chambers of the grotto contain funerary tablets and altars to Ngoc Hoang (the Emperor of Jade), Quan The Am Bo Tat (the Goddess of Mercy) and the two Buddhist monks who founded the temples of Thach Dong. The wind creates extraordinary sounds as it blows through the grotto's passageways. Openings in several branches of the cave afford views of nearby Cambodia.

Dong Ho
Dong Ho (*dong* means 'east'; *ho* means 'lake') is a body of water just east of Ha Tien on Ben Tran Hau St. The lake is bounded to the east by a chain of granite hills known at the Ngu Ho (five tigers) and to the west by hills known as To Chan. Dong Ho is said to be most beautiful on nights when there is a full or almost-full moon. According to legend, it is on such nights that fairies dance here in the moonlight.

Beaches & Grottoes
Beaches Near Town Mui Nai (Stag's Head Peninsula) is 4 km west of Ha Tien; it is said to resemble the head of a stag with its mouth pointing upward. On top is a lighthouse; there are sand beaches on both sides of the peninsula. Mui Nai is accessible by road from both the town of Ha Tien and from Thach Dong.

No Beach (Bai No), lined with coconut palms, is several km west of Ha Tien near a fishing village. Bang Beach (Bai Bang) is a long stretch of dark sand shaded by *bang* trees.

Mo So Grotto Located about 17 km towards Rach Gia from Ha Tien and 3 km from the road, Mo So Grotto consists of three large rooms and a labyrinth of tunnels. The cave is accessible on foot during the dry season and by small boat during the wet season. Visitors should have torches and a local guide.

Hang Tien Grotto Hang Tien Grotto, 25 km towards Rach Gia from Ha Tien, served as a hide-out for Nguyen Anh (later Emperor Gia Long) in 1784, when he was being pursued by the Tay Son Rebels. His fighters found zinc coins buried here, a discovery which gave the cave its name, which means 'Coin Grotto'. Hang Tien Grotto is accessible by boat.

Chua Hang Grotto & Duong Beach

Chua Hang Grotto and Duong Beach are about 32 km towards Rach Gia from Ha Tien. To get here, you may have to hire a car or motorbike.

. Chua Hang Grotto is entered through a Buddhist pagoda set against the base of the hill. Visitors light joss sticks and offer prayers here before entering the grotto itself, whose entrance is behind the altar. Inside is a plaster statue of Quan The Am Bo Tat (the Goddess of Mercy). The thick stalactites are hollow and resonate like bells when tapped.

From Chua Hang Grotto, you can see Father and Son Isle (Hon Phu Tu) several hundred metres offshore; it is said to be shaped like a father embracing his son. The island, a column of stone, is perched on a 'foot' worn away by the pounding of the waves; the foot is most fully exposed at low tide.

Duong Beach (Bai Duong), next to Chua Hang Grotto, is one of the nicest beaches in the Ha Tien area. It is known for its *duong* trees, white sand, clear water and absence of underwater rocks. The beach is bounded by the Hon Trem peninsula.

Offshore Islands

Hon Giang Island, which is about 15 km from Ha Tien and can be reached by small boat, has a lovely, secluded beach. There are numerous other islands off the coast between Rach Gia and the Cambodian border. Some local people make a living gathering precious salangane or swifts' nests (the most important ingredient of that famous Chinese delicacy, bird's nest soup) on the islands' rocky cliffs.

Places to Stay

The *Dong Ho Hotel* (18 rooms) is near the floating bridge at the corner of Ben Tran Hau St and To Chau St; doubles/triples cost 7000/10,000d. The *To Chau Hotel* (tel 80; 8 rooms), across To Chau St from the Dong Ho Hotel, has doubles for 6400d, triples for 9600d and quads for 12,800d. Rooms may lack ceiling fans; all toilets are common. The *Ha Tien Hotel* is at the corner of Ben Tran Hau St and Phuong Thanh St.

Places to Eat

Hoa Hiep Restaurant, perhaps the best in town, is on the corner of Than Thuong Sanh and Sam Son streets; it serves Chinese and Vietnamese food. *Xuan Thanh Restaurant* is around the block at the corner of Ben Tran Hau and Tham Tuong Sanh streets; this place has a few Western dishes. *Ha Tien Restaurant* is on Ben Tran Hau St next to the Dong Ho Hotel.

Getting There & Away

Ha Tien is 92 km from Rach Gia, 95 km from Chau Doc, 206 km from Cantho, 338 km from Saigon and 225 km from Phnom Penh (via Kampot). The road between Rach Gia and Ha Tien is in a dismal state of repair.

Bus Buses from Ho Chi Minh City to Ha Tien leave from the Mien Tay Bus Station in An Lac; the trip takes 9 to 10 hours.

Ha Tien Bus Station (Ben Xe Ha Tien) is on the other side of the floating toll bridge from the centre of town. Buses leave from here to An Giang Province, Cantho (departs 5.50 am and 9.10 am), Cuu Long Province, Ho Chi Minh City (departs at 2 am) and Rach Gia (five times a day). The bus trip from Rach Gia to Ha Tien takes about 5 hours.

Boat Passenger ferries dock at the Ferry Terminal, which is not far from the To Chau Hotel next to the floating bridge. Daily ferries depart for Chau Doc at 6 am and for Tinh Bien at 11 am and 12 noon.

It may be possible to travel between Rach Gia and Ha Tien by scheduled or chartered

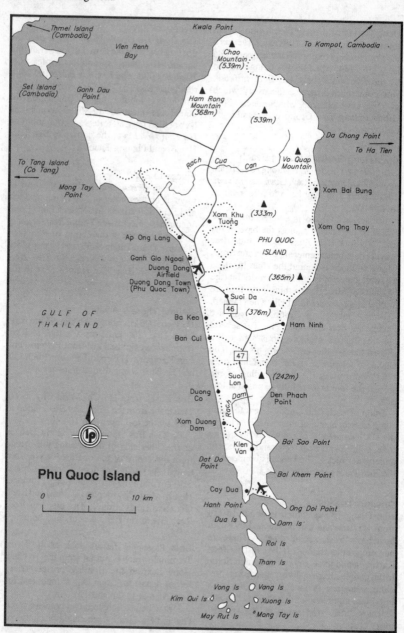

Phu Quoc Island

boat; for more information, ask around each town's quay.

Getting Around
The tolls for the floating bridge across the To Chau River are 100d for a person, 50d for a bicycle and 200d for a motorbike.

The main form of local transport is the *xe dap loi* (a trailer pulled by a bicycle).

PHU QUOC ISLAND
Mountainous and forested Phu Quoc Island (Dao Phu Quoc; population 18,000) is in the Gulf of Thailand 45 km west of Ha Tien and 15 km south of the coast of Cambodia. The tear-shape island, which is 48 km long and has an area of 1320 sq km, is governed as a district of Kien Giang Province. The island's fishing industry is centred in the village of Duong Dong. Phu Quoc is claimed by Cambodia; its Khmer name is usually rendered Ko Tral.

Phu Quoc is known for its production of high-quality *nuoc mam* (fish sauce), its rich fishing grounds and the unspoiled beaches that ring the island. There are fantastic views of underwater marine life through the transparent blue-green waters off some of the beaches around the southern part of the island. A number of small islands near Phu Quoc are great for fishing and swimming.

Phu Quoc Island served as a base of operations for the French missionary Pigneau de Behaine from the 1760s to the 1780s. Prince Nguyen Anh, later Emperor Gia Long, was sheltered here by Behaine when he was being hunted by the Tay Son Rebels.

Getting There & Away
Air Air Vietnam flies from Saigon to Duong Dong, Phu Quoc's main town, every Friday; the flight costs US$62.

Boat There may be a ferry service from Rach Gia to Duong To (on the southern tip of the island; a 100 km trip) and Duong Dong (on the west coast; a 140 km trip). When the Cambodian civil war is settled, it may be possible to reach Phu Quoc from Cambodia.

CAMAU
Camau, situated on the Ganh Hao River, is the largest town in the Camau Peninsula, an area at the southern tip of Vietnam which includes all of Minh Hai Province and parts of Kien Giang and Hau Giang provinces. The town of Camau is in the middle of the U-Minh Forest, a huge mangrove swamp covering 1000 sq km of Minh Hai and Kien Giang provinces. Local people use certain species of mangrove as a source of timber, charcoal, thatch and tannin. When the mangroves flower, bees feed on the blossoms, providing both honey and wax. The area is also an important habitat for waterfowl.

The U-Minh Forest, which is the largest mangrove swamp in the world outside of the Amazon basin, was serious damaged during the Vietnam War by American aerial defoliation. Despite replanting efforts, 20% of Camau's tidal mangrove forests are still a wasteland of rotting stumps protruding from the murky waters.

The population of Camau includes many ethnic-Khmers. The area has the lowest population density in southern Vietnam.

Getting There & Away
Camau is 179 km from Cantho and 348 km from Saigon.

Bus Buses from Ho Chi Minh City to Camau leave from Mien Tay Bus Station in An Lac. The trip takes 10 hours by regular bus and 8 hours by express bus.

South-Central Coast

This section covers the littoral provinces of Thuan Hai, Khanh Hoa, Phu Yen, Binh Dinh, Quang Ngai and southern Quang Nam-Danang. The cities, towns, beaches and historical sites in this region, most of which are along National Highway 1, are listed from south to north..

Phan Thiet

Phan Thiet (population 76,000) is best known for its *nuoc mam* (fish sauce) and fishing industry. The population includes descendants of the Chams, who controlled this area until 1692. During the colonial period, the Europeans lived in their own segregated quarter, which stretched along the north bank of the Phan Thiet River, while the Vietnamese, Chams, South Chinese, Malays and Indonesians lived along the river's south bank.

Thuan Hai Province is one of the most arid regions of Vietnam. The nearby plains, which are dominated by rocky, roundish mountains, support a bit of irrigated rice agriculture.

Orientation
Phan Thiet is built along both banks of the Phan Thiet River, which is also known as the Ca Ti River and the Muong Man River. National Highway 1 runs right through town; south of the river, it is known as Tran Hung Dao St while north of the river it is called Le Hong Phong St.

Information
Tourist Office The office of Thuan Hai Province Tourism (Cong Ty Du Lich Thuan Hai; tel 2474, 2475) is at 82 Trung Trac St (corner Tran Hung Dao St), which is just south of the bridge over the Phan Thiet River.

Phan Thiet Beach
To get to Phan Thiet's beachfront, turn east (right if you're heading north) at Victory Monument, an arrow-shaped, concrete tower with victorious cement people at the base.

Cham Music
Performances of Cham music are sometimes held at the Vinh Thuy Hotel, which is at Phan Thiet Beach.

Mui Ne Beach
Mui Ne Beach, famous for its sand dunes, is 22 km east of Phan Thiet near a fishing village at the tip of Mui Ne Peninsula. There are plans to build a hotel here. Between 8.30 am and 4 pm, a local bus makes six daily round trips between Phan Thiet Bus Station and Mui Ne.

Places to Stay
Thuan Hai Tourism's basic *Phan Thiet Hotel* (tel 2573) is at 40 Tran Hung Dao St. Foreigners are charged US$24 for a room with air-con and bath; cheaper rooms are also available.

Provinces of South Central Vietnam

1	Quang Tri
2	Thua Thien-Hué
3	Quang Nam-Danang
4	Gia Lai-Kon Tum
5	Quang Ngai
6	Binh Dinh
7	Dak Lak
8	Phu Yen
9	Khanh Hoa
10	Lam Dong
11	Thuan Hai
12	Song Be
13	Dong Nai
14	Tay Ninh
15	Long An

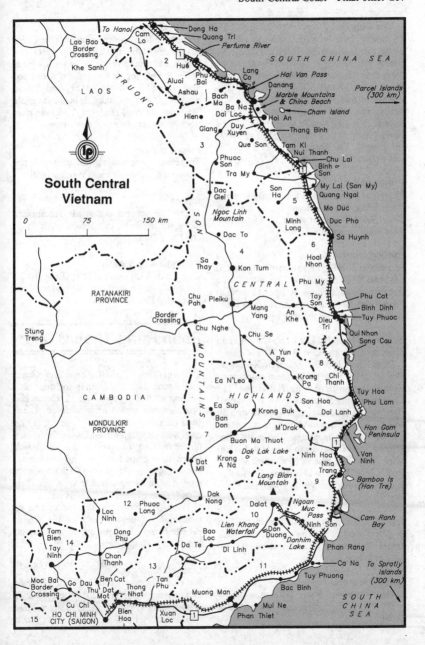

South Central Vietnam

0   75   150 km

To Hanoi
Lao Bao Border Crossing
Khe Sanh
Cam Lo
Dong Ha
Quang Tri
Perfume River
LAOS
TRUONG
Aluoi
Ashau
Hue
Phu Bai
Lang Co
Hai Van Pass
Danang
Marble Mountains & China Beach
Cham Island
SOUTH CHINA SEA
Parcel Islands (300 km)
Bach Ma
Ba Na
Dai Loc
Hoi An
Hien
Giang
Duy Xuyen
Thang Binh
Que Son
Tam Ki
Nui Thanh
Chu Lai
Binh Son
Phuoc Son
Tra My
Son Ha
My Lai (Son My)
Quang Ngai
Mo Duc
Duc Pho
Sa Huynh
Dac Glei
Ngoc Linh Mountain
Minh Long
Dac To
Sa Thay
Kon Tum
Hoai Nhon
Phu My
CENTRAL
RATANAKIRI PROVINCE
Chu Pah
Pleiku
Mang Yang
An Khe
Tay Son
Phu Cat
Binh Dinh
Tuy Phuoc
Border Crossing
Chu Nghe
Chu Se
Dieu Tri
Qui Nhon
Song Cau
Stung Treng
A Yun Pa
Krong Pa
Chi Thanh
Tuy Hoa
Phu Lam
CAMBODIA
Ea N'Leo
HIGHLANDS
Son Hoa
Ea Sup
Krong Buk
Dai Lanh
Hon Gom Peninsula
MONDULKIRI PROVINCE
Ban Don
M'Drak
Buon Ma Thuot
Ninh Hoa
Van Ninh
Dat Mil
Krong A Na
Dak Lak Lake
Nha Trang
Bamboo Is (Hon Tre)
Lang Bian Mountain
Dak Nong
Dalat
Ngoan Muc Pass
Cam Ranh Bay
Phuoc Long
Loc Ninh
Lien Khang Waterfall
Don Duong
Ninh Son
Tam Bien
Tay Ninh
Dong Phu
Bao Loc
Da Te
Danhim Lake
Phan Rang
Chon Thanh
Di Linh
Ca Na
To Spratly Islands (300 km)
Moc Bai Border Crossing
Go Dau
Ben Cat
Tan Phu
Muong Man
Tuy Phuong
Bac Binh
Cu Chi
Thu Dat Mot
Thong Nhat
Mui Ne
HO CHI MINH CITY (SAIGON)
Bien Hoa
Xuan Loc
Phan Thiet
SOUTH CHINA SEA

MOUNTAINS
SON

The *Vinh Thuy Hotel* (tel 2622 and 2655; 66 rooms), built between 1985 and 1989, is along the seashore on Ton Tuc Thang St; rooms cost 12,000 to 20,000d. To get to the Vinh Thuy Hotel, turn towards the sea (eastward) at the Victory Monument.

Khach San 19-4 (tel 2460), which is across the street from Phan Thiet Bus Station, is at 1 Tu Van Tu St (just past 217 Le Hong Phong St). Locals pay 5500 to 7500d for a triple. The hotel overlooks a vista of salt-evaporation pools.

Places to Eat
There is a restaurant on the 3rd floor of the *Phan Thiet Hotel* and another at the *Vinh Thuy Hotel*. The restaurant at *Khach San 19-4* may not serve full meals.

Getting There & Away
Phan Thiet is 198 km due east of Saigon, 250 km from Nha Trang and 247 km from Dalat. Because National Highway 1 passes through Phan Thiet, all vehicles going north or south along the coast pass through the town.

Bus Buses from Ho Chi Minh City to Phan Thiet depart from Mien Dong Bus Station.

Phan Thiet Bus Station (Ben Xe Thuan Hai; tel 2590) is on the northern outskirts of town at Tu Van Tu St, which is just past 217 Le Hong Phong St (also known as National Highway 1). The station is open from 5.30 am to 3.30 pm; tickets should be purchased the day before departure. There are nonexpress buses from here to Bien Hoa, Ho Chi Minh City, Long Khanh, Madagoui, Mui Ne Beach, Phan Rang and Phu Cuong as well as to other destinations within Thuan Hai Province.

Train The nearest train station to Phan Thiet is 12 km west of the town at Muong Man. Trains TN1 and TN2 and autorails AR1 and AR2 stop here.

Getting Around
Local Transport Phan Thiet has a few cyclos, some of which always seem to be at the bus station.

CA NA BEACH
During the 16th century, princes of the Cham royal family would fish and hunt tigers, elephants and rhinoceros here. Today, Ca Na is better known for its turquoise waters lined with splendid white-sand beaches dotted with huge boulders. Rau Cau Island is visible offshore. National Highway 1 and the train tracks pass very near the water here.

Places to Stay
There are several bungalows for rent near the restaurants. A beach resort is being built.

Places to Eat
There are several oceanside restaurants along the highway, including *Ca Na Quan* and *Rang Dong*.

Getting There & Away
Ca Na is 114 km north of Phan Thiet and 32 km south of Phan Rang. Many long-haul buses stop here for a break.

Phan Rang-Thap Cham

The twin cities of Phan Rang and Thap Cham (population 38,000), famous for their production of table grapes, are in Thuan Hai Province in a region of semi-desert. Local flora include poinciana trees and sabra-like cacti with vicious thorns. Many of the houses on the outskirts of town are decorated with Greek-style grape trellises. The area's best-known sight is the group of Cham towers known as Po Klong Garai, from which Thap Cham (Cham Tower) derives its name.

Thuan Hai Province is home to tens of thousands of descendants of the Cham people, many of whom live in and around Phan Rang-Thap Cham.

Orientation
National Highway 1 is called Thong Nhat St as it runs through Phan Rang. Thong Nhat St is Phan Rang's main commercial street. Thap Cham is strung out along Highway 20, which

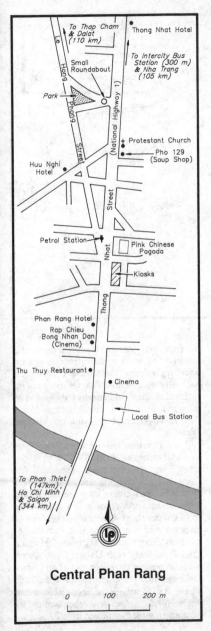

Central Phan Rang

0   100   200 m

heads west from Phan Rang towards Ninh Son and Dalat.

Information

Tourist Office The office of Thuan Hai Tourism (Cong Ty Du Lich Thuan Hai; tel 74) is in the Huu Nghi Hotel at 1 Huong Vuong St. If you're heading north, turn left off Thong Nhat St between numbers 267 and 269 and go 100 metres.

Po Klong Garai Cham Towers

Phan Rang-Thap Cham's most famous landmark is Po Klong Garai, four brick towers constructed at the end of the 13th century during the reign of the Cham monarch Jaya Simhavarman III. The towers, built as Hindu temples, stand on a brick platform at the top of Cho'k Hala, a crumbly granite hill covered with some of the most ornery cacti this side of the Rio Grande.

Over the entrance to the largest tower (the *kalan*, or sanctuary) is a carving of a dancing Shiva with six arms. Note the inscriptions on the doorposts. Inside the vestibule is a statue of the bull Nandin, symbol of the agricultural productivity of the countryside. To ensure a good crop, farmers would place an offering of fresh greens in front of Nandin's muzzle. Under the main tower is a *mukha-linga*, a linga (a stylised phallus which symbolises maleness and creative power and which represents the Hindu god Shiva) with a painted human face on it. A wooden pyramid has been constructed above the *mukha-linga*.

Inside the tower opposite the entrance to the *kalan* you can get a good look at some of the Cham's sophisticated masonry technology. The structure attached to it was originally the main entrance to the complex.

On a nearby hill is a rock with an inscription from the year 1050 commemorating the erection of a linga by a Cham prince.

On the hill directly south of Cho'k Hala there is a concrete water tank built by the Americans in 1965. It is encircled by French pillboxes, which were built during the Franco-Vietminh War to protect the nearby rail yards. To the north of Cho'k Hala you can see the concrete revetments of Thanh

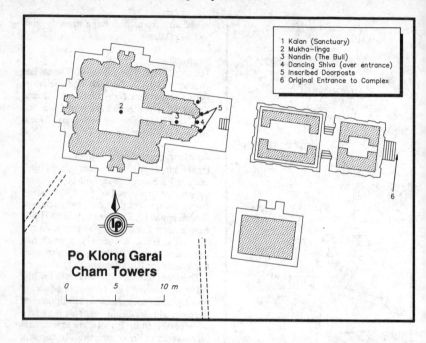

1 Kalan (Sanctuary)
2 Mukha–linga
3 Nandin (The Bull)
4 Dancing Shiva (over entrance)
5 Inscribed Doorposts
6 Original Entrance to Complex

Po Klong Garai Cham Towers

0   5   10 m

Son Airbase, used since 1975 by the Soviet-built MiGs of the Vietnamese Air Force.

Po Klong Garai is several hundred metres north of National Highway 20, at a point 7 km towards Dalat from Phan Rang. The towers are on the other side of the tracks from Thap Cham Railroad Station.

Thap Cham Rail Yards

The Thap Cham Rail Yards are 300 metres south-east of Po Klong Garai and across the tracks from the Thap Cham Railway Station. The main function of the yards, which were founded by the French about 80 years ago, is the repair of Vietnamese Railways' ancient 1 metre gauge engines and rolling stock. Spare parts are made either by hand or with antique machine tools and metal presses. Each pair of railroad wheels you see lying about weighs 500 kg.

It may be possible to tour the yards, but judging by the small armoury (which includes a 50 calibre machine gun!) kept at the front gate, it seems clear that the area is deemed to have a certain strategic import-ance. Indeed, the Vietnamese Communists are well aware of how vital railroads are for national security – that's why they used to go to so much trouble to sabotage them during the Franco-Vietminh War and the Vietnam War.

The 86 km long rail line from Thap Cham to Dalat operated from 1930 until 1964, when it was closed because of repeated Viet Cong attacks. The line used a *crémaillère* system in which chains were used to pull the trains up the mountainside at a grade of up to 12 cm per metre. The steepest sections of track are visible at Ngoan Muc Pass (Belle-vue Pass) from National Highway 20 (which links Phan Rang with Dalat). There are no plans at present to reopen the Thap Cham-Dalat rail line. The oldest engine at the Thap Cham Rail Yards is an inoperable steam engine for the *crémaillère* manufactured by Machinenfabrik Esselingen in 1929.

Po Ro Me Cham Tower

Po Ro Me Cham Tower (Thap Po Ro Me), among the newest of Vietnam's Cham towers, is about 15 km south of Phan Rang on a rocky hill 5 km towards the mountains from National Highway 1. The *kalan* (sanctuary), which is decorated with paintings, is said to have two inscribed doorposts, two stone statues of the bull Nandin, a bas-relief representing a deified king in the form of Shiva and two statues of queens, one of whom has an inscription on her chest. The towers are named after the last ruler of an independent Champa, King Po Ro Me (ruled 1629-51), who died a prisoner of the Vietnamese.

Tuan Tu Hamlet

There is a minaretless Cham mosque, which is closed to visitors, in the Cham hamlet of Tuan Tu (population 1000). This Muslim community is governed by elected religious leaders (*Thay Mun*), who can easily be identified by their traditional costume, which includes a white robe and an elaborate white turban with red tassels. In keeping with Islamic precepts governing modesty, Cham women often wear head coverings and skirts. The Chams, like other ethnic minorities in Vietnam, suffer from discrimination and are even poorer than their ethnic-Vietnamese neighbours.

To get to Tuan Tu Hamlet, head south from town along National Highway 1. Go 250 metres south of the large bridge to a small bridge. Cross it and turn left (to the southeast) onto a dirt track. At the market (just past the Buddhist pagoda on the right), turn right and follow the road, part of which is lined with hedgerows of cacti, for about 2 km, crossing two white concrete footbridges. Ask villagers for directions along the way. Tuan Tu is 3 km from National Highway 1.

Ninh Chu Beach

Ninh Chu Beach (Bai Tam Ninh Chu) is 5 km south of Phan Rang.

Places to Stay

The main tourist hotel in Phan Rang is the *Huu Nghi Hotel* (tel 74; 25 rooms) at 1 Huong Vuong St. Foreigners are charged US$25 for a double; for Vietnamese, doubles cost between 8000 and 15,000d. To get there, turn east (left if you are heading north) off Thong Nhat St between numbers 267 and 269 and go 100 metres.

The *Phan Rang Hotel* (20 rooms) is at 354 Thong Nhat St, which is 150 metres south of the pink pagoda in the market area; a single costs 4000d.

Four storey *Thong Nhat Hotel* (tel 2049; 16 rooms) at 164 Thong Nhat St is a modern, run-down place with more than its fair share of vermin. Vietnamese pay 9000/11,500d for doubles/triples; foreigners are asked to pay 54,000d for exactly the same double!

Places to Eat

A local delicacy is roasted or baked gecko (*dong*) served with fresh green mango.

Thu Thuy Restaurant is a three storey eatery at 404 Thong Nhat St. *Nha Hang 426* is across the street from the Bus Station. *Nha Hang 404* is at 404 Thong Nhat St. For soup, try *Pho 129* at 231 Thong Nhat St (just south of the Protestant church).

Getting There & Away

Phan Rang is 344 km from Saigon, 147 km from Phan Thiet, 105 km from Nha Trang and 110 km from Dalat.

Bus Buses from Ho Chi Minh City to Phan Rang-Thap Cham depart from Mien Dong Bus Station.

Phan Rang Intercity Bus Station (Ben Xe Phan Rang; tel 2031) is on the northern outskirts of town opposite 64 Thong Nhat St. There is bus service from here to Ca Na Beach, Cam Ranh Bay, Dalat, Danang, Don Duong, Ho Chi Minh City, Long Huong, Phan Ri, Phan Thiet, Nha Trang, Nhi Ha, Noi Huyen, Son Hai, Song Dan and Song My.

The Local Bus Station (Ben Xe) is at the southern end of town across the street from 426 Thong Nhat St.

Train The Thap Cham Railroad Station is about 6 km west of National Highway 1 within sight of Po Klong Garai Cham Towers. Thap Cham is served by Trains TN1 and TN2 and autorails AR1 and AR2.

Getting Around

There is a bicycle parts store at 118 Thong Nhat St.

CAM RANH BAY

Cam Ranh Bay is an excellent natural harbour 56 km north of Phan Rang-Thap Cham. The Russian fleet of Admiral Rodjestvenski used it in 1905 at the end of the Russo-Japanese War as did the Japanese during WWII, when the area was still considered an excellent place for tiger hunting. In the mid-1960s, the Americans constructed a vast base here, including an extensive port, ship repair facilities and an airstrip.

After reunification, the Russians and their fleet came back, enjoying far better facilities than they had found 7 decades before. Continued Soviet use of the base, which is the largest Soviet naval installation outside the Soviet Union, is seen by observers as contingent on Moscow's support for Vietnam's domestic and foreign policies. Indeed, despite Soviet requests, the Vietnamese have refused to grant them permanent rights to the base.

In 1988, Mikhail Gorbachev offered to abandon the installation if the Americans would do the same with their six bases across the South China Sea in the Philippines. The following year, however, the Vietnamese, evidently annoyed with the Soviets, appeared to offer the Americans renewed use of Cam Ranh Bay. According to the *New York Times*, the Soviet presence at Cam Ranh Bay was significantly reduced in 1990 as part of the Kremlin's cost-cutting measures.

There are said to be beautiful beaches around Cam Ranh Bay, but why deliberately spend your vacation near one of the most strategically sensitive places in all of Vietnam? There are lots of other great beaches that don't have the Soviet navy docked nearby.

Nha Trang

Nha Trang (population 200,000), the capital of Khanh Hoa Province, has what is probably the nicest municipal beach in all of Vietnam. It is the ideal place for the sort of lazy seaside vacation Caribbean resorts are famous for. The turquoise waters around Nha Trang are almost transparent, making for excellent fishing, snorkelling and scuba diving. Of late, lots of 'massage' signs have been popping up around town, a sure sign that visitors are expected.

Nha Trang's dry season, unlike that of Saigon, runs from June to October. The wettest months are October and November, but rain usually falls only at night or in the morning.

The combined fishing fleet of Khanh Hoa Province and neighbouring Phu Yen Province numbers about 10,000 trawlers and junks; they are able to fish during the 250 days of calm seas per year. The area's seafood products include abalone, lobster, prawns, cuttle-fish, mackerel, pomfret, scallops, shrimps, snapper and tuna. Exportable agricultural products from the area include cashew nuts, coconuts, coffee and sesame seeds. Salt production employs 4000 people.

Orientation

Tran Phu Blvd runs along Nha Tranh Beach, becoming Tu Do St south of the airport. The centre of Nha Trang is around the Nha Trang Hotel on Thong Nhat St.

Information

Tourist Office Khanh Hoa Province Tourism (Cong Ty Du Lich Khanh Hoa; tel 22753) can provide cars, drivers and guides and may also rent out diving and underwater fishing equipment. Their office is on the second floor of a yellow two storey building on the grounds of the Hai Yen Hotel. To get there, enter the Hai Yen Hotel through the front entrance (at 40 Tran Phu Blvd) and walk all the way through the main building. Alternatively, you can use the Hai Yen

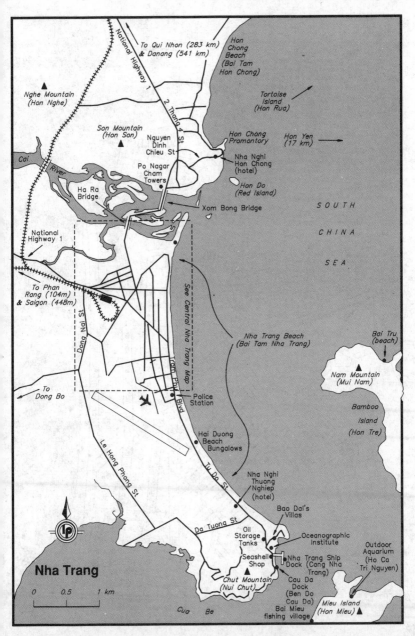

Nha Trang

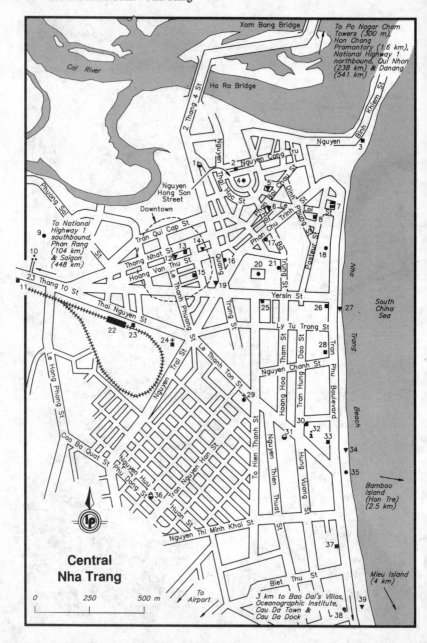

Xom Bong Bridge

Cai River

Ha Ra Bridge

To Po Nagar Cham
Towers (300 m),
Hon Chong
Promontory (1.6 km),
National Highway 1
northbound, Qui Nhon
(238 km) & Danang
(541 km)

Nguyen · 3

Nguyen Cong Tru

Nguyen
Hong Son
Street

Downtown

Phuong Sg

To National
Highway 1
southbound,
Phan Rang
(104 km)
& Saigon
(448 km)

9

10

Tran Qui Cap St

Thong Nhat St

Hoang Van Thu St

11

23 Thang 10 St

Thai Nguyen St

22   23

24

Le Hong Phong St

Cao Ba Quat St

Nguyen Trai St

Le Thanh Ton St

Nguyen Hong

Nguyen Thi Minh Khai St

Phu Dong St

Tran Nguyen Han

Thuan St

36

Le Thanh Phuong

Quang

To Hien Thanh St

Nguyen Thien Thuat St

Hung Vuong St

Biet Thu St

To
Airport

3 km to Bao Dai's Villas,
Oceanographic Institute,
Cau Da Town &
Cau Da Dock

1

4

5

6   Le

Phan   Chu Trinh

Phan

17

Trung St

20 21

Yersin St

25   26   27

Ly Tu Trong St

Hoang Hoa Dao St

Tham St

28

Nguyen Chanh St

Tran Hung

Tran Phu Boulevard

29

30

31   32
1   33

34

35

37

38

39

Bac Chau St

Dinh Phung

Loi

Phan

Pasteur St

Binh Khiem St

Nguyen

Thai Hoc St

2 Thang 4 St

16

18

19

13 14

12

15

Nha

Trang

Beach

South
China
Sea

Bamboo
Island
(Hon Tre)
(2.5 km)

Mieu Island
(4 km)

7

8

**Central
Nha Trang**

0   250   500 m

■ PLACES TO STAY		● OTHER	
3	Nha Nghi 378 Bo Noi Vu (hotel)	1	Short-Haul Bus Station
8	Thang Loi Hotel	2	Dam Market Lambretta Station
11	Viet Ngu Hotel	4	Dam Market
13	Nha Tranh Hotel	7	GPO
15	Kuong Hai Hotel	9	Giant Seated Buddha
17	Nha Khach 25 Phan Chu Trinh (hotel)	10	Long Son Pagoda
23	Railway Station Dormitory (Nha Tro)	16	Foreign Trade Bank
26	Thong Nhat Hotel	18	Pasteur Institute & Yersin
28	Nha KhachNha Trang Hotel		Museum
30	Hung Dao Hotel	20	Stadium
33	Hai Yen Hotel	21	Youth Tourism Express Bus
37	Khach San 58 Tran Phu (hotel)		Office
		22	Nha Trang Railway Station
▼ PLACES TO EAT		24	Nha Trang Cathedral
		25	Bien Vien Tinh (hospital)
5	Lac Canh Restaurant	29	Church
6	Nha Hang 33 Le Loi (restaurant)	31	Express Bus Station
12	Pho Hanoi (soup shop)	32	Phu Khanh Province Tourism
14	Binh Minh Restaurant	35	War Memorial Obelisk
19	Ice Cream Shops	36	Lien Tinh Bus Station
27	Cafes	38	Nha Trang Ship Chandler
34	Cafes		Company
39	Cafes		

Hotel's back gate at 1 Tran Hung Dao St (next to the Hung Dao Hotel). The office is open from 7 to 11.30 am and 1.30 to 5 pm Monday to Saturday.

The Nha Trang Ship Chandler Company (Cung Ung Tau Bien; tel 21195) is at 74 Tran Phu Blvd. This concern, which is also known as Nha Trang Ship Chanco, rents snorkelling, underwater fishing and skin-diving gear and hires out cars, buses, boats and guides. The Ship Chandler Company also supplies food for ships, does minor marine repairs, runs restaurants and provides entertainment for sailors, including massages and dancing at the villa in which their office is located.

Nha Trang Tourism (tel 21231), which runs various cafes and restaurants around town, has its office in the Hung Dao Hotel, which is at 3 Tran Hung Dao St. Rental cars cost US$0.25 per km with minimum charges of US$12.50 for a half day and US$25 for a full day.

Post & Telecommunications The GPO (telex 500 GDDB NT) is at 2 Tran Phu Blvd, which is near the northern end of Nha Trang Beach one block from the Thang Loi Hotel; it is open daily from 6.30 am to 8.30 pm. International telephone calls can be placed via Saigon or Hanoi. The GPO also offers international telex and domestic fax services.

Money The Bank for Foreign Trade (Ngan Hang Ngoai Thuong; tel 21054) at 17 Quang Trung St offers the standard bank rate. It is open from 7 to 11.30 am and 1 to 5 pm Monday to Saturday except Thursday afternoons. The bank says it will accept Australian dollars, Deutchmarks, French francs, Hong Kong dollars, Japanese yen, Singapore dollars, Soviet roubles and United States dollars as well as travellers cheques denominated in US dollars and Japanese yen. They also say they will exchange Vietnamese dong for US dollars (for 5% less than their dong-for-dollars rate) provided you can supply proof of having bought the dong legally.

Emergency An American-built hospital, Benh Vien Tinh (tel 22175), is on Yersin St.

Po Nagar Cham Towers

The Cham towers of Po Nagar (The Lady of the City) were built between the 7th and 12th centuries on a site used for Hindu worship as early as the 2nd century AD. Today, both ethnic-Chinese and Vietnamese Buddhists come to Po Nagar to pray and make offerings according to their respective traditions. Out of deference to the continuing religious significance of this site, shoes should be removed before entering the towers.

There were once seven or eight towers at Po Nagar, four of which remain. All the temples face the east, as did the original entrance to the complex, which is to the right as you ascend the hillock. In centuries past, a person coming to pray passed through the pillared *mandapa* (meditation hall), ten of whose pillars can still be seen, before proceeding up the staircase to the towers.

The 23 metre high North Tower (Thap Chinh), with its terraced pyramidal roof, vaulted interior masonry and vestibule, is a superb example of Cham architecture. It was built in 817 AD by Pangro, a minister of King Harivarman I, 43 years after the temples here were sacked and burned by Malay corsairs who probably came from Srivijaya on Sumatra. The raiders also carried off a linga made of precious metal. In 918 AD, King Indravarman III placed a gold *mukha-linga* in the North Tower, but it was taken by the Khmers. In 965 AD, King Jaya Indravarman I replaced the gold *mukha-linga* with the stone figure of Uma (a shakti of Shiva) which remains to this day.

Above the entrance to the North Tower, two musicians flank a dancing four armed Shiva, one of whose feet is on the head of the bull Nandin. The sandstone doorposts are covered with inscriptions, as are parts of the walls of the vestibule. A gong and a drum stand under the pyramid-shaped ceiling of

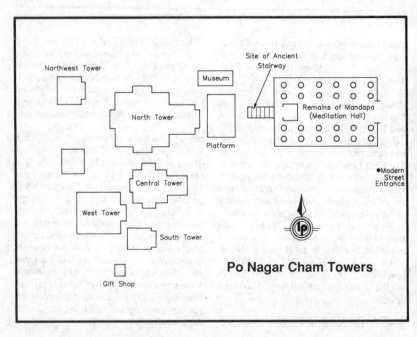

Po Nagar Cham Towers

the antechamber. In the 28 metre high pyramidal main chamber there is a black stone statue of the goddess Uma (in the shape of Bhagavati) with ten arms, two of which are hidden under her vest; she is seated leaning back against some sort of monstrous animal.

The Central Tower (Thap Nam) was built partly of recycled bricks in the 12th century on the site of a structure dating from the 7th century. It is less finely constructed than the other towers and has little ornamentation; the pyramidal roof lacks terracing or pilasters. Note the inscription on the left-hand wall of the vestibule. The interior altars were once covered with silver. There is a linga inside the main chamber.

The South Tower (Mieu Dong Nam), at one time dedicated to Sandhaka (Shiva), now shelters a linga.

The richly ornamented North-East Tower (Thap Tay Bac) was originally dedicated to Ganesha. The pyramid-shaped summit of the roof of the North-East Tower has disappeared.

The West Tower, of which almost nothing remains, was constructed by King Vikrantavarman during the first half of the 9th century.

Near the North Tower is a small museum with a few mediocre examples of Cham stonework; the explanatory signs are in Vietnamese only. At one time there was a small temple on this site. If you are heading north, be sure to visit the Cham Museum in Danang, which has the finest collection of Cham statuary.

The towers of Po Nagar stand on a granite knoll 2 km north of Nha Trang on the left bank of the Cai River. To get there from Nha Trang, take Quang Trung St (which becomes 2 Thang 4 St) north across Ha Ra Bridge and Xom Bong Bridge, which span the mouth of the Cai River.

Hon Chong Promontory

Hon Chong is a narrow granite promontory that juts out into the turquoise waters of the South China Sea. The superb views of the mountainous coastline north of Nha Trang and nearby islands can be enjoyed while sipping something cool at one of the shaded refreshment kiosks located on a bluff overlooking the promontory.

To the north-west is Nui Co Tien (Fairy Mountain), whose three summits are believed to resemble a reclining female fairy. The peak on the right is her face, which is gazing up towards the sky; the middle peak is her breasts; and the summit on the left (the highest) forms her crossed legs.

To the north-east is Hon Rua (Tortoise Island), which really does resemble a tortoise. The two islands of Hon Yen are off in the distance to the east. A bit south of Hon Chong (that is, towards Nha Trang) and a few dozen metres from the beach is tiny Hon Do (Red Island), which has a Buddhist temple on top.

There is a gargantuan handprint on the massive boulder balanced at the tip of the promontory. According to local legend, it was made by a drunk male giant fairy when he fell down upon spying a female fairy bathing nude at Bai Tien (Fairy Beach), which is the point of land closest to Hon Rua. Despite the force of his fall, the giant managed to get up and eventually catch the fairy. The two began a life together but soon the gods intervened and punished the male fairy, sending him off to a 're-education camp' (this is evidently a post-1975 version of the story) for an indefinite sentence.

The love-sick female fairy waited patiently for her husband to come back, but after a very long time, despairing that he might never return, she lay down in sorrow and turned into Nui Co Tien (Fairy Mountain). When the giant male fairy finally returned and saw what had become of his wife, he prostrated himself in grief next to the boulder with his handprint on it. He, too, turned to stone and can be seen to this day.

Hon Chong is 3.5 km from central Nha Trang. To get there from Po Nagar, head north on 2 Thang 4 St for 400 metres. Just before 15 2 Thang 4 St, turn right onto Nguyen Dinh Chieu St and follow the road for about 700 metres. If you prefer to travel to Hon Chong by Lambretta, catch one heading to Dong De at the Dam Market Lambretta Station.

Beaches

Nha Trang Beach Coconut palms provide shelter for both bathers and strollers along most of Nha Trang's 6 km of beachfront. Three clusters of refreshment stalls sell drinks and light food. The water is usually remarkably clear.

Hon Chong Beach Hon Chong Beach (Bai Tam Hon Chong) is a series of beaches that begin just north of Hon Chong Promontory; fishers live here among the coconut palms. Behind the beaches are steep mountains whose lower reaches support crops that include mangoes and bananas.

Pasteur Institute

Nha Trang's Pasteur Institute was founded in 1895 by Dr Alexandre Yersin (1863-1943), who was – from among the tens of thousands of colonists who spent time in Vietnam – probably the Frenchman most beloved by the Vietnamese. Born in Sweden of French parents, Dr Yersin came to Vietnam in 1889 after working under Louis Pasteur in Paris. He spent the next 4 years travelling throughout the Central Highlands and recording his observations. During this period he came upon the site of what is now Dalat and recommended to the government that a hill station be established there. In 1894, in Hong Kong, he discovered the rat-borne microbe that causes bubonic plague. Dr Yersin was the first to introduce rubber and quinine-producing trees to Vietnam.

Today, the Pasteur Institute in Nha Trang coordinates vaccination and hygiene programmes for the country's southern coastal region. Despite its minuscule budget and antiquated equipment (the labs look much as they did half a century ago), the Institute produces vaccines (eg rabies, diphtheria, pertussis, typhoid) and tries to carry out research in microbiology, virology and epidemiology. Vietnam's two other Pasteur Institutes are in Saigon and Dalat.

Dr Yersin's library and office are now a museum; items on display include laboratory equipment (such as his astronomical instruments) and some of his personal effects. There is a picture of Dr Yersin above the door to the veranda. The model boat was given to him by local fishermen, with whom he spent a great deal of time. The Institute library, which is across the landing from the museum, houses many of Dr Yersin's books as well as modern scientific journals, mostly from Eastern Europe. At his request, Dr Yersin is buried near Nha Trang.

To find someone to show you the museum (Vien Bao Tang), ask around in the main building (a mauve-coloured two storey structure) during working hours (except at lunchtime). The museum is on the 2nd floor of the back wing of the main building. To get there, go up the stairs near the sign that reads Thu Vien (Library).

Long Son Pagoda

Long Son Pagoda (also known as Tinh Hoi Khanh Hoa Pagoda and An Nam Phat Hoc Hoi Pagoda), a sight popular with domestic tourists, is about 500 metres west of the railroad station opposite 15 23 Thang 10 St. The pagoda, now home to nine monks, was founded in the late 19th century and has been rebuilt several times over the years. The entrance and roofs are decorated with mosaic dragons made of glass and bits of ceramic tile. The main sanctuary is an attractive hall adorned with modern interpretations of traditional motifs. Note the ferocious nose hairs on the colourful dragons which are wrapped around the pillars on either side of the main altar.

At the top of the hill behind the pagoda is the huge white Buddha, seated on a lotus blossom, which is visible from all over the city. There are great views of Nha Trang and nearby rural areas from the platform around the 14 metre high figure, which was built in 1963. As you approach the pagoda from the street, the 152 stone steps up the hill to the Buddha begin to the right of the structure.

Nha Trang Cathedral

Nha Trang Cathedral, built in French Gothic

style and complete with medieval-looking stained glass windows, stands on a small hill overlooking the railway station. It was constructed of simple cement blocks between 1928 and 1933. Today, the Cathedral is the seat of the bishop of Nha Trang. In 1988, a Catholic cemetery not far from the church was disinterred to make room for a new building for the railway station. The ashes were brought to the Cathedral and reburied in cavities behind the wall of plaques lining the ramp up the hill.

Masses are held daily at 5 am and 4.30 pm and on Sundays at 5 am, 7 am and 4.30 pm. If the main gate on Thai Nguyen St is closed, go up the ramp opposite 17 Nguyen Trai St to the back of the building.

Oceanographic Institute
The Oceanographic Institute (Vien Nghiem Cuu Bien; tel 22536), founded in 1923, has an aquarium (*ho ca*) and specimen room open to the public; it also has a library. The ground-floor aquarium's 23 tanks are home to a variety of colourful live specimens of local marine life, including seahorses. It is open daily from 7 to 11.30 am and 1.30 to 5 pm; the admission fee is 1000d.

Behind the main building and across the volleyball court is a large hall filled with 60,000 dead specimens of sea life including stuffed sea birds and fish, corals and the corporeal remains of various marine creatures preserved in glass jars.

The Oceanographic Institute is 6 km south of Nha Trang in the port village of Cau Da (also called Cau Be). To get there, go south on Tran Phu St (which becomes Tu Do St south of the airport) all the way to the end of the street. Lambrettas to Cau Da (fare: 400d) leave from Dam Market Lambretta Station.

Mieu Island
Mieu Island (Tri Nguyen Island) is touted in tourist literature as the site of an 'outdoor aquarium' (Ho Ca Tri Nguyen). In fact, the 'aquarium' is an important fish-breeding farm where over 40 species of fish, crustaceans and other marine creatures are raised in three separate compartments. There is a cafe built on stilts over the water; canoes, it is said, can be rented nearby.

The main village on Mieu Island is Tri Nguyen. Bai Soai is a gravel beach on the far side of Mieu Island from Cau Da.

Getting There & Away If you have lots of money and little time, you can book an expensive tourist boat with Khanh Hoa Tourism or the Ship Chandler Company. Impoverished and less-hurried travellers might catch one of the regular ferries that go to Tri Nguyen village from Cau Da Dock, which is a few hundred metres south of the Oceanographic Institute.

Bao Dai's Villas
Between the mid-'50s and 1975, Bao Dai's Villas (tel 22449, 21124) were used by high-ranking officials of the South Vietnamese government, including President Thieu. This all changed in 1975, when the villas were taken over for use by high-ranking Communist officials, who included Prime Minister Pham Van Dong. Today, low-ranking 'capitalist tourists' can rent a room in the Villas for US$35 a night (for details, see 'Places to Stay').

Bao Dai's five villas, built in the 1920s, are set on three hills with brilliant views of the South China Sea, Nha Trang Bay (to the north) and Cau Da port (to the south). Between the buildings wind paths lined with tropical bushes and trees. Most of the villas' furnishings have not been changed in decades.

To get to Bao Dai's Villas from Nha Trang, turn left off Tu Do St (the continuation of Tran Phu Blvd) a bit past the white cement oil storage tanks (but before reaching Cau Da village). The Villas are several hundred metres north of the Oceanographic Institute.

Bamboo Island (Hon Tre)
Bamboo Island (Hon Tre), several km from the southern part of Nha Trang Beach, is the largest island in the Nha Trang area. Tru Beach (Bai Tru) is at the northern end of the island. Ebony Island (Hon Mun), just south of Bamboo Island, is known for its snorkell-

ing. To get to either island, you'll probably have to hire a boat.

Hon Yen

Hon Yen (Salangane Island) is the name of two lump-shaped islands visible in the distance from Nha Trang Beach. Hon Yen and other islands off Khanh Hoa Province are the source of Vietnam's finest salangane (swifts') nests. The nests are used in birds' nest soup as well as in traditional medicine, and are considered an aphrodisiac. It is said that Emperor Minh Mang, who ruled Vietnam from 1820 to 1840, derived his extraordinary virility from the consumption of salangane nests.

The nests, which the salanganes (or swifts) build out of their silk-like salivary secretions, are semi-oval and about 5 to 8 cm in diameter. They are usually harvested twice a year. Red nests are the most highly prized. Annual production in Khanh Hoa and Phu Yen provinces is about 1000 kg. At present, salangane nests fetch US$2000 per kilo in the international marketplace!

There is a small, secluded beach at Hon Yen. The 17 km trip out to the islands takes 3 to 4 hours by small boat.

Thung Chai Basket Boats

The 2-metre-wide round baskets used by fishers to transport themselves from the shore to their boats (and between boats) are made of woven bamboo strips covered with pitch. They are known in Vietnamese as *thung chai* (*thung* means 'basket', *chai* means 'pitch'). Rowed standing up, a *thung chai* can carry four or five people.

Nha Trang's fishing fleet operates mostly at night, spending the days in port for rest and equipment repair.

Dien Khanh Citadel

Dien Khanh Citadel dates from the 17th century Trinh Dynasty. It was rebuilt by Prince Nguyen Anh (later Emperor Gia Long) in 1793 during his successful offensive against the Tay Son Rebels. Only a few sections of the walls and gates are extant. Dien Khanh Citadel is 11 km west of Nha Trang near the villages of Dien Toan and Dien Thanh. The best way to get to Dien Khanh Citadel is to take a Lambretta to Thanh from Dam Market Lambretta Station.

Ba Ho Falls

Ba Ho Falls, with its three waterfalls and three pools, is in a forested area 19 km north of Nha Trang and about 1 km from the road; it is a great place for a picnic. Ba Ho Falls is near Ninh Ich Xa in Vinh Xuong District and not far from Phu Huu village. To get there, take the bus to Ninh Hoa from the Short-Haul Bus Station.

Places to Stay

Nha Trang Beach The following hotels along Nha Trang's municipal beach are listed from north to south:

Four storey *Nha Nghi 378 Bo Noi Vu* (tel 22216; 59 rooms) is at 48 Nguyen Binh Khiem St at the northern tip of Nha Trang Beach; rooms cost between 6000 and 30,000d. This establishment is frequented by domestic tour groups.

The tourist-class *Thang Loi Hotel* (tel 22241), which resembles an American-style motel, is 100 metres from the beach at 4 Pasteur St, one of the few streets in Vietnam to retain its French name.

The *Thong Nhat Hotel* (tel 22966) is at 18 Tran Phu St (corner Yersin St); doubles cost between US$24 and US$40.

Nha Khach Nha Trang (tel 22671; 83 rooms) is at 24 Tran Phu Blvd. Foreigners are charged US$12.50 for a double with a fan and US$14.50 to US$17 for a double with air-con. Guests have reported that the management is uncooperative and that maintenance is poor.

The *Hai Yen Hotel* (tel 22828, 22974; over 100 rooms), whose name means 'sea swift', has two entrances, the main one at 40 Tran Phu Blvd and the other at 1 Tran Hung Dao St. Foreigners are charged US$10/17.25 for doubles without/with air-conditioning; the deluxe suite costs US$35. Locals pay 13,400d for a double with a fan. The office of Khanh Hoa Tourism is around back.

The *Hung Dao Hotel* (tel 22246; 27

rooms) is at 3 Tran Hung Dao St (next to the Tran Hung Dao St entrance of the Hai Yen Hotel); triples with fans cost US$10. The office of Nha Trang Tourism (tel 21231) is here.

Four storey *Khach San 58 Tran Phu* (tel 22997; 35 rooms), set 50 metres off the street at 58 Tran Phu Blvd, is across from a particularly nice section of the beach; doubles without/with air-con go for 10,000d/20,000d. This place belongs to the Vietnamese Naval Ministry.

The *Hai Duong Beach Bungalows* (tel 21150; 20 bungalows) are on Tran Phu Blvd a few hundred metres south of one of the gates to the airport. The steep-roofed bungalows, which are often booked up, are in a grove of casuarina trees right along the beach; each has two beds and costs 10,000d a night. If you're staying here during the rainy season, make sure your bungalow doesn't leak. The Hai Duong complex includes a volleyball court and a restaurant.

Nha Nghi Thuong Nghiep (tel 22867; 30 rooms) at 36 Tu Do St (the continuation of Tran Phu Blvd) is a guest house for workers' groups, but if they have a spare room they'll rent it out to travellers. Beds here cost 2500d. The seashore opposite the hotel is occupied by commercial buildings, but there is a nice beach 500 metres to the north.

City Centre *Nha Khach 25 Phan Chu Trinh* (tel 22897; 43 rooms) is 500 metres from the beach at 25 Phan Chu Trinh St; domestic tourists pay 6000d for doubles.

The *Nha Trang Hotel* (Chi Nhanh Khach San Nha Trang; tel 22347 and 22224; 74 rooms) is a seven storey building at 133 Thong Nhat St; doubles cost between 6000 and 12,000d.

The *Khuong Hai Hotel* (tel 22470; 30 rooms) at 36 Yet Kieu St has doubles for 6000d. To get to reception, go through the hallway on the left side of the building and up the stairs.

Hon Chong Promontory *Nha Nghi Hon Chong* (tel 22188; 48 rooms) on Nguyen Dinh Chieu St is at the summit of a hillock

150 metres from Hon Chong Promontory. Housed in the buildings of what was, before 1975, the American-supported Protestant Theological Seminary, Nha Nghi Hon Chong has quadruples with mattresses, mosquito nets and private bathrooms for 10,000d. This place is popular with domestic tour groups. The rooms are fairly clean and there is a huge on-site dining hall.

Cau Da *Bao Dai's Villas* (tel 22449, 21124) near Cau Da (on the coast 6 km south of Nha Trang) are by far the nicest accommodation in the area. For US$35 per night, you can sleep in a spacious double room with high-ceilings and huge bathrooms where Vietnam's ruling elite has rested itself since the days of French rule. The villas have recently been renovated and new air-conditioning units have been installed. To get to Bao Dai's Villas from Nha Trang, go south on Tran Phu Blvd (which becomes Tu Do St) and turn left just past the white cement oil storage tanks.

Other *Viet Ngu Hotel* (no telephone; 20 rooms) is 50 metres from the entrance to Long Son Pagoda at 25 23 Thang 10 St; doubles cost only 6500d. This privately owned hotel is only half a km from the railway station but quite a way from the water.

The *Nha Trang Railroad Station Dormitory* (Nha Tro Duong Sat Ga Nha Trang) is in the first building to your right as you exit the railway terminal; they offer cheap dormitory accommodation. There is also dormitory accommodation (*phong tro*) at *Lien Tinh Bus Station (Ben Xe Lien Tinh)*.

Places to Eat
Local Specialties Nha Trang is known for its excellent seafood.

Green dragon fruit (*thanh long*), which is the size and shape of a small pineapple and has an almost-smooth magenta skin, grows only in the Nha Trang area. Its delicious white meat is speckled with black seeds and tastes a bit like kiwifruit. Green dragon fruit grows on a kind of creeping cactus – said to resemble a green dragon – that climbs up the trunks and branches of trees and flourishes on parched hillsides that get very little water. *Thanh long* is in season from May to September and can be purchased at Dam Market.

Locals often make a refreshing drink out of crushed green dragon fruit, ice, sugar and sweetened condensed milk. They also use it to make jam.

Nha Trang Beach The restaurant at the *Hai Yen Hotel* is open from 5 am to midnight. The *Thong Nhat Hotel* also has a restaurant.

There are three clusters of cafes, serving mostly refreshments, along the beach. They are across Tran Phu Blvd from the Thong Nhat Hotel (18 Tran Phu Blvd), the Hai Yen Hotel (40 Tran Phu Blvd) and the Ship Chandler Company office (74 Tran Phu Blvd).

Dam Market Area One of the best seafood restaurants in town is the *Lac Canh Restaurant*, which is a block east of Dam Market at 11 Hang Ca St. Giant shrimps, lobsters and the like are grilled right at your table (if you so order).

Nha Hang 33 Le Loi at 33 Le Loi St (corner Nguyen Du St) is opposite the main gate to Dam Market. *Nha Hang 31 Le Loi* is next door.

Vegetarian There is a vegetarian restaurant, *Quay Hang Com Chay*, in the covered semi-circular food pavilion north-east of the main building of Dam Market. The restaurant is right across from stall number 117 (as indicated by little blue tags with red numbers on them displayed on each of the stalls that encircle the main market building). The food here is made of beans and vegetables and is prepared to look and taste like popular meat dishes.

Downtown The *Binh Minh Restaurant*, founded in 1953, is at 64 Hoang Van Thu St (corner Yet Kieu St); their Vietnamese dishes are excellent. *Pho Hanoi* at 21 Le Thanh Phuong St is open from 5.30 to 10 am and from 3 to 10 pm; this place's speciality is tasty cinnamon-flavoured *pho*. There are

several cafes and restaurants in the vicinity of the Nha Trang Hotel.

For ice cream, try the shops around 52 Quang Trung St (corner Ly Thanh Ton St).

Snorkelling, Skin Diving & Boats
Khanh Hoa Province's 71 offshore islands are renowned for the remarkably clear water surrounding them. The Ship Chandler Company (tel 21195; at 74 Tran Phu Blvd) and Khanh Hoa Province Tourism (tel 22753; at 1 Tran Hung Dao St) plan to begin renting out underwater fishing and skin-diving gear. Boats can be hired from both, but you'll probably get a much better deal on the docks at Cau Da (see 'Getting Around'). Snorkelling equipment can be purchased at Dam Market or rented from the Ship Chandler Company.

Things to Buy
There are a number of shops selling beautiful seashells (and items made from seashells) near the Oceanographic Institute in Cau Da village. As a brochure of Nha Trang Tourism put it, 'Before leaving Nha Trang, tourists had better call at Cau Da to get some souvenirs of the sea ... for their dears at home'. Inexpensive guitars are on sale at 24 Hai Ba Trung St (corner Phan Chu Trinh St). The Hai Yen Hotel has a small gift shop.

The wonderful green dragon fruit (*thanh long*) is sold in and around Dam Market from May to September.

Getting There & Away
Road distances from Nha Trang:

Ho Chi Minh City	448 km
Phan Rang	104 km
Buon Ma Thuot	205 km
Qui Nhon	238 km
Quang Ngai	412 km
Pleiku	424 km
Danang	541 km

A series of roughly parallel roads head inland from near Nha Trang, linking Vietnam's deltas and coastal regions with the Central Highlands.

Air Vietnam Airlines flies from Saigon to Nha Trang every Sunday; the one-way fare is US$39. There are also regular flights to Nha Trang from Danang and Hanoi. Vietnam Airlines' Nha Trang office (tel 21147) is at 82 Tran Phu St.

Bus Express and regular buses from Saigon to Nha Trang depart from Mien Dong Bus Station. By express bus, the trip takes 11 to 12 hours.

Lien Tinh Bus Station (Ben Xe Lien Tinh; tel 22192), Nha Trang's main intercity bus terminal, is opposite 212 Ngo Gia Tu St; there are dormitory accommodation (*phong tro*) here. Non-express buses from Lien Tinh Bus Station go to:

Bao Loc
Bien Hoa (11 hours)
Buon Ma Thuot (6 hours)
Dalat (6 hours)
Danang (14 hours)
Di Linh
Ho Chi Minh City (12 hours)
Phan Rang (2½ hours)
Quang Ngai
Qui Nhon (7 hours)
Pleiku (10 hours)

Express buses leave from two different stations. The Youth Tourism Express Bus Office (Du Lich Thanh Nien; tel 22010) is just off Yersin St at 6 Hoang Hoa Tham St; tickets are sold daily from 4 am to 6 pm. There are buses from here to:

Destination	Days	Departs	Duration
Buon Ma Thuot	daily	5 am	5 hours
Dalat	Tu/Th/St	5 am	5 hours
Danang	M/W/F	5 am	3 hours
Saigon	daily	5 am 4.30 pm	11 hours

The Express Bus Station (Tram Xe Toc Hanh; tel 22397, 22884) is about 150 metres from the Hung Dao Hotel at 46 Le Thanh Ton St; the ticket office is open every day from 6 am to 4.30 pm. Tickets for early morning buses must be purchased 1 to 3 days before departure. Tickets for most buses leaving from the Express Bus Station are also sold at Lien Tinh Bus Station. Buses depart at 5 am (unless otherwise indicated) to:

Buon Ma Thuot (5.30 am; 5 hours)
Dalat (5 hours),
Danang (13 hours),
Hanoi (40 hours)
Ho Chi Minh City (5 am & 4.30 pm; 12 hours)
Hué (15 hours)
Quang Binh
Quang Ngai (10 hours)
Qui Nhon (6 hours)
Vinh (35 hours)

The Short-Haul Bus Station (Ben Xe Noi Tinh; tel 22191) is opposite 111 2 Thang 4 St. Aged Renault and DeSoto omnibuses depart from here to Cam Ranh, Nhieu Giang, Ninh Hoa, Tuy Hoa, Tu Bong, Song Cau, Song Hinh, Tay Son and Van Gia.

Train The Nha Trang Railway Station (Ga Nha Trang; tel 22113), overlooked by the nearby Cathedral, is across the street from 26 Thai Nguyen St; the ticket office is open between 7 am and 2 pm only.

Northward-bound TN2 leaves Nha Trang at 9.45 am every day for its 43 hour trip to Hanoi; either STN2 or STN4 departs each day at 10 pm. Both take 39 hours to Hanoi. On even days of the month, NH2 leaves Nha Trang at 3 pm, arriving in Danang at 8 am the next day and in Hué at noon. A local train departs at 9.30 pm, arriving in Qui Nhon 10 hours later.

Southward-bound TN1 leaves Nha Trang every day at 5 pm and takes 14 hours to get to Ho Chi Minh City; either STN3 or STN5 departs every day at 2 am, arriving in Saigon at 2 pm. On Tuesdays, Thursdays and Sundays, AR1 (an autorail) leaves Nha Trang at 6 pm, arriving in Ho Chi Minh City at 6 am the next day; its alter ego, AR2, departs from Ho Chi Minh City on Mondays, Wednesdays and Fridays.

Getting Around

Local Transport Dam Market Lambretta Station (Ben Xe Lam Cho Dam) is on Nguyen Hong Son St near the corner of Nguyen Thai Hoc St. It is due north of the main building of Dam Market, which is a round modern structure several stories high. Lambrettas from Dam Market Lambretta Station go to Cau Da (or Cau Be, also known as Chut), where the Oceanographic Institute and the fishing boat dock are located; Dong De (near Hon Chong); and Thanh (take this one to get to Dien Khanh Citadel).

There are bicycle parts shops around 49 Ngo Gia Tu St and in the vicinity of Dam Market.

Boat The best place in the Nha Trang area to hire boats is the fishing boat dock at Cau Da (Ben Do Cau Da), which is 6 km due south of Nha Trang. Motorised 7 metre boats cost 35,000d per hour; a round-trip to Mieu Island costs about 20,000d. Boats with a 50 person capacity cost 40,000d for the round-trip to Mieu Island. Small boats rowed standing up can be hired here as well. It may also be possible to hire boats a few hundred metres away at the larger Nha Trang Ship Dock (Cang Nha Trang).

Tourist boats can be rented from both Khanh Hoa Tourism and the Ship Chandler Company (see the 'Information' section for details).

Ferries to Tri Nguyen village on Mieu Island depart from Cau Da when full; the fare is 500d.

DAI LANH BEACH

Semicircular casuarina-shaded Dai Lanh Beach is 83 km north of Nha Trang and 153 km south of Qui Nhon on National Highway 1. At the southern end of the beach is a vast sand-dune causeway; it connects the mainland to Hon Gom, a mountainous peninsula almost 30 km in length. The main village on Hon Gom is Dam Mon (known to the French as Port Dayot), which is on a sheltered bay facing the island of Hon Lon.

At the northern end of Dai Lanh Beach is Dai Lanh Promontory (Mui Dai Lanh), named Cap Varella by the French.

Places to Stay

There is a tourist hotel just off National Highway 1, a few hundred metres south of the fishing village of Dai Lanh.

Getting There & Away

Dai Lanh Beach runs along National Highway 1, so any vehicle travelling along the coast between Nha Trang and Tuy Hoa (or Qui Nhon) will get you there.

Qui Nhon

Qui Nhon (or Quy Nhon; population 188,000) is the capital of Binh Dinh Province and one of Vietnam's more active second-string seaports. The beaches in the immediate vicinity of the city are nothing to write home about and the city itself is a bit dingy, but Qui Nhon is a convenient and

■	PLACES TO STAY
1	Viet Cuong Hotel
5	Thanh Binh Hotel
6	Dong Phuong Hotel
8	Nha Khach Ngan Hang Dau Tu (hotel)
9	Qui Nhon Peace Hotel
12	Nha Khach Huu Nghi (Hotel)
21	Quy Nhon Tourist Hotel

▼	PLACES TO EAT
3	Pho 350 (soup shop)
4	Soup Shops
10	Ngoc Lien Restaurant
11	Olympic Hotel & Vu Hung Restaurant
20	Cang Tin (restaurant)

●	OTHER
2	Qui Nhon Bus Station
7	Short-Haul Transport Station
13	Long Khanh Pagoda
14	GPO
15	Foreign Trade Bank
16	Lon Market
17	Church
18	War Memorial
19	Express Bus Station
22	Zoo
23	Binh Dinh Tourism

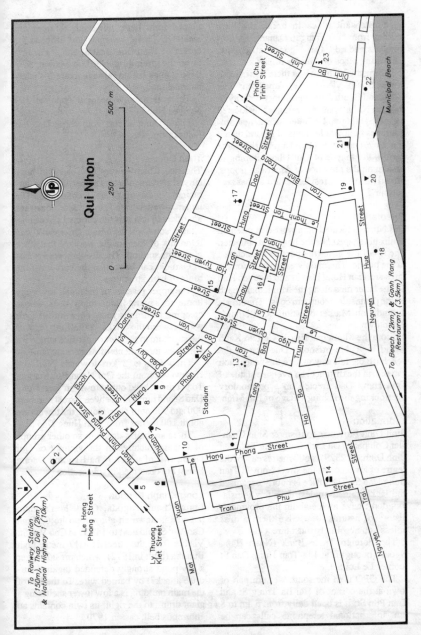

Qui Nhon

500 m

250

0

To Railway Station
(150m), Thap Doi (2km)
& National Highway 1 (10km)

Le Hong
Phong Street

Ly Thuong
Kiet Street

To Beach (2km) & Ganh Rang
Restaurant (3.5km)

Municipal Beach

Phan Chu
Trinh Street

Stadium

not-unpleasant place to break the long journey from Nha Trang to Danang. By provincial standards, Qui Nhon is a hopping, happening place on Sunday nights.

During the Vietnam War there was considerable South Vietnamese, American, Viet Cong and South Korean military activity in the Qui Nhon area, and refugees dislocated by the fighting and counter-insurgency programmes built whole slums of tin and thatch shacks around the city. During the same period, the mayor of Qui Nhon, hoping to cash in on the presence of American troops, turned his official residence into a 'massage parlour'.

Orientation
Qui Nhon is located on a west-east oriented peninsula shaped like the nose of an anteater. The tip of the nose (the port area) is closed to the public. The main west-east thoroughfares are Tran Hung Dao St and Nguyen Hue St; the latter runs along the Municipal Beach on the peninsula's southern coast. The streets around Lon Market constitute Qui Nhon's downtown.

From the Municipal Beach, Cu Lao Xanh Island is visible offshore. Due east of the beach (to the left as you face the water) you can see, in the distance, an oversize statue of Tran Hung Dao erected on a promontory overlooking the fishing village of Hai Minh.

Information
Binh Dinh Province Tourism & Ship Chandler Company (Du Lich Cung Ung Tau Bien Binh Dinh; tel 2329) is 600 metres east of the centre of town across the street from 78 Tran Hung Dao St. The office is poorly organised and lacks trained guides; their few translators don't have a clue about the province's history or natural sites. Give them a miss unless you absolutely must hire a car.

The Foreign Trade Bank (Ngan Hang Ngoai Thuong) is at 148 Tran Hung Dao St (corner Le Loi St).

The GPO is in the south-western part of town at the corner of Hai Ba Trung St and Tran Phu St; it is open daily from 6 am to 8 pm. International telephone calls can be placed from here; telegraph services are available. There is a small post office at the corner of Phan Boi Chau St and 1 Thang 4 St on the ground floor of Lon Market; they have stamps but no postage metre for international mail.

There is a large hospital opposite 309 Nguyen Hue St.

Photo Dung at 305 Tran Hung Dao has Kodak print film.

Thap Doi
The two Cham towers of Thap Doi have curved pyramidal roofs rather than the terracing typical of Cham architecture. The larger tower, whose four granite doorways are oriented towards the cardinal directions, retains some of its ornate brickwork and remnants of the granite statuary that once graced its summit. The dismembered torsos of Garudas can be seen at the corners of the roofs of both structures.

The upper reaches of the small tower are home to several flourishing trees whose creeping tendrilous roots have forced their way between the bricks, enmeshing parts of the structure in the sort of net-like tangle for which the monuments of Angkor are famous.

Thap Doi is 2 km towards National Highway 1 from the Qui Nhon Bus Station. To get there, head out of town on Tran Hung Dao St and turn right between street numbers 900 and 906 onto Thap Doi St; the towers are about 100 metres from Tran Hung Dao St.

There are half-a-dozen or so other groups of Cham structures in the vicinity of Qui Nhon, two of which (Cha Ban and Duong Long) are described in this section.

Long Khanh Pagoda
Long Khanh Pagoda, Qui Nhon's main pagoda, is down an alley opposite 62 Tran Cao Van St and next to 143 Tran Cao Van St. Visible from the street is a 17 metre high Buddha (built in 1972), which presides over a lily pond strongly defended (against surprise attack?) by barbed wire. To the left of the main building is a low tower sheltering a giant drum; to the right, its twin contains an enormous bell, cast in 1970.

The main sanctuary was completed in 1946 but was damaged during the Franco-Viet Minh War; repairs were completed in 1957. In front of the large copper Thich Ca Buddha (with its multi-coloured neon halo) is a drawing of multi-armed and multi-eyed Chuan De. There is a colourfully painted Buddha at the edge of the raised platform. In the corridor which passes behind the main altar is a bronze bell with Chinese inscriptions; it dates from 1805.

Under the eaves of the left-hand building of the courtyard behind the sanctuary hangs a blow-up of the famous photograph of the bonze Thich Quang Duc immolating himself in Saigon in June 1963 to protest the policies of the Diem regime. The 2nd level of the two storey building behind the courtyard contains memorial plaques for deceased monks (on the middle altar) and laypeople.

Long Khanh Pagoda was founded around 1700 by a Chinese merchant, Duc Son (1679-1741). The seven monks who live here preside over the religious affairs of Qui Nhon's relatively active Buddhist community. Single-sex religion classes for children are held on Sundays.

Qui Nhon Municipal Beach

Qui Nhon Municipal Beach, which extends along the southern side of the anteater's nose, consists of a few hundred metres of clean sand shaded by a coconut grove. The nicest section of beach is across from the Qui Nhon Tourist Hotel. Farther west, the shore is lined with the boats and shacks of fishing families.

A longer, quieter bathing beach begins about 2 km south-west of the Municipal Beach. To get there, follow Nguyen Hue St away from the tip of the peninsula westward. Part of the seafront near here is lined with industrial plants, some of which belong to the military. Ganh Rang Restaurant is at the far end of the beach.

Binh Dinh-Xiem Riep-Ratanakiri Zoo

This small seaside zoo, whose inhabitants include monkeys, crocodiles, porcupines and bears, is named for the two Cambodian provinces the animals came from. Siem Reap (Vietnamese: *Xiem Riep*) Province, where the monuments of Angkor are located, is in the north-western part of the country. Ratanakiri is in Cambodia's far north-eastern corner and borders both Laos and Vietnam. The uncharitable might classify the animals here as war booty (or prisoners of war). The zoo is at 2B Nguyen Hue St.

Lon Market

Lon Market (Cho Lon), Qui Nhon's central market, is a large modern building enclosing a courtyard in which fruits and vegetables are sold. Most goods one can reasonably expect to find in the provinces can be purchased here. Tu Hai Restaurant is on the 3rd floor facing Phan Boi Chau St.

Cha Ban

The ruins of the former Cham capital of Cha Ban (also known at various times as Vijaya and Qui Nhon) are 26 km north of Qui Nhon and 5 km from Binh Dinh. The city was built within a rectangular wall measuring 1400 metres by 1100 metres. Canh Tien Tower (Tower of Brass) stands in the centre of the enclosure. The tomb of General Vu Tinh is nearby.

Cha Ban, which served as the seat of the royal government of Champa from the year 1000 (after the loss of Indrapura, also known as Dong Duong) until 1471, was attacked and plundered repeatedly by the Vietnamese, Khmers and Chinese. In 1044, the Vietnamese prince Phat Ma occupied the city and carried off a great deal of booty as well as the Cham king's wives, harem and female dancers, musicians and singers. Cha Ban was under the control of a Khmer overseer from 1190 to 1220.

In 1377, the Vietnamese were defeated in an attempt to capture Cha Ban and their king was killed. The Vietnamese Emperor Le Thanh Ton breached the eastern gate of the city in 1471 and captured the Cham king and 50 members of the royal family. During this, the last great battle fought by the Chams, 60,000 Chams were killed and 30,000 more were taken prisoner by the Vietnamese.

During the Tay Son Rebellion, Cha Ban served as the capital of the region of central Vietnam ruled by the eldest of the three Tay Son brothers. It was attacked in 1793 by the forces of Nguyen Anh (later Emperor Gia Long) but the assault failed. In 1799, the forces of Nguyen Anh, under the command of General Vu Tinh, lay siege to the city and captured it. The Tay Son soon re-occupied the port of Thi Nai (modern-day Qui Nhon) and then lay siege to Cha Ban themselves. The siege continued for over a year, and by June 1801, Vu Tinh's provisions were gone. Food was in short supply; all the horses and elephants had long before been eaten. Refusing to consider the ignominy of surrender, Vu Tinh had an octagonal wood tower constructed. He filled it with gunpowder and, arrayed in his ceremonial robes, went inside and blew himself up. Upon hearing the news of the death of his dedicated general, Nguyen Anh wept.

Duong Long Cham Towers

The Duong Long Cham Towers (Thap Duong Long, the 'Towers of Ivory') are 8 km from Cha Ban. The largest of the three brick towers is embellished with granite ornamentation representing nagas and elephants. Over the doors are bas-reliefs of women, dancers, standing lions, monsters and various animals. The corners of the structure are formed by enormous dragon heads.

Hoi Van Hot Springs

The famous hot springs of Hoi Van are north of Qui Nhon in Phu Cat District.

Quang Trung Museum

The Quang Trung Museum is dedicated to Nguyen Hue, the second-oldest of the three brothers who led the Tay Son Rebellion, who crowned himself Emperor Quang Trung in 1788. In 1789 (a few months before a Parisian mob stormed the Bastille), Quang Trung led the campaign that overwhelmingly defeated a Chinese invasion force of 200,000 troops near Hanoi. This epic battle is still celebrated as one of the greatest triumphs in Vietnamese history. Quang Trung died in 1792 at the age of 40.

During his reign, Quang Trung was something of a social reformer. He encouraged land reform, revised the system of taxation, improved the army and emphasised education, opening numerous schools and encouraging the development of Vietnamese poetry and literature. Indeed, Communist literature often portrays him as the leader of a peasant revolution whose progressive policies were crushed by the reactionary Nguyen Dynasty, which came to power in 1802 and was overthrown by Ho Chi Minh in 1945.

The Quang Trung Museum is known for its demonstrations of *binh dinh vo*, a traditional martial art that is performed with a bamboo stick. To get there take National Highway 19 towards Pleiku. The museum, which is 48 km from Qui Nhon, is in Tay Son District 5 km off the highway. The Tay Son area produces a wine made of sticky rice.

Vinh Son Falls

Vinh Son Falls is 18 km off National Highway 19, which links Binh Dinh and Pleiku. To get there, you might try taking a Vinh Thanh-bound truck from the Short-Haul Transport Station in Qui Nhon and changing vehicles in Vinh Thanh.

Places to Stay

Nha Khach Ngan Hang Dau Tu (tel 2012; 15 rooms) is two blocks from the bus station at 399 Tran Hung Dao St. This place is centrally located (though it's a bit far from the beach), the rooms are clean and quiet and the management is friendly. Rooms with fans range from 5000d for a single to 15,000d for a quadruple with private bath. To get to the reception desk, go almost to the back of the building and turn up the stairs to the right. The *Qui Nhon Peace Hotel* (Khach San Hoa Binh; tel 2900; 64 rooms) is half a block from Nha Khach Ngan Hang Dau Tu opposite 266 Tran Hung Dao St; doubles cost 12,000d.

Nha Khach Huu Nghi (tel 2152; 22 rooms) at 210 Phan Boi Chau St is a bit grimy but remains popular with domestic travellers. Doubles go for 5000d (with fan) and 6000d (with air-con); most rooms come with private bath. There is a restaurant on the ground floor.

The *Viet Cuong Hotel* (tel 2434; 22 rooms), a basic but serviceable place midway between the bus station and the railroad station (about 100 metres from each), is at 460 Tran Hung Dao St. Doubles cost between 4000d and 6000d; the more expensive rooms have attached bath.

The modern *Dong Phuong Hotel* (tel 2915, 2562; 20 rooms) at 39-41 Mai Xuan Thuong St (near the corner of Le Hong Phong St) has doubles starting at 8000d. There is a restaurant on the ground floor.

The *Olympic Hotel* (Khach San Lien Doanh; tel 2375; 23 rooms) is next to the stadium; singles start at 6000d; doubles range from 7500 to 15,000d. The entrance is opposite 167 Le Hong Phong St (corner Tang Bat Ho St). Vu Hung Restaurant is upstairs.

The *Thanh Binh Hotel* (tel 2041; 80 rooms) is 300 metres from the bus station at 17 Ly Thuong Kiet St. This place, which belongs to the Provincial People's Committee, is frequented by government officials so certain standards of cleanliness are maintained. Doubles with fan cost between 4500d (with a mat) to 12,000d; a double room with air-conditioning costs 18,000d.

The four storey *Trade Union Guest House* (Nha Khach Lien Doan Lao Dong; tel 2247; 18 double rooms) is inconveniently located at 686 Tran Hung Dao St, just over 1 km towards National Highway 1 from the bus station; doubles with mats, fans and common toilets cost 6000d. This new but poorly maintained place is used mostly by trade union delegations and truck drivers.

The *Quy Nhon Tourist Hotel* (Khach San Du Lich Quy Nhon; tel 2401, 2329; 47 rooms) is right on Qui Nhon Municipal Beach at 8 Nguyen Hue St. Foreigners, who must pay in US dollars, are charged between US$21 and US$31 for a double; locals pay only about one-sixth these prices. The rooms and common areas are grimy and dimly lit. The only thing this place has going for it is

its proximity to the beach, which is partially offset by its distance from the centre of town. Unless you can figure out a way to convince them to let you pay in dong, the prices are highway robbery. There are few places to eat in the vicinity.

Places to Eat

There are only a handful of proper restaurants in Qui Nhon. One of the best is *Vu Hung Restaurant* (tel 2375, 2908), which is on the roof of the Olympic Hotel. The entrance is opposite 167 Le Hong Phong St (corner Tang Bat Ho St).

Huu Nghi Restaurant is on the ground floor of Nha Khach Huu Nghi at 210 Phan Boi Chau St. They have quite a variety of Vietnamese food and some good Western dishes (stuffed crab, onion soup) as well. The *Dong Phuong Restaurant* at 39-41 Mai Xuan Thuong St is on the ground floor of the Dong Phuong Hotel; it is open from 6 am to 11 pm. They have a rather limited menu of Vietnamese food and only a few Western dishes.

Tu Hai Restaurant (tel 2582) is on the 3rd floor of Lon Market (on the side overlooking Phan Boi Chau St); it is open from 6.30 am to 10 pm. The management is friendly and the menu is in English, but the food is indifferently prepared. Nearby *Bien Sanh Dancing*, an enterprise run as part of Tu Hai Restaurant, offers dancing with a live band from 8 to 10 pm every Tuesday, Thursday and Saturday night.

For tasty food at rock-bottom prices, try the *Ngoc Lien Restaurant*, a favourite with Qui Nhonians, at 288 Le Hong Phong. There are several other homey restaurants in the immediate vicinity.

The *Ganh Rang Restaurant* is 3.5 km west of town along Nguyen Hue St. Built on pylons and set among palms, this privately run restaurant is right on the water at a site said to have been a favourite of Bao Dai's wife.

Soup There is a line of soup shops along Phan Boi Chau St at numbers 286, 288, 290 and 292; they are open from 6 am to 10 pm. *Pho 350*, also open 6 am to 10 pm, is a soup restaurant at 350 Tran Hung Dao St. The *Cang Tin* (restaurant) along the Municipal Beach at 14 Nguyen Hue St sells soup in the morning.

Getting There & Away

Road distances from Qui Nhon:

Hi Chi Minh City	677 km
Nha Trang	238 km
Pleiku	186 km
Kontum	198 km
Quang Ngai	174 km
Danang	303 km

Qui Nhon is 10 km off National Highway 1. It is the nearest coastal city to Pleiku, Kontum and the rest of the northern section of the Central Highlands. National Highway 19 to Tay Son and Pleiku heads westward from Binh Dinh, which is 18 km north of Qui Nhon.

There is a border crossing to Cambodia's remote Ratanakiri Province about 250 km due west of Qui Nhon near the village of Chu Nghe. At present, the crossing is used by Vietnamese companies to bring Ratanakiri's forest products to the coast for export. When the Cambodian civil war ends, it may be possible to visit Ratanakiri, which is not accessible by land from Phnom Penh (the bridges are out), from Qui Nhon.

Air Weekly flights link Ho Chi Minh City and Hanoi with Phu Cat, an airfield 36 km north of Qui Nhon.

In Qui Nhon, the Vietnam Airlines Booking Office (tel 2953) is near the Thanh Binh Hotel in the building next to 30 Nguyen Thai Hoc St. Tickets must be purchased at least 2 days in advance. For airline passengers, transport to and from Phu Cat is provided by Vietnam Airlines. Small trucks to Phu Cat depart from the Short-Haul Transport Station.

Bus Qui Nhon Bus Station (Ben Xe Khach Qui Nhon; tel 2246) is opposite 543 Tran Hung Dao St (across from where Le Hong Phong St hits Tran Hung Dao St). The non-express ticket windows are open from 5 am

to 4 pm; the express ticket window (Khach Di Xe Toc Hanh), which is in the fenced-in enclosure next to the non-express windows, is open from 4 am to 4 pm. Tickets should be purchased the day before departure.

Express buses, all of which leave at 5 am, go to Buon Ma Thuot, Dalat, Danang, Hanoi, Ho Chi Minh City, Hué, Nha Trang, Quang Tri and Vinh.

Non-express buses leave from here to:

Destination	Departs	Duration
An Khe		
An Lao	6 am	
Bong Son	6 am	
Buon Ma Thuot	5 am	8 hrs
Cam Ranh		
Dalat	6 am	10 hrs
Danang	6 am	6 hrs
Hanoi	5 am	39 hrs
Hoai An	6 am	
Ho Chi Minh City	5 am	16 hrs
Hué	6 am	
Kontum	8 am	11 hrs
Nha Trang	5 am	5½ hrs
Phu My	6 am	
Pleiku	6 am	6 hrs
Quang Ngai	6 am	5 hrs
Tam Quan	6 am	
Tuy Hoa		
Van Canh		
Vinh Thanh	6 am	

The Express Bus Station (tel 2172) is 100 metres from the Quy Nhon Tourist Hotel at 14 Nguyen Hue St. There are express buses from here to Buon Ma Thuot, Dalat, Danang, Dong Hoi, Hanoi, Ho Chi Minh City, Hué, Nha Trang, Ninh Binh, Quang Tri, Thanh Hoa and Vinh. All buses depart at 5 am. The ticket window (Phong Ban Ve Xe Toc Hanh Cac Tuyen Duong) is open from 6.30 to 11 am and 1.30 to 5 pm.

Vehicles to places within a 50 km radius of Qui Nhon depart from the Short-Haul Transport Station (Ben Xe 1 Thang 4), which is at the intersection of Phan Boi Chau St and Mai Xuan Thuong St (near 280 Phan Boi Chau St and 60 Mai Xuan Thuong St). Tickets are sold in a kerbside wood and corrugated iron kiosk. Small trucks leave from here to Binh Dinh (6 km from Cha Ban), Dap Da, Dieu Tri (the railway station),

Phu Cat (the airport), Tay Son (vehicles from Tay Son go to within about 5 km of the Quang Trung Museum), Tuy Phuoc and Vinh Thanh.

Train The city of Qui Nhon is poorly served by rail. Qui Nhon Railway Station (Ga Qui Nhon; tel 2036) is at the end of a 10 km spur line off the main north-south track. The station is 70 metres from Tran Hung Dao St on Hoang Hoa Tham St, which intersects Tran Hung Dao St between numbers 661 and 663. There is primitive dormitory accommodation (*nha tro*) at the station for 500d a night.

Only two very slow local trains stop at Qui Nhon Railroad Station. Train DS departs for points south at 9.45 am on even days of the month (its northward-bound twin leaves Saigon on odd days of the month); the trip all the way to Saigon takes 24 hours. Northward-bound 172 leaves at 5 am daily, arriving in Danang about 13 hours later.

The nearest the Reunification Trains (TN and STN) get to Qui Nhon is Dieu Tri, 10 km from the city. Tickets for trains departing from Dieu Tri can be purchased at the Qui Nhon Railroad Station, though if you arrive in Dieu Tri by train, your best bet is to purchase an onward ticket before leaving the station.

Northbound, TN2 departs from Dieu Tri at 4 pm; STN4 pulls out at 4.34 am. Southbound, TN1 departs at 9.55 am; STN3 leaves at 7.40 pm. STN5 and STN6 do not stop at Dieu Tri, which means that Dieu Tri does not have STN service every day of the week. I suggest you double-check the schedule of STN3 and STN4 at the Qui Nhon Railroad Station before making the trip out there. Small trucks from Qui Nhon to Dieu Tri leave from the Short-Haul Transport Station.

SA HUYNH

Sa Huynh is a prosperous little seaside town whose beautiful semicircular beach is bordered by rice paddies and coconut palms. The town is also known for its salt marshes and salt evaporation ponds. In the vicinity of Sa Huynh, archaeologists have unearthed remains of the Dong Son Civilisation dating from the 1st century AD.

Place to Stay

There is a small beach-side hotel, the *Sa Huynh Hotel*, just off National Highway 1.

Getting There & Away

Sa Huynh is on National Highway 1 114 km north of Qui Nhon and 60 km south of Quang Ngai. Non-express trains may stop at the Sa Huynh Railway Station (Ga Sa Huynh).

QUANG NGAI CITY

Quang Ngai City, the capital of Quang Ngai Province, is something of a backwater. Built on the south bank of the Tra Khuc River (known for its oversized water-wheels), the city is about 15 km from the coast, which is lined with beautiful beaches. The city and province of Quang Ngai are also known as Quang Nghia; the name is sometimes abbreviated as Quangai.

Even before WW II, Quang Ngai was an important centre of resistance to the French. During the Franco-Vietminh War, the area was a Viet Minh stronghold. In 1962, the South Vietnamese Government introduced its disastrous strategic hamlet programme to the area. Villagers were forcibly removed from their homes and resettled in fortified hamlets, infuriating and alienating the local population and increasing popular support for the Viet Cong. Some of the bitterest fighting of the Vietnam War took place in Quang Ngai Province.

Son My sub-district, 14 km from Quang Ngai City, was the scene of the infamous My Lai Massacre of 1968, in which hundreds of civilians were slaughtered by American soldiers. A memorial has been erected on the site of the killings.

As a result of the wars, very few bridges in Quang Ngai Province remain intact. At many river crossings, the rust-streaked concrete pylons of the old French bridges, probably destroyed by the Viet Minh, stand next to the ruins of their replacements, blown up by the VC. As it has for 15 or more years, traffic crosses the river on a third bridge,

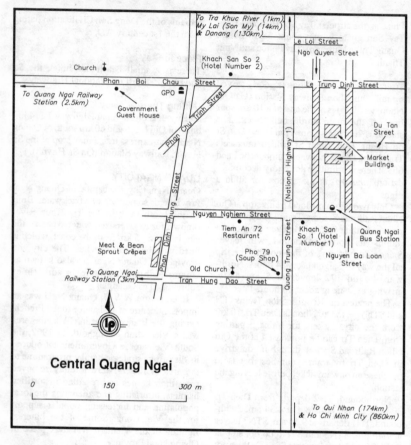

Central Quang Ngai

0   150   300 m

(Map labels:)

To Tra Khuc River (1km), My Lai (Son My) (14km) & Danang (130km)

Le Loi Street
Ngo Quyen Street

Church

Khach San So 2 (Hotel Number 2)

Phan Boi Chau Street
GPO

Le Trung Dinh Street

To Quang Ngai Railway Station (2.5km)

Government Guest House

Phan Chu Trinh Street

Du Tan Street

Market Buildings

(National Highway 1)

Phan Dinh Phung Street

Nguyen Nghiem Street

Tiem An 72 Restaurant

Khach San So 1 (Hotel Number1)

Quang Ngai Bus Station

Meat & Bean Sprout Crêpes

Pho 79 (Soup Shop)

Quang Trung Street

Nguyen Ba Loan Street

To Quang Ngai Railway Station (3km)

Old Church

Tran Hung Dao Street

To Qui Nhon (174km) & Ho Chi Minh City (860km)

---

made of steel girders, of the sort that army engineering corps put up in a pinch.

Orientation

National Highway 1 is called Quang Trung St as it passes through Quang Ngai City. The railroad station is 3 km west of town out Phan Boi Chau St. The market area is between Ngo Quyen St and Nguyen Ba Loan St.

Information

The GPO is 150 metres off Quang Trung St at the corner of Phan Boi Chau St and Phan Dinh Phung St.

Site of the My Lai Massacre

Son My sub-district was the site of the most horrific war crimes committed by American ground forces during the Vietnam War. The My Lai Massacre consisted of a series of atrocities carried out all over Son My sub-district, which is divided into four hamlets, one of which is named My Lai. The largest mass killing took place in Tu Cung Hamlet in Xom Lang sub-hamlet (also known as Thuan Yen sub-hamlet), where the Son My Memorial was later erected.

Son My sub-district was a known Viet Cong stronghold, and several American soldiers had been killed and wounded in the area in the days preceding the 'search-and-destroy operation' that began on the morning of 16 March 1968. The operation was carried out by Task Force Barker, which consisted of three companies of United States Army infantry. At about 7.30 am – after the area around Xom Lang sub-hamlet had been bombarded with artillery and the landing zone raked with rocket and machine gun fire from helicopter gunships – the three platoons of Charlie Company (commanded by Captain Ernest Medina) were landed by helicopter. They encountered no resistance during the 'combat-assault', nor did they come under fire at any time during the entire operation; but as soon as Charlie Company's sweep eastward began, so did the atrocities.

As the soldiers of Lieutenant William Calley's 1st Platoon moved through Xom Lang, they shot and bayonetted fleeing villagers, threw hand grenades into houses and family bomb shelters, slaughtered livestock and burned dwellings. Somewhere between 75 and 150 unarmed local people were rounded up and herded to a ditch, where they were mowed down by machine-gun fire.

In the next few hours, as command helicopters circled overhead and US Navy boats patrolled offshore, the 2nd Platoon (under Lieutenant Stephen Brooks), the 3rd platoon (under Lieutenant Jeffrey La Cross) and the company headquarters group also committed unspeakable crimes. At least half-a-dozen groups of civilians, including women and children, were assembled and executed. Local people fleeing towards Quang Ngai along the road were machine-gunned, and wounded civilians (including young children) were summarily shot. As these massacres were taking place, at least four girls and women were raped or gang-raped by groups of soldiers. In one case, a rapist from 2nd Company is reported to have shoved the muzzle of his assault rifle into the vagina of his victim and pulled the trigger.

One American soldier is reported to have shot himself in the foot to get himself out of the slaughter; he was the only American casualty that day in the entire operation.

Action to cover up the atrocities at Son My was undertaken at every level of the US Army command, but eventually there were several investigations. Though a number of officers were disciplined, only one, Lieutenant Calley, was court-marshalled and found guilty of the murders of 22 unarmed civilians. He was paroled in 1974.

The Son My Memorial is set in a park where Xom Lang sub-hamlet once stood. Around it, among the trees and rice paddies, are the graves of some of the victims, buried in family groups. Near the memorial is a small museum which is opened for official delegations.

The site of the My Lai Massacre is 14 km from Quang Ngai. To get there from town, head north (towards Danang) on Quang Trung St (National Highway 1) and cross the long bridge over the Tra Khuc River. A few metres from the northern end of the bridge you will come to a triangular concrete stele indicating the way to the Son My Memorial. Turn right (eastward, parallel to the river) on the dirt road and continue for 12 km. The road to Son My passes through particularly beautiful countryside of rice paddies, manioc patches and vegetable gardens shaded by casuarinas and eucalyptus trees.

If you don't have a car, the best way to get to Son My District from Quang Ngai is to hire a motorbike (Honda ong) near the bus station or along Quang Trung St.

Bien Khe Ky Beach

Bien Khe Ky Beach (Bai Bien Khe Ky) is a long, secluded beach of fine sand 17 km from Quang Ngai and several km past (east of) the Son My Memorial. The beach stretches for many km along a long, thin casuarina-lined spit of sand separated from the mainland by Song Kinh Giang, a body of water about 150 metres inland from the beach.

As the mass killings in and around Xom Lang were taking place a couple of km to the west, another massacre was committed by Bravo Company just east and south of the bridge across Song Kinh Giang. Huts were indiscriminately fired on and burned, fleeing civilians were gunned down on the sand ridge and as they ran towards the beach, and family bomb shelters were blown up without giving the people in them the chance to escape. Women and children who did manage to run out of the shelters were shot; captured VC suspects were tortured. This whole incident, in which up to 90 civilians may have been killed, was completely covered up, and the charges filed against Bravo Company's commanding officer, 1st Lieutenant Thomas Willingham, were eventually dismissed.

Places to Stay

There are only three hotels in Quang Ngai City; a fourth is being built. *Khach San So 1* (Hotel Number 1) is 50 metres from the bus station at 42 Nguyen Nghiem St; rooms cost 4000 to 5000d. This is the sort of place that does not change the sheets very often. *Khach San So 2* (Hotel Number 2; 13 rooms) is about 100 metres west of Quang Trung St at 41 Phan Boi Chau St; rooms go for 4000 to 6000d. Khach San So 2, which is about 400 metres from the bus station, is probably a bit nicer than Khach San So 1.

The only proper hotel in town is *Nha Khach Uy Ban Thi* (tel 2109), which is in fact a guest house used mostly by government officials. Foreigners are charged US$20 for a double. Nha Khach Uy Ban Thi is approximately 300 metres from Quang Trung St at about number 52 Phan Boi Chau St.

A large, five storey hotel is slowly being constructed on the northern outskirts of the city next to the bridge over the Tra Khuc River.

Places to Eat

A local speciality is *bo gan*, bits of beef topped with ground peanuts and eaten on pieces of giant rice crackers.

The restaurant at *Nha Khach Uy Ban Thi*, the government guest house, is the only real restaurant in Quang Ngai. *Tiem An 72 Restaurant* at 72 Nguyen Nghiem St is about 150 metres from the bus station. Despite its modern façade, *Nha Hang 155* at 155 Quang Trung St is a place to avoid. There are cafes at numbers 47, 51 and 53 Phan Boi Chau St

(near Hotel Number 2) but they don't have much to eat. Meat and bean sprout crêpes fried over open fires are sold in the evenings on Phan Dinh Phung St between Tran Hung Dao St and Nguyen Nghiem St. *Pho 79* at the corner of Quang Trung St and Tran Hung Dao St has soup.

Getting There & Away

Road distances from Quang Ngai are:

Saigon	860 km
Nha Trang	412 km
Qui Nhon	174 km
Danang	131 km

Bus Quang Ngai City Bus Station (Ben Xe Khach Quang Ngai) is opposite 32 Nguyen Nghiem St, which is about 100 metres east of Quang Trung St (National Highway 1). Buses from here go to Buon Ma Thuot (and other places in Dac Lac Province), Dalat, Danang, Ho Chi Minh City, Hoi An, Kontum (and other destinations in Gia Lai-Kon Tum Province), Nha Trang and Qui Nhon.

There is no express bus from Quang Ngai City to Danang. Old Renault buses, which take 4 hours to cover the 130 km to Danang, begin their daily runs around 6 am.

Train The Quang Ngai Railway Station (Ga Quang Nghia or Ga Quang Ngai) is 3 km west of the centre of town. To get there, take Phan Boi Chau St west from Quang Trung St (National Highway 1) and continue going in the same direction after the street name changes to Nguyen Chanh St. At 389 Nguyen Chanh St (which you'll come to as Nguyen Chanh St curves left), continue straight on down a side street. The railroad station is at the end of the street.

Northbound, TN2 departs at 9 pm, arriving in Danang 3½ hours later. Train 172 to Danang leaves at 1.34 pm; NH2 to Hué departs at 1.20 pm. Southbound, TN1 pulls out of the station at 4.35 am and takes a bit over 5 hours to get to Qui Nhon. Train 171 to Qui Nhon leaves at 10.20 am; NH1 to Nha Trang departs just after midnight (at 12.15 am).

CHU LAI

About 30 km north of Quang Ngai, the buildings and concrete aircraft revetments of the huge American base at Chu Lai stretch along several km of sand to the east of National Highway 1. Despite the obvious dangers, collecting and selling scrap metal from old ordnance has become a thriving local industry. During the war, there was a huge shantytown made of packing crates and waste tin from canning factories next to the base. The inhabitants of the shantytown sup-

ported themselves by providing services to the Americans: doing laundry, selling soft drinks and engaging in prostitution.

CHIEN DANG CHAM TOWERS

Three Cham towers, enclosed by a wall, stand at Chien Dang, which is 5 km north of Tam Ki, 69 km north of Quang Ngai and 62 km south of Danang. A broken stele here dates from the 13th century reign of King Harivarman.

Central Highlands

The Central Highlands (Cao Nguyen Trung Phan) cover the southern part of the Truong Son Mountain Range (Annamite Cordillera) and include the provinces of Lam Dong, Dac Lac (Dak Lak) and Gia Lai-Kon Tum (Gia Lai-Con Tum). The region, which is home to many ethno-linguistic minority groups (montagnards), is renowned for its cool climate, beautiful mountain scenery and innumerable streams, lakes and waterfalls.

Though the population of the Central Highlands is only about 2 million, the area has always been considered strategically important. During the Vietnam War, considerable fighting took place around Buon Ma Thuot, Pleiku and Kontum.

With the exception of Lam Dong Province (in which Dalat is located), the Central Highlands are closed to foreigners. Even Westerners with legitimate business in the area have been arrested and sent back to Saigon. This extreme sensitivity may stem from the limited nature of central government control of remote areas as well as a concern that secret 're-education camps' (rumoured to be located in the region) will be discovered and publicised. In addition, Hanoi is known to be concerned that China may be trying to foment rebellion against Hanoi by exploiting the ethnic affinities between Vietnam's montagnards and related ethnic groups in southern China.

Small-scale guerrilla attacks are sometimes carried out by an organisation known as FULRO *(Front Unifié de Lutte des Races Opprimés*, or the United Front for the Struggle of the Oppressed Races), which was supported by the French and later the Americans and still receives assistance from Thailand and China. FULRO's support comes mainly from montagnards who feel threatened by Hanoi's policies of: 1) populating the highlands with ethnic-Vietnamese settlers, especially in New Economic Zones (NEZs); 2) encouraging the replacement of traditional slash-and-burn agriculture with sedentary farming; 3) promoting Vietnamese language and culture (Vietnamisation); and 4) forcibly introducing Communist social structures (collectivisation, etc).

BAO LOC

The town of Bao Loc (also known as B'Lao; elevation 850 metres) is a convenient place to break the trip between Saigon and Dalat. National Highway 20 is called Tran Phu St as it passes through town. Tea, mulberry leaves (for the silkworm industry) and silk are the major local industries.

For a while after reunification, this area was placed under an 8 pm to dawn curfew because of the FULRO insurgency.

Bay Tung Falls

The trail to the Bay Tung Falls (Thac Bay Tung, which means 'Seven Steps') begins 7 km towards Saigon from the Bao Loc Hotel along National Highway 20 (and 3 km from the Dai Lao Bridge over the Dai Binh River). The trailhead is in Ap Dai Lao, a hamlet in the village of Xa Loc Chau, behind a refreshments shop run by Ba Hai. The shop is on the right as you travel towards Saigon.

Suoi Mo (the stream of dreaming) is 400 metres west of Ba Hai's place along a path that passes among wood and thatch houses set amidst tea bushes, coffee trees and banana and pineapple plants. The path veers left at the stream and becomes torturously slippery as it makes its way along the bamboo and fern-lined bank. The first cascade is about 100 metres straight ahead. Several of the pools along Suoi Mo are swimmable but the water is of uncertain purity.

Bao Loc Church

Bao Loc Church is several hundred metres towards Dalat along the highway from the Bao Loc Hotel. There is an old Shell filling station across the road. Masses are held on Sundays.

Tea Factories

If you've ever wondered how tea is prepared, you might try getting someone to show you around one of Bao Loc's tea-processing plants. The largest is Nha May Che 19/5, which is 2 km towards Dalat from the Bao Loc Hotel. The factory, which produces tea for export, is on the top of a low hill next to a modern yellow water tower. The second largest tea factory is named 28/3. A joint Vietnamese and Soviet concern named Vietso (formerly Bisinée) is another place where you might inquire.

Place to Stay

The Bao Loc Hotel (tel 105 via the Dalat telephone exchange; 6 rooms), built in 1940, is at 14 Tran Phu St; a single costs 15,000d. The large covered dining area is used to screen videos every evening from 6.30 to 9 pm.

Place to Eat

Local products, sold in shops along Tran Phu St, include avocados, strawberries, jams and honey. Buy a French roll or two and you've got a meal.

The restaurant of the *Bao Loc Hotel* serves Vietnamese food, including dishes featuring venison; European-style food can be special-ordered. There is a restaurant called *Nha Hang 28/3* on National Highway 20 about 2 km towards Saigon from the Bao Loc Hotel. Other places to eat are strung out along Tran Phu St (National Highway 20) in both directions from the hotel.

Getting There & Away

Bao Loc is 177 km north-east of Saigon, 49 km west of Di Linh and 131 km south-west of Dalat.

The bus station is 2 km from the Bao Loc Hotel.

DI LINH

The town of Di Linh (pronounced 'Zee Ling'), also known as Djiring, is 1010 metres above sea level. The area's main product is tea, which is grown on giant plantations founded by the French and now run by the government. The Di Linh Plateau, sometimes compared to the Cameron Highlands of Malaysia, is a great place for day hikes. Only a few decades ago, the region was famous for its tiger hunting.

Bo Bla Waterfall

Thirty-two metre high Bo Bla Waterfall is 7 km west of town.

Getting There & Away

Di Linh is 226 km north-east of Saigon and 82 km south-west of Dalat on the main Saigon-Dalat highway. The town is 96 km from Phan Thiet by a secondary road.

WATERFALLS
Pongour Falls

Pongour Falls, the largest in the Dalat area, is about 55 km towards Saigon from Dalat and 7 km off the highway. During the rainy season, the falls form a full semicircle.

Gougah Falls

Gougah Falls is approximately 40 km from Dalat towards Saigon. It is only 500 metres from the highway and is easily accessible.

Lien Khang Falls

At Lien Khang Falls, the Danhim River, 100 metre wide at this point, drops 15 metres over an outcrop of volcanic rock. The site, which can be seen from the highway, is 35 km towards Saigon from Dalat. Lien Khang Falls is not far from Lien Khang airport.

DANHIM LAKE & POWER STATION

Danhim Lake (elevation 1042 metres) was created by a dam built between 1962 and 1964 by the Japanese as part of its war reparations. The huge Danhim hydroelectric project supplies electricity to much of the south.

The surface of the lake (which is often used by Saigon movie studios for filming romantic lakeside scenes) is 9.3 sq km. With a permit, hiking may be possible in the forested hills around the Danhim Lake, which, though said to be a great place for fishing, seems to be closed to the public, perhaps for security reasons.

The power station is at the western edge of the coastal plain. Water drawn from Danhim Lake gathers speed as it rushes almost a vertical km down from Ngoan Muc Pass in two enormous pipes.

Danhim Lake is about 38 km from Dalat in Don Duong District of Lam Dong Province. As you head towards Phan Rang, the dam is about a km to the left of the Dalat-Phan Rang highway. The power station is at the base of Ngoan Muc Pass near the town of Ninh Son.

Place to Stay

There is a hotel in Ninh Son.

NGOAN MUC PASS

Ngoan Muc Pass (Deo Ngoan Muc; altitude 980 metres), known to the French as Bellevue Pass, is about 5 km towards Phan Rang from Danhim Lake and 64 km west of Phan Rang. On a clear day, you can see all the way across the coastal plain to the Pacific Ocean, an aerial distance of 55 km. As the highway winds down the mountain in a series of switchbacks, it passes under the two gargantuan pipes – still guarded by armed troops in concrete fortifications – which link Danhim Lake with the power station. To the south of the road (to the right as you face the ocean) you can see the steep tracks of the *crémaillère* cog-wheel railway linking Cham with Dalat. This railway was completed in 1928 but closed in 1964 because of repeated Viet Cong attacks.

Sites of interest at the top of Ngoan Muc Pass include a waterfall next to the highway, pine forests and the old Bellevue Railway Station.

Dalat

Dalat (elevation: 1475 metres), which is situated in a temperate region dotted with lakes and waterfalls and surrounded by evergreen forests, is the most delightful city in all of Vietnam. That it was once called *La Petite Paris* is a great compliment to the capital of France. Not surprisingly, Dalat is a favourite honeymooning spot.

The city's population of 125,000 includes about 5000 members of ethno-linguistic minorities (*Dan Toc*), of which there are said to be 33 distinct groups in Lam Dong Province. Members of these 'hilltribes' – who still refer to themselves by the French word 'montagnards', which means 'mountain dwellers' – can often be seen in the marketplaces wearing their traditional dress. Hilltribe women of this area carry their infants on their backs in a long piece of cloth worn over one shoulder and tied in the front.

The economy of Dalat is based on tourism (300,000 domestic tourists visit every year) as well as growing garden vegetables and flowers, which are sold all over southern Vietnam. The area was once famous for its big-game hunting, and a 1950s brochure boasted that 'a 2-hour drive from the town leads to several game-rich areas abounding in deer, roes, peacocks, pheasants, wild boar, black bear, wild caws, panthers, tigers, gaurs and elephants'.

There is a New Economic Zone (a planned rural settlement where southern refugees and people from the overcrowded north were semi-forcibly resettled after reunification) 14 km from Dalat in Lam Ha District; it has a population of about 10,000.

History

The site of Dalat was 'discovered' in 1897 by Dr Alexandre Yersin (1863-1943), a protégé of Louis Pasteur who was the first person to identify the plague bacillus. The city itself was established in 1912 and quickly became popular with Europeans as a cool retreat from the sweltering heat of the coastal plains and the Mekong Delta. In the local Lat language, 'Da Lat' means 'the river of the Lat tribe'.

During the Vietnam War, Dalat was, by the tacit agreement of all parties concerned, largely spared the ravages of war. Indeed, it seems that while South Vietnamese Army officers were being trained at the city's Mil-

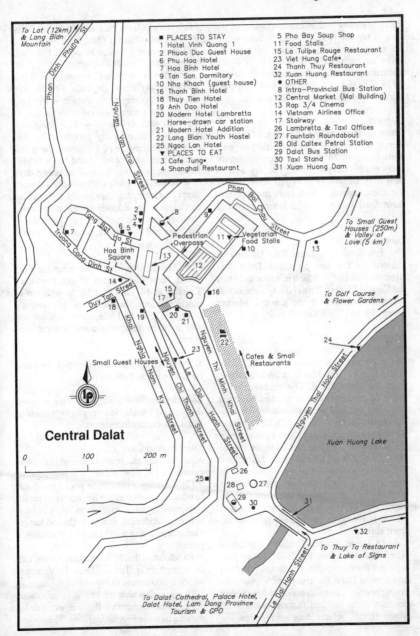

■ PLACES TO STAY
1 Hotel Vinh Quang 1
2 Phuoc Duc Guest House
6 Phu Hoa Hotel
7 Hoa Binh Hotel
9 Tan Son Dormitory
10 Nha Khach (guest house)
16 Thanh Binh Hotel
18 Thuy Tien Hotel
19 Anh Dao Hotel
20 Modern Hotel Lambretta
   Horse-drawn car station
21 Modern Hotel Addition
22 Lang Bian Youth Hostel
25 Ngoc Lan Hotel
▼ PLACES TO EAT
3 Cafe Tung*
4 Shanghai Restaurant

5 Pho Bay Soup Shop
11 Food Stalls
15 La Tulipe Rouge Restaurant
23 Viet Hung Cafe*
24 Thanh Thuy Restaurant
32 Xuan Huong Restaurant
● OTHER
8 Intra-Provincial Bus Station
12 Central Market (Mai Building)
13 Rap 3/4 Cinema
14 Vietnam Airlines Office
17 Stairway
26 Lambretta & Taxi Offices
27 Fountain Roundabout
28 Old Caltex Petrol Station
29 Dalat Bus Station
30 Taxi Stand
31 Xuan Huong Dam

To Lat (12km) & Lang Bidn Mountain

Phan Dinh Phung St
Nguyen Van Troi Street
Tang Bat Ho St
Truong Cong Dinh St
Duy Tan Street
Khoi
Nguyen Nghia Nam Ky Street
Le Dai Hanh Street
Nguyen Chi Thanh Street
Nguyen Thi Minh Khai Street
Phan Boi Chau Street
Nguyen Thai Hoc Street
Le Dai Hanh Street

Pedestrian Overpass
Vegetarian Food Stalls
Hoa Binh Square

To Small Guest Houses (250m) & Valley of Love (5 km)

To Golf Course & Flower Gardens

Small Guest Houses

Cafes & Small Restaurants

Central Dalat

0   100   200 m

Xuan Huong Lake

To Thuy Ta Restaurant & Lake of Signs

To Dalat Cathedral, Palace Hotel, Dalat Hotel, Lam Dong Province Tourism & GPO itary Academy and affluent officials of the Saigon regime were relaxing in their villas, VC cadre were doing the same thing not far away in *their* villas. Dalat fell to North Vietnamese forces without a fight on 3 April 1975. There is no problem with left-over mines and ordnance in the Dalat area.

Climate
Dalat is often called the City of Eternal Spring. The average maximum daily temperature is a cool 24°C; the average minimum daily temperature is 15°C. The dry season runs from December to March. Even during the rainy season, which lasts more-or-less from April to November, it is sunny most of the time.

Orientation
The city centre is around Rap 3/4 cinema (named for the date on which Dalat was 'liberated' in 1975), which is up the hill from the Central Market. Xuan Huong Lake is 500 metres south-east of the Central Market along Nguyen Thi Minh Khai St.

Information
Tourist Office The headquarters of of Lam Dong Province Tourism (tel 2125, 2366, 2021) is at 12 Tran Phu St, across the street from the Dalat Hotel. The organisation is eager to promote foreign tourism to Dalat and may be able to help with getting an internal travel permit to Lam Dong Province. To arrange transport or to hire a guide, go to the part of the building closest to the Palace Hotel, which is on a nearby hill. Lam Dong Tourism is well aware of the importance of preserving Dalat's unique charm and is working on a programme to ensure that the city is well-served by development, most of which is likely to be funded by investors from abroad.

Lam Dong Youth Tourism Company (Hiep Hoi Du Lich; tel 2136, 2318) runs sight-seeing excursions and camping trips in and around Dalat for groups of Vietnamese young people. The main office of this private concern is on the 2nd floor of Lang Bian Youth Hostel, which is down Nguyen Thi

Minh Khai St from the Central Market. They have another office at 7 Hoa Binh Square and will soon open a Saigon branch at 123 Cach Mang Thang Tam St in District 3.

The Youth Tourism Company, which has guides who speak English, French and Russian, is planning to introduce trekking expeditions lasting several days or longer that will include camping with the Chill, Koho and Lat minority peoples. The cost depends on the size of the group, the transport required and food expenses. Reservations should be made at least 5 days in advance. The company has only a limited supply of camping equipment for hire so participants should bring their own warm clothing, medical supplies, rain gear, sleeping bags and backpacks; the company does have nylon tents.

Post The GPO is across the street from the Dalat Hotel and Lam Dong Province Tourism at 14 Tran Phu St. In addition to postal services, the GPO has international telegraph, telex and telephone facilities and will soon be able to transmit international faxes.

Money Dollars can be changed at the usual hotel rate in the Palace Hotel.

Laundry Because of the cool temperatures, drip-drying laundry is a very slow process in Dalat, especially indoors.

Xuan Huong Lake
Xuan Huong Lake in the centre of Dalat was created in 1919 by a dam. It is named after a 17th-century Vietnamese poet known for her daring attacks on the hypocrisy of social conventions and the foibles of scholars, bonzes, mandarins, feudal lords and kings. The lake is circumnavigated by a strollable path.

Paddleboats that look like giant swans can be rented near Thanh Thuy Restaurant, which is 200 metres north-east of the dam. A golf course, which is being refurbished, occupies 50 hectares on the northern side of the lake near the Flower Gardens. The majestic hilltop Palace Hotel overlooks Xuan Huong Lake from the south.

French District

The area between Rap 3/4 cinema and Phan Dinh Phung St hasn't changed in decades. If, in the year 1934, someone had evacuated a provincial town in France and repopulated it with Vietnamese, this is what it would have looked like 20 years later. This is a delightful area for walking around.

Central Market

Dalat's Central Market, built in 1958, is at the northern end of Nguyen Thi Minh Khai St. The finest, freshest vegetables in Vietnam (as well as cut flowers and the usual merchandise) are available here. There are dozens of food stalls in the roofed-over section behind the main building.

Governor-General's Residence

The old French Governor-General's Residence (Dinh Toan Quyen, or Dinh 2; tel 2093), now used as a guest house and for official receptions, is a dignified building of modernist design built in 1933. The original style of furnishing has been retained in most of the structure's 25 rooms. Shoes must be taken off at the front door.

The Governor-General's Residence is about 2 km from the centre of town up the hill from the intersection of Tran Hung Dao St and Khoi Nghia Bac Son St; it is open to the public from 7 to 11 am and 1.30 to 4 pm. Entrance tickets are sold at an outbuilding (once servants' quarters) several hundred metres from the residence itself. They may try to charge extra if you want to take photographs inside the building.

Guests can stay in the upstairs bedroom suites, with their balconies and huge bathrooms, for US$30 per person per night; for details, contact Lam Dong Province Tourism.

Bao Dai's Summer Palace

Emperor Bao Dai's Summer Palace (Biet Dien Quoc Truong, or Dinh 3) is a tan, 25 room villa constructed in 1933. The decor has not changed in decades except for the addition of Ho Chi Minh's portrait over the fireplace. The palace, filled with artefacts from decades and governments past, is extremely interesting.

The engraved glass map of Vietnam was given to Emperor Bao Dai (born 1913; reigned 1926-45; he has lived in France since the mid-50s) in 1942 by Vietnamese students in France. In Bao Dai's office, the life-size white bust above the bookcase is of Bao Dai himself; the smaller gold and brown busts are of his father, Emperor Khai Dinh. Note the heavy brass royal seal (on the right) and military seal (on the left). The photographs over the fireplace are of (from left to right) Bao Dai, his eldest son Bao Long (in uniform) and Empress Nam Phuong, who died in 1963.

Upstairs are the royal living quarters. The room of Bao Long, who now lives in England, is decorated in yellow, the royal colour. The huge semicircular couch was used by the Emperor and Empress for family meetings, during which their three daughters were seated in the yellow chairs and their two sons in the pink chairs. Check out the ancient tan Rouathermique infra-red sauna machine near the top of the stairs.

Bao Dai's Summer Palace is set in a pine grove 500 metres south-east of the Pasteur Institute, which is on Le Hong Phong St 2 km from the city centre. The palace is open to the public from 7 to 11 am and 1.30 to 4 pm. Shoes must be removed at the door.

Tourists can stay here for US$30 per person per night; for more information, contact Lam Dong Province Tourism.

Flower Gardens

The Dalat Flower Gardens (Vuon Hoa Dalat; tel 2151) were established in 1966 by the South Vietnamese Agriculture Service and renovated in 1985. Flowers represented include hydrangeas, fuchsias and orchids (*hoa lan*). Most of the latter are in special shaded buildings off to the right from the entrance. The orchids are grown in blocks of coconut palm trunk and in terracotta pots with lots of ventilation holes. Severa' monkeys live in cages on the grounds of the Flower Gardens.

Near the gate you can buy *cu ly*, reddish-brown animal-shaped pieces of fern stems whose fibres are used to stop bleeding in traditional medicine. Cold drinks are available nearby.

The Flower Gardens front Xuan Huong Lake at 2 Phu Dong Thien Vuong St, which leads from the lake to Dalat University; they are open from 7.30 am to 4 pm. Ticket sales are suspended for a while around noon.

Dalat University

Dalat University (tel 2246) was founded as a Catholic university in 1957 by Hué Archbishop Ngo Dinh Thuc, older brother of President Ngo Dinh Diem (assassinated in 1963), with the help of Cardinal Spelman of New York. The university, which was closed in 1975 and reopened 2 years later, has 1200 students from south-central Vietnam. The students live in off-campus boarding houses. The university library contains 10,000 books, including some in English and other Western languages. The US-Indochina Reconciliation Project of Philadelphia, Pennsylvania, USA is interested in holding summer programmes in intensive Vietnamese language study here.

Dalat University is at 1 Phu Dong Thien Vuong St (corner Dinh Tien Hoang St). The 38 hectare campus can easily be identified by the red-star-topped triangular tower, which once held aloft a cross. Permission for foreigners to visit the university can be arranged by calling 2246.

Nuclear Research Centre

Dalat's Nuclear Research Centre uses its American-built Triga Mark II reactor for radioactive medicine, to train scientists and to analyse samples collected for geological and agricultural research. The centre, financed under the United States' Atoms for Peace programme, was formally dedicated in 1963 by President Ngo Dinh Diem (who was assassinated 4 days later) and US Ambassador Henry Cabot Lodge. In 1975, as the South was collapsing, the US spirited away the reactor's nuclear fuel elements; the centre was reopened in 1984.

The Nuclear Research Centre, with its tall, thin chimney, can easily be seen from the Palace Hotel as well as from the Dragon Water Pumping Station.

Tomb of Nguyen Huu Hao

Nguyen Huu Hao, who died in 1939, was the father of Nam Phuong, Bao Dai's wife. He was the richest person in Go Cong District of the Mekong Delta. Nguyen Huu Hao's tomb is on a hilltop 400 metres north-west of Cam Ly Falls.

Former Petite Lycée Yersin

The former Petite Lycée Yersin at 1 Hoang Van Thu St is now a cultural centre (tel 2511) run by the provincial government. Lessons in electric and acoustic guitar, piano, violin, clarinet, saxophone, etc are held here, making this a good place to meet local musicians. A new music centre is being established on Tang Bat Ho St.

Cam Ly Falls

Cam Ly Falls, opened as a tourist site in 1911, is one of those must-see spots for domestic visitors. The grassy areas around the 15 metre high cascades are decorated with stuffed jungle animals which Vietnamese tourists love to be photographed with. Refreshments are available. The waterfall is between numbers 57 and 59 Hoang Van Thu St; it is open from 7 am to 6 pm.

Valley of Love

Named the Valley of Peace by Emperor Bao Dai, the Valley of Love (Thung Lung Tinh Yeu, or Vallée d'Amour in French), had its name changed in 1972 (the year Da Thien Lake was created) by romantically-minded students from Dalat University. Paddleboats cost 1500d per hour; 15 person canoes cost 15,000d an hour. Horses can be hired for 6000d per hour. Refreshments and local delicacies (jams, candied fruits, etc) are on sale near the lookout.

The Valley of Love is 5 km north of Xuan

Huong Lake out Phu Dong Thien Vuong St. The entrance fee is 200d.

Dragon Water Pumping Station

Guarded by a fanciful cement dragon, the Dragon Water Pumping Station was built in 1977-78. The statue of the Virgin Mary holding baby Jesus and gazing towards Dalat dates from 1974. Thong Nhat Reservoir is on top of the hill just west of the pumping station.

The Dragon Water Pumping Station is on top of a low rise 500 metres west of the entrance to the Valley of Love.

Lake of Sighs

The Lake of Sighs (Ho Than Tho) is a natural lake enlarged by a French-built dam; the forests in the area are hardly Dalat's finest. There are several small restaurants up the hill from the dam. Horses can be hired near the restaurants for 6000d an hour.

According to legend, Mai Nuong and Hoang Tung met here in 1788 while he was hunting and she picking mushrooms. They fell in love and sought their parents' permission to marry. But at that time Vietnam was threatened by a Chinese invasion and Hoang Tung, heeding Emperor Quang Trung's call-to-arms, joined the army without waiting to tell Mai Nuong. Unaware that he was off fighting and afraid that his absence meant that he no longer loved her, Mai Nuong sent word for him to meet her at the lake. When he did not come she was overcome with sorrow and, to prove her love, threw herself into the lake and drowned. Thereafter, the lake has been known as the Lake of Sighs.

The Lake of Sighs is 6 km north-east of the centre of Dalat out Phan Chu Trinh St.

Pagodas & Churches

Lam Ty Ni Pagoda Lam Ty Ni Pagoda, also known as Quan Am Tu, was founded in 1961. The decorative front gate was constructed by the pagoda's one monk, Vien Thuc, an industrious man who learned English, French, Khmer and Thai at Dalat University. During his 20 years here, he has built flower beds and gardens in several different styles, including a miniature Japanese garden complete with a bridge. Nearby are trellis-shaded paths decorated with hanging plants. Signs list the Chinese name of each garden. Vien Thuc also built much of the pagoda's wooden furniture.

Lam Ty Ni Pagoda is about 500 metres north of the Pasteur Institute at 2 Thien My St. A visit here can easily be combined with a stop at Bao Dai's Summer Palace.

Linh Son Pagoda Linh Son Pagoda was founded in 1938. The giant bell is said to be made of bronze with gold mixed in, its great weight making it too heavy for thieves to carry off. Behind the pagoda are coffee and tea plants tended by the 15 monks, who range in age from 20 to 80, and half-a-dozen novices.

One of the monks here has led a fascinating and tragic life whose peculiar course reflects the vagaries of Vietnam's modern history. Born in 1926 of a Japanese father and a Vietnamese mother, during WW II he was pressed into the service of the Japanese occupation forces as a translator. He got his secondary school degree from a French-language Franciscan convent in 1959 at the age of 35. His interest later turned to American literature, in which he received a masters degree (his thesis was on William Faulkner) from Dalat University in 1975. The monk speaks half-a-dozen East Asian and European languages with fluent precision.

Linh Son Pagoda is about 1 km from the town centre on Phan Dinh Phung St; the street address is 120 Nguyen Van Troi St.

Dalat Cathedral Dalat Cathedral, which is on Tran Phu St next to the Dalat Hotel, was built between 1931 and 1942 for use by French residents and vacationers. The cross on the spire is 47 metres above the ground. Inside, the stained glass windows bring a bit of medieval Europe to Dalat. The first church built on this site (in the 1920s) is to the left of the cathedral; it has a light blue arched door.

There are three priests here. Masses are held at 5.30 am and 5.15 pm every day and on Sundays at 5.30 am, 7 am and 4 pm. The parish's three choirs (one for each Sunday mass) practise on Thursdays and Saturdays from 5 to 6 pm.

Vietnamese Evangelical Church

Dalat's pink Evangelical Church, the main Protestant church in the city, was built in 1940. Until 1975, it was affiliated with the Christian and Missionary Alliance. The minister here was trained at Nha Trang Bible College.

Since reunification, Vietnam's Protestants have been persecuted even more than have Catholics, in part because many Protestant clergymen were trained by American missionaries. Although religious activities at this church are still restricted by the government, Sunday is a busy day: there is Bible study from 7 to 8 am followed by worship from 8 to 10 am; a youth service is held from 1.30 to 3.30 pm.

Most of the 25,000 Protestants in Lam Dong Province, who are served by over 100 churches, are hilltribe people. Dalat's Vietnamese Evangelical Church is one of only six churches in the province whose membership is ethnic-Vietnamese.

The Vietnamese Evangelical Church is 300 metres from Rap 3/4 at 72 Nguyen Van Troi St.

Domaine de Marie Convent

The pink, tile-roofed structures of the Domaine de Marie Convent (Nha Tho Domaine), constructed between 1940 and 1942, were once home to 300 nuns. Today, the eight remaining nuns support themselves by making ginger candies and by selling the fruit grown in the orchard out the back.

Suzanne Humbert, wife of Admiral Jean Decoux, Vichy-French Governor-General of Indochina from 1940 to 1945, is buried at the base of the outside back wall of the chapel. A benefactress of the chapel, she was killed in an auto accident in 1944.

Masses are held in the large chapel every day at 5.30 am and on Sundays at 5.30 am and 4.15 pm.

The Domaine de Marie Convent is on a hilltop at 6 Ngo Quyen St, which is also called Mai Hac De St.

Du Sinh Church Du Sinh Church was built in 1955 by Catholic refugees from the North. The four post Sino-Vietnamese-style steeple was constructed at the insistence of a Hué-born priest of royal lineage. The church is on a hilltop with beautiful views in all directions, making this a great place for a picnic.

To get to Du Sinh Church, go 500 metres south-west along Huyen Tran Cong Chua St from the former Couvent des Oiseaux, which is now a teachers' training high school.

Thien Vuong Pagoda Thien Vuong Pagoda, also known simply as Chua Tau (the Chinese pagoda), is popular with domestic tourists, especially ethnic-Chinese. Set on a hilltop amidst pine trees, the pagoda was built by the Trieu Chau Chinese Congregation. Tho Da, the monk who initiated the construction of the pagoda in 1958, emigrated to the United States; there are pictures of his 1988 visit on display. The stalls out the front are a good place to buy local candied fruit and preserves.

The pagoda itself consists of three yellow buildings made of wood. In the first building is a gilded wooden statue of Ho Phap, one of the Buddha's protectors. On the other side of Ho Phap's glass case is a gilded wooden statue of Pho Hien, a helper of A Di Da Buddha (the Buddha of the Past). Shoes should be removed before entering the third building, in which there are three 4 metre high standing Buddhas donated by a British Buddhist and brought from Hong Kong in 1960. Made of gilded sandalwood and weighing 1400 kg each, the figures – said to be the largest sandalwood statues in Vietnam – represent Thich Ca Buddha (Sakyamuni, the historical Buddha; in the centre); Quan The Am Bo Tat (Avalokiteçvara; on the right); and Dai The Chi Bo Tat (an assistant of A Di Da; on the left).

Thien Vuong Pagoda is about 5 km from the centre of town out Khe Sanh St.

Minh Nguyet Cu Sy Lam Pagoda A second Chinese Buddhist pagoda, Minh Nguyet Cu Sy Lam Pagoda, is reached by a path beginning across the road from the gate of Thien Vuong Pagoda. It was built by the Quang Dong (Cantonese) Chinese Congregation in 1962. The main sanctuary of the pagoda is a round structure constructed on a platform representing a lotus blossom. Inside is a painted cement statue of Quan The Am Bo Tat (Avalokiteçvara, the Goddess of Mercy) flanked by two other figures. Shoes should be taken off before entering. Notice the repetition of the lotus motif in the window bars, railings, gateposts, etc. There is a giant red gourd-shaped incense oven near the main sanctuary. The pagoda is open all day long.

Su Nu Pagoda Su Nu Pagoda, also known as Chua Linh Phong, is a Buddhist nunnery built in 1952. The nuns here – who, according to Buddhist regulations, are bald – wear grey or brown robes except when praying, at which time they don saffron raiment. Men are allowed to visit, but only women live here. The nunnery is open all day, but it is considered impolite to come around lunch time, when the nuns sing their prayers a cappella before eating. Across the driveway from the pagoda's buildings and set among tea plants is the grave-marker of Head Nun Thich Nu Dieu Huong, who is still alive and going strong at the age of almost 80.

Su Nu Pagoda is about 1 km south of Le Thai To St at 72 Hoang Hoa Tham St.

Places to Stay – bottom end

Because of its popularity with domestic travellers, Dalat has an extensive network of cheap, well-run hotels, guest houses and dormitories. Make sure they have hot water before you check in. There are 100 or so places to stay in Dalat.

Town Centre The *Thuy Tien Hotel* (tel 2444; 8 rooms) is in the heart of the old French section at 7 3 Thang 2 St; doubles cost 10,000 to 12,000d; quads go for 16,000 to 20,000d. This place, whose spacious rooms are equipped with balconies and hot water,

is often full. The *Phu Hoa Hotel* (Khach San Phu Hoa; tel 2482) is a block away at 16 Tang Bat Ho St; they charge 2500d per bed. *Phuoc Duc Guest House* (Nha Nghi Phuoc Duc; tel 2200) is near Rap 3/4 cinema at 4 Khu Hoa Binh St; singles, doubles and triples cost 2500d per person. The owners of this crowded but homey place speak fluent French. Café Tung is next door. *Hotel Vinh Quang 1* (no telephone; 17 rooms) is a block away at 11 Nguyen Van Troi St; doubles are 6000d.

The *Anh Dao Hotel* (tel 2384; 11 rooms), whose management is rather uncooperative, is up the hill from the Central Market on Nguyen Chi Thanh St; the address is 54 Khu Hoa Binh Quarter. For locals, singles/doubles start at 6000/9000d; foreigners and Overseas Vietnamese pay twice as much. The *Ngoc Lan Hotel* (tel 2136; 25 rooms), a big place overlooking the bus station and the lake, is down the street at 42 Nguyen Chi Thanh St; doubles go for 10,200d.

There are small guest houses along Nguyen Chi Thanh St at numbers 6, 12, 14, 20, 22, 34, 36, 40 and 80.

Central Market Area Though the *Modern Hotel* (tel 2379; 30 rooms), which is on Nguyen Thi Minh Khai St across the roundabout from the Central Market, hardly lives up to its name (which dates from the 1960s), the new section being constructed next door might. Doubles with bath cost between 6000d and 20,000d; they also have quads and rooms for six. Out the front is a Lambretta and horse-cart station.

The *Thanh Binh Hotel* (tel 0325; 42 rooms) is across the street from the main building of the Central Market at 40-42 Nguyen Chi Minh Khai St; doubles/quads are 7000/12,000d. Around the corner is *Nha Khach* ('Guest House'; tel 2375; 5 rooms) at 27A Nguyen Thi Minh Khai St. A dorm bed in a six person room costs 1500d. Also on the loop of road that goes around the Central Market complex is *Tan Son Dormitory* (no telephone; 6 rooms) at 20B Nguyen Thi Minh Khai St; each room has six beds.

Nha Khach 90 (tel 2468), which is up

behind the Central Market area on a hilltop above Xuan Huong Lake, is at 12 Phan Boi Chau St. There are half a dozen small guest houses a few hundred metres down Phan Boi Chau St at numbers 4, 4C, 4F, 1/3 and 1 Bui Thi Xuan St.

Phan Dinh Phung St There are several hotels along Phan Dinh Phung St, which is down Truong Cong Dinh St from the town centre. The *Hoa Binh Hotel* (no telephone; 20 rooms) is opposite 64 Truong Cong Dinh St at 127 Phan Dinh Phung St; a quad costs 10,000d. The *Cao Nguyen Hotel* (Khach San Cao Nguyen; 14 rooms) is at 90 Phan Dinh Phung St; a room for four costs 10,000d. Across the street is the *Lien Hiep Hotel* (Nha Khach Lien Hiep; tel 0319; 13 rooms) at 147 Phan Dinh Phung St; rooms cost 2500d per person. The *Thanh The Hotel* (tel 2180; 15 rooms) is a modern four storey building at 118 Phan Dinh Phung St; a quad costs 12,000d. *Khach San Van Hue* is next door. The *Mimosa Hotel* (tel 0320; 24 rooms) at 170 Phan Dinh Phung St charges 3000d per person. *Lan Huong Guest House* (Nha Nghi Lan Huong) is at 190 Phan Dinh Phung St.

The *Lam Son Hotel* (tel 2362; 12 rooms) is about 1 km west of the centre of town in an old French villa at 5 Hai Thuong St; singles/doubles cost 5000/7000d for 2nd class and 6000/8000d for 1st class. The rooms are clean and equipped with hot water and the management is friendly.

Youth Hostel The *Lang Bian Youth Hostel* (tel 2419; 15 rooms) is 100 metres from the Central Market at 6B Nguyen Thi Minh Khai St. A big sign out the front reads 'Festival' in English. This place is run by the Ho Chi Minh Communist Youth Union Committee of Lam Dong Province (Doan Thanh Nien Cong San Ho Chi Minh Tinh Doan Lam Dong). The hostel is usually full, especially during school holidays. Triples with common toilets go for 6000d; each additional person costs 1000d.

Camping Camping is permitted on the out-of-service golf course, at the Dalat Flower Gardens, in the Valley of Love (Da Thien Lake) area, around Quang Trung Reservoir (Tuyen Lam Lake) and near Datanla and Prenn waterfalls. I am told that security is not a problem. Only limited equipment can be hired locally, so the more of your own you have the better. Sleeping bags, unnecessary in Vietnam's coastal areas, are well worth bringing – the nights are often chilly.

For information on camping and trekking to hill-tribe areas around Dalat, contact Lam Dong Youth Tourism Company (Hiep Hoi Du Lich; tel 2136, 2318) on the 2nd floor of the Lang Bian Youth Hostel.

Places to Stay – top end
Hotels Without a doubt, the classiest accommodation in town is at the *Palace Hotel* (Khach San Palace; tel 2203; 43 rooms), a grand old place built between 1916 and 1922. Panoramic views of Xuan Huong Lake can be enjoyed in the hotel's expansive ground-floor public areas, where one can sit in a rattan chair sipping tea or soda while gazing out through a wall of windows. For foreigners, singles/doubles cost US$18/23 in 2nd class, US$20/27 in 1st class, US$24/33 for a deluxe room and US$37/45 for a suite; adding another person to a double costs between US$8 and US$14. The restaurant is open from 6.30 to 8.30 am, 11.30 am to 1.30 pm and 6 to 8 pm. There are tennis courts nearby. The hotel's street address is 2 Tran Phu St. A joint Franco-Vietnamese venture to upgrade the Palace Hotel is in the works.

Another vintage hostelry is the *Dalat Hotel* (Khach San Da Lat; tel 2363; 65 rooms), built in 1907. Though the building, which is at 7 Tran Phu St (opposite the driveway of the Palace Hotel), is a bit run-down there are said to be plans to renovate it. Singles/doubles cost from US$13/16 to US$24/30; adding a third person to a double costs an additional US$6 to US$12. All rooms are supposed to have hot water. There is a billiard room on the ground floor. Though the Dalat Hotel has a restaurant, you'll probably do better to eat across the street at the Palace Hotel.

The *Duy Tan Hotel* (tel 2216; 26 rooms)

at 82 3 Thang 2 St (corner Hoang Van Thu St) is an unimaginatively-managed place built in the style of an American motel. First class singles/doubles cost US$12/15 plus 10% service; a 2nd class single costs US$8.

The *Minh Tam Hotel* (tel 2447; 17 rooms) is 3 km out of town at 20A Khe Sanh St. There are nice views from here of the surrounding landscape of forested hills and cultivated valleys. Formerly the summer house of Tran Le Xuan (the sister-in-law of President Ngo Dinh Diem), the villa, constructed in 1936, was renovated in 1984. This place would be a peaceful retreat were it not for the busloads of domestic tourists continually parading through the flower garden on the hotel's grounds. For 'capitalist tourists', doubles cost US$20 or US$24.

Villas Many of Dalat's 2500 chalet-style villas can be rented. Prime villas are located along the ridge south of Tran Hung Dao St and Le Thai To St, and there is a whole neighbourhood of villas near the Pasteur Institute (around Le Hong Phong St). If you don't mind the tourists tramping through, you can even stay in the old Governor-General's Residence and Bao Dai's Summer Palace for US$30 per person per night. For more information, inquire at Lam Dong Province Tourism.

Places to Eat

Local Specialties Dalat is a paradise for lovers of fresh garden vegetables, which are grown locally and sold all over the south. The abundance of just-picked peas, carrots, tomatoes, cucumbers, avocados, green peppers, lettuce, Chinese cabbage, bean sprouts, beets, green beans, potatoes, corn, bamboo shoots, garlic, spinach, squash and yams makes for meals unavailable anywhere else in the country. Persimmons and cherries are in season from November to January. Avocados are eaten for desert with either sugar or salt and pepper. Apples are known here as *bom* after the French *pomme*. Because of fierce competition in the domestic tourism market, restaurant prices are very reasonable.

The Dalat area is famous for its strawberry jam, dried blackcurrants and candied plums and peaches, which cost 2500d per kg. Other local delicacies include avocado ice cream, sweet beans (*mut dao*) and strawberry, blackberry and artichoke squashes (syrups for making drinks). The region also produces grape and strawberry wines. Artichoke tea, another local speciality, is made from the root of the artichoke plant. Most of these products can be purchased at the central market and at stalls in front of Thien Vuong Pagoda.

Dau hu, a type of pudding, is a Dalat speciality. Made from soymilk, sugar and a bit of ginger, *dau hu* is sold by itinerant women vendors who walk around carrying a large bowl of the stuff and a small stand suspended from either end of a bamboo pole.

Town Centre The *Shanghai Restaurant* is a privately-owned place on the other side of Rap 3/4 cinema from the Central Market; the address is 8 Khu Hoa Binh Quarter. They serve Chinese, Vietnamese and French food from 8 am to 9.30 pm. Around the corner at 2 Tang Bat Ho St is *Pho Bay*, which specialises in *pho* (soup).

Central Market Area Recently-privatised *La Tulipe Rouge Restaurant* (tel 2394) is across the square from the main building of the Central Market at 1 Nguyen Thi Minh Khai St; it is open from 6 am to 9 pm. The fare includes Vietnamese, Chinese and European dishes.

There are dozens of food stalls in the covered area behind the main Central Market building. A number of cafes and small restaurants are located along Nguyen Thi Minh Khai St between the Central Market and Xuan Huong Lake.

Xuan Huong Lake *Thuy Ta Restaurant* (tel 2268), formerly *La Grenouillère* (roughly translated, 'The Froggery'), is built on piles over the waters of Xuan Huong Lake. The panoramic view from the veranda encompasses almost the whole of the lake's forested coastline. Thuy Ta Restaurant, which is at the tip of a perfectly round island reached by a bridge, is directly below the Palace Hotel; it is open from 6 am to 9 pm and makes a great place for breakfast.

Across the lake is *Thanh Thuy Restaurant* (Cua Hang Thanh Thuy), which is on the water 200 metres along Nguyen Thai Hoc St from the Xuan Huong Dam.

Hotels There is a good restaurant in the *Palace Hotel*. The *Dalat Hotel* also has an in-house restaurant.

Vegetarian There are three vegetarian food stalls, each signposted *com chay* (vegetarian food), in the area of covered food stalls behind the main building of the Central Market. They are right across the street from Nha Khach, a hotel at 27A Nguyen Thi Minh Khai St. All three serve delicious 100% vegetarian food prepared to resemble and taste like traditional Vietnamese meat dishes; a full multi-course meal costs only about 2500d.

Cafes *Café Tung* at 6 Khu Hoa Binh St was a famous hang-out of Saigonese intellectuals during the 1950s. Old-timers swear that the place remains exactly as it was when they were young. As it did then, Café Tung serves only tea, coffee, hot cocoa, lemon soda and orange soda to the accompaniment of mellow French music. This is a marvellous place to warm up and unwind on a chilly evening.

Viet Hung Café (Kem Viet Hung) specialities are ice cream and iced coffee. The cafe has entrances across from 22 Nguyen Chi Thanh St and on Le Dai Hanh St up the hill from the Lang Bian Youth Hostel.

Nightlife
At the Lang Bian Youth Hostel, video shows begin at 1 pm and run until the evening. Dancing at the ground-floor club starts at 7.30 pm. The Dalat Hotel has dancing nightly (except Mondays) beginning at 7.30 pm.

Things to Buy
In addition to the edible delights listed under 'Places to Eat,' Dalat is known for its *kim mao cau tich*, a kind of fern whose fibres are used to stop bleeding in traditional Chinese medicine. The stuff is also known as *cu ly* (animals) because the fibrous matter is sold attached to branches pruned to resemble reddish-brown hairy animals.

The hilltribes of Lam Dong Province make handicrafts for their own use only. Lat products include dyed rush mats and rice baskets that roll up when empty. The Koho and Chill produce the split-bamboo baskets used by all the national minorities in this area to carry things on their backs. The Chill also weave cloth, including the dark blue cotton shawls worn by some montagnard women. The hilltribe people carry water in a hollow gourd with a corn-cob stopper that is sometimes wrapped in a leaf for a tighter fit. A market for such goods has not yet developed so there are no stores in town selling them. If you are interested in montagnard handicrafts, you might ask around Lat Village, which is 12 km north of Dalat.

Getting There & Away
Road distances from Dalat:

Buon Ma Thuot	396 km
Danang	746 km
Di Linh	82 km
Nha Trang	205 km
Phan Rang	101 km
Phan Thiet	247 km
Ho Chi Minh City	308 km

Air Dalat is served by Lien Khang Airport, which is about 30 km south of the city. At present there are weekly flights to and from Ho Chi Minh City (US$28 one-way) and Hanoi (US$143 one-way). There are plans to begin daily service to and from Ho Chi Minh City. Lien Khang Airport is authorised to accept light aircraft which, the provincial government hopes, will be carrying well-heeled visitors from other South-East Asian countries; when the 1500-metre runway is lengthened to 2500 metres, the airport will be able to handle larger aircraft. Cam Ly

Airstrip, situated only 3 km from the centre of Dalat, is not in use.

The Vietnam Airlines office in Dalat (tel 0330) is at 5 Truong Cong Dinh St, which is across the street from Rap 3/4 cinema.

Bus Dalat Bus Station (Ben Xe Dalat; tel 2077) is next to the old Caltex petrol station, which is 100 metres towards the Central Market from Xuan Huong Dam; the ticket office is open from 4.30 am to 5.30 pm. There is daily express service from Dalat to Ho Chi Minh City (6 to 7 hours) and Nha Trang. Express buses also run two or three times a week to Danang (19 hours), Quang Ngai and Qui Nhon. All the express buses, most of which are new Czech-built Karosas, depart at 5 am.

Non-express buses, which depart when full starting at 6 am, link Dalat with:

Bao Loc (B'Lao)
Cat Tien
Da Hoai
Danang
Da Teh
Di Linh (Djiring)
Don Duong (Darang)
Dong Van
Duc Trong
Hanoi (with a change of buses)
Ho Chi Minh City (8 to 9 hours)
Nam Bang
Phan Rang
Phan Thiet
Phu Son
Quang Ngai
Qui Nhon
Tan My

The Intra-Provincial Bus Station (Ben Xe Khach Noi Thanh) is one block north of Rap 3/4 cinema. Buses departing from here connect Dalat with destinations within Lam Dong Province, including Bao L'ao, Cau Dat, Di Linh (Djiring), Da Thien, Lac Duong, Ta In and Ta Nun. The administrative offices of the Intra-Provincial Bus Station are near the main bus station.

Train There are no plans at present to rebuild the *crémaillère* cog-wheel railroad line that linked Dalat and Thap Cham (Phan Rang) from 1928 and 1964, though the idea has been suggested. The old train station is now a lorry depot.

Getting Around
Hiking & Cycling The best way to enjoy the forests and cultivated countryside around Dalat is either on foot, seated on horseback or pedalling a bicycle. Suggested routes include:

1) Heading out 3 Thang 4 St, which becomes National Highway 20, to the pine forests of Prenn Pass and Quang Trung Reservoir.
2) Going via the Governor-General's Residence out Khe Sanh St to Thien Vuong Pagoda.
3) Taking Phu Dong Thien Huong St from Dalat University to the Valley of Love.
4) Going out to Bao Dai's Summer Palace and from there, after stopping at Lam Ty Ni Pagoda, via Thien My St and Huyen Tran Cong Chua St to Du Sinh Church.

Cyclo Dalat is too hilly for cyclos.

Lambrettas & Horse-Drawn Carts There is a Lambretta and horse-cart station on Nguyen Thi Minh Khai St in front of the Modern Hotel, which is across the roundabout from the main building of the Central Market. The Lambretta office (Xe Lam Dalat) is next to the Caltex petrol station and the bus station.

Motorbikes Motorbikes and motorcycles (*Honda ong*), which can carry one passenger in addition to the driver, stop in front of the Caltex petrol station next to Dalat Bus Station.

Taxi Rentable Peugeot 203s – all of them black with white roofs – park on the Central Market side of Xuan Huong Dam (near the bus station) and near Rap 3/4 cinema; it costs only 40,000d to rent one for a full day. The taxi office is next to the main bus station and is signposted as Xe Taxi Dalat. Automobiles with drivers can also be hired through Lam Dong Province Tourism.

AROUND DALAT
Prenn Pass
The area along National Highway 20 between Dalat and Datanla Waterfall is known as Prenn Pass. The hillsides support mature pine forests while the valleys are used to cultivate vegetables. This is a great area for hiking and horseback riding.

Quang Trung Reservoir
Quang Trung Reservoir (Tuyen Lam Lake) is an artificial lake crated by a dam in 1980. It is named after Emperor Quang Trung (also known as Nguyen Hue), a leader of the Tay Son Rebellion who is considered a great hero for vanquishing a Chinese invasion force in 1789. The area is being developed for tourism; there are several cafes not far from the dam and paddleboats, rowboats and canoes are for rent nearby. The hillscape around the reservoir is covered with pine trees, most of them newly planted. There is a switchback path up the hill due south-west of the water intake tower. Minority farmers live and raise crops in the vicinity of the lake.

To get to Quang Trung Reservoir, head out of Dalat on National Route 20. At a point 5 km from town turn right and continue for 2 km.

Datanla Falls
Datanla is, in my opinion, the most beautiful waterfall in the Dalat area, largely because of the lush vegetation which surrounds it. The falls are 350 metres from Highway 20 on a path that first passes through a forest of pines and then continues steeply down the hill into a rain forest.

To get to Datanla, turn off Highway 20 about 200 metres past the turn-off to Quang Trung Reservoir; the entrance fee is 200d. There is a second entrance to the falls several hundred metres farther down the road.

Prenn Falls
Prenn Waterfall (elevation 1124 metres) consists of a 15-metre free fall over a wide rock outcrop. A path goes under the outcrop, affording a view of the pool and surrounding rainforest through the curtain of falling water. The path is often impassable after a rainstorm, when the waterfall becomes a raging brown torrent. Refreshments are sold at kiosks near the falls. The park around the falls was dedicated by the Queen of Thailand in 1959.

The entrance to Prenn Falls is near the Prenn Restaurant, which is 13 km from Dalat towards Saigon and Phan Rang; the entrance fee is 200d.

Lat Village
The nine hamlets of Lat Village (population 6000), whose name is pronounced *Lac* by the locals, are about 12 km from Dalat at the base of Lang Bian Mountain. The inhabitants of five of the hamlets are of the Lat ethnic group; the residents of the other four are members of the Chill, Ma and Koho tribes, each of which speaks a different dialect.

Traditionally, Lat houses are built on piles with rough plank walls and a thatch roof. The people of Lat Village eke out a living growing rice, coffee, black beans and sweet potatoes. The villages have 300 hectares of land and produce one rice crop per year. Many residents of Lat have been forced by economic circumstances into the business of producing charcoal, a lowly task often performed by members of Vietnam's minorities. Before 1975, many men from Lat worked with the Americans, as did montagnards elsewhere in the Central Highlands.

Classes in the village's primary and secondary schools, successors of the École Franco-Koho in Dalat in 1948, are conducted in Vietnamese rather than tribal languages. Lat has one Catholic church and one Protestant church. A Koho-language Bible (*Sra Goh*) was published by Protestants in 1971; a Lat-language Bible, prepared by Catholics, appeared the following year. Both montagnard dialects, which are quite similar to each other, are written in a Latin-based script.

Places to Eat There are no restaurants in Lat, just a few food stalls.

Getting There & Away A small, usually

packed bus makes two daily round trips between Dalat and Lat. The bus departs from Dalat at 12 noon and sometime between 4.30 and 5 pm; it leaves Lat at 7 am and (for the last time of the day) at 12.30 pm.

To get to Lat from Dalat, head north on Xo Viet Nghe Tinh St. At Tung Lam Hamlet there is a fork in the road marked by a shot-up cement street sign. Continue straight on (that is, north-westward) rather than to the left (which leads to Suoi Vang, the 'Golden Stream', 14 km away). By bicycle, the 12 km trip to from Dalat to Lat takes about 40 minutes. On foot, it's a 2-hour walk. The road is in poor repair.

Lang Bian Mountain

Lang Bian Mountain (known in Vietnamese as Lam Vien Mountain) has five volcanic peaks ranging in altitude from 2100 to 2400 metres. Of the two highest peaks, the eastern one is known to locals by the woman's name K'Lang; the western one bears a man's name, K'Biang. The upper reaches of the mountain are forested. Only half-a-century ago, the verdant foothills of Lang Bian Mountain, now defoliated, sheltered wild oxen, deer, boars, elephants, rhinoceros and tigers.

The hike up to the top of Lang Bian Mountain, from where the views are truly spectacular, takes 3 to 4 hours from Lat Village. The path begins due north of Lat and is easily recognisable as a red gash in the green mountainside. It is possible to hire young locals as guides.

Ankroët Falls & Lakes

The two Ankroët Lakes were created as part of a hydro-electric project. The waterfall (Thac Ankroët) is about 15 metres high. The Ankroët Lakes are 18 km north-west of Dalat in an area inhabited by hill tribes.

BUON MA THUOT

Buon Ma Thuot (or Ban Me Thuot; population 65,000; elevation 451 metres) is the capital of Dac Lac (Dak Lak) Province. A large percentage of the area's population is made up of ethnic minorities. One of the region's main crops is coffee, which is grown on plantations run by East German managers who are said to be as imperiously demanding as were their French predecessors. Before WW II, the city was a centre of big-game hunting.

The rainy season in this area lasts from April to November, though downpours are usually of short duration. Because of its lower elevation, Buon Ma Thuot is warmer and more humid than Dalat.

At present, it is difficult to get permission to visit Buon Ma Thuot.

Information

Dac Lac Province Tourism (tel 2322) is at 3 Phan Chu Trinh St. The exchange bank is on Ama Tranglon St.

Drai Sap Falls

Drai Sap Falls, about 12 km from Buon Ma Thuot, is in the middle of a hardwood rainforest.

Hilltribe Museum

Displays at the museum feature traditional montagnard dress as well as agricultural implements, fishing gear, bows and arrows, weaving looms and musical instruments. There are said to be 31 distinct ethnic groups in Dac Lac Province.

The Hilltribe Museum is near the Thang Loi Hotel at 1 Me Mai St.

Tua

The Rhade (or Ede) hamlet of Tua is 13 km from Buon Ma Thuot. The people here make a living raising animals and growing manioc, sweet potatoes and maize.

Rhade society is matrilineal and matrilocal (centred around the household of the wife's family). Extended families live in long-houses, each section of which houses a nuclear family. Each long-house is presided over by a man, often the husband of the senior woman of the family. The property of the extended family is owned and controlled by the oldest woman in the group.

The religion of the Rhade is animistic. In

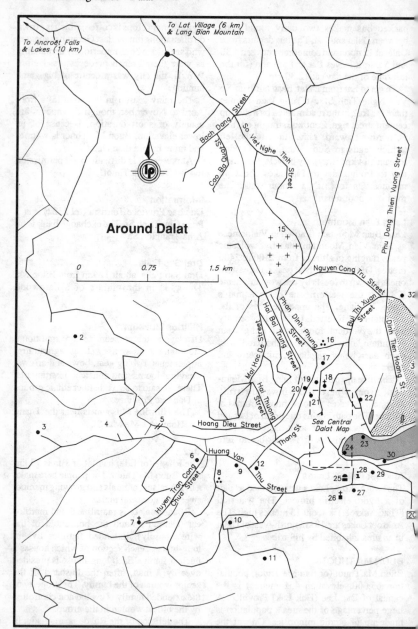

To Lat Village (6 km)
& Lang Bian Mountain

To Ancroet Falls
& Lakes (10 km)

Around Dalat

0   0.75   1.5 km

Bach Dang Street

So Viet Nghe Tinh Street

Cao Ba St

Phu Dong Thien Vuong Street

Nguyen Cong Tru Street

Bui Thi Xuan Street

Dinh Tien Hoang St

Phan Dinh Phung Street

Hai Ba Trung Street

Mai Hoc De Street

Hai Thuong Street

Hoang Dieu Street

Thang St

See Central
Dalat Map

Huong Van

Huyen Tran Cong Chua Street

Thu Street

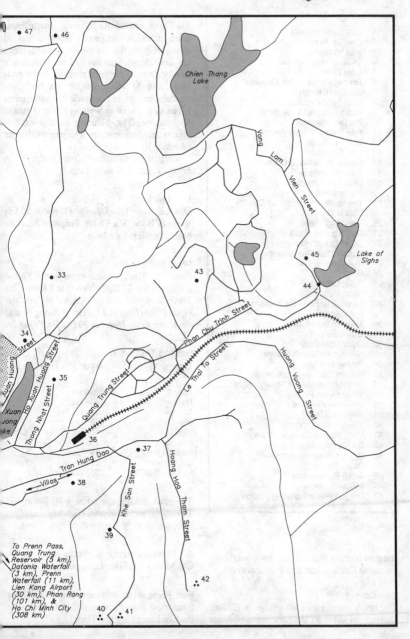

To Prenn Pass,
Quang Trung
Reservoir (5 km),
Datania Waterfall
(3 km), Prenn
Waterfall (11 km),
Lien Kang Airport
(30 km), Phan Rang
(101 km), &
Ho Chi Minh City
(308 km)

1 Tung Lam Hamlet
2 Cam Ly Airstrip (unused)
3 War Memorial
4 Tomb of Nguyen Huu Hao
5 Cam Ly Waterfall
6 Former Couvent des Oiseaux
7 Du Sinh Church
8 Lam Ty Ni Pagoda
9 Former Petite Lycée Yersin
10 Pasteur Institute
11 Bao Dai's Summer Palace
12 Duy Tan Hotel
13 Lam Son Hotel
14 Domaine de Marie Convent
15 Dalat Cemetary
16 Linh Son Pagoda
17 Mimosa Hotel
18 Vietnamese Evangelical Church
19 Thanh The Hotel
20 Lien Hiep Hotel
21 Cao Nguyen Hotel
22 Small Guest Houses
23 Thanh Thuy Restaurant
24 Xuan Huong Dam
25 GPO
26 Dalat Cathedral
27 Dalat Hotel
28 Lam Dong Province Tourism
29 Palace Hotel
30 Thuy Ta Restaurant
31 Golf Course
32 Dalat University
33 Nuclear Research Centre
34 Flower Gardens
35 Former Grande Lyceé Yersin
36 Former Crémaillére Railway Station
37 Villa of Nam Phung
38 Governor-General's Residence
39 Minh Tam Hotel
40 Thien Vuong Pagoda
41 Minh Nguyet Cu Sy Lam Pagoda
42 Su Nu Pagoda
43 Military Academy (off-limits)
44 Dam
45 Small Restaurants
46 Valley of Love
47 Dragon Water Pumping Station

Ma Thuot, are mostly M'nong, a matrilineal tribe in which the family name is passed down through the female line and children are considered members of their mother's family. Despite feminist theories to the contrary, the M'nong are known for their fiercely belligerent attitude towards other tribes in the area as well as towards ethnic Vietnamese. The M'nong hunt wild elephants using domesticated elephants, dozens of which live in Ban Don.

There is a 13th century Cham tower 36 km north of Ban Don at Ya Liao.

Dak Lak Lake

Dak Lak Lake (Ho Dac Lac) is about 50 km south of Buon Ma Thuot. Emperor Bao Dai built a small palace here.

Places to Stay

Buon Ma Thuot's main hotel is the *Thang Loi Hotel* (tel 2322), which is at 1 Phan Chu Trinh St. Other places in town include the *Hoang Gia Hotel* at 2 Le Hong Phong St and the *Hong Kong Hotel* at 30 Hai Ba Trung St.

Getting There & Away

Land distances from Buon Ma Thuot:

Dalat	396 km
Danang	666 km
Kontum	246 km
Nha Trang	191 km
Ninh Hoa	160 km
Phan Rang	295 km
Pleiku	197 km
Qui Nhon	223 km
Ho Chi Minh City	352 km

The road linking the coast with Buon Ma Thuot intersects National Highway 1 at Ninh Hoa, which is 34 km north of Nha Trang.

Air There are weekly flights to and from Ho Chi Minh City, Hanoi and perhaps Danang.

Bus There is bus service to Buon Ma Thuot from most major towns and cities between Ho Chi Minh City and Hanoi.

the past century many Rhade have been converted to Catholicism and Protestantism.

Ban Don

The residents of Ban Don village in Ea Sup District, which is 55 km north-west of Buon

PLEIKU

Pleiku (or Playcu; elevation 785 metres) is a market town in the centre of a vast, fertile plateau whose red soil is of volcanic origin. Many of the 35,000 inhabitants of the city, which is 785 metres above sea level, are members of ethnic minorities.

Getting There & Away

Road distances from Pleiku:

Buon Ma Thuot	197 km
Nha Trang	424 km
Qui Nhon	186 km
Ho Chi Minh City	550 km

Pleiku is linked by road to Buon Ma Thuot, Qui Nhon (via An Khe), Kontum and Cambodia's Ratanakiri Province (via Chu Nghe).

Air There are weekly Vietnam Airlines flights to Pleiku from both Ho Chi Minh City and Hanoi.

Bus There is non-express bus service to Pleiku from most coastal cities between Nha Tranh and Danang.

KONTUM

Kontum (population 35,000; altitude 525 metres) is in a region inhabited primarily by ethnic minority groups, including the Bahnar, Jarai, Rengao and Sedeng.

During the course of a major battle between South Vietnamese forces and the North Vietnamese that took place in and around Kontum in the spring of 1972, the area was devastated by hundreds of US B-52 raids.

Jrai Li Falls

Forty-two metre high Jrai Li Falls (Thac Ya Li) are 22 km south-west of Kontum.

Getting There & Away

Land distances from Kontum:

Buon Ma Thuot	246 km
Nha Trang	436 km
Pleiku	46 km
Qui Nhon	198 km
Ho Chi Minh City	896 km

Danang

The complexes that afflict Hanoi, the nation's capital, and Saigon, itself once a capital city, seem far, far away in Danang (population 400,000), Vietnam's fourth-largest city. Danang's distance from other centres of power, its natural endowments (the port, its proximity to Laos and Thailand) and the high degree of provincial autonomy afforded by Vietnam's political structure allow for considerable local initiative. Of late, the city has become a leader in implementing economic reforms and has shown itself eager to demonstrate the sort of dynamism and economic pragmatism likely to attract foreign investment. In addition, Danang serves as the main seaport for the southern part of land-locked Laos.

Among the Danang-area sites of interest to visitors are the Marble Mountains, China Beach (Bai Non Nuoc), the ancient port town of Hoi An (Faifo), the Cham towers at My Son, Ba Na hill station, Hai Van Pass (Col des Nuages) and Lang Co Beach.

History
Danang, known under the French as Tourane, succeeded Hoi An (Faifo) as the most important port in central Vietnam during the 19th century.

In late March 1975, Danang, the second-largest city in South Vietnam, was the scene of utter chaos after Saigon government forces were ordered to abandon Hué and Quang Ngai had fallen to the Communists, cutting South Vietnam in two. Desperate civilians tried to flee the city as soldiers of the disintegrating South Vietnamese Army engaged in an orgy of looting, pillage and rape. On 29 March 1975, two truckloads of Communist guerrillas, more than half of

■ PLACES TO STAY

1 Nha Nghi Du Lich Thanh Binh (hotel)
2 Dong Da Hotel (Khach San Huu Nghi)
3 Danang Hotel
4 Hai Van Hotel
5 Song Han Hotel
6 Railway Hotel
10 Nha Khach (hotel)
13 Khach San 32 (hotel)
20 Dong Kinh Hotel
26 Thu Do Hotel
29 Khach San Yen Hanh (hotel)
35 Hai Chau Hotel
36 Pacific Hotel (Thai Binh Duong Hotel)
37 Orient Hotel (Phuong Dong Hotel)

▼ PLACES TO EAT

15 Thanh Lich Restaurant
17 Seamen's Club (cafe)
19 Nha Hang 72 (restaurant)
25 Chin Den Restaurant
27 Dac San Restaurant
28 Nha Hang So 10 (restaurant)
31 Thanh Huong Restaurant
34 Thoi Dai Restaurant

38 Tiem An Binh Dan (restaurant)
39 Tu Do Restaurant
40 Quan Chay Vegetarian Restaurant

● OTHER

7 Foreign Trade Bank (Vietcombank)
8 People's Committee of Quang Nam-Danang Province
9 Market
11 Cao Dai Temple
12 Ancient Renault Buses
14 Vietnam Airlines Booking Office
16 GPO
18 Danang Tourism
21 Former US Consulate
22 Ferries across the Han River
23 Short-Haul Pickup Truck Station
24 Con Market
30 Municipal Theatre
32 Cho Han (market)
33 Danang Cathedral
41 Phap Lam Pagoda (Chua Tinh Hoi)
42 Cham Museum
43 Tam Bao Pagoda
44 Pho Da Pagoda

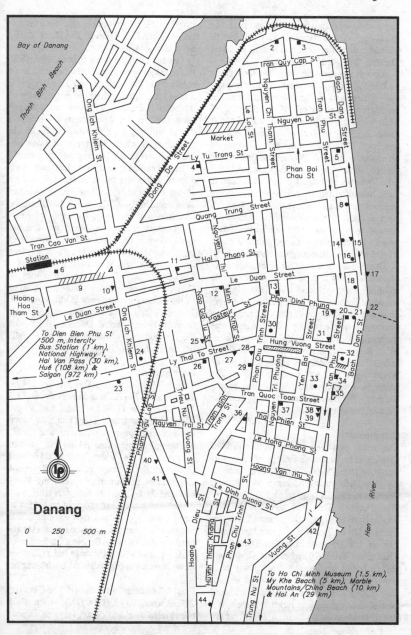

Bay of Danang

Thanh Binh Beach

To Dien Bien Phu St
(500 m), Intercity
Bus Station (1 km),
National Highway 1,
Hai Van Pass (30 km),
Hué (108 km) &
Saigon (972 km)

Danang

0   250   500 m

To Ho Chi Minh Museum (1.5 km),
My Khe Beach (5 km), Marble
Mountains/China Beach (10 km)
& Hoi An (29 km)

Han River

them women, drove into what had been the most heavily defended city in South Vietnam, and without firing a shot, declared Danang 'liberated'.

Almost the only fighting that took place as Danang fell was between South Vietnamese soldiers and civilians battling for space on flights and ships out of the city. On 27 March, the president of World Airways, Ed Daly, ignoring explicit government orders, sent two 727s from Saigon to Danang to evacuate refugees. When the first plane landed, about a thousand desperate and panicked people mobbed the tarmac. Soldiers fired assault rifles at each other and at the plane as they tried to shove their way through the rear door. As the aircraft taxied down the runway trying to take off, people climbed up into the landing-gear wells and someone threw a hand grenade, damaging the right wing.

Those who managed to fight their way aboard, kicking and punching aside anyone in their way, included over 200 soldiers, mostly members of the elite Black Panthers company. The only civilians on board were two women and one baby – and the baby was there only because it had been thrown aboard by its desperate mother, who was left on the tarmac. Several of the stowaways in the wheel wells couldn't hold on, and as the plane flew southward, TV cameras on the second 727 filmed them falling into the South China Sea.

Orientation

The main east-west artery in the city of Danang is known at various points along its length as Hung Vuong St (in the city centre), Ly Thai To St (near the Central Market) and Dien Bien Phu St (out around the Intercity Bus Station). This thoroughfare is intersected by Bach Dang St, which runs along the Han River; Tran Phu St, one block west of Bach Dang St; and Phan Chu Trinh St (or Phan Chau Trinh St), where the Orient and Palace hotels are located. Bach Dang St is one-way going north; Tran Phu St is one-way going south. The municipal stadium, with its four tall cement lighting towers, is a good landmark by which to navigate

between the city centre (around the intersection of Phan Chu Trinh St and Hung Vuong St) and huge Con Market.

Danang is on the western bank of the Han River. Along the eastern bank, which can be reached via the Nguyen Van Troi Bridge, is a long, thin peninsula at the northern tip of which is Nui Son Tra, known as 'Monkey Mountain' to the Americans. It is now a closed military area. To the south, 11 km from the city, are the Marble Mountains. Hai Van Pass overlooks Danang from the north.

In recent years, an attempt has been made to rationalise the numeration of Danang's streets, many of which received new names after reunification. The result has been the simultaneous listing of two sets of street numbers, with some buildings using either one system or the other and other structures signposted for both. This is particularly true of Ong Ich Khiem St and Hung Vuong St.

The process of bringing the names of Danang's streets in line with the sensitivities of the present government is still going on. The city's distinctive cement street signs date from the French period. Occasionally, one of the new white-on-blue metal plaques falls off, revealing the old French name.

Information

Tourist Office Danang Tourism (tel 21423, 22213) at 48 Bach Dang St near the GPO is open from 7 to 11.30 am and 1 to 4.30 pm Monday to Saturday. They can't do much beyond providing you with a car and guide.

Foreigners interested in business, trade or investment in the Danang area would do well to contact the Foreign Economic Relations Department of Quang Nam-Danang Province (tel 21092) at 136 Ong Ich Khiem St. The dynamic staff are efficient and eager to be of assistance. Indeed, they exemplify this province's pragmatic, pro-business orientation. The offices of the People's Committee of Quang Nam-Danang Province (tel 21238) are in the French-era city hall at 34 Bach Dang St.

Post & Telecommunications The GPO (tel 21499; telex 704 PUBLIC DN), which offers telex, telephone and postal services, is next to 46 Bach Dang St (corner of Le Duan St); it is open daily from 6 am to 8.30 pm.

Money The Foreign Trade Bank, Vietcombank, is at 46A Le Loi St near the corner of Hai Phong St; it is open from 7.30 to 11.30 am and 1 to 3.30 pm Monday to Saturday except Thursday and Saturday afternoons.

Consulate The Consulate General of the USSR (tel 22543) is at 5 Dong Da St.

Cham Museum

The Cham Museum (Bao Tang Cham), founded in 1915 by the École Française d'Extrême Orient, has the finest collection of Cham sculpture in the world. Many of the sandstone carvings (altars, lingas, garudas, ganeshas and images of Shiva, Brahma and Vishnu) are absolutely stunning; this is the sort of place you can easily visit again and again. It is well worth it to get a knowledge-able guide (a scarce commodity in these parts) to show you around. The Cham Museum is near the intersection of Tran Phu St and Le Dinh Duong St and is open daily from 8 to 11 am and 1 to 5 pm.

A trilingual guidebook to the museum written by its director, Tran Ky Phuong, Vietnam's most eminent scholar of Cham civilisation, gives excellent background on the art of Champa; it also includes some information on the museum's exhibits. The booklet, entitled *Museum of Cham Sculpture – Danang* and *Bao Tang Dieu Khac Cham Da Nang* (Foreign Languages Publishing House, Hanoi, 1987), is usually on sale where you buy your entrance ticket.

Cham art can be divided into two main periods. Before the 10th century, it was very emotionally expressive, reflecting contact with seafaring cultures from Indonesia. From the 10th to the 14th centuries, as Champa fell into decline because of unend-ing wars with the Vietnamese, Cham art came under Khmer influence and became more formalistic.

The museum's artefacts, which date from the 7th to 15th centuries, were discovered at Dong Duong (Indrapura), Khuong My, My Son, Tra Kieu (Simhapura), Thap Mam (Binh Dinh) and other sites, mostly in Quang Nam-Danang Province. The rooms in the museum are named after the localities in which the objects displayed in them were discovered.

A recurring image in Cham art is that of Uroja, the 'Mother of the Country', who gave birth to the dynasties that ruled Champa. Uroja, whose name means 'woman's breast' in the Cham language, was worshipped in the form of the nipples one often sees in Cham sculpture. Also common is the linga, phallic symbol of Shiva, which came to prominence after Champa's contact with Hinduism. Cham religious beliefs (and thus Cham architecture and sculpture) were influenced by Mahayana Buddhism as early as the 4th century. In addition to its clear Indian elements, Cham art shows Javanese, Khmer and Dai Viet (Vietnamese) influ-ences.

The four scenes carved around the base of the 7th century Tra Kieu Altar tell part of the Ramayana epic in a style influenced by the Amaravati style of South India. Scene A (see diagram), in which 16 characters appear, tells the story of Prince Rama, who broke the sacred bow, Rudra, at the citadel of Videha and thus won from King Janak the right to wed his daughter, Princess Sita. Scene B, which also comprises 16 characters, shows the ambassadors sent by King Janak to Prince Rama's father, King Dasaratha, at Ayodhya. The emissaries inform King Dasaratha of the exploits of his son, present him with gifts, and invite him to Videha to celebrate his son's wedding. In Scene C (which has 18 characters), the royal wedding ceremony (and that of three of Prince Rama's brothers, who marry three of Princess Sita's cousins) is shown. In Scene D, 11 apsaras dance and present flowers to the newlyweds under the guidance of the two gandhara musicians who appear at the beginning of Scene A.

Former US Consulate

After reunification, the former US Consulate

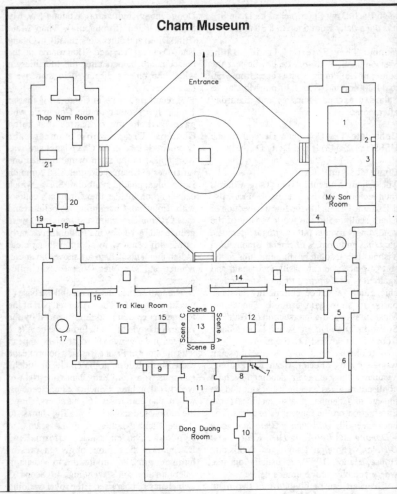

Cham Museum

1 My Son Altar; from My Son, 8th–9th centuries
2 Ganesha (seated elephant); from My Son, 8th–9th centuries
3 Birthday of Brahma; from My Son, 8th–9th centuries
4 Polo players; from Thach An, 7th century
5 Altar ornaments; from Khuong My, 10th century
6 The Goddess Sarasvati; from Chanh Lo, 11th century
7 Vishnu, from Tra Kieu, 10th century
8 A deity; from Dong Duong, 9th–10th centuries
9 A deity; from Dong Duong, 9th–10th centuries
10 Dong Duong Altar ornaments; from Dong Duong, 9th–10th centuries
11 Dong Duong Altar; from Dong Duong, 9th–10th centuries
12 Linga
13 Tra Kieu Altar; from Tra Kieu, 7th century
14 Dancing Shiva; from Phong Le, 10th century
15 Linga
16 Dancing female apsaras; from Quang Nam–Danang Province, 10th century
17 Altar ornaments; from Binh Dinh, 12th–14th centuries
18 Lions; from Thap Mam, 12th–14th centuries
19 Shiva; from Thap Mam, 12th–14th centuries
20 The elephant–lion Gajasimha; from Thap Mam, 12th–14th centuries
21 The sea monster Makara; from Thap Mam, 12th–14th centuries

building was turned into Danang's Museum of American War Crimes; that's why a Huey helicopter with its door gun still attached is sitting in the courtyard. In 1975, during the chaos that reigned in the days before the Communist take-over, evacuation barges docked right across the street from the consulate. The consulate was later looted, and mobs of Vietnamese – furious at having been 'abandoned' by the Americans – tried to burn it down. Today, the brick structure is considered beyond repair and may be torn down.

The former US Consulate is on the corner of Bach Dang St and Phan Dinh Phung St.

Danang Cathedral

Danang Cathedral (Chinh Toa Da Nang), known to locals as Con Ga Church (the Rooster Church) because of the weathercock on top of the steeple, was built for the city's French residents in 1923. Today, it serves a Catholic community of 4000. The Cathedral's extraordinary architecture is well worth a look, as are the medieval-style stained glass windows of various saints.

Next door to the cathedral are the offices of the diocese of Danang and Saint Paul Convent. About 100 nuns – who, when praying, wear white habits in the summer and black habits in the winter – live here and at another convent building across the Han River.

Danang Cathedral is on Tran Phu St across from the Hai Chau Hotel. If the main gate is locked, try the back entrance, which is opposite 14 Yen Bai St. Masses are held daily at 5 am and 5 pm and on Sundays at 5 am, 6.30 am and 4.30 pm.

Pagodas & Temples

Caodai Temple Danang's main Caodai Temple (Chua Cao Dai), built in 1956 and now home to six priests, is the largest such structure outside of the sect's headquarters in Tay Ninh. There are 50,000 Caodais in Quang Nam-Danang Province, 20,000 in Danang itself. The temple is across the street from Hospital C (Benh Vien C), which is at 74 Hai Phong St. As at all Caodai temples,

prayers are held four times a day at 6 am, noon, 6 pm and midnight.

The left-hand gate to the complex, marked *Nu Phai*, is for women; the right gate, marked Nam Phai, is for men. The doors to the sanctuary are also segregated: women to the left, men to the right, and priests of either sex through the central door. Behind the main altar sits an enormous globe with the 'divine eye', symbol of Caodaism, on it.

Hanging from the ceiling in front of the altar is a sign reading *Van Giao Nhat Ly*, which means 'All Religions have the same reason'. Behind the gilded letters is a picture of the founders of five of the world's great religions. Left-to-right, they are: Lao Tze; either Moses or Mohammed (wearing blue robes cut in the style of the Greek Orthodox); Jesus (portrayed as he is in French icons); the Buddha (who has a distinctly South-East Asian appearance); and Confucius (looking as Chinese as could be).

Portraits of early Caodai leaders, dressed in turbans and white robes, are displayed in the building behind the main sanctuary. Ngo Van Chieu, founder of Caodaism, is shown standing wearing a pointed white turban and a long white robe with blue markings.

Phap Lam Pagoda Phap Lam Pagoda (Chua Phap Lam, also known as Chua Tinh Hoi) is opposite 373 Ong Ich Khiem St (123 Ong Ich Khiem St according to the old numbering). Built in 1936, this pagoda has a brass statue of Dia Tang, the Chief of Hell, near the entrance. Six monks live here. Quan Chay Vegetarian Restaurant is just up the street.

Tam Bao Pagoda The main building of Tam Bao Pagoda (Chua Tam Bao) at 253 Phan Chu Trinh St is topped with a five tiered tower. Only four *bonzes* live at this large pagoda, which was built in 1953.

Pho Da Pagoda Pho Da Pagoda (Pho Da Tu), which is across from 293 Phan Chu Trinh St, was built in 1923 in a traditional architectural configuration. Today, about 40 *bonzes*, most of them young, live and study here. Local laypeople and their children participate actively in the pagoda's lively religious life.

Ho Chi Minh Museum

The Ho Chi Minh Museum (Bao Tang Ho Chi Minh; tel 5656) has three sections: a museum of military history in front of which American, Soviet and Chinese weaponry are displayed; a replica of Ho Chi Minh's house in Hanoi (complete with a small lake); and, on the other side of the pond from the house, a museum about Uncle Ho.

The museum, which is on Nguyen Van Troi St 250 metres west of Nui Thanh St, is open Tuesday to Sunday from 7 to 11 am and 1 to 4.30 pm.

Tombs of Spanish & French Soldiers

Spanish-led Philippine and French troops attacked Danang in August 1858, ostensibly to end the mistreatment of Vietnamese Catholics and Catholic missionaries by the government of Emperor Tu Duc. The city quickly fell, but the invaders soon had to contend with cholera, dysentery, scurvy, typhus and mysterious fevers. By the summer of 1859, twenty times as many of the invaders had died of illness as had been killed in combat. Many of these soldiers are buried in a chapel (Bai Mo Phap Va Ta Ban Nha) about 15 km from the city. The names of the dead are written on the walls.

To get there, cross Nguyen Van Troi Bridge and turn left onto Ngo Quyen St. Continue north to Tien Sa Port (Cang Tien Sa). The chapel, a white building, stands on the right on a low hill about half a km past the gate of the port.

Beaches

My Khe Beach My Khe Beach (Bai Tam My Khe) is about 6 km by road from downtown Danang. The beach drops off sharply to deep water; the undertow is dangerous, especially in winter.

To get there by car, cross Nguyen Van Troi Bridge and continue straight (eastwards) across the big intersection (instead of turning right (southwards) to the Marble Moun-

tains). If you don't have a car, you might try hopping a ferry across the Han River from the foot of Phan Dinh Phung St and catching a ride south-eastward to Nguyen Cong Tru St.

Thanh Binh Beach Thanh Binh Beach is only a couple of km from the centre of Danang. It is often crowded, notwithstanding the fact that the water is not the cleanest. To get there from Con Market, head all the way to the northern end of Ong Ich Khiem St.

Nam O Beach Nam O Beach is on the Bay of Danang about 15 km from the city towards Hai Van Pass. Vehicles to Nam O depart from the Short-Haul Pickup Truck Station. Kim Lien Railway Station is a few km from the beach.

China Beach For information on China Beach, see the 'Marble Mountains & China Beach' section .

Hai Van Pass

Hai Van Pass (Deo Hai Van), whose name means 'Pass of the Ocean Clouds' (the French knew it as the Col des Nuages) crosses over a spur of the Truong Son Mountain Range that juts into the South China Sea. About 30 km north of Danang, National Highway 1 climbs to an elevation of 496 metres, passing south of the peak Ai Van Son (altitude 1172 metres). The railroad track, with its many tunnels, goes around the peninsula, following the shoreline.

In the 15th century, Hai Van Pass formed the boundary between Vietnam and the Kingdom of Champa. Until the Vietnam War, the pass was heavily forested. At the top of the Hai Van Pass is an old French fort later used by the South Vietnamese Army and the Americans. The views from near the fortress are quite spectacular. Watch out for the live mortar shells left lying about in the undergrowth!

Lang Co

Lang Co is a paradisiacal peninsula of palm-shaded sand with a crystal-clear turquoise blue lagoon on one side and many km of beachfront facing the South China Sea on the other. This is one of the most idyllic places in all of Vietnam. There are spectacular views of Lang Co, which is just north of Hai Van Pass, from both National Highway 1 and the train linking Danang and Hu.

Getting There & Away Lang Co Railway Station, served by non-express trains, is almost exactly midway between Danang and Hué.

Places to Stay A hotel is being built at Lang Co.

Ba Na Hill Station

Ba Na, the 'Dalat of Quang Nam-Danang Province', is a hill station along the crest of Mount Ba Na (or Nui Chua), which rises 1467 metres above the coastal plain. The view in all directions is truly spectacular, and the air is fresh and cool: though it may be 36°C on the coast, the temperature is likely to be between 15° and 26°C at Ba Na. Rain often falls at altitudes of 700 to 1200 metres above sea level, but around the hill station itself the sky is usually clear. Mountain paths in the area lead to a variety of waterfalls and viewpoints.

Ba Na, founded in 1919 for use by French settlers, is not presently in any condition to welcome visitors; but the provincial government has high hopes of making Ba Na once again a magnet for tourists.

By road Ba Na is 48 km west of Danang (as the crow flies, the distance is 27 km). Until WWII, French vacationers travelled the last 20 km by sedan chair!

Ho Chi Minh Trail

Remnants of the Ho Chi Minh Trail can be seen about 60 km west of Danang near the mountain town of Giang. Other areas through which the Ho Chi Minh Trail passed include Hien District and Phuoc Son District. The population of these mountainous parts of Quang Nam-Danang Province includes many montagnards (hill-tribe people) such as the Katu, some of whom still live as they have for generations.

Places to Stay – bottom end

City Centre Danang's ever-entrepreneurial People's Committee has discovered that decent accommodation at fair prices will keep visitors around (and spending money) longer. Towards this end, they have made sure that all sectors of the hotel market in the city are adequately covered. Among their hotel projects in town is the *Hai Chau Hotel* (tel 22722), which since its opening in early 1989 has quickly become a favourite with Overseas Vietnamese and budget travellers. Though it looked at least 10 years old on the day it opened (thanks to typically shoddy construction and finishing work), the plumbing is operable and so are the air conditioners, which grace every room. The Hai Chau Hotel charges foreigners and Overseas Vietnamese 20,000d (plus 10% service) for a single, 32,000d for a double and 40,000d for a triple. Local Vietnamese pay exactly half these prices, but don't bother arguing: they won't budge, in part because the place is so often full up. The Hai Chau Hotel is conveniently located near the centre of town at 215 Tran Phu St, which is across the street from Danang Cathedral (Chinh Toa Da Nang).

Central Danang has several rock-bottom places where you get what you pay for but little more. *Khach San Dong Kinh* (21 rooms) is at 87 Tran Phu St, an extremely convenient location, especially if you just found out that the Hai Chau Hotel is full. Basic rooms with fans cost 5000 to 6000d. *Khach San Yen Hanh* (tel 21230; 25 rooms) is right in the city centre at 42 Phan Chu Trinh St. It is a basic hotel for domestic travellers, with rooms going for 6000 or 7000d. The staff here is friendly; in fact, it is sometimes *too* friendly, and one traveller reports having been run out of the hotel by prostitutes. Two blocks away at 32 Phan Dinh Phung St is *Khach San 32* (tel 22491). Doubles/triples with fan cost 7000/8000d; a triple with air-con goes for 18,000d. Reception is up the stairs from the entrance on Chi Thanh St.

Khach San Thu Do at 65 Hung Vuong St (107 Hung Vuong St by the old numbering) is a rather grimy place with rooms in the 5000 to 8000d range. It is only a few blocks from Con Market (Cho Con).

Railway Station Area To the left of the parking lot as you exit the railway station building is the four storey *Khach San Duong Sat 29-3* (tel 22794). The name means '29th of March Railway Hotel' and commemorates the day Danang was 'liberated' in 1975. The 200 dorm beds come with mats only and cost 2000d per night; a room for three or four people costs 8000d. One hundred metres away is a tiny place simply called *Nha Khach* (tel 22948) at 124 Ong Ich Khiem (15 Ong Ich Khiem by the new numbering system); doubles go for 5000d and come with mats only.

Intercity Bus Station Area There are a number of places around the Intercity Bus Station offering extremely basic dormitory accommodation. They are probably worth considering only if you're really hard up or if you arrive in town by bus in the wee hours of the morning. *Nha Tro Ben Xe* (Bus Station Dormitory) is a two storey yellow building on the east side of the bus station parking lot; it is across the street from 208 Dien Bien Phu St.

There are two establishments simply called *Nha Tro* at numbers 196 and 198 Dien Bien Phu St. *Phong Tro So 1* is at 194 Dien Bien Phu St. *Phong Tro So 2* is down the block at 214 Dien Bien Phu St. *Nha Khach* is at 186 Dien Bien Phu St.

Northern Neighbourhoods Several large hotels are located, rather inconveniently, in the residential area at the northern tip of the peninsula on which the city of Danang is located. The *Danang Hotel* (tel 21179; about 100 rooms) at 3 Dong Da St is popular with budget travellers as a dong-denominated alternative to the Hai Chau Hotel; doubles cost 20,000d. The building was constructed

in the late 1960s to house American military personnel. The Danang Hotel has an in-house restaurant, one of the few in the vicinity.

Next door at 7 Dong Da St is the *Dong Da Hotel* (tel 22563; 68 rooms), also known as *Khach San Huu Nghi*. Vietnamese pay between 6000 and 12,000d for a room; foreigners are charged 20,000d for a 1st class room. The Dong Da Hotel has its own restaurant.

A bit closer to the railroad station is the *Hai Van Hotel* (tel 21300; 47 rooms) at 2 Nguyen Thi Minh Khai St. Locals pay 16,000 to 18,000d for doubles with air-conditioning; foreigners are charged 26,000d. The *Song Han Hotel* (tel 22540; about 30 rooms) is along the Han River at 26 Bach Dang St. Rooms, some with air-con, cost between 15,000 and 20,000d for Vietnamese but US$15 to US$20 for foreigners.

Nha Nghi Du Lich Thanh Binh (tel 21319) at 5 Ong Ich Khiem St is right on Thanh Binh Beach, known for its crowds and polluted water. This place is reserved for Vietnamese workers on organised union vacations but they might agree to rent out an unbooked room.

Places to Stay – top end
If you book a tour with Vietnam Tourism, chances are they'll lodge you at one of the two relatively expensive high-rise hotels in town. Otherwise, there is little reason to stay at these places unless you simply must have a 8th floor view of Danang. The *Phuong Dong Hotel* (tel 21266, 22854), also known as the *Orient Hotel*, is at 93 Phan Chu Trinh St. Singles with private bath cost US$25; there is a decent restaurant on the top. The *Thai Binh Hotel* (tel 22137, 22921), also called the *Pacific Hotel*, is across the street; singles/doubles cost US$15/17 to US$18/20 while a triple goes for US$25. The food at the 7th floor restaurant is cheap but dismal.

Places to Eat
City Centre The best restaurant in Danang (and one of the best in Vietnam) is the *Tu Do Restaurant* (tel 22039) at 180 Tran Phu St,

100 metres from the Hai Chau Hotel; it is open from 7 am to 9 pm. The menu is extensive, the service is punctilious and the food is in fact quite good, but some of the prices are a lot higher than you'd reasonably expect to pay. Next door at 174 Tran Phu St is *Tiem An Binh Dan Restaurant*, a modest place with reasonable prices.

Nha Hang So 10 is on Phan Chu Trinh St (corner Hung Vuong St). *Dac San Restaurant* is nearby at 95 Hung Vuong St.

Thoi Dai Restaurant (tel 21495, 21441) at 171 Tran Phu St is crowded with locals in the evenings. *Thanh Huong Restaurant* (tel 22101) at 40 Hung Vuong St (corner Tran Phu St) is a small, friendly place with a local clientele; it's a good place for morning *pho* (soup). Avoid *Nha Hang 72*, an indifferently run greasy spoon at 72 Tran Phu St.

A breakfast of fried beef and eggs with fresh French bread and salad is available from 6 to 11 am daily at the *Chin Den Restaurant* (the name means 'Black Nine'), which is near the stadium at 32 Ngo Gia Tu St.

Thanh Lich Restaurant, near the GPO at 42 Bach Dang St, has an extensive menu in English, French and Vietnamese. This place has received good reviews from foreign businesspeople.

The *Orient* and *Palace* hotels each have restaurants, though the food at both is rather mediocre.

Con Market There are dozens of food stalls behind the main market building. *An Vong Restaurant* is at 137 Hung Vuong St.

Northern Neighbourhoods There are a number of small restaurants along Dong Da St towards the train station from the *Danang* and the *Dong Da* hotels, both of which have their own restaurants.

Vegetarian *Quan Chay*, a vegetarian food stall, serves the usual selection of Vietnamese-style vegetarian dishes prepared to look and taste like meat dishes. The food here is very, very inexpensive; a filling, multi-course meal for three may cost 4000d or so.

Quan Chay, open daily 7 am to 4 pm, is half a block from Phap Lam Pagoda (Chua Tinh Hoi) and about a km from the city centre. The street address is 484 Ong Ich Khiem St (162 Ong Ich Khiem by the old numbers).

Prepared vegetarian food is sold on the 1st and 15th of each lunar month at *Cho Han*, a vegetable market off Hung Vuong St between Bach Dang St and Tran Phu St.

Entertainment

Danang's night life centres around Tran Phu, Hung Vuong, Le Loi and Phan Chu Trinh streets.

The Municipal Theatre, which offers a wide variety of performances depending on which troupes are in town, is on the corner of Hung Vuong and Le Loi streets. *Hat Tuong*, a form of classical drama, is performed by a provincial troupe that tours all around Quang Nam-Danang Province.

There are a number of cinemas along Tran Phu St near the Vietnam Airlines office. Liberation Day Cinema (Rap 29-3) is on Phan Chu Trinh St near the corner of Tran Quoc Toan St.

Things to Buy

Danang seems particularly well-endowed with tailors, many of whom have shops along Hung Vuong St. For a pittance over the cost of the cloth, you can have high-quality shirts, pants, skirts, etc tailored to fit your exact proportions. Cloth is available either from the tailors' stock or at the cloth stalls near the intersection of Hung Vuong and Yen Bai streets.

Film and photo supplies can be purchased at 86 Phan Chu Trinh St and 136 Hung Vuong St.

Danang's central marketplace, Con Market (Cho Con) is at the intersection of Hung Vuong and Ong Ich Khiem streets. The front section was built in 1985. Con Market has a huge selection of just about everything sold in Vietnam: household items, ceramics, fresh vegetables, stationary, cutlery, fruit, flowers, polyester clothes, etc. Dozens of food stalls are located in the back part of the market.

Getting There & Away
Road distances from Danang:

Ho Chi Minh City	972 km
Nha Trang	541 km
Qui Nhon	303 km
Quang Ngai	130 km
Hué	108 km
Lao Bao	350 km
(Lao-Vietnam border)	
Savannakhet, Laos	500 km
(Lao-Thai border)	
Hanoi	764 km

Air The Danang office of Vietnam Airlines (tel 21130) is at 35 Tran Phu St.

Flights from Ho Chi Minh City to Danang depart Tan Son Nhut Airport at 6.30 am on Mondays, Wednesdays and Saturdays. These flights continue on to Hanoi, departing Danang at 8.25 am. Flights to Danang from Hanoi depart at 6.30 am on Tuesdays, Fridays and Sundays, continuing on to Ho Chi Minh City from Danang at 8.20 am.

With high hopes of attracting regular flights from abroad, Danang Airport became Danang International Airport in 1989, joining Tan Son Nhut and Noi Bai as Vietnam's third point of entry by air. The airport can handle most types of aircraft and is being outfitted with modern all-weather navigation equipment with an eye toward making the city a transit stop for international flights. Visitors arriving in Danang on domestic flights are registered with the police and asked for what can charitably be called a registration fee.

During the Vietnam War, Danang had one of the busiest airports in the world. Dozens of American-built cement revetments, some of which are now used to house Vietnamese Air Force MiGs, still line the runways.

Bus The Danang Intercity Bus Station (Ben Xe Khach Da Nang; tel 21265) is about 3 km from the city centre on the thoroughfare known, at various points along its length, as Hung Vuong St, Ly Thai To St and Dien Bien Phu St. The ticket office for express buses is across the street from 200 Dien Bien Phu St; it is open from 7 to 11 am and 1 to 5 pm. Express bus service is available to Buon Ma Thuot (17 hours), Dalat, Gia Lai, Haiphong, Hanoi (24 hours), Ho Chi Minh City (24 hours), Hon Gai, Lang Son, Nam Dinh and Nha Trang (14 hours). Tickets for non-express buses to Kontum, Sathay and Vinh (12 hours) are also sold here. All express buses depart at 5 am.

The non-express ticket office is open from 5 am until the late afternoon. There is non-express bus service from Danang Bus Station to:

Ai Nghia	Kham Duc
An Hoa	Kiem Lam
Chu Lai	Quang Ngai
Dong Ha	Que Son
Giang	Qui Nhon
Giao Thuy	Tam Ky
Go Noi	Thanh My
Ha Lam	Tien Phuoc
Ha Tan	Tra My
Hoi An	Trao
Hiep Duc	Trung Mang
Hué	Trung Phuoc

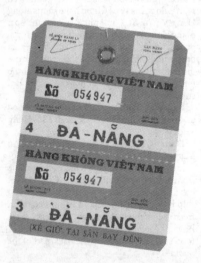

Upon arrival at the Danang Intercity Bus Station, be prepared for aggressive touting by cyclo drivers. A cyclo ride to the city centre should cost about 1500d.

Ancient Renault buses to Cam Lam, Kim Lien, Mui Bai and Vinh Diem leave from a small local bus station about half a km from the city centre at the corner of Le Duan and Nguyen Thi Minh Khai streets. The station is in operation from 5 am to about 6 pm.

Short-Haul Pickup Truck Station

Lambrettas and small passenger trucks to places in the vicinity of Danang leave from the Short-Haul Pickup Truck Station opposite 80 Hung Vuong St, which is about a block west of Con Market (Cho Con). There is service from here to Cam Le, Cau Do, Hoa Khanh, Hoi An (Faifo), Kim Lien, Nam O (there's a beach here), Non Nuoc (the Marble Mountains and China Beach), Phuoc Tuong and Son Cha. The trip to Non Nuoc takes approximately 20 minutes; the ride to Hoi An takes about 1 hour. Vehicles leave when full (ie when packed with people). The station opens at about 5 am and closes around 5 pm.

Train Danang Train Station (Ga Da Nang) is about 1.5 km from the city centre on Haiphong St at the northern end of Hoang Hoa Tham St. The train ride to Hué is one of the nicest in the country (though driving up and over Hai Van Pass is also spectacular).

Northbound, the quickest ride is on TN2, STN4 and STN6, which take 3¼ hours to Hué. Other trains to Hué include DH2 (4 hours) and 166 (6 hours). The DH trains stop at Danang, Lang Co, Cau Hai, Da Bac and Hué. Watch your belongings as you pass through the pitch-black tunnels.

The fastest train service to points south is on TN1, STN 3 and STN 5, which take 14 hours to Nha Trang and 26 to 29 hours to Saigon. Train 172 goes to Qui Nhon, and NH2 will take you (very slowly) to Nha Trang.

For details on the Vietnamese rail system (schedules, travel times, etc), see the 'Getting Around' chapter.

Getting Around

Ferries across the Han River depart from a dock at the foot of Phan Dinh Phung St.

MARBLE MOUNTAINS & CHINA BEACH

Marble Mountains

The Marble Mountains (Ngu Hanh Son or Nui Non Nuoc) consist of five stone hillocks, once islands, made of marble. Each is said to represent one of the five elements of the universe and is named accordingly: Thuy Son (water), Moc Son (wood), Hoa Son (fire), Kim So (metal or gold) and Tho Son (earth). The largest and most famous, Thuy Son, has a number of natural caves (*dong*) in which Buddhist sanctuaries have been built over the centuries. When Champa ruled this area, these same caves were used as Hindu shrines. Thuy Son is a popular pilgrimage site, especially on days of the full and sliver moons and during Tet.

Local children have learned that foreign tourists buy souvenirs and sometimes leave tips for unsolicited guided tours, so you are not likely to begin your visit alone. But the kids are generally good-natured, and some of the caves are difficult to find without their assistance. A flashlight is useful inside the caves.

Of the two paths leading up Thuy Son, the one closer to the beach (at the end of the village) makes for a better circuit once you get up the top. So unless you want to follow this entry backwards, don't go up the staircase with concrete kiosks and a black cement sign at its base.

At the top of the staircase (from which Cham Island is visible) is a gate, Ung Chon, which is pockmarked with bullets. Behind Ung Chon is Linh Ung Pagoda. As you enter the sanctuary, you'll see on the left a fantastic figure with a huge tongue. To the right of Linh Ung are monks' quarters and a small orchid garden.

Behind Linh Ung and to the left a path leads through two short tunnels to several caverns known as Tang Chon Dong. There are a number of concrete Buddhas and blocks of carved stone of Cham origin in these caves. Near one of the altars there is a flight of steps leading up to another cave, partially open to the sky, with two seated Buddhas in it.

To the left of the small building which is

to the left of Linh Ung (ie immediately to the left as you enter Ung Chon gate) is the main path to the rest of Thuy Son. Stairs off the main pathway lead to Vong Hai Da, a viewpoint from which a brilliant panorama of China Beach and the South China Sea is visible.

The stone-paved path continues on to the right and into a canyon. On the left is Van Thong Cave. Opposite the entrance is a cement Buddha behind which a narrow passage leads up to a natural chimney open to the sky.

After you exit the canyon and pass through a battle-scarred masonry gate, a rocky path to the right goes to Linh Nham, a tall chimney-cave with a small altar inside. Nearby, another path leads to Hoa Nghiem, a shallow cave with a Buddha in it. But if you go down the passageway to the left of the Buddha you come to cathedral-like Huyen Khong Cave, lit by an opening to the sky. The entrance to this spectacular chamber is guarded by two administrative mandarins (to the left of the doorway) and two military mandarins (to the right). Scattered about the cave are Buddhist and Confucian shrines; note the inscriptions carved into the stone walls. On the right a door leads to two stalactites dripping water that local legend says comes from heaven. Actually, only one stalactite drips; the other one supposedly ran dry when Emperor Tu Duc (ruled 1848-83) touched it. During the Vietnam War, this chamber was used by the VC as a field hospital while American soldiers on R & R lounged on nearby China Beach.

A bit to the left of the battle-scarred masonry gate is Tam Thai Tu, a pagoda restored by Emperor Minh Mang in 1826. A path heading obliquely to the right goes to monks' residences beyond which are two shrines from which a red dirt path leads to five small pagodas. Before you arrive at the monks' residences, stairs on the left-hand side of the path lead to Vong Giang Dai, which offers a fantastic 180° view of the other Marble Mountains and the surrounding countryside. To get to the stairway down, follow the path straight on from the masonry gate.

Non Nuoc Hamlet
Non Nuoc Hamlet is on the southern side of Thuy Son and is a few hundred metres west of China Beach. The marble carvings made here by skilled (and not-so-skilled) craftspeople would make great gifts if they didn't weigh so much. The town was recently spruced up by Danang Tourism.

China Beach
China Beach (Non Nuoc Beach, or Bai Tam Non Nuoc), made famous in the US TV serial of the same name, stretches for many km north and south of the Marble Mountains. During the Vietnam War, American soldiers were airlifted here for 'rest-and-relaxation' (often including a picnic on the beach) before being returned by helicopter to combat. The Viet Cong cadres hiding in Thuy Son must have had a great view of the proceedings.

Places to Stay
The *Non Nuoc Hotel* (tel 21470, 22137; 40 rooms) is right on China Beach. Built in 1985, rooms in the light-green semicircular hotel are clean and pleasant. A new building with 60 more rooms is being constructed next door. Singles/doubles equipped with both air-con and fans cost US$22/25 (plus 10% service). The restaurant will change dollars. The Non Nuoc Hotel is often full so call first if you don't have reservations.

To get to the Non Nuoc Hotel, drive to the Marble Mountains and turn left into Non Nuoc hamlet. Follow the road past the largest Marble Mountain and keep going as it curves around to the right (almost parallel to the beach). Before you hit the sand, turn right towards the casuarina grove (and away from the beach) and follow the road around to the left.

Places to Eat
There is a restaurant at the *Non Nuoc Hotel*.

Getting There & Away

Pickup trucks to the Marble Mountains (Ngu Hanh Son), Non Nuoc Hamlet and nearby China Beach (Bai Tam Non Nuoc) depart when full from the Short-Haul Pickup Truck Station in Danang. The trip takes about 20 minutes.

The 11 km route from Danang to the Marble Mountains passes by the remains of a 2 km long complex of former American military bases; aircraft revetments are still visible.

It is possible to get to the Marble Mountains from Danang by chartered boat. The 8.5 km trip up the Han River and the Vinh Diem River takes about 1¼ hours.

The Marble Mountains are 19 km north of the Hoi An (Faifo) along the 'Korean Highway'.

Around Danang

HOI AN

Hoi An is a riverine town 30 km south of Danang. Known as Faifo to early Western traders, it was one of South-East Asia's major international ports during the 17th, 18th and 19th centuries. In its heyday, Hoi An, a contemporary of Macau and Malacca, was an important port of call for Dutch, Portuguese, Chinese, Japanese and other trading vessels. Vietnamese ships and sailors based in Hoi An sailed to Thailand and Indonesia as well as to all sections of Vietnam. Today, parts of Hoi An look exactly as they did a century-and-a-half ago. More than perhaps any other place in Vietnam, Hoi An retains the feel of centuries past, making it the sort of place that grows on you the more you explore it. If you've got the time, Hoi An is worth at least a couple of days.

History

Recently excavated ceramic fragments from 2200 years ago constitute the earliest evidence of human habitation in the Hoi An area. They are thought to belong to the late-Iron Age Sa Huynh civilisation, which is related to the Dong Son culture of northern Vietnam.

From the 2nd to the 10th centuries, when this region was the heartland of the Kingdom of Champa – this is when the nearby Cham capital of Simhapura (Tra Kieu) and the temples of Indrapura (Dong Duong) and My Son were built – there was a bustling seaport at Hoi An. Persian and Arab documents from the latter part of the period mention Hoi An as a provisioning stop. Archaeologists have uncovered the foundations of numerous Cham towers in the vicinity of Hoi An (the bricks and stones of the towers themselves were reused by later Vietnamese settlers).

In 1307, the Cham king married the daughter of a Vietnamese monarch of the Tran Dynasty, presenting Quang Nam Province to the Vietnamese as a gift. When the Cham king died, his successor refused to recognise the deal and fighting broke out; for the next century, chaos reigned. By the 15th century, peace had been restored, allowing normal commerce to resume. During the next 4 centuries, Chinese, Japanese, Portuguese, Dutch, Spanish, Indian, Filipino, Indonesian, Thai, French, English and American ships called at Hoi An to purchase high-grade silk (for which the area is famous), fabrics, paper, porcelain, tea, sugar, molasses, areca nuts, pepper, Chinese medicines, elephant tusks, beeswax, mother-of-pearl, lacquer, sulphur and lead.

The Chinese and Japanese traders sailed south in the spring, driven by winds out of the north-east. They would stay in Hoi An until the summer, when southerly winds would blow them home. During their 4 month sojourn in Hoi An, the merchants rented waterfront houses for use as warehouses and living quarters. Some traders began leaving full-time agents in Hoi An to take care of off-season business affairs. This is how the foreigners' colonies got started. The Japanese ceased coming to Hoi An after 1637, when the Japanese government forbade all contact with the outside world.

Hoi An was the first place in Vietnam to be exposed to Christianity. Among the 17th century missionary visitors was the French

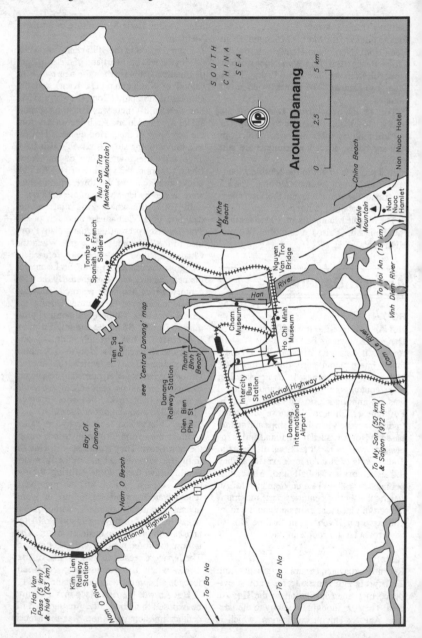

Around Danang

SOUTH CHINA SEA

0   2.5   5 km

Nui Son Tra (Monkey Mountain)

Tombs of Spanish & French Soldiers

China Beach

Nan Nuoc Hotel

Marble Mountain

Non Nuoc Hamlet

My Khe Beach

Nguyen Van Troi Bridge

Tien Sa Port

Han River

Cham Museum

Ho Chi Minh Museum

To Hoi An (19 km)

Vinh Diem River

see 'Central Danang' map

Danang Railway Station

Thanh Binh Beach

Cam Le River

Dien Bien Phu St

Intercity Bus Station

National Highway 1

To My Son (50 km) & Saigon (972 km)

Bay Of Danang

Nam O Beach

Danang International Airport

To Ba Na

To Ba Na

National Highway 1

Nam O River

Kim Lien Railway Station

To Hai Van Pass (5 km) & Hué (8.3 km)

priest Alexandre de Rhodes, who devised the Latin-based *quoc ngu* script for the Vietnamese language.

Hoi An was almost completely destroyed during the Tay Son Rebellion in the 1770s and 1780s but was rebuilt and continued to serve as an important port for foreign trade until the late 19th century, when the Thu Bon River (Cai River), which links Hoi An with the sea, silted up and became too shallow for navigation. During this period Danang (Tourane) began to eclipse Hoi An as a port and centre of commerce. In 1916, a rail line linking Danang with Hoi An was destroyed by a terrible storm; it was never rebuilt.

The French chose Hoi An as an administrative centre. During the American war, Hoi An remained almost completely undamaged.

Hoi An was the site of the first Chinese settlement in southern Vietnam. The town's Chinese congregational assembly halls (*hoi quan*) still play a special role among southern Vietnam's ethnic-Chinese, some of whom travel to Hoi An from all over the south to participate in congregation-wide celebrations. Today, 1300 of the Hoi An area's present population of about 60,000 are ethnic-Chinese. Relations between ethnic-Vietnamese and ethnic-Chinese in Hoi An are excellent, in part because the Chinese here, unlike their countryfolk elsewhere in the country, have become culturally assimilated to the point that they even speak Vietnamese among themselves.

A number of Hoi An's wooden buildings date from the first part of the 19th century or earlier, giving visitors who have just a bit of imagination the feeling that they have been transported back a couple of centuries to a time when the wharf was crowded with sailing ships, the streets teemed with porters transporting goods to and from wharehouses, and traders from a dozen countries haggled in a babble of languages.

Architecture

So far, 844 structures of historical significance have been identified in Hoi An. These structures are of nine types:

1) Houses & shops
2) Wells
3) Family chapels for ancestor worship
4) Pagodas
5) Vietnamese & Chinese temples
6) Bridges
7) Communal buildings
8) Assembly halls (*hoi quan*) of various Chinese congregations
9) Tombs (Vietnamese, Chinese & Japanese; no original European tombs survive)

Many of Hoi An's older structures exhibit features of traditional architecture rarely seen today. The fronts of some shops, which are open during the day to display the wares, are shuttered at night, as they have been for centuries, by inserting horizontal planks into grooves cut into the columns that support the roof. Some roofs are made of thousands of brick-coloured 'Yin & Yang' roof tiles, so called because of the way the alternating rows of concave and convex tiles fit together. During the rainy season, the lichens and mosses that live on the tiles spring to life, turning entire rooftops bright green.

Many of Hoi An's houses have round pieces of wood with a Yin & Yang symbol in the middle surrounded by a spiral design over the doorway. These 'watchful eyes' (*mat cua*) are supposed to protect the residents of the house from harm.

Every year during the rainy season, Hoi An has problems with flooding, especially near the waterfront. The greatest flood Hoi An has ever known took place in 1964, when the water reached all the way up to the roof-beams of the houses.

Plans are under way to restore Hoi An's historic structures and to preserve the unique character of the city. Assistance is being provided to local authorities by the Archaeological Institute in Hanoi, the Japan-Vietnam Friendship Association and experts from Europe and Japan.

Orientation

Bach Dang St runs along the Thu Bon River, which is also known as the Hoi An River and

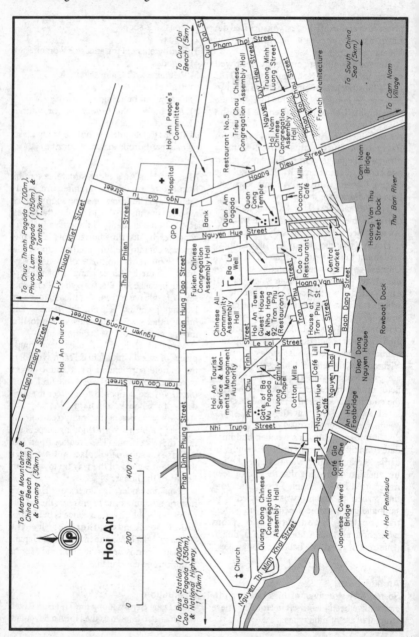

Hoi An

To Chuc Thanh Pagoda (700m), Phuoc Lam Pagoda (1050m) & Japanese Tombs (1.2km)

To Marble Mountains & China Beach (19km) & Danang (30km)

To Bus Station (400m), Cao Dai Pagoda (350m) & National Highway (10km)

To Cua Dai Beach (5km)

To South China Sea (5km)

To Cam Nam Village

Pham Thai Street

Qua Dai St

Truong Minh Luong Street

Duy Hieu Street

Phan Boi Chau Street

French Architecture

Hoi An People's Committee

Triev Chau Chinese Congregation Assembly Hall

Restaurant No.5

Nguyen Thai Chinese Congregation Assembly Hall

Hoang Dieu Street

Hospital

Ly Thuong Kiet Street

Gia Tu Street

Thoi Phien Street

Cam Nam Bridge

Thu Ban River

Bank

Quan Am Pagoda

Quan Cong Temple

Coconut Milk Café

GPO

Nguyen Hue Street

Cao Lau Restaurant

Central Market

Hoang Van Thu Street Dock

Tran Hung Dao Street

Ba Le Well

Fukien Chinese Congregation Assembly Hall

Chinese All-Community Assembly Hall

Hoang Van Thu Street

Rowboat Dock

Hoi An Church

Nguyen Truong To Street

Tran Phu Street

Hoi An Town Guest House & Nha Hang 92 Tran Phu (Restaurant)

House at 77 Tran Phu St

Hoc Street

Bach Dang Street

Tran Cao Van Street

Le Loi Street

Hoi An Tourist Service & Monuments Managment Authority

Phan Chu Trinh Street

Gate of Ba Mu Pagoda

Truong Family Chapel

Cotton Mills

Café Lili

Nguyen Thai Street

Diep Dong Nguyen House

Nguyen Hue Café

An Hoi Footbridge

Phan Dinh Phung Street

Nhi Trung Street

Café Gia Khat Ghe

Quang Dong Chinese Congregation Assembly Hall

Church

Nguyen Thi Minh Khai Street

Japanese Covered Bridge

An Hoi Peninsula

400 m

200

0

the Cai River. Many of Hoi An's most interesting sites are along Tran Phu St.

Information

Tourist Office The Hoi An Tourist Service and Monuments Management Authority (*Ban Quan Ly Di Tich*; tel K72), which can provide a tour guide if contacted before your arrival, is at 100 Tran Phu St. When a separate authority is set up to provide services to tourists, this outfit will revert back to its primary job of preserving Hoi An's historical sites. On the 2nd floor are several display cases filled with antiques of Cham and Faifo origin.

Post The GPO is across from 11 Tran Hung Dao St (on the north-west corner of Ngo Gia Tu and Tran Hung Dao streets).

Money The bank, which does not yet accept foreign currency, is 50 metres south of the GPO at 2 Hoang Dieu St.

Film Film is on sale at 43 Tran Phu St.

Emergency The hospital is across the street from the GPO at 10 Tran Hung Dao St (on the north-east corner of Ngo Gia Tu and Tran Hung Dao streets).

Japanese Covered Bridge

The Japanese Covered Bridge (Cau Nhat Ban, or Lai Vien Kieu) connects 155 Tran Phu St with 1 Nguyen Thi Minh Khai St. The first bridge on this site was constructed in 1593 by the Japanese community of Hoi An to link their neighbourhood with the Chinese quarters across the stream. The bridge was provided with a roof so it could be used as a shelter from both the rain and the sun.

The Japanese Covered Bridge is very solidly built, apparently because the original builders were afraid of earthquakes, which are common in Japan. Over the centuries, the ornamentation of the bridge has remained relatively faithful to the original Japanese design, reflecting the Japanese preference for understatement, which contrasts greatly with the Vietnamese and Chinese penchant

for wild decoration. The French flattened out the roadway to make it more suitable for their motorcars but the original arched shape was restored during the major renovation work carried out in 1986.

Built into the northern side of the bridge is a small temple, Chua Cau. Over the door is written the name given to the bridge in 1719 to replace the name then in use, which meant 'the Japanese Bridge'. The new name, Lai Vien Kieu (Bridge for Passers-By From Afar), never caught on.

According to legend, there once lived an enormous monster called Cu whose head was in India, its tail in Japan and its body in Vietnam. Whenever the monster moved, terrible disasters, such as floods and earthquakes, befell Vietnam. This bridge was built on the monster's weakest point – its 'Achilles' heel', so to speak – killing it. But the people of Hoi An took pity on the slain monster and built this temple to pray for its soul.

The two entrances to the bridge are guarded by a pair of monkeys on one side and a pair of dogs on the other. According to one story, these animals were popularly revered because many of Japan's emperors were born in years of the dog and monkey. Another tale relates that construction of the bridge was begun in the year of the monkey and finished in the year of the dog.

The steles listing Vietnamese and Chinese contributors to a subsequent restoration of the bridge are written in Chinese characters (*chu nho*), the *nom* script not yet having become popular in these parts.

Tan Ky House

The Tan Ky House was built almost 2 centuries ago as the home of a well-to-do ethnic-Vietnamese merchant. The house has been lovingly preserved and today it looks almost exactly as it did in the early 19th century.

The design of the Tan Ky House shows evidence of the influence Japanese and Chinese styles had on local architecture. Japanese elements include the crabshell-shaped ceiling (in the section immediately before the courtyard), which is supported by three progressively shorter beams one on top of the other. There are similar beams in the salon. Under the crabshell ceiling are carvings of crossed sabres enwrapped by a ribbon of silk. The sabres symbolise force; the silk represents flexibility.

Chinese poems written in inlaid mother-of-pearl are hung from a number of the columns that hold up the roof. The Chinese characters on these 150 year old panels are formed entirely out of birds gracefully portrayed in various positions of flight.

The courtyard has four functions: to let in light; to provide ventilation; to bring a bit of nature into the home; and to collect rainwater and provide drainage. The stone tiles covering the patio floor were brought from Thanh Hoa Province in north-central Vietnam. The carved wooden balcony supports around the courtyard are decorated with grape leaves, a European import, further evidence of the unique mingling of cultures that took place in Hoi An.

The back of the house, in which several families now live, fronts the river. In olden times, this section of the building was rented out to foreign merchants.

That the house was a place of commerce as well as a residence is indicated by the two pulleys attached to a beam in the storage loft located just inside the front door.

The exterior of the roof is made of tiles; inside, the ceiling consists of wood. This design keeps the house cool in the summer and warm in the winter. The house's floor tiles were brought from near Hanoi.

The Tan Ky House is a private home at 101 Nguyen Thai Hoc St, not far from Café Lili. It is open to visitors for a small fee. The owner, whose family has lived here for six generations, speaks fluent French and English. The house is open every day from 8 am to 12 noon and from 2 to 4.30 pm.

Diep Dong Nguyen House
The Diep Dong Nguyen House was built for a Chinese merchant, an ancestor of the present inhabitants, in the late 19th century. The front room on the ground floor was once

a dispensary for Chinese medicines (*thuoc bac*), which were stored in the glass-enclosed cases lining the walls. The owner's private collection of antiques, which includes photographs, porcelain and furniture, is on display upstairs. The objects are not for sale! Two of the chairs were once lent by the family to Emperor Bao Dai.

The house, which is at 80 Nguyen Thai Hoc St (by the new numbering system) and 58 Nguyen Thai Hoc St (by the old system) is open every day from 8 am to 12 noon and from 2 to 4.30 pm.

House at 77 Tran Phu St
This private house, which is across the street from the Hoi An Town Guest House, is about 3 centuries old. There is some especially fine carving on the wooden walls of the rooms around the courtyard, on the roofbeams and under the crabshell roof (in the salon next to the courtyard). Note the green ceramic tiles built into the railing around the courtyard balcony. The house is open to visitors for a small fee.

Assembly Hall of the Quang Dong Chinese Congregation
The Assembly Hall of the Quang Dong (Guangdong, or Cantonese) Chinese Congregation, founded in 1786, is at 176 Tran Phu St and is open daily from 6 to 7.30 am and from 1 to 5.30 pm. The main altar is dedicated to Quan Cong (Chinese: *Kuan Kung*). Note the long-handled brass 'fans' to either side of the altar. The lintel and door-posts of the main entrance and a number of the columns supporting the roof are made of single blocks of granite. The other columns were carved out of the durable wood of the jackfruit tree. There are some interesting carvings on the wooden beams that support the roof in front of the main entrance.

Chinese All-Community Assembly Hall
The Chinese All-Community Assembly Hall (Chua Ba), founded in 1773, was used by all five Chinese congregations in Hoi An: Fukien, Quang Dong (Cantonese), Hai Nam (from Hainan Island), Trieu Chau and Gia

Ung. The pavilions off the main courtyard incorporate 19th century French elements.

At present, various parts of the complex are used for the manufacture of hand-tied carpets and hanging blinds made of bamboo beads. The women who work here make between US$7.50 and US$12.50 per month.

The main entrance is on Tran Phu St at the end of Hoang Van Thu St, but the only way in these days is around the back at 31 Phan Chu Trinh St.

Assembly Hall of the Fukien Chinese Congregation

The Assembly Hall of the Fukien (Phuoc Kien) Chinese Congregation was founded as a place to hold community meetings. Later, it was transformed into a temple for the worship of Thien Hau, Goddess of the Sea and Protectress of Fishermen and Sailors, who was born in Fukien Province. The triple gate to the complex was built in 1975.

The mural near the entrance to the main hall on the right-hand wall depicts Thien Hau, her way lit by lantern light, crossing a stormy sea to rescue a foundering ship. On the wall opposite is a mural of the heads of the six Fukien families who fled from China to Hoi An in the 17th century following the overthrow of the Ming Dynasty.

The second-to-last chamber contains a statue of Thien Hau. To either side of the entrance stand red-skinned Thuan Phong Nhi, who can hear for great distances, and green-skinned Thien Ly Nhan, who can see for a 1000 miles. When either sees or hears sailors in distress, they inform Thien Hau, who then sets off to effect a rescue. The replica of a Chinese boat along the right-hand wall is in 1:20 scale. The four sets of triple beams which support the roof are typically Japanese.

The central altar in the last chamber contains seated figures of the heads of the six Fukien families who immigrated to Hoi An in the 17th century. The smaller figures below them represent their successors as clan leaders. In a 30 cm high glass dome is a figurine of Le Huu Trac, a Vietnamese physician renowned in both Vietnam and China for his curative abilities.

Behind the altar on the left is the God of Prosperity. On the right are three fairies and smaller figures representing the 12 'midwives' (ba mu), each of whom teaches newborns a different skill necessary for the first year of life: smiling, sucking, lying on their stomachs and so forth. Childless couples often come here to pray for offspring. The three groups of figures in this chamber represent the elements most central to life: one's ancestors, one's children and economic well-being.

The middle altar of the room to the right of the courtyard commemorates deceased leaders of the Fukien congregation. On either side are lists of contributors, women on the left and men on the right. The wall panels represent the four seasons:

The Assembly Hall of the Fukien Chinese Congregation, which is opposite 35 Tran Phu St (near the corner of Hoang Van Thu St), is open from 7.30 am to 12 noon and from 2 to 5.30 pm. It is fairly well lit and can be visited after dark. Shoes should be removed upon mounting the platform just past the naves.

Quan Cong Temple

Quan Cong Temple, also known as Chua Ong, is at 24 Tran Phu St (according to the new numbers) and 168 Tran Phu St (according to the old numbering system). Founded in 1653, this Chinese temple is dedicated to Quan Cong, whose partially gilt statue – made of papier mâché on a wood frame – is in the central altar at the back of the sanctuary. On the left is a statue of General Chau Xuong, one of Quan Cong's guardians, striking a tough-guy pose Oliver North can only dream about. On the right is the rather plump administrative mandarin Quan Binh. The life-size white horse recalls a mount ridden by Quan Cong until he was given a red horse of extraordinary endurance, representations of which are common in Chinese pagodas.

Stone plaques on the walls list contributors to the construction and repair of the temple. Check out the carp-shaped rain spouts on the roof surrounding the courtyard.

The carp, symbol of patience in Chinese mythology, is a popular symbol in Hoi An.

Shoes should be removed when mounting the platform in front of the statue of Quang Cong.

Hai Nam Assembly Hall

The Assembly Hall of the Hai Nam Chinese Congregation was built in 1883 as a memorial to 108 merchants from Hainan Island in southern China who were mistaken for pirates and killed in Quang Nam Province during the reign of Emperor Tu Duc (ruled 1848-83). The elaborate dais contains plaques in their memory. In front of the central altar is a fine gilded wood carving of Chinese court life.

The Hai Nam Congregation Hall is on the north side of Tran Phu St, near the corner of Hoang Dieu St.

Trieu Chau Assembly Hall

In 1776, as the American Revolutionary War was heating up, the Trieu Chau Chinese here in Hoi An were busy building their congregational hall. There is some outstanding woodcarving on the beams, walls and altar. On the doors in front of the altar are carvings of two Chinese girls wearing their hair in the Japanese manner.

The Trieu Chau Congregation Hall is across from 157 Nguyen Duy Hieu St (near the corner of Hoang Dieu St).

Truong Family Chapel

The Truong Family Chapel (Nha Tho Toc Truong), founded about 2 centuries ago, is a shrine dedicated to the ancestors of this ethnic-Chinese family. Some of the memorial plaques were presented by the emperors of Vietnam to honour members of the Truong family who served as local officials and as mandarins at the imperial court. To get there, turn into the alley next to 69 Phan Chu Trinh St.

Gate of Ba Mu Pagoda

Though Ba Mu Pagoda, founded in 1628, was demolished by the South Vietnamese government during the 1960s to make room for a three storey school building, the gate (Phat Tu) remains standing. Enormous representations of pieces of fruit form part of the wall between the two doorways.

The gate of Ba Mu Pagoda is opposite 68 Phan Chu Trinh St.

Ba Le Well

Water for the preparation of authentic *cao lau* (see Places to Eat) must be drawn from Ba Le Well and no other. The well itself, which is said to date from Cham times, is square in shape. To get there, turn down the alleyway opposite 35 Phan Chu Trinh St. Hang a right before reaching number 45/17.

French Architecture

There is a whole city block of colonnaded French buildings on Phan Boi Chau St between numbers 22 and 73.

Cotton Weaving

Hoi An is known for its production of cotton cloth. All over the city there are cotton mills with rows of fantastic wooden looms that make a rhythmic clackety-clack clackety-clack sound as a whirring cycloidal drive wheel shoots the shuttle back and forth under the watchful eyes of the machine attendant. The elegant technology used in building these domestically produced machines dates from the Industrial Revolution. Indeed, this is what mills in Victorian England must have looked like.

There are cloth mills at numbers 140 and 151 Tran Phu St.

Caodai Pagoda

Serving Hoi An's Caodai community, many of whose members live along the path out to the Japanese tombs, is the small Caodai Pagoda (built 1952) between numbers 64 and 70 Huynh Thuc Khang St (near the bus station). One priest lives here. Sugar and corn are grown in the front yard to raise a bit of extra cash.

Hoi An Church

The only tombs of Europeans in Hoi An are in the yard of the Hoi An Church, which is at the corner of Nguyen Truong To St and Le Hong Phong St. When this modern building was constructed to replace an earlier structure at another site, several 18th-century missionaries were reburied here.

Chuc Thanh Pagoda

Chuc Thanh Pagoda is the oldest pagoda in Hoi An. It was founded in 1454 by Minh Hai, a Buddhist monk from China. Among the antique ritual objects still in use are several bells, a stone gong 2 centuries old and a carp-shaped wooden gong said to be even older. Today, five elderly monks live here.

In the main sanctuary, gilt Chinese characters inscribed on a red roof-beam give details of the pagoda's construction. Under a wooden canopy on the central dais sits an A Di Da Buddha flanked by two Thich Ca Buddhas (Sakyamuni). In front of them is a statue of Thich Ca as a boy flanked by his servants.

To get to Chuc Thanh Pagoda, go all the way to the end of Nguyen Truong To St and turn left. Follow the sandy path for 500 metres.

Phuoc Lam Pagoda

Phuoc Lam Pagoda was founded in the mid-17th century. Late in the century, the head *bonze* was An Thiem, a Vietnamese prodigy who became a monk at the age of 8. When he was 18, the king drafted An Thiem's brothers into his army to put down a rebellion. Am Thiem volunteered to take the places of the other men in his family and eventually rose to the rank of general. After the war, he returned to the monkhood but felt guilty about the many people he had slain. To atone for his sins, he volunteered to clean the Hoi An Market for a period of 20 years. When the 20 years were up, he was asked to come to Phuoc Lam Pagoda as head monk.

To get to Phuoc Lam Pagoda, continue past Chuc Thanh Pagoda for 350 metres. The path passes by an obelisk erected over the tomb of 13 ethnic-Chinese decapitated by the Japanese during WW II for resistance activities.

Tomb of the Japanese Merchant Yajirobei

The tombstone of the Japanese merchant Yajirobei, who died in 1647, is clearly inscribed with Japanese characters. The stele, which faces north-east towards Japan, is held in place by the tomb's original covering, which is made of an especially hard kind of cement whose ingredients include powdered seashells, the leaves of the *boi loi* tree and cane sugar. Yajirobei may have been a Christian who came to Vietnam to escape persecution in his native land.

To get to Yajirobei's tomb, go north to the end of Nguyen Truong Tu St and follow the sand path around to the left (west) for 40 metres until you get to a fork. The path that continues straight on leads to Chuc Thanh Pagoda, but you should turn right (northward). Keep going for just over 1 km, turning left (to the north) at the first fork and left (to the north-west) at the second fork. When you arrive at the open fields, keep going until you cross the irrigation channel. Just on the other side of the channel turn right (south-east) onto a raised path. After going for 150 metres, turn left (north-east) into the paddies and walk 100 metres. The tomb, which is on a platform surrounded by a low stone wall, stands surrounded by rice paddies.

The tombstone of a Japanese named Masai, who died in 1629, is a few hundred metres back towards Hoi An. To get there, turn left (south-east) at a point about 100 metres towards town from the edge of the rice fields. The tombstone is on the right-hand side of the trail about 30 metres from the main path.

For help in finding the Japanese tombs, show the locals the following words: *Ma Nhat* (or *Mo Nhat*), which means 'Japanese tombs'.

There are other Japanese tombs in Duy Xuyen District, which is across the delta of the Thu Bon River from Hoi An.

Cam Kim Island

The master woodcarvers who, in previous centuries, produced the fine carvings that graced the homes of Hoi An's merchants and the town's public buildings came from Kim Bong village on Cam Kim Island. These days, some of the villagers build wooden boats. To get there, catch one of the frequent boats from the Hoang Van Thu Street Dock.

Cua Dai Beach

The fine sands of Cua Dai Beach (Bai Tam Cua Dai) are usually deserted. When there is a full moon, people come here to hang out until late at night. Changing booths are provided; refreshments are sold in the shaded kiosks.

Cham Island is offshore. If it's clear, visible to the north-west are the Marble Mountains and, behind them, the peaks around Hai Van Pass.

Cua Dai Beach is 5 km east of Hoi An out Cua Dai St, which is the continuation of Tran Hung Dao and Phan Dinh Phung streets. The road passes shrimp hatching pools built with Australian assistance. There are plans for a team of Australian submarine archaeologists to excavate sunken ships near here.

Cham Island

Cham Island (Culao Cham) is in the South China Sea 21 km from Hoi An; by boat, the trip takes about 2 hours. The island is famous as a source of swifts' nests, which are exported to Hong Kong, Singapore and elsewhere for use in bird's nest soup.

Both foreigners and Vietnamese need authorisation to visit the island because recent attempts to flee the country have been disguised as excursions to Cham Island. A motorised ferry to Cham Island's two fishing villages departs from the Hoang Van Thu Street Dock at about 7 am; it returns in the afternoon.

Place to Stay

The Hoi An Town Guest House (Nha Khach Thi Xa Hoi An; tel K131; 3 rooms) is at 92 Tran Phu St. A room with four of five beds costs 6000d. Mattresses are available upon request; bathrooms are communal.

Places to Eat

Hoi An's contribution to Vietnamese cuisine is *cao lau*, which consists of doughy flat noodles mixed with croutons, bean sprouts and greens and topped with pork slices. It is mixed with crumbled crispy rice paper immediately before eating. Hoi An is the *only* place genuine *cao lau* can be made because the water used in the preparation of the authentic article must come from a particular well in town. The best *cau lao* in Hoi An is served at *Cao Lau Restaurant* at 42 Tran Phu St, which is run by several elderly ladies who were young lasses when the place was furnished.

Nha Hang 92 Tran Phu is a restaurant on the ground floor of the Hoi An Town Guest House (Nha Khach Thi Xa Hoi An). *Nha Hang So Nam* (Restaurant Number 5) is a government-owned place at 5 Hoang Dieu St.

For something to drink, such as a thirst-quenching glass of iced coconut milk (*nuoc dua*), try one of Hoi An's refreshment shops. The *Coconut Milk Café* is across from the Assembly Hall of the Hai Nam Chinese Congregation at 7 Tran Phu St. *Café Lili* is at 109 Tran Phu St. Near the Japanese Covered Bridge you'll find the *Nguyen Hue Café* (across from 174 Tran Phu St) and *Café Gia Khat Che*, which is next to 151 Tran Phu St in the old French-era post office building. There are several cafes along Le Loi St near the intersection with Phan Chu Trinh St.

Getting There & Away

Bus Buses from Danang to Hoi An (via the Marble Mountains and China Beach) leave from both the Intercity Bus Station and the Short-Haul Pickup Truck Station, which has more frequent service. The ride takes an hour once the vehicle actually gets going.

The Hoi An Bus Station (Ben Quoc Doanh Xe Khach; tel 84) is 1 km west of the centre of town at 74 Huynh Thuc Khang St. Small truck-buses from here go to Dai Loc (Ai Nghia), Danang, Quang Ngai (once a day departing in the early morning), Que Son, Tam Ky and Tra My. Service to Danang begins at 5 am; the last bus to Danang departs in the late afternoon.

Boat Small motorised ferries leave Hoi An for nearby districts and Cham Island from the Hoang Van Thu Street Dock, which is across from 50 Bach Dang St. The daily boat to Cham Island usually departs between 7 and 8 am. The daily boat to Duy Xuyen leaves at 5 am. There is also frequent service to Cam Kim Island.

Chartered boat trips along the Thu Bon River (the Cai River), the largest in Quang Nam-Danang Province, can be arranged at the Hoang Van Thu Street Dock. It may be possible to take an all-day boat ride from Hoi An all the way to Simhapura (Tra Kieu) and the My Son area.

Driving There are two land routes from Danang to Hoi An. The shortest way is to drive to the Marble Mountains (11 km from Danang) and continue south along the 'Korean Highway' for another 19 km. Alternatively, you can head south from Danang on National Highway 1 and, at a signposted intersection 27 km from the city, turn left (east) for 10 km.

Getting Around

The best way to get around Hoi An and to surrounding areas is by bicycle. No one is renting the things out yet, but you might try borrowing one. There are bicycle parts shops on Nguyen Hue St near the Central Market.

MY SON

My Son is Vietnam's most important Cham site. During the centuries when Simhapura (Tra Kieu) served as the political capital of Champa, My Son was the site of the most important Cham intellectual and religious centre and may also have served as a burial place for Cham monarchs. My Son is considered to be Champa's counterpart to the grand cities of South-East Asia's other Indian-influenced civilisations: Angkor (Cambodia), Pagan (Myanmar), Ayuthaya (Thailand) and Borobudur (Java).

The monuments are set in a verdant valley surrounded by hills and overlooked by massive Cat's Tooth Mountain (Hon Quap). Clear brooks (in which visitors can take a dip) run between the structures and past nearby coffee plantations. The entrance fee is 5000d; it is used for upkeep of the site.

My Son became a religious centre under King Bhadravarman in the late 4th century. The site was occupied until the 13th century, the longest period of development of any monument in South-East Asia (by comparison, Angkor's period of development lasted only 3 centuries, as did that of Pagan). Most of the temples were dedicated to Cham kings associated with divinities, especially Shiva, who was regarded as the founder and protector of Champa's dynasties.

Champa's contact with Java was extensive. Cham scholars were sent to Java to study, and there was a great deal of commerce between the two empires; Cham pottery has been found on Java. In the 12th century, the Cham king wed a Javanese wife.

Because some of the ornamentation work at My Son was never finished, archaeologists know that the Chams first built their structures and only then carved decorations into the brickwork. Researchers have yet to figure out for certain how the Chams managed to get the baked bricks to stick together. According to one theory, they used a paste prepared with a botanical oil indigenous to Central Vietnam. During one period in their history, the summits of some of the towers were covered with a layer of gold.

During the Vietnam War, the vicinity of My Son was completely devastated and depopulated in extended bitter fighting. Finding it a convenient staging ground, Viet Cong guerrillas used My Son as a base; in response the Americans bombed the monuments. Of the 68 structures of which traces have been found, 25 survived repeated pillagings in previous centuries by the Chinese, Khmer and Vietnamese. The American bombings spared about 20 of these, some of which sustained damage. Today, Vietnamese authorities are being helped in their restoration work by experts from Poland.

Elements of Cham civilisation can still be seen in the life of the people of Quang Nam-

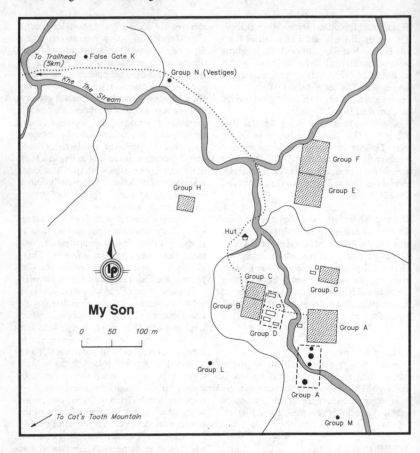

To Trailhead (5km) • False Gate K

• Group N (Vestiges)

Khe The Stream

Group F

Group E

Group H

Hut

Group C

Group G

Group B

Group A

My Son

0   50   100 m

Group D

Group L

Group A

To Cat's Tooth Mountain

Group M

Danang and Quang Ngai provinces whose forebears assimilated many Cham innovations into their daily lives. These include techniques for pottery-making, fishing, sugar production, rice farming, irrigation, silk production and construction.

Warning!

During the Vietnam war, the hills and valleys around the My Son site were extensively mined. When mine clearing operations were carried out in 1977, six Vietnamese sappers were killed in this vicinity. Today, grazing cows are sometimes blown up, which means that as the years pass and the poor beasts locate the mines one by one, the hills around here are becoming less and less unsafe ... For your own safety, do *not* stray from marked paths.

If you are so inclined, you might try looking at the bright side: during French restoration work here in the 1930s, one person was eaten by a tiger. Nowadays, after so many years of war, the largest undomesticated animals in the area are wild pigs, which pose no danger to humans. Maneating animals or mines...it's always something.

The Site

The monuments of My Son have been divided by archaeologists into ten main groups, lettered A, A', B, C, D, E, F, G, H and K. Each structure has been given a name consisting of a letter followed by a number.

The first structure you encounter along the trail is the false gate K, which dates from the 11th century. Between K and the other groups is a coffee plantation begun in 1986; among the coffee bushes, peanuts and beans are grown.

Group B B1, the main sanctuary (*kalan*), was dedicated to Bhadresvara, which is a contraction of the name of the king who built the first temple at My Son with '-esvara,' which means Shiva. The first building on this site was erected in the 4th century, destroyed in the 6th century and rebuilt in the 7th century. Only the 11th century base, made of large sandstone blocks, remains; the brick-work walls have disappeared. The niches in the wall were used to hold lamps (Cham sanctuaries had no windows). The linga inside was discovered during excavations in 1985 one metre beneath where it is now displayed.

B5, built in the 10th century, was used for storing sacred books and precious ritual objects, some made of gold, which were used in ceremonies performed in B1. The boat-shaped roof (the 'bow' and 'stern' have fallen off) shows the influence of Malayo-Polynesian architecture. Unlike the sanctuaries, this building has windows. The fine Cham masonry inside is all original. Over the window on the wall facing B4 is a bas relief in brick of two elephants under a tree with two birds in it.

The ornamentation on the exterior walls of B4 are an excellent example of a Cham decorative style, typical of the 9th century,

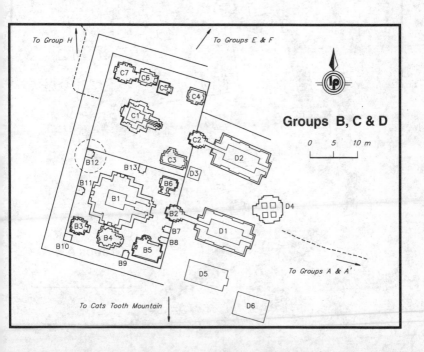

Groups B, C & D

said to resemble worms. This style is unlike anything found in other South-East Asian cultures.

B3 has an Indian-influenced pyramidal roof typical of Cham towers. Inside B6 is a bathtub-shaped basin for keeping the sacred water that was poured over the linga in B1; this basin is the only one of its kind of Cham origin known.

B2 is a gate. Around the perimeter of Group B (structures B7 through B13) are small temples dedicated to the gods of the directions of the compass (*dikpalaka*).

Group C The 8th century sanctuary C1 was used to worship Shiva portrayed in human form (rather than in the form of a linga, as in B1). Inside is an altar where a statue of Shiva, now in the Cham Museum in Danang, used to stand. On either side of the stone doorway you can see, bored into the lintel and the floor, the holes in which two wooden doors once swung. Note the motifs, characteristic of the 8th century, carved into the brickwork of the exterior walls.

Group D Building D1, once a *mandapa*

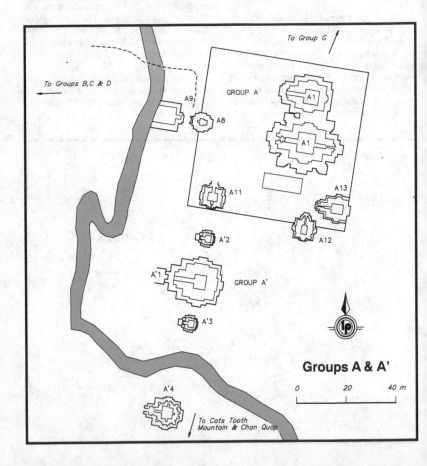

(meditation house), is now used as a store-room. It is slated to become a small museum of Cham sculpture. Objects to be displayed include a large panel of Shiva dancing on a platform above the bull Nandin: to Shiva's left is Skanda (under a tree), his son Uma, his wife and a worshipper; to Shiva's right is a dancing saint and two musicians under a tree, one with two drums, the other with a flute. The display will also include a finely carved lion – symbol of the power of the king (the lion was believed to be an incarnation of Vishnu and the protector of kings) – whose style belies Javanese influence.

Group A The path from groups B, C and D to Group A leads eastward from near D4.

Group A was almost completely destroyed by US attacks. According to locals, massive A1, considered the most important monument at My Son, remained impervious to aerial bombing and was finally finished off by a helicopter-borne sapper team. All that remains of A1 today is a pile of collapsed brick walls. After the destruction of A1, Philippe Stern, an expert on Cham art and curator of the Guimet Museum in Paris, wrote a letter of protest to President Nixon, who ordered US forces to keep on killing Vietnamese but not to do any further damage to Cham monuments.

A1 was the only Cham sanctuary with two doors. One faced the east, direction of the Hindu gods; the other door faced west towards groups B, C and D and the spirits of the ancestor-kings that may have been buried there. Inside A1 is a stone altar pieced back together in 1988. Among the ruins some of the brilliant brickwork, which is of a style typical of the 10th century, is still visible. At the base of A1 on the side facing A10 (which is decorated in 9th century style) is a carving of a worshipping figure, flanked by round columns, with a Javanese *kala-makara* (sea-monster god) above. There may be some connection between the presence of this Javanese motif and the studies in Java of a great 10th century Cham scholar. There are plans to partially restore A1 and A10 as soon as possible.

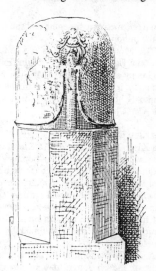

A Lingam (phallic symbol of Shiva)

Other Groups Group A', which dates from the 8th century, is at present overgrown and is thus inaccessible. Group E was built during the 8th to 11th centuries. Group F dates from the 8th century. Group G, which has been damaged by time rather than war, is from the 12th century. There are long-term plans to restore these monuments.

Simhapura (Tra Kieu)

Simhapura (Tra Kieu), the 'Lion Citadel', was the first capital city of Champa, serving in that capacity from the 4th to the 8th centuries. Today, nothing remains of the city except the rectangular ramparts. A large number of artefacts, including some of the finest carvings in the Cham Museum in Danang, were found here.

You can get a good view of the city's outlines from the Mountain Church (Nha Tho Nui), which is on the top of Buu Chau Hill in Tra Kieu. This modern open-air structure was built in 1970 to replace an earlier church destroyed by time and war. A Cham tower once stood on this spot. Simhapura is about 500 metres to the south and south-west of the hilltop.

The Mountain Church is 6.5 km from National Highway 1 and 19.5 km from the beginning of the footpath to My Son. Within Tra Kieu, it is 200 metres from the morning market (Cho Tra Kieu) and 550 metres from Tra Kieu Church.

Tra Kieu Church

Tra Kieu Church (Dia So Tra Kieu), which serves the town's Catholic population of 3000, was built a century ago (though obviously, the border of the semicircular patio, which is made of upturned artillery shells, was added later). The priest here is interested in Cham civilisation and has amassed a collection of Cham artefacts found by local people.

A 2nd floor room in the building to the right of the church is due to open as a museum in 1990. The round ceramic objects with faces on them, which date from the 8th to 10th centuries, were affixed to the ends of tile roofs. The face is that of Kala, the God of Time.

Tra Kieu Church is 7 km from National Highway 1 and 19 km from the trail to My Son. It is 150 metres down an alley opposite the town's clinic of occidental medicine (Quay Thuoc Tay Y), 350 metres from the morning market (Cho Tra Kieu) and 550 metres from the Mountain Church.

Indrapura (Dong Duong)

The Cham religious centre of Indrapura (Dong Duong) was the site of an important Mahayana Buddhist monastery, the Monastery of Lakshmindra-Lokeshvara, founded in 875. Indrapura served as the capital of Champa from 860 to 986, when the capital was transferred to Cha Ban (near Qui Nhon). Tragically, as a result of the devastation wrought by the French and American wars, only part of the gate to Indrapura is extant.

Indrapura is 21 km from My Son as the crow flies and 55 km from Danang.

Places to Stay

Unless you have equipment to camp out at

My Son, the nearest hotels are in Hoi An and Danang.

Getting There & Away

Bus There are two daily bus runs between the Danang Intercity Bus Station and Trung Phuoc, departing Danang at 7 am and 1 pm and leaving Trung Phuoc at 7 am and 11 am. Unfortunately, Trung Phuoc is quite a way from the path to My Son. Before trying this, get definite information on exactly how close to My Son the bus will bring you. Note that there is no transport back to Danang in the afternoon.

Boat If you have lots of time and either hate walking or love boat rides, you might try hiring a small boat (*ghe*) to take you from Duy Phu hamlet across the Khe The reservoir (Ho Khe The) to where the Khe The River feeds into the reservoir, which is still 3 km from My Son. Ask the locals for a *ghe den My Son*. The ride takes about 30 minutes.

Driving The trailhead to My Son is 60 km from Danang. To get there from Danang, head south on National Highway 1. The turnoff to Hoi An is 27 km south of Danang; at a point 6.8 km south of the turnoff (and 2 km south of the long bridge over the Thu Bon River), turn right towards Tra Kieu. Buu Chau Hill, on which the Mountain Church sits, is 6.5 km from National Highway 1 on the left. The alleyway leading to Tra Kieu Church and its small museum is 400 metres down the road (past the marketplace).

Twelve km past Tra Kieu (and 8.6 km beyond the Chiem Son Railroad Bridge) is Kim Lam. Turn left here (going straight will lead you to a destroyed bridge). The footpath to the My Son site is on the left-hand side of the road 6.8 km from Kim Lam.

Walking It's a bit of a hike (about 5 km) from the road to My Son. The trail heads due south toward Cat's Tooth Mountain (Hon Quap), whose shape does in fact resemble a cat's tooth. When the dirt road is upgraded, vehicles will be able to bring visitors to a point about 3 km from the monuments. About 2 km from the main road the path crosses the Khe The River. If you prefer to cross without swimming, take the detour, which goes up the side of the hill to the left. After rejoining the main path, the trail crosses a stream fed by a spring said to have been a favourite stopping place of the famous French archaeologist Henri Parmentier.

Hué

Hué (population 200,000) served as Vietnam's political capital from 1802 to 1945 under the 13 emperors of the Nguyen Dynasty. Traditionally, the city has been one of Vietnam's cultural, religious and educational centres. Today, Hué's main attractions are the splendid tombs of the Nguyen emperors, several notable pagodas and the remains of the Citadel. As locals will tell you repeatedly, the women of Hué are renowned for their beauty.

History

The citadel-city of Phu Xuan was built on the site of present-day Hué in 1687. In 1744, Phu Xuan became the capital of the southern part of Vietnam, which was under the rule of the Nguyen Lords. The Tay Son Rebels occupied the city from 1786 until 1802, when it fell to Nguyen Anh. He renamed the city Hué and crowned himself Emperor Gia Long, thus founding the Nguyen Dynasty, which ruled the country – at least in name – until 1945. Immediately upon his accession, Gia Long began the decades-long construction of the Citadel, the Imperial City and the Forbidden Purple City.

In 1885, when the advisors of 13 year old Emperor Ham Nghi objected to French activities in Tonkin, French forces encircled the city. Unwisely, the outnumbered Vietnamese forces launched an attack; the French responded mercilessly. According to a contemporary French account, the French forces took 3 days to burn the imperial library and remove from the palace every object of value, including everything from gold and silver ornaments to mosquito nets and toothpicks. Ham Nghi fled to Laos but was eventually captured and exiled to Algeria. The French replaced him with the more pliable Dong Khanh, thus ending any pretence of genuine Vietnamese independence.

Hué was the site of the bloodiest battles of the 1968 Tet Offensive and was the only city

in South Vietnam to be held by the Communists for more than a few days. While the American command was concentrating its energies on relieving the siege of Khe Sanh, North Vietnamese and VC troops skirted the American stronghold and walked right into Hué, South Vietnam's third-largest city. When the Communists arrived, they hoisted their flag from the Citadel's flag tower, where it flew for the next 25 days; the local South Vietnamese governmental apparatus completely collapsed.

Immediately upon taking Hué, Communist political cadres implemented detailed plans to liquidate Hué's 'uncooperative' elements. Thousands of people were rounded up in extensive house-to-house searches conducted according to lists of names meticulously prepared months in advance. During the 3½ weeks Hué remained under Communist control, approximately 3000 civilians – including merchants, Buddhist monks, Catholic priests, intellectuals and a number of foreigners as well as people with ties to the South Vietnamese government – were summarily shot, clubbed to death or buried alive. The victims were buried in shallow mass graves, which were discovered around the city over the course of the next few years.

When South Vietnamese Army units proved unable to dislodge the North Vietnamese and VC forces, General Westmoreland ordered US troops to recapture the city. During the next few weeks, whole neighbourhoods were levelled by VC rockets and American bombs. In 10 days of bitter combat, the VC were slowly forced to retreat from the New City. During the next 2 weeks, most of the area inside the Citadel (where two thirds of the population lived), including the Imperial Enclosure and the Forbidden Purple City, was flattened by the South Vietnamese Air Force, US artillery and brutal house-to-house fighting. Approximately 10,000 people died in Hué during the Tet Offensive. Thousands of VC troops, 400

South Vietnamese soldiers and 150 American Marines were among the dead, but most of those killed were civilians.

Orientation

Hué, which is 16 km inland from the South China Sea, is bisected by the Perfume River (Huong Giang, or Song Huong). Inside the Citadel, which is on the left bank of the river, is the Imperial Enclosure, which surrounds the Forbidden Purple City, former residence of the royal family. Wide areas within the Citadel are devoted to agriculture, a legacy of the destruction of 1968.

Dong Ba Market is near the eastern corner of the Citadel. Nearby, a commercial district stretches along the Dong Ba Canal. Tran Hung Dao St runs along the river from Dong Ba Market to Phu Xuan Bridge. Le Duan St goes from Phu Xuan Bridge to the corner of the Citadel, where it turns westward, following the moat. Across the Dong Ba Canal from Dong Ba Market are the sub-districts of Phu Cat and Phu Hiep, known for their Chinese pagodas.

On the right bank of the Perfume River is the New City, once known as the European Quarter. Le Loi St runs along the river. The Imperial Tombs are spread out over a large area to the south of the New City.

Information

Tourist Office The offices of Thua Thien-Hué Province Tourism (Cong Ty Du Lich Thua Thien-Hué; tel 2369, 2288, 2355) are in the building to the right as you enter the gate of the Huong Giang Hotel, which is at 51 Le Loi St. Thua Thien-Hué Tourism can supply guides and cars (including 4WD). Tours of the DMZ, which is in neighbouring Quang Tri Province, can be arranged here. The office is open from 7 to 11.30 am and 1.30 to 5 pm.

Hué City Tourism (Cong Ty Du Lich Thanh Pho Hué; tel 3577) is at 18 Le Loi St (corner Ha Noi St). Hué City Tourism runs several tourist villas on Ly Thuong Kiet St and can rent cars and arrange traditional theatre (*Cai Luong*) and music performances.

It may be possible to hire English, French, German and Russian-speaking guides at the Foreign Language Teachers' Club (Club des Enseignants de Langues Étrangéres, abbreviated CENLET; in Vietnamese: Cau Lac Bo Giao Vien Ngoai Ngu; tel 2599), which recently moved from its temporary quarters at 4 Hoang Hoa Tham St (corner Le Loi St). To find the new address, show the French acronym or Vietnamese name to a local person.

Hué's largest hospital is at 16 Le Loi St. The offices of the Provincial People's Committee are at 14 Le Loi St. The Hué University library is at 18 Le Loi St.

Post International postal and telephone services are available at the GPO, which is opposite 7 Hoang Hoa Tham St and is open from 6.30 am to 9 pm. International postal, telephone and telex services are available at the 2nd floor post office (tel 3093; telex 755 NGU VT) in the Huong Giang Hotel (tel 2122), which is at 51 Le Loi St. The postal windows are supposed to be open from 9 am to 1 pm and 5 to 9 pm.

Money Hué's only foreign exchange bank is the Industrial & Commercial Bank (Nhan Hang Cong Thuong; tel 3275) at 2A Le Quy Don St; it is open from Monday to Saturday 7 to 11.30 am and 1.30 to 4 pm. The exchange windows are on the far left as you enter. Foreign currency can be changed at an inferior rate at the front desk of the Huong Giang Hotel. The bank (Ngan Hang Nha Nuoc Thua Thien-Hué; tel 2572) on Hoang Hoa Tham St does not yet conduct foreign currency transactions.

The Citadel

Construction of the moated Citadel (Kinh Thanh), whose perimeter is 10 km, was begun in 1804 by Emperor Gia Long on a site chosen by geomancers. The Citadel was originally made of earth, but during the first few decades of the 19th century, tens of thousands of workers laboured to cover the ramparts, built in the style of the French

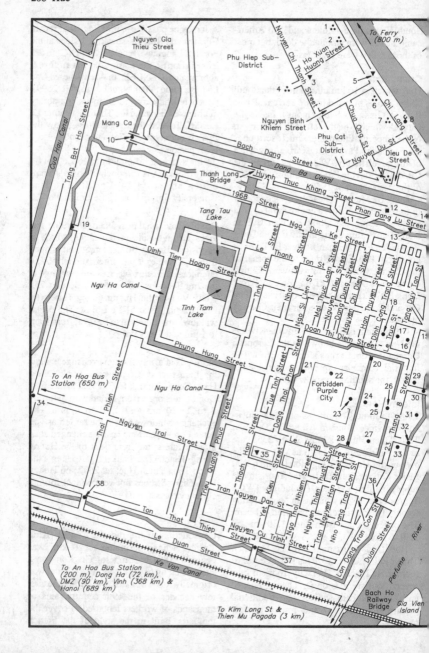

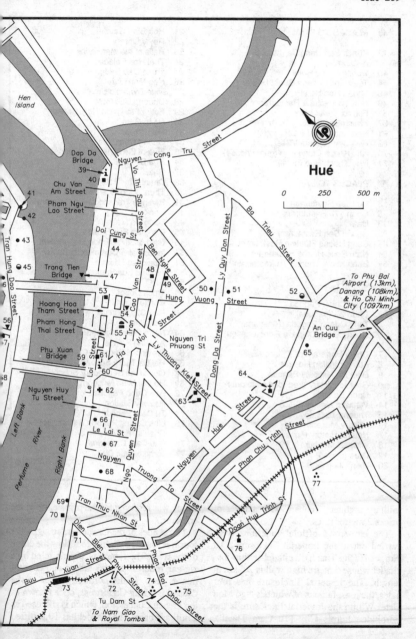

Hué

0   250   500 m

Hen Island

Dap Da Bridge
39
40
Chu Van Am Street
Pham Ngu Lao Street
41
42
43
Dai Cung St
44
45
Trang Tien Bridge   47
48
49
53
Hoang Hoa Tham Street
54
Pham Hong Thai Street
55
Phu Xuan Bridge   59
61
60
62
Nguyen Huy Tu Street
63
66
Le Lai St
67
Nguyen
68
69
70
Dien Bien
71
Bui Thi Xuan Street
73
72
74
75
Tu Dam St
To Nam Giao & Royal Tombs
76
77

Nguyen Cong Tru Street
Vo Thi Sau Street
Ben Nghe Street
Ly Quy Don Street
Ba Trieu Street
50   51   52
To Phu Bai Airport (13km), Danang (108km), & Ho Chi Minh City (1097km)
An Cuu Bridge
65
64
Hung Vuong Street
Dong Da Street
Tran Cao Van Street
Nguyen Tri Phuong St
Hai Ba Trung Street
Ly Thuong Kiet Street
Hue Street
Phan Chu Trinh Street
Nguyen Truong To Street
Doan Huu Trinh St
Phan Boi Chau Street

Tran Hung Dao Street
Le Loi Street
Ngo Quyen Street
Tran Thuc Nhan St

Perfume River
Left Bank
Right Bank
56
57
58
6
8

■ PLACES TO STAY

12	Khach San Hang Be (hotel & restaurant)
40	Huong Giang Hotel
44	Teachers' College Guest House
48	Thuan Hoa Hotel
49	Nua Thu Hotel & Restaurant
53	Former Hotel Morin
57	Khach San Thuong Tu (hotel)
61	Nha Khach 18 Le Loi (hotel)
63	Hué City Tourism Villas
70	Nha Khach Chinh Phu (guest house)
71	Nha Khach Hué (hotel)

▼ PLACES TO EAT

3	Hu Hiep Restaurant
5	Quan 176 Restaurant
13	Cafe
35	Huong Sen Restaurant
47	Song Huong Floating Restaurant
54	Nam Song Huong Restaurant
56	Banh Khoai Thuong Tu (restaurant)

● OTHER

1	Trieu Chieu Pagoda
2	Chua Ba (pagoda)
4	Tang Quang Pagoda (Hinayana)
6	Quang Dong Chinese Congregation Hall
7	Chieu Ung Pagoda
8	Former Indian Mosque
9	Dieu De National Pagoda
10	Gate to military area (closed to public)
11	Dong Ba Gate
14	Vietnam Airlines Office
15	Thuong Tu Gate
16	Military Museum
17	Natural History Museum
18	Imperial Museum
19	Gate (closed)
20	Hien Nhon Gate

21	Hoa Binh Gate
22	Royal Library
23	Halls of the Mandarins
24	Thai Hoa Palace
25	Trung Dao Bridge
26	Ngo Mon Gate
27	Nine Dynastic Urns
28	Chuong Duc Gate
29	Four of the Nine Holy Cannons
30	Ngan Gate
31	Flag Tower
32	Quang Duc Gate
33	Five of the Nine Holy Cannons
34	Nha Do Gate
37	Gate
38	Chanh Tay Gate
39	Thua Thien-Hué Province Tourism
41	Riverine Transportation Cooperative
42	Dock
43	Dong Ba Market
45	Dong Ba Bus Station
46	Gold & Silver Trade Department
50	Industrial & Commercial Bank
51	Municipal Theatre
52	An Cuu Bus Station
55	GPO
58	Truck Depot
59	Cercle Sportif
60	Hué City Tourism
62	Hospital
64	Notre Dame Cathedral
65	An Dinh Palace
66	Provincial People's Committee
67	Hai Ba Trung Secondary School
68	Quoc Hoc Secondary School
69	Ho Chi Minh Museum
72	Bao Quoc Pagoda
73	Railway Station
74	Tu Dam Pagoda
75	Linh Quang Pagoda & Phan Boi Chau's Tomb
76	Phu Cam Cathedral
77	Tomb of Duc Duc

military architect Vauban, with a layer of bricks 2 metres thick.

The emperor's official functions were carried out in the Imperial Enclosure (Dai Noi, or Hoang Thanh), a citadel-within-the-citadel whose 6 metre high wall is 2.5 km in length. The Imperial Enclosure has four gates, the most famous of which is Ngo Mon Gate. Within the Imperial Enclosure is the Forbidden Purple City (Tu Cam Thanh), which was reserved for the private life of the emperor.

Three sides of the Citadel are straight; the fourth is rounded slightly to follow the curve of the river. The ramparts are encircled by a zig-zag moat 30 metres across and about 4 metres deep. In the northern corner of the Citadel is Mang Ca fortress, once known as the French Concession, which is still used as a military base. The Citadel has 10 fortified gates, each of which is reached by a bridge across the moat.

The Flag Tower The 37 metre high Flag Tower (Cot Co), also known as the King's Knight, is Vietnam's tallest flagpole. Erected in 1809 and increased in size in 1831, a terrific typhoon (which devastated the whole city of Hué) knocked it down in 1904. The tower was rebuilt in 1915, only to be destroyed again in 1947. It was re-erected in its present form in 1949. During the VC occupation of Hué in 1968, the National Liberation Front flag flew defiantly from the tower for 3½ weeks.

The Nine Holy Cannons Located just inside the Citadel ramparts near the gates to either side of the Flag Tower, the Nine Holy Cannons, symbolic protectors of the Palace and Kingdom, were cast from brass articles captured from the Tay Son Rebels. The cannons, whose casting on the orders of Emperor Gia Long was completed in 1804, were never intended to be fired. Each is 5 metres long, has a bore of 23 cm and weighs about 10 tonnes. The four cannons near Ngan Gate represent the four seasons; the five cannons next to Quang Duc Gate represent the five elements: metal, wood, water, fire and soil.

Ngo Mon Gate The principle gate to the Imperial Enclosure is Ngo Mon Gate (Noontime Gate), which faces the Flag Tower. It is open from 6.30 am to 5.30 pm; the entrance fee for foreigners is US$1.

The central passageway, with its yellow doors, was reserved for use by the emperor, as was the bridge across the lotus pond. Everyone else had to use the gates to either side and the paths around the lotus pond.

On top of the gate is Ngu Phung (the Belvedere of the Five Phoenixes), where the emperor appeared on important occasions, notably for the promulgation of the lunar calendar. Emperor Bao Dai ended the Nguyen Dynasty here on 30 August 1945, when he abdicated to a delegation sent by Ho Chi Minh's Provisional Revolutionary

The outer walls of The Citadel

Government. The middle section of the roof is covered with yellow tiles; the roofs to either side are green.

Thai Hoa Palace Thai Hoa Palace (the Palace of Supreme Peace), built in 1803 and moved to its present site in 1833, is a spacious hall with an ornate roof of huge timbers supported by 80 carved and lacquered columns. Reached from the Ngo Mon Gate via Trung Dao Bridge, it was used for the emperor's official receptions and other important court ceremonies, such as anniversaries and coronations. During state occasions, the king sat on his elevated throne and received homage from ranks of mandarins. Nine steles divide the bi-level courtyard into areas for officials of each of the nine ranks in the mandarinate; administrative mandarins stood to one side and military mandarins to the other.

Halls of the Mandarins The buildings in which the mandarins prepared for court ceremonies, held in Can Chanh Reception Hall, were restored in 1977. The structures are directly behind Thai Hoa Palace on either side of a courtyard in which there are two gargantuan bronze cauldrons (*vac dong*) dating from the 17th century.

The Nine Dynastic Urns The Nine Dynastic Urns (*dinh*) were cast in 1835-36. Traditional ornamentation was then chiselled into the sides of the urns, each of which is dedicated to a different Nguyen sovereign. The designs, some of which are of Chinese origin and date back 4000 years, include the sun, the moon, meteors, clouds, mountains, rivers and various landscapes. About 2 metres in height and weighing 1900 to 2600 kg each, the urns symbolise the power and stability of the Nguyen throne. The central urn, which is the largest and most ornate, is dedicated to the founder of the Nguyen Dynasty, Emperor Gia Long.

Forbidden Purple City The Forbidden Purple City (Tu Cam Thanh) was reserved for the personal use of the emperor. The only servants allowed into the compound were eunuchs, who would have no temptation to molest the royal concubines.

The Forbidden Purple City was almost entirely destroyed during the Tet Offensive. The area is now given over to vegetable plots, between which touch-sensitive mimosa plants flourish. The two storey Library (Thai Binh Lau) was recently partly restored. The foundations of the Royal Theatre (Duyen Thi Duong), begun in 1826 and later home of the National Conservatory of Music, can be seen nearby.

Imperial Museum The beautiful hall which houses the Imperial Museum (formerly the Khai Dinh Museum) was built in 1845 and restored when the museum was founded in 1923. The walls are inscribed with poems written in Vietnamese *nom* characters. The most precious artefacts were lost during the war, but the ceramics, furniture and royal clothing that remain are well worth a look. On the left side of the hall are a royal sedan chair, a gong and a musical instrument consisting of stones hung on a bi-level rack. On the other side of the hall is the equipment for a favourite game of the emperors, the idea of which was to bounce a stick off a wooden platform and into a tall, thin jug.

Across the street what was once a former school for princes and the sons of high-ranking mandarins. Behind the school is the Military Museum, with its usual assortment of American and Soviet-made weapons, including a MiG 17. Nearby is a small natural history exhibit.

The Imperial Museum is open from 6.30 am to 5.30 pm.

Tinh Tam Lake In the middle of Tinh Tam Lake, which is 500 metres north of the Imperial Enclosure, are two islands connected by bridges. The emperors used to come here with their retinues to relax.

Tang Tau Lake An island in Tang Tau Lake, which is a few hundred metres from Tinh Tam Lake, was once the site of a royal library. It is now occupied by a small Hinayana pagoda, Ngoc Huong Pagoda.

Royal Tombs

The tombs (*lang tam*) of the Nguyen Dynasty (1802-1945) are 7 to 16 km to the south of Hué. They are open from 6.30 am to 5 pm daily; the entrance fee to each tomb is US$1.

Most of the tomb complexes consist of five parts: 1) A Stele Pavilion in which the accomplishments, exploits and virtues of the deceased emperor are engraved on a marble tablet. The testaments were usually written by the dead ruler's successor (though Tu Duc chose to compose his own). 2) A temple for the worship of the emperor and empress. In front of each altar, on which the deceased rulers' funerary tablets were placed, is an ornate dais that once held items the emperor used every day: his tea and betel trays, cigarette cases, etc, most of which have disappeared. 3) A sepulchre, usually inside a square or circular enclosure, where the emperor's remains are buried. 4) An Honour Courtyard paved with dark-brown *bat trang* bricks along the sides of which stand stone elephants, horses and civil and military mandarins. The civil mandarins wear square hats and hold the symbol of their authority, an ivory sceptre; the military mandarins wear round hats and hold swords. 5) A lotus-pond surrounded by frangipani and pine trees. Almost all the tombs, which are situated in walled compounds, were planned by the Nguyen emperors during their lifetimes. Many of the precious ornaments once reposited in the tombs disappeared during the war.

The best way to tour the Royal Tombs is on bicycle. The quiet paved roads between the tombs pass among the solid little homes of peasants; peaceful groves of trees; rice, vegetable, manioc and sugar cane plots; and newly reafforested hills.

Nam Giao Nam Giao (Temple of Heaven) was once the most important religious site in all Vietnam. It was here that every 3 years, the emperor solemnly offered elaborate sacrifices to the All-Highest Emperor of the August Heaven (Thuong De). The topmost esplanade, which represents Heaven, is round; the middle terrace, representing the Earth, is square, as is the lowest terrace.

After reunification, the provincial government erected – on the site where the sacrificial altar once stood – an obelisk in memory of soldiers killed in the war against the South Vietnamese government and the Americans. There was strong public sentiment in Hué against the obelisk and the Hué Municipal People's Committee proposed tearing down the memorial and erecting another elsewhere, but the weathered and faded column is still there.

Tomb of Dong Khanh Emperor Dong Khanh, nephew and adopted son of Tu Duc, was placed on the throne by the French after they captured his predecessor, Ham Nghi (who had fled after the French sacking of the royal palace in 1885), and exiled him to Algeria. Predictably, Dong Khanh proved docile; he ruled from 1886 until his death 2 years later.

Dong Khanh's mausoleum, the smallest of the Royal Tombs, was built in 1889. It is 7 km from the city.

Tomb of Tu Duc The majestic and serene tomb of Emperor Tu Duc is set amidst frangipani trees and a grove of pines. Tu Duc designed the exquisitely harmonious tomb, which was constructed between 1864 and 1867, for use both before and after his death. The enormous expense of the tomb and the forced labour (*corvée*) used in its construction spawned a coup plot which was discovered and suppressed in 1866.

It is said that Tu Duc, who ruled from 1848 to 1883 (the longest reign of any Nguyen monarch), lived a life of truly imperial luxury: at every meal, 50 chefs prepared 50 dishes served by 50 servants; and his tea was made of drops of dew that had condensed overnight on the leaves of lotus plants. Though Tu Duc had 104 wives and countless concubines, he had no offspring. One theory has it that he became sterile after contracting smallpox.

Tu Duc's Tomb, which is surrounded by a solid octagonal wall, is entered from the east via Vu Khiem Gate. A path paved with *bat trang* tiles leads to Du Khiem Boat Landing, which is on the shore of Luu Khiem Lake. From the boat landing, Tinh Khiem Island, where Tu Duc used to hunt small game, is off to the right. Across the water to the left is Xung Khiem Pavilion, where the Emperor would sit among the columns with his concubines composing or reciting poetry. The pavilion, built over the water on piles, was restored in 1986.

Across Khiem Cung Courtyard from Du Khiem Boat Landing are steps leading through a gate to Hoa Khiem Temple, where Emperor Tu Duc and Empress Hoang Le Thien Anh are worshipped. Before his death, Tu Duc used Hoa Khiem Temple as a palace, staying here during his long visits to the complex. Hoa Khiem Temple contains a number of interesting items, including a mirror used by the Emperor's concubines; a clock and other objects given to Tu Duc by the French; the Emperor and Empress's funerary tablets; and two thrones, the larger of which was for the Empress (Tu Duc was only 153 cm tall).

Minh Khiem Chamber, to the right behind Hoa Khiem Temple, was built for use as a theatre. Tu Duc's mother, the Queen Mother Tu Du, is worshipped in Luong Khiem Temple, which is directly behind Hoa Khiem Temple.

Back down at the bottom of the stairway, the brick path continues along the shore of the pond to the Honour Courtyard. Across the lake from the Honour Courtyard are the tombs of Tu Duc's adopted son, Emperor Kien Phuc, who ruled for only 7 months in 1883, and the Empress Le Thien Anh, Tu Duc's wife.

After walking between the honour guard of elephants, horses and diminutive civil and military mandarins (the stone mandarins were made even shorter than the emperor), you reach the masonry Stele Pavilion, which shelters a massive stone tablet weighing about 20 tonnes. It took 4 years to transport the stele, the largest in Vietnam, from the area of Thanh Hoa, 500 km to the north. Tu Duc drafted the inscriptions on the stele himself in order to clarify certain aspects of his reign. He freely admitted that he had made mistakes and chose to name his tomb Khiem, which means modest. The two nearby towers symbolise the emperor's power.

Tu Duc's sepulchre, enclosed by a wall, is on the other side of a half-moon-shaped lake. In fact, Tu Duc was never actually interred here, and the site where his remains were buried along with great treasure is not known. Because of the danger of grave robbers, extreme measures were taken to keep the location secret: every one of the 200 servants who buried the king were beheaded.

Tu Duc's Tomb is 7 km from Hué on Van Nien hill in Duong Xuan Thuong village.

Tomb of Thieu Tri Construction of the tomb of Thieu Tri, who ruled from 1841 to 1847, was completed in 1848. It is the only one of the Royal Tombs not enclosed by a wall. Thieu Tri's tomb, which is similar in layout to that of Minh Mang (though smaller), is about 7 km from Hué.

Tomb of Khai Dinh The gaudy and crumbling tomb of Emperor Khai Dinh, who ruled from 1916 to 1925, is perhaps symptomatic of the decline of Vietnamese culture during the colonial period. Begun in 1920 and completed in 1931, the grandiose reinforced concrete structure makes no pretence of trying to blend in with the surrounding countryside. The architecture, completely unlike that of Hué's other tombs, is an unfortunate synthesis of Vietnamese and European elements. Even the stone faces of the mandarin honour guards are endowed with a mixture of Vietnamese and European features.

After climbing 36 steps between four dragon banisters, you get to the first courtyard, flanked by two pavilions. The Honour Courtyard, with its rows of elephants, horses and civil and military mandarins, is 26 steps further up the hillside. In the centre of the Honour Courtyard is an octagonal Stele Pavilion.

Up three more flights of stairs is the main

building, Thien Dinh, which is divided into three halls. The walls and ceiling are decorated with murals of the 'Four Seasons', the 'Eight Precious Objects', the 'Eight Fairies' and other designs made out of colourful bits of broken porcelain and glass embedded in cement. Under a graceless 1 tonne concrete canopy is a gilt bronze statue of Khai Dinh in royal regalia. Behind the statue is the symbol of the sun. The Emperor's remains are interred 18 metres below the statue. Khai Dinh is worshipped in the last hall.

The Tomb of Khai Dinh is 10 km from Hué in Chau Chu village.

Tomb of Minh Mang Perhaps the most majestic of the Royal Tombs is that of Minh Mang, who ruled from 1820 to 1840. Known for the harmonious blending of its architecture with the natural surroundings, the tomb was planned during Minh Mang's lifetime and built between 1841 and 1843 by his successor.

The Honour Courtyard is reached via three gates on the eastern side of the wall: Dai Hong Mon (Great Red Gate; in the centre), Ta Hong Mon (Left Red Gate; on the left) and Huu Hong Mon (Right Red Gate; on the right). Three granite staircases lead from the Honour Courtyard to the square Stele Pavilion, Dinh Vuong. Nearby there once stood an altar on which buffaloes, horses and pigs were sacrificed.

Sung An Temple, dedicated to Minh Mang and his Empress, is reached via three terraces and Hien Duc Gate. On the other side of the temple, three stone bridges span Trung Minh Ho (The Lake of Impeccable Clarity). The central bridge, Cau Trung Dao, constructed of marble, was used only by the emperor. Minh Lau Pavilion stands on the top of three superimposed terraces representing the 'three powers': the heavens, the earth and water. Visible off to the left is the Fresh Air Pavilion; the Angling Pavilion is off to the right.

From a stone bridge across crescent-shaped Tan Nguyet Lake (Lake of the New Moon), a monumental staircase with dragon banisters leads to the sepulchre, which is surrounded by a circular wall symbolising the sun. In the middle of the enclosure, reached through a bronze door, is the Emperor's burial place, a mound of earth covered with mature pine trees and dense shrubbery.

The Tomb of Minh Mang, which is on Cam Ke hill in An Bang village, is on the left bank of the Perfume River 12 km from Hué. To get there, take a boat across the river from a point about 1.5 km south-west of Khai Dinh's tomb. Visitors have reported gross overcharging by the boat operator.

Tomb of Gia Long Emperor Gia Long, who founded the Nguyen Dynasty in 1802 and ruled until 1820, ordered the construction of his tomb in 1814. According to the royal annals, the Emperor himself chose the site after scouting the area on elephant-back. The rarely visited tomb, which is presently in a state of ruin, is 14 km from Hué on the left bank of the Perfume River.

Pagodas, Temples & Churches

Thien Mu Pagoda Thien Mu Pagoda (also known as Linh Mu Pagoda), built on a hillock overlooking the Perfume River, is one of the most famous structures in all of Vietnam. Its 21 metre high octagonal tower, seven storey Thap Phuoc Duyen, was built by Emperor Thieu Tri in 1844 and has become the unofficial symbol of Hué. Each of the seven storeys is dedicated to a Buddha who appeared in human form (*manushi-buddha*).

Thien Mu Pagoda was founded in 1601 by the Nguyen Lord Nguyen Hoang, governor of Thuan Hoa Province. According to legend, a Fairy Woman (Thien Mu) appeared to Nguyen Hoang and told him to construct a pagoda here. Over the centuries, the pagoda's buildings have been destroyed and rebuilt several times. Eight bonzes and two nuns now live at the pagoda, which was a hotbed of anti-government protest during the early 1960s.

To the right of the tower is a pavilion containing a stele dating from 1715. It is set on the back of a massive marble turtle,

Thien Mu Pagoda

symbol of longevity. To the left of the tower is another six sided pavilion, this one sheltering an enormous bell, Dai Hong Chung, which was cast in 1710 and weighs 2052 kg; it is said to be audible 10 km away. In the main sanctuary, in a case behind the bronze laughing Buddha, are three statues: A Di Da (pronounced 'AH-zee-dah'), the Buddha of the Past; Thich Ca (Sakyamuni), the historical Buddha; and Di Lac Buddha, the Buddha of the Future.

Behind the main sanctuary is the Austin motorcar which transported the bonze Thich Quang to the site in Saigon of his 1963 self-immolation, which was seen around the world in a famous photograph. Around the back are vegetable gardens in which the monks grow their own food.

Thien Mu Pagoda is on the banks of the Perfume River 4 km south-west of the Citadel. To get there from Dong Ba Market,

head south-west (parallel to the river) on Tran Hung Dao St, which turns into Le Duan St after Phu Xuan Bridge. Cross the railway tracks and keep going on Kim Long St. Thien Mu Pagoda can also be reached by sampan.

Bao Quoc Pagoda Bao Quoc Pagoda was founded in 1670 by a Buddhist monk from China, Giac Phong. It was given its present name, which means 'pagoda which serves the country', in 1824 by Emperor Minh Mang, who celebrated his 40th birthday here in 1830. A school for training monks was opened at Bao Quoc Pagoda in 1940. The pagoda was last renovated in 1957.

In the orchid-lined courtyard behind the sanctuary is the cage of a most extraordinary parrot (*nhong*). The male bonzes taught the bird, which was born in 1977, to say (with impeccable intonation, of course) *'Thua thay co khach '*(Master, there is a guest) and *'A Di Da Phat '*(A Di Da Buddha). But female visitors also spoke to the bird, and in time it began imitating their higher-pitched voices as well. Now the poor confused creature alternates between male and female renditions of its repertoire of sayings.

The central altar in the main sanctuary contains three identical statues, which represent (from left to right) Di Lac, the Buddha of the Future; Thich Ca, the historical Buddha (Sakyamuni); and A Di Da (pronounced 'AH-zee-dah'), the Buddha of the Past. Behind the three figures is a memorial room for deceased monks. Around the main building are monks' tombs, including a three storey, red-and-grey stupa built for the pagoda's founder.

Bao Quoc Pagoda is on Ham Long Hill in Phuong Duc District. To get there, head south from Le Loi St on Dien Bien Phu St and turn right immediately after crossing the railroad tracks.

Tu Dam Pagoda Tu Dam Pagoda, which is about 600 metres south of Bao Quoc Pagoda at the corner of Dien Bien Phu St and Tu Dam St, is one of Vietnam's best-known pagodas. Unfortunately, the present buildings were constructed in 1936 and are of little interest.

Tu Dam Pagoda was founded around 1695 by Minh Hoang Tu Dung, a Chinese monk. It was given its present name by Emperor Thieu Tri in 1841. The Unified Vietnamese Buddhist Association was established at a meeting held here in 1951. During the early 1960s, Tu Dam Pagoda was a major centre of the Buddhist anti-Diem and anti-war movement. In 1968, it was the scene of heavy fighting, scars of which remain.

Today, Tu Dam Pagoda, home to six monks, is the seat of the provincial Buddhist Association. The peculiar bronze Thich Ca Buddha in the sanctuary was cast in Hué in 1966.

Just east of the pagoda down Tu Dam St is Linh Quang Pagoda and the tomb of the scholar and anti-colonialist revolutionary Phan Boi Chau (1867-1940).

Notre Dame Cathedral Notre Dame Cathedral (Dong Chua Cuu The) at 80 Nguyen Hue St is an impressive modern building combining the functional aspects of a European cathedral with traditional Vietnamese elements, including a distinctly Oriental spire. At present, the huge cathedral, which was constructed between 1959 and 1962, has 1600 members. The two French-speaking priests hold daily masses at 5 am and 5 pm and on Sunday at 5 am, 7 am and 5 pm; children's catechism classes are conducted on Sunday mornings. Visitors who find the front gate locked should ring the bell of the yellow building next door.

Phu Cam Cathedral Phu Cam Cathedral, whose construction began in 1963 and was halted in 1975 before completion of the bell tower is the eighth church built on this site since 1682. The Hué diocese, which is based here, hopes eventually to complete the structure if funds can be found. Phu Cam Cathedral is at 20 Doan Huu Trinh St, which is at the southern end of Nguyen Thruong Tu St. Masses are held daily at 5 am and 6.45 pm and on Sundays at 5 am, 7 am, 2 pm and 7 pm.

Phu Cat & Phu Hiep Sub-districts
The island on which Phu Cat & Phu Hiep sub-districts are located can be reached by crossing the Dong Ba Canal near Dong Ba Market. The area is known for its numerous Chinese pagodas and congregational halls, many of which are along Chi Lang St.

Dieu De National Pagoda The entrance to Dieu De National Pagoda (Quoc Tu Dieu De), built under Emperor Thieu Tri (ruled 1841-47), is along Dong Ba Canal at 102 Bach Dang St. It is one of the city's three 'national pagodas' (pagodas that were once under the direct patronage of the Emperor). Dieu De National Pagoda is famous for its four low towers, one to either side of the gate and two flanking the sanctuary. There are bells in two of the towers; the others contain a drum and a stele dedicated to the pagoda's founder.

During the regime of Ngo Dinh Diem (ruled 1955-63) and through the mid-1960s, Dieu De National Pagoda was a stronghold of Buddhist and student opposition to the South Vietnamese government and the war. In 1966, the pagoda was stormed by the police, who arrested many *bonzes*, Buddhist laypeople and students and confiscated the opposition movement's radio equipment. Today, three *bonzes* live at the pagoda.

The pavilions on either side of the entrance to the main sanctuary contain the 18 La Ha, whose rank is just below that of Bodhisattva, and the 8 Kim Cang, protectors of Buddha. In the back row of the main dais is Thich Ca Buddha (Sakyamuni) flanked by two assistants, Pho Hien Bo Tat (to his right) and Van Thu Bo Tat (to his left).

Former Indian Mosque Hué's Indian Muslim community constructed the mosque at 120 Chi Lang St in 1932. The structure was used as a house of worship until 1975, when the Indian community fled. It is now a private residence.

Chieu Ung Pagoda Chieu Ung Pagoda (Chieu Ung Tu), opposite 138 Chi Lang St, was founded by the Hai Nam Chinese congregation in the mid-19th century and rebuilt in 1908. It was last repaired in 1940. The sanctuary retains its original ornamentation, which is a bit faded but mercifully unaffected by the third-rate modernistic renovations that have marred other such structures. The pagoda was built as a memorial for 108 Hai Nam merchants who were mistaken for pirates and killed in Vietnam in 1851.

Hall of the Quang Dong Chinese Congregation

The Quang Dong Chinese Congregational Hall (Chua Quang Dong), founded almost a century ago, is opposite 154 Chi Lang St. Against the right-hand wall is a small altar holding a statue of Confucius (in Vietnamese: *Khong Tu*) with a gold beard. On the main altar is red-faced Quan Cong (in Chinese: *Kuan Kung*) flanked by Trung Phi (on the left) and Luu Bi (on the right). On the altar to the left is Lao Tze with disciples to either side. On the altar to the right is Phat Ba, a female Buddha.

Chua Ba Chua Ba, across the street from 216 Chi Lang St, was founded by the Hai Nam Chinese Congregation almost a century ago. It was damaged in the 1968 Tet Offensive and was subsequently reconstructed. On the central altar is Thien Hau Thanh Mau, Goddess of the Sea and Protectress of Sailors. To the right is a glass case in which Quan Cong (in Chinese: *Kuan Kung*) sits flanked by his usual companions, the mandarin general Chau Xuong (to his right) and the administrative mandarin Quang Binh (to his left).

Chua Ong Chua Ong, which is opposite 224 Chi Lang St, is a large pagoda founded by the Fukien Chinese Congregation during the reign of Vietnamese Emperor Tu Duc (ruled 1848-83). The building was severely damaged during the 1968 Tet Offensive when an ammunition ship blew up nearby. A gold Buddha sits in a glass case opposite the main doors of the sanctuary. The left-hand altar is dedicated to Thien Hau Thanh Mau, Goddess of the Sea and Protectress of Sailors; she is flanked by her two assistants,

thousand-eyed Thien Ly Nhan and red-faced Thuan Phong Nhi, who can hear for 1000 miles. On the altar to the right is Quan Cong.

Next door is a pagoda of the Trieu Chieu Congregation.

Tang Quang Pagoda Tang Quang Pagoda (Tang Quang Tu), which is just down the road from 80 Nguyen Chi Thanh St, is the largest of the three Hinayana (Theravada, or *Nam Tong*) pagodas in Hué. Built in 1957, it owes its distinctive architecture to Hinayana Buddhism's historical links to Sri Lanka and India (rather than China). The pagoda's Pali name, Sangharansyarama (the light coming from the Buddha), is inscribed on the front of the building.

Quoc Hoc Secondary School

Quoc Hoc Secondary School (the Lycée Nationale) is one of the most famous secondary schools in Vietnam. Founded in 1896 and run by Ngo Dinh Kha, the father of South Vietnamese President Ngo Dinh Diem, many of the school's pupils later rose to prominence in both North and South Vietnam. Numbered among Quoc Hoc Secondary School's former students are General Vo Nguyen Giap, strategist of the Viet Minh victory at Dien Bien Phu and North Vietnam's long-serving deputy premier, defence minister and commander-in-chief; Pham Van Dong, North Vietnam's Prime Minister for over a quarter of a century; and Ho Chi Minh himself, who attended the school briefly in 1908.

Next door to Quoc Hoc Secondary School, which is at 10 Le Loi St, is Hai Ba Trung Secondary School.

Ho Chi Minh Museum

On display at the Ho Chi Minh Museum (Bao Tang Ho Chi Minh) at 9 Le Loi St are photographs, some of Ho's personal effects and documents relating to his life and accomplishments. The museum is down the block and across the street from Quoc Hoc Secondary School.

Trang Tien Bridge

The Trang Tien Bridge (formerly the Nguyen Hoang Bridge) across the Perfume River was blown up in 1968 and later repaired. The newer Phu Xuan Bridge was built in 1971.

Municipal Theatre

The Municipal Theatre (Nha Van Hoa Trung Tam) is on Huong Vuong St (corner of Ly Quy Don and Dong Da streets).

Thuan An Beach

Thuan An Beach (Bai Tam Thuan An), 13 km north-east of Hué, is on a splendid lagoon near the mouth of the Perfume River. Lambrettas and old Renaults from Hué to Thuan An depart from the Dong Ba Bus Station. You might also try hiring a sampan to make the trip by river. At Thuan An, you can stay at the Tan My Hotel.

Bach Ma

Bach Ma, a French-era hill station known for its superb weather, is 55 km south-west of Hué. Bach Ma is 1200 metres above sea level but only 20 km from Canh Duong Beach. At present, there are no functioning hotels and the access road is in poor condition. There are plans to redevelop Bach Ma if the requisite capital can be found.

Places to Stay – bottom end

Right Bank Nha Khach Hué (tel 2153; 37 rooms) is 200 metres from the railroad station at 2 Le Loi St; doubles cost from 15,000d (with fan and communal bath) to 30,000d (with air-con and private bath). Cars and bicycles can be hired here, or so they say. Nha Khach 18 Le Loi (tel 3720; 6 rooms) at 18 Le Loi St (corner Hung Vuong St) is run by Hué City Tourism; doubles go for between 8000 and 15,000d.

The Nua Thu Hotel (tel 3929; 6 rooms) at 26 Nguyen Thi Phuong St was just renovated by its owners, entrepreneurially-minded State Transport Company Number 3. Doubles cost in the neighbourhood of 20,000d. The restaurant here is very good.

The Hué Teachers' College Guest House,

signposted as simply Nha Khach, is at 36 Le Loi St (corner Doi Cung St).

Left Bank Khach San Thuong Tu (no telephone; 8 rooms) is not far from Phu Xuan Bridge at 1 Dinh Tien Hoang St; a single costs 8000d, a quad goes for 10,000d. Khach San Hang Be (tel 3752) fronts Dong Ba Canal at 73 Huynh Thuc Khang St, which is several blocks north-west of Dong Ba Market. Singles/doubles cost 12,000/20,000d for foreigners. There is a restaurant on the ground floor.

Places to Stay – top end

Right Bank The Huong Giang Hotel (tel 2122) is at 51 Le Loi St, which is almost directly across the Perfume River from Dong Ba Market; doubles cost between US$25.50 and US$32 (plus 10% service). The post office on the 2nd floor is supposed to be open from 9 am to 1 pm and 5 to 9 pm. There is a decent restaurant on the 4th floor. The American-style plugs here deliver 220 volts. The Huong Giang II Hotel under construction next door will have 260 beds.

The most delightful accommodation to be had in Hué are three small villas (Nha Khach) along Ly Thuong Kiet St. Run by Hué City Tourism, they each have a homey living room and some of the nicest rooms in town; meals are prepared on request for US$8 per day. Doubles/triples in the villa at 18 Ly Thuong Kiet St (tel 3889; 5 rooms) cost US$16/20. Next door at 16 Ly Thuong Kiet St is a slightly larger villa (tel 3679). The villa at 11 Ly Thuong Kiet St (4 rooms) charges US$16 for a double, US$18 for a triple and US$20 for a quad.

Nha Khach Chinh Phu at 5 Le Loi St, only recently opened to tourists, is a palatial villa right on the river. Built during the rule of Emperor Bao Dai, it once served as the Palace of the Governor of Central Vietnam (Phu Thu Hien Trung Viet). After reunification, the building was turned into a guest house for high-ranking official guests.

An Dinh Palace, which is on Nguyen Hue St a few hundred metres from Hung Vuong St, was built during the reign of Emperor

Khai Dinh for his wife, mother of Emperor Bao Dai. There are plans to turn the palace into a tourist hotel.

The *Thuan Hoa Hotel* (tel 2576; about 50 rooms) is at 7B Nguyen Tri Phuong St, a few blocks from the Huong Giang Hotel. Foreigners are charged US$30 to US$35 for a room (Vietnamese pay one-sixth that).

There are plans to renovate the colonial-style building on the corner of Le Loi St and Hung Vuong St that once housed the *Hotel Morin*. The structure is now part of Hué University.

Places to Eat

Left Bank *Ban Khoai Thuong Tu* is a few blocks from the Flagpole at 6 Dinh Tien Hoang St; it is open from 7 am to 8 pm. This restaurant, which has the words Lac Thien written in cement on the façade, serves a traditional Hué speciality, *banh khoai*, which is a crêpe with bean sprouts, shrimp and meat inside. It is eaten with greens, starfruit slices and *nuoc leo*, a thick brown sauce made with peanuts, sesame seeds and spices. Another Hué speciality available here is *bun thit nuong*, which is noodles, greens, fruit and fried dried meat eaten with *nuoc leo*. You might wash down your *banh khoai* with the mild local beer, '22'.

Delicious sweet soups (*che*) made with such ingredients as beans and bananas are served either hot or iced in shops at numbers 10 and 12 Dinh Tien Hoang St.

The *Café* is in an interesting old building at 51 Phan Dinh Phung St, a few blocks north-east of Dong Ba Market; they serve only drinks.

Quan 176 is a small place in Phu Cat sub-district at 176 Chi Lang St. They serve traditional Hué pastries, including *banh nam* (a flat cake of rice flour, meat and shrimp fried in a banana leaf), *banh loc* (a chewy cake made of rice flour and shrimp and baked in a banana leaf) and *cha tom* (a flat cake made of meat, shrimp and egg).

The *Hang Be Restaurant* (tel 3752) is on the ground floor of the Hang Be Hotel at 73 Huynh Thuc Khang St.

Within the Citadel, the *Huong Sen Restaurant* (tel 3201) is at 42 Nguyen Trai St (corner Thach Hau St). This 16 sided pavilion, built on pylons in the middle of a lotus pond, is open from 9 am to midnight. The fare is mostly Vietnamese.

Phu Hiep Restaurant (tel 3560) in Phu Hiep District is at 19 Ho Xuan Huong St (opposite 53 Nguyen Chi Thanh St).

Right Bank The restaurant on the 4th floor of the Huong Giang Hotel at 51 Le Loi St serves Vietnamese, European and vegetarian dishes. The food is decent and the prices are surprisingly reasonable.

Nua Thu Restaurant, which is on the ground floor of the Nha Thu Hotel (tel 3929), is at 26 Nguyen Thi Phuong St. The food here is really good, a fact reflected in its popularity with local people.

The *Song Huong Floating Restaurant* is on the bank of the Perfume River just north of the Trang Tien Bridge (near the intersection of Le Loi St and Hung Vuong St).

The *Nam Song Huong Restaurant* is opposite the GPO at 7 Hoang Hoa Tham St. It is open from 8.30 am to 9 pm. This large, airy place serves excellent soup and egg rolls (this far north they're called *nem Sai Gon* rather than *chia gio*).

There is a restaurant in the *Cercle Sportif*, which is on Le Loi St next to the Phu Xuan Bridge. The Cercle Sportif has tennis courts and rents paddle boats.

Vegetarian Vegetarian food, which has a long tradition in Hué, is prepared at pagodas for consumption by the bonzes. Small groups of visitors might be invited to join the monks for a meal. Stalls in the marketplaces serve vegetarian food on the 1st and 15th days of the lunar month.

Things to Buy

Hué is known for producing the finest conical hats in Vietnam. The city's speciality are 'poem hats' which, when held up to the light, reveal black cut-out scenes sandwiched between the layers of translucent palm leaves.

Dong Ba Market, which is on the left bank

of the Perfume River a few hundred metres north of Trang Tien Bridge, is Hué's main market. It was recently rebuilt after much of the structure was destroyed by a typhoon in 1986. Nearby are several photography stores. Near the Huong Giang Hotel, film is sold in a shop at 54 Le Loi St.

Gold and silver objects are available at the Gold and Silver Trade Department (Cua Hang My Nghe Vang Bac Hué; tel 3949), which is at 55 Tran Hung Dao St.

Getting There & Away

Ground distances from Hué:

Ho Chi Minh City	1097 km
Danang	108 km
Aluoi	60 km
Quang Tri	56 km
Dong Ha	72 km
Lao Bao (Lao border)	152 km
Savannakhet, Laos (Thai border)	400 km
Ben Hai River	94 km
Dong Hoi	166 km
Vinh	368 km
Hanoi	689 km

The road to Aluoi is negotiable only by 4WD. It may soon be possible to reach Hué by land from Thailand via Savannakhet, Lao Bao and Dong Ha.

Air The Vietnam Airlines Booking Office (tel 2249) is a block from Dong Ba Market at 16 Phan Dang Luu St; it is open Monday to Saturday from 7 to 11 am and 1.30 to 5 pm.

Hué is served by Phu Bai Airport, once an important American air base, which is 14 km south of the city centre. There are flights from Phu Bai to Ho Chi Minh City (US$90) every Saturday and to Hanoi (US$67) each Wednesday. Flights to Hué depart from Ho Chi Minh City on Wednesdays and from Hanoi on Saturdays. There are flights from Phu Bai to Danang every Tuesday, Friday and Saturday. Lambrettas from Dong Ba Bus Station link Hué with Phu Bai.

Train Hué Railway Station (Ga Hué; tel 2175) is on the right bank at the south-west end of Le Loi St. The ticket office is open from 6.30 am to 5 pm. There is no accommodation at the station.

Heading north, trains DH4 and 164 serve Dong Hoi and TN2, STN 4 and STN6 go all the way to Hanoi. Heading south, DH1 and 165 serve Danang, NH1 goes to Nha Trang and TN1, STN3 and STN5 go all the way to Saigon. For more information on the Vietnamese rail network (including travel times and TN and STN schedules) see the 'Getting Around' section.

Bus Hué has three main bus stations, one to destinations south (An Cuu Bus Station), another to destinations north (An Hoa Bus Station) and a short-haul bus station (Dong Ba Bus Station). Fifteen years after reunification, the people of Hué still look to the south for trade and other ties, a fact reflected in the sparseness of traffic passing through the old Demilitarised Zone (DMZ).

Buses to places north of Hué depart from An Hoa Bus Station (Ben Xe An Hoa, or Ben Xe So 1; tel 3014), which is at the western tip of the Citadel across from 499 Le Duan St (corner Tang Bat Ho St). Non-express buses from here go to:

Aluoi
Ba Don
Dien Sanh
Dong Ha (3 hours)
Dong Hoi
Hanoi
Hoan Lao
Ho Xa
Khe Sanh (twice a day; 7 hours)
Ky Anh
Quang Tri
Thanh Khe
Thuong Phong
Vinh

Almost all of the buses depart at 5 or 5.30 am. Dorm beds are available for 500d at the *Phong Tro* in the station and at places across Tang Bat Ho St also marked *Phong Tro*. Tickets for some buses (eg to Aluoi, Ba Don, Dong Hoi, Hanoi, Hoan Lao, Thuong Phong and Vinh) can be purchased at An Cuu Bus Station.

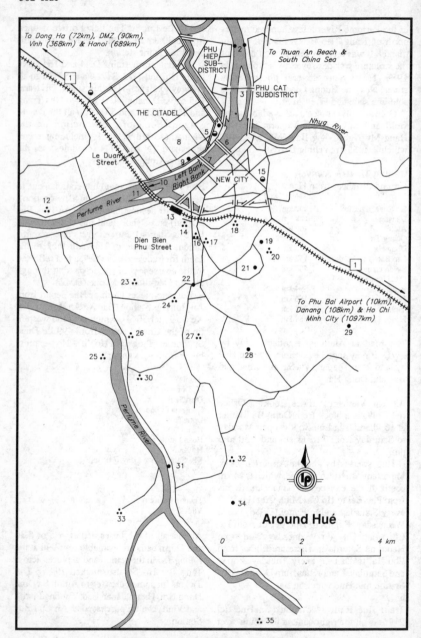

To Dong Ha (72km), DMZ (90km), Vinh (368km) & Hanoi (689km)

PHU HIEP SUB-DISTRICT

To Thuan An Beach & South China Sea

PHU CAT SUBDISTRICT

THE CITADEL

Nhug River

Le Duan Street

Left Bank
Right Bank

NEW CITY

Perfume River

Dien Bien Phu Street

To Phu Bai Airport (10km), Danang (108km) & Ho Chi Minh City (1097km)

Perfume River

Around Hué

0   2   4 km

1	An Hoa Bus Station
2	Ferry Terminals
3	Hen Island
4	Dong Ba Market
5	Dong Ba Bus Station
6	Trang Tien Bridge
7	Phu Xuan Bridge
8	Imperial Enclosure
9	Flag Tower
10	Bach Ho Railway Bridge
11	Gia Vien Island
12	Thien Mu Pagoda
13	Railway Station
14	Bao Quoc Pagoda
15	An Cuu Bus Station
16	Tu Dam Pagoda
17	Linh Quang Pagoda & Phan Boi Chau's Tomb
18	Duc Duc's Tomb
19	Tam Thai Hill
20	Tra Am Pagoda
21	Ngu Binh Hill
22	Nam Giao
23	Tu Hieu Pagoda
24	Tomb of Dong Khanh
25	Hon Chen Temple
26	Tomb of Tu Duc
27	Truc Lam Pagoda
28	Thien Thai Hill
29	Dong Tranh Hill
30	Tomb of Thieu Tri
31	Ferry
32	Tomb of Khai Dinh
33	Tomb of Minh Mang
34	Vung Hill
35	Tomb of Gia Long

Buses to points south of Hué leave from An Cuu Bus Station (tel 3817), which is opposite 46 Hung Vuong St (corner Nguyen Hue St); the ticket windows are open from 5 to 11 am and 1 to 6 pm. There is daily (or more frequent) service from here to:

Buon Ma Thuot
Cau Hai
Danang
Ho Chi Minh City
Khe Tre
Kontum
Pleiku
Nha Trang (once every 2 days)
Qui Nhon
Truoi
Vien Trinh

Tickets for buses from An Hoa Bus Station to Aluoi, Ba Don, Dong Hoi, Hanoi, Hoan Lao, Thuong Phong and Vinh can be purchased at An Cuu Bus Station.

Vehicles to destinations in the vicinity of Hué depart from Dong Ba Bus Station (Ben Xe Dong Ba; tel 3055), which is on the left bank of the Perfume River between Trang Tien Bridge and Dong Ba Market. There are entrances at numbers 85 and 103 Tran Hung Dao St. Signs listing destinations mark the spots from which various vehicles depart.

Ancient black Citroën 'Traction' service taxis leave for Dong Ha about every 2 hours between 5 am and 5 pm. Old Renaults serve La Chu, Phong Loc, Phong Son, Sia, Thuan An Beach and Vu Diem (all of which are in Huong Dien District) between 4 am and 5 pm. Lambrettas go to An Cuu Bus Station, An Hoa Bus Station, An Lo, Bao Vinh, Cho Dinh, Cho No, Kim Long, La Chu, Phu Bai Airport, Phu Luong, Tay Loc, Thuan An Beach and Van Thanh. Dodge trucks go to Binh Dien, which is 30 km from Hué.

Hitching To hitch a ride, you might try asking around the truck parking area at 1 Le Duan St (near the left-bank end of Phu Xuan Bridge).

Getting Around
Boat Many sights in the vicinity of Hué, including Thuan An Beach, Thien Mu Pagoda and several of the Royal Tombs, can be reached by river. You might try hiring a boat behind Dong Ba Market or at the Riverine Transportation Cooperative (Van Tai Gioi Duong Song), whose office is right across Dong Ba Canal from Dong Ba Market. Boats may also be available near Dap Da Bridge, which is a bit east of the Huong Giang Hotel. Hué Tourism and Thua Thien-Hué Province Tourism can arrange outings on the Perfume River.

Driving Cars with drivers can be hired from Hué City Tourism (tel 3577) and Thua Thien-Hué Province Tourism (tel 2369). The offices of Transport Company Number 3 (Cong Ty Van Tai So 3; tel 3922, 3622) are on Dien Bien Phu St and at the Nua Thu Hotel (tel 3929), which the cooperative runs. The Hué City Transport Cooperative (Hop Tac O To) has offices at 1 Le Duan St (near the Citadel-side end of Phu Xuan Bridge) and on Nguyen Thai Hoc St. Nha Khach Hué (tel 2153) at 2 Le Loi St may also be able to rent out passenger vehicles.

Motorbikes There is no set place to hire a chauffeur-driven motorbike (*Honda ong*), which is the cheapest motor-driven way to get out to the tombs. Ask around and someone interested in earning a bit of extra cash will turn up.

Bicycles If it's not raining, the most pleasant way to tour the Hué area is by bicycle. Nha Khach Hué at 2 Le Loi St has plans to hire out bicycles, but if they haven't gotten around to doing it yet, you might try to borrow one.

DMZ & Vicinity

From 1954 to 1975, the Ben Hai River served as the demarcation line between the Republic of Vietnam (South Vietnam) and the Democratic Republic of Vietnam (North Vietnam). The Demilitarised Zone (DMZ) consisted of an area 5 km to either side of the demarcation line.

The idea of partitioning Vietnam had its origins in a series of agreements concluded between the United States, Great Britain and the Soviet Union at the Potsdam Conference, which was held in Berlin in July 1945. For logistical reasons, the Allies decided that Japanese occupation forces to the south of the 16th parallel would surrender to the British while those to the north would surrender to the Nationalist Chinese (Kuomintang) Army under Chiang Kai-Shek.

In April 1954 in Geneva, Ho Chi Minh's government and the French agreed to an armistice among whose provisions was the creation of a demilitarised zone at the Ben Hai River. The agreement stated explicitly that the division of Vietnam into two zones was merely a temporary expediency and that the demarcation line did not constitute a political boundary. But when nationwide general elections planned for July 1956 were not held, Vietnam found itself divided into two states with the Ben Hai River, which is almost exactly at the 17th parallel, as their de facto border.

During the Vietnam War, the area just south of the DMZ was the scene of some of the bloodiest battles of the conflict. Dong Ha, Quang Tri, Con Thien, Camlo, Camp Carroll, the Rockpile, Khe Sanh, Lang Vei, the Ashau Valley, Hamburger Hill – these became almost household names in the USA as, year after year, television pictures and casualty figures provided Americans with their daily evening dose of the war.

Since 1975, 5000 people have been injured or killed in and around the DMZ by mines and ordnance left over from the war. Despite the risk, impoverished peasants still dig for chunks of left-over metal to sell as scrap. The locals are paid the equivalent of 2.5 US cents (!) per kg of steel, US$0.38 per kg of aluminium and US$0.77 per kg of brass. Much of the metal is sold to Japan.

Orientation

The old DMZ extends from the coast westward to the Lao border; National Highway 9 (Quoc Lo 9) runs more-or-less parallel to the DMZ. The Ho Chi Minh Trail (Duong Truong Son), actually a series of roads, trails and paths, ran from North Vietnam southward (perpendicular to National Highway 9) through the Truong Son Mountains and western Laos. To prevent infiltrations and to interdict the flow of troops and matériel via the Ho Chi Minh Trail, the Americans established a line of bases along National Highway 9, including (from east to west) Cua Viet, Gio Linh, Dong Ha, Con Thien, Cam Lo, Ca Lu, Camp Carroll, the Rockpile, Khe Sanh Combat Base and Lang Vei.

The old bases along National Highway 9 can be visited in a day trip from Dong Ha. The road leading south-east from the Dakrong Bridge goes to the Ashau Valley (site of infamous Hamburger Hill) and Aluoi. With a 4WD it is possible to drive the 60 rough km from Aluoi to Hué.

WARNING

At many of the places listed in this section you will find live mortar rounds, artillery projectiles and mines strewn about. *Never* touch any left-over ordnance. Watch where you step. If the locals have not carted it off for scrap it means that even they are afraid to disturb it. Bear in mind that white phosphorus shells – whose contents burn fiercely when exposed to air and will, if they get on your flesh, eat all the way through your hands, feet, limbs or torso – are remarkably impervious to the effects of prolonged exposure and are likely to remain extremely

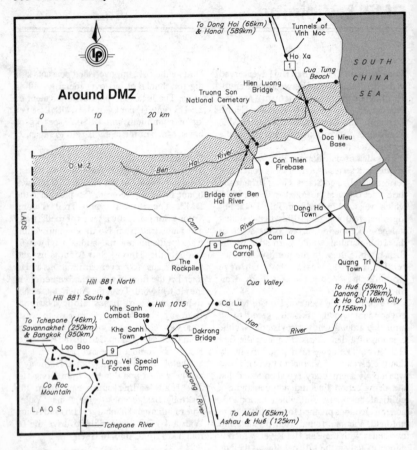

Around DMZ

0   10   20 km

To Dong Hoi (66km)
& Hanoi (589km)

Tunnels of
Vinh Moc

Ho Xa

SOUTH
CHINA
SEA

Cua Tung
Beach

Hien Luong
Bridge

Truong Son
National Cemetary

Doc Mieu
Base

D.M.Z   Ben   Hai   River

Con Thien
Firebase

Bridge over Ben
Hai River

Dong Ha
Town

Cam   Lo   River

LAOS

Cam Lo

9

Camp
Carroll

The
Rockpile

Cua Valley

Quang Tri
Town

Hill 881 North

Hill 881 South   Hill 1015

Ca Lu

To Hué (59km),
Danang (178km),
& Ho Chi Minh City
(1156km)

Khe Sanh
Combat Base

Khe Sanh
Town

Dakrong
Bridge

Han   River

To Tchepone (46km),
Savannakhet (250km)
& Bangkok (950km)

Lao Bao

9

Lang Vei Special
Forces Camp

Co Roc
Mountain

LAOS

Dakrong   River

Tchepone River

To Aluoi (65km),
Ashau & Hué (125km)

dangerous for many more years. Don't become a statistic!

DONG HA

Dong Ha, the capital of newly reconstituted Quang Tri Province, is at the intersection of National Highway 1 and National Highway 9. Dong Ha served as a US Marines command and logistics centre in 1968-69. In the spring of 1968, a division of North Vietnamese troops crossed the DMZ and attacked Dong Ha. The city was later the site of a South Vietnamese Army base.

Orientation

National Highway 1 is called Le Duan St as it passes through Dong Ha. The orientation of Le Duan St is more or less east-west. National Highway 9 (the new American-built branch), signposted as going to Lao Bao, intersects National Highway 1 next to the bus station. Tran Phu St (old National Highway 9) intersects Le Duan St 600 metres west of (towards the river from) the bus station. Tran Phu St runs south for 400 metres until the blockhouse, where it turns westward.

There is a market area along National

Highway 1 between Tran Phu St and the river.

Information
The office of Quang Tri Province Tourism (Du Lich Quang Tri; tel 239) is at the Dong Truong Son Hotel, which is 3 km from the city out on Tran Phu St. Cars and guides are said to be available here, but you'd do better to arrange a guided visit to the area through Thua Thien-Hué Tourism in Hué.

French Blockhouse
Surrounded by captured American tanks and artillery pieces, the old French-built blockhouse (Lo Khot) was used by the French and later the American and South Vietnamese armies. The blockhouse is on Tran Phu St 400 metres from National Highway 1.

Places to Stay
Nha Khach Dong Ha (tel 361; 24 rooms) is a pleasant official guest house 300 metres west of the French blockhouse (Lo Khot) on Tran Phu St. Rooms cost US$12 for foreigners.

Dong Truong Son Hotel (Khach San Dong Truong Son; tel 239), which only recently began accepting guests, is 3 km out Tran Phu St from the old French blockhouse (Lo Khot). When the entire structure is completed, there will be 75 rooms.

Decrepit and filthy *Khach San Dong Ha* (tel 213; 20 rooms) is next to the bus station. It is not the sort of place you'd want to stay without a flashlight. Rooms for four with mats and mosquito nets but without fans cost 8000d. The only good thing about this place is its proximity to the bus station.

Places to Eat
There are a number of eateries along National Highway 1 (Le Duan St) between the bus station and Tran Phu St. These places look rather run-down but the food is pretty good because of the fierce competition for the lucrative patronage of truckers. There are more places to eat on Tran Phu St between the blockhouse and Nha Khach Dong Ha.

There is a nice restaurant at the Dong Truong Son Hotel.

Getting There & Away
Road distances from Dong Ha:

Ben Hai River	22 km
Danang	190 km
Dong Hoi	94 km
Hanoi	617 km
Hué	72 km
Khe Sanh	65 km
Lao Bao (Lao border)	80 km
Saigon	1169 km
Savannakhet, Laos (Thai border)	327 km
Truong Son National Cemetery	30 km
Vinh	294 km
Vinh Moc	41 km

Train Dong Ha Railway Station (Ga Dong Ha) has very limited local train service. Heading north, DH4 departs at 3.10 pm and takes 3 hours to get to Dong Hoi. Train 164 leaves at 8.20 am, taking 4 hours to Dong Hoi. Going south, DH3 leaves at 9.15 am and arrives in Hué 2 hours later. Train 163 departs at 6.54 pm, arriving in Hué 2½ hours later.

To get to the train station from the bus station, head south-east on National Highway 1 for 1 km. The railway station is 150 metres across a field to the right (south-west) of the highway.

Bus Buses from Hué to Dong Ha depart from An Hoa Bus Station. Citroën Tractions to Dong Ha leave from Dong Ba Bus Station.

In Dong Ha, Dong Ha Bus Station (Ben Xe Khach Dong Ha; tel 211) is at the intersection of National Highway 1 and National Highway 9. Vehicles to Hué depart between 5 am and 5 pm. There are buses to Khe Sanh at 8 am and 11 am; to get to Lao Bao, change buses in Khe Sanh. There is service every Monday and Thursday to Hanoi; the bus departs at 5 am, arriving in Vinh at 6 or 7 pm and in Hanoi at 5 am the next day. Buses also link Dong Ha with Danang, Contien, Cua, Dien Sanh, Hai Tri and Ho Xa, which is

Remains of Russian-built T-54 in DMZ

along National Highway 1 13 km west of Vinh Moc.

QUANG TRI

The town of Quang Tri, which is 59 km north of Hué and 12.5 km south of Dong Ha Bus Station, was once an important citadel-city. In the spring of 1972, four divisions of North Vietnamese regulars backed by tanks, artillery and rockets, poured across the Demilitarised Zone into Quang Tri Province in what became known as the Eastertide Offensive. They lay siege to Quang Tri City, shelling it heavily before capturing it along with the rest of the province. During the next 4 months, the city was almost completely obliterated by South Vietnamese artillery and massive carpet bombing by American fighter-bombers and B-52s. The South Vietnamese Army suffered 5000 casualties in the rubble-to-rubble fighting to retake Quang Tri City.

Today, there is little to see in the town of Quang Tri except a memorial and a few remains of the moat, ramparts and gates of the citadel, once a South Vietnamese army headquarters. The Citadel is 1.6 km from National Highway 1 on Le Duan St (not to be confused with Le Duan St in Dong Ha), which runs perpendicular to National Highway 1. The ruined two storey building between National Highway 1 and the bus station used to be a Buddhist high school. Along National Highway 1 near the turnoff to Quang Tri is the skeleton of a church.

Cua Viet Beach, once the site of an important American landing dock, is 16 km north-east of Quang Tri. Gia Dang Beach is 13 km east of town.

Place to Stay

There are no hotels in Quang Tri, but the local People's Committee runs a guest house (*Nha Khach Uy Ban Huyen Trieu Hai*) on Le Duan St.

Getting There & Away

The bus station is on Le Duan St (Quang Tri's north-south oriented main street) 600 metres from National Highway 1. Renault buses to An Hoa Bus Station in Hué leave at 5.30 am, 6.30 am, 8 am and 12 noon. A Citroën Traction to Dong Ba Bus Station in Hué departs daily at 6.30 am. The daily bus to Khe Sanh leaves at 8 am. There is also service to Ho Xa.

DOC MIEU BASE

Doc Mieu Base, which is next to National Highway 1 on a low rise 8 km south of the Ben Hai River, was once part of an elaborate electronic system (McNamara's Wall) intended to prevent infiltration across the DMZ. Today, it is a lunar landscape of bunkers, craters, shrapnel and live mortar rounds. Bits of cloth and decaying military boots are strewn about on the red earth. This devastation was created not by the war but by scrap-metal hunters, who have found excavations at this site particularly reward-ing.

BEN HAI RIVER

Twenty-two km north of Dong Ha, National Highway 1 crosses the Ben Hai River, once the demarcation line between North and South Vietnam, over the decrepit Hien Luong Bridge. Until 1967 (when it was bombed by the Americans), the northern half of the bridge that stood on this site was painted red while the southern half was yellow. Following the signing of the Paris Cease-Fire Agreements in 1973, the present bridge and the two flag towers were built. A typhoon knocked over the flag pole on the northern bank of the river in 1985.

CUA TUNG BEACH

Cua Tung Beach, a long, secluded stretch of sand where Vietnam's last emperor, Bao Dai, used to vacation, is just north of the mouth of the Ben Hai River. There are beaches on the southern side of the Ben Hai River as well. Every bit of land in the area not levelled for planting is pockmarked with bomb craters of all sizes. Offshore is Con Co Island, which can be reached by motorised boat; the trip takes 2½ hours or so.

Place to Stay

There is a convalescent home (*Nha Dien Duong Cua Tung*; tel 03 from the Cho Gio Post Office exchange) on a bluff overlooking the beach. Though as of this writing none have ever done so, travellers are welcome to use its very basic facilities. There are no fans (though the home does have a generator) and rooms are outfitted with mats rather than mattresses.

Getting There & Away

There are no buses to Cua Tung Beach, which can be reached by turning right (east-ward) off National Highway 1 at a point 1.2 km north of the Ben Hai River. Cua Tung Beach is about 7 km south of Vinh Moc via the dirt road that runs along the coast.

THE TUNNELS OF VINH MOC

The remarkable tunnels of Vinh Moc are yet another monument to the tenaciousness of North Vietnamese determination to perse-vere and triumph – at all costs and despite incredible difficulties – in the war against South Vietnam and the USA. The 2.8 km of tunnels here, all of which can be visited, are the real thing, unadulterated (unlike the tunnels at Cu Chi) for viewing by tourists. A museum is being constructed on the site. A visit to the tunnels can be combined with bathing at the beautiful beaches which extend for many km north and south of Vinh Moc.

Local authorities, who prefer not to lose any foreigners in the maze of forks, branches and identical weaving passageways, are adamant that visitors enter the tunnels only if accompanied by a local guide. The tunnels have been chemically treated to keep snakes away. The entrance fee is 3000d. Bring a flashlight.

In 1966, the villagers of Vinh Moc, facing incessant US aerial and artillery attacks which rendered small family shelters inef-fective, began tunnelling by hand into the red clay earth. After 18 months of work (during which the excavated earth was camouflaged to prevent its detection from the air), the entire village of 1200 persons was relocated underground. The adults would go outside to fish and work in the fields; the old people and children stayed inside all the time. Supplies were delivered to the village on bicycles and by boat.

Later, the young and old were evacuated and the local young people, who continued to fish and plant, were joined by soldiers whose mission was to keep communications and supply lines to nearby Con Co Island open. People began moving above-ground in 1969 but returned to the tunnels in 1972-73. A total of 11,500 tons of supplies reached Con Co Island and a further 300 tons were shipped to the south thanks to the Vinh Moc tunnels.

Other villages in the vicinity also built tunnel systems but none were as elaborate as the one at Vinh Moc. The poorly constructed tunnels of Vinh Quang village (at the mouth of the Ben Hai River) were crushed by bombs, killing everyone inside.

The tunnel network at Vinh Moc remains essentially as it looked 20 years ago, though some of the 12 entrances, seven of which exit onto the palm-lined beach, have been retimbered and others have become overgrown with foliage. The tunnels, which average 1.2 metres wide and are from 1.2 to 1.7 metres in height, were built on three levels ranging from 15 to 26 metres below the crest of the bluff. The deepest level was used by the military.

On both sides of the passageways are tiny chambers with arched ceilings, each of which housed a family. Water was drawn from wells (the water table is only 5 metres below the deepest tunnel). The centrepiece of the network is a long, narrow room on the middle level. It was used as a warehouse and conference hall and was big enough to seat 150 people, who would gather to sing or, from 1972 onwards, watch movies. Electric lighting was also added in 1972. The network included a medical clinic with obstetric facilities; over the years, 17 children were born in the tunnels.

The tunnels were repeatedly hit by American bombs, but the only ordnance that posed a real threat was the feared 'drilling bomb'. Only once did such a bomb score a direct hit, but it failed to explode and no one was injured; the inhabitants adapted the hole for use as an air shaft. The mouths of the complex that faced the sea were sometimes hit by naval gunfire.

Offshore is vegetation-covered Con Co Island, which during the war was an important supply depot. Today, the island, which is ringed by rocky beaches, houses a small military base. The trip from Vinh Moc to Con Co takes 2½ to 3 hours by motorised fishing boat.

Places to Stay

There is no hotel at Vinh Moc but if you have a letter of introduction from Quang Tri Tourism you may be able to stay in a private house. Accommodation is available at Cua Tung Beach, 7 km to the south.

Getting There & Away

The turnoff to Vinh Moc from National Highway 1 is 6.5 km north of the Ben Hai River in the village of Ho Xa. Vinh Moc is 13 km from National Highway 1.

TRUONG SON NATIONAL CEMETERY

Truong Son National Cemetery (Nghia Trang Liet Si Truong Son) is a memorial to tens of thousands of North Vietnamese soldiers from transport, construction and anti-aircraft units who were killed in the Truong Son Mountains (the Annamite Cordillera) along the Ho Chi Minh Trail (Duong Truong Son). Row after row of white tombstones stretch across the hillsides in a scene eerily reminiscent of the endless lines of crosses and Stars of David in US military cemeteries. The cemetery is maintained by disabled war veterans.

The soldiers are buried in five zones according to the part of Vietnam they came from; within each zone, the tombs are arranged by province of origin. The gravestones of five colonels (*Trung Ta* and *Dia Ta*) and seven decorated heroes, of whom one is a woman, are in a separate area. Each headstone bears the inscription *Liet Si*, which means 'martyr'. The soldiers whose remains are interred here were originally buried near where they were killed and were brought here after reunification, but many of the graves are empty, bearing the names of a small portion of Vietnam's 300,000 MIAs.

On the hilltop above the sculpture garden is a three sided stele. On one face are engraved the tributes of high-ranking Vietnamese leaders to the people who worked on the Ho Chi Minh Trail. At the bottom is a poem by the poet To Huu. Another side tells the history of the May 1959 Army Corps (*Doang 5.59*) which is said to have been founded on Ho Chi Minh's birthday in 1959 with the mission of constructing and maintaining a supply line to the South. The third side lists the constituent units of the May 1959 Army Corps, which eventually included five divisions. The site where the cemetery now stands was used as a base of the May 1959 Army Corps from 1972 to 1975.

Getting There & Away

The road to Truong Son National Cemetery intersects National Route 1 13 km north of Dong Ha and 9 km south of the Ben Hai River; the distance from the highway to the cemetery is 17 km. A rocky cart-path, passable (but just barely) by motorcar, links Cam Lo (on National Route 9) with Truong Son National Cemetery. The 18 km drive from Cam Lo to the cemetery passes by newly planted rubber plantations and the homes of Bru (Van Kieu) tribal people who raise, among other crops, black pepper.

CON THIEN FIREBASE

In September 1967, North Vietnamese forces backed by long range artillery and rockets crossed the DMZ and besieged the US Marine base of Con Thien, which had been established to stop infiltrations across the DMZ and as part of 'McNamara's Wall' (named after the US Secretary of Defense 1961-68), an abortive electronic barrier to detect infiltrators. The Americans responded with 4000 bombing sorties (including 800 by B-52s) during which more than 40,000 tons of bombs were dropped on the North Vietnamese forces around Con Thien, transforming the gently sloping brush-covered hills that surrounded the base into a smoking moonscape of craters and ashes. As a result of the bombing, the siege was lifted, but the battle had accomplished its real purpose: to divert US attention from South Vietnam's cities in preparation for the Tet Offensive. The area around the base is still considered too dangerous even for scrap metal hunters to approach.

Con Thien Firebase is 10 km west of National Highway 1 and 7 km east of Truong Son National Cemetery along the road linking National Highway 1 with the cemetery. Concrete bunkers mark the spot a few hundred metres to the south of the road where the base once stood.

Con Thien is 12 km from National Highway 9 and 6 km from Truong Son National Cemetery on the road that links Cam Lo with the cemetery. As you head towards the cemetery, the base is visible off to the right (east).

Six km towards National Highway 1 from Con Thien (and 4 km from the highway) is another US base, C-3, the rectangular ramparts of which are still visible just north of the road. It is inaccessible due to mines.

CAMP CARROLL

Established in 1966, Camp Carroll was named for a US Marine captain who was killed trying to seize a nearby ridge. The gargantuan 175 mm cannons at Camp Carroll were used to shell targets as far away as Khe Sanh. In 1972, the South Vietnamese commander of Camp Carroll, Lieutenant Colonel Ton That Dinh, surrendered and joined the North Vietnamese army; he is now a high-ranking official in Hué.

These days there is not that much to see at Camp Carroll except a few overgrown trenches and the remains of their timber roofs. Bits of military hardware and lots of rusty shell casings litter the ground. The concrete bunkers were destroyed by local people seeking to extract the steel reinforcing rods to sell as scrap; concrete chunks from the bunkers were hauled off for use in construction. Locals out prospecting for scrap metal can point out what little of the base is left.

The area around Camp Carroll now belongs to the State Pepper Enterprises (Xi Nghiep Ho Tieu Tan Lam). The pepper plants are trained so that they climb up the trunks of jackfruit trees. There are also rubber plantations nearby. The road to Camp Carroll leads on to the fertile Cua Valley, once home to a number of French settlers.

The turnoff to Camp Carroll is 11 km west of Cam Lo, 24 km east of the Dakrong Bridge and 37 km east of the Khe Sanh Bus Station. The base is 3 km from National Highway 9.

THE ROCKPILE

The Rockpile was named for what can only be described as a 230 metre high pile of rocks. There was a US Marines lookout on top of the Rockpile and a base for American long-range artillery nearby. The local tribal people, who live in houses built on stilts, engage in slash-and-burn agriculture.

The Rockpile is 26 km towards Khe Sanh from Dong Ha.

DAKRONG BRIDGE

The Dakrong Bridge, which is 13 km east of the Khe Sanh Bus Station, was built in 1975-76 with assistance from the Cubans. The bridge crosses the Dakrong River (also known as the Ta Rin River). Hill-tribe people in the area live by slash-and-burn agriculture. Some of the tribesmen openly carry assault rifles left over from the war; this is against the law but the government seems unwilling or unable to do anything about it.

The road that heads south-east from the bridge to Aluoi was once a branch of the Ho Chi Minh Trail. Constructed with Cuban help, it passes by the stilted homes of the Brus.

ALUOI

Aluoi is approximately 65 km south-east of the Dakrong Bridge and 60 km west of Hué. There are a number of waterfalls and cascades in the area. Tribes living in the mountainous Aluoi area include the Ba Co, Ba Hy, Ca Tu and Taoi. US Army Special Forces bases in Aluoi and Ashau were overrun and abandoned in 1966; the area then became an important trans-shipment centre for supplies coming down the Ho Chi Minh Trail.

Among the better-known military sites in the vicinity of Aluoi are landing zones Cunningham, Erskine and Razor, Hill 1175 (west of the valley) and Hill 521 (in Laos). Farther south in the Ashau Valley is 'Hamburger Hill' (Apbia Mountain). In May 1969, American forces on a search and destroy operation near the Lao border fought one of the fiercest engagements of the war here, suffering terrible casualties (hence the name); in less than a week of fighting, 241 American soldiers died at Hamburger Hill, a fact well publicised in the American media. A month later, after US forces withdrew from the area to continue operations elsewhere, the hill was reoccupied by the North Vietnamese.

KHE SANH COMBAT BASE

Khe Sanh Combat Base, site of the most famous siege (and one of the most controversial battles) of the Vietnam War, sits silently on a barren plateau surrounded by vegetation-covered hills often obscured by mist and fog. It is hard to imagine as you stand in this peaceful, verdant land, with the neat homes and vegetable plots of local tribespeople and Vietnamese settlers all around, that in this very place in early 1968 about 500 Americans (the official figure of 205 American dead was arrived at by statistical sleight-of-hand) and uncounted thousands of North Vietnamese and local people died amidst the din of machine-guns and the fiery explosions of 1000 kg bombs, white phosphorus shells, napalm, mortars and artillery rounds of all sorts.

But little things help you to picture what the history books say happened here. The outline of the airfield remains distinct (to this day nothing will grow on it). In places, the ground is literally carpeted with bullets and rusting shell casings. And all around are little groups of local people digging holes in their relentless search for scrap metal (once, local scavengers say proudly, they unearthed an entire bulldozer!). And the US MIA Team, which is charged with finding the remains of Americans listed as 'missing-in-action', still visits the area to search for the bodies of the Americans who disappeared during the fierce battles in the surrounding hills. Most of the remains they find are Vietnamese.

History

Despite opposition from Marine Corps brass to General Westmoreland's attrition strategy (they thought it futile), the small US Army Special Forces (Green Beret) base at Khe Sanh, built to recruit and train local tribesmen, was turned into a Marine stronghold in ate 1966. In April 1967, there began a series of 'Hill Fights' between the US forces and the well-dug-in North Vietnamese Army infantry who held the surrounding hills. In the period of a few weeks, 155 Marines and perhaps thousands of North Vietnamese were killed. The fighting centred on hills 881 South and 881 North, both of which are about 8 km north-west of Khe Sanh Combat Base.

In late 1967, American intelligence detected the movement of tens of thousands of North Vietnamese regulars armed with mortars, rockets and artillery into the hills around Khe Sanh. The commander of American forces in Vietnam, General Westmoreland, became convinced that the North Vietnamese were planning another Dien Bien Phu, a preposterous analogy given American firepower and the proximity of Khe Sanh to supply lines and other American bases. President Johnson himself became obsessed by the spectre of Dien Bien Phu: to follow the course of the battle, he had a sand-table model of the Khe Sanh plateau constructed in the White House Situation Room, and he took the unprecedented step of requiring a written guarantee from the Joint Chiefs of Staff that Khe Sanh could be held. Westmoreland, determined to avoid another Dien Bien Phu' at all costs, assembled an armada of 5000 aeroplanes and helicopters and increased the number of troops at Khe Sanh to 6000. He even ordered his staff to study the feasibility of using tactical nuclear weapons (!).

The 75-day Siege of Khe Sanh began on 21 January 1968 with a small-scale assault on the base perimeter. As the Marines and the South Vietnamese Rangers with them braced for a full-scale ground attack, Khe Sanh became the focus of global media attention. It was the cover story for both *Newsweek* and *Life* magazines and appeared on the front pages of countless newspapers around the world. During the next 2 months, the base was subject to continuous ground attacks and artillery fire. US aircraft dropped 100,000 tons of explosives on the immediate vicinity of Khe Sanh Combat Base. The expected attempt to overrun the base never came, and on 7 April 1968 after heavy fighting, US Army troops reopened National Route 9 and linked up with the Marines, ending the siege.

It now seems clear that the Siege of Khe Sanh, in which an estimated 10,000 North Vietnamese died, was merely an enormous diversion intended to draw US forces and the attention of their commanders away from South Vietnam's population centres in preparation for the Tet Offensive, which began a week after the siege did. At the time, however, Westmoreland considered the entire Tet Offensive to be a 'diversionary effort' to distract attention from Khe Sanh!

A few days after Westmoreland's tour of duty in Vietnam ended in July 1968, American forces in the area were redeployed. Policy, it seemed, had been reassessed and holding Khe Sanh, for which so many men had died, was deemed unnecessary. After everything at Khe Sanh was buried, trucked out or blown up – nothing recognisable that could be used in a North Vietnamese propaganda film was to remain – US forces up and left Khe Sanh Combat Base under a curtain of secrecy. The American command had finally realised what a Marine officer had long before expressed this way: 'When you're at Khe Sanh, you're not really anywhere ... You could lose it and you really haven't lost a damn thing'.

Getting There & Away

To get to Khe Sanh Combat Base, turn northwestward at the triangular intersection 600 metres towards Dong Ha from Khe Sanh Bus Station. The base is on the right-hand side of the road 2.5 km from the intersection.

KHE SANH TOWN

Set amidst beautiful hills, valleys and fields at an elevation of about 600 metres, the town of Khe Sanh (Huong Hoa) is a pleasant district capital once known for its French-run coffee plantations. Many of the inhabitants are Bru tribespeople who have moved here from the surrounding hills. A popular pastime among the hill-tribe women is smoking long-stemmed pipes.

Place to Stay

The guest house of the District People's Committee (Nha Khach Huyen Huong Hoa; tel 27 from the Dong Ha telephone exchange) has five rooms and about 20 beds. It is 300 metres south (towards Laos) from Khe Sanh Bus Station.

Getting There & Away

Khe Sanh Bus Station (Ben Xe Huong Hoa) is on National Highway 9600 metres south-west (towards the Lao frontier) from the triangular intersection where the road to Khe Sanh Combat Base branches off. Buses to Dong Ha depart at 7 am and around 12 noon; the daily bus to Hué leaves at 7 am. There are two buses a day to Lao Bao; the first leaves at 6 am, the second whenever it is full. The ticket window is open from 6 to 7 am; tickets for later buses are sold on board. If and when the border with Laos is opened for trade and travel, the public transport situation in the area is likely to improve significantly.

LANG VEI SPECIAL FORCES CAMP

In February 1968, Lang Vei Special Forces Camp, established in 1962, was attacked and overrun by North Vietnamese infantry backed by nine tanks. Of the base's 500 South Vietnamese, Bru and Montagnard defenders, 316 were killed. Ten of the 24 Americans at the base were killed; 11 of the survivors were wounded.

All that remains of dog-bone shaped Lang Vei Base are the overgrown remains of numerous concrete bunkers. Locals can show you around. The base is on a ridge just south-west of National Highway 9 at a point 9.2 km towards Laos from the Khe Sanh Bus Station and 7.3 km towards Khe Sanh from Lao Bao Market.

LAO BAO

Lao Bao is right on the Tchepone River (Song Xe Pon), which marks the Vietnam-Laos border. Towering above Lao Bao on the Lao side of the border is Co Roc Mountain, once a North Vietnamese artillery stronghold.

Two km from the border post is Lao Bao Market, where Thai goods smuggled through the bush from Laos to Vietnam are readily available. Merchants accept either Vietnamese dong or Lao kip.

Lao Bao is 18 km west of Khe Sanh, 80 km from Dong Ha, 152 km from Hué, 46 km east of Tchepone (Laos), 250 km east of Savannakhet, Laos (on the Thai frontier) and 950 km from Bangkok (via Ubon Ratchathani). Lao Bao may soon become an important border crossing for trade and tourism between Thailand and central Vietnam.

North-Central Vietnam

DONG HOI

The fishing port of Dong Hoi is the capital of Quang Binh Province. Important archaeological finds from the neolithic period have been made in the vicinity. During the Vietnam War, the city suffered extensive damage from US bombing. When travelling on National Highway 1 north of the DMZ, note the old French bunkers and US bomb craters lining the route; both are especially numerous near road and rail bridges. The Vietnam-Cuba Hospital is 1 km north of town.

Beaches

Most of Quang Binh Province is lined with sand dunes and beaches. There are tens of km of beaches and dunes north of town and on a long spit of sand south of town. Nhat Le Beach is at the mouth of the Nhat Le River; another bathing site in the region is Ly Hoa Beach.

Places to Stay

Khach San Chuyen Gia (Hotel for Foreign Experts) was built by the Cubans. The new *Nhat Le Hotel* is 200 metres east of National Highway 1. The *Ngoai Thuong Guest House* is frequented by domestic business travellers.

Getting There & Away

Dong Hoi is 166 km from Hué, 94 km from Dong Ha, 197 km from Vinh and 489 km from Hanoi.

Dong Hoi is on both National Highway 1 and the Saigon-Hanoi railway line. Road traffic between Dong Ha and Dong Hoi is very light, especially after the early morning. North of the DMZ, National Highway 1 is narrow and poorly paved.

There is a ferry crossing at Cua Gianh, which is 33 km north of Dong Hoi.

PHONG NHA CAVE

Phong Nha Cave, which is about 45 km north-west of Dong Hoi, is remarkable for its thousands of metres of passageways lined with a great variety of stalactites and stalagmites. The main tunnel is 1451 metres in length and has 14 halls. Travel within the cave is by boat and on foot. The Chams utilised the grottoes of Phong Nha Cave as Buddhist sanctuaries in the 9th and 10th centuries; the remains of Cham altars and inscriptions can still be seen. Vietnamese Buddhists continue to venerate these sanctuaries, as they do other Cham religious sites.

DEO NGANG

Deo Ngang is a mountainous coastal area that constitutes the easternmost section of the Hoanh Son Mountains (Transversal Range), which stretches from the Lao border to the sea along the 18th parallel. Until the 11th century, the range formed Vietnam's frontier with the Kingdom of Champa. Later, the French used it as the border between their protectorates of Annam and Tonkin; Annam Gate (Porte d'Annam) is still visible at Deo Ngang from National Highway 1. The Hoanh Son Mountains now demarcate the border between Quang Binh Province and Nghe Tinh Province. There are a number of islands offshore.

CAM XUYEN

The town of Cam Xuyen is about 150 km north of Dong Hoi and 45 km south of Vinh. There is a guest house, *Nha Khach Cam Xuyen*, on the west side of the road.

Vinh

Nghe Tinh Province is endowed with poor soil and some of the worst weather in Vietnam. The area frequently suffers from floods and devastating typhoons. Nghe Tinh is one of the places about which the locals say: 'The typhoon was born here and comes

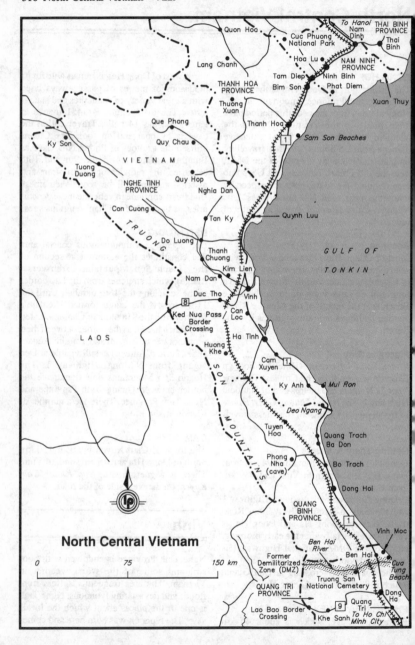

North Central Vietnam

0   75   150 km

back often to visit'. The summers are very hot and dry while during the winter the cold and rain are made all the more unpleasant by biting winds from the north.

The upland and highland regions of Nghe Tinh, much of which is thickly forested, cover 80% of the province's territory and are home to Muong, Tai (Thai or Thay), Khmer, Meo and Tho hill-tribe people. Mountain fauna includes tigers, leopards, elephants, rhinoceros, deer, monkeys, gibbons and flying squirrels. Nghe Tinh's agricultural products include wet-grown rice, sugar cane, tea, mulberry leaves, areca and pomelo.

Nghe Tinh Province is famous for its revolutionary spirit. Both Phan Boi Chau (1867-1940) and Ho Chi Minh (1890-1969) were natives of Nghe Tinh Province. The Nghe Tinh Uprising (1893-95) against the French was led by the scholar Phan Dinh Phung (1847-95). The Nghe Tinh Soviets Movement (1930-31) began with a series of workers' strikes and demonstrations encouraged by the newly-formed Indochinese Communist Party; by the summer of 1930, peasant associations (or soviets) had seized power in some areas. The French moved swiftly to suppress the unrest, employing aircraft to attack crowds of demonstrators. The Ho Chi Minh Trail began in Nghe Tinh Province, and much of the war matériel transported on the Ho Chi Minh Trail was shipped via the port of Vinh.

A good source of information on Nghe Tinh Province is *Nghe Tinh: Native Province of Ho Chi Minh*, which is volume 59 of the *Vietnamese Studies* series published in English and French in Hanoi by XUNHASABA.

VINH

The port city of Vinh is the capital of Vietnam's most populous province, Nghe Tinh, which is the second largest in the country. While there is almost nothing of interest in the city, it is a convenient place to stop for the night if you are going overland between Hué and Hanoi. Westerners in the city have reported being warned about a crime wave that began in the wake of the

discharge from the army of tens of thousands of young men who had been serving in Cambodia. Authorities in Hanoi have been refusing to grant permits for visits to Vinh to individual travellers.

Vinh would have been poor even if the pleasant citadel-city of colonial days had not been destroyed in the early 1950s as a result of French aerial bombing and the Viet Minh's scorched earth policy. Vinh would have been poor even if it had not subsequently been devastated by a huge fire. And Vinh would have been poor even if the United States had not obliterated the city in hundreds of air attacks and naval artillery bombardments from 1964 to 1972 which left only two buildings (one of which comprises part of the Nghe Tinh Guest House) intact (the Americans paid a high price for the bombings – more US aircraft and airmen were shot down over Nghe Tinh Province than over any other part of North Vietnam).

The combination of these factors with the poor soil and harsh climate has made Vinh and all of Nghe Tinh Province one of the most destitute regions of one of the poorest countries in the world. Of the province's children, 72% (!) are malnourished. In the markets, 30d and 50d notes are still widely used; despite their infinitesimal value, such bills still mean something here. The peasants who can be seen begging along National Highway 1 in Nghe Tinh Province are known to be so utterly destitute that even domestic travellers give them money.

After the war, Vinh was rebuilt with East German financial and technical assistance, which perhaps explains why the city's grim and rapidly dilapidating buildings suffer from a uniform lack of imagination.

Orientation

As National Highway 1 enters Vinh from the south, it crosses the mouth of the Lam River (Ca River), also known as Cua Hoi Estuary. North of the soon-to-be replaced pontoon bridge (built after American bombing destroyed the old bridge in 1972) National Highway 1 is called Nguyen Du St; it becomes Tran Phu St in town. As National

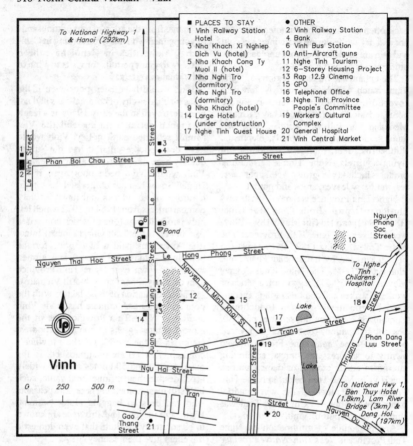

To National Highway 1 & Hanoi (292km)

PLACES TO STAY
1 Vinh Railway Station Hotel
3 Nha Khach Xi Nghiep Dich Vu (hotel)
5 Nha Khach Cong Ty Muoi II (hotel)
7 Nha Nghi Tro (dormitory)
8 Nha Nghi Tro (dormitory)
9 Nha Khach (hotel)
14 Large Hotel (under construction)
17 Nghe Tinh Guest House

OTHER
2 Vinh Railway Station
4 Bank
6 Vinh Bus Station
10 Anti-Aircraft guns
11 Nghe Tinh Tourism
12 6-Storey Housing Project
13 Rap 12.9 Cinema
15 GPO
16 Telephone Office
18 Nghe Tinh Province People's Committee
19 Workers' Cultural Complex
20 General Hospital
21 Vinh Central Market

Vinh

0   250   500 m

Highway 1 enters Vinh from the north, it becomes Le Loi St and then Quang Trung St. Quang Trung St (which runs north-south) and Tran Phu St intersect one block north of Vinh Central Market.

Street address numbers are not used in Vinh.

Information

Tourist Office The office of Nghe Tinh Tourism (Cong Ty Du Lich Nghe Tinh; tel 4692, 2285) is on the 3rd storey of a six storey building in the housing project on Quang Trung St between Le Hong Phong St and Rap 12.9 cinema. The office is about 700 metres north of Vinh Central Market.

Post The post office is on Nguyen Thi Minh Khai St 300 metres north-west of Dinh Cong Trang St; it is open from 6.30 am to 9 pm.

Telephone International and domestic telephone calls can be made from the calling office (Cong Ty Dien Bao Dien Thoai), which is in a little building on Dinh Cong Trung St near the corner of Nguyen Thi Minh Khai St. The office, which is across the street from the Workers' Cultural Complex and

100 metres west of the gate to the Nghe Tinh Guest House, is supposed to be open from 7 am to 9 pm. If no one is there, inquire at the cigarette stall next door or go into the telephone exchange building, which is across the field behind the calling office.

Money The bank is in a brand new building at the corner of Le Loi St and Nguyen Si Sach St.

Emergency The general hospital is on the corner of Tran Phu St and Le Mao St.

Vinh Central Market
Vinh's main marketplace, Cho Vinh, is noteworthy for the limited selection of goods offered for sale. There are food stalls around the back. Vinh Central Market is at the end of Cao Thang St, which is the southern continuation of Quang Trung St.

Veterans' Vietnam Restoration Project Clinic
A building for surgery and physical therapy was built on the grounds of Nghe Tinh Children's Hospital in the fall of 1989 by a team from the Veterans' Vietnam Restoration Project (based in Garberville, California) working alongside Vietnamese war veterans. The same group also constructed a medical clinic in Vung Tau. Nghe Tinh Children's Hospital (Benh Vien Nhi Nghe Tinh) is out Nguyen Phong Sac St (the continuation of Truong Thi St) and down a side street on the right (towards the south-east).

Workers' Cultural Complex
The Workers' Cultural Complex (Cau Lac Bo Cong Nhan), a huge structure at the corner of Le Mao St and Dinh Cong Trang St, is the centre of Vinh's cultural life. It includes a cinema, a theatre and a dancing hall in which concerts, plays, film screenings, dances and other events are held.

Anti-Aircraft Guns
Don't try to visit the field of anti-aircraft guns on Le Hong Phong St. It is not a museum dedicated to the glorious exploits of the people of Vinh in resisting the American imperialists. The guns, with their double barrels pointed skyward, are loaded and still ready to defend the city against aerial attack.

Birthplace of Ho Chi Minh
Kim Lien Village, where Ho Chi Minh was born in 1890, is 14 km from Vinh. The house in which he was born can be visited; nearby there is a museum.

Beaches
Vinh is 15 km from the sea. Cua Lo Beach is 20 km from the city.

Places to Stay
Bus Station Area Within the precincts of the bus station, dormitory beds are available for 700d at *Nha Nghi Tro* (tel 4127), which is next to the ticket office on the southern edge of the bus parking area. *Nha Khach* is across Le Loi St from the bus station next to the pond; a room costs 6000d. *Nha Nghi Tro* (tel 2362; 6 rooms) is on Le Loi St 60 metres south (to the right as you exit) of the bus station gate; a bed costs 1000d, a room 4000d.

Railway Station Area As you exit the railroad station terminal building, the *Vinh Railway Station Hotel* (Khach San Duong Sat Ga Vinh; tel 24; 5 rooms), a modern two storey building, is to the left; a room costs 7500d. *Nha Khach Xi Nghiep Dich Vu* (tel 4705) is a modern three storey structure just north of the intersection of Le Loi St and Phan Boi Chau St, which is about 1 km due east of the railway station; singles/doubles are 12,000/24,000d. *Nha Khach Cong Ty Muoi II* (tel 2425; 5 rooms) is down an alleyway that intersects Le Loi St 150 metres south of Phan Boi Chau St.

Elsewhere in Town The nicest place to stay in Vinh is the *Nghe Tinh Guest House* (Nha Khach Nghe Tinh; tel 3175), which is on Dinh Cong Truong St 200 metres north-east of Le Mao St. Rooms range from 8000d (3rd class; in Vietnamese: *loai 3*) to 25,000d; dollar prices are US$10 to US$20. Don't stay in the poorly constructed new building out the back if you can avoid it; though it is only a few years old, it is infested with rats, bedbugs and fleas and is more spookily decrepit than the older structures (one of which survived the American bombings). There is an old bomb shelter next to the new building.

The *Ben Thuy Hotel* (Khach San Ben Thuy; tel 4892) is on Nguyen Du St (National Highway 1) 1.3 km towards the centre of Vinh from the bridge over the Lam River and 1.8 km towards the bridge from the intersection of Nguyen Du St and Truong Thi St.

A large hotel is being built on the west side of Le Loi Street about 600 metres north of the Central Market and across the street from the six storey housing project.

Places to Eat

There is a restaurant on Dinh Cong Trang St next door to the reception building of the Nghe Tinh Guest House complex. There are a number of small restaurants on Le Ninh St just outside the gate to the railway station. The food stalls in Vinh Central Market are behind the main building.

Getting There & Away

Road distances from Vinh:

Danang	468 km
Dong Hoi	197 km
Hanoi	292 km
Hué	363 km
Lao border	97 km
Thanh Hoa	139 km

National Highway 8, which begins in Vinh, crosses into Laos at 734 metre high Keo Nua Pass.

Air Vietnam Airlines may have flights from Hanoi to Vinh.

Train Vinh Railway Station (Ga Vinh; tel 4924) is 1 km west of the intersection of Le Loi St and Phan Boi Chau St, which is 1.5 km north of the Central Market.

Trains heading North

Train	Departs	Duration (hours)
STN4	4.14 am	9.45 (Hanoi)
TN2	6.40 pm	10.45 (Hanoi)
V2	2.05 pm	13.40 (Hanoi)
V82	9 pm	16 (ThuongTinh)

Trains heading South

Train	Departs	Duration (hours)
STN3	7.35 pm	11.25 (Hué)
TN1	6.25 am	12.10 (Hué)

Trains VD1 & VD2 link Vinh and Dong Hoi.

Bus Vinh Bus Station (Ben Xe Vinh; tel 4127, 4924) is on Le Loi St about 1 km north of the Central Market; the ticket office is open from 4.30 am to 5 pm daily. Express buses to Buon Ma Thuot, Danang, Hanoi and Saigon depart every day at 5 am; express buses to Hanoi leave at other times of the day as well. Non-express buses link Vinh with:

Bahai	Huong Son (Pho Chau)
Cam Xuyen	Ky Anh
Cau Giat	Lat
Con Cuong	Muong Xen
Cua	Nghia Dan
Do Luong	Phuc Son
Dung	Pleiku (Playcu)
Gia Lam	Que Phong
Hanoi	Quy Chau
Ha Tinh	Quy Hop
Hoa Binh	Trung Tam
Hué	Yen Thanh

Getting Around

There are almost no passenger cyclos in Vinh because the people can't afford to ride them. To get around, you might try hiring an over-size cargo cyclo.

THANH HOA CITY

Thanh Hoa City is the capital of Thanh Hoa Province; in this region, National Highway 1 is lined with bomb craters, particularly near bridges and railway stations. There is a large and attractive church on the northern out-skirts of town.

Thanh Hoa Province was the site of the Lam Son Uprising (1418-28), in which Vietnamese forces led by Le Loi (later Emperor Ly Thai To) expelled the Chinese

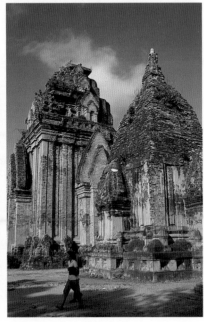

Top: View from Ngoan Muc Pass, between Dalat and Phan Rang (DR)
Left: The northern highlands (PS)
Right: Cham Towers near Nha Trang (OT)

Top: China Beach, Danang (RM)
Left: Imperial City, Hué (TA)
Right: Thien Mu Pagoda, Hué (DR)

and re-established the country's independence.

Muong and Red Tai (Thai) hilltribes live in the western part of the province.

Information
Thanh Hoa Province Tourism (tel 298) is at 21A Quang Trung St.

Places to Stay
There are two hotels along National Highway 1, *Khach San 25A* and *Khach San 25B*.

Places to Eat
Soup shops, tea shops and a few restaurants can be found along National Highway 1, especially near the southern entrance to town.

Getting There & Away
Thanh Hoa City is 502 km from Hué, 139 km from Vinh and 153 km from Hanoi.

Trains T83 and T84 link Thanh Hoa with Thuong Tinh, which is 17.5 km south of Hanoi Railway Station.

SAM SON BEACHES
The two Sam Son Beaches, among the nicest in the north, are 16 km south-east of Thanh Hoa City; they are a favourite vacation spot of Hanoi residents who can afford such luxuries. Near the bridge, which the US repeatedly bombed, are extensive fortifications and trenchworks. Accommodation ranges from basic bungalows to multi-storey hotels.

NINH BINH
Ninh Binh is 200 km north of Vinh, 61 km north of Thanh Hoa and 114 km south of Hanoi. The *Ninh Binh Hotel* (Khach San Ninh Binh) is a new place along National Highway 1.

Hanoi

Hanoi, the capital of the Socialist Republic of Vietnam, is a drab but pleasant and even charming city, in large part because of its famous lakes, shaded boulevards and verdant public parks. The city centre is an architectural museum piece, its blocks of ochre buildings retaining the air of a provincial French town of the 1930s. The people of Hanoi are known for being more reserved – and at the same time more traditionally hospitable – than their southern compatriots.

The city of Hanoi (population 925,000) is a small part of Greater Hanoi, which has a land area of 2139 sq km and a population of 2,800,000. The city is 72 km inland from the Gulf of Tonkin.

Hanoi may not be quite ready for an influx of 'capitalist tourists'. Many Westerners, (both backpackers and businesspeople) report being harassed by the police, especially at the airport, where the officials have a propensity to detain and fine foreigners as they leave. And there seems to be a certain amount of anti-Americanism – so absent in most of the rest of the country – especially among mid-level government officials.

Getting anything done in Hanoi is much more difficult than in the south, which is a major reason why the city, along with the rest of the north, is shunned by businesspeople, most of whom come here, if at all, only to deal with government ministries. Despite the recent economic liberalisation, entrepreneurship seems confined to the little shops and sidewalk stalls that have sprung up around town.

Whatever else Ho Chi Minh may have done, he created in North Vietnam a very effective police state. For almost 4 decades, the people of Hanoi and the north have suffered under a regime characterised by the ruthless exercise of police power; anonymous denunciations by a huge network of informers; the detention without trial of *bonzes*, priests, landowners and anyone else

seen as a potential threat to the government; and the blacklisting of dissidents and their children and their children's children. This legacy of human rights violations, which Amnesty International reports is continuing, has left its mark on the people of Hanoi, who seem strangely complacent and even cowed compared to the dissatisfied and outspoken Saigonese. Perhaps they are less discontented because the north has never experienced the war-time affluence US aid brought to the south; but then again, it can hardly be a coincidence that most of the boat people who fled Vietnam in the late 1980s were northerners.

History

The site where Hanoi now stands has been inhabited since the Neolithic period. Emperor Ly Thai To moved his capital here in 1010 AD, renaming the site Thang Long (City of the Soaring Dragon). Hanoi served as the capital of the Later Le Dynasty, founded by Le Loi, from its establishment in 1428 until 1788, when it was overthrown by Nguyen Hue, founder of the Tay Son Dynasty. The decision by Emperor Gia Long, founder of the Nguyen Dynasty, to rule from Hué relegated Hanoi to the status of a regional capital.

Over the centuries, Hanoi has borne a variety of names, including Dong Kinh (Eastern Capital), from which the Europeans derived the name they eventually applied to all of northern Vietnam, Tonkin. The city was named Hanoi (The City in a Bend of the River) by Emperor Tu Duc in 1831. From 1902 to 1953, Hanoi served as the capital of French Indochina.

Hanoi was proclaimed the capital of Vietnam after the August Revolution of 1945, but it was not until the Geneva Agreements of 1954 that the Viet Minh, driven from the city by the French in 1946, were able to return. During the Vietnam War, US bombing destroyed parts of Hanoi and killed many hundreds of civilians; almost all the damage has since been repaired.

Orientation

Hanoi is situated on the right bank of the Red River (Song Hong), which is spanned by two bridges, the old Long Bien Bridge (now used only by two-wheeled vehicles and pedestrians) and the new Chuong Duong Bridge.

In the centre of downtown Hanoi is Hoan Kiem Lake (also called the Lake of the Restored Sword and the Small Lake). To the north of the lake is the Old Quarter (known to the French as the *Cité Indigéne*), delineated by the Citadel to the west, Dong Xuan Market to the north and the ramparts of the Red River to the east. The Old Quarter is characterised by narrow streets whose names change every two blocks. South and southwest of the lake is the modern city centre, known as the *Ville Française* to the French. The colonial-era buildings in this area house many of Hanoi's hotels, state stores and non-Socialist embassies.

Ho Chi Minh's Mausoleum is to the west of the Citadel, which is still used as a military base. In front of the mausoleum is Ba Dinh Square. Most of the city's Socialist embassies are nearby in beautiful old mansions (Western late-comers had to settle for far less attractive embassy quarters elsewhere). West Lake (Ho Tay), another of Hanoi's famous lakes, is north of Ho Chi Minh's Mausoleum.

The Swedish Embassy is 3.5 km west of Hoan Kiem Lake near Giang Vo Lake. Other embassies in this area include Finland, Malaysia and Myanmar. Two large hotels, the Giang Vo Hotel and the Thang Long Hotel, are near Giang Vo Lake.

The city of Hanoi consists of four districts (*quan*): Hoan Kiem District (around the Lake of the Restored Sword); Ba Dinh District (which includes the Citadel, Ho Chi Minh's Mausoleum and the Swedish Embassy); Hai Ba Trung District (along the river south of Hoan Kiem District); and Dong Da District (south of Ba Dinh District). Greater Hanoi includes 11 suburban districts.

Information

Tourist Office The head office of Vietnam Tourism is at 54 Nguyen Du St (tel 57080, 52986, 55963; telex 4269 TOURISM VT, 4552 TOURISM VT). It can arrange organised tours for one or more persons but not much else. Coordination between people within the office is so poor that what you agree on with one official may not be communicated to the people who will be assigned to actually carry out what you have hired them to do.

Get *everything* – especially the itinerary and all costs – in writing. Keep a carbon or photocopy of your contract and itinerary with you at all times; if they ask to see it, make sure to keep a copy for yourself.

You should also insist upon paying no more than one-third of your bill as a down payment and the balance at the end of the trip. Unfortunately, travellers' experiences indicate that during the tour, you may need the added bit of leverage which you'll lack if you're all paid up.

The Hanoi Tourism & Service Company, better known by its acronym TOSERCO (tel 52937, 63541; telex 4535 HOTELO VT), is at 8 To Hien Thanh St (corner Mai Hac De St). As of this writing, this is the best place in all of Vietnam for individual travellers to get visa extensions and internal travel permits. TOSERCO is run by the Hanoi People's Committee.

Hanoi Tourism (tel 54209, 57886) is a rather useless organisation; it has an office at 18 Ly Thuong Kiet St and another in the Thong Nhat Hotel.

The Immigration Police Office is at 83 Tran Hung Dao St; it is open Monday to Saturday from 8 to 11 am and 1 to 5 pm.

Post & Telecommunications The GPO (Buu Dien Trung Vong; tel 54413), which occupies a full city block facing Hoan Kiem Lake, is at 75 Dinh Tien Hoang St (between Dinh Le St and Le Thach St). The entrance in the middle of the block leads to the postal services windows, where you can send letters, pick up domestic packages and pur-

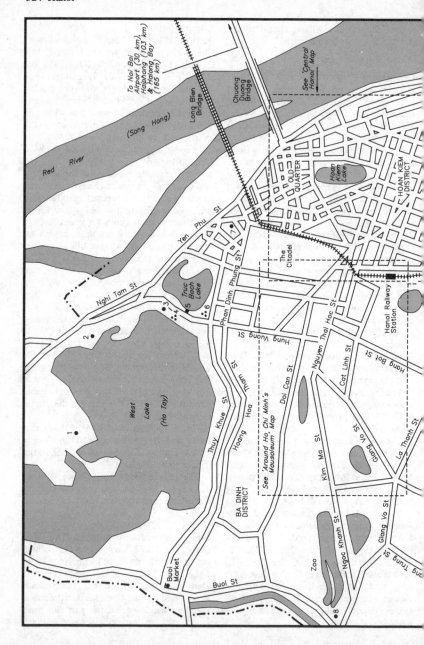

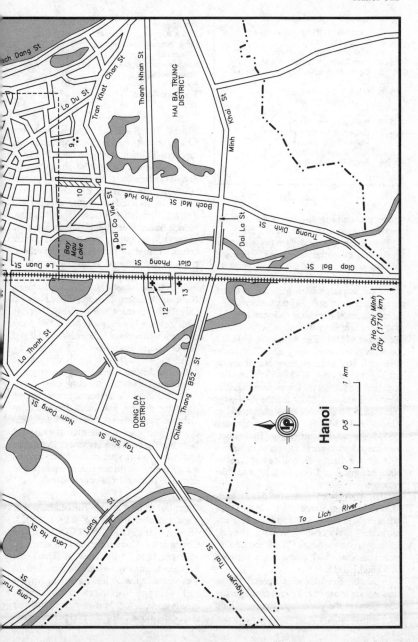

1	Communist Party Guest House
2	Thang Loi Hotel
3	Nha Noi Ho Tay Restaurant
4	Tran Quoc Pagoda
5	Commemorative Plaque to downed US pilot
6	Quan Thanh Pagoda
7	Dong Xuan Market
8	Thu Le Park & Zoo Entrance
9	Hai Ba Trung Temple
10	Bicycle & Motorbike Shops
11	Polytechnic University
12	International Hospital
13	Bach Mai Hospital

Fire Brigade	08
First Aid	05
Long-Distance Operator (Domestic)	00
Long-Distance Operator (International)	01
Police	03
Telephone Repairs	09
Time	07

chase philatelic items; the postal services section is open from 6.30 am to 8 pm.

The same entrance leads to the telex, telegram and domestic telephone office (tel 55918), which is to the left as you enter the building. Telex and domestic telephone services are available from 6.30 am to 8 pm; telegrams can be sent 24 hours a day.

International telephone calls can be made and faxes sent from the office (tel 52030) at the corner of Dinh Tien Hoang St and Dinh Le St, which is open daily from 7.30 am to 9.30 pm. Fax charges from Hanoi are as follows: to the USA, US$25.50 for the first page and US$20.50 for subsequent pages; to Western Europe, US$20 for the first page and US$16.50 for additional pages; and to Australia, US$15 for the first page and US$12 for subsequent pages. Both international telephone and fax services have a 10% service charge. This office also handles both incoming and outgoing international packages.

DHL Worldwide Express (tel 57124; telex 4324 HN), whose Hanoi office is in the GPO, offers express parcel and document delivery to virtually every country on earth. The first 500 grams costs between US$50 and US$70; each additional 500 grams costs between US$5 and US$15.

In Hanoi, the following special phone numbers are in use (don't count on the person who answers the phone speaking anything but Vietnamese):

Money The Bank for Foreign Trade (tel 52831) at 47-49 Le Thai To St offers the best legal rate in town; it is open daily from 8 to 11.30 am and 1.30 to 3.30 pm except on Saturday afternoons, Sundays and national holidays. The currency exchange counter, which is at window eight, accepts US dollars, British pounds, Deutchmarks, French francs, Hong Kong dollars, Japanese yen and Swiss francs; they do not at present accept Australian dollars. Only travellers' cheques denominated in US dollars will be cashed. Acceptable travellers' cheques include those issued by American Express, Bank of America, Citicorp, First National City Bank, Thomas Cook and Visa. The early 20th century interior decor of the bank makes it well worth a look inside even if you do not require its services.

All the major tourist hotels can change dollars at the front desk but will give you a rate 5% to 10% below the bank rate.

To find someone interested in exchanging dong for dollars, ask other foreigners or mention your interest to one of the cyclo drivers who wait outside the major hotels. Now that the bank rate is more or less in line with what you can get on the black market, it may not be worth the risk to squeeze that extra few percent from your dollars.

Chamber of Commerce The head office of Vietcochamber (tel 25961, 25962, 53023, 56446; telex 4257 VIETCO VT), the Chamber of Commerce and Industry of Vietnam, is at 33 Ba Trieu St. The Trade Service Company, which is attached to Vietcochamber, also has its offices here. It can arrange business trips, assist businesspeople with bureaucratic formalities (visa extensions, internal travel permits, etc), book hotel accommodation anywhere in the country, arrange land transport of all sorts and provide translation services.

Some Useful Addresses The Ministry of Foreign Affairs is at 1 Ton That Dam St, near Ho Chi Minh's Mausoleum. English-speaking personnel can always be found at the North America Department (tel 57279, 58201, extension 314 or 312). The Foreign Press Centre of the Ministry of Foreign Affairs (tel 54697) is at 10 Le Phung Hieu St. The International Relations Department of the Ministry of Information (tel 53152; telex 4532 VNRT VT) is at 58 Quan Su St.

Registration & Internal Travel Permits At some point, the Interior Ministry decided to try out more liberal policies on individual travel, but as in Laos, their policies keep changing. It is therefore impossible to predict the kind of a reception your requests for internal travel permits and visa extensions will receive in Hanoi. I should add that the circumstances of my own detention and expulsion from Vietnam do not bode well for individual travel in the north. You may have no problems at all, but it is conceivable that you will have to fly back to Bangkok after your 3-day tourist visa expires. To find out up-to-date information on government policies concerning independent travel before arriving, your best bet is to ask around the guests houses of Khao San Road in Bangkok.

If you are not being hosted by an official body that is taking care of the paperwork, do not forget to register with the Immigration Police either via TOSERCO or Vietcochamber or at the Immigration Police Office. You must re-register each time you enter the country. Your registration documents allow you to overnight in Hanoi only. In general, special permission is not required for day trips out of the city, but an internal travel permit is necessary if you want to spend the night outside of Hanoi.

Businesspeople may be able to extend their visas and receive internal travel permits through the Chamber of Commerce, Vietcochamber.

TOSERCO issues internal travel permits (including permits to go overland to Saigon) and visa extensions to individual travellers with tourist visas. It charges US$5 for registration, US$10 for an internal travel permit and US$20 each visa extension. Visa extensions of up to 2 weeks are available; don't count on being able to extend your visa for an additional 2 weeks, though this may in fact prove possible.

Internal travel permits are available for travel to the Sam Son Beaches, Hué, Danang, Nha Trang, Saigon and Vung Tau and may be given for trips to Haiphong and Halong Bay. To get an internal travel permit, you will need to supply a complete itinerary including exact dates, but no one seems to mind if your actual travel dates vary slightly. Paperwork done through TOSERCO takes 2 days to clear. TOSERCO can also arrange for cars, guides and hotels.

The Hanoi office of Vietnam Tourism has consistently been obstructive when tourists have sought to do anything other than fork out lots of cash for guided tours. Many travellers have reported being told that without a tour they could not extend their 3-day visas, and that when visa extensions for individual travel were approved, they had to pay US$50.

Foreign Embassies The following are the addresses of foreign embassies in Hanoi:

Afghanistan
    Khu Van Phuc – D1 (tel 53249)
Albania
    49 Dien Bien Phu St (tel 54490)
Algeria
    13 Phan Chu Trinh St (tel 53865)
Australia
    66 Ly Thuong Kiet St (tel 52763, 52703). The chancery is open weekdays from 8 am to 12 noon and 1 to 4.30 pm.
Belgium
    51 Nguyen Du St (tel 52176) or Khu Van Phuc – B3, suites 201 and 202 (tel 52263)
Bulgaria
    41-43 Tran Phu St (tel 52908, 57923)

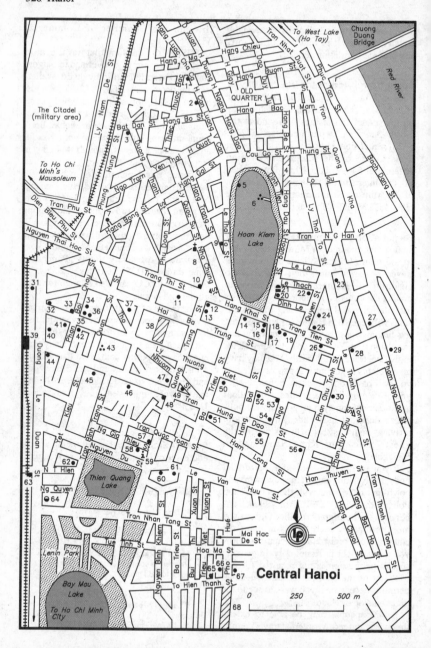

Central Hanoi

0   250   500 m

■ PLACES TO STAY

3 Phung Hung Hotel
22 Government Guest House
24 Thong Nhat Hotel
26 Dan Chu Hotel
32 Dong Loi Hotel
33 Railway Service Company Hotel
40 Railway Station Hotel
42 Ministry of Transportation Guest House
44 Khach San 30-4 (hotel)
53 Hoa Binh Hotel
56 Hoan Kiem Hotel
63 Nha Tro (dormitory)

▼ PLACES TO EAT

1 Cha Ca Restaurant
2 Restaurant 22
5 Thuy Ta Restaurant
7 Food Stalls
14 Bo Ho Restaurant
16 Sophia Hotel & Restaurant
18 Bodega Café
31 Huong Sen Restaurant
52 Small Restaurants
66 Restaurant 202
67 Hoa Binh Restaurant

● OTHER

4 Shoe Market
6 Ngoc Son Temple & Huc Bridge
8 Saint Joseph Cathedral
9 Vietnam Airlines Domestic Office
10 Aeroflot Office
11 National Library
12 Vietnam Airlines International Office

13 Air France Office
15 Traditional Medicines Pharmacy
17 State General Department Store
19 Foreign Language Bookstore
20 International Telephone Office
21 GPO
23 Foreign Trade Bank
25 Thong Nhat Bookstore
27 Revolutionary Museum
28 Municipal Theatre
29 History Museum
30 Algerian Embassy
34 West German Embassy
35 UNDP & UNICEF
36 Australian Embassy
37 'Hanoi Hilton' Prison
38 19th December Market
39 Hanoi Railway Station
41 Egyptian Embassy
43 Ambassadors' Pagoda
45 Workers' Cultural Palace
46 Immigration Police Office
47 Iraqi Embassy
48 Cambodian Embassy
49 Indian Embassy
50 Vietcochamber
51 French Embassy
54 Indonesian Embassy
55 Finnish Embassy
57 Lao Embassy Consular Section
58 FAO Office
59 Vietnam Tourism Head Office
60 Belgian Embassy
61 Japanese Embassy
62 Lao Embassy
64 Kim Lien Bus Station
65 TOSERCO
68 Bicycle & Motorbike Shops

Cambodia
71 Tran Hung Dao St (tel 53788, 53789); it is open from 8 to 11 am and 2 to 4.30 pm daily except Sunday. Visas applied for here can be picked up at the Cambodian Consulate in Saigon.
China
46 Hoang Dieu St (tel 53736, 53737)
Cuba
65 Ly Thuong Kiet St (tel 52281, 54775, 52426)
Czechoslovakia
13 Chu Van An St (tel 54131/32)
Egypt
26 Ly Thuong Kiet St (corner Ly Thuong Kiet St; tel 52944, 52909, 56944)

Federal Republic of Germany
25 Phan Boi Chau St, which is next to the UNDP compound (tel 53663, 55402); it is open from 7.30 am to 12 noon and 1 to 3.30 pm.
Finland
43 Tran Hung Dao St (tel 57096) or B3b Giang Vo – F1, 2 (tel 56754, 57096)
France
49 Ba Trieu St or 57 Tran Hung Dao St (tel 52719, 54367/68)
Hungary
47 Dien Bien Phu St (tel 52748, 52858, 52742)
India
58-60 Tran Hung Dao St (tel 53406, 55975)

Indonesia
  50 Ngo Quyen St or 38 Tran Hung Dao St (tel 53353, 57969)
Iraq
  66 Tran Hung Dao St (tel 55111, 54141)
Italy
  9 Le Phung Hieu St (tel 56246/56; telex 4416)
Japan
  49 Nguyen Du St or Khu Trung Tu – E3 (tel 57902, 57924)
Korea (North)
  25 Cao Ba Quat St (tel 53008)
Laos
  22 Tran Binh Trong St (tel 54576). The consular section is on the 2nd floor of an unmarked yellow building opposite the FAO office at 40 Quang Trung St (tel 52588); it is theoretically open Monday to Friday from 8 to 11 am and from 2 to 4.30 pm. Three photos and plane tickets are required for a 5-day transit visa, which costs US$10 and takes at least 24 hours to issue.
Libya
  Khu Van Phuc – A3 (tel 53379)
Malaysia
  Khu Van Phuc – A3 (tel 53371; telex 4412)
Mongolia
  39 Tran Phu St (tel 52151, 53009)
Myanmar
  Khu Van Phuc – A3 (tel 53369)
Netherlands
  53 Ly Thai To St
Nicaragua
  Khu Trung Tu – E1 (tel 62214/16)
Philippines
  4 Ho Xuan Huong or Khu Trung Tu – E1 (tel 57948, 57873)
Poland
  3 Chua Mot Cot St (tel 52027, 53728, 52207)
Romania
  5 Le Hong Phong St (tel 52014)
Sweden
  So 2, Duong 358, Khu Van Phuc, Quan Ba Dinh (tel 54824, 54825; telex 4420)
Thailand
  Khu Trung Tu – E1 (tel 56043, 56053, 62644)
United Kingdom
  16 Ly Thuong Kiet St (tel 52349, 52510, 52319)
USSR
  58 Tran Phu St (tel 54631, 54632)
Yugoslavia
  29B Tran Hung Dao St (tel 52343, 53677)

Aid Organisations There are a number of foreign aid organisations with offices in Hanoi. These include:

FAO (Food & Agriculture Organisation)
  3 Nguyen Gia Thieu St (tel 57208, 57239)

International Committee of the Red Cross (ICRC)
  Thong Nhat Hotel (tel 54454)
OMS
  Khu Van Phuc – A1 (tel 57901, 52148)
PAM
  27-29 Phan Boi Chau St (tel 57495, 57318, 54254)
UNDP (United Nations Development Programme)
  27-29 Phan Boi Chau St, which is at the corner of Ly Thuong Kiet St (tel 57495, 54254, 57318)
UNFPA (United Nations Fund for Population Control)
  Khu Giang Vo – Khoi 3 (tel 54763)
UNHCR (United Nations High Commission for Refugees)
  60 Nguyen Thai Hoc St (tel 57871, 56785)
UNICEF (United Nations Children's Fund)
  72 Ly Thuong Kiet St, which is next to the Australian embassy (tel 53440, 54222, 52109)
World Food Programme
  27-29 Phan Boi Chau St (in the UNDP compound)

Airline Offices The Vietnam Airlines Domestic Booking Office is next to Hoan Kiem Lake at 16 Le Thai To St (corner Hang Trong St); it is open from 7.30 to 11 am and 1 to 3 pm.

The Vietnam Airlines International Booking Office handles reservations (tel 55284) and ticketing (tel 53842) for all airlines serving Hanoi, including Aeroflot, Air France (in the near future), Czechoslovak Airlines (CSA), Interflug, Lao Aviation, Kampuchean Airlines and THAI. The International Booking Office is the only place in the city where you can actually purchase international airline tickets, though reservations can be made at the Air France and Aeroflot offices. Upstairs is a computer link-up with the SITA international reservations system. The International Booking Office is on the corner of Trang Thi St and Quang Trung St; it is open from 8 to 11.30 am and 1 to 3.30 pm except Saturday afternoons and Sundays.

The Air France office (tel 53484) is next door to the Vietnam Airlines International Booking Office at 1 Quang Trung St; it is open from 8 to 11.30 am and 2 to 4.30 pm daily except Saturday afternoons and Sundays. Reservations for any Air France flight in the world can be made here.

The Aeroflot office (tel 56184) is diagonally opposite the International Booking Office; it is open from 8 to 11.30 am and 3.30 to 6 pm Monday to Saturday, though on Saturday it's not fully staffed. Cheap tickets to Europe may be available here for US dollars cash.

Bookshops The Thong Nhat Book Store is near the Thong Nhat Hotel on the corner of Ngo Quyen and Trang Tien streets. It has a limited selection of books in Western languages published in Vietnam as well as postage stamps, posters, greeting cards and Soviet-produced art books and propaganda treatises. The Thong Nhat Book Store is open daily from 8 am to 12 noon and 1 to 8.30 pm except on Mondays and Thursdays, when the store closes at 4.30 pm.

The Foreign Language Bookshop (tel 57043) at 61 Trang Tien St is open daily from 8 to 11.30 am and 2 to 4.30 pm; it has Soviet art books and a lot of material in Russian. Similar published items are available at the State Bookshop (tel 54282), which is at 40 Trang Tien St. It is open Monday to Saturday from 8 to 11.30 am and 2 to 8 pm except on Mondays and Thursdays, when it closes at 5 pm. The State Enterprise for the Import & Export of Books & Periodicals (tel 54067), better known by its acronym Xunhasaba, has a shop at 32 Hai Ba Trung St. Xunhasaba publishes the English and French-language *Vietnamese Studies* series.

The office of the Foreign Languages Publishing House (tel 53841) is at 46 Tran Hung Dao St. The offices of the State Company for the Distribution of Foreign Language Books (tel 55376) are at 66 Trang Tien St.

Libraries The National Library (tel 52643) is at 31 Trang Tien St; the Technical & Social Sciences Library (tel 52345) is at 26 Ly Thuong Kiet St; the Army Library (tel 58101) is on Ly Nam St.

Prostitutes It is said that there are 1000 government-registered prostitutes in Hanoi.

Emergency Both the French and Swedish embassies have physicians attached to their staffs.

The International Hospital (*Benh Vien Quoc Te*; tel 62042), where foreigners are usually referred, is on the western side of Kiem Lien St a bit south of the Polytechnic University (*Dai Hoc Bach Khoa*). To get there, take bus Nos 4, 7 or 15 from the city centre. In winter, the hospital's out-patient clinic is open from 8 am to 12.30 pm and 1 to 4.30 pm; in summer, it is open from 7.30 am to 12 noon and 1 to 4.30 pm. The staff speak English and French and are very helpful. There is an on-site pharmacy. Westerners must pay in US dollars.

Other hospitals in Hanoi include the Bach Mai Hospital (tel 53731) on Nam Bo St; the K Hospital at 43 Quan Su St; the E Hospital in Co Nhue; the Institute of Ophthalmology at 38 Tran Nhan Tong St; the Traditional Medicine Hospital (tel 52850) on Nguyen Binh Khiem St; the Vietnam-Germany Friendship Hospital (*Benh Vien Viet-Duc*; tel 53531) on Trang Thi St; and the Vietnam-Soviet Union Friendship Hospital at 92 Tran Hung Dao St and 37 Hai Ba Trung St.

If you need a dentist, ask at the Thang Loi Hotel or Thang Long Hotel.

Lakes, Temples & Pagodas
One Pillar Pagoda Hanoi's famous One Pillar Pagoda (Chua Mot Cot) was built by the Emperor Ly Thai Tong, who ruled from 1028 to 1054. According to the annals, the heirless emperor dreamed that he had met the Quan The Am Bo Tat (Goddess of Mercy), who, while seated on a lotus flower, handed him a male child. Ly Thai Tong then married a young peasant girl he met by chance and had a son and heir by her. To express his gratitude for this event, he constructed the One Pillar Pagoda in 1049.

The One Pillar Pagoda, built of wood on a stone pillar 1.25 metres in diameter, is designed to resemble a lotus blossom, symbol of purity, rising out of a sea of sorrow. One of the last acts of the French before quitting Hanoi in 1954 was to destroy the One Pillar Pagoda; the structure was rebuilt by the new government.

One Pillar Pagoda

The entrance to Dien Huu Pagoda is a few metres from the staircase of the One Pillar Pagoda. This small pagoda, which surrounds a garden courtyard, is one of the most delightful in Hanoi. The old wood and ceramic statues on the altar are very different to those common in the south. An elderly monk can often be seen performing acupuncture on the front porch of the pagoda.

Tours of Ho Chi Minh's Mausoleum end up at the One Pillar Pagoda.

Temple of Literature The Temple of Literature (Van Mieu) was founded in 1070 – 4 years after the Norman Invasion of England – by Emperor Ly Thanh Tong, who dedicated it to Confucius (in Vietnamese, Khong Tu) in order to honour scholars and men of literary accomplishment. The temple constitutes a rare example of well-preserved traditional Vietnamese architecture.

Vietnam's first university was established here in 1076 to educate the sons of mandarins. In 1484, Emperor Le Thanh Tong ordered that steles be erected in the temple premises recording the names, places of birth and achievements of men who received doctorates (*Thai Hoc Sinh*) in each triennial examination, beginning in 1442. Though 116 examinations were held between 1442 and 1778, when the practice was discontinued, only 82 stelae are extant. In 1802, Emperor Gia Long transferred the National University to his new capital, Hué. Major repairs were last carried out here in 1920 and 1956.

The Temple of Literature consists of five courtyards divided by walls. The central pathways and gates between courtyards were reserved for the king. The walkways on one side were for the use of administrative mandarins; those on the other side were for military mandarins.

The main entrance is preceded by a gate on which an inscription requests that visitors dismount their horses before entering. Khue Van Pavilion, which is at the far side of the second courtyard, was constructed in 1802 and is considered a fine example of Vietnamese architecture. The 82 stelae, considered the most precious artefacts in the temple, are arrayed to either side of the third enclosure; each stele sits on a stone tortoise.

The Temple of Literature is 2 km west of Hoan Kiem Lake. The complex, which is 350 by 70 metres, is bounded by Nguyen

Thai Hoc St, Hang Bot St, Quoc Tu Giam St and Van Mieu St. It is open from 8.30 to 11.30 am and 1.30 to 4.30 pm Tuesday to Sunday; the entrance fee is 200d. There is a small gift shop inside the temple.

Hoan Kiem Lake Hoan Kiem Lake is an enchanting body of water right in the heart of Hanoi. Legend has it that in the mid-15th century, Heaven gave Emperor Le Thai To (Le Loi) a magical sword which he used to drive the Chinese out of Vietnam. One day after the war, while out boating, he came upon a giant golden tortoise swimming on the surface of the water; the creature grabbed the sword and disappeared into the depths of the lake. Since that time, the lake has been known as Ho Hoan Kiem (Lake of the Restored Sword) because the tortoise restored the sword to its divine owners.

The tiny Tortoise Pagoda, topped with a red star, is on an islet in the middle of the lake; it is often used as an emblem of Hanoi. Every morning around 6 am, local residents can be seen around Hoan Kiem Lake doing their traditional morning exercises, jogging and playing badminton.

Ngoc Son Temple Ngoc Son (Jade Mountain) Temple, founded in the 18th century, is on an island in the northern part of Hoan Kiem Lake. Surrounded by water and shaded by trees, it is a delightfully quiet place to rest. The temple is dedicated to the scholar Van Xuong, General Tran Hung Dao (who defeated the Mongols in the 13th century) and La To, patron saint of physicians.

Ngoc Son Temple is reached via wooden The Huc (Rising Sun) Bridge, painted red, which was constructed in 1885. To the left of the gate stands an obelisk whose top is shaped like a paintbrush. The temple is open daily from 8 am to 5 pm; the entrance fee is 200d.

West Lake (Ho Tay) Two legends explain the origins of West Lake (Ho Tay), which covers an area of 5 sq km. According to one, West Lake was created when the Dragon King drowned an evil nine-tailed fox in his lair, which was in a forest on this site. Another legend relates that in the 11th century, a Vietnamese bonze, Khong Lo, rendered a great service to the emperor of China, who rewarded him with a vast quantity of bronze from which he cast a huge bell. The sound of the bell could be heard all the way to China, where the Golden Buffalo Calf, mistaking the ringing for its mother's call, ran southward, trampling on the site of Ho Tay and turning it into a lake.

West Lake, also known as the Lake of Mist and the Big Lake, was once ringed with magnificent palaces and pavilions. These were destroyed in the course of various feudal wars. The circumference of West Lake is about 13 km.

Tran Quoc Pagoda is on the shore of West Lake just off Tranh Nien St, which divides West Lake from Truc Bach Lake. A stele here dating from 1639 tells the history of this site. The pagoda was rebuilt in the 15th century and in 1842. There are a number of monks' funerary monuments in the garden.

Truc Bach Lake Truc Bach (White Silk) Lake is separated from West Lake by Thanh Nien St, which is lined with flame trees. In the 18th century, the Trinh Lords built a palace on this site; it was later turned into a reformatory for deviant royal concubines, who were condemned to weave a very fine white silk.

Quan Thanh Pagoda (also called Tran Vo Temple) is on the shore of Truc Bach Lake near the intersection of Thanh Nein St and Quan Thanh St. The pagoda, shaded by huge trees, was established during the Ly Dynasty (ruled 1010 to 1225) and was dedicated to Tran Vo (God of the North), whose symbols of power are the tortoise and the snake. A bronze statue and bell here date from 1677.

Ambassadors' Pagoda The Ambassadors' Pagoda (Quan Su; tel 52427) is the official centre of Buddhism in Hanoi, attracting quite a crowd – mostly old women – on holidays. During the 17th century, there was a guest house here for the ambassadors of Buddhist countries. Today, there are about a dozen monks and nuns at the Ambassadors' Pagoda. Next to the pagoda is a store selling Buddhist ritual objects.

The Ambassadors' Pagoda is at 73 Quan Su St (between Ly Thuong Kiet and Tran Hung Dao streets); it is open to the public every day from 7.30 to 11.30 am and 1.30 to 5.30 pm.

Hai Ba Trung Temple The Hai Ba Trung Temple, founded in 1142, is 2 km south of Hoan Kiem Lake on Tho Lao St. A statue here shows the two Trung sisters (1st century AD) kneeling with their arms raised, as if to address a crowd. Some people say the statue shows the sisters, who had been proclaimed queens of the Vietnamese, about to dive into a river in order to drown themselves, which they are said to have done rather than surrender following their defeat at the hands of the Chinese.

Museums

History Museum The History Museum (Bao Tang Lich Su), once the museum of the École Française d'Extrême Orient, is one block east of the Municipal Theatre at 1 Pham Ngu Lao St. The building, constructed of reinforced concrete, was completed in 1930.

Exhibits include artefacts from Vietnam's prehistory (Palaeolithic and Neolithic periods); proto-Vietnamese civilisations (1st and 2nd millennia BC); the Dong Son Civilisation (7th century BC to 3rd century AD); the Oc-Eo (Funan) culture of the Mekong Delta (1st to 6th centuries AD); the Indianised kingdom of Champa (1st to 15th centuries); the Khmer kingdoms; various Vietnamese dynasties and their resistance to Chinese attempts at domination; the struggle against the French; and the history of the Communist Party.

Army Museum The Army Museum (Bao Tang Quan Doi) is on Dien Bien Phu St; it is open daily except Mondays from 7.30 to 11.30 am only. Outside, Soviet and Chinese weaponry supplied to the North are on display alongside French and US-made weapons captured in the Franco-Vietminh War and the Vietnam War. The centrepiece is a Soviet-built MiG-21 jet fighter triumphant amidst the wreckage of French aircraft downed at Dien Bien Phu and a US F-111. The displays include scale models of various epic battles from Vietnam's long military history, including Dien Bien Phu and the capture of Saigon.

Next to the Army Museum is the hexagonal Flag Tower, which has become one of the symbols of the city. It is part of a Vauban-style citadel constructed by Emperor Gia Long (ruled 1802-19).

Ho Chi Minh Museum As of this writing, a huge cement structure that is to house the Ho Chi Minh Museum is under construction a few hundred metres from Ho Chi Minh's Mausoleum and the One Pillar Pagoda.

Fine Arts Museum The building housing the Fine Arts Museum (Bao Tang My Thuat; tel 52830) served as the Ministry of Information under the French. It continues its propaganda function today: the museum's exhibits consist almost exclusively of politically correct folk art, sculpture, engravings and lacquerware by contemporary artists.

Most of the works on display are revolutionary in style and content, depicting heroic figures waving red flags, children with rifles, a wounded soldier joining the Communist Party, innumerable tanks and weaponry, and grotesque Americans. One lacquerware work depicts artillery pieces being hauled up a mountainside. Upstairs are a few examples of traditional crafts along with an incredibly intricate embroidery of Ho Chi Minh reading.

The Fine Arts Museum is at 66 Nguyen Thai Hoc St (corner Cao Ba Quai St), which is across the street from the back wall of the Temple of Literature; it is open from 8 am to 12 noon and 1.30 to 4 pm Tuesday to Sunday.

Revolutionary Museum The Revolutionary Museum (Bao Tang Cach Manh) at 25 Tong Dan St presents the history of the Vietnamese Revolution.

Independence Museum The house at 48 Hang Ngang St, in which Ho Chi Minh drafted Vietnam's Declaration of Independence in 1945, has been turned into a museum.

Ho Chi Minh's Mausoleum

In the tradition of Lenin and Stalin before him and Mao after him, the final resting place of Ho Chi Minh is a glass sarcophagus set deep inside a monumental edifice that has become a site of pilgrimage. Ho Chi Minh's Mausoleum – built despite the fact that in his will, Ho requested to be cremated – was constructed between 1973 and 1975 of native materials gathered from all over Vietnam; the roof and peristyle are said to evoke either a traditional communal house or a lotus flower. While reviewing parades and ceremonies taking place on the grassy expanses of Ba Dinh Square, high-ranking party and government leaders stand in front of the mausoleum.

Ho Chi Minh's Mausoleum is open to the public on Tuesday, Wednesday, Thursday and Saturday mornings from 8 to 11 am; on Sundays and holidays, it is open from 7.30 to 11.30 am. The mausoleum is closed for 2 months a year (usually from September to early November) while Ho Chi Minh's embalmed corpse is in the USSR for maintenance.

All visitors must register and check their bags and cameras at a reception hall on Chua Mot Cot St; if possible, bring your passport for identification. Soundtracks for a 20-minute video about Ho Chi Minh are available in Vietnamese, English, French, Khmer, Lao, Russian and Spanish.

The following rules are strictly applied to all visitors to the mausoleum: 1) People wearing shorts, tank-tops, etc will not be admitted. 2) Nothing (including day packs and cameras) may be taken into the mausoleum. 3) A respectful demeanour must be maintained at all times. 4) For obvious reasons of decorum, photography is absolutely prohibited inside the mausoleum. 5) It is forbidden to put your hands in your pockets. 6) Hats must be taken off inside the mausoleum building.

To ensure that these directives are carried out, honour guards will accompany you as you march single-file from near reception to the mausoleum entrance. Inside the building, more guards – wearing Eastern European-style chocolate-brown uniforms complete with Sam Browne belts – are stationed at intervals of five paces, giving an eerily authoritarian aspect to the macabre spectacle of the embalmed, helpless body with its wispy white hair.

After exiting from the mausoleum, the tour will pass by the Presidential Palace, constructed in 1906 as the Palace of the Governor General of Indochina; it is now used for official receptions. Ho Chi Minh's house, built of the finest materials in 1958, is next to a carp-filled pond. Nearby is what was once Hanoi's botanical garden, now a park. The tour ends up at the One Pillar Pagoda (see 'Lakes, Temples & Pagodas').

History Ho Chi Minh is the best known of some 50 aliases assumed over the course of his long career by Nguyen Tat Thanh (1890-1969), founder of the Vietnamese Communist Party and President of the Democratic Republic of Vietnam from 1946 until his death. The son of a fiercely nationalistic scholar-official of humble means, he was educated in the Quoc Hoc Secondary School in Hué before working briefly as a teacher in Phan Thiet. In 1911, he signed on as a cook's apprentice on a French ship, sailing to North America, Africa and Europe. He remained in Europe, where, while working as a gardener, snow sweeper, waiter, photo retoucher and stoker, his political consciousness began to develop.

After living briefly in London, Ho Chi Minh moved to Paris, where he adopted the name Nguyen Ai Quoc (Nguyen the Patriot). During this period, he mastered a number of languages (including English, French, German and Mandarin) and began to write about and debate the issue of Indochinese independence. During the 1919 Versailles

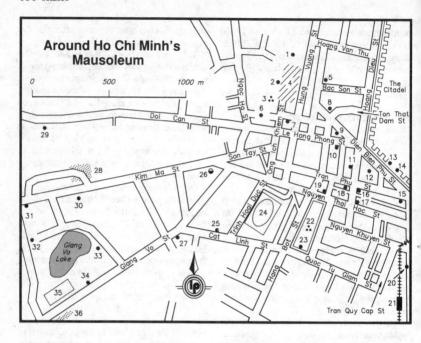

Around Ho Chi Minh's Mausoleum

Peace Conference, he tried to present an independence plan for Vietnam to American President Woodrow Wilson. Ho was a founding member of the French Communist Party, which was established in 1920. In 1923, he was summoned to Moscow for training by the Communist International, which later sent him to Canton (Guangzhou), where he founded the Revolutionary Youth League of Vietnam, a precursor to the Indochinese Communist Party and the Vietnamese Communist Party.

After spending time in a Hong Kong jail in the early '30s and more time in the USSR and China, Ho Chi Minh returned to Vietnam in 1941 for the first time in 30 years. That same year – at the age of 51 – he helped found the Viet Minh Front, the goal of which was the independence of Vietnam from French colonial rule and Japanese occupation. In 1942, he was arrested and held for a year by the Nationalist Chinese. As Japan prepared to surrender in August 1945, Ho

Chi Minh led the August Revolution, which took control of much of the country; and it was he who composed Vietnam's Declaration of Independence (modelled in part on the American Declaration of Independence) and read it publicly very near the site of his mausoleum. The return of the French shortly thereafter forced Ho Chi Minh and the Viet Minh to flee Hanoi and take up armed resistance.

Old Quarter

The Old Quarter is demarcated, roughly speaking, by Hoan Kiem Lake, the Citadel, Dong Xuan Market and the ramparts of the Red River. As they have since the 15th century, the narrow streets of the Old Quarter bear names that reflect the business once conducted there: Silk St, Rice St, Paper St, Broiled Fish St, Vermicelli St, Jewellers' St, Paper Votive Objects St and so forth. The area now houses a variety of small shops.

Dong Xuan Market

Dong Xuan Market is 1.3 km north of the northern end of Hoan Kiem Lake. State stores near the entrance offer a limited selection of outmoded goods; out the back are shops selling potted plants and live animals, including monkeys, mynah birds and parrots. Nearby are food stalls and vendors selling fresh vegetables. Near the main entrance there is a pharmacy specialising in traditional medicines, including alcohol-based snake syrups.

St Joseph Cathedral

Stepping inside neo-Gothic St Joseph Cathedral (inaugurated in 1886) is like being instantly transported to medieval Europe. The cathedral is noteworthy for its square towers, elaborate altar and stained-glass windows. The first Catholic mission in Hanoi was founded in 1679.

The main gate to St Joseph Cathedral is open daily from 5 to 7 am and 5 to 7 pm, the hours when masses are held. At other times of the day guests are welcome but must enter the cathedral via the compound of the Diocese of Hanoi, the entrance to which is a block away at 40 Nha Chung St. After walking through the gate, go straight and then turn right. When you reach the side door to the cathedral, ring the small bell high up to the right of the door to call the priest to let you in. Across Nha Chung St from the diocese compound is a nunnery where about 30 older nuns live.

Hanoi Hilton

The 'Hanoi Hilton' is the nickname given to a prison in which US prisoners-of-war – mostly aircraft crewmen – were held during the Vietnam War. The high walls of the forbidding triangular building, officially known as Hoa Lo Prison, are pierced by precious few barred windows. The structure, which was constructed by the French in the early 20th century, is bounded by Hai Ba Trung, Tho Nhuom and Hoa Lo streets. Photography is forbidden.

Long Bien Bridge

The Long Bien Bridge, crosses the Red River 600 metres north of the new Chuong Duong Bridge, is a fantastic hodge-podge of repairs dating from the Vietnam War. American aircraft repeatedly bombed the strategic Long Bien Bridge (which at one time was defended by 300 anti-aircraft guns and 84 SAM missiles), yet after each attack the Vietnamese somehow managed to improvise replacement spans and return it to road and rail service. It is said that when US POWs were put to work repairing the bridge, the US military, fearing for their safety, ended the attacks.

The 1682-metre Long Bien Bridge was opened in 1902. It was once known as the Paul Doumer Bridge after the turn-of-the-century French Governor General of Indochina, Paul Doumer (1857-1932), who was assassinated a year after becoming President of France.

Government Guest House
Formerly the Palace of the Governor of Tonkin, the ornate Government Guest House (tel 55853) was stormed during the August Revolution of 1945; the wrought-iron fence surrounding the ornate building still shows marks from bullets fired during the battle. The guest house, which is now used to house highly favoured official guests, is at 2 Le Thach St, across Ngo Quyen St from the Thong Nhat Hotel.

Thu Le Park & Zoo
Thu Le Park & Zoo (Bach Thu Thu Le), with its expanses of shaded grass and ponds, is 6 km west of Hoan Kiem Lake. The entrance is on Buoi St a few hundred metres north of Ngoc Khanh St. The zoo is open daily from 6 am to 6 pm; the entrance fee is 200d.

Co Loa Citadel
Co Loa Citadel (Co Loa Thanh), the first fortified citadel recorded in Vietnamese history, dates from the 3rd century BC. Only vestiges of the massive ancient ramparts, which enclosed an area of about 5 sq km, are extant. Co Loa again became the national capital under Ngo Quyen (reigned 939 to 944). In the centre of the citadel are temples dedicated to King An Duong Vuong (ruled 257 to 208 BC), who founded the legendary Thuc Dynasty, and his daughter My Nuong (Mi Chau). When My Nuong showed her father's magic crossbow trigger – which

made the Vietnamese king invincible in battle – to her husband (who was the son of a Chinese general) he stole it and gave it to his father. With its help, the Chinese were able to defeat An Duong Vuong and his forces, depriving Vietnam of its independence.

Co Loa Citadel is 16 km from Hanoi in Dong Anh district.

Festivals

Tet, the Vietnamese New Year, falls in late January or early February. In Hanoi, Tet is celebrated in a variety of ways. A flower market is held during the week before the beginning of Tet on Hang Luoc St, which is near Dong Xuan Market. A 2 week flower exhibition and competition takes place in Lenin Park beginning on the 1st day of the new year. On the 4th day of the new year, there is a firecracker festival in Dong Ky, a village 3 km north of Hanoi. A competition for the loudest firecracker is held, attracting gargantuan firecrackers up to 16 metres in length! On the 13th day of the 1st lunar month in the village of Lim in Ha Bac Province, boys and girl engage in *hat doi*, a traditional game in which groups conduct a sung dialogue with each other; other activities include chess, cock-fighting and firecrackers. Wrestling matches are held on the 15th day of the 1st lunar month at Dong Da Mound, site of the uprising against Chinese invaders led by Emperor Quang Trung (Nguyen Hue) in 1788.

Vietnam's National Day, 2 September, is celebrated at Ba Dinh Square (the expanse of grass in front of Ho Chi Minh's Mausoleum) with a rally and fireworks; boat races are held on Hoan Kiem Lake.

Places to Stay

If Vietnam Tourism has anything to do with your visit to Hanoi, they may try to put you up in a hotel far from the city centre, such as the Thang Loi or the Thang Long. If you prefer to be downtown, insist on it. Because Hanoi has relatively few decent hotels, there is likely to be a severe shortage of hotel rooms when tourism and international business pick up.

Places to Stay – bottom end
Downtown The *Sophia Hotel* (tel 55069), which is upstairs from Sophia Restaurant, is at 6 Hang Bai St (between Hai Ba Trung St and Hoan Kiem Lake); singles/doubles cost 10,000/20,000d. The location and prices have made this place a favourite with backpackers.

Railway Station Area The old but eminently serviceable *Dong Loi Hotel* (Khach San Dong Loi; tel 55721) is on the corner of Le Duan and Ly Thuong Kiet streets; rooms without/with bath cost US$6/12. The *Railway Station Hotel* (Khach San Ga; tel 57171; 10 rooms) is right across from the railway station at 113 Le Duan St; a single costs 2500d, a room with 19 beds goes for 14,400d. I am told that these prices are likely to go up. *Khach San 30-4* (tel 52611; 6 rooms) is down the block at 115 Tran Hung Dao St; a single costs 10,000d.

The *Railway Service Company Hotel* (Cong Ty Phuc Vu Duong Sat Khach San Cong Nhan Duong Sat So 1; tel 52842; 80 beds) is across the street from the UNDP complex at 80 Ly Thuong Kiet St. Reception is upstairs. Singles/triples cost 8000/7000d (why a triple is cheaper than a single I'm not sure). A single dorm bed costs 2500d; a room for six costs 15,000d. Diagonally across from here at 83B Ly Thuong Kiet St is the *Ministry of Transportation Guest House* (Nha Khach Bo Giao Thong Van Tai), but good luck getting past the front door.

The *Phung Hung Hotel* (tel 52614) is a bit over 1 km north of the railway station on Phung Hung St (at the corner of Duong Thanh St); foreigners are charged US$5 each. It is very near the Old Quarter.

Kim Lien Bus Station Area *Nha Tro* (tel 52405; 42 beds), whose name simply means 'dormitory,' is across the street from the Kim Lien Bus Station. It is one of the many buildings bearing the address 100 Le Duan St (corner Kham Thien St). This place is open

24 hours a day, so if your bus comes in very late at night (when the city's other hotels are closed), it's a good place to crash until morning. A dorm bed with a mat (rather than a mattress) costs 1500d. The rooms here, which are equipped with fans, have four, six or 10 beds; if you want a single, you'll have to hire all the beds in a room.

Swedish Embassy Area The *Giang Vo Hotel* (tel 53407, 56598; about 300 rooms) consists of several five-storey apartment blocks. One entrance to the hotel, which is 3.5 km west of the city centre, faces Giang Vo Lake; there is another entrance on Ngoc Khanh St. Rooms cost 8000 to 15,000d. The Giang Vo Hotel is run by TOSERCO.

The *Ministry of Foodstuffs Guest House* (Nha Khach Cong Nghiep Truc Pham; tel 55302) is at 40 Cat Linh St; at present it accepts only Ministry of Foodstuffs personnel.

Places to Stay – top end

City Centre The *Thong Nhat Hotel* (tel 58221, 52785), formerly Hotel Metropole, is at 15 Ngo Quyen St; singles/doubles cost from US$24/29 to US$44/49. The postal services counter is open from 10 am to 6 pm. The restaurant is – as was common decades ago – ventilated by some three dozen ceiling fans; if they cranked them all up at once the food would get blown away. There are plans to renovate the Thong Nhat Hotel, which is known for its cranky plumbing and the occasional rat.

The *Dan Chu Hotel* (tel 53323) is at 29 Trang Tien St. A single costs US$36 plus 10% for service; the restaurant is quite good. Once called the Hanoi Hotel, it was built in the late 19th century. The *Hoan Kiem Hotel* (tel 54204) is at 25 Tran Hung Dao St (corner Phan Chu Trinh St); a single costs US$36. The *Hoa Binh Hotel* (tel 53315) at 27 Ly Thuong Kiet St charges US$30.50 for a single.

Swedish Embassy Area One of the least expensive of the major hotels in Hanoi is the *Thang Long Hotel* (tel 57796, 52270), a 10-storey building which overlooks Giang Vo, a small lake 3.5 km west of the city centre. There is a reason for the reasonable prices: not only is it located well out of the city centre, but almost every cliché about shoddy and grim Eastern Bloc design and construction holds true about this place. The silver lining of this grey cloud is that rooms on the upper floors are offered at reduced rates because the lifts are so often out of order. In other words, if you don't mind climbing up eight or 10 flights of stairs, you can get a pretty good deal. A single/double on the first few floors costs US$20/US$24 and a suite goes for US$34; on the upper floors, a double may go for as little as US$14.

The hotel has two restaurants, dourly named Restaurant A and Restaurant B. In case you have forgotten that you are in Hanoi (rather than somewhere where customer service means something), a stern sign reminds you that meals are served only at certain hours. Other facilities here include a telex office (open from 7 am to 9 pm), gift shops, a dentist, boat rentals (on the nearby lake) and bicycle rental (1000d an hour).

West Lake Area The most expensive hotel in Hanoi is the *Thang Loi Hotel* (tel 58211/2/3/4/5 and 52004; telex 4276 KSTL VT; 140 rooms), also known as 'the Cuban Hotel' because it was built in the mid-1970s with Cuban assistance. The floor plan of each level is said to have been copied from a one-storey Cuban building, which explains the doors that lead nowhere. Around the main building are bungalows. Foreign airline crews overnighting in Hanoi usually come here to sleep and drink.

The hotel is built on pylons over West Lake and is surrounded by attractive landscaping. Singles/doubles with air-con cost US$42/48; nicer rooms cost US$56/64 (plus 10% for service). Among the amenities available are postal and telex services, a barber, a hairdresser, massage, tennis courts, gift shops and a swimming pool. The Thang Long Hotel is on Yen Phu St 3.5 km from the city centre.

The *Communist Party Guest House* (Nha

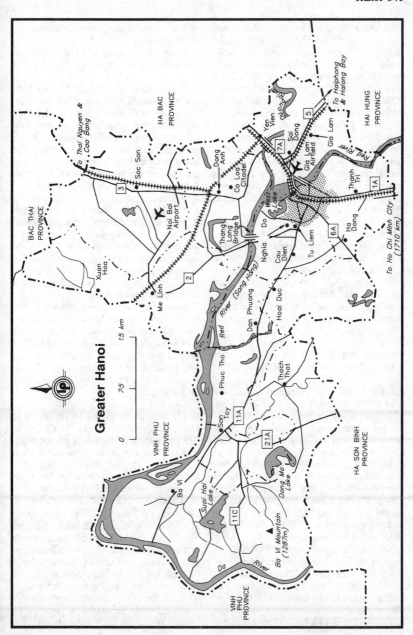

Greater Hanoi

Khach Cua Dang, also known as Nha Khach Ho Tay; tel 58241, 54165) has recently turned itself into a tourist hotel. The well-designed, spacious villas, set amidst a beautifully landscaped area on West Lake were once the exclusive preserve of top party officials; but now, visitors bearing US dollars are welcome to avail themselves of the great facilities, excellent food and friendly staff. The greatest disadvantage of the Communist Party Guest House is its distance from the city centre and the lack of public transport from Nghi Tam St to the complex. The 5.5 km trip from downtown Hanoi to the hotel takes about half an hour by bicycle.

Other Areas The *La Thanh Hotel* (tel 54321; about 100 rooms) is inconveniently located 2 km west of Ho Chi Minh's Mausoleum at 218 Doi Can St; a double with air-con, hot water, private bath and a refrigerator costs US$16 to US$18. Only 15 of the rooms are available to tourists (the rest of the building is used for offices). The French-era structure was renovated in 1959.

Places to Eat

Hanoi is famous for its *pho* (breakfast soup).

Central Hanoi The restaurants in the *Dan Chu Hotel* and the *Thong Nhat Hotel* are quite decent and the prices are surprisingly moderate (meals start at US$2). The *Hoan Kiem Hotel* and the *Hoa Binh Hotel* also have in-house restaurants.

Sophia Restaurant (tel 55069), which has a small hotel above it, is at 6 Hang Bai St (between Hai Ba Trung St and Hoan Kiem Lake). Downstairs is a cafe; the restaurant proper is on the 2nd floor. The *Bodega Café* is down the street at 57 Trang Tien St; this place serves pastries and drinks.

Bo Ho Restaurant (tel 56418, 52075) faces Hoan Kiem Lake on the corner of Hang Khay St and Ba Trieu St. The main hall, with its high ceilings and 16 ancient fans, has hardly changed in 40 years. Bo Ho is one of the few places in Vietnam where you can get cheese and milk (the latter is served either

with or without sugar). There is dancing here every Thursday night.

There are a number of small eateries on Hang Bai St at the corner of Ly Thuong Kiet St.

Restaurant 202 (Nha Hang 202) is 1.5 km south of Hoan Kiem Lake at 202 Pho Hué. One of the best restaurants in the city, it is a favourite of the diplomatic community. Restaurant 202 has a vaguely French atmosphere and a good selection of foreign beers. The menu includes both Vietnamese and European dishes; serving sizes are small. Across the street at 163 Pho Hué is the *Hoa Binh Restaurant*.

Near the railway station, the *Huong Sen Restaurant* (tel 52805), run by Hanoi Tourism, is at 52 Le Duan St. There are a number of other places to eat in the immediate vicinity of the railway station, including a restaurant next to the lobby of the *Dong Loi Hotel*. There are quite a few small restaurants around Kim Lien Bus Station.

Fresh vegetables can be purchased at *19th of December Market* (Cho 19-12), whose two entrances are opposite 61 Ly Thuong Kiet St and next to 41 Hai Ba Trung St. Dog meat is available from curb-side vendors a few hundred metres north of the History Museum on Le Phung Hieu St near Trang Quang Kha St.

Old Quarter *Restaurant 22* (also known as Quang An Restaurant) is at 22 Hang Can St. The entrance is through a narrow passageway and up the stairs. It has menus in Vietnamese, English, French, Italian and Swedish. Another favourite of the expat community is *Cha Ca Restaurant*, which is at 14 Cha Ca St; it specialises in fish (in fact, *cha ca* means 'fried fish'). Cha Ca St, which is a two-block-long continuation of Luong Van Can St, begins about 500 metres north of Hoan Kiem Lake. *Nha Thinh Restaurant* is at 28 Luong Van Can St. Not far away at 50 Hang Vai St is the *Piano Restaurant*. One of its specialties is boiled crab. As the name suggests, there is live music every evening.

Chau Thanh Restaurant, a favourite of visiting journalists, is 350 metres north of the

Hang Dau St shoe market at 60 Ngo Phat Loc St (near the intersection of Hang Be St and Hang Bac St). The best way to find the restaurant, which is down an unmarked alleyway, is to ask a cyclo driver or a native of the neighbourhood. The food is excellent. This is one of the few places in Hanoi open late at night (ie after 9 pm).

There are a number of food stalls in the alleyway between numbers 202 and 204 Hang Bong St. Nearby at 192 Hang Bong St is a small restaurant. *Bittek Restaurant*, also known as *Le Français*, is off Hang Gai St at 17 Ly Quoc Su St; *bittek* means 'beefsteak'.

In Dong Xuan Market there are food stalls as well as fresh produce vendors.

Thuy Ta Restaurant at 1 Le Thai To St is a two-storey place overlooking Hoan Kiem Lake. It is about 200 metres south of the intersection of Le Thai To and Hang Gai streets. The fare is limited to Vietnamese food, including what can best be described as Vietnamese chop suey.

Swedish Embassy Area *Restaurant 79* is at 79 Kim Ma St, which is a few hundred metres west of the Swedish Embassy. There are two restaurants on the ground floor of the Thang Long Hotel. The excellent *Phuong Nam Restaurant* is on Giang Vo St in Block I1, which is near the corner of Cat Linh St. *Dong Do Restaurant* is on Giang Vo St next to the exhibition hall (Trien Lam Giang Vo); the food is mediocre. There are several small places to eat across Giang Vo St from the exhibition hall.

West Lake *Nha Noi Ho Tay Restaurant* is on West Lake (Ho Tay) just off of Duong Thanh Nien St; it is very near Tran Quoc Pagoda. Farther north, *Thy Ho Restaurant* is on the ground floor of the Thang Loi Hotel.

Entertainment

Municipal Theatre The 900 seat Municipal Theatre (tel 54312), which faces eastward up Trang Tien St, was built in 1911 as an opera house. It was from a balcony of this building that a Viet Minh-run committee of citizens announced that it had taken over the city on 16 August 1945. These days, performances are held here in the evenings.

Workers' Cultural Palace The huge Workers' Cultural Palace complex (Nha Van Hoa Cong Nhan), built with Soviet aid and completed in 1985, houses libraries, classrooms, sports facilities, and a 1200-seat theatre. There are great views from the roof. It is on Tran Hung Dao St three blocks east of the railway station.

Dancing Dancing – both ballroom and disco – is all the rage with young Hanoi residents who can afford it. '*Soirées Dansantes*' are held at the Thong Nhat Hotel every Saturday and Sunday night from 8 to 11.30 pm. There is dancing every Thursday night at the Bo Ho Restaurant (tel 56418, 52075), which is next to Hoan Kiem Lake on the corner of Hang Khay St and Ba Trieu St. The Dan Chu Hotel also has dancing.

Water Puppets Invitations to performances of water puppetry, a fantastic art form unique to Vietnam, can sometimes be procured through Vietnam Tourism, TOSERCO, Vietcochamber or a foreign embassy. An opportunity to see water puppets is a treat not to be missed.

Circus The endearingly amateurish State Circus often performs in the evenings in a huge tent near the entrance to Lenin Park (Cong Vien Le Nin). Many of the performers (gymnasts, jugglers, animal trainers, etc) were trained in Eastern Europe.

Billabong Club The Australian embassy's famous Billabong Club meets every Friday night from 8 to 12 pm in a clubhouse next to the Australian Embassy's swimming pool, which is behind the chancery building (tel 52763, 52703) at 66 Ly Thuong Kiet St. The club offers a grand selection of Australian beers and the chance to meet much of the English-speaking community in Hanoi. Each guest must buy a US$10 book of tickets for drinks and snacks (Australian dollars are not accepted). All Australians are welcome;

other nationalities are admitted by invitation only.

Things to Buy

There are a number of photo stores on Hang Khay St, which fronts the southern shore of Hoan Kiem Lake. You might also try Anh Mau, a store at 18 Hang Gai St.

Greeting cards with traditional Vietnamese designs hand-painted on silk covers, are available around town for 400d or so. Souvenir tee-shirts with permanent colours can be purchased or special-ordered at 45 Hang Bong St. The shop at 1A Ly Quoc Su St sells poor-quality tee-shirts with water-soluble designs.

Attractive gold-on-scarlet banners, usually given as awards for service to the party or state, can be ordered to your specifications (with your name or date of visit, for instance) at shops at 13 Hang Bong St and 40 Hang Bong St. Souvenir patches, sewn by hand, can also be commissioned at 13 Hang Bong St. Hang Gai St and its continuation, Hang Bong St, are a good place to look for embroidered tablecloths and hangings; one shop you might try is Tan My at 109 Hang Gai St. There are a number of antique shops in the vicinity. Hanoi is a good place to have informal clothes custom tailored.

There are quite a number of stores in Hanoi offering new and antique Vietnamese handicrafts (lacquerware, mother-of-pearl inlay, ceramics, sandalwood statuettes, etc) as well as watercolours, oil paintings, prints and assorted antiques. Hanart (tel 53045) at 43 Trang Tien St offers old ceramics, wood and stone figurines, lacquerware, mother-of-pearl inlay, ivory objects, carpets, etc. The Galerie d'Art at 61 Thi Trang Tien St is open from 8 am to 12 noon and 2 to 7 pm daily; its specialties include watercolours, oils, puppets and prints. My Thuat Art Gallery is at 61 Trang Tien St. Another store offering typical products of traditional Vietnamese artisanship faces Hoan Kiem Lake at 25 Hang Khay St. Studio 31, which is two stores away at 31 Hang Khay St, has a selection of paintings. There are small crafts shops at 53 and 55 Ba Trieu St. There is a souvenir shop

for foreigners on the corner of Ly Thuong Kiet and Hang Bai streets; it is open Tuesday to Sunday from 8.30 am to 12 noon and 1.30 to 5.30 pm.

Tapes of Vietnamese music are available at Sun Ashaba, which is at 32 Hai Ba Trung St. There is a pharmacy (Hieu Thuoc Quan Hoan Kiem; tel 54212) specialising in traditional medicines – including something called Gecko Elixir – at 2 Hang Bai St (corner Hang Khay St).

For philatelic items, try the philatelic counter at the GPO (in the main postal services hall); it is run by the government philatelic corporation, Cotevina (Cong Ty Tem Viet Nam).

Hanoi's largest store is the State General Department Store (Bach Hoa Tong Hop), which is on Hang Bai St between Hai Ba Trung St and Hoan Kiem Lake. There's not much to buy here, but the store is worth a look to see what isn't for sale and what hasn't changed here since independence.

Watercolour paints and brushes are available at a store at 216 Hang Bong St (corner Phung Hung St). Musical instruments can be purchased from shops at 24 and 36 Hang Gai St, and 76 and 85 Hang Bong St.

Getting There & Away

Land distances from Hanoi:

Ba Be Lakes	240 km
Bac Giang	51 km
Bac Ninh	29 km
Bach Thong (Bac Can)	162 km
Cam Pha	190 km
Cao Bang	272 km
Da Bac (Cho Bo)	104 km
Danang	763 km
Dien Bien Phu	420 km
Ha Dong	11 km
Ha Giang	343 km
Hai Duong	58 km
Haiphong	103 km
Halong Bay (Hon Gai)	165 km
Hoa Binh City	74 km
Hué	658 km
Lai Chau	490 km
Lang Son	151 km
Nam Dinh	90 km
Ninh Binh	42 km
Phat Diem	121 km

Phnom Penh, Cambodia	1964 km
Saigon	1710 km
Son La	308 km
Tam Dao Hill Station	85 km
Thai Binh	109 km
Thai Nguyen	80 km
Thakhek, Laos	576 km
Thanh Hoa	153 km
Tuyen Quang	165 km
Viet Tri	291 km
Yen Bai	182 km

Air Aeroflot, Czechoslovak Airlines (CSA), Kampuchean Airlines, Interflug, Lao Aviation, Thai Airways International (THAI) and Air Vietnam link Hanoi with Bangkok (US$160 one-way), Dubai, East Berlin, Karachi, Moscow, Phnom Penh (US$175 one-way), Prague and Vientiane (US$80 one-way). Air France may begin serving Hanoi soon. At present, only THAI and Vietnam Airlines fly the Bangkok-Hanoi route. For details on reservations and ticketing in Hanoi, see Airline Offices in the Information section earlier.

It is essential to reconfirm all reservations for flights out of the country.

Hanoi's Noi Bai Airport – which, as you will see before landing or after taking off, is ringed with the craters of American bombs – is about 30 km from the city. Road traffic from Noi Bai Airport to Hanoi crosses the Red River on the Chuong Duong Bridge, which runs parallel to the old road-and-rail Long Bien Bridge.

As in Saigon, checked baggage arriving in Hanoi is often x-rayed to check for contraband. The x-ray machines at Hanoi's Noi Bai Airport are *not* film-safe. *Never* put exposed or unexposed film into your checked luggage when entering or exiting Vietnam by air.

Visitors arriving in Hanoi from Vientiane have reported having things disappear from checked baggage.

Customs and police officials at the airport have a reputation for arbitrariness and unpleasantness. Getting visibly angry is a social no-no and is likely to make them even more obstinate.

Train The Hanoi Railway Station (Ga Ha Noi; tel 52628) is opposite 115 Le Duan St at the western end of Tran Hung Dao St; the ticket office is open from 7.30 to 11.30 am and 1.30 to 3.30 pm only. Windows 2, 4 and 6 handle trains heading southward; tickets for trains to the east and north are available at windows 1 and 3. Tickets should be purchased at least 1 day before departure.

The following trains serve destinations south of Hanoi:

Train	Dep	Dest	Dur	Type
TN1	7 pm	Saigon	58 hrs	Exp
STN3/5	10 am	Saigon	52 hrs	Exp
V1	2.05 pm	Vinh	4 hrs	Exp
V81*	10 pm	Vinh	16 hrs	Reg
T83*	5.05 am	Thanh Hoa	8 hrs	Reg
ND1*	4.30 pm	Nam Dinh	4 hrs	Reg

*Departs from Truong Tin, which is 17.5 km south of Hanoi Railway Station.

The following trains link Hanoi with points west and north of the city:

Train No	Route	Duration
HP1 & HP2	Hanoi-Haiphong	3 hrs(Exp)
H61 & H62	Hanoi-Haiphong	5 hrs
H63 & H65	Hanoi-Haiphong	5 hrs
91 & 92	Hanoi-Quan Trieu	4 hrs
93 & 94	Hanoi-Quan Trieu	4 hrs
LS1 & LS2	Hanoi-Lang Son	6 hrs

Train	Route	Duration
LS3 & LS4	Hanoi-Lang Son	7 hrs
PL1 & PL	Hanoi-Pho Lu (via Yen Bai)	10 hrs
PL3 & PL4	Hanoi-Pho Lu (via Yen Bai)	11 hrs

For more information on the Vietnamese train network, see the Getting Around chapter.

Bus Hanoi has several main bus terminals. Kim Lien Bus Station serves points south of Hanoi. Kim Ma Bus Station serves destinations that are north-west of the capital. Buses to points north-east of Hanoi leave from Long Bien Bus Station, which recently moved to the east bank of the Red River. Soviet-built buses seating 24 people can be chartered from the Kim Ma Bus Station; for more information, have a

Vietnamese-speaker call 44227 or 43808. Buses can also be hired from Vietcochamber.

Kim Lien Bus Station (Ben Xe Kim Lien; tel 55230) is 800 metres south of the railway station at 100 Le Duan St (corner Nguyen Quyen St). The express bus *(toc hanh)* ticket office, which is open every day from 4.30 am to 5 pm, is across the street from 6B Nguyen Quyen St. There are express buses to:

Binh Dinh
Buon Ma Thuot (42 hours)
Danang (24 hours)
Gia Lai
Ho Chi Minh City (49 hours)
Kontum
Nha Trang (39 hours)
Quang Ngai (27 hours)
Qui Nhon (35 hours)

All the express buses leave daily at 5 or 5.30 am. According to a new incentive plan, the driver must refund 10% of the ticket price if an express bus is 2 hours late and 20% if the bus is 3 or more hours late.

There are non-express buses from Kim Lien Bus Station to:

Bac Son
Bim Son (3½ hours)
Chi Ne
Danang (about 24 hours)
Do Luong
Dong Ha (20 hours)
Dong Van
Guot
Ha Tinh
Ho Chi Minh City (60 hours)
Hoa Binh (3½ hours)
Hoa Mac (1½ hours)
Hué (24 hours)
Kim Bang
Ky Anh (12 hours)
Nghia Dan
Phu Ly (12 hours)
Sam Son Beaches (5 hours)
Thai Nguyen (2½ hours)
Thanh Hoa (4 hours)
Thuong Tin (trains V81, T83 & ND1 depart from here)
Tuyen Quang (6½ hours)
Vinh (8 to 10 hours)

Most non-express buses depart between 4.30

and 5.30 am, though some, especially on shorter routes, leave later in the day.

Kim Ma Bus Station (Ben Xe Kim Ma; tel 52846) is opposite 166 Nguyen Thai Hoc St (corner Giang Vo St). Tickets should be purchased the day before departure for buses to:

Chi Ne	Tho Tang
Co Tuyet	Thuan Chau
Ha Giang	Tuan Giao
Hat Lot	Tuyen Quang
Hoa Binh	Viet Tri
Moc Chau	Vinh Yen
Phu Tho	Yen Bai
Son La	

Tickets for the following shorter runs are sold 15 minutes before departure: Bac Ninh, Bat Bat, Da Chong, Dap Cau, Ni, Phuc Tho, Phuc Yen, Quang Oai, Son Tay, Tan Hong, Trung Ha and Xuan Hoa.

Getting Around

Airport Transport Buses from Hanoi to Noi Bai Airport depart from the Vietnam Airlines Domestic Booking Office at 16 Le Thai To St (corner Hang Trong St). The schedule depends on the departure and arrival times of domestic flights; buses leave daily at 4.30 am and sometimes at 6, 7, 8 and 9 am and 12 noon as well. The trip to Noi Bai takes 50 minutes. Bus tickets are sold inside the Domestic Booking Office in the room to your right as you enter; look for the sign that includes the word *oto*.

There may also be buses to the airport from the International Booking Office (tel 55284), which is at the corner of Trang Thi and Quang Trung streets.

Vietnam Tourism charges US$20 for a taxi ride to Noi Bai Airport; the same service costs US$33 from Hanoi Tourism.

Bus The map of Hanoi issued in 1987 includes bus lines (in red) and tram lines (in blue); some of the information is outdated. Service on many of the bus routes is rather infrequent.

Tram Hanoi's antiquated electric tram system is one of the slowest urban transit

systems in the world (and also one of the cheapest – a ride costs only 100d). But the snail's pace at which the ancient, rickety cars wend their way through the city's traffic in no way detracts from the miracle that they are running at all. One tram line links Lenin Park (Cong Vien Le Nin) with Hoan Kiem Lake via Le Duan, Hang Bong and Hang Gai streets. A second line goes northward from Hoan Kiem Lake and then westward along Thuy Khue St to Dong Xuan Market and Buoi Market.

Taxi There are no taxis to be hailed in Hanoi, nor are there taxi stands as yet. To hire a car with a driver, contact a major hotel, Vietnam Tourism, Hanoi Tourism, TOSERCO or Vietcochamber.

Cyclo Cyclos are generally cheaper in Hanoi than in Saigon, though not if you take one you find sitting in front of a major tourist hotel.

Bicycle The best way to get around Hanoi is by bicycle. The only place renting out bicycles is the Thang Long Hotel (tel 57796) on Giang Vo St; it charges 1000d per hour.

If you'll be in town for more than a few days, you might consider buying a cheap Vietnamese-made bicycle, which costs only about US$25. There are dozens upon dozens of bicycle and motorbike shops along Pho Hué (Hué St) south of Restaurant 202, which is at 202 Pho Hué. Bicycle parts are also available at shops near the intersection of Dien Bien Phu and Nguyen Thai Hoc streets.

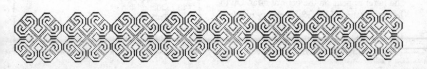

The North

Stretching from the Hoang Lien Mountains (Tonkinese Alps) eastward across the Red River Delta to the islands of Halong Bay, the northern part of Vietnam (Bac Bo), known to the French as Tonkin, includes some of the country's most spectacular scenery. The mountainous areas are home to many distinct hill-tribe groups, some of which remain relatively untouched by Vietnamising and Westernising influences.

Unfortunately, most of the north is closed to tourism (or at least to individual travellers). The areas near the Chinese border, where heavy fighting took place during the Chinese invasion of 1979, are considered militarily sensitive, but elsewhere the reason for keeping Westerners out seems to have more to do with the attitude of Hanoi's bureaucrats, who can't stand having people do things independent of official supervision. However, foreign aid officials regularly travel to projects in outlying areas, and Western journalists (especially cash-laden TV crews), accompanied by officials from the ministries of Information or Foreign Affairs, have managed to get around a bit. For tourists with sufficient funds to hire a car, driver and guide, it may be possible to arrange a private guided tour of Bac Bo through Vietnam Tourism's Hanoi office.

Around Hanoi

THAY PAGODA

Thay Pagoda (the Master's Pagoda), also known as Thien Phuc (Heavenly Blessing), is dedicated to Thich Ca Buddha (Sakyamuni, the historical Buddha) and 18 arhats (monks who have attained Nirvana); the latter appear on the central altar. On the left is a statue of the 12th-century monk Tu Dao Hanh, the 'Master' after whom the pagoda is named; on the right is a statue of King Ly Nhan Tong, who is believed to be a reincarnation of Tu Dao Hanh. In front of the pagoda is a small stage built on stilts in the middle of a pond; water puppet shows are staged here during festivals.

The pagoda's annual festival is held from the 5th to the 7th days of the 3rd lunar month. Pilgrims and other visitors enjoy watching water-puppet shows, hiking and exploring caves in the area.

Thay Pagoda is about 40 km south-west of Hanoi in Ha Son Binh Province.

TAY PHUONG PAGODA

Tay Phuong Pagoda (Pagoda of the West), also known as Sung Phuc Pagoda, consists of three parallel single-level structures built on a hillock said to resemble a buffalo. The 76 figures carved from jackfruit wood, many from the 18th century, are the pagoda's most celebrated feature. The earliest construction here dates from the 8th century.

Tay Phuong Pagoda is approximately 40 km south-west of Hanoi in Tay Phuong hamlet of Ha Son Binh Province. A visit here can easily be combined with a stop at Thay Pagoda.

Provinces of Northern Vietnam

1 Lai Chau
2 Son La
3 Hoang Lien Son
4 Ha Tuyen
5 Bac Thai
6 Cao Bang
7 Lang Son
8 Vinh Phu
9 Greater Hanoi
10 Ha Son Binh
11 Hai Hung
12 Greater Haiphong
13 Quang Ninh
14 Thai Binh
15 Nam Ninh
16 Thanh Hoa

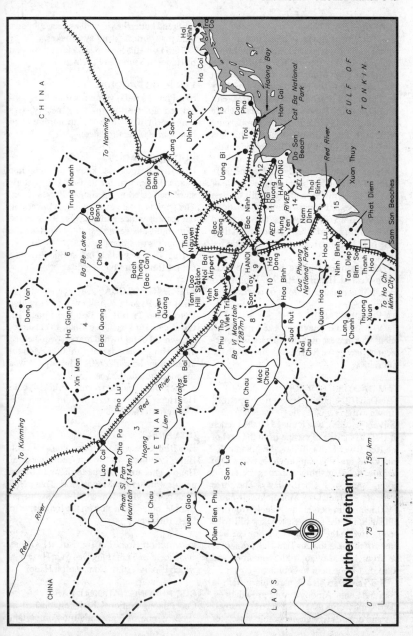

Northern Vietnam

PERFUME PAGODA

The Perfume Pagoda (Chua Huong) is a complex of pagodas and Buddhist shrines built into the limestone cliffs of Huong Tich Mountain (the Mountain of the Fragrant Traces). Among the better-known sites here are Thien Chu (Pagoda Leading to Heaven); Giai Oan Chu (Purgatorial Pagoda), where the faithful believe deities purify souls, cure sufferings and grant offspring to childless families; and Huong Tich Chu (Pagoda of the Perfumed Vestige).

Great numbers of pilgrims come here during a festival that begins in the middle of the 2nd lunar month and lasts until the last week of the 3rd lunar month; these dates usually end up corresponding to March and April. Pilgrims and other visitors spend their time here boating, hiking and exploring the caves.

The Perfume Pagoda is about 60 km south-west of Hanoi in Ha Son Binh Province. It is accessible by road or river.

BA VI MOUNTAIN

Ba Vi Mountain (elevation 1287 metres) is about 65 km west of Hanoi. There is a spectacular view of the Red River valley from the summit.

TAM DAO HILL STATION

Tam Dao Hill Station (elevation 930 metres), known to the French as the Cascade d'Argent (Silver Cascade), was founded by the French in 1907 as a place of escape from the heat of the Red River Delta. Today, the grand colonial villas are a bit run-down, but Tam Dao retains its refreshing weather, beautiful hiking areas and superb views. The three summits of Tam Dao Mountain, all about 1400 metres in height, are visible from the hill station to the north-east. Many hill-tribe people live in the Tam Dao region. The best times of the year to visit Tam Dao are said to be from late-May to mid-September and from mid-December to February.

The Tam Dao area is particularly rich in flora and fauna. Among the old-growth trees, giant ferns (some as tall as 9 metres), camellias and orchids live an incredible variety of

birds and butterflies as well as deer, gibbons, wild pigs, tortoises and rare snakes.

Tam Dao Hill Station is 85 km north-west of Hanoi in Vinh Phu Province.

VAN PHUC PAGODA

Van Phuc Pagoda, surrounded by hills considered noteworthy for their beauty, was founded in 1037. It is 27 km north-east of Hanoi in Ha Bac Province.

BUC THAP PAGODA

Buc Thap Pagoda, also known as Ninh Phuc Pagoda, is known for its four storey stone stupa dedicated to the monk Chuyet Cong. The pagoda's date of founding is uncertain, but records indicate that it was rebuilt in the 17th and 18th centuries; the layout of the structure is traditional.

Buc Thap Pagoda is in Ha Bac Province not far from Van Phuc Pagoda.

KIEP BAC PAGODA

Kiep Bac Pagoda, also known as Ho Quoc Pagoda and Tran Hung Dao Dai Vuong Tu, is dedicated to Tran Quoc Tuan, an outstanding general of renowned bravery who helped Tran Hung Dao defeat 300,000 Mongol invaders in the mid-1280s. The pagoda was founded around the year 1300.

Kiep Bac Pagoda, recently restored, is in Hai Hung Province 61 km from Hanoi and 32 km from Bac Ninh.

HOA BINH

Hoa Binh City, which is the capital of Ha Son Binh Province, is 74 km south-west of Hanoi. This area is home to many hill-tribe people, including Muong and Thai. Hoa Binh can be visited on an all-day excursion from Hanoi, or as a stop on the long drive to Dien Bien Phu.

Information Hoa Binh Tourism (tel 37) has an office at 24 Tran Hung Dao St in Ha Dong, which is only 11 km from central Hanoi.

CUC PHUONG NATIONAL PARK

Cuc Phuong National Park, established in 1962, is one of Vietnam's most important

Butterfly

nature preserves. Though wildlife has suffered a precipitous decline in Vietnam in recent decades, the park's 222 sq km of primary tropical forest remain home to an amazing variety of wildlife, including 1967 species of flora from 217 families and 749 genera; 1800 species of insects from 30 orders and 200 families; 137 species of birds; 64 species of animals; and 33 species of reptiles. Among the extraordinary variety of life forms in the park are several species discovered here, including a tree known as *Bressiaopsis Cucphuongensis* and the endemic red-bellied squirrel *Callosciurus erythrinaceus Cucphuongensis*. Larger animals you may encounter range from the yellow macaque (*Macaca mullata*) to the spotted deer (*Cevus nippon*).

In Con Moong Cave, one of the park's many grottoes, the stone tools of prehistoric humans have been discovered.

Cuc Phuong National Park, which is 70 km from the sea, covers an area about 25 km long and 11 km wide in the provinces of Ha Nam Ninh, Ha Son Binh and Thanh Hoa. The elevation of the highest peak in the park is 648 metres. At the park's lower elevations, the climate is sub-tropical.

Place to Stay
The rest house at park headquarters charges US$12 per night.

Getting There & Away
Cuc Phuong National Park is 140 km from Hanoi (via Ninh Binh); sections of the road are in poor condition. With a car, it is possible to visit the forest as a day trip from Hanoi.

KEO PAGODA
Keo Pagoda (Chua Keo) was founded in the 12th century to honour the Buddha and the monk Khong Minh Khong, who miraculously cured Emperor Ly Than Ton (ruled 1128-38) of leprosy. The finely carved wooden bell tower is considered a masterpiece of traditional Vietnamese architecture. The nearby dike is a good place to get a general view of the pagoda complex.

Keo Pagoda is in Thai Binh Province 9.5 km from the town of Thai Binh near Thai Bac.

HOA LU
Hoa Lu was the capital of Vietnam under the Dinh Dynasty (ruled 968 to 980) and the Early Le Dynasty (ruled 980 to 1009). The site was an attractive place for a capital city because of both its distance from China and the natural protection afforded by the region's landscape, parts of which are said to resemble Halong Bay without the water.

The ancient citadel of Hoa Lu, most of which has been destroyed, covered an area of about 3 sq km. The outer ramparts encompassed temples, shrines and the place where the king held court. The royal family lived in the inner citadel.

Today, there are two sanctuaries at Hoa Lu. Dinh Tien Hoang, restored in the 17th century, is dedicated to the Dinh Dynasty. Out the front is the stone pedestal of a royal throne; inside are bronze bells and a statue of Emperor Dinh Tien Hoang with his three sons. The second temple, Dai Hanh (or Dung Van Nga), commemorates the rulers of the

Early Le Dynasty. Inside the main hall are all sorts of drums, gongs, incense burners, candle holders and weapons; to the left of the entrance is a sanctuary dedicated to Confucius.

Bic Dong Cave is in the village of Van Lam, a short boat trip away. The three sanctuaries here date from the 17th century.

Hoa Lu is at the southern edge of the Red River Delta in Truong Yen Village, which it in Gia Khanh District of Ha Nam Ninh Province. By car, the trip from Hanoi to Hoa Lu takes about 2 hours.

PHAT DIEM

Phat Diem (Kim Son) is the site of a cathedral remarkable for its vast dimensions and unique Sino-Vietnamese architecture. The vaulted ceiling is supported by massive limwood columns almost 1 metre in diameter and 10 metres tall. In the lateral naves, there are a number of curious wood and stone sculptures. The main altar is made of a single block of granite.

Before 1954, the cathedral, founded by a Vietnamese priest named Six, was an important centre of Catholicism in the north, and there was a seminary here. Six's tomb is in the square in front of the cathedral. Nearby is a covered bridge dating from the late 19th century.

Phat Diem is 121 km south of Hanoi and 29 km south-east of Ninh Binh.

Haiphong

Haiphong, Vietnam's third most populous city, is the north's main industrial centre and one of the country's most important seaports. Greater Haiphong has an area of 1515 sq km and a population of 1,300,000; Haiphong proper covers 21 sq km and is home to 370,000 inhabitants.

The French took possession of Haiphong, then a small market town, in 1874. The city soon became a major port; industrial concerns were established here in part because of the proximity of coal supplies.

One of the immediate causes of the Franco-Vietminh War was the infamous French bombardment of the 'native quarters' of Haiphong in 1946 in which hundreds of civilians were killed and injured (a contemporary French account estimated civilian deaths at 'no more than 6000').

Haiphong came under American air and naval attacks between 1965 and 1972. In May 1972, President Nixon ordered the mining of Haiphong harbour to cut the flow of Soviet military supplies to North Vietnam. As part of the Paris Cease-Fire accords of 1973, the US agreed to help clear the mines from Haiphong harbour; 10 US Navy minesweepers were involved in the effort.

Since the late 1970s, Haiphong has seen a massive outflux of refugees, including many ethnic Chinese, who have taken with them much of the city's fishing fleet.

Information
Useful Addresses The following addresses may be of use:

Haiphong Tourism
  15 Le Dai Hanh St (tel 47486)
GPO
  3 Nguyen Tri Phuong St (corner Hoang Van Thu St)
Soviet Consulate
  14 Minh Khai St (tel 47611)
Municipal Museum
  Dien Bien St
Municipal Theatre
  Tran Hung Dao St
Municipal Library
  On the corner of Minh Khai and Dien Bien streets
Municipal People's Committee
  Hoang Dieu St
Communist Party offices
  Dinh Tien Hoang St
Vietnam-Czechoslovakia Friendship Hospital (*Benh Vien Viet-Tiep*)
  Nha Thuong St
Traditional Medicine Hospital (*Benh Vien Dong Y*)
  Nguyen Duc Canh St

Du Hang Pagoda

Du Hang Pagoda, which is at 121 Du Hang St, was founded 3 centuries ago. Though it has been rebuilt several times since, it

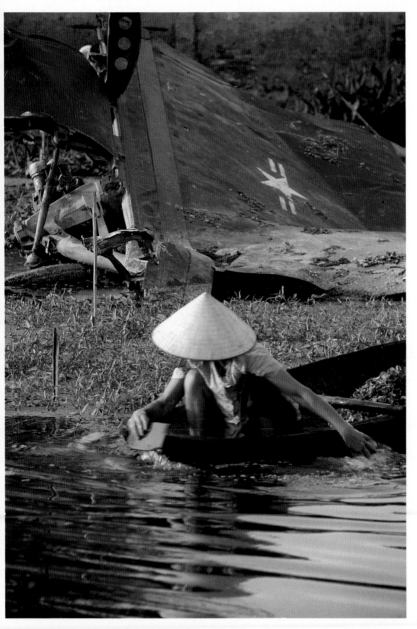

Wreckage of a US B52, Hanoi (LG)

Left: Street market, Hanoi (TA)
Right: Rickshaw transport, Hanoi (RM)
Bottom: Junk, Halong Bay (PS)

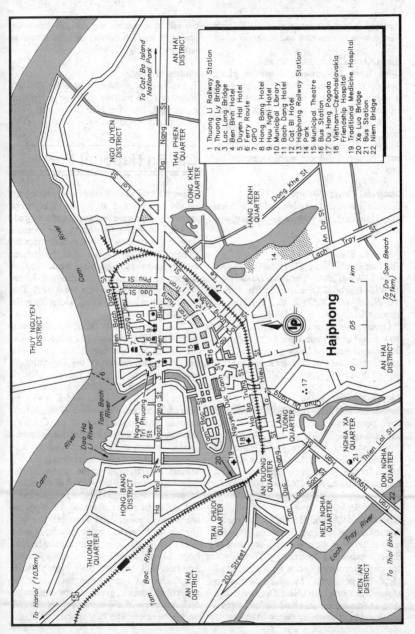

1	Thuong Li Railway Station
2	Thuong Ly Bridge
3	Lac Long Bridge
4	Ben Binh Hotel
5	Duyen Hai Hotel
6	Ferry Route
7	GPO
8	Hong Bang Hotel
9	Huu Nghi Hotel
10	Municipal Library
11	Bach Dang Hotel
12	Cat Bi Hotel
13	Haiphong Railway Station
14	Park
15	Municipal Theatre
16	Bus Station
17	Du Hang Pagoda
18	Vietnam–Czechoslovakia Friendship Hospital
19	Traditional Medicine Hospital
20	Xe Lua Bridge
21	Bus Station
22	Niem Bridge

Haiphong

remains a good example of traditional Vietnamese architecture and sculpture.

Hang Kenh Communal House
Hang Kenh Communal House on Hang Kenh St is known for its 500 relief sculptures in wood. The area in which the structure is located was once part of the village of Kenh.

Hang Kenh Tapestry Factory
Founded 65 years ago, the Hang Kenh Tapestry Factory produces wool tapestries for export.

Dang Hai Flower Village
Flowers grown at Dang Hai, which is 5 km from Haiphong, are sold on the international market.

Places to Stay
The French-era *Huu Nghi Hotel* (tel 47206) is at 62 Dien Bien St. The *Bach Dang Hotel* (tel 47244) is at 42 Dien Bien St. The *Duyen Hai Hotel* (tel 47657) is at 5 Nguyen Tri Phuong St.

Other hotels you might try include the *Ben Binh Hotel* on the corner of Dien Bien and Ben Binh streets; the *Hong Bang Hotel* at 64 Dien Bien St; the *Cat Bi Hotel* at 29 Tran Phu St; and the *Cat Bi Hotel* at 29 Tran Phu St.

Getting There & Away
Authorities in Hanoi have been refusing to grant permits for individual travel to Haiphong.

Haiphong is 103 km from Hanoi on National Highway 5. The two cities are also linked by rail (by express trains HP1/HP2 and regular trains H61/H62 and H63/H64).

DO SON BEACH
Palm-shaded Do Son Beach, 21 km southeast of Haiphong, is the most popular sea-side resort in the north and a favourite of Hanoi's expatriate community. The hilly 4 km long promontory ends with a string of islets. The peninsula's nine hills are known as the Cuu Long Son (Nine Dragons). The town is famous for its ritual buffalo fights, which are held annually on the 10th day of the 8th lunar month, the date on which the leader of an 18th century peasant rebellion here was killed.

Places to Stay
Places to stay in town include the *Do Son Hotel* (tel 10 via the Do Son telephone exchange), the *Van Hoa Hotel*, the *Hoa Phuong Hotel* and the *Hai Au Hotel*.

Cat Ba National Park

About half of Cat Ba Island (whose total area is 354 sq km) and 90 sq km of adjacent inshore waters were declared a national park in 1986 in order to protect the island's diverse ecosystems. These include tropical evergreen forests on the hills, freshwater swamp forests at the base of the hills, coastal mangrove forests, small freshwater lakes, sandy beaches and offshore coral reefs. The main beaches are Cai Vieng, Hong Xoai Be and Hong Xoai Lon.

There are numerous lakes, waterfalls and grottoes in the spectacular limestone hills, the highest of which rises 331 metres above sea level. The growth of the vegetation is stunted near the summits because of high winds. The largest permanent body of water on the island is Ech Lake, which covers an area of 3 hectares. Almost all of the surface streams are seasonal; most of the Cat Ba's rainwater flows into caves, following underground streams to the sea and resulting in a severe shortage of fresh water during the dry season. Though parts of the interior of the island are below sea level, most of the island is between 50 and 200 metres in elevation.

Cat Ba Island is home to 15 types of mammals, such as the Francois monkey (*Presbytis francoisi poliocephalus*), wild boar (*Sus scrofa*), deer, squirrels and hedgehogs; 21 species of birds, including hawks, hornbills and cuckoos, have been sighted. Cat Ba lies on a major migration route for waterfowl (ducks, geese, shorebirds) who feed and roost in the mangrove forests and on the beaches. The 620 species of plants

Sampan, Halong Bay

recorded on Cat Ba include 118 timber species and 160 plants with medicinal value.

The waters off Cat Ba Island are home to 200 species of fishes, 500 species of molluscs and 400 species of arthropods. Larger marine animals in the area include seals and three species of dolphin.

Stone tools and bones left by human beings who lived between 6000 and 7000 years ago have been found at 17 sites on the island. The most thoroughly studied site is Cai Beo Cave, discovered by a French archaeologist in 1938, which is 1.5 km from Cat Ba Town.

Today, the island's human population of 12,000 is concentrated in the southern part of the island, including the town of Cat Ba (Cat Hai). They live by fishing, forest exploitation and agriculture, including the growing of rice, cassava, oranges, apples and lychees.

During February, March and April Cat Ba's weather is often cold and drizzly, though the temperature rarely falls below 10°C. Tropical storms and typhoons are frequent.

Getting There & Away

Cat Ba National Park is 133 km from Hanoi and 30 km east of Haiphong. A boat to Cat Ba is supposed to depart from Haiphong every day at 6 am; the trip takes about 3½ hours. The park headquarters is at Trung Trang.

HALONG BAY

Magnificent Halong Bay, with its 3,000 islands rising from the clear, emerald waters of the Gulf of Tonkin, is one of the natural marvels of Vietnam. The vegetation-covered islands, which are spread out over an area of 1500 sq km, are dotted with innumerable beaches and grottoes created by the wind and the waves. Visitors have compared the area's magical landscape of carboniferous chalk islets to Guilin, China and Krabi in southern Thailand. The bay is said to be inhabited by a mysterious marine creature of gargantuan proportions known as the Tarasque.

The name 'Ha Long' means 'where the dragon descends into the sea'. Legend has it that the islands of Halong Bay were created by a great dragon who lived in the moun-

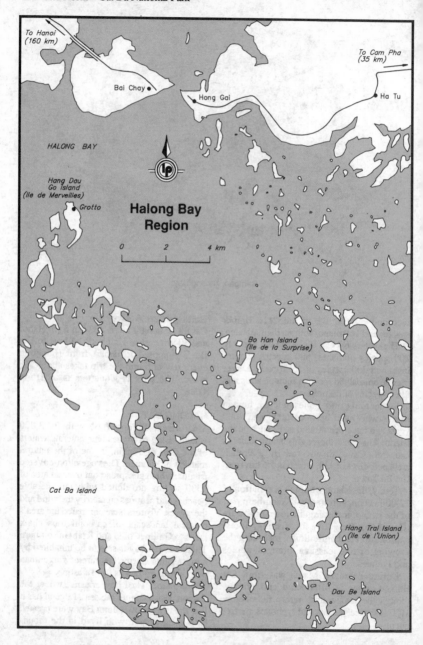

To Hanoi
(160 km)

To Cam Pha
(35 km)

Bai Chay

Hong Gai

Ha Tu

HALONG BAY

Hang Dau
Go Island
(Ile de Merveilles)

Grotto

**Halong Bay
Region**

0   2   4 km

Bo Han Island
(Ile de la Surprise)

Cat Ba Island

Hang Trai Island
(Ile de l'Union)

Dau Be Island

tains. As he ran towards the coast, his flailing tail gouged out valleys and crevasses; as he plunged into the sea, the areas dug up by his tail became filled with water, leaving only bits of high land visible.

Quang Ninh Province, whose major towns are Hong Gai and Cam Pha, is Vietnam's foremost coal-producing region.

Information

There is an office of Quang Ninh Tourism (tel 08 via the Halong telephone exchange) in the town of Bai Chay, which is across the water from Hong Gai.

Grottoes

Because of the type of rock the islands of Halong Bay consisit of, the area is dotted with thousands of caves of all sizes and shapes.

Hang Dau Go (Grotto of Wooden Stakes), known to the French as the Grotte des Merveilles (Cave of Marvels), is a huge cave consisting of three chambers which you reach via 90 steps. Among the stalactites of the first hall, scores of gnomes appear to be holding a meeting. The walls of the second chamber sparkle if bright light is shined on them. The cave derives its Vietnamese name from the third of the chambers, which is said to have been used during the 13th century to store the sharp bamboo stakes which Tran Hung Dao planted in the bed of the Bach Dang River to impale the Kublai Khan's invasion fleet.

Other well-known caves in Halong Bay include the Grotto of Bo Nau and 2 km long Hang Hanh Cave.

Beaches

Bai Chay is a dirt and pebble beach northeast of Haiphong popular with Hanoi residents. There are a number of climbable hills in the vicinity.

There is a beach resort at Tra Co, which is very near the Chinese border; it is off limits to foreigners.

Places to Stay

In the town of Bai Chay, the *Ha Long Hotel* (tel 238) charges Westerners US$35 for a room; the place next door costs only 15,000d. Other hotels you might try include the *Bach Long Hotel* (tel 281), the *Hoang Long Hotel* (tel 264) and the *Son Long Hotel* (tel 254).

Getting There & Away

Hong Gai (Hon Gay) is 165 km from Hanoi, 60 km from Haiphong and 40 km from Cam Pha; Bai Chay is across the water a few km west of Hong Gai. The trip from Hanoi to Halong Bay takes about 3 hours by car and 5 hours by public bus.

Bus Buses from Hanoi to Halong Bay depart from the Long Bien Bus Station, which is on the east side of the Red River.

The Bai Chay Bus Station is about 1 km from the Ha Long Hotel.

Tours Vietnam Tourism in Hanoi offers rather expensive 3 day tours to Halong Bay: it costs US$88 to hire a car (which can seat up to three people in addition to the driver and guide) for the round-trip from Hanoi; room and board cost US$48 per person for 3 days; and Vietnam Tourism charges US$28 per hour (!) for a boat out to the island grottoes.

Getting Around

It is possible to hire a motorised launch to tour the islands and their grottoes. To find a boat, ask around the quays of Bay Chay or Hong Gai.

The Far North

LANG SON

The town of Lang Son (elevation: 270 metres), the capital of mountainous Lang Son Province, has long served as an important crossing point into China. Much of the area's population is made up of ethnic minorities (Tho, Nung, Man and Dao), many of whom continue their traditional way of life.

Natural resources of the area include coal and wood.

Lang Son was partially destroyed in February 1979 by invading Chinese forces; the ruins of the town and the devastated frontier village of Dong Dang, 14 km to the north, are often shown to foreign journalists as evidence of Chinese aggression. Today, though the border region is still mined, fortified and heavily guarded, Sino-Vietnamese trade continues, and peasants can be seen walking across the border carrying bottles of Chinese beer to sell in Vietnam.

There are caves 3.5 km from Lang Son near the village of Ky Lua.

Getting There & Away
Lang Son is the last stop on the railway line that once continued on to Nanning, China. By road, the city is 151 km from Hanoi.

CAO BANG
Cao Bang City is the capital of Cao Bang Province, many of whose inhabitants are members of the Tho, Nung, Dao and Meo national minorities. Principal products of the region include beef, pork, goats, zinc and lumber. The area is known for its waterfalls and grottoes.

Getting There & Away
Cao Bang is 272 km north of Hanoi.

BA BE LAKES
The Ba Be Lakes are an area of waterfalls, rivers, deep valleys, lakes and caves set amidst towering peaks. The lakes, which are about 145 metres above sea level, are surrounded by steep mountains up to 1754 metres high. The 1939 Madrolle Guide to Indochina suggests getting around the area 'in a car, on horseback, or, for ladies, in a chair', meaning, of course, a sedan chair.

Ba Be (three bays) is the name of the southern part of a narrow body of water 7 km long; the northern section of the lake, separated from Ba Be by a 100 metre wide strip of water sandwiched between high walls of chalk rock, is called Be Kam. The Nam Nang River is navigable for 23 km between a point

4 km above Cho Ra and the Falls of Dau Dang, which consist of a series of cascades between sheer walls of rock. Pong Tunnel is almost 300 metres in length and 30 to 40 metres high.

Getting There & Away
The Ba Be Lakes are in Cao Bang Province not far from the borders of Bac Thai Province and Ha Tuyen Province. Ba Be is 240 km from Hanoi, 61 km from Bach Thong (Bac Can) and 17 km from Cho Ra.

The North-West

SON LA
Son La, capital of a province of the same name, is 308 km west of Hanoi. The area is populated mainly by hill tribes, including the Black Tai (Thai or Tay), Meo, Muong and White Tai. Vietnamese influence in the area was minimal until this century; from 1959 to 1980, the region was part of the Tay Bac Autonomous Region *(Khu Tay Bac Tu Tri)*.

Son La was once the site of a French penal colony where anti-colonialist revolutionaries were held.

There is a basic hotel in the town of Son La, which is on the road from Hanoi to Dien Bien Phu.

DIEN BIEN PHU
Dien Bien Phu was the site of that rarest of military events, a battle that can be called truly decisive. On 6 May 1954, the day before the Geneva Conference on Indochina was set to begin half a world away, Viet Minh forces overran the beleaguered French garrison at Dien Bien Phu after a 57-day siege, shattering French morale and forcing the French government to abandon its attempts to re-establish colonial control of Indochina.

Dien Bien Phu (population 10,000), capital of Dien Bien District of Lai Chau Province, is in one of the remotest parts of Vietnam. The town is 16 km from the Lao border in flat, heart-shaped Muong Thanh Valley, which is about 20 km long and 5 km wide and is surrounded by steep, heavily-forested hills. The area is inhabited by hill-tribe people, most notably the Tai and Hmong. Ethnic Vietnamese, whom the government has been encouraging to settle in the region, currently comprise about one-third of the Muong Thanh Valley's population of 60,000.

For centuries, Dien Bien was a transit stop on the caravan route from Burma and China to northern Vietnam. Dien Bien Phu was established in 1841 by the Nguyen Dynasty to prevent raids on the Red River Delta by bandits.

In early 1954, General Henri Navarre, commander of French forces in Indochina, sent a force of 12 battalions to occupy the Muong Thanh Valley in order to prevent the Viet Minh from crossing into Laos and threatening the Lao capital of Luang Phabang. The French units, one-third of whose members were ethnic-Vietnamese, were soon surrounded by a Viet Minh force under General Vo Nguyen Giap consisting of 33 infantry battalions, six artillery regiments and a regiment of engineers. The Viet Minh force, which outnumbered the French by five to one, was equipped with 105 mm artillery pieces and anti-aircraft guns carried by porters through jungles and across rivers in an unbelievable feat of logistics. The guns were emplaced in carefully camouflaged positions dug deep into the hills that overlooked the French positions.

A failed Viet Minh human-wave assault against the French was followed by weeks of intense artillery bombardments. Six battalions of French paratroops were parachuted into Dien Bien Phu as the situation worsened, but bad weather and the Viet Minh artillery, impervious to French air and artillery attacks, prevented sufficient reinforcements and supplies from arriving by air. An elaborate system of trenches and tunnels allowed Viet Minh soldiers to reach French positions without coming under fire. After the idea of employing American conventional bombers was rejected – as was a Pentagon proposal to use tactical atomic bombs – the French trenches and bunkers were overrun. All 13,000 men of the French garrison were either killed or taken prisoner; Viet Minh casualties are estimated at 25,000.

Today, the site of the battle is marked by a small museum. The headquarters of the French commander, Colonel Christian de Castries, has been recreated and nearby there are old French tanks and artillery pieces. One of the two landing strips used by the French is extant. There is a monument to Viet Minh casualties on the site of the former French position known as Eliane, where bitter fighting took place. A memorial to the 3000 French troops buried under the rice paddies was erected in 1984 on the 30th anniversary of the battle.

At present, the Vietnamese government is considering a request by French veterans of Dien Bien Phu that they be allowed to restage their paratroop drop of almost 4 decades ago.

Getting There & Away

Though there is no regularly scheduled air service to Dien Bien Phu, it is sometimes possible to catch the odd flight out there.

The 420 km drive from Hanoi to Dien Bien Phu takes 2 full days. In other words, a minimum of 5 days is required for an overland expedition from Hanoi to Dien Bien Phu: 2 days to get there, a day to visit the area, and 2 days to come back. Visitors report that getting there is half the fun: as it nears Dien Bien, the road winds through beautiful mountains and high plains inhabited by hill tribes (notably the Black Tai and Hmong) who still live as they have for generations. Between Hoa Binh and Son La, the road passes through tea plantations and orchards.

LAO CAI

The Hoang Lien Mountains, named the Tonkinese Alps by the French, include Vietnam's highest peaks. The altitude of the tallest, Phan Si Pan Mountain (also spelled Fan Si Pan), is 3143 metres. Lao Cai is the major town in the Hoang Lien Mountains region.

The old hill station of Cha Pa (altitude: 1600 metres) is 29 km from Lao Cai.

Laos

Introduction

Laos has harboured a variety of cultures - Lao, Hmong-Mien, Khmer and Thai - for centuries and remains one of Asia's most undeveloped and undiscovered countries. From the fertile lowlands of the Mekong River Valley to the rugged Annamite highlands, legendary Lao hospitality and natural scenery have survived decades of war and offer travellers an unparalleled glimpse of old South-East Asia.

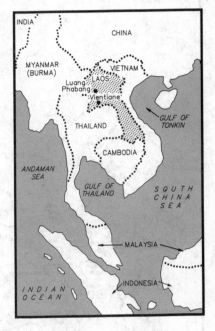

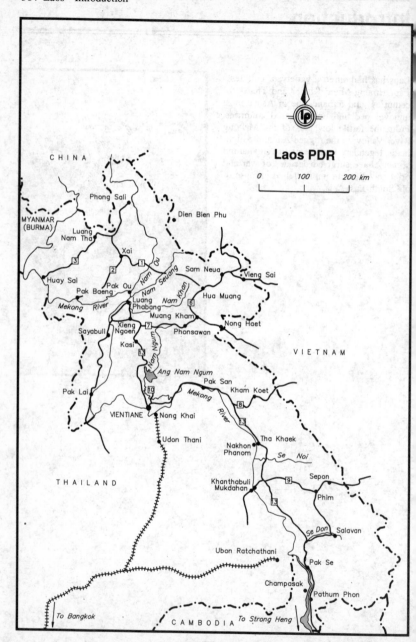

Facts about the Country

HISTORY
Prehistory

The Mekong River Valley and Khorat Plateau areas which today encompass significant parts of Laos, Cambodia and Thailand were inhabited as far back as 10,000 years. Virtually all ethnic groups in these areas, both indigenous and immigrant, belong to the Austro-Thai ethno-linguistic family. In Laos, historically speaking, these are mostly subgroups identified with the Thai-Kadai and Miao-Yao, or Hmong-Mien, language families.

The Thai-Kadai is the most significant ethno-linguistic group in all of South-East Asia, with 72 million speakers extending from the Brahmaputra River in India's Assam state to the Gulf of Tonkin and China's Hainan Island. To the north, there are Thai-Kadai speakers well into the Chinese provinces of Yunnan and Guangxi, and to the south they extend as far as the northern Malaysian state of Kedah. In Thailand and Laos, they are the majority populations, and in China, Vietnam and Myanmar (Burma) they are the largest minorities. The major Thai-Kadai groups are the Ahom (Assam), the Siamese (Thailand), the Black Thai (Laos and Thailand), the Shan (Myanmar and Thailand), the Lü (Laos, Thailand and China) and the Yuan (Laos and Thailand). All of these groups belong to the Thai half of Thai-Kadai; the Kadai groups are relatively small (numbering less than a million) and include such comparatively obscure languages in South China as Kelao, Lati, Laha, Laqua and Li.

When trying to trace the origins of the current inhabitants of Laos, one must consider the fact that their predecessors belonged to a vast, nonunified zone of Austro-Thai influence that involved periodic migrations along several different geographic lines.

Thai Migration

A linguistic map of South China, North-West India and South-East Asia clearly shows that the preferred zones of occupation by the Thai peoples (including various Lao groups) have been river valleys, from the Red River (Hong River) in South China and Vietnam to the Brahmaputra River in Assam. At one time, the access points into what is now Thailand and Laos were the Yuan Jiang and other river areas in Yunnan and Guangxi and the Chao Phraya River in Thailand. These are areas where the populations remain quite concentrated today. Areas between Thailand and Laos were intermediate zones and have always been far less populated.

The Mekong River Valley between Thailand and Laos was one such intermediate migrational zone, as were river valleys along the Nam Ou, Nam Seng and other rivers in modern Laos (Myanmar's Shan States also fall into this category). As far as historians have been able to piece together from scant linguistic and anthropological evidence, significant numbers of Thai peoples in South China began migrating southward in small groups as early as the 8th century AD, but most certainly by the 10th century. These groups established local polities along traditional Thai lines according to *muang* (roughly 'principality' or 'district') under the hereditary rule of chieftains or sovereigns called *chao muang*.

Each *muang* was based in a river valley or section of a valley. Some *muang* were loosely collected under one *chao muang* or an alliance of several. One of the largest collections of *muang* (though not necessarily united) was in South China and was known as Nam Chao (often corrupted as Nan Chao in modern texts) or Lord(s) of the River(s).

In the mid-13th century, the rise to power of the Mongols under Kublai Khan in Sung Dynasty China caused a more dramatic southward migration of Thai peoples. Wherever Thais met indigenous populations of Tibeto-Burmans and Mon-Khmers in the move south (into what is now Myanmar,

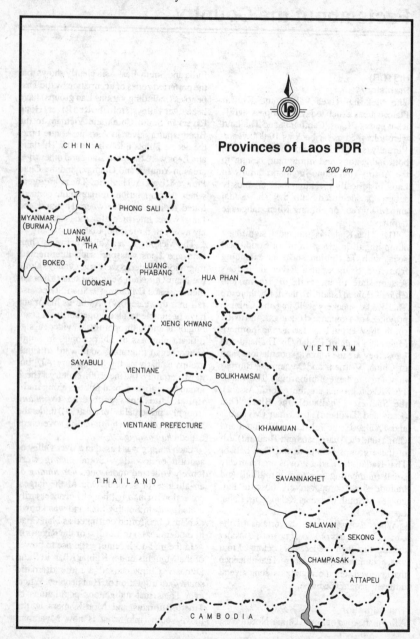

Provinces of Laos PDR

0   100   200 km

CHINA

MYANMAR (BURMA)

PHONG SALI

LUANG NAM THA

BOKEO

UDOMSAI

LUANG PHABANG

HUA PHAN

XIENG KHWANG

VIETNAM

SAYABULI

VIENTIANE

BOLIKHAMSAI

VIENTIANE PREFECTURE

KHAMMUAN

THAILAND

SAVANNAKHET

SALAVAN

SEKONG

CHAMPASAK

ATTAPEU

CAMBODIA

Thailand, Laos and Cambodia), they were somehow able to displace, assimilate or co-opt them without force. This seems to puzzle many historians, but the most simple reason is probably that there were already Thai peoples in the area. This supposition finds considerable support in current research on the development of Austro-Thai language and culture.

Lan Na Thai & Lan Xang

Until the 13th century, there were several small, independent Thai *muang* in what is today northern Thailand and Laos. In the mid-13th century, a Thai rebellion against the Khmers resulted in the consolidation of several *muang* to create the famous Sukhothai kingdom in northern Thailand. Sukhothai's King Ram Khamhaeng supported Chao Mengrai of Chiang Mai and Chao Khun Ngam Muang of Phayao (Chiang Mai and Phayao were both *muang* in northern Thailand) in the formation of Lan Na Thai (Million Thai Rice Fields), sometimes written simply as Lanna. Lanna extended across north central Thailand to include the *muang* of Wieng Chan (Vientiane).

In the 14th century, Wieng Chan was taken from Lanna by Chao Fa Ngum (also spelt Fa Ngoum) of Muang Sawa (later known as Luang Phabang). Fa Ngum conquered Muang Sawa and Wieng Chan with the assistance of the Khmers, as he was raised in the Khmer courts of Angkor and had married a Khmer princess. He also managed to bring much of the Khorat Plateau in north-eastern Thailand under his control as well, and in 1353 he named these territories Lan Xang (Million Elephants). Geographically, it was one of the largest kingdoms in mainland South-East Asia, although then, as now, it was sparsely populated. Although Lan Xang is considered by many present-day Lao to have been the first truly Lao nation, it was originally created as a Khmer client state.

Fa Ngum made Theravada Buddhism the state religion and accepted the Pha Bang, a gold Buddha image said to have been cast in

Sri Lanka, from the Khmers. The Pha Bang became a talismanic symbol for the sovereignty of the Lao kingdom of Lan Xang and has remained so in the Lao People's Democratic Republic today. The image was kept in Muang Sawa, which is how the city's name later became changed to Luang Phabang, Great Pha Bang.

Within 20 years of its founding, Lan Xang's frontiers had expanded eastward to Champa and along the Annamite mountains in Vietnam. Fa Ngum became known as 'the Conqueror' because of his constant preoccupation with warfare. Unable to tolerate his ruthlessness any longer, Fa Ngum's ministers finally drove him into exile in 1373.

Phaya Samsenthai (Lord of 300,000 Thai – derived from a census of adult males living in Lan Xang in 1376) succeeded Fa Ngum. Samsenthai reorganised and consolidated the royal administration of Lan Xang along Siamese lines, building many *wat* (temple-monasteries) and schools. He also developed the economy and during his reign Lan Xang became an important trade centre.

Samsenthai was succeeded in 1520 by King Phothisarat, who moved the capital to Wieng Chan. In 1545, Phothisarat subdued the kingdom of Lanna and gained the throne of that kingdom for his son, Setthathirat. When Setthathirat inherited the kingship of Lan Xang two years later, he brought with him the Pha Kaew or so-called Emerald Buddha from Lanna (the Lanna equivalent to Lan Xang's Pha Bang). He had Wat Pha Kaew built in Wieng Chan to house the Pha Kaew (the image was later taken back by the Thais) and also ordered the construction of That Luang, the country's largest Buddhist stupa.

Although Lan Xang was a large and powerful kingdom, its rulers were never able to fully subjugate the highland tribes of mountain Laos. States in north-eastern Laos, such as Xieng Khwang and Sam Neua, remained independent of Lan Xang rule. In 1571, King Setthathirat disappeared somewhere in the mountains on the way back from a military expedition into Cambodia, and it is thought that his troops may have met with rebellious highlanders on an excursion into southern Laos.

Leaderless, Lan Xang declined rapidly over the next 60 years, dissolving into warring factions and subject to intermittent Burmese domination. Finally in 1637, King Suliya Vongsa ascended the throne following a dynastic war. He ruled for 60 years, the longest reign of any Lao monarch, and was able to further expand Lan Xang's frontiers. These years are regarded as Laos' 'golden age' – a historic pinnacle in terms of territory and power.

Fragmentation & the War with Siam

When King Suliya Vongsa died without an heir in 1694, there was a three-way struggle for the throne that led to the break-up of Lan Xang. By the early 18th century, Suliya's nephew, under the stewardship of Annam (Vietnam), had taken control of the middle Mekong River Valley around Wieng Chan. A second, independent kingdom emerged in Luang Phabang under Suliya's grandsons. A prince in the lower Mekong River area established a third kingdom, Champasak, under Siamese influence.

By the end of the 18th century, the Siamese had expanded their influence to include the Kingdom of Wieng Chan and were also exacting tribute from Luang Phabang. Wieng Chan was further pressured by the Vietnamese into paying tribute to Emperor Gia Long's Annamite empire. Unable or unwilling to serve two masters, Wieng Chan's Prince Anou went to war with Siam in the 1820s, an unsuccessful challenge that resulted in the virtual razing of the Wieng Chan capital and the forced resettlement of many of its residents to Siam. Eventually the same fate overtook Luang Phabang and Champasak. By the late 1800s, practically the entire region between the Mekong and the Annamite Chain had been defeated and depopulated (which is one reason there are more Lao in Thailand today than in Laos).

Wieng Chan, Luang Phabang and Champasak, then became Siamese satellite states by the late 19th century. In 1885, the Siamese

also occupied the neutral states of Xieng Khwang and Hua Phan as buffers against the expanding influence of the French in Vietnam.

French Rule

In the late 19th century, the French were busy making inroads toward the establishment of a French Indochina. After creating French protectorates in Tonkin and Annam, France secured a consulate at Luang Phabang (with Siamese permission) and was soon able to convince that state to ask for protectorate status as well.

Through a succession of Siamese-French treaties between 1893 and 1907, the Siamese eventually relinquished control of all territory east of the Mekong River, keeping everything to the west for themselves. The French united all of the remaining Lao principalities as one nation according to the Western custom of territorial boundaries. Like the British, they assumed they had little to fear from uniting separate entities that had never been able to integrate successfully.

It was the French who gave the country its modern name, Laos, an apparent misapprehension of le Laos for les Laos, the plural of Lao (in the Lao language, the country and people are both simply 'Lao'). Laos was never very important to France except as a buffer between British-influenced Thailand (and British-occupied Burma) and the more economically important Annam and Tonkin. But the presence of the French undermined the traditional flexibility of Lao interstate relations and severed the most populous part of the country by conceding Isan (northeastern Thailand, predominantly Lao in population) to Siam. Hence, the French involvement in Laos, however benign it may have initially appeared (there was never any French military action against the Lao people until 1964), resulted in a weakening of Lao states that probably could not have been achieved even by warfare.

The French also stifled the indigenous modernisation of Laos by imposing a Vietnamese-staffed French civil service (just as the British did in Burma with their Indian-staffed civil service). Even the present-day Lao government labours under the influences of French and Vietnamese administrative styles.

WW II & Independence

In 1941, the Japanese occupied French Indochina with the support of the Vichy regime. The Lao mounted very little resistance against the occupation but were able to gain more local autonomy than they enjoyed under the French.

Towards the end of the war, the Japanese forced the French-installed King Sisavang Vong to declare independence in spite of his loyalty to France. Prime Minister and Viceroy Phetsarat didn't trust the King and formed a resistance movement called *Lao Issara* (Free Lao) to ensure that the country remained free of French colonial rule once the Japanese left.

When French paratroopers landed in Wieng Chan and Luang Phabang in 1945, they had King Sisavang Vong relieve Prince Phetsarat of his official positions and once again declared Laos to be a French protectorate. Phetsarat and the Lao Issara formed the Committee of the People and in October 1945 drew up a new constitution proclaiming Laos independent of French rule. When the King at first refused to recognise the new document, he was deposed by the National Assembly.

Eventually Sisavang Vong came around to the Lao Issara view of things and was reinstated as King in April 1946. Two days after his coronation, French and Lao guerrillas who called themselves the 'Free French' took Wieng Chan and smashed Lao Issara forces (as well as resistance forces sent by Ho Chi Minh from Vietnam). Phetsarat and many of the Lao Issara fled to Thailand, where they set up a government-in-exile with Phetsarat as Regent.

By late 1946, the French were willing to concede autonomy to Laos and invited the Lao Issara to enter into formal negotiations. But the Lao Issara split into three factions in response to the offer. One faction, under Phetsarat, refused to negotiate with the French, insisting on immediate independence according to Lao Issara terms only. The second was headed by Phetsarat's half-brother, Prince Souvanna Phouma, who wanted to negotiate with the French in forming an independent Laos. The third faction was led by another half-brother, Prince Souphanouvong, who wanted to work out a deal with the Viet Minh under Ho Chi Minh.

The French proceeded without the cooperation of the Lao Issara and in 1949 held a French-Lao convention in which Laos was recognised as an 'independent associate state' that remained part of the French Union. The treaty gave Laos the right to become an independent member of the United Nations and for the first time Laos was recognised by the West as a separate nation. The Lao Issara dissolved, but Phetsarat remained in Thailand.

Four years later, France granted full sovereignty to Laos via the Franco-Laotian Treaty of 1953. By this time, the French were heavily preoccupied with the Viet Minh offensives in Vietnam and were looking to reduce their colonial burden in an attempt to preserve what little remained of the French Empire.

The Rise of the Pathet Lao

Prior to the late '40s and early '50s, the only Lao association with the communist liberation movement had been through the membership of Prince Souphanouvong and Kaysone Phomvihane memberships in Ho Chi Minh's Indochinese Communist Party (ICP). In 1948, Prince Souphanouvong went to Hanoi to gain support from the Viet Minh for a Lao communist movement. At about the same time, a Viet Minh organiser named Kaysone Phomvihane (who later became Secretary-General of the Lao People's Revolutionary Party and Prime Minister of the LPDR) was also making headway among tribal minorities in the mountain districts of eastern Laos on behalf of the ICP.

In 1950, the Viet Minh-supported Free Lao Front (Neo Lao Issara, often incorrectly translated as 'Lao Freedom Front') and the

Lao Resistance Government under Prince Souphanouvong were founded in eastern Laos to fight French colonial influences in Laos.

The 25 years that led to the Lao communist takeover in 1975 encompassed a somewhat bewildering succession of political changes – just keeping track of all the name changes requires an almost prodigious memory. First, the ICP reconstituted itself as the Vietnamese Workers Party in 1951, with plans to organise separate covert parties in Laos (the Lao People's Party) and Cambodia (the Cambodian People's Party) as well. The first use of the term Pathet Lao (Land of the Lao) came in an international communiqué released by the Free Lao Front in 1954 and referred specifically to the tactical forces of the FLF (and later the Patriotic Lao Front). In 1965, the name was changed to the Lao People's Liberation Army (LPRA), but for the international media, the term Pathet Lao (PL) became generally applied to the Vietnamese-supported liberation movement in Laos.

In 1953-4, the Kingdom of Laos was governed by a constitutional monarchy along European lines. A French-educated elite ran the government, while the Lao resistance in the countryside increased. The US government, anxious to counter the Viet Minh influence in South-East Asia, began pouring aid into Laos to assure loyalty to the 'democratic cause'. During this same period, Viet Minh and PL troops claimed the northeastern Lao provinces of Hua Phan and Phong Sali following the Geneva Conference of 1954, which sanctioned the takeover 'pending political settlement'.

In 1955 a clandestine Communist party was officially formed in Sam Neua (Hua Phan Province) under the name Lao People's Party (LPP), consisting of 25 former ICP members. In reality, this group had existed since 1951 when the ICP split into three groups representing Vietnam, Laos and Cambodia. The LPP set up a national front in early '56 called the Lao Patriotic Front (LPF, known in Lao as Neo Lao Hak Sat or NLHS – which ought really to be translated as Patriotic Lao Front). The LPP, like its counterpart in Cambodia, was a member of the Indochinese United Front, which was led by the Vietnamese Workers Party.

Coalition & Dissolution

In 1957, the participants at the Geneva Conference had finally reached a settlement. The LPF and the Royal Lao Government agreed to a coalition government (under the RLG's Prince Souvanna Phouma) called the Government of National Union. Two LPF ministers and their deputies were admitted at the national level.

According to the Geneva agreement, the 1500 PL troops in the north-east were supposed to be absorbed into the Royal Lao Army, but disagreements over rank precluded a successful merger. When a 1958 National Assembly election in the two northeastern provinces demonstrated unexpected LPF support among the general populace (13 out of 21 seats), there was a right-wing reaction that led to the arrest of LPF ministers and deputies, and the re-entrenchment of PL troops in the countryside. This government reaction was undoubtedly fuelled by the US government's withdrawal of all aid to Laos (which by this point made up the bulk of the Lao national budget) following the electoral results.

The fall of the Government of National Union left the Wieng Chan government under the dominance of the Committee for the Defense of National Interests (CDNI), which was made up of extreme right-wing military officers and French-educated elites. The CDNI had strong US backing. Phoui Sananikone was installed as prime minister and Prince Souvanna Phouma was made the Lao ambassador to France. But within a year of their arrest, Prince Souphanouvong and his LPF colleagues had escaped and were again leading the resistance in the countryside.

When a 1959 UN investigation declared that the PL were not using regular North Vietnamese troops, the Wieng Chan government was strongly advised to adopt a more neutral policy toward the LPF.

The PL was definitely receiving North Vietnamese support in the form of resident political and military advisors throughout this period, however. The North Vietnamese, in fact, took virtual control of the sparsely populated eastern Laos to use as a supply route (the 'Ho Chi Minh Trail') to the Viet Cong in South Vietnam. In the north and north-east, the North Vietnamese assisted the PL in gaining control over the tribal mountain-dwellers. Once again, to counter the North Vietnamese presence, the USA began pouring aid into Laos, this time mostly for direct military use.

Coup & Counter-Coup

In August 1960, a neutralist military faction led by Kong Le seized Wieng Chan in a coup d'état and recalled Prince Souvanna Phouma from France to serve as prime minister. Rightist General Phoumi Novasan at first agreed to support the new government and to allow LPF participation but in a few months changed his mind and withdrew with his troops to southern Laos. In December he launched an attack on Wieng Chan and wrested control from the neutralists. Kong Le and his troops retreated to Xieng Khwang, where they joined forces with the PL and North Vietnamese. The Soviet Union supplied this new coalition with armaments and by 1961 they held virtually all of northern and eastern Laos.

A superpower confrontation threatened to erupt when the USA announced that it would intervene with US troops to prevent what was perceived as a communist takeover of Laos. A 14-nation conference convened in Geneva in May 1961 to try and abate the crisis. Both sides held their ground, awaiting the outcome of the conference. In May 1962, after long internal and international negotiations, a set of agreements were signed which provided for an independent, neutral Laos. The observance of these agreements were to be monitored by the International Commission for Supervision & Control (ICSC). A second Government of National Union was formed the following month, a coalition of Prince Boun Oum (representing the rightist

military), Prince Souphanouvong (for the PL) and Prince Souvanna Phouma (for the neutralist military).

This second attempt at a coalition government didn't last long. Minor skirmishes occurred between PL and neutralist troops over the administration of the north-east. The PL seriously upset the tripartite balance of power by attacking Kong Le's neutralist headquarters in Xieng Khwang, thus forcing Kong Le into an alliance with the rightists to avoid defeat.

In 1964, there was a rapid series of coups and counter-coups that resulted in the final alignment of the PL on the one side and the neutralist and right-wing factions on the other. From this point on, the PL leadership refused to participate in any offers of coalition or national elections, quite justifiably believing that they would never be given a voice in governing the country as long as either of the other two factions were in power.

The War of Resistance

From 1964 to 1973, the war in Indochina heated up. US air bases were established in Thailand, and US bombers were soon crisscrossing eastern and north-eastern Laos on their way to and from bombing missions in North Vietnam and along the Ho Chi Minh trail. Secret saturation bombing of PL strongholds was carried out, but the PL simply moved their headquarters into caves near Sam Neua. Even without specific targets, B-52 captains would empty their bomb bays over civilian centres in eastern Laos when returning from Vietnamese air strikes so that their orders to release all bombs would be fulfilled. The USA, in fact, dropped more bombs on Laos than they did worldwide during WW II; Laos has thus earned the distinction of being the most heavily bombed nation, on a per capita basis, in the history of warfare.

As guerrilla resistance in South Vietnam increased, the US military leadership feared that bombing Laos wasn't enough, so they began forming a special CIA-trained army in the country to counter the growing influence of the Pathet Lao. This army of 10,000 was largely made up of Hmong tribesmen under the direct command of the Royal Lao Army General Vang Pao, himself a Hmong. These troops were a division of the RLA that was trained for mountain warfare and were not, as has been claimed, mercenaries in the true sense of the term. Like the South Vietnamese army, however, they were US-trained (in the case of Laos, also Thai-trained) and US-paid. By the end of the '60s, there were more Thais and Lao Theung than Hmong in the RLA.

Revolution & Reform

In 1973, as the USA began negotiating its way out of Vietnam, a cease-fire agreement was reached in Laos. The country was effectively divided into PL and non-PL zones, just as it had been in 1954. Only this time the communists controlled eleven of thirteen provinces instead of two. A Provisional Government of National Union (PGNU) was formed after long negotiations and the two sides began trying to form yet another coalition government. Popular support for the PL grew as the non-PL Wieng Chan leadership showed increasing signs of corruption and US manipulation.

The unexpectedly rapid fall of Saigon and Phnom Penh following US withdrawal in April 1975 led the PL to seize Sala Phou Khoun, a strategic crossroads between Luang Phabang and Wieng Chan. The LPP applied political pressure to non-PL ministers and generals as well, urging them to resign. Luang Phabang and Wieng Chan were papered over with threatening PL posters that left little to the imagination as to what the alternative to resignation might be.

On the 4 May 1975, four ministers and seven generals resigned and an exodus of the Lao political and commercial elite across the Mekong into Thailand began. PL forces then seized the southern provincial capitals of Pak Se, Champasak and Savannakhet without opposition and on 23 August they took Vientiane in a similar manner. Over the following months, the PGNU was quietly dismantled and in December the Lao People's Revolu-

tionary Party (LPRP) was declared the ruling party of the newly christened Lao People's Democratic Republic. Kaysone Phomvihane, a long-time protegé of the North Vietnamese, has served as the Prime Minister of the LPDR ever since.

Observers of East European politics may notice a close similarity between the 1975 revolution in Laos and the communist takeover in Czechoslovakia in 1948. Both involved national fronts, supported by covert Marxist-Leninist parties, which effected semilegal changes of power through a combination of popular support and armed threats. Furthermore, both countries were in the shadow of intimidating foreign armies stationed at nearby borders, ready to intervene at any moment (the Soviets in the case of Czechoslovakia, the Vietnamese in the case of Laos).

During the first 2 years of LPRP rule, harsh political and economic policies caused thousands of refugees to leave the country. The government followed the Vietnamese policy of 'accelerated socialisation' through a rapid reduction of the private sector and a steep increase in agricultural cooperativisation.

The practice of the traditional Lao religion, Buddhism, was also severely curtailed (see the Religion section in this chapter for more detail).

At first King Savang Vatthana was given a figurehead role in the new government. But in early 1977, anti-communist rebels briefly seized Muang Non, 50 km south of Luang Phabang. When government forces regained the village, the captured rebels supposedly implicated the monarchy. Immediately thereafter, the king and his family were banished to Viengsai, a village in northern Laos on the Vietnamese border. Although it was announced that the King would be attending a *samana*, or re-education camp, neither he nor anyone in his family has been heard of since.

By mid-1979, this repression had resulted in widespread unrest among the peasants, the traditional power base for Lao communism. As in Vietnam, liberal reforms were undertaken, but in Laos the liberalisation went further (see the Economics & Religion sections in this chapter). But the gradual reforms were unfortunately too little, too late to prevent the further reduction of an already small population. By the end of the '70s, Lao refugees (including hill tribes) in Thailand constituted 85% of all Indochinese with official refugee status. Unlike the Vietnamese, who had to undertake perilous sea journeys, or the Cambodians, who braved the equally perilous Dang Rek Mountains and the 'killing fields' of the Khmer Rouge, Lao refugees had but to cross the Mekong to escape the change of governments. The UN estimated that over 150,000 refugees from Laos were still in Thailand in the '80s, while tens of thousands have been resettled in other countries. In Laos, as many as 40,000 people have been sent to re-education camps and 30,000 imprisoned since the PL takeover.

The influence of the USSR's glasnost and perestroika policies undoubtedly contributed to further reform in the LPDR during the '80s. As in other socialist nations, there has been an on-going power struggle between the old hard-liners and the younger Party and non-Party leadership, who seek further liberalisation. In Laos, this is compounded by two conflicting tendencies for policy development. One tendency has been for the Lao leadership to follow the Vietnamese example, the other to implement policies that are developed specifically for the Lao situation. The second tendency has appeared to gain more and more strength during recent years. But the flourishing of a truly Lao socialism, if such is possible, is still hampered by the direct and (at this point) unavoidable Vietnamese influence on Lao affairs. Those who push for liberalisation always run the risk of being labelled *patikan* (reactionaries).

Historically, virtually all Lao polities from the early *muang* to the LPDR have been dependent on some greater Asian power, whether it be the Siamese, Burmese, Khmer, or Vietnamese. Sometimes as many as three of these at one time have exacted tribute, as in the case of 16th-century Lan Xang – a vassal of Siam, Burma and Vietnam. Add to this the fact that three Western powers (France, the USA and the USSR) have contributed greatly to the destabilisation of the Asian balance of power, and the result has been a Laos that has never quite been able to establish a stable, separate national entity.

When compared with the country's long history of civil and international war, however, the current state of Lao affairs seems relatively peaceful and stable. A repatriation program has been agreed upon by Thai and Lao authorities in an effort to see that many of the Lao refugees still in Thailand will return to Laos over the next few years. Following the serendipitous events of 1989-90 in Eastern Europe, perhaps we can expect a similar progression of pluralism and self-determination among Indochinese states.

For the moment, however, Vietnamese party officials have announced that absolutely no nonparty members will ever be allowed a share in governing any part of Vietnam, Cambodia and Laos. It remains to be seen whether the Lao will continue to tolerate an externally directed, one-party system on behalf of the Vietnamese.

GEOGRAPHY

Laos is a landlocked country which shares borders with Thailand, Cambodia, Vietnam, China and Myanmar. It covers 235,000 sq km, an area slightly larger than Great Britain. All of Laos is within the tropics, between latitudes 14° and 23° and longitudes 100° and 108°. Two main physical features, rivers and mountains, dominate the topography. Mountains and plateaus cover well over 70% of the country. All rivers and tributaries west of the Annamite Chain of mountains drain into the Mekong River, which flows from Laos through Cambodia and into the South China Sea via the Mekong Delta in southern Vietnam. Waterways east of the Annamites, in the provinces of Hua Phan and Xieng Khwang, eventually flow into the Gulf of Tonkin.

The Mekong River (Mae Nam Khong) has its source far away in China's Qinghai Province and forms the country's borders with Thailand as well as Myanmar. The Mekong flows over 1800 km along these borders and has traditionally served as the country's lifeline (especially when Lao principalities ruled both sides of the river prior to French and Siamese political surgery). The river is navigable year-round between Luang Phabang and Savannakhet, and hence is a major transportation link between the north and the south. The Mekong River Valley and its fertile flood plains form the country's primary agricultural zones as well, including virtually all of the country's wet-rice lands. The two largest valley sections are near Vientiane and Savannakhet, and these are, as a result, the major population centres. The Mekong and its tributaries are also an important source of fish, a mainstay of the Lao diet.

Major tributaries of the Mekong include the Nam Ou and the Nam Tha, both of which flow through deep, narrow limestone valleys from the north, and the Nam Ngum, which flows into the Mekong across a broad alluvial plain in Vientiane Province. This latter river is the site of a large hydroelectric plant that is a primary source of power for Vientiane area towns. Electricity generated at the plant is also sold to Thailand and is an important source of revenue for the country.

Running about half the length of Laos, parallel to the course of the Mekong River, is the Annamite Chain, a rugged mountain range with peaks averaging 1600 to 3000 metres in height. Roughly in the centre of the range is the Khammuan Plateau, an area of striking limestone grottoes and gorges. At the southern end of the Annamite Chain is the 10,000 sq km Boloven Plateau, an important area for the cultivation of high-yield mountain rice, coffee, tea and other crops that flourish at higher altitudes.

The larger, northern half of Laos is made up almost entirely of broken, steep-sloped mountain ranges. The highest mountains are found in Xieng Khwang Province, where peaks exceeding 2000 metres are not unusual. Phu Bia, the country's highest peak at about 3000 metres, is in Xieng Khwang.

Just north of Phu Bia is the country's largest mountain plateau, the Xieng Khwang Plateau, which rises 1200 metres above sea level. The most famous part of the plateau is the Plain of Jars, an area dotted with huge prehistoric stone jars of unknown origin.

CLIMATE

The annual Asian monsoon cycles that affect all of mainland South-East Asia produce two general seasons in Laos: the wet from May to October and the dry from November to April. Average precipitation varies considerably according to latitude and altitude, with southern Laos getting the most rain overall. The peaks of the Annamite Chain receive the heaviest rainfall, over 300 cm annually. The provinces of Luang Phabang, Sayabuli and Xieng Khwang, for the most part, receive only 100 to 150 cm a year. Vientiane and Savannakhet get about 150 to 200 cm, as do Phong Sali, Luang Nam Tha and Bokeo.

Temperatures vary according to altitude as well. In the Mekong River Valley from Bokeo Province to Champasak Province, as in most of Thailand and Myanmar, the highest temperatures occur in March and April (with temperatures approaching 38°C), the lowest in December and January (dropping as low as 15°C). In the mountains of Xieng Khwang, however, December-January temperatures can easily drop to 0° C at night; in mountainous provinces of lesser elevation, temperatures may be 5 to 10 degrees higher. During most of the rainy season, daytime temperatures average around 29°C in the lowlands, and around 25°C in mountain valleys.

GOVERNMENT

Since 2 December 1975, the official name of the country has been the Lao People's Democratic Republic (Sathalanalat Pasathipatai Pasason Lao). Informally, it is acceptable to call the country Laos, which in the Lao language is *Pathet Lao* – *pathet* means 'land' or 'country', from the Sanskrit *pradesha*.

Following the 1975 takeover, the former pro-Western, monarchical regime was replaced by a government which espoused a

Marxist-Leninist political philosophy in alignment with other communist states, most explicitly the Socialist Republic of Vietnam, the People's Republic of Kampuchea (now the State of Cambodia) and the USSR.

The Party

The central ruling body in Laos is the Lao People's Revolutionary Party (LPRP), which is modelled on the Vietnamese Communist Party. The LPRP is directed by the Party Congress, which meets every 4 or 5 years to elect party leaders. Other important party organs include the Political Bureau (Politburo), the Central Committee and the Permanent Secretariat.

The party ideal is a 'proletarian dictatorship', as proclaimed by Secretary-General Kaysone Phomvihane in 1977:

To lead the revolution, the working class must act with the help of its general staff, that is to say the political party of the working class, the Marxist-Leninist Party. In our country it is the LPRP which is the sole authentic representative of the interests of the working class, of the working masses of all ethnic groups in the Lao nation.

Despite the claim to proletarianism, membership in the LPRP has consisted mainly of peasant farmers and tribespeople from various ethnic groups, though urban worker membership has increased since the 1975 Revolution. Before the revolution, party membership was about 60% Lao Theung (hill tribes also known as *Kha*), 36% Lao Lum (lowland Lao) and 4% Lao Sung (Hmong and Mien hill tribes). Percentages are not known by anyone outside Laos.

The main seat of LPRP power, as in most communist parties, is the Politburo, which officially makes all policy decisions. In theory, members of the Politburo are selected by the Party Central Committee. In practice, since the Secretary-General of the Politburo, the Secretariat and the Central Committee are all one man, Kaysone Phomvihane (who is also the Prime Minister of the Council of Government), virtually all members of these major party organs are coopted by Kaysone,

who has enjoyed the full support of the Vietnamese since the '40s.

Kaysone was born in 1920 in Savannakhet of a Vietnamese father and Lao mother. Much of his early life was spent in Hanoi, where he studied law. Assisted by the Viet Minh, he helped organise the Lao Issara resistance movement in the '40s. His role in modern Lao politics cannot be overestimated. Nor can the role of the Vietnamese, who at last count still had 50,000 troops stationed in Laos.

Administration

The LPDR government is structured along Socialist Republic of Vietnam (SRV) lines. The Council of Government, like the SRV's Council of Ministers, consists of twelve ministries (eg, the Ministry of Propaganda, Information, Culture and Tourism). In addition to the Council of Government, there is the Office of the Prime Minister, the National Bank, the National Planning Committee and the Nationalities Committee.

The Supreme People's Assembly (SPA) serves as the government's legislative body and is modelled on the SRV's National Assembly and the USSR's Supreme Soviet. Since the revolution, total membership in the SPA has varied between 40 and 45. About two-thirds of the members are drawn from the LPRP, the Lao Front for National Construction and the Alliance of Lao Patriotic Neutralist Forces (a group of military officers aligned with the Lao People's Revolutionary Army); the remaining third is drawn from groups sympathetic to the left. The SPA's main function thus far has been to meet once a year to approve declarations of the prime minister.

For 15 years following the revolution, the LPDR had no constitution. The first official Constitution was drafted in mid-1990 by the Party for the approval of the Supreme People's Assembly. Interestingly enough, it contains no reference to socialism in the economy but formalises private trade and foreign investment. The Constitution also removed the hammer and sickle from the official national symbol to be used on government signs and stationery.

The LPDR's first legal code wasn't enacted until 1988, the same year that Vientiane began looking abroad for foreign capital. The new canon established a court system, prosecutor's office, criminal trial rules and one of the most liberal foreign investment codes in Asia.

Lao Front for National Construction

The Lao Front for National Construction (LFNC) was formed in 1979 to take the place of the old Lao Patriotic Front, which had been in existence since 1956 as a political cover for the clandestine Lao People's Party. It's new incarnation was intended to quell unrest among the general population by providing mass participation in a nationalistic effort, much like the Fatherland Front in the SRV. In other words, you don't have to be a Party member to join, as long as you follow Party principles.

The LFNC is comprised of the LPRP, the Federation of Lao Trade Unions, the Federation of Lao Peasants, the Association of Women and other groups originally organised by the Party. The Front is administered by a National Congress (the general membership), a Presidium (headed by ageing President Souphanouvong), a Secretariat, a Central Committee and local committees at the village, canton, district and provincial levels.

Like the SPA, the LFNC has no real power and appears mainly to serve as a rubber stamp apparatus for LPDR policies. There is a potential for pluralism in the Lao government structure, however, which may eventually be realised (assuming current East European trends are paralleled).

Political Divisions

Laos is divided into 16 provinces (*khwaeng*): Wieng Chan (Vientiane), Sayabuli, Luang Phabang, Luang Nam Tha, Xieng Khwang, Hua Phan (Houa Phan), Phong Sali, Bokeo, Udomsai (Udomxai), Bolikhamsai, Khammuan (Khammouane), Savannakhet, Salavan (Saravan), Sekong, Attapeu and

Champasak. In addition, Vientiane (Kamphaeng Nakhon Wieng Chan) is an independent prefecture on an administrative parity with the provinces.

Below the province is the *muang* or district, which is comprised of two or more *tasseng* (sub-districts or cantons), which are in turn divided into *ban*, or villages.

ECONOMY

About 80% of the Lao population is engaged in agriculture, fishing and forestry; another 10% is employed in the armed forces or in the civil service. This breakdown remained virtually the same before and after the 1975 Revolution. Laos has been dependent on foreign aid since the '50s, however, and the amounts and sources of aid have varied greatly over the intervening years.

Between 1968 and 1973, when US aid to the Royal Government of Laos was at is peak (averaging about US\$74.4 million a year), the Lao were among the highest recipients of aid per capita in the world. This aid of course, was enjoyed by those in the RLG Vientiane zone and not by those in the Pathet Lao 'liberated zone' (who got falling US bombs instead). During this period (and back as far as 1964, when the War of Resistance really began), the 11 provinces of the liberated zone existed on a subsistence economy supplemented by commodity assistance from the USSR, China and North Vietnam.

After the termination of US aid in 1975, the Vientiane economy collapsed and the new government found itself struggling to manage a virtually bankrupt state. Until 1979, policies of 'accelerated socialisation' (nationalisation of private sector businesses and collectivisation of all agriculture) only made conditions worse. In July 1979, however, the government stopped the creation of new collectives and ordered the consolidation of existing ones, admitting that most Lao peasants were dissatisfied with the system.

Under the new policy, a certain amount of free enterprise was allowed at the village level. For example, families were given permission to cultivate individual rice fields, although major farming activities (clearing fields, planting, weeding and harvesting) were to be carried out cooperatively. Anyone familiar with rice farming in mainland South-East Asia knows that this is exactly how it's done traditionally, even in capitalist countries like Thailand. Rice harvests in Laos are divided into three portions: one for the state, one for the village rice bank, and one for the family (according to a per capita ration system) for sale or consumption.

The LPRP has also made radical changes in monetary policy (allowing a free-floating currency) and commodity pricing (bringing prices closer to free market rates), with the result that by the end of the '80s the economy appeared to be relatively stable. Both consumer goods and agricultural products are widely available. The exception is in the rural areas of the south, where temporary rice shortages are still common.

In 1987, the government further loosened restrictions on private enterprise. Prior to that year, only about half of the shophouses along Vientiane's main commercial avenue, Thanon Samsenthai, were open. By the end of 1989, at least three-quarters had opened their doors. Foreign, private investment is now welcome in Laos, most of which comes from Thailand. Laos and Thailand have even opened a jointly owned and operated bank in Vientiane. Japan, Australia and France have also shown interest in investing in Laos.

But the credit for economic stabilisation can't go all to the lionisation of the economy per se. Foreign aid has also greatly increased since 1980, making up as much as 78% of the national budget in certain years. Asian Development Bank loans and other kinds of credit have also increased as the country's credit image has improved. UN agencies like UNESCO and the United Nations Development Programme are pouring funds and personnel into Laos as the country again becomes a player in the development game. Non-governmental organisations such as Save the Children and World Concern are also present.

Yet another reason the economy is doing comparatively well is due to the tolerance of the free, or 'black', market (*talat meut*). Markets everywhere in Laos trade freely in untaxed goods smuggled from Thailand (and elsewhere) and the changing of currency (mostly US dollars and Thai baht) at free market rates is quite open. Moneychangers even have street stalls in Vientiane.

On an international scale, however, Laos is still one of the poorest countries in the world. The annual per capita income in 1989 was US$135, which placed Laos ahead of Vietnam (US$130) and Cambodia (less than US$130) but below Bangladesh (US$175) and Bhutan (US$160). Gross National Product growth in 1989 was estimated to be 4.5% per annum. On the bright side, Laos has one of the lowest foreign debts in Asia – US$0.7 billion (compared with US$10 billion in Vietnam, US$6 billion in Burma, US$15.5 billion in Thailand or US$0.6 billion in Cambodia).

Inflation in Laos, when measured according to the national currency (*kip*), is running at a high 65%. However, in US dollar terms, which along with the Thai baht is for all intents and purposes the currency standard in the LPDR, inflation is much more modest – perhaps around 30% per annum.

Laos' greatest economic potential lies in its natural resources, which have yet to be fully exploited.

Agriculture & Forestry

Only around 10% of the total land area in Laos is considered suitable for agriculture. Cultivation is carried out according to dual patterns, one for the lowlands and one for the highlands. Lowland agriculture involves permanent farming communities which employ irrigated fields; in the highlands, farming communities are to some extent migrational, preferring to use swidden ('slash-and-burn') methods in which forest areas are cut to the ground and burned in preparation for planting. Laos is currently trying to discourage swidden agriculture among the highland peoples, in order to prevent deforestation.

Important crops in the lowlands include wet rice, corn, wheat, cotton, fruits and vegetables. In the mountains, dry rice, tobacco, tea, coffee and opium are the major cash crops.

Opium is a major source of income for Laos, since it is the only country in South-East Asia that permits legal cultivation and sale. It is estimated that in 1987 the total production of opium in Laos approached 300 tons (compared with 100 tonnes in colonial Laos 35 years earlier). The legal sale of opium is a government monopoly, but much (perhaps most) of the product leaves the country along smuggling routes through Thailand. Some is also refined into heroin in semiclandestine laboratories in the north, and then smuggled out of the country. The government disclaims any knowledge of the heroin refineries, but curiously the very areas which drug trafficking experts indicate as lab locations are absolutely off limits to any tourist or foreign resident.

Since about two-thirds of the country is forested, timber is also an important product and is developing into one of Laos' biggest exports. Teak is the most important wood for export earnings, followed by secondary forest products like benzoin, a resin used to manufacture perfume, and cardamom, a spice.

Minerals

Laos is rich in mineral resources, including tin, coal, oil, iron, copper, gold, phosphorite, gypsum, zinc and salt, which are just starting to be exploited.

Hydroelectric Power

The Nam Ngum Dam, 70 km north of Vientiane, generates most of the electricity used in the Vientiane Valley. In addition, Thailand buys about 850 million kilowatt-hours per year from Laos, via high power lines that stretch across the Mekong and as far away as the Udon Thani, Thailand.

Fishing

The rivers in Laos yield a steady supply of fish, an important source of nutrition for the general population. The huge lake (370 sq km) created by the damming of the Nam Ngum is being used for a number of experimental fisheries. If these and other fishery projects are successful, Laos will probably begin exporting freshwater fish to Thailand in the future.

Manufacturing

So far in Laos there is little manufacturing to speak of. Though most manufactured goods used in the country are imported from Thailand or elsewhere, there are a few factories in Vientiane that produce soft drinks, beer, cigarettes, bricks and cement. Increased foreign investment may eventually involve joint manufacturing ventures, though Laos doesn't have as large and skilled a labour force as Vietnam, which is currently a target of such ventures.

POPULATION

An accurate census of the Laos population hasn't been taken since the early '60s. The current total is estimated to be around 3.8 million, with an average annual growth rate of 2.9%. As many as 10% of the population may have fled the country since 1975. The population density is one of the lowest in Asia, about 15 people per sq km.

Roughly half the population are ethnic Lao. Of the remaining half, 10% to 20% are estimated to be tribal Thai, 20 % to 30% are Lao Theung (lower mountain-dwellers mostly of proto-Malay or Mon-Khmer descent) and 10% to 20% are Lao Sung (Hmong or Mien tribes who live at higher altitudes).

PEOPLE

The people of Laos traditionally divide themselves into four categories: Lao Lum, Lao Thai, Lao Theung and Lao Sung. This classification follows a stepwise increase in elevation according to traditional habitat, beginning in the alluvial plains of the Mekong River and arriving finally at the highest peaks of the northern mountain ranges.

Lao Lum

The Lao Lum (Low Lao) are the ethnic Lao

who have traditionally resided in the Mekong River Valley or along lower tributaries of the Mekong and who speak the Lao language. They are an ethnic subgroup of the Thai peoples who have proliferated throughout South-East Asia, south China, and the north-eastern Indian subcontinent (see the History section of this chapter for more detail on Thai migration routes). The Lao Lum culture has traditionally consisted of a sedentary, subsistence lifestyle based on wet-rice (with glutinous rice or *khao nio* the preferred variety) cultivation. The Lao, like all Thais, were originally animists (followers of earth spirit cults) who took on Theravada Buddhism as their main religion in the middle of the first Christian millennium.

Lao Thai

These are Thai subgroups closely related to the Lao who are more 'tribal' in character; that is, they have resisted absorption into mainstream Lao culture and tend to subdivide themselves according to smaller group distinctions. Like the Lao Lum, they live along river valleys, but the Lao Thai have chosen to reside in upland valleys rather than in the lowlands of the Mekong flood plains.

The Lao Thai cultivate dry or mountain rice as well as wet, or irrigated, rice. Some still practise swidden agriculture. In general, they have maintained animist beliefs and eschewed conversion to Buddhism or Christianity.

The various Lao Thai groups are distinguished from one another by the colour of their clothing or general area of habitation, eg Black Thai, White Thai, Red Thai, Forest Thai, North Thai and so on.

Thai Dam

The most predominant tribe is the Thai Dam (Black Thai), who live in the upland valleys of north and eastern Laos, especially Xieng Khwang and Hua Phan provinces. As their name suggests, black is the preponderant colour of their traditional garb. A fairly large number of Thai Dam, 1950s refugees from North Vietnam's Dien Bien Phu, also live in Vientiane Province.

The Thai Dam have a caste system that divides them into three classes: the *phu tao*, or nobility; the *phu noi*, or commoners; and the *maw*, or priests. Of all the Lao Thai groups, the Thai Dam are considered the most archetypical since their traditions have been so well preserved over the centuries. Among the Lao, they are known for their honesty and industriousness.

Lao Theung

The Lao Theung (Approaching-the-Top Lao) are a loose affiliation of mostly Mon-Khmer peoples who live on mid-altitude mountain slopes in northern Laos. The most numerous group is the Khamu, followed by the Lamet. The Lao Theung are also known by the pejorative term *Kha*, which means 'slave' or 'servant' in the Lao language. This is because they were used as indentured labour by migrating Thai peoples in earlier centuries and more recently by the Lao monarchy. Today, they still often work as labourers for the Lao Sung. The Lao Theung have a much lower standard of living than any of the three other groups described here. Most trade between the Lao Theung and other Lao is carried out by barter. Metal tools are not common among the Khamu and Lamet, who rely mostly on wood, bamboo and stone implements.

Most of the Khamu are swidden agriculturists who grow mountain rice, coffee, tobacco and cotton. Traditionally they are animists, though many of those living near Lao centres have converted to Theravada Buddhism and a few are Christians.

Other ethnic groups included under the Lao Theung rubric include small groups of proto-Malays and Tibeto-Burmans living in northern and southern Laos.

Lao Sung

The Lao Sung (High Lao), include those hill tribes who make their residence at altitudes greater than 1000 metres above sea level. Of all the peoples of Laos, they are the most recent immigrants, having come from Burma (now Myanmar), Tibet and southern China within the last century.

The largest group are the Hmong, also called Miao or Meo, who probably number around 200,000. The agricultural staples of the Hmong are dry rice and corn raised by the slash-and-burn method. They also are adroit at raising cattle, pigs, water buffalo and chickens. For the most part, theirs is a barter economy in which iron is the medium of exchange. Iron is important for the crafting of machetes and flintlock rifles for land-clearing and hunting. Their one cash crop is opium, which they manufacture more of than any other group in Laos. The Hmong are most numerous in the provinces of Hua Phan, Xieng Khwang and Luang Phabang.

The second largest group are the Mien (also called Iu Mien, Yao and Man), who number 30,000 to 50,000 and live mainly in Luang Nam Tha Province. The Mien and Hmong have many ethnic and linguistic similarities but intermarriage is rare. Both groups have a sophisticated social structure that extends beyond the village level and both groups are predominantly animist. The Mien, like the Hmong, are poppy cultivators.

The Hmong are considered more aggressive and war-like, however, and as such were perfect for the CIA-trained special RLG forces under General Vang Pao in the '60s and early '70s. The anti-communist resistance groups that still exist today in Laos are mostly Hmong.

Large numbers of Hmong and Mien left Laos following the 1975 takeover and are now living as refugees in France, the USA and other Western countries. Although it is often claimed that this is because they were 'mercenaries' of the USA (see the History section for more detail), the fact is that the vast majority of Hmong and Mien who left Laos had no involvement in the war. However, it's possible they left out of fear that they would be persecuted because of the active Hmong participation that did occur.

Other much smaller Tibeto-Burman hill-tribe groups in Laos include the Akha, Lisu and Lahu. Sometimes these are included under the heading of Lao Theung since they live at slightly lower elevations than the Hmong and Mien. Like the Hmong and the Mien, they live in the mountains of northern Laos.

Other Asians

As elsewhere in South-East Asia, the Chinese have been migrating to Laos for centuries to work as merchants and traders. Most came direct from Yunnan but more recently, many have been arriving from Vietnam. Estimates of their presence varies from 2% to 5% per cent of the total population but at least half of all Chinese in Laos are said to live in Vientiane and Savannakhet. Most restaurants, cinemas, hotels, repair shops and jewellery shops in these towns are owned by ethnic Chinese.

In recent decades, many Thais have come to Laos as well. Unlike the Chinese, they tend not to settle in Laos but to come for short intervals during which they engage in business or aid and education projects. Since the Thai-Lao rapprochement of the '80s, Thais are coming in ever-increasing numbers; like the Chinese, they tend to be found in the cities, but it's not unusual to run into Thais upcountry as well, working on rural aid projects.

In Vientiane there is also a small but visible number of north Indians and Pakistanis who run tailor and fabric shops. For some reason, they also seem to make up a good portion of FAO, WHO and UN teams working in Laos as well (along with Bangladeshis and Burmese).

In southern Laos, especially in Champasak Province, live small numbers of Cambodians. Most commonly they work as truck drivers and boatmen involved in legal and illegal trade between Laos, Cambodia and Thailand. A few Cambodians are stationed in Vientiane as members of Indochinese political committees.

Europeans

Most of the expatriate Europeans living in Laos (less than 300 in all) are temporary contract employees of nongovernmental organisations such as UNESCO, FAO, the Red Cross, the Mennonite Central Committee, the Mekong Committee, or various bilateral aid programmes such as the Lao-Australian Irrigation Project, the Lao-Swedish Forestry Programme and so on. Virtually all of them live in huge government-provided mansions in east Vientiane, just like they did before 1975. The exceptions are the aid workers from the USSR and Eastern Europe, who generally are on much lower stipends than their Western counterparts – they tend to live in nondescript housing projects on the outskirts of Vientiane.

Very few people of European descent, whether from the West or the East, have been allowed permanent residence in the Laos. For some nationalities, quotas limit the total number from one nation that can be working in Laos at a given time (eg Americans, whose numbers are limited to 30).

CULTURE
Architecture

In architecture, Laos never really distinguished itself. Partially this is because many structures were built of wood: fire, weather and invading armies have left few wooden structures in Laos that hail from the pre-eminent 16th to 18th centuries.

The most unique edifice in Laos is the That Luang, or Great Stupa, in Vientiane (see Vientiane section for more specific detail). A *that* (from the Pali-Sanskrit *dhatu*, meaning 'element' or 'component part') is a spire or dome-like structure that commemorates the life of the Buddha. The distinctive shape may have been inspired by the staff and begging bowl of the wandering Buddha. Many *that* are said to contain sacred relics (*dhatu*) – parts of the Buddha's body, eg a hair, nail or piece of bone. Considering the number of *that* throughout Buddhist Asia, it is very unlikely that all those which claim to contain Buddha relics actually do.

The curvilinear, four-cornered superstructure at That Luang is the Lao standard – most stupas of truly Lao origin are modelled on this one (you'll also see Lao stupas in northeastern Thailand, which is mostly populated by ethnic Lao). Other types of stupas in Laos are either Siamese or Khmer-inspired. An

exception is the That Mak Mo, or Watermelon Stupa, in Luang Phabang which is semi-spherical in shape – of possible Sinhalese influence but still distinctive.

The *uposatha*, or 'chapel' (*Lao: sim*), where new monks are ordained is always the most important structure in any Theravada Buddhist *wat*, or temple. In Laos, there are basically two architectural styles for such buildings – the Vientiane style and the Luang Phabang style (Xieng Khwang had its own unique temple architecture but unfortunately no examples have survived the war). In Vientiane, *sim* are large rectangular buildings constructed of brick and covered with stucco, much like their counterparts in Thailand. The high-peaked roofs are layered to present several levels (always odd in number – three, five, or seven, occasionally nine) corresponding to various Buddhist doctrines which have been codified into groups of these numbers (the three characteristics of existence, the seven levels of enlightenment, etc). The edges of the roofs almost always feature a repeated flame motif, with long, finger-like hooks at the corners called *chao fa*, or 'sky lords'. Legend has it that these hooks are for catching evil spirits that descend on the *sim* from above.

The front of a Vientiane-style *sim* usually features a large veranda with heavy columns which support an ornamented, overhanging roof. Some Lao *sim* will also have a less-ornamented rear veranda, while those that have a surrounding terrace are Bangkok-influenced. One of the best features of the Vientiane style is the carved wooden shade that often appears along the top portion of the front veranda. Usually the carving depicts a mythical figure such as the half-bird, half-human *kinnari*, or sometimes the Buddha himself, against a background of dense, stylised foliage. The artisans of Lan Xang were extremely adept at this type of woodcarving. Carved porticoes like these represent one of the highlights of Lao art and provide links to sculptural and musical motifs that are seen throughout South-East Asia, from Myanmar to Bali.

In Luang Phabang, the architectural style

is akin to northern Siamese or Lanna style, which is hardly surprising as for several centuries Laos and northern Thailand shared the same kingdoms. As in Vientiane, roofs are layered, but in Luang Phabang they sweep very low, almost reaching the ground in some instances. The overall effect is quite dramatic, as if the *sim* were about to take flight. Luang Phabang temples are also admired for the gold relief on the doors and outside walls of some temple structures. Wat Xieng Thong is a prime example (see the Luang Phabang section for details).

What's a Wat Technically speaking, a *wat* is a Buddhist compound where monks reside; without monks it isn't a *wat*. The word derives from the Pali-Sanskrit term *avasa* which means 'dwelling'. Anywhere in Laos, a typical *wat* will contain the following structures: a *sim*, or *uposatha*; a *haw trai*, or tripitika library where Buddhist scriptures are stored; *kuti*, or monastic quarters; a *haw kawng*, or drum tower; a *sala long tham*, or open-air meeting place where monks and laity listen to *tham* (Sanskrit: *dharma*) or Buddhist doctrine; and various *that* or stupas (the smaller stupas are *that kraduk* or 'bone stupas', where the ashes of worshippers are interred). Many *wats* also have a *haw phii khun wat*, or spirit house, for the temple's reigning earth spirit – in spite of the fact that spirit worship is illegal in Laos today. Various other buildings may be added as needed for *wat* administration, but these are the basics.

Sculpture

As in Thailand, Burma and Cambodia, the focus of most traditional art in Lao culture has been religious, specifically Buddhist. Unlike the art of these other three countries, Lao art never encompassed a broad range of styles and periods, mainly because Laos has had a much more modest history in terms of power and longevity. Furthermore, since Laos was intermittently dominated by its neighbours, much Lao art was destroyed or carried off by the Burmese, Siamese or Khmers.

This doesn't mean, however, that what remains isn't worthy of admiration. Though limited in range, Lao art and architecture can be unique and expressive. Most impressive is Lao sculpture of the 16th to 18th centuries, the heyday of the kingdom of Lan Xang (Million Elephants). Lao sculpture was usually bronze, stone or wood and the subject was invariably the Lord Buddha. Like other Buddhist sculptors, the Lao artisans emphasised features thought to be peculiar to the historical Buddha, including a beak-like nose, extended earlobes, tightly curled hair and so on.

Two types of standing Buddha images are distinctively Lao. The first is the 'Calling for Rain' posture, which depicts the Buddha standing with his hands held rigidly at his side, fingers pointing toward the ground. This posture is never seen in other South-East Asian Buddhist art traditions. The slightly rounded, 'boneless' look of the image recalls Thailand's Sukhothai style, and the way the lower robe is sculpted over the hips looks vaguely Khmer. But the flat, slab-like earlobes, arched eyebrows and very aquiline nose are uniquely Lao. The bottom of the figure's robe curls upward on both sides in a perfectly symmetrical fashion (also uniquely Lao). The whole image gives the distinct impression of a rocket in flight. Considering that the Lao custom at the end of the dry season is to fire bamboo rockets into the sky in a plea for rain, this is probably the artists' desired effect.

The other original Lao image type is the 'Contemplating the Bodhi Tree' Buddha. The Bodhi tree, or 'Tree of Enlightenment', refers to the large banyan tree that the historical Buddha purportedly was sitting beneath when he attained enlightenment in Bodhgaya, India in the 6th century BC. In this image the Buddha is standing in much the same way as in the 'Calling for Rain' pose except that his hands are crossed at the wrists in front of his body.

The finest examples of Lao sculpture are found in Vientiane's Wat Pha Keo and Wat Si Saket and in Luang Phabang's National Museum.

Though uncommon overall, other styles of sculpture from Siam and Angkor can be seen occasionally in Laos.

Folk Crafts

As already noted, the Lao are skilful carvers. This applies not only to *sim* porticoes and gold relief, but to the everyday folk art. Wood and bone are the most popular carving mediums.

Among the Hmong and Mien hill tribes, silversmithing plays an important role in the maintenance of 'portable wealth' and inheritance. Silversmithing and goldsmithing is a traditional Lao art as well but in recent years has been in decline.

Lao weavers are still in top form, however. Traditional wooden looms are in common use in lowland villages, with both cotton and silk as weaving mediums. Woven cloth is sewn into various kinds of clothing and can be used for decoration or in socio-religious ceremonies as well. The most common type of weaving is for the *pha sin*, a long wraparound skirt worn by almost all Lao women. Synthetic dyes are replacing natural, but the resulting materials are always colourful. Gold or silver thread is frequently woven into the borders of fabrics, reminiscent of the *songket* fabric of Malaysia.

Mats and baskets woven of various kinds of straw and reed are also common and are becoming a small but important export to Thailand.

Music & Dance

As in other South-East Asian cultures, music in Laos can be divided into classical and folk traditions. The classical music of Laos is the least interesting, simply because it is so imitative of (but generally inferior to) the classical traditions of Thailand and Cambodia. Lao classical music was originally developed as court music for royal ceremonies and classical dance-drama. The standard ensemble for this genre is called the *sep nyai* and consists of a set of tuned gongs called *khong vong*, a xylophone-like instrument called the *ranynat*, the *khui*, or bamboo flute, and the *pi*, a double-reed wind instrument similar to the oboe. Nowadays, the only time you'll generally hear this type of music is during the occasional public performance of the *Ramakien*, a dance-drama based on the Hindu epic *Ramayana*. The practice of classical Lao music and drama has been in decline for some time now – 40 years of intermittent war and revolution has simply made this kind of entertainment a low priority among most Lao.

Not so with Lao folk music, which has always stayed close to the people. The principal instrument in the folk genre is the *khaen* (French spelling: *khene*), a wind instrument that is devised of a double row of bamboo-like reeds fitted into a hardwood soundbox. The rows can be as few as four or as many as eight. The khaen player blows (as with a harmonica, sound is produced whether the breath is moving in or out of the instrument) into the soundbox while covering or uncovering small holes in the reeds that determine the pitch for each. An adept player is able to produce a churning, calliope-like music that is quite danceable. The most popular folk dance is the *lam wong*, or 'circle dance', in which couples dance circles around one another until there are three circles in all: a circle danced by the individual, the circle danced by the couple, and one danced by the whole crowd.

The *khaen* is often accompanied by the *saw* (sometimes written *so*), a bowed string instrument. In more elaborate ensembles the *khui* and *khong vong* may be added, as well as various hand drums. *Khaen* music can also incorporate a vocalist. Most Lao pop music is based on vocal *khaen* music. Melodies are almost always pentatonic, ie they feature five-note scales.

The Lao folk idiom also has its own theatre, based on the *maw lam* (*mo lam*) tradition. Maw lam is difficult to translate but means something like 'master, or priest, of dance'. Performances always feature a witty, topical combination of talking and singing that ranges across themes as diverse as politics and sex. Very colloquial, even bawdy language is employed; this is one art form that has always bypassed government censors, whether it's the French or the LPRP.

There are four basic types of *maw lam*. The first, *maw lam luang* ('great *maw lam*'), involves an ensemble of performers in costume, on stage. *Maw lam khu* (couple *maw lam)* features a man and woman who engage in flirtation and verbal repartee. *Maw lam chot* ('juxtaposed *maw lam*') has two performers of the same gender who 'duel' by answering questions or finishing an incomplete story issued as a challenge. Finally, *maw lam dio* ('solo *maw lam*') involves only one performer. All types of *maw lam* are most commonly performed at temple fairs and on other festive occasions. You can also commonly hear *maw lam khu* and *maw lam dio* on Lao or north-eastern Thai radio stations.

RELIGION
Theravada Buddhism
About half of the people of the LPDR are Theravada Buddhists. This proportion is mostly lowland Lao, along with a sprinkling of tribal Thais. Buddhism was apparently introduced to Luang Phabang (then Muang Sawa) in the late 13th or early 14th centuries. The first monarch of Lan Xang, King Fa Ngum, was the first to declare Buddhism the state religion, which he did by accepting the Pha Bang Buddha image from his Khmer father-in-law. In 1356 AD, he built a wat in Muang Sawa to house this famous image.

But Buddhism was fairly slow in spreading throughout Laos, even among the lowland peoples, who were reluctant to accept the faith instead or even alongside *phii* or earth spirit worship. King Setthathirat, who ruled Lan Xang from 1547 to 1571, attempted to make Vientiane a regional Buddhist centre, but it wasn't until the reign of King Suliya Vongsa in the mid to late 17th century that Buddhism began to be taught in Lao schools. Since the 17th century, Laos has maintained a continuous Theravadin tradition.

Basically, the Theravada school of Buddhism is an earlier and, according to its followers, less corrupted form of Buddhism than the Mahayana schools found in East Asia or in the Himalayan lands. The Theravada (Teaching of the Elders) school is also called the 'Southern' school since it took the southern route from India, its place of origin, through South-East Asia (Myanmar, Thailand, Laos and Cambodia in this case), while the 'Northern' school proceeded north into Nepal, Tibet, China, Korea, Mongolia, Vietnam and Japan. Because the southern school tried to preserve or limit the Buddhist doctrines to only those canons codified in the early Buddhist era, the northern school gave Theravada Buddhism the name Hinayana, or the 'Lesser Vehicle'. They considered themselves Mahayana, the 'Great Vehicle', because they built upon the earlier teachings, 'expanding' the doctrine in such a way so as to respond more to the needs of lay people, or so it is claimed.

Theravada or Hinayana doctrine stresses the three principal aspects of existence; *dukkha* (suffering, unsatisfactoriness, disease), *anicca* (impermanency, transiency of all things) and *anatta* (non-substantiality or non-essentiality of reality: no permanent 'soul'). These concepts, when 'discovered' by Siddhartha Gautama in the 6th century BC, were in direct contrast to the Hindu belief in an eternal, blissful, Self or *Paramatman*, hence Buddhism was originally a 'heresy' against India's Brahmanic religion.

Gautama, an Indian prince-turned-ascetic, subjected himself to many years of severe austerities to arrive at this vision of the world and was given the title Buddha, 'the Enlightened' or 'the Awakened'. Gautama Buddha spoke of four noble truths which had the power to liberate any human being who could realise them. These four noble truths are:

1) The truth of suffering – 'Existence is suffering'.
2) The truth of the cause of suffering – 'Suffering is caused by desire'.
3) The truth of the cessation of suffering – 'Eliminate the cause of suffering (desire) and suffering will cease to arise'.

4) The truth of the path – 'The eight-fold path is the way to eliminate desire/extinguish suffering'.

The 'eight-fold path' (*atthangika-magga*) consists of: (1) right understanding, (2) right mindedness (or 'right thought'), (3) right speech, (4) right bodily conduct, (5) right livelihood, (6) right effort, (7) right attentiveness and (8) right concentration. These eight limbs belong to three different 'pillars' of practice: morality or *sila* (3 - 5); concentration or *samadhi* (7 & 8); and wisdom or *panna* (1 & 2). Some Buddhists believe the path, called the Middle Way since ideally it avoids both extreme austerity as well as extreme sensuality, is to be taken in successive stages, while others say the pillars are interdependent.

The ultimate goal of Theravada Buddhism is *nibbana* (Sanskrit: *nirvana)* which literally means the 'blowing-out' or 'extinction' of all causes of *dukkha*. Effectively it means an end to all corporeal existence – an end to that which is forever subject to suffering and which is conditioned from moment to moment by *karma* or action. In reality, most Lao Buddhists aim for rebirth in a 'better' existence rather than the supramundane goal of *nibbana*, which is highly misunderstood by Asians as well as Westerners. Many Lao express the feeling that they are somehow unworthy of nibbana. By feeding monks, giving donations to temples and performing regular worship at the local wat they hope to improve their lot, acquiring enough merit (Pali: *punña*; Lao: *bun*) to prevent or at least lessen the number of rebirths. The making of merit (*het bun*) is an important social as well as religious activity in Laos. The concept of reincarnation is almost universally accepted by Lao Buddhists, and to some extent even by non-Buddhists, and the Buddhist theory of karma (*kam*) is well-expressed in the Lao proverb '*het dii, dai dii; het sua, dai sua*' – 'do good and receive good; do evil and receive evil'.

The *Trilatna* (*triratna*), or Triple Gems, highly respected by Lao Buddhists, include the Buddha, the Dhamma (the teachings) and the Sangha (the Buddhist brotherhood). Each is visible in Lao towns, particularly in the Mekong Valley. The Buddha in his sculptural form is found on high shelves or altars in homes and shops as well as in temples. The Dhamma is chanted morning and evening in every wat. The Sangha is represented by the street presence of orange-robed monks, especially in the early morning hours when they perform their alms-rounds, in what has almost become a travel-guide cliche in motion.

Socially, every Lao Buddhist male is expected to become a monk for a short period in his life, optimally between the time he finishes school and starts a career or marries. Men or boys under 20 years of age may enter the Sangha as novices and this is not unusual since a family earns great merit when one of its sons takes robe and bowl. Traditionally the length of time spent in the wat is 3 months, during the Buddhist lent (*phansaa* or *watsa*) beginning in July, which coincides with the rainy season. However, nowadays men may spend as little as a week or 15 days to accrue merit as monks.

Monks must follow 227 vows or precepts as part of the monastic discipline. Many monks ordain for a lifetime. Of these a large percentage become scholars and teachers, while some specialise in healing and/or folk magic (although the latter is greatly discouraged by the current ruling party). There is no similar hermetic order for nuns, but women are welcome to reside in temples as lay nuns, with shaved heads and white robes.

The women only have to follow eight precepts. Because discipline for these 'nuns' is much less strenuous than it is for monks, they don't attain quite as high a social status as do monks. However, aside from the fact that they don't perform ceremonies on behalf of other lay persons, they engage in the same basic religious activities (meditation and dharma study) as monks. The reality is that wats which draw sizeable contingents of eight-precept nuns are highly respected because women don't choose temples for reasons of clerical status – when more than a few reside at one temple it's because the teachings there are considered particularly strong.

Post-1975 Buddhism

During the 1964-73 war years, both sides sought to use Buddhism for their own propaganda purposes. In 1968 the LPF included as part of its platform a resolution

To respect and preserve the Buddhist religion, the purity and freedom of public worship and preaching by monks, to maintain pagodas, to promote unity and mutual assistance between monks and lay followers of different Buddhist sects...

By the early '70s, the LPF was winning the propaganda war in the religious sphere, as more and more monks threw their support behind the communist cause.

But major changes were in store for the Sangha following the 1975 takeover. Initially, Buddhism was banned as a primary school subject and people were forbidden to make merit by feeding monks. Monks were also forced to till the land and raise animals in direct violation of their monastic vows.

Mass dissatisfaction among the faithful prompted the government to rescind their total ban on the feeding of monks in 1976. The giving of rice only was allowed but still the laity was not satisfied, since it was felt that not much merit was to be obtained from the mere offering of rice (which also meant that monks had to continue the cultivation of the soil). By the end of 1976, the LPDR government was not only allowing the traditional alms-giving, it was offering a daily ration of rice directly to the Sangha.

The Department of Religious Affairs controls the Sangha and ensures that the teaching of Buddhism is in accordance with Marxist principles. All monks now have to undergo political indoctrination as part of their monastic training. All canonical and extra-canonical Buddhist texts have been subject to 'editing' by the DRA, who make sure that everything contained therein is congruent with the development of socialism in Laos. Monks are also forbidden to promote *phii* worship, which has been officially banned in Laos along with *sayasat* or folk magic.

One of the more major changes in Lao Buddhism has been the abolition of the Thammayut sect. Formerly the Sangha in Laos was divided into two sects, the Mahanikai and the Thammayut (as in Thailand). The Thammayut is a minority sect that was begun by Thailand's King Mongkut and patterned after an early Mon form of monastic discipline which the King had practised as a *bhikkhu*. Discipline for Thammayut monks is generally stricter than that of the Mahanikai sect. Thammayut monks are expected to attain proficiency in meditation as well as Buddhist scholarship or scripture-study; the Mahanikai monks typically 'specialise' in one or the other.

The Pathet Lao historically objected to the Thammayut sect because it was seen as a tool of the Thai monarchy (and hence US imperialism – even though the Thammayut were in Laos long before the Americans were in Thailand) for infiltrating Lao political culture. The LPRP has not only banned the Thammayut sect but have also banned all Buddhist literature written in the Thai language. This has severely curtailed the availability of Buddhist literature in Laos since Thailand has always been a major source of religious material (just as it is for every other kind of written material).

In Laos nowadays there is only one official sect, 'the Lao Sangha' (*Song Lao*). Former Thammayut monks have either fled to Thailand or renounced their sectarian affiliation. Whether it is due to this exodus or because of the general strictness of policy, the total number of Buddhist monks in Laos declined from 15,000 in 1975 to 12,000 by 1980.

Other Religions

In spite of the fact that *phii* worship has been officially banned, it remains the dominant non-Buddhist belief system in the country. Even in Vientiane, Lao citizens openly perform the ceremony called *sukwan* or *ba si* (*baci*) in which the 32 guardian spirits known as *khwan* are bound to the guest of honour by white strings tied around the wrists. Each of the 32 *khwan* are thought to be guardians over different organs in a person's body.

Khwan occasionally wander away from their owner, which isn't thought to be much of a problem except when that person is about to embark on a new project or on a journey away from home, or when they're very ill. Then it's best to perform the *ba si* to ensure that all the khwan are present and attached to the person's body. Nowadays, the ceremony appears to have become more of a cheerful formality than a serious ritual, but few Lao would dare to undertake a long journey without participating. Another obvious sign of the popular Lao devotion to *phii* can be witnessed in Vientiane at Wat Si Muang. The central image at the temple is not a Buddha figure but the *lak muang* or 'city pillar', in which the guardian spirit for the city is believed to reside. Many local residents make daily offerings before the pillar.

Outside the Mekong River Valley, the *phii* cult is particularly strong among the tribal Thai, especially the Black Thai (Thai Dam), who pay special attention to a class of *phii* called *ten*. The *ten* are earth spirits that preside not only over the plants and soil, but over entire districts as well. The Black Thai also believe in the 32 *khwan* or guardian spirits. Priests, *maw*, who are specially trained in the propitiation and exorcism of spirits preside at important Black Thai festivals and ceremonies.

The Khamu tribes have a similar hierarchy of spirits they call *hrooi*. The most important *hrooi* are those associated with house and village guardianship. Ceremonies involving *hrooi* are closed to non-Khamu observers so little has been written about them. During the '60s some Khamu participated in a 'cargo cult' that believed in the millennial arrival of a messiah figure who would bring them all the trappings of Western civilisation.

The Hmong-Mien tribes also practise animism, along with ancestral worship. Some Hmong groups recognise a pre-eminent spirit that presides over all earth spirits; others do not. Some Hmong also follow a Christian version of the cargo cult in which they believe Jesus Christ will arrive in a jeep, dressed in combat fatigues. The Akha, Lisu and other Tibeto-Burman groups mix animism and ancestor cults, except for the Lahu, who worship a supreme deity called Geusha.

HOLIDAYS & FESTIVALS

The traditional Lao calendar, like the calendars of China, Vietnam, Cambodia and Thailand, is a solar-lunar mix. The year itself is reckoned by solar phases, while the months are divided according to lunar phases (unlike the Western calendar in which months as well as years are reckoned by the sun). The Lao Buddhist Era (BE) calendar figures year one as 638 BC (not 543 BC as in Thailand), which means that you must subtract 638 from the Lao calendar year to arrive at the Christian calendar familiar in the West (eg 1990 AD is 2628 BE according to the Lao Buddhist calendar).

Festivals in Laos are mostly linked to agricultural seasons or historical Buddhist holidays. The general word for festival in Lao is *bun* (or *boun*).

April

Pi Mai The lunar new year begins in mid-April and practically the entire country comes to a halt and celebrates. Houses are cleaned, people put on new clothes and Buddha images are washed with lustral water. In the wats, offerings of fruit and flowers are made at various altars and votive mounds of sand or stone are fashioned in the courtyards. Later the citizens take to the streets and dowse one another with water, which is an appropriate activity as April is usually the hottest month of the year. This festival is particularly picturesque in Luang Phabang, where it includes elephant processions. The 15th, 16th and 17th of April are official public holidays.

May

International Labour Day (1st) This honours workers all over the world. In Vientane there are parades, but elsewhere not much happens. Public holiday.

Visakha Bu-saa (Visakha Puja) (Full Moon) This falls on the 15th day of the 6th lunar month, which is considered the day of the Buddha's birth, enlightenment and *parinibbana* or passing away. Activities are centred around the wat, with much chanting, sermonising and, at night, beautiful candlelit processions.

Bun Bang Fai (Rocket Festival) This is a pre-Buddhist rain ceremony that is now celebrated alongside Visakha Puja in Laos and north-east Thailand. This can be one of the wildest festivals in the country, with plenty of music and dance (especially the irreverent *maw lam* performances), processions and general merry-making, culminating in the firing of bamboo rockets into the sky. The firing of the rockets is supposed to prompt the heavens to initiate the rainy season and bring much-needed water to the rice fields.

July

Khao Phansaa (also *Khao Watsa*) (Full Moon) This is the beginning of the traditional 3-month 'rains retreat', during which Buddhist monks are expected to station themselves in a single monastery. At other times of year they are allowed to travel from wat to wat or simply to wander in the countryside, but during the rainy season they forego the wandering so as not to damage fields of rice or other crops. This is also the traditional time of year for men to enter the monkhood temporarily, hence many ordinations take place.

August/September

Haw Khao Padap Din (Full Moon) This is a sombre festival in which the living pay respect to the dead. Many cremations take place during this time and gifts are presented to the Sangha so that monks will chant on behalf of the deceased.

October/November

Awk Phansaa (*Awk Watsa*) (Full Moon) This celebrates the end of the 3-month rains retreat. Monks are allowed to leave the monasteries to travel and are presented with robes, alms-bowls and other requisites of the renunciative life.

A second festival held in association with Awk Phansaa is the *Bun Nam* (Water Festival). Boat races are commonly held in towns located on rivers, such as Vientiane, Luang Phabang and Savannakhet.

November

That Luang Festival (Full Moon) This takes place at Pha That Luang in Vientiane. Hundreds of monks assemble to receive alms and floral votives early in the morning on the first day of the festival. There is a colourful procession between Pha That Luang and Wat Si Muang. The celebration lasts a week and includes fireworks and music, culminating in a candlelit circumambulation (*wien thien*) of That Luang.

December

Lao National Day (2nd) This celebrates the 1975 victory of the proletariat over the monarchy with parades, speeches etc. It is a Public holiday.

December/January

Bun Pha Wet This is a temple-centred festival in which the *jataka* or birth-tale of Prince Vessantara, the Buddha's penultimate life, is recited. This is also a favoured time (second to Khao Phansaa) for Lao males to be ordained into the monkhood. The scheduling of Bun Pha Wet is staggered so that it is held on different days in different villages. This is so that relatives and friends living in different villages can invite one another to their respective celebrations.

February

Magha Puja (*Makkha Bu-saa*) (Full Moon) This commemorates a speech given by the Buddha to 1250 enlightened monks who came to hear him without prior summons. In the talk, the Buddha laid down the first monastic regulations and predicted his own death. Chanting and offerings mark the festival, culminating in the candlelit circumambulation of wats throughout the country (celebrated most fervently in Vientiane and at the Khmer ruins of Wat Phu, near Champasak).

Vietnamese Tet & Chinese New Year This is celebrated in Vientiane with parties, fireworks and visits to Vietnamese and Chinese temples. Chinese and Vietnamese-run businesses usually close for 3 days.

LANGUAGE
Language Milieu

The official language of the LPDR is Lao as spoken and written in Vientiane. As an official language, it has successfully become the lingua franca between all Lao and non-Lao ethnic groups in Laos. Of course, native Lao is spoken with differing accents and with slightly differing vocabularies as you move from one part of the country to the next, especially in a north to south direction. But it is the Vientiane dialect that is most widely understood.

All dialects of Lao are members of the Thai half of the Thai-Kadai family of languages and are closely related to languages spoken in Thailand, northern Myanmar and pockets of China's Yunnan Province. Standard Lao is indeed close enough to Standard Thai (as spoken in central Thailand) that, for native speakers, the two are mutually intelligible. In fact, virtually all speakers of Lao can easily understand spoken Thai, since the bulk of the television and radio they listen to is broadcast from Thailand. Among educated Lao, written Thai is also easily understood, in spite of the fact that the two scripts differ (to about the same degree that the Greek and Roman scripts differ). This is because many of the textbooks used at the college and university level in Laos are actually Thai texts.

Even closer to Standard Lao are Thailand's Northern and North-Eastern Thai dialects. North-Eastern Thai (also called Isan) is virtually 100% Lao in vocabulary and intonation; in fact there are more Lao speakers living in Thailand than in Laos. Hence if you are travelling to Laos after a spell in Thailand (especially the north-east), you should be able to put whatever you learned in Thailand to good use in Laos. (It doesn't work as well in the opposite direction; native Thais can't always understand Lao since they've had less exposure.)

In the cities and towns of Luang Phabang Province and the Mekong River Valley, French is widely understood. In spite of its colonial history, French remains the official second language of the government and many official documents are written in French as well as Lao. Shop signs sometimes appear in French (alongside Lao, as mandated by law), though signs in English and Russian are nearly as common these days. English is sometimes understood, but to a much lesser extent than French (young Lao students are an exception, since English is now more popular with them than French).

Many USSR-trained Lao also speak Russian. Although these Lao have spent enough time in Russia to recognise a Soviet when they see one, kids sometimes assume that any Caucasian walking down the street is a Soviet, and they may greet you in halting Russian.

But it pays to learn as much Lao as possible during your stay in the country, since speaking and understanding the language not only enhances verbal communication but garners a great deal of respect from the Lao you come into contact with.

Pronunciation & Tones

Basically, Lao is a monosyllabic, tonal language, like various dialects of Thai and Chinese. Consequently, the word *sao*, for example, can mean 'girl', 'morning', 'pillar' or 'twenty' depending on the tone. For people from non-tonal language backgrounds, it can be very hard to learn at first. Even when we 'know' the correct tone, our tendency to denote emotion, emphasis and questions through tone modulation often interferes with uttering the correct tone. So the first rule in learning and using the tone system is to avoid overlaying your native intonation patterns onto the Lao.

Vientiane Lao has six tones (compared with five in Standard Thai, four in Mandarin and nine in Cantonese). Three of the tones are level (low, mid and high) while three follow pitch inclines (rising, high falling and low falling). All six variations in pitch are *relative to the speaker's natural vocal range*, so that one person's low tone is not necessarily the same pitch as another person's. Hence, keen pitch recognition is not a prerequisite for learning a tonal language like Lao. A relative distinction between pitch contours is all that is necessary, just as it is with all languages (English and other European languages use intonation, too, just in a different way).

The low tone is produced at the relative bottom of your conversational tonal range – but flat and level. Example: *dīi* (good).

The mid tone is flat like the low tone, but spoken at the relative middle of the speaker's vocal range. No tone mark used. Example: *het* (do).

The high tone is flat again, this time at the relative top of your vocal range. Example: *heúa* (boat).

The rising tone begins a bit below the mid tone and rises to just at or above the high tone. Example: *saăm* (three).

The high falling tone begins at or above the high tone and falls to the mid level. Example: *sâo* (morning).

The low falling tone begins at about the mid level and falls to the level of the low tone. Example: *khào* (rice).

On a visual curve the tones might look like this:

— ⁻ ⌒ — ⌣
Mid   Low   Falling   High   Rising

Script Prior to the consolidation of various Lao *muang* in the 14th century, there was little demand for a written language. When a written language was deemed necessary by the Lan Xang monarchy, Lao scholars based their script on an early alphabet devised by the Thais (which in turn had been created by Khmer scholars who used South Indian scripts as models!). The alphabet used in Laos is closer to the original prototype; the original Thai script was later extensively revised (which is why Lao looks 'older' than Thai, even though it is newer as a written language).

The Lao script consists of 32 consonants (but only 20 separate *sounds*) and 28 vowel and diphthong possibilities (15 separate *symbols* in varying combinations). In addition to the consonant and vowel symbols are four tone marks, only two of which are commonly used to create the six different tones (in combination with all the other symbols). Written Lao proceeds from left to right, though vowel-signs may be written before, above, below, 'around' (before, above *and* after), *or* after consonants, depending on the sign. Although learning the alphabet is not difficult, the writing system itself is fairly complex, so unless you are planning a lengthy stay in Laos it should perhaps be foregone in favour of learning actually to speak the language. Included in this book is a list of prominent place-names in Lao script as well as in Roman script, so that you can at least 'read' the names of destinations in a pinch, or point to them if necessary.

Transliteration

The rendering of Lao words into Roman script is a major problem, since many of the Lao sounds, especially certain vowels, do not occur in English. The problem is compounded by the fact that because of Laos' colonial history, transcribed words most commonly seen in Laos are based on the old colonial French system of transliteration, which bears little relation to the way an English speaker would usually choose to write a Lao word.

A prime example is the capital of Laos, Vientiane. The Lao pronunciation, following a fairly logical English-Roman transliteration, would be Wieng Chan (some might hear it more as Wieng Jan). Since the French don't have a written consonant that corresponds to 'w', they chose to use a 'v' to represent all 'w' sounds, even though there is no actual 'v' sound in Lao. The same goes for 'ch' (or 'j'), which for the French was best rendered 'ti-'; hence Wieng Chan (which means 'City of the Moon') comes out 'Vientiane' in the French transliteration. The 'e' is added so that the final 'n' sound isn't partially lost, as it is in French words ending with 'n'.

Since there is no official method of transliterating the Lao language (the Lao government is incredibly inconsistent in this respect, though they tend to follow the old French methods), I am basically following the transcription system used in Lonely Planet's Thailand guide since the languages have virtually identical phonemes. Elsewhere in the Laos section of this guide, I've used the same system, except in instances where it differs greatly from common transliteration (eg Vientiane). The public and private sectors in Laos are gradually moving towards a more internationally recognisable system along the lines of the Royal Thai General Transcription (which is fairly readable across a large number of language types). This can also be problematic, however, as when an 'r' is used where an 'h' or 'l' is the actual sound, simply because the Lao symbols for these sounds look so much like the Thai 'r' (spoken Lao has no 'r' sound).

Here is a guide to the phonetic system:

Consonants
th   't' as in English 'tea'.

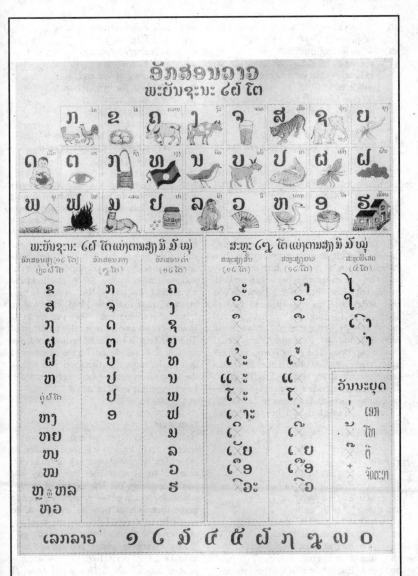

Chart featuring Lao alphabet and numbers

ph   'p 'as in English 'put' (but never as in 'phone').

kh   'k' as in English 'kite'.

k   similar to 'g' in English 'good' or 'k' in 'cuckoo' but unaspirated and unvoiced.

t   't' as in English 'forty' – unaspirated or 'unexploded'; close to 'd' but unvoiced.

p   similar to the 'p' in 'stopper', unvoiced, unaspirated (but not like the 'p' in 'put').

ng   as in English 'sing'; used as an initial consonant in Thai. Practice by saying 'sing' without the 'si'.

ny   similar to the 'ni' in 'onion'; used as an initial consonant in Lao.

All the remaining consonants correspond closely to their English counterparts. Two exceptions are 'x' and 'v', which commonly occur on Lao street signs but which are both misleading. Elsewhere in this book, a V is sometimes used in transliterated Lao to conform with common spellings. All instances of 'v' in transcribed Lao words are pronounced as 'w'. Example: 'Vang Vieng' should be pronounced Wang Wieng. Furthermore, many standard place names in Roman script use an 'x' for what in English is 's'. There is no difference in pronunciation of the two; pronounce all instances of 'x' as 's'. Example: 'Xieng' should be pronounced Sieng.

Vowels

i   as in English 'it'

ii   as in English 'feet' or 'tea'

ai   as in English 'pipe' or 'I'

aa   long 'a' as in 'father'

a   half as long as 'aa' above

ae   as in English 'bat' or 'tab'

e   as in English 'hen'

eh   like 'a' in English 'hate'

oe   as in English 'rut' or 'hut' but more closed

u   as in English 'flute'

uu   as in English 'food'

eu   as in French 'deux'

ao   as in English 'now' or 'cow'

aw   as in English 'jaw'

o   as in English 'phone'

oh   as in English 'toe'

eua   diphthong of 'eu' and 'a'

ie   'i-a' as in the French *rien*

ua   'u-a' as in 'tour'

uay   'u-a-i' (as in 'Dewey')

iu   'i-u' (as in 'yew')

io   actually a triphthong of 'i-a-w' (but very similar in pronunciation to Italian *mio* or *dio*)

In Laos you may come across many instances where the transliteration of vowels and consonants differs significantly, as in 'Louang' for Luang, 'Khouang' for Khwang or 'Xaignabouli' for Sayabouli. The French spellings are particularly inconsistent in the use of the vowel 'ou', which in their transcriptions sometimes corresponds to a 'u' and sometimes to 'w'. An 'o' is often used for a short 'aw', as in 'Bo', which is pronounced more like Baw. Finally, there is no 'r' sound in spoken Lao. When you see an 'r' in transcribed Lao, it is usually a borrowed Thai spelling; it should be pronounced like an 'l' in this case. Again, for the purposes of this guide, most transliteration will follow the English system – only very common French spellings will be noted.

Grammar

Neither spoken nor written Lao words change according to number, gender or tense. The word *wat* (temple), for example, never changes no matter how many *wat* you're speaking of. The exception is pronouns, for which *phuak* is usually added to make them plural (*lao* is 'she/he' while *phuak lao* is 'they'). Likewise, the word *pai* (go) stays the same whether you mean 'go', 'going', 'went' or 'gone'. You can add *laew* to make a verb perfective (to show accomplished action), as in *khawy pai laew*, 'I went' or 'I've gone'.

Adjectives always follow the nouns they modify as in *wat nyai* or 'big temple'. Adjectives in Lao have a stative aspect which means you don't need to insert the verb 'to be' when describing something, eg *lao puay* means 'he *(lao)* (is) sick *(puay)*'. When identifying two things, use *maen* for equivalence, *pen* for a class or condition. For example, you say *an-nii maen sam-law* (This is a pedicab) but *khawy pen nak-dontii* (I'm a musician).

To make an adjective or verb negative, insert *baw* before the word, as in *baw dii*, 'not good'. *Baw* can also be used at the end of an utterance to form a tag question, as in *dii baw*, 'Is it good?'. Don't make the mistake of raising your voice to indicate a question; *baw* is always spoken with a level mid tone. Another way to make a question is to add *maen baw* at the end – this is when you expect an affirmative answer, eg *wat nii nyai, maen baw*, which means 'This temple is big, isn't it?' or *laa-khaa jet phan kip, maen baw*, 'The price is 7000 kip, right?'.

Useful Words & Phrases
Do you have...?
   Mìi...baw (subject goes in the middle)
   ມີ....ບໍ?
Don't have.
   Daw mìi
   ບໍ່ມີ.
Isn't it?
   Maen baw
   ແມ່ນບໍ?
It isn't.
   Baw maen
   ບໍ່ແມ່ນ.
It doesn't matter.
   Baw pēn nyāng (used to mean 'you're welcome', 'no problem', etc)
   ບໍ່ເປັນຫຍັງ.
What day?
   Meua dāi
   ມື້ໃດ?
What do you call this in Lao?
   Pháa-sāa láo ôen ăn-nîi waa nyāng
   ພາສາລາວເອີ້ນ ເອິ້ນວ່າຫຍັງ?
What is this?
   ăn-nîi maen nyāng
   ອັນນີ້ແມ່ນຫຍັງ?

What time?
   Wéh-láa dāi
   ຈັກໂມງ?
Where is...?
   ...yuu sāi (subject first)
   ...ຢູ່ໃສ?
will go
   já pāi or *si pāi*
   ຈະໄປ ຊິໄປ
come
   máa
   ມາ
go
   pāi
   ໄປ
this
   ăn-nîi (noun)
   ອັນນີ້
   nîi (adjective)
   ນີ້
that
   ăn-nân (noun)
   ອັນນັ້ນ
   nân (adjective)
   ນັ້ນ
no (or not)
   baw
   ບໍ່
went or has gone
   pāi lâew
   ໄປແລ້ວ

Greetings & Civilities
Greeting
   Sa-bāi-dīi
   ສະບາຍດີ
How are you?
   Sa-bāi-dīi baw
   ສະບາຍດີບໍ?
(I'm) fine.
   (Khàwy) sa-bāi-dīi
   (ຂ້ອຍ)ສະບາຍດີ.
Where (are you) going?
   Pai sāi (commonly used as a greeting on the street)
   ໄປໃສ?
he/she
   láo or *khāo* (when speaking of most people)
   ລາວ ເຂົາ

he/she
  poen (when speaking of elders)
  ເພິ່ນ

I
  khàwy (to most people)
  ຂ້ອຍ
  kha-nâwy (to elders)
  ຂະນ້ອຍ

thank you
  khàwp jãi
  ຂອບໃຈ

thank you very much
  khàwp jãi lãi lãi
  ຂອບໃຈຫລາຍໆ

we
  háo or *phûak khàwy*
  (ເຮົາ) ພວກຂ້ອຍ

you (singular)
  jâo
  ເຈົ້າ

you (plural)
  phûak jâo
  ພວກເຈົ້າ

they
  add *phûak* before *láo*, *khão* or
  ພວກ
  poen as with 'you' (plural)
  ລາວ, ເຂົາ

Small Talk

Can you speak Lao?
  Jâo pàak phàa-sãa lào dâi baw
  ເຈົ້າປາກພາສາລາວໄດ້ບໍ?

I can't.
  Khàwy baw dâi
  ຂ້ອຍບໍ່ໄດ້

I can speak a little Lao.
  Khàwy pàak phàa-sãa lào dâi nâwy neung
  ຂ້ອຍປາກພາສາລາວໄດ້ນ້ອຍໜຶ່ງ.

I come from...
  Khàwy mãa tae...
  ຂ້ອຍມາແຕ່...

(I) like...
  Mak...
  ມັກ

(I) don't like...
  Baw mak...
  ບໍ່ມັກ...

My name is...
  Khàwy seu...
  ຂ້ອຍຊື່...

understand
  Khào jãi
  ເຂົ້າໃຈ

(Do you) understand?
  Khào jãi baw
  ເຂົ້າໃຈບໍ?

(I don't) understand.
  Baw khào jãi
  ບໍ່ເຂົ້າໃຈ.

What is your name?
  Jâo seu nyãng
  ເຈົ້າຊື່ຫຍັງ?

Where do you come from?
  Jâo màa tae sãi
  ເຈົ້າມາແຕ່ໃສ?

(I) want (+ verb)...
  Yàak...
  ຢາກ...

(I) don't want (+ verb)...
  Baw yàak...
  ບໍ່ຢາກ...

(I) want (+ noun)...
  Yàak dâi
  ຢາກໄດ້

(I) want to go...
  Yàak pãi
  ຢາກໄປ

(I) want a ticket.
  Yàak dâi pîi
  ຢາກໄດ້ປີ້.

(I) need (+ verb or noun)...
  Tawng-kāan...
  ຕ້ອງການ...

Accommodation

bath/shower
  àap nâm
  ອາບນ້ຳ

cold
  não
  ເຢັນ

hot
  hâwn
  ຮ້ອນ

hotel
  hóhng háem
  ໂຮງແຮມ

room
hàwng
ຫ້ອງ

toilet
hàwng nâm (rest room)
ຫ້ອງນ້ຳ
sùam (commode)
ສ້ວມ

towel
phàa set tōh
ຜ້າເຊັດໂຕ

Around Town

bus
lot pa-jām tháang
ລົດປະ   ລົດເມ

cafe
hâan kīn deum
ຮ້ານກິນດື່ມ

fast
wái wái
ໄວ

market
talàat
ຕະຫຼາດ

pedicab
sāam-lâw
ສາມລໍ້

post office
pāi-sá-nii
ໄປສະນີ

restaurant
hâan āahāan
ຮ້ານອາຫານ

slow
sâa sâa
ຊ້າ

station
sá-thāa-nii
ສະຖານີ

Shopping

How much?
Thao dāi
ເທົ່າໃດ?

a little
nâwy neung
ນ້ອຍໜຶ່ງ

big
nyai
ໃຫຍ່

buy
sêu
ຊື້

expensive
pháeng
ແພງ

give
āo hài
ເອົາໃຫ້

inexpensive, cheap
thèuk
ຖືກ

really expensive
pháeng thâe
ແພງແທ້

sell
khāi
ຂາຍ

small
nâwy
ນ້ອຍ

Emergencies

(I) need a doctor
Tâwng-kāan māw
ຕ້ອງການໝໍ

doctor
māw
ໝໍ

hospital
hóhng pha-yáa-bāan
ໂຮງພະຍາບານ

Time & Dates

now
dìo nîi
ດຽວນີ້

today
mêu nîi
ມື້ນີ້

tomorrow
mêu eun
ມື້ອື່ນ

yesterday
mêu wáan nîi
ມື້ວານນີ້

Numbers

1
neung
ນຶ່ງ

2
sǎwng
ສອງ

3
sǎam
ສາມ

4
sii
ສີ່

5
hâa
ຫ້າ

6
hók
ຫົກ

7
jèt
ເຈັດ

8
pàet
ແປດ

9
kâo
ເກົ້າ

10
síp
ສິບ

11
síp-ét
ສິບເອັດ

12
síp-sǎwng
ສິບສອງ

13
síp-sǎam
ສິບສາມ

14
síp-sii
ສິບສີ່

20
sáo
ຊາວ

21
sáo-ét
ຊາວເອັດ

22
sáo-sǎwng
ຊາວສອງ

23
sáo-sǎam
ຊາວສາມ

30
sam-síp
ສາມສິບ

40
sii-síp
ສີ່ສິບ

50
hâa-síp
ຫ້າສິບ

100
neung hâwy
ນຶ່ງຮ້ອຍ

200
sǎwng hâwy
ສອງຮ້ອຍ

6 − 1 = 5

ບົດເຝິກຫັດ

ຈົ່ງແບ່ງເມັດເຂົ້າທ່ານເມັດອອກເປັນສອງໆ. ຈຸທົ່ວມີຈັກເມັດ?   ແບ່ງໄດ້ຈັກ
ວິທີ?

2+1	1+3	5+2	5−1	4−2
4+1	2+3	5−4	6−1	2+3
5−1	3−2	5−3	1+5	3+3

Page from a Lao number primer

300
sǎam hâwy
ສາມຮ້ອຍ
1000
neung phán
ນຶ່ງພັນ
10,000
neung méun
ນຶ່ງໝື່ນ ສິບພັນ
100,000
neung sǎen
ນຶ່ງແສນ ຮ້ອຍພັນ
million
lâan
ລ້ານ
billion
phán lâan
ພັນລ້ານ

Books for Language Study

The *English-Lao, Lao-English Dictionary* by Russell Marcus (Charles Tuttle Co, Suido 1-chome, 1-6 Bunkyo-chu, Tokyo, Japan) is a handy book to have in Laos. Of course you won't be able to read the Lao-English section, but the English-Lao definitions are fairly extensive and the transliteration is more or less consistent. Transliterated Lao words are also accompanied by tone marks (the authors use numbers for the six tones), which are really necessary for any dictionary or phrasebook to be of real use.

The same company also publishes *Lao for Beginners: An Introduction to the Spoken and Written Language of Laos* by Tatsuo Hoshino and Russell Marcus. This 200-page primer is organised by situations (eg 'Coming & Going', 'Touring Vientiane', 'Bargaining at the Market'), so the lessons are mostly quite relevant to everyday language use. The primer uses the same transliteration system as the dictionary described above, so the two go together nicely.

For more serious students, little else is available. Probably the most complete text is the US Foreign Service Institute's *Lao Basic Course, Volumes 1 & 2* (Superintendent of Documents, Washington, DC 20402, USA, 1971). Volume 1 takes students step by step through the rudiments of pronunciation, grammar and writing. Volume 2 is a Lao reader (all written Lao with no translation) for advanced students. Both books are oriented toward pre-1975 Laos, with many references to the monarchy and so on.

All of the above books can be purchased in Bangkok as well, at Asia Books, Sukhumvit Rd Soi 15. In Laos, about the only thing available is *Basic Spoken Laos in Sixteen Lessons*, which can be purchased at the Australian Embassy in Vientiane for US$2. It's a flimsy 26-page booklet with a good, if limited, range of basic words and phrases used in everyday Lao life. Two serious drawbacks are that tones are not indicated for Roman transcriptions and the transliteration system is inconsistent and difficult to follow.

In Vientiane's government bookshops you can also purchase children's first language primers, which aren't a bad way to start for those who will be staying a long time in Laos and want to master the written language.

Facts for the Visitor

VISAS & TRAVEL RESTRICTIONS

Visas for foreigners who want to visit the LPDR are of four types. For all types of visas, the Lao Embassy requires that the official one-page visa application form be filled out in triplicate and submitted along with three passport photos and the appropriate fee. When applying from abroad (except Thailand), you should allow at least 2 months for the visa process. This is because for all visas except the Tourist Visa, the embassies must await approval from authorities in Laos before they can issue them. In Thailand, the process is much faster since all they have to do is phone or telex Vientiane for approval.

Most travellers to Laos will be going on a Tourist Visa. At this writing, these visas are usually issued only to those who are members of package tours. Tours can only be booked through agencies who are registered with Lao Tourism. The agencies take care of visa arrangements, so if you're going on a Tourist Visa you won't be getting directly involved with Lao embassies at all. See the Guided Tours section for more information.

Lao embassies abroad will occasionally issue Tourist Visas to individuals – the only way to know for sure is to apply, as their decisions seem to be made on a case by case basis (it's never automatic). The Lao Embassy in Bangkok is very strict though – to get a visa in Bangkok you'll have to book a minimum 2-day tour.

When Laos first opened to tourists in February 1989, several small Thai travel agencies in Bangkok and Nong Khai (across the Mekong River from Vientiane) were acting as brokers for the larger, officially sanctioned agencies. For a fee of around US$100, you could arrange a minimal 2-night package deal for Vientiane, fly in on your own, then extend your visa up to 14 days without much fuss. No one really checked to see whether you were staying at the pre-arranged hotel or not.

Although you weren't supposed to venture outside Vientiane prefecture without a travel pass, travellers roamed the country anyway, hitching on trucks to Luang Phabang and riding river ferries up and down the Mekong between Luang Phabang and Savannakhet. The LPDR Ministry of the Interior didn't like this wandering at all. Worse, Lao Tourism wasn't getting its payment for the package tour arrangements since the small Thai agencies were just keeping the money they earned from selling visas.

By August 1989, the Lao government began cracking down a bit. At this writing, the small agencies aren't allowed to broker visas anymore without putting up a substantial bond. This means that in all likelihood the only way you'll be able to obtain a Tourist Visa in Bangkok is by buying the minimum 2-night Vientiane package from an officially registered agency. This type of visa can still be extended up to 14 days, however, without booking further package tours (see the Visa Extension section). Travel is permitted outside Vientiane prefecture upon issuance, in Vientiane, of a travel pass that is good only for one intended destination at a time (see the Visa Extension section for more information on travelling outside Vientiane).

The Short-Stay Visa or *petit sejour* is good for up to 15 days and is the type usually issued to family or friends of foreigners who are working in Laos. Expatriates in Laos must apply on their relative's or friend's behalf from within the country. The application fee for this visa is US$35. It is extendible for a second 15 days.

A person who has a short-term professional or volunteer assignment in Laos is generally issued a Non-Immigrant Visa that is good for 30 days and extendible for another 30 days. As with the Short-Stay Visa, the application fee is US$35.

The Transit Visa is the easiest of all the visas to get but is the most restricted. It is intended for stopovers in Vientiane for air passengers travelling between two other countries. It's common to ask for such a visa when travelling between Hanoi and Bangkok (either direction), for example. The visa is granted upon presentation of a confirmed ticket between the two destinations. The maximum length of stay for the Transit

Visa is 5 days, no extension allowed. No travel outside the town of Vientiane is permitted on this visa. In Vietnam, the fee for this visa is US$10.

Other Restrictions

Visa Validation Once you arrive in Laos, you *must* report to Immigration within 3 days of your arrival to have your visa validated. This requirement applies for all visa types. If you fail to show up within the 3-day period, you risk having your visa revoked and being deported. At the Immigration Office (same location as for visa extensions), you have to fill in some forms, hand over another photo, and pay a small fee in kip (less than US$0.50). If you take your passport to Immigration in the morning, it's usually ready by early afternoon. There are a couple of photo studios on Thanon Samsenthai that take passport photos but it's cheaper to have them made in Bangkok than in Vientiane.

Travel Passes Travel passes (*bai anuyaat doen thaang* in Lao or *laissez passer* in French) are sometimes checked by local police when foreigners show up unannounced in towns outside Vientiane. They are also sometimes checked when boarding domestic flights or long-distance river ferries. Travel passes are issued to tourists (when they purchase a tour package – see the Tour section) for only the following provinces outside Vientiane: Luang Phabang, Xieng Khwang, Savannakhet, Salavan and Champasak. Lao Tourism has plans to add Hua Phan, Phong Sali and Luang Nam Tha to the permitted list within the next few years.

Port of Arrival Note that most Lao visas require that visitors enter Laos by air. The words 'By Air – Wattay' will appear next to your visa if this is the case. If you want to enter Laos by ferry across the Mekong River (from Nong Khai, Thailand, the only permissible crossing point for non-Thai foreigners), you'll have to stipulate that in advance. Most tour agencies will not arrange this since it means lost revenue on the ticket price. If you

Lao Tourism travel pass

get the Tourist Visa on your own (from a Lao embassy in another country besides Thailand), the request usually seems to be granted (the visa will be notated 'By Land at Tha Deua'). Also, if you're getting a visa other than the Tourist Visa, you should be able to get permission.

Visa Extensions

The Immigration Office of the Ministry of the Interior in Vientiane is on Thanon Talat Sao off Thanon Lan Xang, opposite the Morning Market (the only Roman-scripted sign reads 'Ministère d'Intérieur'). This is where you get your visa validated (within 3 days, as noted in the Other Restrictions section) or extended. An extension requires the filling out of forms and three passport photos. The application takes about 24 hours to process, during which time you must leave your passport with Immigration.

The Short-Stay Visa can be extended for a second 15 days and the Non-Immigrant Visa for a second 30 days. The Transit Visa can not be extended beyond 5 days.

A Tourist Visa can be extended up to a maximum of 14 days. This means that if you arrive in Vientiane on a '3-day' package (actually 2 nights and 2 half-days, for a total of 2 days in the country), you are allowed to apply for an extension and stay on in Vientiane for a combined total of 14 days, without having to buy another package tour (obviously, this is the most economical way to spend some time in Vientiane).

Those on Tourist Visas who want to go to another province, however, are technically required to purchase a minimum 2-night package in that province as well; you aren't supposed to extend your visa in Vientiane and then take off for Luang Phabang on your own, for example (as people were doing in 1989). The way the authorities monitor this is by requiring that you carry a travel pass when going to any other province besides Vientiane. Lao citizens are also required to carry travel passes when leaving their assigned domiciles. The only way for a tourist to get a travel pass is by arranging a tour package through Lao Tourism.

No matter how many short tours within the country you choose to arrange, you aren't allowed to exceed the maximum of 14 days. You can, however, return to Bangkok and start over again.

The Immigration Office is open weekdays 8 to 11 am and 2 to 5 pm.

Thai Visas

If you're returning to Thailand and plan to stay there beyond 15 days, or if you plan to enter Thailand via the Nong Khai river ferry, you'll need a Thai visa. You can apply for one at the Thai Embassy in Vientiane, which is located on Thanon Phon Kheng, a couple of hundred metres north-east of the Pratuxai monument. A 60-day tourist visa costs 300 baht, payable in Thai currency only. The application process requires three passport photos and takes 1 to 3 days to come through (3 is normal; 1 if you can convince them it's urgent).

The Thai Embassy is open from 9 am to 12 noon and 2 to 4 pm weekdays.

Overseas Embassies

If you're going to Laos on a package tour, you won't deal directly with any Lao embassy, since tour agencies handle all visa arrangements. To apply for a visa on your own, you can try one of these embassies:

LPDR Embassy
    193 Sathon Tai Rd, Bangkok (tel 286-0010)
LPDR Consular Office
    40 Quang Trung St (on 2nd floor of unmarked building across from offices of the Food & Agriculture Organization), Hanoi (tel 52588)
LPDR Chancellery
    111 214th St, Phnom Penh (tel 251821)

You can also check with Lao embassies or consulates in other countries (those that have relations with Laos), but your chances of getting a visa from an embassy or consulate outside Thailand or Vietnam are somewhat slim. The exception, of course, is when you go through an authorised tour agency. If you have plenty of lead time, however, it is worth trying an overseas embassy (it's not unusual for visas to take 2 months to come through) because they do occasionally issue Tourist Visas to individuals, contrary to announced policy.

Australia
    1 Dalman Crescent, O'Malley, Canberra, ACT
    2606
China
    11 E 4th St, Sunli-Tun, Chao Yang, Beijing
Czechoslovakia
    Zitna 2, 125 41 Praha 2
Federal Republic of Germany
    1100 Berlin Esplanade 17, Berlin
Hungary
    Josefhegy UT 28-30, G/6 1025, Budapest
India
    7 West End Colony, New Delhi 110021
Japan
    3-21, 3-Chome, Nishi Azabu, Minato-ku, Tokyo
Mongolia
    27 Stalin Ave, 2nd Floor, Apartment 10-11,Ulan
    Batur
Myanmar
    A1 Diplomatic Headquarters, Fraser Rd, Yangon
    (Rangoon)
Poland
    2/1 Marconich St, Warsaw 02-954
Sweden
    Nornsgatan 82-B, 1 TR, 11721 Stockholm
USA
    2222 S St NW, Washington, DC 20008
USSR
    Sis 18, Katchalova, Moscow

TOURS

Ordinarily Lonely Planet doesn't recommend buying package tours, but for Laos
it's the only way in – for the moment. All
tours in Laos are handled by the state-run
Lao Tourism (Thawng Thio Lao). Lao
Tourism has a standard set of packages (16
different itineraries in all) that it sells,
ranging from 2 nights in Vientiane to 14 days
in Vientiane, Luang Phabang, the Plain of
Jars, Savannakhet, Pak Se and Champasak.
In each destination, Lao Tourism arranges all
accommodation (double occupancy), all
meals, a tour guide and all domestic transport.

When you book a tour outside Laos, you
must deal with an authorised agent of Lao
Tourism (eg Indoswiss in Bangkok,
Orbitours in Australia, etc). Lao Tourism sets
base fees that they charge all tour agencies
and the agencies in turn mark up the price to
include their minimal expenses and what
they want to take in as profit.

The costs can vary widely from agency to

agency. Deithelm Travel in Bangkok, for
example, charges US$590 (based on a seven-
person minimum) for their 3-day Vientiane
package. Out of this fee, it pays Lao Tourism
around US$169 per person for the tour and
shell out a maximum of US$160 per person
(probably less) for the Vientiane-Bangkok-
Vientiane flight, for a total of $329. The
difference (US$261 or more per person)
goes in its pockets, and it don't even have to
handle any of the tour arrangements beyond
getting you to and from Bangkok International Airport. Deithelm's 6-day tour of
Vientiane and Luang Phabang (the only
other tour it offers) costs US$950 per person,
for an approximate net profit of US$342 per
person.

The least expensive way to tour Laos then,
is to take the cheapest, shortest Vientiane
tour you can find, then extend your Tourist
Visa and book further tours (if you want to
leave Vientiane Province) directly through
Lao Tourism. The average cost for one of
Lao Tourism's 3-day tours outside of Vientiane is US$200 (regardless of the province
visited), which includes domestic flights, all
meals and accommodation, and a guide.
Once you arrive at an approved destination,
you are allowed to stay beyond the duration
of the tour (up to the limits of your visa) as
long as you arrange this beforehand. In this
way, you could spend a week each in Vientiane and Luang Phabang and only have to
purchase two 3-day tours. Or you could do
four different tours within Laos for less then
the cost of one 6-day, two-city tour through
Deithelm.

Finding an inexpensive tour to Vientiane
is the difficult part, especially since the
crackdown in 1989. All of the authorised
foreign companies (Akiou in France, Artou
in Switzerland, Going in Italy, Indoculture in
Germany, Chippewa and Wings of the World
in Canada, Sai and Sayu in Tokyo, and
Orbitours in Sydney) are about as expensive
as Bangkok's Deithelm, sometimes more so
when they require you to purchase your air
ticket to/from Bangkok through them.

The least expensive tour company in
Bangkok at the moment is Indoswiss (tel

236-7655), Suite 1102B, 11th Floor, Dusit Thani Building, 946 Rama IV Rd. A minimal 3-day Vientiane tour through Indoswiss costs around US$180 to US$200, depending on the number of people going at one time. If the small brokers start operating again (a definite possibility) such a package might go as low as US$130.

Rumour has it that a couple of agencies will be up and running again in Nong Khai in the very near future. Before the '89 crackdown, Tourist Visas could be arranged in Nong Khai for as little as US$50. When they start up again, rates will probably be more in line with the small Bangkok brokers, ie around US$120 to US$130. If you plan to go to Nong Khai anyway, it's worth checking out. Inquire at any of the guest houses in town, eg Mut-Mee Guest House, Niyana Guest House or Mekong Guest House.

All Vientiane tours, no matter who books them, require that you fly into Laos via Wattay Airport in Vientiane. Departure from Laos by ferry (to Thailand) is allowed, however. See the Vientiane chapter for more details.

Tourism Policy in Laos

Officials at Lao Tourism would most prefer to see tourism in Laos become a sort of private club (as in Bhutan) to which only wealthy tourists can gain membership. They hold the perspective that a policy of unrestricted individual entry into Laos would result in 'cultural pollution'. They also claim that the country will derive maximum economic benefit from restricted, package tourism.

From the perspective of the dedicated traveller, on the other hand, the package tour approach tends to insulate tourists from the people and culture of Laos. Travellers who saw the country during the 6-month 'window of opportunity' that occurred in 1989 (when many individuals were able to travel around Laos freely) say that the Lao they met along the way were practically unanimous in their preference for the individual (as opposed to the package) tourist. Naturally, when travellers move through the country on their own,

Lao Tourism seal

the average Lao peasant or small tradesperson derives more of a monetary benefit than when prearranged package tours hurry through with Lao Tourism officials. The bulk of the money from package tours goes directly into the hands of Lao Tourism, who operate the hotels and restaurants used by the tour groups (not to mention the huge cut they receive from selling packages in the first place).

As to the question of cultural integrity, it's not easy to say which kind of tourism is potentially more harmful. It would seem that the parading of wealthy tourists through such a comparatively undeveloped country would create more of an obvious socio-cultural disparity (thus leading to unreasonably high economic expectations on the part of the locals) than allowing individuals of varying economic backgrounds the chance to interact with the people on a more natural basis. On the other hand, such one-to-one contact could lead to 'subversive' thinking, in the perception of the Lao government, so perhaps freedom of thought is the real issue here.

At any rate, this kind of narrow thinking may give way to a more moderate policy with time. In 1990, the Tourist Authority of Thailand began conducting tourism research in Laos on behalf of the LPDR government.

Obviously, the Lao are to some degree seeking to follow Thailand's example in successfully attracting millions of visitors. Regardless of the results of the study, Laos is not likely to get very far with tourism unless it loosens up. A 3-day, one-city package that costs upwards of US$600 (from outside Laos) is just not going to sell when right next door in Thailand a person can travel in some style for a month (several months for the frugal traveller) on that same amount.

Lao Tourism

In all fairness, it should be mentioned that the tours led by Lao Tourism are not bad value as far as package tours go (when booked directly through their Vientiane office). Except for the obvious inconvenience of having to put up with a group (although sometimes the group is as small as two to four people) and follow a guide around, the tours are generally well planned and genuinely informative. Guides are usually flexible when it comes to the itinerary, adding or deleting bits (within obvious time, distance and cost limits) according to the needs of the group.

Unlike early China tours in which visitors were herded from factory to agricultural collective, Lao Tourism itineraries do not try to present visitors with a proletarian paradise – political rhetoric is in fact relatively absent from guide commentary.

Meals are plentiful if a bit on the bland side, but you can sometimes request local specialties. Or simply inform your guide that you want to eat real Lao food during the tour, not the ersatz version usually offered to Westerners.

Hotel accommodation varies considerably from destination to destination (see the Accommodation section for detail), but Lao Tourism tries to see that tourists get the best that's available in each location. Of course, this is another reason why you might be uncomfortable with the package tour set-up.

MONEY

US$1	=	K600
Thai B 1	=	K24
A$1	=	K498
UK£1	=	K1128
FFr1	=	K114
DM1	=	K384

Currency

The official national currency in the LPDR

is the *kip*. In reality, the people of Laos use three currencies in day-to-day commerce: kip, Thai baht and US dollars. In larger towns such as Vientiane, Luang Phabang and Savannakhet, baht and dollars are readily acceptable at all business establishments, including hotels, restaurants and shops. In smaller towns and villages kip or baht seem to be preferred.

Kip notes come in denominations of 1, 5, 10, 20, 50 and 100 kip. Kip coins (*aat*) are available but rarely seen since anything below 1 kip is virtually worthless.

Changing Money

The kip is on a constant downward spiral like the Mexican peso. In early '89, US$1 bought K470; 6 months later you could get K740 per dollar. Hence, to quote kip exchange rates here would be meaningless. Since the dollar figure is more stable, most prices in this book are quoted in US dollars rather than kip. When figuring US dollar prices in kip, use the current black market rate.

Dollars and baht can be exchanged for kip at the official National Bank rate or at the free-market rate. The official rate tends to be about 30% lower than the free rate, hence you're better off changing money on the black market. There's no legal requirement that you change money at the bank – money-changers operate openly in the outdoor markets of Vientiane. Most shop owners will be glad to give you kip in exchange for baht or dollars, too.

How do you find out the going black market rate? Your best bet is to ask travellers who have been in Laos for a couple of weeks already. Better yet, ask a Thai who is in Laos on business – the Thais will know the rate down to the last kip.

A Lonely Planet reader wrote to say that the best kip exchange is in Poland! You can also buy kip in Thailand at the black-market rate.

Laos has no currency restrictions on the amount of money you're required to exchange at the official rate (as in Myanmar) or any 'foreign exchange certificates' (as in China).

Banking

The only bank that foreigners are allowed to use is La Banque pour le Commerce Extérieur Lao on Thanon Pang Kham near the Lane Xang Hotel in Vientiane. They will cash US dollar travellers' cheques but require that you take half the cash back in kip at the official rate. In other words, you can't simply sign over a travellers' cheque for cash US dollars and then go out and change dollars for kip on the black market. None of the hotels in Laos will take travellers' cheques at this writing.

Hence it is better to bring enough cash for your entire visit to Laos rather than bring travellers cheques (unless you don't mind losing 5% to 30% on every bank exchange). It doesn't really matter whether you bring Thai baht or US dollars – both have about the same purchasing power in Laos. Security is not generally a problem, though of course you should keep your money in a safe place (eg a money belt).

At the end of 1989 a joint Thai-Lao bank opened on Lan Xang Ave in Vientiane. It would be worth checking to see what their foreign exchange situation is.

Foreign residents of Laos are permitted to open US dollar accounts at La Banque pour le Commerce Exéterieur Lao. They are also permitted to receive cash US dollars back when they close the account, but only on the day before their departure from Laos (it's necessary to show bank officials an exit visa and confirmed air ticket).

La Banque pour le Commerce Extérieur Lao is open from 8.30 to 4 pm Monday to Friday.

COSTS

If it wasn't for the current tour requirement, Laos would be a very inexpensive country to visit by most standards. The Lao Tourism tours to provinces outside Vientiane are actually pretty decent value when you add up everything that's included, though you could still do it more cheaply on your own (especially if you use ground transport rather than air).

In general, food is cheap, hotels are not.

The average meal in a Lao restaurant costs less than US$1 per person. A cup of coffee costs about US$0.13, and draft beer is only US$0.30 a litre. On the other hand, the Lan Xang Hotel in Vientiane costs US$40 a night for a room that in Thailand would go for half that. The cheapest hotel in Vientiane, the Vieng Vilay, costs US$5 a night for a single.

Estimating a per diem cost for Laos is difficult since it depends on how much you try to see (ie how many Lao Tourism packages you purchase). The average Lao Tourism package costs about $100 a day, all inclusive. If you stay in Vientiane, you could get by for about US$8 to US$10 a day, not counting the cost of the initial package into Vientiane (see the Tour section). Towns in south Laos like Pak Se or Savannakhet would cost about the same, perhaps a bit lower, while Luang Phabang is a bit costlier due to the high rates at the two hotels there.

In places where you're not permitted to go, per diem costs would be much lower, since the average guest lodging only costs around US$2. Food is also cheaper off the beaten path – more like US$0.50 per meal.

TIPPING
Tipping is not customary in Laos, not even in the tourist hotels.

TOURIST INFORMATION
Local Tourist Offices
The state-run Lao Tourism runs all package tours in Laos. It has offices in both Vientiane and Luang Phabang.

Overseas Representatives
To book a tour outside of Laos you must deal with an authorised agent of Lao Tourism. For a list of travel agents see the Tour section in the Vietnam Facts for the Visitor chapter.

Foreign Embassies
For details of which countries have embassies and consulates in Laos see the Vientiane chapter.

GENERAL INFORMATION
Post
Outgoing mail is fairly reliable and inexpensive. The safe arrival of incoming mail is less certain, especially for packages.

The GPO in Vientiane has a poste restante service – be sure that those who write to you use the full name of the country, 'Lao People's Democratic Republic' or at least 'Lao PDR'.

A bit of philatelist trivia – Lao stamps are printed in Cuba.

The GPO is open from from 8 am to 5 pm Monday to Saturday and from 8 am to 12 noon on Sunday.

Telephone
Telephone service in Laos, both domestic and international, is on-again, off-again at best. Heavy rains often stop service altogether for hours.

The best place to make international calls is the International Telephone Office (Cabines Télécommuniques Internationales) on Thanon Setthathirat in Vientiane, which is open 24 hours a day. Sometimes there's a long wait, since Laos has only two international lines – one to Western countries via Hong Kong and another to socialist countries via Moscow. The operators cannot place collect calls or reverse phone charges – you must pay for the call when it is completed.

In provincial capitals, international telephone service is available at the GPO.

Calls to Bangkok cost US$4 for the first 3 minutes, US$1.08 per minute thereafter. For calls to the USA, it's US$15 for the first 3 minutes, then US$5 a minute. Europe and Australia each cost US$14 for the first 3 minutes, then US$4.43 per minute.

Telex & Telegraph

Telex and telegraph services are handled at the GPO in each provincial capital.

Electricity

The LPDR uses 220-volt circuitry. Bring adapters and transformers as necessary for any appliances you bring along. Adapters for common European plugs are available at shops in Vientiane.

Blackouts are common during the rainy season, so it's a good idea to bring a torch (flashlight).

Time

Laos, like Thailand, is 7 hours ahead of Greenwich Mean Time. Thus 12 noon in Vientiane is 1 am in New York, 10 pm (the previous day) in Los Angeles, 3 pm in Sydney, 1 pm in Perth and 5 am in London.

Business Hours

Government offices are generally open from 8 to 11 am and 2 to 5 pm. Shops and private businesses open and close a bit later and either stay open during lunch or close for just an hour.

Weights & Measures

The international metric system is the official system for weights and measures in the LPDR. Shops, markets and highway signs for the most part conform to the system. In rural areas distances are occasionally quoted in *meun*; 1 *meun* is equivalent to 12 km. Gold and silver are sometimes weighed in *baht*; a *baht* is 15 grams.

MEDIA
Newspapers & Magazines

The only English-language periodical legally distributed in Laos is the English edition of a Soviet newspaper that's not really worth reading. Thailand's *Bangkok Post* is occasionally seen in markets.

Foreign embassies and consulates are a good source of reading material in Vientiane, however. The Australian, British and American posts all welcome visitors to their respective lounges, where dated newspapers and magazines are available for perusal.

At the Lao Embassy in Bangkok you can get free copies of a large English-language pictorial simply entitled *Lao People's Democratic Republic*. Features typically cover such fascinating topics as irrigation, animal husbandry or the Lao People's Revolutionary Youth Union, along with the occasional history and geography of a selected province. More interesting is the 'Lao PDR News Bulletin' that is issued periodically by the embassy. This contains brief press statements on new government policies, Thai-Lao joint communiqués and so on.

Radio & Television

The LPDR has one radio station, Lao National Radio. English-language news is broadcast daily at 1 pm and 8.30 pm. All the usual short-wave radio programming (BBC, VOA and Radio Australia) can be received if you have a short-wave radio.

Vientiane and Savannakhet have one television station (Channel 8) but it's not much to watch and is limited to 3 hours in the evening (usually 7.30 to 10.30 pm). Most Lao watch Thai television, which can be received anywhere in the Mekong River Valley. Russian TV is also beamed in by satellite. In the north, mountains prevent the reception of TV broadcasts.

HEALTH

Refer to the general Health section in the Vietnam Facts for the Visitor chapter for overall health preparations for Vietnam, Laos and Cambodia.

Opisthorchiasis

One additional health warning specific to Laos is to be on guard against 'liver flukes' (opisthorchiasis). These are tiny worms that are occasionally present in freshwater fish in Laos. The main risk comes from eating raw or under-cooked fish. Travellers should in particular avoid eating *paa daek* (*padek*), which is a fermented fish used as an accompaniment for rice. It's often carried around in bamboo tubes – slung over the shoulders of farmers. *Paa daek* is not commonly served in city restaurants, but is quite common in rural Laos. Since it's considered a great delicacy, it's often offered to guests – this is one case where you have to weigh carefully the possible health consequences against the risk of offending your hosts.

A much less common way to contract liver flukes is by swimming in rivers. According to a Czech parasitologist who spent several months researching opisthorchiasis in Laos, the only known area where the flukes might be contracted by swimming in contaminated waters is in the Mekong River around Khong Island in southern Laos.

Symptoms The intensity of symptoms depends very much on how many of the flukes get into your body. At low levels, there are virtually no symptoms at all; at higher levels, an overall fatigue, low-grade fever and swollen or tender liver (or general abdominal pain) are the usual symptoms, along with worms or worm eggs in the faeces.

Treatment Persons suspected of having liver flukes should have a stool sample analysed by a competent doctor or clinic in Vientiane or Bangkok. The usual medication is 750 mg of praziquantel (often sold as Biltricide) three times daily for a week.

DANGERS & ANNOYANCES

On the whole, the Lao are trustworthy people and theft is not much of a problem. Still, it's best if you keep your hotel room locked when you're out and while sleeping at night. If you ride a crowded bus, watch your luggage and don't keep money in your trouser pockets.

Most areas of the country are secure in the military sense. The only exceptions are those places where you're not permitted to go as a tourist. One such area is near Kasi, on the road between Vientiane and Luang Phabang, where anti-government rebels occasionally attack truck convoys (the only way to get to Luang Phabang by road is via truck). In 1989, at least 15 people were killed in attacks near Kasi.

The two provinces on the Laos-Myanmar border, Bokeo and Luang Nam Tha, should also be considered insecure because of the opium trade. Any stranger seen in the countryside of these provinces might be suspected of being an international drug enforcement agent; there are also occasional skirmishes here between different opium armies. The area around the capital of Luang Nam Tha (Muang Luang Nam Tha) is probably secure, however, and Lao Tourism has plans to allow tourist visits at some point in the future.

FILM & PHOTOGRAPHY

Film is reasonably priced in Laos (Vientiane, Luang Phabang and Savannakhet) but the selection is limited to Agfa or Kodak colour print films (ASA 100 or 200 only) and one slide film, Ektachrome 100HC. For black & white film or other slide films, you'd best stock up in Bangkok, where film is relatively cheap, before you come to Laos.

As in other tropical countries, the best times of day for photography are early to mid morning and late afternoon. A polarising filter would be helpful for cutting glare and improving contrast.

ACCOMMODATION

Laos is not blessed (or cursed) with a great number or variety of hotels. If you book a tour through Lao Tourism or one of its agents, you'll not usually have a choice. For Vientiane and Luang Phabang, you can sometimes specify '1st class' or 'standard'. Choosing 1st class puts you in the Lan Xang Hotel in Vientiane and the Luang Phabang

Hotel in Luang Phabang, the country's top hotels at the moment. Elsewhere, the accommodation falls into the 'standard' class, which can be anything from a rustic government guest house without running water to a multi-storey tourist hotel.

Hotel rooms in Vientiane and Luang Phabang have private bathrooms (cold water only) and ceiling fans as standard features. Higher cost rooms have air-con and a very few feature air-con and hot water. Hot water is hardly a necessity in lowland Laos (where it is most likely to be available), but would be nice in the mountains (where it's almost never available).

If you have extra days after a tour is finished (or if you're lucky enough to have come on a non-tourist visa), you can choose your own hotel. Unlike in China or Myanmar, foreigners aren't restricted to certain hotels. But even when you're on your own, the choice is limited outside Vientiane. Most provincial capitals have only one or two hotels at best. Where there aren't any hotels, you can usually arrange to stay in government guest houses, which feature small rooms and shared bath facilities. The tariff at government guest houses is only about US$2 a night.

The LPDR government has plans to build several more hotels over the next decade, mostly using Thai capital. For the most part, these new hotels will be designed to serve the needs of package tour groups and as such will probably cost around US$20 to US$30 a night for individuals. The cheap guest house phenomenon that is so widespread in Thailand and Indonesia has not come to Laos and it's not likely that it will. Nor does Laos have any student or worker dormitories that are open to foreigners, as in China.

Most hotels, especially those in Vientiane, Luang Phabang and Savannakhet, will require that you fill out a police report (*fiche de police*) when checking in so that your passport and visa numbers will be on file.

FOOD

Lao cuisine is very similar to Thai cuisine in many ways. Like Thai food, almost all dishes are cooked with fresh ingredients, including vegetables (*phak*), fish (*paa*), poultry (*kai* – chicken, *pet* – duck), pork (*muu*) and beef (*sin wua*) or water buffalo (*sin khwai*). In Luang Phabang, dried water-buffalo skin (*nang khwai haeng*) is a quite popular ingredient in local dishes.

Because of Laos' distance from the sea, freshwater fish is more commonly used than saltwater fish or shellfish. Lime juice, lemon grass and fresh coriander leaf are added to give the food its characteristic tang. To salt the food, various fermented fish concoctions are used, most commonly *nam paa*, which is a thin sauce of fermented anchovies (usually imported from Thailand), and *paa daek*, a coarser, native Lao preparation that includes chunks of fermented freshwater fish, rice husks and rice 'dust'. *Nam paa daek* is the sauce poured from *paa daek*. (See the Health section for warnings on eating *paa daek*.)

Other common seasonings include the galingale root (Lao: *khaa*), hot chillies (*maak phet*), ground peanuts (more often a condiment), tamarind juice (*nam maak khaam*), ginger (*khing*) and coconut milk (*nam maak phao*). Chillies are sometimes served on the side in hot pepper sauces called *jaew*.

Many Lao dishes are quite spicy because of the Lao penchant for *maak phet*. But the Lao also eat a lot of what could be called Chinese food which is generally, but not always, less spicy. Rice noodles (*foe*) are quite popular as a snack or even for breakfast. *Khao pun*, flour noodles topped with a sweet/spicy sauce, is often called 'Lao spaghetti'. One of the most common Lao dishes is *laap*, which is a Lao-style salad of minced meat, fish or vegetables tossed with lime juice, garlic, *khao khua* (roast, powdered rice), green onions and chillies. It can be very hot or rather mild, depending on the cook.

Rice is the foundation for all Lao meals (as opposed to snacks), as elsewhere in South-East Asia. In general, the Lao eat 'sticky' or glutinous rice (*khao nio*), although ordinary white rice (*khao jao*) is also common. Sticky rice is eaten with the hands: the general practice is to grab a small fistful from the woven container that sits on the table, then roll it into a rough ball which is used to dip into the various dishes. *Khao jao*, on the other hand, is eaten with a fork and spoon. The fork is only used to prod food onto the spoon, which is the main utensil for eating this type of rice.

Where to Eat

Many restaurants or foodstalls, especially outside Vientiane, do not have menus, so it is worthwhile memorising a standard 'repertoire' of dishes. Those restaurants that do offer written menus don't always have an English version (in fact, it's rare when they do). Most provinces have their own local specialities in addition to the standards and you might try asking for *aahaan phi-set* (special food), allowing the proprietors to choose for you. In remote areas like Xieng Khwang Province, choices can be rather limited.

The most economical places to eat and the most dependable are noodle-shops and night markets. Most towns and villages have at least one night market and several noodle-shops. The next step up is the Lao-style cafe or *haan kheuang deum* (drink shop), where a slightly more varied selection of dishes is usually served. Most expensive is the *haan aahaan* (food shop), where the menu is usually posted on the wall or on a blackboard (in Lao).

What to Eat

Except for the 'rice plates' and noodle dishes, Lao meals are usually ordered family style, which is to say that two or more people order together, sharing different dishes. Traditionally, the party orders one of each kind of dish, eg one chicken, one fish, one soup, etc. One dish is generally large enough for two people. One or two extras may be ordered for a large party. If you come to eat at a Lao restaurant alone and order one of these 'entrees', you had better be hungry or know enough Lao to order a small portion. The latter is not a particularly acceptable alternative; the Lao generally consider eating alone in a restaurant unusual. But then

as a *falang* (foreigner) you're an exception anyway. A cheaper alternative is to order dishes 'over rice' or *laat khao*.

In Vientiane, Luang Phabang and Savannakhet, French bread is a popular breakfast food. Sometimes it's eaten plain with hot milk coffee (*kafae nom hawn*), sometimes it's eaten with eggs (*khai*) or in a baguette sandwich that contains Lao-style paté and vegetables. When they're fresh, Lao baguettes are superb. Excellent croissants are also available, especially in the bakeries of Vientiane.

A list of standard dishes follows. Opposite the English is a transliterated pronunciation of the Lao names using the system outlined in the Language section, along with the Lao script so you can point to the name if necessary.

Soups

mild soup with vegetables & pork
  kāeng jèut
  ແກງຈືດ
same as above, with bean curd
  kāeng jèut tâo-hûu
  ແກງຈືດເຕົາຮູ້
soup with chicken, *khaa* & coconut
  tôm kháa kài
  ຕົ້ມຂ່າໄກ່
fish & lemon grass soup with mushrooms
  tôm yám pāa
  ຕົ້ມຍໍາປາ
rice soup with fish/chicken
  khào tôm pāa/kai
  ເຂົ້າຕົ້ມປາ / ໄກ່

Eggs

hard-boiled egg
  khai tôm
  ໄຂ່ຕົ້ມ
fried egg
  khai dāo
  ໄຂ່ດາວ
plain omelette
  khai jīaw
  ຈືນໄຂ່
omelette stuffed with vegetables & pork
  khai yat sai
  ໄຂ່ຍັດໄສ້

Bread

plain bread (usually French-style)
khào jii
ເຂົ້າຈີ່

baguette sandwich
khào jii pa-te
ເຂົ້າຈີ່ປະເຕ

croissants
khwaa-song
ກຣົວຊົງ

Noodles

rice noodle soup with vegetables & meat
fõe nâm
ເຟີ

rice noodle soup without broth
fõe hàeng
ເຟີແຫ້ງ

rice noodles served on plate with gravy
lâat naa
ລາດໜ້າ

fried noodles with soy sauce
phát siyu
ຜັດສະອິ້ວ

yellow wheat noodles in broth, with vegetables & meat
mii nam
ໝີ່ນ້ຳ

yellow wheat noodles without broth
mii hàeng
ໝີ່ແຫ້ງ

white flour noodles, served with sauce
khào pùn
ເຂົ້າປຸ້ນ

Fish

crisp-fried fish
pãa jẽun
ປາ

fried prawns
kûng jẽun
ກຸ້ງ

grilled prawns
kûng pîng
ກຸ້ງປີ້ງ

steamed fish
pãa nèung
ປານຶ່ງ

grilled fish
pãa jii
ປາຈີ່

catfish
pãa dúk
ປາດຸກ

eel
pãa lãi
ປາໄຫຼ

giant Mekong catfish
pãa béuk
ປາເບິກ

sheatfish
pãa sa-ngûa
ປາສະງົວ

carp
pãa waa
ປາຫວາ

serpent fish
pãa khaw
ປາຄໍ

freshwater sting ray
pãa faa lái
ປາຟາໄລ

Miscellaneous

fried rice
khào phát
ເຂົ້າຜັດ

stir-fried vegetables
phát phák
ຜັດຜັກ

roast duck
pét pîng
ເປັດປີ້ງ

roast chicken
kai piîng
ໄກ່ປີ້ງ

chicken fried with chillies
kai phát màak phét
ໄກ່ຜັດໝາກເຜັດ ຫລື ວ້າໄກໃສໝາກເຜັດ

fried chicken
kai jẽun
ໄກ່

spicy green papaya salad
tam-sòm or *sòm màak-hung*
ຕຳໝາກຫຸ່ງ

chicken fried with ginger
kai phát khĩng
ໄກ່ຜັດຂີງ

cellophane noodle salad
yám khào pùn jíin
ຍຳເສັ້ນລ້ອນ

spicy beef salad
lâap sîn
ລາບຊີ້ນ

spicy chicken salad
lâap kai
ລາບໄກ່

Sweets

custard
sāngkha-nyáa
ສັງຂະຫຍາ

egg custard
màw kāeng
ເຂົ້າໜົມໝໍແກງ

banana in coconut milk
nâ wāan màak kûay
ນ້ຳຫວານໝາກກ້ວຍ

sticky rice in coconut cream
khào nīo dāeng
ເຂົ້າໜຽວແດງ

sticky rice in coconut cream & ripe mango
khào nīo màak muang
ເຂົ້າໜຽວໝາກມ່ວງ

sticky rice cakes
khào nóm
ເຂົ້າໜົມ

sticky rice in coconut milk cooked in bamboo
khào lāam
ເຂົ້າຫຼາມ

Fruit

mandarin orange
màak kîang
ໝາກກ້ຽງ

watermelon
màak móh
ໝາກໂມ

mangosteen
màak máng-khut
ໝາກມັງຄຸດ

rambutan
màak ngaw
ໝາກເງາະ

rose-apple
màak kîang
ໝາກກ້ຽງ

banana
màak kûay
ໝາກກ້ວຍ

pineapple
màak nat
ໝາກນັດ

mango
màak muang
ໝາກມ່ວງ

durian*
màak thu-rían
ໝາກທຸລຽນ

longan
màak yam yái
ໝາກຍຳໄຍ

papaya
màak hung
ໝາກຫຸ່ງ

custard-apple
màak khìap
ໝາກຂຽບ

lime or lemon
màak náo
ໝາກນາວ

guava
màak sīi-dāa
ໝາກສີດາ

betel nut
màak
ໝາກ

jackfruit
màak mîi
ໝາກມີ້

*durian – is held in high esteem by the Lao and throughout South-East Asia, but most Westerners dislike this fruit. There are several varieties, so keep trying until you find the variety that you find out of this world!

Useful Food Sentences

I eat only vegetarian food.
Khâwy kīn jēh
ຂ້ອຍກິນແຕ່ຜັກເຈ້ນັ້ນ

I can't eat pork.
Khâwy kīn mūu baw dâi
ຂ້ອຍກິນໝູບໍ່ໄດ້

I can't eat beef.
  Khâwy kīn sîn baw dâi
  ຈອຍກິນຊີ້ນບໍ່ໄດ້
(I) don't like it hot & spicy.
  Baw mak phét
  ບໍ່ມັກເຜັດ
(I) like it hot & spicy.
  Mak phét
  ມັກເຜັດ
(I) can eat Lao food.
  Kīn aa-hāan láo pēn
  ກິນອາຫານລາວໄດ້
What do you have that's special?
  Míi nyãng phi-sèt
  ມີຫຍັງເຜີຍເສດ?
I didn't order this.
  Án-nîi khâwy baw dâi sang
  ຈອຍບໍ່ໄດ້ສັ່ງອັນນີ້
Do you have ...?
  Míi .... baw
  ມີ...ບໍ?

DRINKS
Non-alcoholic Drinks
drinking water
  nâm deum
  ນ້ຳດື່ມ
boiled water
  nâm tôm
  ນ້ຳຕົ້ມ
ice
  nâm kâwn
  ນ້ຳກ້ອນ
weak Chinese tea
  nâm sáa
  ນ້ຳຊາ
hot water
  nâm hâwn
  ນ້ຳຮ້ອນ
cold water
  nâm yén
  ນ້ຳເຢັນ
hot Lao tea with sugar
  sáa dãm hâwn
  ຊາຮ້ອນ
hot Lao tea with milk & sugar
  sáa hâwn
  ຊານົມຮ້ອນ

iced Lao tea with milk & sugar
  sáa yén
  ຊານົມເຢັນ
iced Lao tea with sugar only
  sáa dãm yén
  ຊາດຳເຢັນ
no sugar (command)
  baw sai nâm-tãan
  ບໍ່ໃສ່ນ້ຳຕານ
hot Lao coffee with milk & sugar
  kāa-fáe nóm hâwn
  ກາເຟນົມຮ້ອນ
hot Lao coffee with sugar, no milk
  kāa-fáe dãm
  ກາເຟດຳ
hot Nescafe with milk & sugar
  net nóm
  ເນັສນົມ
hot Nescafe with sugar, no milk
  net dãm
  ເນັສດຳ
Ovaltine
  oh-wantin
  ໂອວັນຕິນ
orange soda
  nâm mák kang
  ນ້ຳໝາກກ້ຽງ
plain milk
  nóm jèut
  ນົມຈືດ
yoghurt
  nóm sôm
  ນົມສົ້ມ
beer
  bīa
  ເບຍ
rice whiskey
  lâo láo
  ເຫຼົ້າລາວ
soda water
  nâm sōh-dãa
  ນ້ຳໂຊດາ

Implements
glass
  jàwk
  ຈອກ
bottle
  kâew
  ແກ້ວ

Alcohol

Beer Three kinds of beer are brewed by the Lao Government Brewery (abbreviated BGL after the French) on the outskirts of Vientiane. Least expensive but very drinkable is BGL's draft beer (*bia sot*), which is only available in beer bars in Vientiane. The price is standard – at about US$0.35 per litre.

BGL also bottles a *Bia Lao* (Bière Lao in French) that sells for a standard US$0.40 for a small bottle (360 ml) or US$0.75 for a large (700 ml). Look for the tiger's head on the label with the letters BGL above. Then there's *33 Export*, which costs a few more pennies per bottle than Biere Lao. Both are good beers by Asian standards.

Imported canned beer from Singapore is also available, including Heineken (brewed in Singapore under Dutch licence) and Tiger. From Australia comes Swan and the occasional Foster's. These imported beers cost about US$0.70 for a small can.

Distilled Spirits Rice whisky or *lao lao* (Lao alcohol) is a popular drink among lowland Lao. The government distils two brands, *Phan Thong* (the label reads Chevreuil d'Or in French) and *Sing Thong* (Gold Tiger). Both are very similar in taste to Thailand's famous 'Mekong whisky'. A 750 ml bottle of either costs about US$2.20. It's best taken over ice with a splash of soda and a squeeze of lime, though some prefer to mix it with Coke imported from Thailand.

In rural provinces, a weaker version of *lao lao* is fermented by households or villages. Strictly speaking, it's not legal but no one seems to care. It's not always safe to drink, however, since unboiled water is often added to it during and after the fermentation process.

BOOKS & BOOKSHOPS

Books on Laos can be difficult to find. The government bookshops in Vientiane carry mostly Lao, Vietnamese and Russian books. The only book on the country available in English is a large and poorly done pictorial guide called *Laos* (also available in Spanish, French, Russian and Lao).

Chalermnit Books (Soi Gaysorn, Ploenchit Rd) in Bangkok has a small selection of used books on Laos, mostly in French.

The libraries of universities with Asian Studies departments or faculties often carry some of the following English-language books. If you read French, you'll find others as well. Very few books on Laos in any language have been published since the 1975 Revolution.

General

Laos: A Country Study (US Government Printing Office, 1971) is one of American University's Area Handbook Series, researched and written by the Foreign Area Studies Department. Probably the most comprehensive book available in English about pre-1975 Lao society, politics, history and economics, it's also remarkably objective considering it was commissioned by the US Army. You can sense the authors holding back, though, when recounting the events of the early '60s leading to US involvement in Laos.

History

History of Laos by Maha Sila Viravong (Paragon Book Reprint Corp, New York, 1964) is a fairly complete early (pre-War of Resistance) history written by a Thai.

A New History of Laos by ML Manich Jumsai (Chalermnit Books, Bangkok, 1971) is basically a slight expansion and update of Viravong's work.

Laos: War & Revolution by Nina Adams & Alfred McCoy (Harper Colophon Books, New York, 1970) was commissioned by the Committee of Concerned Asian Scholars. This book represents the Western academic left-wing view of pre-1975 Laos.

Politics & Society

Contemporary Laos: Studies in the Politics & Society of the Lao People's Democratic Republic edited by Martin Stuart-Fox (University of Queensland Press, St Lucia &

London, 1982). A collection of academic essays on Laos, including detailed discussions of the history and workings of the Lao People's Party, minority politics, Buddhism since the 1975 Revolution, Lao-Thai and Lao-Vietnamese relations and Lao refugees. Some essays are quite well researched while others seem somewhat removed from the Lao reality.

Laos: Politics, Economics, & Society by Martin Stuart-Fox (Pinter Publishers, New York & London or Lynne Riemer Publishers, Boulder, Colorado, 1983) A good overview of Laos since the 1975 Revolution, with details on the post-1979 economic reforms. Stuart-Fox is obviously cornering the market on Lao studies in the English-speaking world.

Travel Guides

What you hold in your hand is the only up-to-date guide on Laos available in English. The classic two-volume Guide Madrolle guide to Indochina, last updated in 1939, is worth reading in the original French (if you can find it). The volume that includes Laos is entitled *Indochine du Nord* (Société d'Éditions Géographiques, Maritimes et Coloniales, Paris, 1939). Of course, many of the place names have changed several times since 1939 (and some places were bombed out of existence), but for guidebook buffs it's a must-read.

An English version of the Guide Madrolle was also issued in 1939 (entitled *Indochina*) by the same publisher, but the two volumes were condensed into one so it's not nearly as complete as the French.

MAPS

The State Geographic Service (*Kom Phaen Thii Haeng Lat* in Lao or Service Géographique d'État in French) has produced a few adequate maps of Laos and the major provincial capitals. Some were originally done by the RLG's National Geographic Service while some are new, so provincial divisions can differ significantly. The Laos tourist map of Vientiane and administrative map of the whole country (labelled in French only as 'Laos – RDPL Carte Administrative') are available at the Lan Xang Hotel and in some souvenir shops along Thanon Samsenthai. Other maps can be purchased direct from the State Geographical Service, which is located on a side street to the west of the Pratuxai.

The most detailed maps of Laos available are those that were developed by the US Defense Mapping Agency in the '60s and early '70s. These topographic maps are labelled in English and French and are often seen on the walls of LPDR government offices. The State Geographic Service still stocks a few of the US-made maps, but they won't usually sell them to foreigners. Since very little road travel is permitted in Laos, the more general SGS maps are really sufficient for most travel purposes.

THINGS TO BUY

Laos is not a big country for shopping. Many of the handicrafts and arts available in Laos are easily obtainable in Thailand. Hill-tribe crafts can be less expensive in Laos, but only if you bargain. Like elsewhere in South-East Asia, bargaining is a local tradition (originally introduced to the area by early Arab and Indian traders). Although most shops nowadays have fixed prices, fabric, carvings, jewellery and antiques are usually subject to bargaining.

Fabric

Silk and cotton fabrics are woven in many different styles according to the geographic provenance and ethnicity of the weavers. Generally speaking, the fabrics of the north feature a mix of solid colours with simple striped patterns (usually in the form of a *phaa sin* or women's wraparound skirt). Sometimes gold or silver thread is woven in along the borders.

In the south, the style of weaving is marked by the *mat-mii* technique, which involves 'tie-dying' the threads before weaving. The result is a soft, spotted pattern similar to Indonesian *ikat*. *Mat-mii* cloth can be used for different types of clothing or for wall-hangings. Among the Cambodian communities in the south is a tradition of *mat-mii* that features pictographic story lines with a few Khmer words woven into the pattern.

Among the Hmong and Mien tribes, square pieces of cloth are embroidered and quilted to produce strikingly colourful fabrics in apparently abstract patterns that contain ritual meanings. In Hmong these are called *pa ndau* (flower cloth). Some larger quilts feature scenes that represent village life.

Many tribes among both the Lao Sung and Lao Theung groups produce woven shoulder bags in the Thai and Tibetan traditions, like those seen all across the mountains of South and South-East Asia. In Laos, they're called *nyam*. The Lahu make a particularly strong and good-looking bag.

The best place to buy fabric is in the weaving villages themselves, where you can watch how it's made and get 'wholesale' prices. Failing this, you can find a pretty good selection as well as reasonable prices at open markets in provincial towns, including Vientiane. The most expensive places to buy fabric are in tailor shops and handicraft stores.

Carvings

The Lao produce well-crafted carvings in wood, bone and stone. Subjects can be everything from Hindu or Buddhist mythology to themes from everyday life. Opium pipes seem to be plentiful in Laos and sometimes have intricately carved bone or bamboo shafts, along with engraved ceramic bowls.

To shop for carvings, look in antique or handicraft stores.

Jewellery

Gold and silver jewellery are good buys in Laos, although you must search hard for well-made pieces. Some of the best silverwork is done by the hill tribes. Gems are also sometimes available, but you can get better prices in Thailand.

Most provincial towns have a couple of shops that specialise in jewellery. You can also find jewellery in antique and handicraft shops.

Antiques

Vientiane, Luang Phabang and Savannakhet each have a sprinkling of antique shops. Anything that looks old could be up for sale in these shops, including Asian pottery (especially Ming dynasty porcelain), old jewellery, clothes, carved wood, musical instruments, coins and bronze statuettes.

WHAT TO BRING

Pack light, wash-and-wear, natural-fabric clothes, unless you're going to be in the mountains in the cool season, in which case you should have a sweater/pullover and a light jacket.

Sunglasses are a must for most people and are difficult to find in Laos. Slip-on shoes or sandals are highly recommended – they are cool to wear and easy to remove before entering a Lao home or temple. A small torch (flashlight) is a good idea, since power blackouts are common. A couple of other handy things are a compass and a fits-all sink plug.

Toothpaste, soap and most other toiletries can be purchased cheaply almost anywhere in Laos. Sunscreen, mosquito repellent, contraceptives and tampons are hard to find, however, so bring enough to last your trip.

CONDUCT
Visiting Temples
The Lao are very devout Buddhists. When visiting Lao Buddhist temples, you owe a measure of respect to the religion and to the people who so graciously allow you to enter their places of worship. Correct behaviour in temples entails several guidelines, the most important of which is to dress neatly and to take your shoes off when you enter religious buildings such as the *sim*. Buddha images are sacred objects, so don't pose in front of them for pictures and definitely do not climb or sit upon them. When sitting in front of a Buddha image, do not point your feet towards the image. The Lao usually employ the 'mermaid pose' when facing an image, which keeps both feet pointed to the rear of the seated person.

If you want to speak with a monk (the occasional monk can speak English or French), try to keep your head a bit lower than his. If he's sitting, you should sit, too (use the 'mermaid pose' again); if he's standing, you may have to bend down a bit to show proper respect. Women should never touch monks or hand them objects (place an object on a table or other surface in front of a monk instead).

A few of the larger wats in Vientiane charge small entry fees. In other temples, offering a small donation before leaving the compound is appropriate but not mandatory. Usually there are donation boxes near the entry of the *sim* or next to the central Buddha image at the rear. In rural wats, there may be no donation box available; in these, it's OK to leave money on the floor next to the central image or even by the doorway – no one is likely to steal it.

Other Customs
Traditionally, the Lao greet each other not with a handshake but with a prayer-like palms-together gesture known as a *wai*. If someone wais you, you should *wai* back (unless it is a child). But nowadays the Western-style handshake is just as common and most Lao will offer the same to a foreigner.

The feet are the lowest part of the body (spiritually as well as physically) so don't point your feet at people (you shouldn't even point at objects with your feet). In the same context, the head is regarded as the highest part of the body, so don't touch Lao people on the head either.

When things go wrong, don't be quick to anger – it won't help matters, since losing one's temper means loss of face for everyone present. Remember that this is Asia, where keeping your cool is the paramount rule. A smile and *sabai-dii* (Lao greeting) goes a long way toward calming the initial trepidation that locals may feel upon seeing a foreigner, whether in the city or the countryside.

Top: Market stall with parachute roof, Vientiane (RM)
Left: Morning market, Vientiane (JC)
Right: Wat In Paeng, Vientiane (JC)

Top Left: Pratuxai Monument, Vientiane (JC)
Top Right: Pha That Luang, Vientiane (JC)
Bottom Left: Wat Xieng Khwan, Vientiane (KO)
Bottom Right: That Dam, Vientiane (JC)

Getting There

AIR

Vientiane is the only legal port of disembarkation in Laos for foreign air passengers. At the present time, the only regularly scheduled air routes that exist are between Vientiane and Bangkok, Hanoi, Ho Chi Minh City, Phnom Penh and Moscow.

To/From Bangkok

The most frequent flights into Vientiane originate in Bangkok. Flights leave from Bangkok International Airport daily except Wednesday when there are no Bangkok-Vientiane flights. On Mondays, Tuesdays and Saturdays, departures are on Lao Aviation. Lao Aviation uses Soviet-built Antonov 24 prop planes that take about an hour and 20 minutes to reach Wattay Airport (on the outskirts of Vientiane). On Thursdays and Sundays, Thai Airways International (THAI) handles the flights on Boeing 737 jets; these take about 50 minutes to reach Wattay. The fare is the same for both airlines – US$82 each way.

The best place to purchase air tickets to Vientiane in Bangkok is at a THAI office. THAI is the agent for Lao Aviation in Thailand, so they handle ticket stock for both carriers. If you're buying the required Vientiane package, of course, the air ticket will be included. Since the Bangkok-Vientiane ticket price is never discounted, the smaller discount agencies that sell cheap international tickets can't get a better fare than THAI itself. As a matter of fact, they generally charge more for the ticket, adding a surcharge that they collect for themselves or for another intermediary. It's not unusual for a ticket to cost US$40 more than the standard THAI/Lao Aviation fare at another agency.

Unfortunately, you can't buy Bangkok-Vientiane tickets from THAI offices abroad at this time, except as part of a package tour (see Guided Tours in the Facts for the Visitor section).

To/From Hanoi

Direct Vietnam Airlines flights from Hanoi to Vientiane leave every Thursday and cost US$80 each way. Lao Aviation flies from

Hanoi to Vientiane on Tuesdays for the same fare.

To/From Ho Chi Minh City

Lao Aviation flies between Ho Chi Minh City via Pak Se in southern Laos every Thursday for US$155 each way.

To/From Phnom Penh

Lao Aviation flies between Phnom Penh and Vientiane Wednesday and Friday via Pak Se. The flight (as always, an Antonov 24) takes about 3½ hours and costs US$120.

To/From London/Moscow

Aeroflot flies a Tupolev 154 to Vientiane from Moscow every Wednesday that connects with a flight from London. The fare all the way from London is only US$400.

General Agents for Lao Aviation

Following are the agents for Lao Aviation in Thailand, Vietnam and Cambodia:

Bangkok
    Thai Airways International, 89 Vibhavadi Rangsit Rd (tel 233-3810)
Hanoi
    Vietnam Airlines, 25 Trang Thi St (tel 53842)
Phnom Penh
    Kampuchea Airlines, 62 Tou Samlith St (tel 25887)

Airport Arrival

Arrivals at Wattay Airport are generally rather casual events. Customs and immigrations procedures are much less cumbersome than in most other socialist countries. Carry-on bags are not usually inspected at all if that's all you've brought; checked baggage, when claimed at the baggage counter, sometimes is.

The government bank has a foreign exchange counter in the terminal, but you're better off changing money on the free market in town. Since Thai baht and US dollars are just as acceptable as kip in Vientiane, there's no need to rush out and change money.

See Getting Around in the Vientiane chapter for information on transport from Wattay Airport to town.

OVERLAND
To/From Thailand

By River The only place where it is legal for non-Thai foreigners to cross overland into Laos from Thailand is at Nong Khai in northeastern Thailand. It's not actually 'over land' since you cross by ferry over the Mekong River. The ferries leave from Nong Khai's Tha Sadet pier every 5 minutes from 8 to 11.30 am and 2 to 4.30 pm daily except Sunday, when the border is closed. The fare is 30 baht in either direction (payable in baht only – kip or US dollars aren't accepted).

On the other side of the river (a 4-minute trip) is the Lao pier, called Tha Deua. At Tha Deua, you pass through Immigration and into a rustic restaurant area where there's an exchange booth and a duty-free shop. As with airport arrival, there's no reason to

ຂາວທວງະບະວົດ ປະຊາທິປະໄຕ ປະຊາຊົນລາວ
ດ່ານຂະໜາບົມວຽງຈັນ Vientiane Airport

ບັດແຈ້ງອອກ Departure Card P F

ປະຈວັນນີ Date ....
ຊື່ Name .... ☐ຊາຍMale ☐ຍິງFemale
ນາມສະກຸນ Family Name.....................
ວັນເດືອນປີເກີດ Date of Birth...............
ທີ່ເກີດ Place of Birth.......................
ຊົນຊາດ Nationality.........................
ອາຊີບ Profession............................
ທີ່ຢູ່ປະຈຳ Country of Residence ....
....
ໜັງສືຜ່ານແດນເລກທີ Passport No...........
ອອກໃຫ້ທີ່ Place of issue ....
ແຈ້ງເລກທີ Visa No...........................
ອອກໃຫ້ທີ່ Place of issue ....
ທີ່ຢູ່ຄວທ້າຍໃນລາວ Last Address in Laos..,.........

ຜູ້ຕິດຕາມ (ຊື່ອາຍຸ) Accompanied(Name Age)
1 ....
2 ....
....

ລາຍເຊັນຜູ້ໂດຍສານ   ລາຍເຊັນເຈົ້າໜ້າທີ ຕ.ນ
Signature of Passenger   Signature of Police I M M

Lao departure card

change money here when it can be done easily in town.

Most visitors to Laos, whether they're coming with a Tourist Visa or on another type of visa, are required to enter the country by air. This is stamped onto your visa in your passport in advance (By Air – Wattay), so it's unlikely that you'll be allowed to cross at Nong Khai coming into the country unless you arrange for permission in advance – see Visas & Travel Restrictions in the Facts for the Visitor chapter.

Transport to Vientiane You have several choices of transport from Tha Deua into town. Car or motorcycle taxis charge a standard 100 baht per vehicle, a reasonable charge considering that Vientiane is over 20 km away. Or you can catch a bus for 8 baht (or a couple of hundred kip) that terminates at Vientiane's Morning Market (*talaat sao*).

By Road & Rail A Lao-Australian plan to construct a bridge over the Mekong River from the Nong Khai railway head (Thailand) to Tha Na Leng (19 km from Vientiane) is soon to enter the construction phase and is expected to be completed by 1993. Once the bridge is up, buses and taxis will go straight into Vientiane from Nong Khai. The next step in the plan is to build a parallel rail bridge in order to extend the Bangkok-Nong Khai railway into Vientiane.

From Other Countries
Although Laos shares land borders with Burma, China, Cambodia and Vietnam, none of these are currently open to overland crossing for foreigners.

Getting Around

AIR

Lao Aviation handles all domestic flights in Laos with Vientiane as the hub – all flights originate and terminate at Wattay Airport. If you are booking tours to provinces outside Vientiane, Lao Tourism will handle your ticketing. You are allowed to book your own flights only if you possess a valid travel pass issued by the Department of Commerce.

The following provincial capitals can be visited by air from Vientiane: Luang Phabang (daily except Saturday), Savannakhet (daily), Luang Nam Tha (via Luang Phabang, Wednesday and Sunday), Xieng Khwang (daily except Tuesday and Sunday), Pak Se (daily), Sayabouli (Tuesday and Friday), Sam Neua (via Xieng Khwang, Wednesday and Saturday) and Salavan (via Savannakhet, Thursday only).

Flights to Luang Phabang, Luang Nam Tha, Savannakhet, Salavan and Pak Se are on turbo-prop Antonov 24 planes. Xieng Khwang, Sayabouli and Sam Neua flights are on Soviet-built ME-8 helicopters (originally designed as troop and cargo transports). The helicopters flights are noisy (ear plugs are a good idea) but scenic, as they fly at fairly low altitudes. Each ME-8 is designed to carry a maximum of 21 passengers seated on a metal ledge in the cabin surrounding the cargo. But it's not unusual for the copters to fly with several passengers over capacity, along with a full cargo load. Occasionally, a copter has to return to the airfield after lift-off when it becomes obvious there's too much weight!

All departure and arrival times given throughout the section on Laos are *scheduled* flight times. In everyday practice, flights are often delayed an hour or two due to weather conditions in the mountains – which includes all destinations except Vientiane, Savannakhet and Pak Se.

The departure tax for domestic flights is US$0.85 in black market kip or US$1 if you pay in US currency. See chart for fares.

Offices

The head office for Lao Aviation (tel 2093) is at 2 Thanon Pang Kham in Vientiane, alongside the Lane Xang Hotel. The office for domestic bookings (tel 2521) is directly across the street (though foreigners can book domestic flights at the head office as well – assuming they have the correct papers). It's open weekdays from 8 am to 12 noon and 2 to 5 pm, Saturdays from 8 to 11.30 am. Lao Aviation's phone number at Wattay Airport is 3015.

The Aeroflot office (tel 3501) is at the corner of Thanon Samsenthai and Thanon Chanthakumman next to the Hotel Ekkalat Metropole.

BUSES & TRUCKS

The road system in Laos remains very much undeveloped. The roads around the periphery of Vientiane prefecture, as far as the Nam Ngum Lake, are surfaced and adequate for just about any type of vehicle. Elsewhere in the country, unsurfaced roads are the rule. Since Laos is 70% mountains, even relatively short road trips involve incredibly long intervals (eg the 200 km trip from Vientiane to Luang Phabang takes around 18 hours to accomplish).

The Lao often travel long road distances by arranging rides with trucks carrying cargo from one province to another. Of course, if

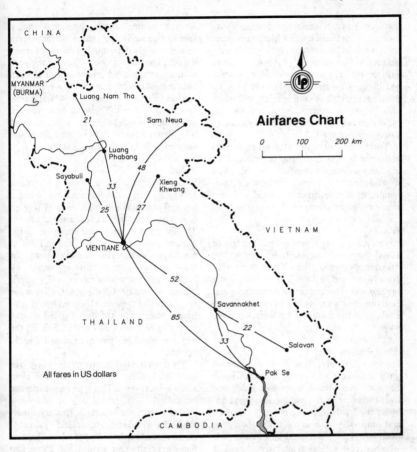

CHINA

MYANMAR
(BURMA)

Luang Nam Tha

Sam Neua

Airfares Chart

0   100   200 km

21

Luang
Phabang

48

Sayabuli

33

Xieng
Khwang

25

27

V I E T N A M

VIENTIANE

52

Savannakhet

T H A I L A N D

85

22

33

Salavan

Pak Se

All fares in US dollars

C A M B O D I A

they can afford it (or the government is paying), they avoid road travel altogether by flying on Lao Aviation planes or helicopters – fares are government-subsidised. The other alternative is river travel (see the Boat section following), which in many ways is the most convenient form of transport in Laos.

Because of road conditions, inter-city bus service is limited to the areas around provincial capitals while inter-province bus service is virtually non-existent.

Around Vientiane, buses are mostly crowded and dilapidated but very cheap (less than US$1 per 50 km). Where the roads are surfaced, they're a very acceptable way to get from one point to another. Outside Vientiane Province, Soviet, Vietnamese or Japanese trucks are often converted into passenger carriers by adding two long benches in the back. These passenger trucks are called *thaek-sii* – 'taxi' – or in some areas *sawng-thaew*, which means 'two rows' in reference to the benches in the back.

If you're waiting by the side of the road for a ride, it helps to know whether approaching vehicles are likely to take on passengers, since one truck looks like the next from a distance. You can identify proprietorship by looking at the licence tags – black tags mean the vehicle is licensed to carry paying passengers; yellow means it's a privately owned vehicle (not very common outside of towns); red is army-owned (not likely to pick up passengers); blue is civil service; and white tags belong to embassies or international organisations (who will sometimes pick up foreign passengers).

Trucks are occasionally stopped and inspected by the Lao army or police. Foreigners on a stopped vehicle may be asked to produce travel passes valid for their destination, as it is technically illegal to board inter-province transport without a pass.

BOAT

Rivers are the true highways and byways of Laos, the main thoroughfares being the Mekong, Nam Ou, Nam Khan, Nam Tha, Nam Ngum and Se Don. The Mekong is the longest and most important water route and is navigable year-round between Luang Phabang in the north and Savannakhet in the south.

River Ferries

For long distances, large diesel river ferries with overnight accommodation are used. Some of these boats have two decks, one over the other, with sleeping areas and onboard foodstalls. Others have only one deck and stop only occasionally for food. For overnight trips, it's a good idea to ascertain whether food will be available on board; if not, be sure to bring food along.

Ferry facilities are quite basic; passengers sit, eat and sleep on wooden decks. The toilet is an enclosed hole in the deck. The fare for a typical 24-hour river ferry trip is US$2.50 to US$3; a 3-day trip (say upriver from Vientiane to Luang Phabang) is about US$7. Fares do not include food if food is available.

As with inter-province travel by air or road, valid travel passes are required for foreign passengers.

River Taxis

For shorter river trips, eg from Luang Phabang to the Pak Ou caves, it's usually best to hire a river taxi since the large river ferries only ply their routes a couple of times a week. The long-tail boats (*heua hang yao*) with engines gimbal-mounted on the stern are the most typical, though for a really short trip, ie crossing a river, a rowboat (*heua phai*) can be hired. The *heua hang yao* are not as inexpensive to hire as you might think – figure on around US$4 an hour for a boat with an eight to 10 person capacity.

TAXIS

Each of the three largest towns – Vientiane, Luang Phabang and Savannakhet – has a handful of car taxis that are used by foreign businesspeople and the occasional tourist. The only place you'll find these are at the airports (arrival times only) and in front of the larger hotels. The cars are usually of Eastern European or Soviet origin, eg Wolgas and Ladas, but occasionally you'll run across an older US car or a new Japanese car. Taxis like these can be hired by the trip, by the hour or by the day. Typical all-day hires cost between US$7 and US$12. By the trip, you shouldn't pay more than US$0.50 per km.

Three-wheeled motorcycle taxis are common in these same towns as well as in some smaller ones. This type of vehicle can be called 'taxi' (*thaek-sii*) or *saam-law* ('samlor' or 'three-wheels'). The larger ones made in Thailand are called 'jumbos' (*jamboh*) and can hold four to six passengers. Fares generally cost about US$0.25 per km per vehicle (you must bargain to get the correct rate). They can go anywhere a regular taxi can go, but aren't usually hired for distances greater than 20 km.

PEDICABS

The bicycle samlor is the mainstay of local transport for hire throughout urban Laos. These used to be commonly called *cyclo* (*sii-khlo*) following the French, but this term is being used less frequently than 'samlor' nowadays. Samlor fares cost about the same as motorcycle taxis but are generally used only for distances less than 2 km or so.

Bargaining is sometimes necessary to get the correct fare, though pedicab drivers seem to be more honest than the motorcycle taxi drivers.

TRANSPORT RESTRICTIONS

As noted above, all inter-province travel (for both foreigners and Lao nationals) requires the possession of a travel pass that is valid for the passenger's destination. This applies whether you're boarding an aeroplane, helicopter, river ferry, bus, truck or car. The travel pass (*bai anuyaat doen thaang*) for foreign tourists is issued by the Department of Commerce; for foreign employees of international organisations it's the Ministry of Foreign Affairs (Lao nationals get theirs from the Provincial Office). The travel pass is not always requested when you board but will almost surely be checked when you arrive at your destination.

If you are discovered by the Lao authorities to have travelled outside of Vientiane without a travel pass, you'll have to undergo a course of questioning and then return to Vientiane for almost immediate deportation – at the very least. You might also end up spending some time in jail.

Within a single province for which you already have travel permission, you are free to travel by any form of transport.

Vientiane Province

VIENTIANE ຈງຈັນ

Vientiane is three entities: province (population 267,000), prefecture (160,000) and city (120,000). Located on a bend in the Mekong River, it was originally one of the early Lao river-valley fiefdoms or *muang* that were consolidated around the time Europe was leaving the Dark Ages. The Lao that settled here chose the area because the surrounding alluvial plains are so incredibly fertile. Early on, the Vientiane *muang* prospered and enjoyed a fragile sovereignty.

At various times over the 10 or so centuries of its history, however, Vientiane lost its standing as an independent kingdom and was controlled by the Burmese, Siamese, Vietnamese and Khmers. When the kingdom of Lan Xang (Million Elephants) was established in the 14th century by the Khmer-supported conqueror Fa Ngum, it was originally centred in Muang Sawa (Luang Phabang), but by the early 16th century the capital had been moved to Vientiane. When Laos became a French protectorate in the late 19th and early 20th centuries, Vientiane was named the capital city and has remained so under communist rule today.

The name means City of the Moon and is actually pronounced Wieng Chan (*Wièng* means 'city' or 'place with walls' in Lao; Chan is the Lao pronunciation of Chandra, a Sanskrit word for 'moon'). The French gave the city its common Roman spelling. It is one of three classic Indochinese cities (including Saigon/Ho Chi Minh City and Phnom Penh) that conjure up images of exotic Eurasian settings. For the most part, Vientiane lives up to these images, with its intriguing mix of Lao, Thai, Chinese, Vietnamese, French, US and Soviet influences.

Although Vientiane is the largest city in the country, it's still small enough that getting to know it is fairly easy. Parts of town are really quite attractive, in particular in the older section of town along the Mekong River. Tree-lined boulevards and old temples impart an atmosphere of timelessness, in spite of passing traffic (which is never very heavy).

Orientation

The city curves along the Mekong River following a bent north-west to south-east axis, with the central district of Chanthabuli at the central bend. Most of the government offices, hotels, restaurants and historic temples are in Muang Chanthabuli near the river. A few old French colonial buildings and Vietnamese-Chinese shophouses remain alongside newer structures built according to the Social Realist school of architecture.

Street signs are mostly written in Lao script only, although signs at major intersections are also written in French. The French designations for street names varies (eg 'route', 'rue' and 'avenue') but the Lao script always reads *thanon*, which means the same as all the French and English variations. Therefore, when asking directions it's always best just to avoid possible confusion and use the Lao word *thanon*.

The main streets in the downtown district are Thanon Samsenthai, which is the pre-eminent shopping area; Thanon Setthathirat (pronounced Setthathilat since there is no 'r' sound in Lao), where several of the most famous temples are located; and Thanon Fa Ngum, which runs along the river and is lined with eucalyptus, pipal and teak trees. Branching off northward, out of Muang Chanthabuli and into Muang Saisettha, is Thanon Lan Xang, Vientiane's widest street.

The main portion of Thanon Lan Xang is a divided boulevard that leads past the Morning Market to the Pratuxai or Victory Gate. After the Pratuxai, it splits into two roads, Thanon Phon Kheng and Thanon That Luang. Thanon Phon Kheng leads to the Unknown Soldiers Memorial, the Lao People's Army Museum and the Thai

Embassy. Thanon That Luang leads to Pha That Luang.

To the north-east of Muang Chanthabuli is Muang Saisettha, where Pha That Luang, Lao Tourism and several embassies are . This is also a residential area of newer French and US-style mansions inhabited by European and Asian expatriates who work for UN agencies or aid programs.

To the south-east of central Vientiane is the mostly local residential *muang* of Sisattanak and to the west is the similarly residential Muang Sikhottabong.

The *muangs* of Vientiane are broken up into neighbourhoods or villages called *ban*. Wattay Airport, for example, is in Ban Wattai, a village in the southern part of Muang Sikhottabong.

Information

Tourist Office The Lao Tourism office is on a hard-to-find side street to the north-east of the Pratuxai monument. This road is apparently unnamed, but it runs between Thanon Nehru and Thanon Phonxai Yai and is almost directly across the street from the offices of the Food & Agriculture Organization. This office is positioned incorrectly on the government's tourist map of Vientiane, so don't waste your time looking for offices on or off Thanon Samsenthai as indicated. (The Immigration Office, on Thanon Talat Sao, has a good wall map showing how to get there, however.)

The only reason to visit Lao Tourism is if you want to book a Lao Tourism package to another province in Laos. The staff at Lao Tourism speaks French and a little English. For information on what to see and do in and around Vientiane, you're better off relying on this guidebook or on tourist information material that is available from the Australian Embassy and various souvenir shops downtown.

You can walk to Lao Tourism from downtown Vientiane, but it's a good 2.5 km distance from the Lane Xang Hotel, for example. A samlor or motorcycle taxi to Lao Tourism costs around US$0.50 one way or slightly more round trip.

There is also a separate Vientiane Tourism office, but they always refer people to the main Lao Tourism office (and none of the staff speaks English).

Post The Post, Telephone & Telegraph office (PTT) is on the corner of Thanon Lan Xang and Thanon Khu Vieng, across the road from the Morning Market. Business hours are from 8 am to 5 pm Monday to Saturday and from 8 am to 12 noon on Sunday.

Telephone The PTT office is only for calls within Laos. Overseas calls can be arranged at the International Telephone Office (Cabines Télécommuniques Internationales) on Thanon Setthathirat. It's open 24 hours a day but lines are sometimes down during heavy rains.

Local calls can be made from any hotel lobby – usually there is no charge. The International Children's Learning Centre (ICLC) off Thanon Samsenthai near Wat Si Muang publishes a local telephone directory called 'How to Call Us & Our Friends' that lists the phone numbers of practically every expat in Vientiane as well as those of embassies, bilateral aid programmes, UN agencies, non-governmental organisations and Lao government offices. The directory can only be purchased at the ICLC and it costs US$5.

Money The Lao Exterior Commerce Bank (La Banque pour le Commerce Extérieur Lao) is the only bank in town equipped to deal with foreigners. It's on Thanon Pang Kham near Lao Aviation and the Lane Xang Hotel. See Banking in the Money section of the Facts for the Visitor chapter for details on exchange restrictions. Bank hours are from 8.30 to 4 pm Monday to Friday.

Foreign Embassies Twenty-three nations have embassies and consulates in Vientiane. Their addresses and telephone numbers are listed and several of the more important ones (embassies that Lonely Planet readers are likely to visit) are indicated on the Vientiane map.

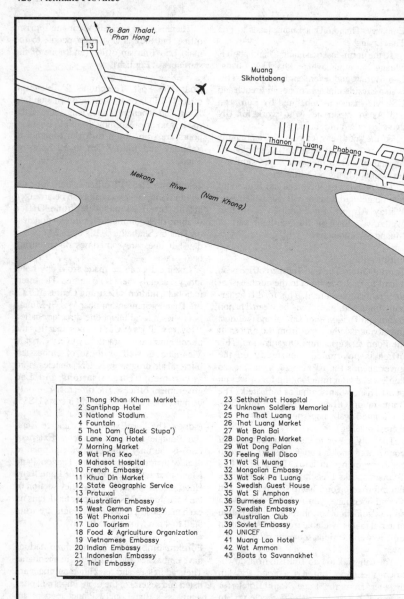

To Ban Thalat, Phan Hong

13

Muang Sikhottabong

Thanon Luang Phabang

Mekong River (Nam Khong)

1 Thong Kham Kham Market
2 Santiphap Hotel
3 National Stadium
4 Fountain
5 That Dam ('Black Stupa')
6 Lane Xang Hotel
7 Morning Market
8 Wat Pha Keo
9 Mahasot Hospital
10 French Embassy
11 Khua Din Market
12 State Geographic Service
13 Pratuxai
14 Australian Embassy
15 West German Embassy
16 Wat Phonxai
17 Lao Tourism
18 Food & Agriculture Organization
19 Vietnamese Embassy
20 Indian Embassy
21 Indonesian Embassy
22 Thai Embassy

23 Setthathirat Hospital
24 Unknown Soldiers Memorial
25 Pha That Luang
26 That Luang Market
27 Wat Ban Bai
28 Dong Palan Market
29 Wat Dong Palan
30 Feeling Well Disco
31 Wat Si Muang
32 Mongolian Embassy
33 Wat Sok Pa Luang
34 Swedish Guest House
35 Wat Si Amphon
36 Burmese Embassy
37 Swedish Embassy
38 Australian Club
39 Soviet Embassy
40 UNICEF
41 Muang Lao Hotel
42 Wat Ammon
43 Boats to Savannakhet

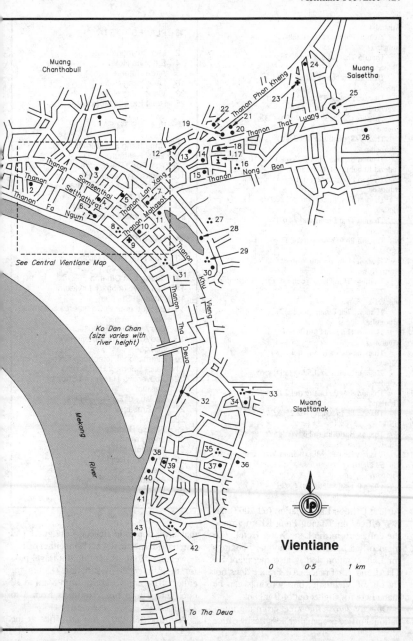

Vientiane

Muang Chanthabuli

Muang Saisettha

Muang Sisattanak

Thanon Phon Kheng

Thanon That Luang

Thanon Nong Bon

Thanon Lan Xang

Thanon Mahasot

Thanon Samsenthai

Thanon Setthathirat

Thanon Fa Ngum

Thanon Khu Vieng

Thanon Tha Deua

Ko Dan Chan
(size varies with
river height)

Mekong
River

See Central Vientiane Map

To Tha Deua

0   0.5   1 km

Australia
  Thanon Phonxai Noi (tel 2477)
Bulgaria
  Thanon That Luang (tel 3236)
China
  Thanon Wat Nak Yai (tel 3494)
Cuba
  Thanon Saphan Thong (tel 3150)
Czechoslovakia
  Thanon Tha Deua (tel 2705, 4423)
France
  Thanon Setthathirat (tel 2642)
Cambodia
  Thanon Saphan Thong Neua (tel 2750, 4527)
Federal Rebublic of Germany
  Thanon Phonxai Noi (tel 2024)
Hungary
  Thanon That Luang Tai (tel 2205/3111)
India
  Thanon That Luang (tel 2410)
Indonesia
  Thanon Phon Kheng (tel 2370/3)
Japan
  Thanon Dong Si Sun Wun (tel 2584)
North Korea
  Thanon Tha Deua (behind Fire Station; tel 2750/4527)
Malaysia
  Thanon That Luang (tel 2662)
Mongolia
  Thanon Tha Deua (tel 3666)
Myanmar
  Thanon Sok Pa Luang (tel 2789)
Poland
  Thanon Talat That Luang (tel 2456)
Sweden
  Thanon Sok Pa Luang (tel 2922/5729)
Thailand
  Thanon Phon Kheng (tel 2508/2765)
USA
  Thanon Bartolini (tel 3570/2357)
USSR
  Thanon Don Pa Mia (behind Wat Ammon) (tel 5339/5012)
Vietnam
  Thanon That Luang (tel 5578)

■	PLACES TO STAY
2	Lao Chaleune Hotel
4	Saysana Hotel
8	Anou Hotel
16	Lane Xang Hotel
23	Vieng Vilay Hotel
25	Hotel Ekkalat Metropole

▼	PLACES TO EAT
1	Nang Bang Restaurant
5	'BGL' Restaurant
9	Thai Food Restaurant
10	Santisouk Restaurant
17	Sukiyaki Bar & Restaurant, Lao Restaurant
18	Nam Phou Restaurant & Government Bookshop

●	OTHER
3	Haan Kin Deum Mixai
6	Vinh Loi Bakery House
7	Saeng Lao Cinema
11	Lao Revolutionary Museum
12	National Stadium
13	Banque pour le Commerce Exterieur Lao
14	Lao Aviation (Domestic)
15	Lao Aviation (International)
19	Mosque
20	International Telephone Office
21	Tailor Shops & Handicrafts
22	Souvenir & Handicraft Shops
24	Aeroflot
26	Ministry of Foreign Affairs
27	US Embassy
28	GPO
29	Bicycle Rentals
30	Immigration
31	Vienglaty Mai Disco
32	Mahasot Hospital
33	French Embassy
34	Le Club France
35	Catholic Church

Airline Offices Lao Aviation (tel 2093) has two offices on Thanon Pang Kham around the corner from the Lane Xang Hotel. The main office handles international bookings for Lao Aviation and is also the agent for THAI and Air France. Air France does not fly out of Vientiane, but bookings can be made here for flights out of Bangkok.

Directly across the street from the international office is a smaller, less flashy office that does domestic tickets. Foreigners can purchase domestic tickets from either office, however, as long as they hold a travel pass for their intended destination. Hours for either office are weekdays from 8 am to 12 noon and 2 to 5 pm, Saturdays from 8 to 11.30 am.

Aeroflot (tel 3501) has an office at the

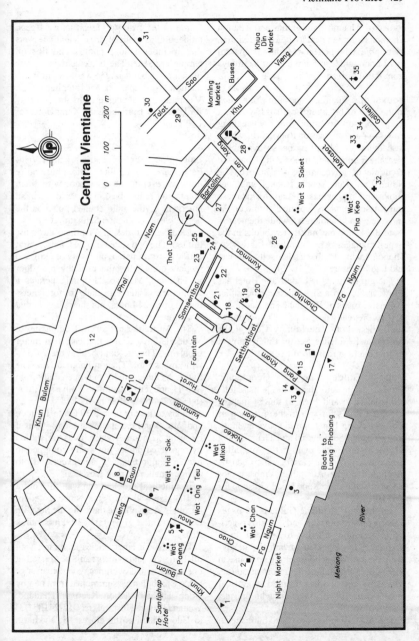

Central Vientiane

0   100   200 m

corner of Thanon Samsenthai and Thanon Chantha Kumman next to the Hotel Ekkalat, Metropole. It is open on weekdays from 8 am to 12 noon and 2 to 5 pm and on Saturdays from 8 to 11.30 am.

Bookshops Vientiane does not offer much in the way of books in English. If you're a reader, be sure to bring your own reading (unless you read Lao or Russian, in which case there are plenty of books available). Near the fountain on Thanon Pang Kham are a couple of government bookstores. The Noum Lao (Lao Youth) Book Centre has books and magazines in Lao, Vietnamese and Russian, posters, political comic books and a few Lao handicrafts, while the nearby State Bookshop has mostly textbooks in the same languages. The Vientiane Library on Thanon Luang Phabang also sells Russian and Lao literature.

The gift shop at the Lane Xang Hotel has a few books in English for sale, and rather expensive maps of Vientiane and Laos.

If you're really desperate for something to read, check with The Library Club at the Australian Residence. See the Entertainment section later for more information.

Maps & Guides The State Geographic Service prints and distributes a passable, bilingual (Lao and French) tourist map of Vientiane that's for sale in the gift shop of the Lane Xang Hotel and in souvenir shops along Thanon Samsenthai and Thanon Pang Kham. Better are the maps in the Australian Embassy's *Vientiane Guide*, which can be purchased at the Australian Embassy for US$8 or at the Lane Xang Hotel gift shop for US$10.

The helpful Vientiane Guide is 46 pages plus five pages of maps and contains practical information on what to see and do in Vientiane. It's oriented toward the newly-arrived expatriate who is setting up house in Vientiane, so not all of the information (eg, where to get pictures framed, electrical repair) is useful for travellers who are just passing through.

The Australian Embassy also publishes *A Guide to the Wats of Vientiane*, a 64-page guidebook to a dozen or so Vientiane wats that includes colour photos and tips on temple etiquette. The book contains a few inaccuracies but is on the whole a fair introduction to temple art and architecture in Vientiane. It's available from the embassy for US$10 or from the Lane Xang Hotel for US$12.

Emergency The six districts within Vientiane each have a police station, but you're unlikely ever to have contact with them unless you're involved in an accident. In an emergency, you could contact police at the police kiosk on Thanon Setthathirat.

Medical facilities in Vientiane are quite limited. The two state hospitals, Setthathirat and Mahasot, operate on levels of skill and hygiene quite below that available next door in Thailand. Mahasot Hospital operates a Diplomatic Clinic 'especially for foreigners' that is open 24 hours, but the reality is that few foreigners use this clinic.

The Australian and Swedish embassies in Vientiane have clinics that can treat minor problems. They're both behind the Australian Embassy off Thanon Phonxai Noi. The Swedish Clinic (tel 4641) is open daily from 8 to 11 am. The Australian Embassy Clinic (tel 2477, 4691; after hours 2183) is open Monday to Friday from 8.30 am to 12 noon and 2 to 4 pm except Wednesday when it closes at 12 noon. These clinics are staffed by registered nurses but aren't equipped to handle major medical emergencies. Both charge small treatment fees.

If a medical problem can wait till you're in Bangkok, all the better, since excellent hospitals are available there (eg the Seventh Day Adventist Hospital, 430 Phitsanulok Rd).

For medical emergencies that can't wait till Bangkok and which can't be treated at one of the embassy clinics, you can arrange to have ambulances summoned from nearby Udon Thani or Khon Kaen in Thailand. Wattana Private Hospital (tel 042-241031/3) in Udon Thani is the closest. Si Nakharin

Hospital (tel 043-237602/6) is farther away in Khon Kaen but is supposed to be the best medical facility in north-eastern Thailand. From either of these hospitals, patients can be transferred to Bangkok as necessary.

Pha That Luang ພະທາດຫລວງ

The Pha That Luang (Great Sacred Stupa) is the most important national monument in Laos, a symbol of both the Buddhist religion and Lao sovereignty. Legend has it that Ashokan missionaries from India erected a stupa here to enclose a breastbone of the Buddha as early as the 3rd century BC, but there is no physical evidence to confirm either the date or the contents of such a monument. But excavations at the site and nearby suggest that a Khmer monastery may have been built here between the 11th and 13th centuries AD.

When King Setthathirat moved the Lan Xang capital from Luang Phabang to Vientiane in the mid-16th century, he ordered the construction of That Luang in its current form, on the site of the Khmer temple. Construction began in 1566 AD and in succeeding years four wats were built around the stupa, one on each side. Only two remain today, Wat That Luang Neua to the north and Wat That Luang Tai to the south. Wat That Luang Neua is the monastic residence of the Supreme Patriarch (Pha Sangkharat) of Lao Buddhism.

In 1641, Gerard van Wuystoff, an envoy of the Dutch East Indies Company, visited Vientiane and was received by King Suliya Vongsa at That Luang in an apparently magnificent ceremony. The Lan Xang kingdom was at the peak of its historical glory and van Wuystoff wrote that he was deeply impressed by the 'enormous pyramid, the top of which was covered with gold leaf weighing about a thousand pounds'(454 kg).

Unfortunately, the glory of Lan Xang and That Luang was only to last another 60 years or so. The stupa and the temples were damaged considerably during the 18th and 19th centuries by invading Burmese and Siamese armies. During a Siamese invasion in 1828, Vientiane was ransacked and depopulated to such an extent that That Luang remained abandoned until it was badly restored under French rule in 1900.

Thirty-three years before the 1900 restoration, a French explorer and architect named Delaporte had stumbled on the abandoned and overgrown That Luang and had made detailed sketches of the monument. Between 1931 and 1935, a French university department reconstructed That Luang according to Delaporte's sketches. Or so say the French; the Lao today claim they carried out the reconstruction because they didn't like the way the French botched the job in 1900. Records to confirm or refute either story are somewhat scarce.

The monument today looks very fortress-like from a distance. Surrounding it is a high-walled cloister with tiny windows. (This was added by King Anouvong in the early 19th century as a defence against invaders.) But even more aggressive-looking than the thick walls are the pointed stupas themselves, which are built in three levels that almost give the appearance of a missile cluster. From a closer perspective, however, the Great Stupa opens up to its admirers and looks much more like a religious monument.

The Great Stupa is designed to be mounted by the faithful, so there are walk-ways around each level, with stairways between. Each level of the monument has different architectural features in which Buddhist doctrine is encoded; devout Buddhists are supposed to contemplate the meaning of these features as they circumambulate. The first level is a square base measuring 68 by 69 metres that supports 323 *sima* or ordination stones. There are also four arched prayer-gates (*haw wai*), one on each side, with short stairways leading up to and beyond them to the second level. The second level is 48 by 48 metres and surrounded by 120 lotus petals. There are 288 *simas* on this level, as well as 30 small stupas symbolising the 30 Buddhist perfections (*palami saamsip that* in Lao, beginning with alms-giving and ending with equanimity). Each of these stupas at one time contained smaller gold stupas and gold leaves, but these were taken by Chinese bandits while That Luang was abandoned in the 19th century.

Arched gates again lead to the next level, which is 30 metres along each side. The tall central stupa, which has a brick core that has been stuccoed over, is supported here by a bowl-shaped base reminiscent of India's first Buddhist stupa at Sanchi. At the top of this mound the superstructure, surrounded by lotus petals, begins.

The curvilinear, four-sided spire resembles an elongated lotus bud and is said to symbolise the growth of a lotus from a seed in a muddy lake bottom to a bloom over the lake's surface, a metaphor for human advancement from ignorance to enlightenment in Buddhism. The stupa is crowned by a stylised banana flower and parasol, but the main part of the spire is no longer gilded. From ground to pinnacle, That Luang is 45 metres tall.

Pha That Luang is about 4 km north-east of the centre of Vientiane at the end of Thanon That Luang. In front of the entrance to the compound is a statue of King Setthathirat.

A small booklet entitled *The Short History of Pha That Luang* can be purchased for a couple of hundred kip at the entrance. The grounds are open to visitors from 8 to 11.30 am and 2 to 4.30 pm, Tuesday to Sunday and are closed Mondays and public holidays. Admission is US$0.25 per person.

If you happen to be in Vientiane in mid-November, don't miss the That Luang Festival (Bun That Luang). See Festivals & Holidays in the Facts About the Country chapter for a brief description.

Cloister The encircling cloister (85 metres on each side) contains various Buddha images. A display of historic sculpture, including not only classic Lao sculpture but also Khmer figures, is on either side of the front entrance (inside). Worshippers sometimes stick balls of rice to the walls (especially during the That Luang Festival in November) to pay respect to the spirit of King Setthathirat.

Wat Si Saket   ວັດສີ່ສະເກດ

This temple is near the Presidential Palace at the north-eastern corner of Thanon Lan Xang and Thanon Setthathirat. Built in 1818 by King Anouvong (Chao Anou), it is the oldest temple still standing in Vientiane today – all others were either built after Wat Si Saket or were rebuilt after destruction by the Siamese in 1828. King Anouvong was more or less a vassal of the Siamese state and had Wat Si Saket constructed in the early Bangkok style. This is probably why the Siamese spared this wat from destruction when they quashed Anouvong's subsequent rebellion against Siamese rule.

In spite of the Siamese architectural influence, Wat Si Saket has several unique features. The interior walls of the cloister are riddled with small niches that contain over 2000 silver and ceramic Buddha images. Over 300 seated and standing Buddhas of varying sizes and materials (wood, stone and bronze) rest on long shelves below the niches, most sculpted or cast in the characteristic Lao style (see Arts in the Facts About the Country chapter for details on Lao religious sculpture). Most of the images are from 16th to 19th century Vientiane but a few hail from 15th to 16th century Luang Phabang. A Khmer-style Naga Buddha – in which the Buddha is seated on a coiled cobra deity whose multi-headed hood shelters the image – is also on display; it was brought from a Khmer site at nearby Hat Sai Fong. Along the western side of the cloister is a pile of broken and half-melted Buddhas from the 1828 Siamese-Lao war.

The *sim* is surrounded by a colonnaded terrace in the Bangkok style and topped by a five-tiered roof. The interior walls have hundreds of Buddha niches similar to those in the cloister, as well as jataka murals depicting the Buddha's life story. Portions of the Bangkok-style painted murals are unrestored 1820s originals, while some parts are a 1913 restoration. UNESCO has plans to do a complete mural restoration by the end of 1991.

The flowered ceiling was inspired by Siamese temples in Ayuthaya, which were in turn inspired by floral designs in the royal palace at Versailles. At the rear interior of the *sim* is an altar with several Buddha images, bringing the total number of Buddhas at Wat Si Saket to 6840! The standing Buddha to the left on the upper altar was cast to the same physical proportions as King Anouvong. The large gilt wood candlestand in front of the altar is an original, carved in 1819.

On the outside veranda at the rear of the *sim* is a 5-metre long wooden trough carved to resemble a *naga* or snake deity. This is the *hang song nam pha* (image-watering rail), which is used during Bun Pi Mai (Lao New Year) to pour water over Buddha images for ritual cleansing.

To the far left of the entrance to the cloister, facing Thanon Lan Xang, is a raised *haw trai* (tripitika library) with a Burmese-style roof. The scriptures that were once contained here are now in Bangkok. Only one of the four doors is original: the other three were restored in 1913.

The hours and admission fee at Wat Si Saket are the same as for Pha That Luang. A Lao guide who speaks French and English is usually on hand to describe the temple and answer questions. There is no charge for the services of the guide.

Wat Pha Keo (Kaew) ວັດພະແກ້ວ

Just down Thanon Setthathirat, about a hundred metres from Wat Si Saket, is the former royal temple of the Lao monarchy, Wat Pha Keo. It has been converted to a museum and is no longer a place of worship.

According to the Lao, the temple was originally built in 1565 by command of King Setthathirat. Setthathirat had been a ruler of the nearby Lanna kingdom in northern Thailand while his father King Phothisarat reigned over Lan Xang. After his father died, he inherited the Lan Xang throne and moved the capital of Lan Xang to Vientiane. From Lanna he brought with him the so-called Emerald Buddha (Pha Keo in Lao, which means 'jewel Buddha image' – but the image is actually made of a type of jade). Wat Pha Keo was built to house this image and to serve as the King's personal place of worship. Following a skirmish with the Lao in 1779, the Siamese recovered the Emerald Buddha and installed it in Bangkok's own Wat Phra Keo (*Phra* is the Thai word for Buddha image; *Pha* is Lao). Later during the Siamese-Lao war of 1828, Vientiane's Wat Pha Keo was razed.

Between 1936 and 1942, the temple was rebuilt, supposedly following the exact same original plan. Herein lies the problem in dating the original temple. If the currently standing structure was restored in the original style, it doesn't seem likely that the original could have been built in the mid-16th century, as it doesn't resemble any known structure in Siam, Laos, Myanmar or Cambodia from that period. In fact it looks very much like a 19th century Bangkok-style *sim*. On the other hand, if the restoration's architects chose to use the more common 19th century style (as exemplified by Wat Si Saket) because they really didn't have the original plans, then it's possible the original was constructed in 1565 as claimed (if it wasn't, it casts the whole Emerald Buddha story into doubt).

At any rate, today's Wat Pha Keo is not that impressive a structure except in size. The rococo ornamentation that runs up and down every door, window and base looks unfinished. But some of the best examples of Buddhist sculpture found in Laos are kept here, so it's worth visiting for that reason alone. A dozen or so prominent sculptures are displayed along the surrounding terrace. These include a 6th to 9th century Dvaravati-style stone Buddha; several bronze standing and sitting Lao-style Buddhas – including the 'Calling for Rain' (standing with hands at his sides), 'Offering Protection' (palms stretched out in front) and 'Contemplating the Tree of Enlightenment' (hands crossed at the wrist in front) poses; and a collection of inscribed Lao and Mon stelae.

Inside the *sim* are royal requisites such as a gilded throne, more Buddhist sculpture (mostly smaller pieces, including a copy of the Pha Bang, the original of which is stored in Luang Phabang), some Khmer stelae, various wooden carvings (door panels, candlestands, lintels) and palm-leaf manuscripts.

The *sim* is surrounded by a garden. At the back of the building is a large stone jar from Xieng Khwang's Plain of Jars (most of the jars that remain in the fields of Xieng Khwang are larger than this one).

Wat Pha Keo is open from 8 to 11.30 am and 2 to 4.30 pm, Tuesday to Sunday and are closed Mondays and public holidays. A French and English-speaking guide is occasionally available at Wat Pha Keo as well. When rains are unusually heavy, the grounds of Wat Pha Keo become flooded and the entrance may be closed until the water level goes down.

Wat Ong Teu Mahawihan ວັດອົງຕື້ມະຫາວິຫານ
Called Wat Ong Teu for short (Temple of the Heavy Buddha), this temple is one of the most important in all of Laos. It was originally built around 1500 AD by King Setthathirat, but like every temple in Vientiane except Wat Si Saket, it was destroyed in later wars with the Siamese, then rebuilt in the 19th and 20th centuries. The Deputy Patriarch (*Hawng Sangkharat*) of the Lao monastic order resides at Wat Ong Teu and presides over the Buddhist Institute, a school for monks who come from all over the country to study dharma in the capital.

The temple's namesake is a large 16th century bronze Buddha of several tons that sits in the rear of the *sim*, flanked by two standing Buddhas. This *sim* is also deservedly famous for the wooden facade over the front terrace, a masterpiece of Lao carving.

Wat Ong Teu is on a shady stretch of Thanon Setthathirat, between Thanon Chao Anou and Thanon Nokeo Kumman.

Wat Hai Sok ວັດຫາຍໂສກ
Across Thanon Setthathirat from Way Ong Teu 'is the lesser acclaimed Wat Hai Sok, which is currently undergoing restoration. It's worth a quick look because of the impressive five-tiered roof (nine if you count the lower terrace roofs).

Wat Mixai ວັດມີໄຊ
Wat Mixai is in the next block east from Wat Ong Teu and Wat Hai Sok along the same street. The *sim* is in the Bangkok style, with a veranda that goes all the way round. The heavy gates, flanked by two *nyak* or guardian giants, are also Bangkok style. An elementary school is in the compound.

Wat In Paeng ວັດອິນແປງ
This temple is in the next block west of Wat Ong Teu. The *sim* is nicely decorated with stucco relief. Over the front veranda gable is an impressive wood and mosaic facade.

Wat Chan ວັດຈັນ
This one's on Fa Ngum Rd near the river, a block south of Wat Ong Teu. The carved wooden panels on the rebuilt *sim* are typically Lao and well executed. Inside the *sim* is a large bronze seated Buddha from the original temple that stood at this site (the Buddha was never moved). In the courtyard are the remains of a stupa that once had standing Buddha images in the 'Calling for Rain' pose on all four sides; one image remains.

Wat Si Muang ວັດສີເມືອງ
These temple grounds are the site of the city pillar (*lak muang*) and are thus considered the home of the guardian spirit of Vientiane. Legend has it that the spot was selected in 1563 as the site for a new wat by a group of sages when King Setthathirat moved his capital to Vientiane. Once the spot was chosen, a large hole was dug to receive the heavy stone pillar (probably taken from an ancient Khmer site nearby), which was suspended over the hole with ropes. Drums and gongs were sounded to summon the townspeople to the area and everyone waited for a volunteer to jump in the hole as a sacrifice to the spirit. A pregnant girl finally leapt in and the ropes were released, thus establishing the town guardianship. (The wat is not, however, named after the girl who was killed, as one guide to Vientiane wats has suggested. Si Muang simply means 'Sacred City'.)

The *sim* (destroyed in 1828 and later

rebuilt in 1915) was built around the *lak muang*, which forms the centre of the altar. The stone pillar is wrapped in sacred cloth, and in front of it is a carved wooden stele with a seated Buddha in relief. The stele is wrapped in blinking red and green lights, as if it were a Christmas decoration.

Several other Buddha images surround the pillar. One worth noting is kept on a cushion a little to the left and in front of the altar. The rather crude, partially damaged stone Buddha survived the 1828 destruction in one of the original *that* on the wat grounds. The locals believe this image has the power to grant wishes or answer troubling questions. If your request is granted, you're supposed to return to Wat Si Muang later with an offering of bananas and coconuts (usually two of each). This is why so many coconuts and bananas are sitting around the *sim*!

In front of the *sim* is a little public park with a statue of King Sisavang Vong.

Wat Si Muang is located at a three-way intersection where Thanon Setthathirat and Thanon Samsenthai converge to become Thanon Tha Deua.

Wat Sok Pa Luang ວັດໂສກປ່າຫຼວງ

Wat Mahaphutthawongsa Pa Luang Pa Yai is the full name for this forest temple (*wat pa*) in south Vientiane's Sisattanak district. It's famous for its rustic herbal saunas, which are usually administered by eight-precept nuns who reside at the temple. Some preparation is involved, so it's wise to make arrangements in advance. After the relaxing sauna, you can take tea while cooling off; expert massage is also available. For optimum medicinal results you're not supposed to wash away your accumulated perspiration for 2 or 3 hours afterwards. Apparently, this allows the herbs to soak into your pores. Nearby Wat Si Amphon also does herbal saunas (see the Getting There & Away section later). Neither temple charges fees for saunas, but you should leave a donation of at least US$2 or US$3 per sauna (the number of bathers doesn't matter).

Wat Sok Pa Luang is also known for its course of instruction in *vipassana*, a type of Buddhist meditation that involves careful mind-body analysis. The abbot and teacher is Ajaan Sali Kantasilo, who was born in Yasothon, Thailand in 1932. Ajaan Sali (Chali in Thai) came to Laos in 1953 at the request of monks and laity in Vientiane who wanted to study vipassana. He accepts foreign students but only speaks Lao and Thai, so interested people will have to arrange for an interpreter if they don't speak either of these languages. Before 1975 he had many Western students; since then he's taught only Lao followers and a small number of interested Russians.

Getting There & Away Taxi, jumbo and samlor drivers all know how to get to Wat Sok Pa Luang. If you're travelling by car or bicycle, take Thanon Khu Vieng south past the Morning Market about 2.5 km until you come to a fairly major road on the left (this is Thanon Sok Pa Luang, but it's unmarked). Turn left here; the entrance to the wat is about half a km on the left. The temple buildings are back in the woods so all you can see from the road is the tall, ornamented gate. If you pass the Swedish Guest House on the left, you've gone too far; the wat is a hundred or so metres before the Swedish Guest House.

Wat Si Amphon is further south off Thanon Si Amphon. A few hundred metres past the Swedish Guest House, turn right on Thanon Si Amphon; Wat Si Amphon is on the left.

That Dam ທາດດໍ

The so-called 'Black Stupa' or That Dam is on Thanon Bartolini, between the Hotel Ekkalat Metropole and the US Embassy. Local mythology says the stupa is the abode of a dormant seven-headed dragon that came to life during the 1828 Siamese-Lao war and protected local citizens. The stupa appears to date from the Lanna or early Lan Xang period and is very similar to stupas in Chiang Saen, Thailand. That Dam is now overgrown and in partial ruins, but it's still impressive-looking.

Wat Xieng Khwan ວັດຊຽງຂວນ

Wat Xieng Khwan (Spirit City Temple), 24 km south of the town centre, is not a true wat since there are no monks in residence and there never have been. Nor is there a *sim* or any other traditional Buddhist architecture. Locals often call it 'Buddha Park', a more apt description since it is a collection of Buddhist (and Hindu) sculpture in a meadow by the side of the Mekong River.

The park was designed and built in 1958 by Luang Pu (Venerable Grandfather) Bunleua Sulilat, a yogi-priest-shaman who merges Hindu and Buddhist philosophy, mythology and iconography into a cryptic whole. He developed a very large following in Laos and north-eastern Thailand, and moved to Thailand around the time of the 1975 revolution. In 1978, he established the similarly inspired Wat Khaek in Nong Khai, Thailand, where he now resides. Originally, Bunleua is supposed to have studied under a Hindu *rishi* in Vietnam.

The cement sculpture at Xieng Khwan is bizarre, yet somehow compelling. It includes statues of Shiva, Vishnu, Arjuna, Buddha and every other Hindu or Buddhist deity imaginable, as well as a few secular figures, all supposedly cast by unskilled artists under Luang Pu's direction. The style of the figures is remarkably uniform.

There is only one building on the grounds, a large pumpkin-shaped monument with three levels joined by interior spiral stairways. It's said that the three levels represent hell, earth and heaven. The rooms inside are filled with small sculptures and are designed so that you can either enter them for viewing or merely look in through windows from an outer hallway at each level. The last spiral stairway leads onto the top of the structure, from where you can view the huge sculptures outside.

Luang Pu doesn't come around the Buddha Park these days, but a caretaker at the gate does take donations.

Pratuxai ປະຕູຊາຍ

The Pratuxai, a large monument very reminiscent of the Arc de Triomphe in Paris, is

Pratuxai Monument, Vientiane

known by a variety of names. The official Lao name, Pratuxai, is roughly equivalent to Arch (*pratu*, also translated as 'door' or 'gate') of Triumph (*xai*, from the Sanskrit *jaya* or 'victory'). Ironically, it was built in 1969 with US-purchased cement that was supposed to have been used for the construction of a new airport.

Since it's purpose was to commemorate the Lao who had died in pre-revolutionary wars, current Lao maps typically label it 'Old Monument' (Ancien Monument in French, or *Anusawali Kao* in Lao) in order to draw attention to the newer Unknown Soldiers Memorial erected since the Revolution. Expats living in Vientiane (who rarely speak Lao) redundantly call it the Anusawali Monument (*anusawali* means 'monument' in Lao). Old French guidebooks sometimes call it the Monument aux Morts, Monument to the Dead.

Whatever you call it, this huge arch at the end of Thanon Lan Xang is within walking distance of the town centre and is worth a quick visit if the weather's agreeable. From a distance, it looks very much like its French source of inspiration. Up close, however, the Lao design starts to come out. The bas-relief on the sides and the temple-like ornamentation along the top and cornices are typically Lao. Beneath the arch is a small outdoor cafe with snacks and cheap beer. A stairway leads to the top of the monument, where for a small entry fee you can look out over the city.

Unknown Soldiers Memorial
ອະນຸສາວະຣີທະຫານບໍ່ຮູ້ນາມ

This white *that*-like structure was built to commemorate the Pathet Lao who died during the 1964-1973 War of Resistance. It's north of Pha That Luang off Thanon Phon Kheng.

Lao Revolutionary Museum
ຫໍພິພິທະພັນປະຕິວັດລາວ

The Lao Revolutionary Museum (Phiphittaphan Patiwat Lao) is in a well-worn classical mansion on Thanon Samsenthai. The hours posted out the front are meaningless; the museum only opens for visiting dignitaries. If you could get in, you'd be able to see a collection of artefacts and photos from the Pathet Lao's lengthy struggle for power.

Morning Market ຕະລາດເຊົ້າ

The Morning Market (Talaat Sao) is on the north-east corner of the intersection of Thanon Lan Xang and Thanon Khu Vieng. It actually runs all day, from 6 am to 6 pm. The sprawling collection of stalls offer fabric, ready-made clothes, hardware, jewellery, tobacco and other smoking material, electronic goods and just about everything else imaginable. Since the loosening of economic restrictions in 1987, the Morning Market has been expanding.

From about 6 to 8 am, vendors along Khu Vieng in front of the Morning Market sell French bread and the Lao breakfast sandwich (*khao jii pa-te*). A few vendors also sell fresh vegetables and fruit during these hours. The rest of the day you don't see much fresh produce except for the occasional street vendor who may wheel a cart through the market.

In the centre of the area is a large building that houses the Vientiane Department Store, which carries mostly imported goods (canned foods, clothes, appliances, handicrafts) from Thailand, China, Vietnam and Singapore. One section of the department store features a small supermarket that sells soap, local and imported foodstuffs and beer.

Other Markets

East of the Morning Market, just across Thanon Mahasot (or Thanon Nong Bon, as it's labelled on some maps) is the Khua Din Market (Talaat Khua Din) which offers fresh produce and fresh meats, as well as flowers and assorted other goods.

A bigger fresh market is Thong Khan Kham Market (Talaat Thong Khan Kham) which is sometimes called the Evening Market since it was originally established to replace the old Evening Market in Ban Nong Duang (which burned in 1987). Like the Morning Market, it's open all day, but is best in the morning. It's the biggest market in Vientiane and has virtually everything. You'll find it north of the town centre in Ban Thong Khan Kham (Gold Bowl Fields Village), at the intersection of Thanon Khan Kham and Thanon Dong Miang.

The That Luang Market is just a little south-east of Pha That Luang on Thanon Talat That Luang. The specialty here is exotic foods like bear paws and snakes that are favoured by the Vietnamese and Chinese.

Dong Dok University ມະຫາວິທະຍາໄລດົງໂດກ

Travellers who'd like to meet Lao university students might want to visit Dong Dok University. It's about 9 km north of the city off the road to Tha Ngon (Route 10). Students at the university's Foreign Language Institute are usually delighted to meet someone who speaks the language that they're studying (Vietnamese, French, Russian and English are common languages of study).

Places to Stay

Vientiane has a choice of around 12 hotels and guest houses to accommodate all tourists, travellers, spies, businesspeople and other visitors who come to town. Foreigners are allowed to stay at any of them, although if you arrive in Vientiane on a Tourist Visa you'll already have paid for 2 nights or more at a pre-assigned place. This is not a bad way to start a stay in Vientiane; the shortage of rooms can make it difficult to find a hotel that's not full. If you plan to extend your stay, you can then seek out a room at your leisure.

Several Vientiane hotels are in the process of upgrading their facilities, which unfortunately means they are also upscaling their rates. Paying more for a room never necessarily means better accommodation, and in Vientiane this is doubly so.

Places to Stay - bottom end

Vieng Vilay Hotel (tel 3287), Thanon Samsenthai, is half a block west of the Aeroflot office. Single/double rooms with fan and private bath are US$5/7. A few air-con rooms are also available for US$7/10 single/double. This is not only the least expensive place in town, it's also one of the most pleasant, once you get used to the dark lobby downstairs. Rooms are relatively well kept and the staff is helpful and efficient, which is why a lot of Thai businessmen stay here. The restaurant downstairs isn't much. In it's pre-revolutionary incarnation, this was the Hotel Constellation (immortalised by John Le Carré's novel *The Honourable Schoolboy*). Most likely the Vieng Vilay will be renovated and upgraded to higher room rates within the next couple of years.

Saysana Hotel (tel 2514/2974), Thanon Chao Anou, has slightly higher rates than at the Vieng Vilay but is not particularly clean or efficient.

Lao Chaleune (tel 2408) at the corner of Thanon Chao Anou and Thanon Fa Ngum is near the river. Rates here are US$10/12 single/double with air-con. Formerly the Inter Hotel, this hotel is well located, clean, not so friendly and often full.

Places to Stay - middle

Anou Hotel (tel 3571), at the corner of Thanon Heng Boun and Thanon Chao Anou, was renovated in late 1989. Since then rates have moved into the US$15-25 range following the example of other recently renovated hotels in the city. The new Anou is clean and a favourite for visiting Asian businesspeople.

Vientiane Hotel (tel 3685) is at Thanon Setthathirat, just before it becomes Thanon Luang Phabang. Fan singles are US$15, air-con doubles are US$18 and air-con doubles with hot water are US$20. Rooms here are not good value by local standards.

Muang Lao Hotel (tel 2278) Thanon Tha Deua, Km 4. This one's a bit out of town, on the way to the Tha Deua ferry, and is on the Mekong River (near the Australian Club). Large, clean, all air-con rooms go for US$16 to US$20. There's a cafe downstairs. If everything else is full in town, this is a good bet.

Santiphap (also Santiphab, Santipharb) *Hotel* (tel 2489, 3305) at 69A Thanon Luang Phabang was formerly the Apollo Hotel. This is the only hotel in Vientiane with a lift (elevator). The atmosphere is very business-like – similar to the average '70s vintage Chinese hotel found throughout urban South-East Asia. Air-con singles/doubles are US$16/18 and two-room suites with refrigerators are US$25. All rooms have hot water.

Villa That Luang (also That Luang Guest House) (tel 3617) is on Thanon That Luang, not far from Pha That Luang. This place was opened in 1989 and has been virtually empty since. It's clean and the staff is eager to please. Large, air-con rooms are a uniform US$20. They offer discounts for long-term stays which start at 5% off the standard rate for 10 days and reach 25% for longer than 2 months.

Hotel Ekkalat Metropole (tel 3179) Thanon Samsenthai near the That Dam or Black Stupa is next door to Aeroflot. This one has undergone at least three incarnations, starting with the pre-1975 Imperial Hotel, followed by the Ekkalat Hotel. After a recent renovation, rates were raised to US$20/26 for a single/double, which includes a complimentary breakfast in the hotel dining room. All rooms are large, clean and have air-conditioning. The Vietnamese couple who run it are very nice but speak only French and Vietnamese. The Ekkalat offers long-term discounts at the same rates as Villa That Luang.

Swedish Guest House (tel 2297) Thanon Sok Pa Luang, is about 3 km south of the town centre. This is where incoming UN employees often stay while waiting to move into a Saisettha district mansion. There are tennis, basketball and badminton courts in the grounds. Rates are US$25 including a Western breakfast.

Places to Stay - top end

Lane Xang Hotel (tel 3672/5346) is on Thanon Fa Ngum, near the river. This four-storey wonder is the LPDR's classiest digs and hence is the hotel of choice for visiting high-rollers. The rooms are really rather ordinary but the hotel does have a swimming pool. If you select a '1st class' Vientiane package tour, this is where you'll be assigned. The Lan Xang doubled its rates in 1989 (but there's still no lift). For walk-ins, rooms are now US$36/46 single/double; two-room suites with TV are US$58 and three-room suites with TV are US$68. A 1-week stay earns a 10% discount off the above rates; for 2 weeks it's 15% and for 3 weeks or more it's 35%.

Places to Eat

Vientiane is a good town for eating, with a wide variety of cafes, street vendors, beer halls and restaurants offering everything from rice noodles to filet mignon.

Breakfast Most of the hotels in Vientiane offer set 'American' breakfasts (two eggs, toast and ham or bacon) for US$1.50 (Villa That Luang) to US$2.30 (Lan Xang Hotel). Or you could get out on the streets and eat where the locals do. One popular breakfast is *khao jii pa-te*, a split French baguette stuffed with Lao-style paté (which is more like English or American luncheon meat than French paté) and various dressings. Vendors who sell these breakfast sandwiches also sell plain baguettes (*khao jii*) – there are several regular bread vendors on Thanon Heng Boun

and also in front of the Morning Market. The fresh baguettes are usually gone by 8.30 am and what's left will be starting to harden.

Across from the Vieng Vilay Hotel at the corner of Thanon Samsenthai and Thanon Chantha Kumman is a little open-air cafe that's only open for breakfast and lunch. The family that runs it prepares a nice *khai ka-ta*, eggs fried and served with French bread on the side. You can also order Chinese dough-nuts (*pa-thong-ko*) or plain bread with *café au lait* (*kaa-fae nom hawn*).

Two side-by-side cafes on Thanon Chao Anou, *Vinh Loi Bakery House* and *Sweet Home Bakery*, sell excellent croissants in the morning. At Vinh Loi, two croissants, a cup of *café au lait* and a glass of *nam saa* (weak Chinese tea), served as a chaser costs about US$0.50 total. The Sweet Home has a menu on the wall in Lao, English and Russian. Other pastries and cakes as well as ice cream are for sale at both cafes.

Noodles Noodles of all kinds are very popular in Vientiane, especially along Thanon Heng Boun, the unofficial China-town. Basically, you can choose between *foe*, a rice noodle that's popular throughout main-land South-East Asia (known as *kwethio* or *kuaythiaw* in Thailand, Malaysia and Singa-pore), and *mii*, the traditional Chinese wheat noodle. Noodles can be ordered as soup (eg *foe nam*), dry-mixed in a bowl (eg *foe haeng*) or fried (eg *foe phat*). A good place for noodles on Heng Boun is the *Nang Suri* at No 12-14. On the corner of Setthathirat and Chao Anou between Wat In Paeng and Wat Ong Teu is a good no-name restaurant (look for the BGL sign) that's always crowded at lunch because of its famous *foe neua* or Vietnamese-style beef noodles.

French There are several commendable French and French-Lao restaurants in Vientiane. Most are expensive by local standards (US$5 to US$7 per meal) but definitely better value than Vientiane hotels. One that is particularly good as well as inexpensive is *Santisouk* (formerly a famous tea-house called *La Pagode*) on Thanon Nokeo

Kumman, near the Lao Revolutionary Museum. The cuisine is of the 'French grill' type and is quite tasty – a filling plate of filet mignon with roast potatoes and vegies costs around US$1.10 using black market kip. A similar plate with filleted fish in a mushroom sauce is US$1.25. It's no wonder Santisouk is one of the most popular restaurants in town.

Of the half dozen or so other more expensive French and French-Lao restaurants, only two are worth noting. *Nam Phou* (Fountain) is on the Fountain Circle off Thanon Pang Kham and is frequented by diplomats and UN types because it has probably the best European food and service in Vientiane. Further down Pang Kham near Lao Aviation is *Le Souriya*, a similarly well-appointed, somewhat pricey place that's owned by a Lao princess.

Lao For real Lao meals, try the Dong Palan night market, off Thanon Ban Fai (marked Thanon Dong Palan on some maps), at the back of the Nong Chan ponds near the Lan Thong Cinema. Vendors sell all the Lao standards, including *laap* and *kai ping*.

The *Haan Kheuang Deum Mixai* (Mixai Eat-Drink Shop) is in a wooden building that's open on three sides and overlooks the Mekong River near the intersection of Fa Ngum and Bokeo Kumman. The menu is not very extensive, but the *laap kai* (chicken *laap*) is very tasty and they have cold draft beer for US$0.30 a litre. This is a great spot to watch the sun set over the Mekong River with the Thai town of Si Chiengmai on the other side. The Mixai is a favourite hang-out for Czechs, Poles and Bulgarians who are working in Laos (sometimes the draft beer runs out by sunset when the place is full). The proprietors play an interesting selection of music on their stereo, from Lao folk to US rockabilly. Goats are usually wandering about below the restaurant.

A similar scene without the goats, river or East Europeans is beneath the Pratuxai (Arch of Triumph) on Thanon Lan Xang. From the outside, this little cafe is practically invisible. But inside are several tables and a couple of vendors who serve the same cheap draft beer (in aluminium Chinese teapots) as at Mixai, plus Lao snacks (buffalo kebab is the starring dish here), while songs like 'Love Me Tender' play on the boom box.

Across from the Lan Xang Hotel on Thanon Fa Ngum are two touristy-looking restaurants side by side: one is the unappealing *Sukiyaki Bar & Restaurant*, while the other is the *Haan Aahaan Lao* (Lao Restaurant). The food at the latter is indeed Lao, but make sure you stipulate *baep Lao thae thae* (true Lao style) or they may serve you Europeanised versions of Lao dishes. The best thing about eating here is that it features live Lao folk music every night except Wednesday.

The restaurant with the best reputation for Lao food among the locals is *Nang Bang* (it may also be called Nam Kham Bang), which is on Thanon Khun Bulom (Khoun Boulom) not far from the Thanon Fa Ngum intersection. It's on the right as you walk north on Khun Bulom. Don't forget to try the *laap*, perhaps its most famous dish.

Thai With all the Thais visiting Vientiane for business and pleasure these days, Thai restaurants are becoming more common. On Thanon Samsenthai just past the Lao Revolutionary Museum is the *Thai Food* restaurant, which has all the Thai standards, including *tom yam kung* (prawn and lemon grass soup) and *kai phat bai kaphrao* (chicken fried in holy basil). Curries are good here – something you don't see much of in Lao cuisine.

The *Food Garden* (*Suan Aahaan* in Lao and Thai) is on Thanon Luang Phabang just before it forks into Setthathirat and Samsenthai. In the typical Thai 'food garden' style, tables are set up in the open air and seafood is the house specialty.

Other Out on Thanon Tha Deua at Km 14, next to the Lao Government Brewery, is a thatched-roof restaurant where you can drink Lao draft beer (*bia sot*, literally 'fresh beer' – and it doesn't get any fresher than this) and eat authentic Lao dishes.

Near the place where you go to get your visa validated on Thanon Talat Sao is a grungy house with a sign out front that says 'Indian Food'. If you can rouse the old man sleeping out the back, he'll serve you an Indian meal for less than US$1.

Entertainment

Dancing Vientiane has a curfew that's in effect from midnight to 6 am. In spite of this, there are at least six discos in town. The curfew isn't strictly enforced – if you're not out past 12.30 or 1 am you should be OK. Disco is rather a misnomer (it's what the Lao call these places), because often the music is live. Although younger Lao tend to predominate, there is usually a mix of generations and the bands or disc jockeys play everything from electrified Lao folk (for *lam wong* dancing) to Western pop.

The newest and most popular place in town is the *Vienglaty Mai* on Thanon Lan Xang, a bit north of the Morning Market on the same side of the street. This place has live bands every night and also serves food. Another local favourite is the *Feeling Well* on Thanon Ban Fai (or Thanon Dong Palan, depending on the map you follow); a couple of hundred metres beyond the Dong Palan night market. Less popular but still cooking on some nights are the *Dao Vieng* at 40 Thanon Heng Boun (above a restaurant) and the *Hanle Discotheque* on the 2nd floor of 2 Thanon Khun Bunlom.

Hotel Clubs The *Lan Xang* and *Santiphap* hotels each have live bands on weekend nights. The *Anou Hotel* used to have a nightly disco which will probably start up again when renovations are completed. The *Saysana Hotel* has a nightly disco but is best attended on weekends. The *Muang Lao Hotel* frequently has live bands.

Bars Outside of the hotels, Vientiane doesn't have too many bars. The ones that do exist seem semi-clandestine, perhaps semi-legal. All serve beer, along with a colonial history of other alcoholic beverages: French champagne, Johnny Walker and Stolichnaya.

Four doors west of the Vieng Vilay Hotel on Thanon Samsenthais is the *Young One's Bar*, which is open till midnight and is typical of other Vientiane bars – small and dimly lit.

Cinema Lao cinemas generally show, in descending order of frequency, Thai, Chinese, Indian, Bulgarian and Russian films. Prints are often in lousy condition but you can hardly argue with the admission charges – less than US$0.15 for the best seat in the house.

The *US Embassy* screens US movies (with popcorn and beverages for sale) every Wednesday at 7 pm for US$2. The theatre is across the street from the main embassy entrance on Thanon Bartolini.

Le Club France shows French films four times a week at the French Embassy off Thanon Setthathirat. Check with the embassy for schedules – the club issues a monthly bulletin.

The Australian Club and Le Club France each have video rental libraries – but you need your own VCR to see them!

Cultural Clubs The Australian Embassy Recreation Club (tel 2275), or the *Australian Club* for short, is out of town on the way to the Thailand ferry pier at Thanon Tha Deua, Km 3. The club has a brilliant pool, right next to the Mekong River, and at sunset many expats (mostly non-Australian!) gather here for an impromptu social hour. On Fridays from 6.30 to 8 pm, there is an official Happy Hour at the snack bar. There are also squash courts, a ping-pong table, billiards and darts. Yearly memberships are US$80 for a family, US$50 for an individual, but shorter-term memberships can be arranged. Or find someone who's a member and go along as their guest. The Club is open from 10 am to 10 pm.

Le Club France is in the French Embassy compound and features a French library (with over 20,000 books and records), French language lessons, and a bar that's open from 9 am to 5 pm.

The Library Club is in the garden of the

Australian Residence in a building called 'the Stockade', which is off Thanon Nehru near the Australian Embassy. It's open to members on Tuesday and Thursday from 4 to 6.30 pm and on Saturday from 9 am to 12 noon. An annual membership is US$10 (plus a refundable US$10 deposit).

Hash House Harriers This is one expat organisation that doesn't charge a membership fee. The Vientiane Hash has a blackboard at the Australian Club that announces the changing location of the weekly hash run, which is held Mondays at 5.30 pm. To participate in the 4 km to 5 km race, you contribute US$3, which pays for the beer, soft drinks and food at the end of the run.

Things to Buy

Just about anything made in Laos is available for purchase in Vientiane, including hill-tribe crafts, jewellery, traditional fabrics and carvings. The main shopping areas are the Morning Market (including shops along Thanon Talat Sao), along west Thanon Samsenthai (near the Vieng Vilay and Ekkalat Hotels) and on Thanon Pang Kham.

Fabrics & Leather The Morning Market is a good place to look for fabrics. Many of the fabric stalls are run by North Indians or Pakistanis. The tailor shops along Thanon Pang Kham (several of which are owned by Indians) also sell fabric and can design and cut clothes to fit. Queen's Beauty Tailor at No 21 has a good reputation but is slow (2 to 3 weeks). Dooley Tailleur around the corner at 314 Samsenthai can cut and sew a pattern in a week.

The Lao Women's Pilot Textile Project, a UNDP-sponsored program, has a shop on Nam Phu Square near the Lao bookshops that's open from 9 am to 6 pm, Monday to Saturday. It specialises in Lao cotton products, both modern and traditional designs.

The Weaving Centre on Thanon Phon Keng is a government weaving collective where you can see handlooms in operation.

Finished weavings are for sale on the premises.

Sun Sae Un Cobbler at 51 Pang Kham makes inexpensive men's leather shoes and also does shoe and luggage repair.

Handicrafts & Antiques Several shops along Thanon Samsenthai and Pang Kham sell Lao and hill-tribe crafts. The Mandalay Boutique in the Nam Phou Restaurant (next to the fountain on Pang Kham) is expensive, but the quality is generally good. Lao Phattana Art and Handicrafts Co-op at 9 Pang Kham has a fair selection of antique and new handwoven silks and cottons, antique silver, wood carvings and other crafts.

Two unmarked shops on Samsenthai specialise in Mien embroidery. Several shops along here sell carved opium pipes (the real thing, not the misrepresented tobacco pipes sold in northern Thailand).

Jewellery Most of the jewellery shops in Vientiane are along Thanon Samsenthai. Gold and silver are the best deals. Saigon Bijou at No 369 is supposedly reputable – it sells and repairs gold and silver jewellery and can also make new pieces on request.

The Indian-owned M M Bari Shop at 370 Thanon Samsenthai is one of the few shops that deals in precious stones as well as gold and silver.

Getting There & Away

Air Vientiane is the only legal port of entry into Laos for foreigners. Air departures from Vientiane are very straightforward. Upstairs in the airport is a restaurant-lounge area with decent enough food. Departure tax is US$5.

Boat Most visitors to Laos, no matter what kind of visa they hold, are required to fly into Vientiane. Upon your departure, however, the Lao government doesn't seem to object if you take the river ferry back to Thailand.

Lao Immigration officials in town may tell you (if you ask) that you need a letter from them to depart by ferry (which they only issue if for some reason you can't make the flight out). In practice, however, the officials at Tha Deua let anyone through. Note that if you decide to leave by ferry, you must obtain a visa (300 baht) from the Thai Embassy on Thanon Phon Keng in advance if you plan to stay more than 15 days in Thailand. It takes up to 3 days to get the Thai visa.

Foot ferries leave from the tiny ferry station at Tha Deua, which is approximately 20 km south-east of Vientiane. Boats leave every 5 minutes or so from 8 to 11.30 am and 2 to 4.30 pm daily except Sunday, when they don't run at all. The boat ticket is 30 baht one way. On Saturday afternoons, Thai Immigration charges a 280 baht 'overtime' fee for stamping your passport on the other side.

There is also a car ferry from Tha Na Leng (at Km 19) but it is highly unlikely that you will leaving by car since tourists aren't allowed to bring cars into Laos. Expats living and working in Laos must clear the paperwork for car exports in advance at the Lao Ministry of Foreign Affairs and at the Thai Embassy. The car ferry costs 200 baht per vehicle (passengers free), plus a 10 baht departure tax in Tha Na Leng, a 20 baht arrival tax in Nong Khai, and a 150 baht important clearance charge in Nong Khai.

Car or motorcycle taxis from Vientiane to Tha Deua charge a standard 100 baht for the trip. You can also ride a bus from the Morning Market out to Tha Deua (departures roughly every half hour) for the kip equivalent of 8 baht.

Getting Around
Central Vientiane is entirely accessible on foot. For explorations in neighbouring districts, however, you'll need vehicular support.

Airport Transport Taxis wait in front of the airport for passengers going into town. The going rate for foreigners seems to be 100 baht, which is overpriced considering it's only a 10 or 15-minute ride to the town centre. If you can catch a motorcycle taxi, the fare is only around 25 baht or about US$1, but motorcycle taxis aren't always available. There are no public buses direct from the airport, but if you walk the hundred metres

south of the terminal to Thanon Luang Phabang, you can catch a bus into town (turn left) for around 8 baht.

Going out to the airport, you can either hire a car or motorcycle taxi as described above, or catch a Phon Hong bus from the Morning Market.

Bus There is a city bus system but it's not oriented toward the central Chanthabuli district where most of the hotels, restaurants, sightseeing and shopping are. Rather, it's for transport to outlying districts to the north, east and west of Chanthabuli. Fares for any distance within Vientiane prefecture are low – about US$0.25 for a 20-km ride.

Car Taxi Only a handful of car taxis operate in Vientiane, and these are stationed in front of the Lane Xang and Santiphap Hotels, as well as at the airport during flight arrival times. For most short trips within town a pedicab or motorcycle is more economical since car taxis are usually reserved for longer trips (to Wattay Airport or to the Thailand ferry pier in Tha Deua) and for hourly or daily hire. In Vientiane, a car and driver for the day costs US$10 to US$12 if you bargain well. At the Lane Xang Hotel, it's a standard US$20 a day.

Motorcycle Taxis The ones in Vientiane are mostly imported from Thailand – basically motorcycles with cabs built around them. The standard size holds two or three passengers; the larger ones (called 'jumbos') have two short benches in the back and can hold four or five, even six passengers if they're not too large. Hire charges are about the same as for samlors but of course they're much speedier. A motorcycle taxi driver will be glad to take passengers on journeys as short as half a km or as far as 20 km. A trip of 20 km would cost US$4 to US$5 one way.

Car & Motorcycle Rental Simply put, there is none, except when you hire the driver, too.

Pedicabs Called *cyclo* in French or *sam-law* (three wheels) in Lao, samlors are one of the most common public conveyances in Vientiane. Charges are about US$0.25 per km (but don't hire a samlor for any distance greater than 2 or 3 km). You can flag down empty samlors passing on the street or pick them up at one of the two main samlor stands, one on Lan Xang near the Morning Market and the other on Chao Anou at the Heng Boun intersection.

Bicycle This is the most convenient and economical way to see Vientiane besides walking. At the moment, there is only one place that rents bikes on a regular basis. This is the bicycle shop across from where you get your visa validated, near the Morning Market, on the south-western corner of Thanon Lan Xang and Thanon Talat Sao. Hire charges depend on the condition of the bike, but usually are around US$2 a day. Come in the morning when the shop opens (around 8.30 am) to ensure you'll get a bike – it only has a few for hire. Some hotels will also occasionally hire bikes belonging to the staff.

AROUND VIENTIANE
Ang Nam Ngum ອ່າງນ້ຳງື່ມ

Approximately 90 km from Vientiane, Ang Nam Ngum is a huge artificial lake that was created by damming the Nam Ngum River. A hydroelectric plant here generates most of the power used in the Vientiane Valley as well as power that's sold to Thailand via high-power wires over the Mekong.

The lake is dotted with picturesque islands and a cruise is well worth arranging. A family from Ban Thalat has a boat that does regular daily cruises for US$3 per person – it's a combination cruise boat for tourists and ferry boat for locals, who use it to go from village to village around the lake. The boat even has video!

Ban Thalat is also worth visiting to see the market, which sells all kinds of edible forest creatures – deer, spiny anteaters, rats and so on.

Places to Stay
A trip to Ang Nam Ngum and back could be done in a day, but if you want to spend a day or two, accommodation is available. Lao Tourism has bungalows near the dam and Vientiane Tourism has some on one of the islands, but for these you would probably have to book a tour from Vientiane. Private accommodation is available for around US$2 a night – ask around. The people who run the cruise-ferry boat can arrange accommodation at villages along the lakeside.

Getting There & Away
Since Ang Nam Ngum is within Vientiane Province, you don't need a travel pass to go there from Vientiane city. From the Morning Market you can catch the 7 am bus all the way to Kheuan Nam Ngum (Nam Ngum Dam) for US$0.50. This trip takes about 3 hours and proceeds along Route 13 through Ban Thalat. If you don't make the 7 am bus, you'll most likely have to take a bus to Ban Thalat (84 km from Vientiane) and then get another one on to the lake.

Taxis in Vientiane charge US$30 round trip to go to the lake. If you hire one, ask the driver to take the more scenic Route 10 through Ban Koen, which is about the same distance as via Ban Thalat, or make a circle route to see both areas.

Northern Laos

LUANG PHABANG ຫລວງພະບາງ

The area that now encompasses Luang Phabang Province was the site of early Thai-Lao *muangs* that were established in the high river valleys along the Mekong River and its major tributaries, the Nam Khan, the Nam Ou and the Nam Seuang (Xeuang). The first Lao kingdom, Lan Xang, was consolidated here in 1353 by the Khmer-supported conqueror Fa Ngum. At that time it was known as Muang Sawa (named after Java, but no one today seems to know why). After King Fa Ngum accepted a Sinhalese Buddha image called Pha Bang (large holy image) as a gift from the Khmer monarchy, the city-state became known as Luang (Great or Royal) Phabang. Luang Phabang remained the capital of Lan Xang until King Phothisarat moved the seat of administration to Vientiane in 1545.

But throughout the Lan Xang period, Luang Phabang was considered the main source of monarchical power. When Lan Xang broke up following the death of King Suliya Vongsa in 1694, one of Suliya's grandsons established an independent kingdom in Luang Phabang that competed alongside kingdoms in Vientiane and Champassak. From then on, the Luang Phabang monarchy was so weak that it was forced to pay tribute at various times to the Siamese and Vietnamese, and finally to the French when Laos became a French protectorate in the early 20th century. The French allowed Laos to retain the Luang Phabang monarchy, however, as did the fledgeling independent governments that followed and it wasn't until the Vietnamese-backed Pathet Lao took over in 1975 that the monarchy was finally dissolved.

Today, Luang Phabang is a sleepy town of 20,000 inhabitants (the province as a whole totals around 300,000) with a handful of historic temples, old French mansions (a French Commissariat was located here) and a beautiful mountain setting.

Orientation

The town sits at the confluence of the Mekong and Nam Khan rivers. A large hill called Phu Si (sometimes spelt Phousy) dominates the town skyline at the upper end of a peninsula formed by the junction of the two rivers. Most of the historic temples are located between Phu Si and the Mekong. Virtually the whole town can be seen on foot in a day or two.

Information

Tourist Office The Lao Tourism office is located at Hotel Luang Phabang on the south-east edge of town. However, their services are geared toward guiding package tours around Luang Phabang, so unless you're part of a tour they're not likely to offer much in the way of assistance.

The standard 2-day Lao Tourism itinerary takes visitors to Wat Chom Si and Wat Xieng Thong on the first day (sometimes other wats if there is time), then the Palace Museum, the Pak Ou caves and a couple of nearby villages on the second. If there are less than four people in the group, Lao Tourism will omit the Pak Ou excursion or ask for a surcharge of US$36.

When Luang Phabang was first opened to tourism in February 1989, as many as 200 to 300 travellers a month were passing through; some arrived by plane, some by boat and some by road. Now that the government has tightened restrictions on travel outside Vientiane, the numbers are more like 20 to 30 a month.

Maps & Guides An excellent French guide-book to the town, if you can find it, is *Louang Prabang* by Thao Boun Souk (pen name for Pierre-Marie Gagneaux), which was published in 1974 by the now-defunct Bulletin des amis du royaume lao. The Lao Tourism guides rely heavily on this little book.

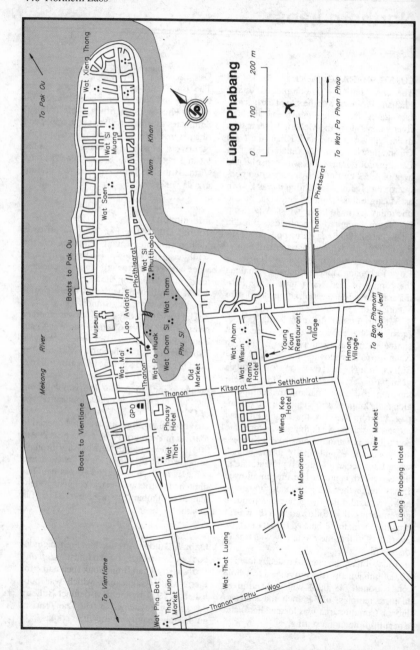

Luang Phabang

0   100   200 m

To Pak Ou

Mekong River

Nam Khan

Boats to Pak Ou

Boats to Vientiane

To Vientiane

Wat Xieng Thong

Wat Si Muang

Wat Saen

Wat Si Phutthabat

Phothisarat

Museum

Lao Aviation

Wat Tham

Wat Mai

Wat Pa Huak

Wat Chom Si

Phu Si

Old Market

Wat That

GPO

Phousy Hotel

Thanon   Kitsarat

Wat Aham

Wat Wisun

Rama Hotel

Setthathirat

Young Koun Restaurant

La Village

Hmong Village

To Ban Phanom & Santi Jedi

Wieng Keo Hotel

Wat Manoram

New Market

Thanon Phetsarat

To Wat Pa Phon Phao

Luang Prabang Hotel

Wat Pha Bat

That Luang Market

Wat That Luang

Thanon Phu Wao

National Museum ຫໍພິພິຕະພັນແຫ່ງຊາດ

This is a good place to start a tour of Luang Phabang since the displays convey some sense of local history. The palace was originally constructed by the side of the Mekong River in 1904 as a residence for King Sisavang Vong and his family. The site for the palace was chosen so that official visitors to Luang Phabang could disembark from their river journeys directly below the palace and be received there. When Sisavang Vong died in 1959, his son Savang Vattana ascended the throne. Shortly after the 1975 Revolution, King Savang Vattana and his family were exiled to northern Laos (never to be heard of again) and the palace was converted into a museum.

The building is laid out in a cruciform shape with the entrance on one side. Various royal religious objects are displayed in the large entry hall, including the dais of the former Supreme Patriarch of Lao Buddhism, a venerable Buddha head presented to the king as a gift from India, a reclining Buddha with the unusual added feature of sculpted mourners at his side, an equally unusual Buddha seated with begging bowl (the bowl is usually only depicted with a standing figure) and a Luang Phabang-style standing Buddha sculpted of marble in the 'Contemplating the Bodhi Tree' pose.

In the right front corner room of the palace, which opens to the outside, is a collection of the museum's most prized art, including the Pha Bang. This gold standing Buddha is 83 cm tall and is said to weigh either 54 kg or 43 kg, depending on which sources you believe. The Khmers presented the image to King Fa Ngum in the 14th century as a Buddhist legitimator of Lao sovereignty. The image is said to have been cast around the 1st century AD in Ceylon. Also in this room are large elephant tusks engraved with Buddhas, several Khmer-crafted sitting Buddhas, Luang Phabang-style standing Buddhas, an excellent Lao frieze taken from a local temple and three beautiful *saew mai khan* (embroidered silk screens with religious imagery) that were crafted by the queen.

To the right of the entry hall is the king's former reception room, where busts of the Lao monarchy are displayed along with two large Ramayana screens. The walls of the room are covered with murals that depict scenes from traditional Lao life. They were painted in 1930 by French artist Alix de Fautereau in such a way that each wall is meant to be viewed at a different time of day – according to the light that enters the windows on one side of the room.

To the left of the entry hall is a room filled with paintings, silver and china that have been presented to Laos as diplomatic gifts from Burma, Cambodia, Thailand, Poland, Hungary, Russia, Japan, Vietnam, China, Nepal, US, Canada and Australia. The objects are grouped according to whether they're from 'socialist' or 'capitalist' countries.

The next room to the left was once the Queen's reception room. Large royal portraits of King Savang Vattana, Queen Kham Phouy and Crown Prince Vong Savang, painted by Russian artist Ilya Glazunov in 1967, are hung on the walls. Also on display in this room are friendship flags from China and Vietnam and replicas of sculpture from New Delhi's Indian National Museum.

Behind the entry hall is the former throne room where royal vestments, gold and silver sabres, and the King's elephant chair (or saddle) are exhibited. Glass cases hold a collection of small crystal and gold Buddhas that were found inside the That Mak Mo stupa. Beyond the throne room are halls that lead to the royal family's residential quarters. The royal bedrooms have been preserved as they were when the King departed, as have the dining hall and a room that contains royal seals and medals. One of the more interesting displays in the museum is a room in the residential section that now contains Lao classical musical instruments and masks for the performance of Ramayana dance-drama – just about the only place in the country where you see these kinds of objects on display.

There is no admission fee and no regular opening hours for the National Museum. To get in, you'll have to ask for someone at Lao Tourism to arrange a visit.

Wat Xieng Thong ວັດຊຽງທອງ(ເມຄງຶສໃກ)

Near the northern tip of the peninsula formed by the Mekong and Nam Khan rivers is Luang Phabang's most magnificent temple, Wat Xieng Thong (Golden City Temple). It was built by King Setthathirat in 1560 and remained under royal patronage until 1975. Like the royal palace, Wat Xieng Thong was placed within easy reach of the Mekong.

The *sim* represents what is considered classic Luang Phabang temple architecture, with roofs that sweep low to the ground (the same style is found in northern Thailand as well). The rear wall of the *sim* features an impressive 'tree of life' mosaic set in a red background. Inside, richly decorated wooden columns support a ceiling vested with *dhammachakkas* (dharma-wheels).

To one side of the *sim*, toward the east, are several small chapels and *that* containing Buddha images of the period. One contains an especially rare reclining Buddha that dates from the construction of the temple. In 1911 it was taken to Paris and displayed at the Paris Exhibition. Gold-leaf votives line the walls on either side of the image. A mosaic on the back exterior wall of this chapel was done in the late 1950s in commemoration of the 2500th anniversary of the Buddha's birth, enlightenment and death. The mosaic is unique because it depicts local village life rather than a religious scene.

Near the compound's east gate stands the royal funeral chapel. Inside is an impressive 12 metre high funeral chariot and various funeral urns for each member of the royal family. (The ashes of King Sisavang Vong, the queen and the king's brother, however, are interred at Wat That Luang in the southern end of Luang Phabang). Gilt panels on the exterior of the chapel depict semi-erotic episodes from the Ramayana.

Wat Wisunarat (Wat Visoun)

This temple to the east of town centre was originally constructed in 1513, making it the oldest operating temple in Luang Phabang,

but was rebuilt in 1898 following a fire 2 years earlier. The original was made of wood, and in the brick and stucco restoration the builders attempted to make the balustraded windows of the *sim* appear to be fashioned of lathed wood (an old South Indian and Khmer contrivance that is uncommon in Lao architecture). The front roof that slopes sideways over the terrace is also unique. Inside the high-ceilinged *sim* is a collection of wooden 'Calling for Rain' Buddhas and 15th to 16th century Luang Phabang *sima* (ordination stones).

In front of the *sim* is That Pathum (Lotus Stupa), which was built in 1514. It's more commonly called That Mak Mo or 'Watermelon Stupa' because of its semi-spherical shape.

Wat Aham

Between Wat Wisun and the Nam Khan is Wat Aham, which was formerly the residence of the Sangkharat (Supreme Patriarch of Lao Buddhism). Two large bodhi trees (pipal or banyan) grace the grounds, which are semi-deserted except for the occasional devotee who comes to make offerings to the town's most important spirit shrine.

Wat Mai ວັດໃໝ່ສຸວັນນະພູມະຣາມ

Close to the Phousy Hotel and the GPO is Wat Mai, or 'New Temple', which was built in 1796 and was at one time a residence of the Sangkharat (succeeding Wat Aham). The five-tiered roof of the wooden *sim* is in the standard Luang Phabang style. The front verandah is remarkable for it's decorated columns and sumptuous gold relief door panels that recount the legend of Vessantara (*Pha Wet*), the Buddha's penultimate incarnation, as well as scenes from the Ramayana and local village life. To one side of the *sim* is a shelter where two long racing boats are kept. These are brought out during Lao New Year in April and again in October during the Water Festival.

The Pha Bang, which is usually housed in Luang Phabang's National Museum, is put on public display at Wat Mai during the Lao new year celebrations.

Top: The Mekong River at sunset (RR)
Left: View of Luang Phabang from Phu Si (JC)
Right: Pha Baen, Luang Phabang (JC)

Top: Fighting beetles, Thai Dam village, Xieng Khwang (JC)
Left: Plain of Jars, Xieng Khwang (JC)
Right: Funeral chapel, Wat Xieng Thong, Luang Phabang (JC)

Wat That Luang ວັດທາດຫລວງ

Legend has it that Wat That Luang was originally established by Ashokan missionaries from India in the 3rd century BC. However, there is no physical evidence to confirm this and the currently standing *sim* was built in 1818. The ashes of King Sisavang Vong are interred inside the large central stupa. Inside the huge *sim* are a few Luang Phabang Buddha images and other artefacts. This temple appears to have the largest contingent of monks in Luang Phabang.

Phu Si ພູສີ

The temples on the slopes of Phu Si are all of rather recent construction, but it is likely there were other temples previously located at this important hill site. None of the temples are particularly distinguished in art or architecture, but there is an excellent view of the town from the top of the hill.

On the lower slopes of the hill are Wat Pa Huak and Wat Pa Thip. At the summit is Wat Chom Si, which is the starting point for a colourful Lao new year procession in mid-April. Behind this temple is a small cave shrine called Wat Thammothayaram or Wat Tham Phu Si. Since it's really nothing more than one large Buddha image and a sheltered area for worshippers, it hardly lives up to its designation as a wat. On a nearby crest is an old Russian anti-aircraft cannon that children use as a makeshift merry-go-round. Below Wat Chom Si is Wat Si Phutthabat, a temple that boasts a Buddha footprint shrine.

Other Temples

Across the Mekong River from central Luang Phabang are several temples that aren't particularly remarkable except that they're in pleasant rural settings. Wat Tham is in a limestone cave that's almost directly across the river from Wat Xieng Thong. Many Buddha images from temples that have burned or otherwise fallen into decay are kept here. There are several other caves nearby that are easily found and explored – bring along a torch (flashlight).

Wat Long Khun is a little to the east of Wat Tham and features a nicely decorated portico of 1937 vintage, plus older sections from the 18th century. When the coronation of a Luang Phabang king was pending, it was customary for him to spend 3 days in retreat at Wat Long Khun before ascending the throne.

At the top of a hill above Wat Long Khun and Wat Than is peaceful Wat Chom Phet, from where there is an undisturbed view of the river.

A few km to the east of town is the recently constructed Santi Jedi or Peace Pagoda. This large yellow stupa contains three levels inside plus an outside, terrace near the top with a view of the surrounding plains. The interior walls are painted with all manner of Buddhists stories and moral admonitions.

Wat Pa Phon Phao is a forest meditation wat about 3 km east of the airport. The teacher, Ajaan Sai Samut, is well respected for his teaching of vipassana or insight meditation. If travellers would like to meet with Ajaan Sai, they should bring along a Lao interpreter.

Behind the That Luang market in town is a modern Vietnamese-Lao Buddhist temple, Wat Pha Bat.

Markets

The main fresh market, Talaat That Luang, is at the intersection of Thanon Phothisarat and Thanon Phu Wao near the river, behind Wat That Luang. Another big market is for dry goods and is held daily off Thanon Setthathirat, the town's broadest avenue. This market will be moving to a new location on the east edge of town within the next couple of years. There is a morning vegetable and fruit market where Thanon Setthathirat terminates at the Mekong River.

Places to Stay

For such an important tourist destination, Luang Phabang has remarkably limited hotel space. In 1989 there were only two hotels in town, both meant for tourists. The *Phousy (Phu Si) Hotel* is well located at the intersection of Setthathirat and Phothisarat (at the site of the former French Commissary). Rooms with fan and bath are US$20/25 single/double. The Phousy has an interior restaurant as well as a garden restaurant out the front. It doesn't get much business, just the occasional businessman from out of town, so is a quiet place to stay in spite of its in-town location.

The *Luang Prabang Hotel* (locally called the Phu Wao) sits on Phu Wao or 'Kite Hill' on the eastern edge of town. Modern rooms here have air-con and non-functioning telephones. There is also a pool, bar and large restaurant. Rates are US$25/35 for a single/double.

The city plans to add two new hotels near Wat Wisunarat, the *Rama* and the *Wieng Keo*. Both will cater mostly to local guests – rooms rates are expected to be around US$10 a night.

Places to Eat

The restaurants in the two tourist hotels are pretty fair. The Luang Prabang Hotel restaurant has the better service and is also a bit of a nightspot – the poolside tables are a popular gathering place on weeknights and on weekends there is usually a live band. There are several small cafes and restaurants along Thanon Phothisarat near the Phousy Hotel, some of which specialise in *laap*. The *Young Koun Restaurant*, across the street from Wat Wisun, has Lao and Chinese food at fairly reasonable prices.

One of the local dining specialities is *jaew bong*, a jam-like condiment made with chillies and dried buffalo skin. A soup called *aw lam*, made with dried meat, mushrooms, eggplant and local herbs, is also a typical Luang Phabang dish. In the markets you may see *phak nam*, a spirulina-like algae that's very high in protein and is rarely found outside the Luang Phabang area.

Getting There & Away

Air Lao Aviation has daily flights to Luang Phabang from Vientiane except Saturday. All flights leave at 8 am except the Tuesday flight, which leaves at 1 pm. From Luang Phabang, departure times are an hour later. The flight is only 40 minutes. The fare is US$33 each way.

During the rainy season, morning departures are often delayed an hour or two (in either direction) because of heavy morning fog in Luang Phabang. When flying into Luang Phabang, try to get a window seat – the view of the town as the plane descends over the mountains in preparation for landing is excellent.

As with all travel outside of Vientiane, passengers are supposed to be in possession of a valid travel pass before boarding flights to Luang Phabang.

Boat Several times a week river ferries leave Vientiane's north jetty on the Mekong River for Luang Phabang. The length of the voyage depends on river height, but is typically 3 nights up and 2 nights down. The fare is US$7 per person and on many boats you must bring your own food. Check at the jetty in advance to see if food will be available. For the boat journey you're supposed to have a travel pass but they don't always check. On the other hand, sometimes they decide to check when the boat is part of the way to Luang Phabang (typically in Pak Lai), in order to extract a bribe from foreigners who don't have the pass.

It's possible to travel by boat along the Mekong River to Ban Huay Sai in Bokeo Province, but this province is currently closed to foreigners.

Bus & Truck Luang Phabang can be reached via Route 13 from Vientiane but it's a trip for the hardy (or perhaps foolhardy, given the array of dangers along the way). Although it's only about 200 km from Vientiane to Luang Phabang by road, it requires 2 long days of travel on buses and trucks on rough roads.

The first step is to catch the 7 am bus to Nam Ngum Dam from Vientiane's Morning Market. The bus takes around 3 hours to reach Nam Ngum and costs US$1 or so. Then you must cross the lake to Bang Tha Huea or Ban Huay Mo which takes 2 to 3 hours depending on the boat. A truck will be waiting to take passengers on to Vang Vieng,

Vang Vieng women

which is 25 km further north. The journey takes about an hour and costs US$0.50.

You can either spend the night in Vang Vieng and start fresh in the morning (recommended) or get another bus or truck for US$0.70 on to Kasi, which is about 50 km and 3 hours further. By that time you've no choice but to spend the night in Kasi, since the last leg, Kasi to Luang Phabang, takes a full day. There is a hotel in Vang Vieng but none in Kasi, so unless you're resourceful you'd best choose to spend the night in Vang Vieng. (Occasionally there are direct buses from Vientiane to Vang Vieng that bypass the lake. These take 7 to 8 hours – check at the Morning Market to see if one's available.)

The last 80 km trip between Kasi and Luang Phabang takes around 11 hours by truck and generally costs US$2 to US$3, depending on the number of passengers. This section of the road is twisty and mountainous – not for the squeamish. On top of the road hazards, vehicles along the road just outside of Kasi are occasionally attacked by anticommunist guerrillas (thought to be ethnic Hmong insurgents). As many as 15 people are estimated to have been killed in truck attacks near Kasi in 1989 alone. Truckers usually carry automatic rifles, grenades and rocket launchers in anticipation of attacks – and they drive slowly to keep an eye out for mines or rockets placed on the road by guerrillas. In 1988, two Russian bridge engineers were driving along this road in a jeep and caught a mortar shell that killed them both – don't even consider taking a private vehicle on this road.

Eventually, if Laos continues to open according to Lao Tourism plans, it will be possible to travel by road from Luang Phabang to Muang Luang Nam Tha along Route 13 and Route 1. For the time being, though, this route is not open. Luang Phabang also connects with Xieng Khwang via Route 6 (which continues east into northern Vietnam), but the road is high and treacherous.

AROUND LUANG PHABANG
Pak Ou Caves ถ้ำปากอู
About 30 km by boat from Luang Phabang along the Mekong River, at the mouth of the

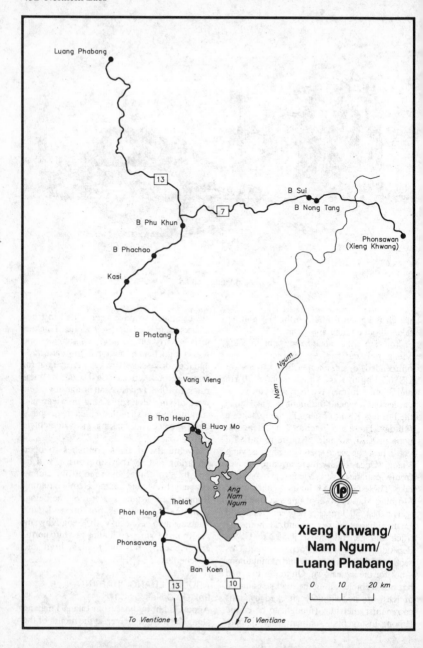

Xieng Khwang/
Nam Ngum/
Luang Phabang

Nam Ou, are the famous Pak Ou caves (Pak Ou means 'Mouth of the Ou'). The basic attraction here is the two caves in the lower part of a limestone cliff which are stuffed with Buddha images of all styles and sizes (but mostly classic Luang Phabang standing Buddhas). The lower cave, called Tham Thing, is entered from the river by a series of steps and can easily be seen in daylight. Stairs to the left of Tham Thing lead round to the upper cave, Tham Phum, which is deeper and therefore requires artificial light for viewing – be sure to bring a torch (flashlight) if you want to see both caves.

On the way to Pak Ou, you can have the boatman stop at small villages on the banks of the Mekong. Opposite the caves, at the mouth of the Nam Ou in front of an impressive limestone cliff called Pha Hen, is a favourite spot for local fishermen.

Getting There & Away You can hire boats to Pak Ou from the pier at the back of the National Palace Museum. A long-tail boat should go for around US$10 for the day, including petrol. The trip takes 1 to 1½ hours each way, depending on the speed of the boat. If you stop at villages along the way, it will naturally take longer.

If you go to Pak Ou as part of a Lao Tourism tour, the guide will most likely stop in at least one village along the way. A picnic lunch is usually brought along to be eaten at the *sala* between the two caves.

Ban Phanom ຊ້ານພະນົມ
This Lü village is east of Luang Phabang, a few km past the airport, and is well known for cotton and silk hand-weaving. On weekends, a small market is set up in the village for the trading of hand-woven cloth, but you can turn up at any time and the villagers will bring out cloth for inspection and purchase. Even if you don't expect to buy anything, it's worth a visit to see the villagers working on their handlooms.

Getting There & Away Buses from Luang Phabang to Ban Phanom leave from Thanon Setthathirat several times a day for a few hundred kip.

XIENG KHWANG PROVINCE ແຂວງຊຽງຂວາງ
Flying into Xieng Khwang Province by helicopter, one is struck at first by the awesome beauty of high green mountains, rugged karst formations and verdant valleys. But as the copter begins to descend, you notice how much of the province is pock-marked with bomb craters in which little or no vegetation grows. Along with Hua Phan, Xieng Khwang is one of the northern provinces that was most devastated by the war. Virtually every town and village in the province was bombed at some point between 1964 and 1973.

The province has a total population of around 120,000 that is comprised of lowland Lao, Thai Dam, Hmong and Phuan. The original capital city, Xieng Khwang, was almost totally bombed out, so the capital was moved to nearby Phonsawan (often spelt Phonsavanh) after the 1975 change of government. Near Phonsawan is the mysterious Plain of Jars (*Thong Hai Hin*). The moderate altitude in central Xieng Khwang, including Phonsawan and the Plain of Jars, means an excellent year-round climate – not too hot in the hot season, not too cold in the cool season and not too wet in the rainy season.

A Xieng Khwang tour is available from Vientiane through Lao Tourism, but they hadn't yet taken any tourists to the province when I researched the area (I was in fact only the second foreigner to have visited the province since 1975). The itinerary is expected to include the Plain of Jars and the Muang Kham area (hot springs, Tham Piu and a Hmong village). For further information contact Lao Tourism in Vientiane.

Phonsawan ໂພນສະວັນ
There's not much to the new capital – an airfield, a semi-paved main street lined with tin-roofed shops, a market and a few government buildings. Among the buildings in town are two small scrap metal warehouses with simple scales hanging in front. This is

where local villagers bring war junk that they find in their fields or in the forests. The warehouses buy the scrap (eg bomb shards, parts of Chinese, Russian and American planes) for US$0.55 a kg, then sell it to larger warehouses in Vientiane, who in turn sell it to the Thais.

Take care when walking in the fields around Phonsawan as undetonated live bombs are not uncommon. The locals use intact bomb casings (without the insides) as pillars for new structures and as fenceposts. Muddy areas are sometimes dotted with 'pineapple bombs' or 'bomblets' – fist-size explosives that are left over from cluster bombs dropped in the '70s. Occasionally, a farmer strikes one with a plough and ends up minus a limb. Children are still occasional victims as well.

Plain of Jars ທົ່ງ ໄຫຫິນ

The Plain of Jars is a large undeveloped area about 12 km outside Phonsawan where huge jars of unknown origin are scattered about. The jars weigh an average of 600 kg to 1 tonne each, though the biggest of them weighs as much as 6 tonnes. They appear to have been fashioned from solid stone, but there is disagreement on this point. Various theories have been advanced as to the functions of the stone jars – that they were used as sarcophagi, as wine fermenters or for rice storage – but no conclusive evidence confirming one theory over the other has yet been uncovered.

The local story is that in the 6th century, a chieftain named Chao Angka ruled the area as part of Muang Pakan. He was supposedly a cruel ruler, and so the heroic Khun Jeuam came down from south China and deposed Angka. To celebrate his victory, Khun Jeuam had the jars constructed for the fermentation of rice wine. According to this version, the jars were cast from a type of cement that was made from buffalo skin, sand, water and sugar cane and fired in a nearby cave kiln. A limestone cave on the Plain of Jars that has smoke holes in the top is said to have been this kiln.

The largest jar on the plain is said to have been the victorious king's and so it's called *Hai Jeuam*. Many of the smaller jars have been taken away by collectors, but there are still several hundred or so on the plain.

Tham Piu ຖ້ຳ ປິວ

Tham Piu is a cave near the former village of Ban Nameun where approximately 400 villagers, many of them women and children, were killed by a single rocket fired into the cave (most likely from a US jet fighter) in 1969. The large cave is in the side of a limestone cliff. But, it's the journey to Tham Piu that is the real attraction, since it passes several Hmong and Thai Dam villages along the way and involves a bit of hiking in the forest.

The cave is just a few km beyond the small town of Muang Kham, which is 30 km east of Phonsawan on Route 6. Also in this area is a hot mineral springs, *Baw Nam Hawn*, that feeds into a stream a few hundred metres off the road. You can sit in the stream right where the hot spring water combines with the cool stream water and 'adjust' the temperature by moving from one area to another.

Further east along the same road, 120 km from Phonsawan, is the market town of Nong Haet, which is only about 25 km short of the Vietnamese border.

Getting There & Away You might be able to hire a jeep and driver in town for around US$20 a day. Buses (actually trucks with benches in back) go from Phonsawan to Muang Kham for US$0.50 or all the way to Nong Haet for US$0.70. To get to Tham Piu, you'd have to take a Nong Haet bus and ask to be let out at the turn-off for Tham Piu. From the turn-off, start walking towards the limestone cliff north of the road until you're within a km of the cliff. At this point you have to plunge into the woods and make your way along a honeycomb of trails to the bottom of the cliff and then mount a steep, narrow trail that leads up to the mouth of the cave. It would be best to ask for directions from villagers along the way or you're liable to get lost. Better still, find someone in Phonsawan who knows the way and invite them to come along for an afternoon hike.

Places to Stay & Eat
There was only one place to stay in Phonsawan in 1989 – the government guest house, which is on a hill overlooking the town. The guest house has 15 rooms with mosquito nets, towels, soap and a shared cold water shower that is sometimes without water. Rooms are US$2 a night per person. Meals are available at the guest house but must be arranged in advance. A new 56-room hotel is under construction in Phonsawan and should be open within the next couple of years.

Along the road that leads from the airfield are several noodle shops. Sometimes they're out of fresh *foe* or *mii*, so they serve instant dried noodles! At night one of the noodle shops has live music.

You can also buy food, including fresh produce, in the market in the centre of town.

Getting There & Away
The only way to get to and from Xieng Khwang is by Lao Aviation helicopter. Flights are scheduled to leave Vientiane at 8 am every day except Tuesday and Sunday, arriving in Phonsawan an hour later. On the return trip, flights are scheduled to leave at 10 am. In either direction, delays are common. The fare is US$27 one way.

HUA PHAN PROVINCE ແຂວງຫົວພັນ
The mountainous north-eastern province of Hua Phan has a total population of 120,000, of whom around 33,000 live in the provincial capital of Sam Neua. At the moment Hua Phan is closed to foreigners, but Lao Tourism has plans to open the province to tourism within the next few years.

The population of Hua Phan is a mixture of Lao, Black Thai (Thai Dam), White Thai (Thai Khao), Northern Thai (Thai Neua) and various Lao Sung and Lao Theung hill tribes. Sam Neua was the headquarters for the Lao People's Party throughout most of the war years.

Getting There & Away
Like Xieng Khwang, the only way to get to Sam Neua is by Lao Aviation helicopter. A Soviet ME-8 helicopter leaves Vientiane's Wattay Airport for Sam Neua every Thursday at 8 am, arriving at 10.50 am – this is the longest domestic flight on Lao Aviation's schedule. The fare is US$48.

Southern Laos

Only three provinces in the south of Laos were open to tourists in late 1989: Savannakhet, Salavan and Champasak. The Mekong River Valley, including the towns of Khanthabuli (Savannakhet), Salavan and Pak Se, are mostly inhabited by lowland Lao. The central highlands are populated by a mixture of Phu Thai, Saek (Sek) and Phu peoples.

Although Lao Tourism has tour itineraries for the south, very few people have booked them – the initial interest has been in Vientiane and Luang Phabang.

SAVANNAKHET PROVINCE ແຂວງສັວັນນະເຂດ

Savannakhet is the country's most populous province (312,000) and is a very active trade junction between Thailand and Vietnam. The rural villages of Savannakhet are among the most typically Lao, especially those near the Vietnam border.

The provincial capital is Muang Khanthabuli, a busy town of 45,000 that's just across the Mekong River from Mukdahan, Thailand.

Places to Stay

Lao Tourism has restored four government villas for use by their tour groups. The *Santiphap Hotel* on Thanon Tha Dan is frequented by businesspeople and has reasonably priced rooms.

Getting There & Away

Air Lao Aviation flies Antonov 24 turboprops to Savannakhet daily at 7 am and returns at 9.05 am. Flights take an hour and 10 minutes one way and cost US$52.

Boat A large river ferry leaves Vientiane's south jetty (Tha Heua Lak Si) every Friday morning at 6 am, arriving in Savannakhet Saturday evening. The fare is around US$3 per person. Food is usually available on board. Coming back to Vientiane, boats leave Tuesday morning and arrive Thursday.

SALAVAN PROVINCE ແຂວງສາລະວັນ

The big attraction in Salavan is the Boloven Plateau, which is actually on the border between Salavan and Champasak. On the Se Set (Xet) River (a tributary of the Se Don) are several waterfalls and traditional Lao villages. Lao Tourism has built new bungalows at one of the falls for use with their tours. Like the Plain of Jars in Xieng Khwang Province, the Boloven Plateau has an excellent climate.

Near the Vietnamese border, on the former Ho Chi Minh Trail, are a few traditional Boloven (Phu Thai) villages. A Boloven village features houses that are arranged in a circle. Once a year, water buffalo sacrifices are held in the middle of the circle.

The provincial capital of Salavan was all but destroyed in the war. The rebuilt town is a collection of brick and wood buildings with a population of around 40,000.

Getting There & Away

Air Lao Aviation only has one weekly flight to Salavan on Thursday which goes via Savannakhet. The flight leaves Vientiane at 7 am, then leaves Savannakhet at 9.05 am, arriving in Salavan at 9.40. In the reverse direction, the flight leaves Salavan at 10.40 am. The fare is US$74 one way from Vientiane or US$22 from Savannakhet.

Bus & Truck You can also get to Salavan by bus or truck from Pak Se in Champasak Province.

CHAMPASAK PROVINCE ແຂວງຈຳປາສັກ

The Champasak area has a long history that began with the Thai *muangs* a thousand years ago. Between the 10th and 13th centuries AD it was part of the Cambodian Angkor Empire. Between the 15th and late 17th centuries it was an important Lan Xang outpost but it later became an independent Lao Kingdom when the Lan Xang Empire broke up at the beginning of 18th century.

Today Champasak Province has a population of around 160,000 that includes lowland Lao, Khmers, and Phu Thai. The province is well known for *mat-mii* silks and cottons that are hand-woven of tie-dyed threads.

Pak Se ປາກເຊ

Pak Se is a relatively new town at the confluence of the Mekong and the Se Don rivers that was founded by the French as an administrative outpost in 1905. It is now the capital of Champasak Province (formerly three separate provinces – Champasak, Xedon and Sithandon) but has little of interest to the traveller apart from a lively market. Lao Tourism accommodation here is in a 30-room restored French colonial villa outside of town towards the Boloven Plateau.

Pak Se is also the gateway for trips to the former royal capital of Champasak and the Angkor temple ruins of Wat Phu.

Getting There & Away Pak Se can be reached by road from Salavan or by air from Vientiane. Lao Aviation flies to Pak Se every day at 7 am. On Mondays, Wednesdays and Saturdays they fly via Savan, arriving in Pak Se at 9.45 am. On all other days the flight is direct and arrives at 8.30 am. The return flights are at 9.30 am and 10.45 am respectively. The fare is US$85 one way.

Friday flights to Pak Se continue on to Phnom Penh at 9.30 am. The fare between Pak Se and Phnom Penh is US$35 one way.

Wat Phu ວັດພູ

This Angkor-period (10th to 13th centuries) Khmer temple site is on the lower slopes of Phu Pasak, about 8 km from the town of Champasak (population 24,000). The government supposedly has plans to restore the site and establish a national museum in Champasak, with international aid. It's badly in need of restoration or it will soon be nothing but scrambled chunks of rock.

The site was probably chosen by the Hindu Khmers of Angkor because of a spring that flows from near the top of the hill (which rises approximately 75 metres above the surrounding plain). Historians say that Phu Pasak was in fact sacred to the pre-Angkor kingdom of Chen La (6th century) and may have been the site of human sacrifices. The site is divided into lower and upper parts which are joined by a stairway. The lower part consists of two ruined palace buildings at the edge of a pond which is used for ritual ablutions.

The upper section is the temple sanctuary itself, which once enclosed a large Shiva phallus (*linga*). It was converted into a Buddhist temple in later centuries but much of the original Hindu sculpture remains in the lintels, which feature various forms of Vishnu and Shiva as well as Kala, the Hindu god of time and death. The *naga* (dragon) stairway leading to the sanctuary is lined with plumeria (*dok jampa*) which is the Lao national tree. There is a good view of the valley from the upper platform. In 1989, some travellers were deterred from ascending to the upper section by local authorities who said that the area wasn't safe. Exactly why the top part wasn't considered safe is not clear.

Festivals Near Wat Phu is a large crocodile stone that may have been the site of the purported Chen La sacrifices. Nowadays, each June, the locals perform a water buffalo sacrifice to the ruling earth spirit for Champasak, Chao Tengkham. The blood of the buffalo is offered to a local shaman who serves as a trance medium for the appearance of Chao Tengkham.

Another important local festival is Bun Wat Phu, when pilgrims from throughout southern Laos come to worship at Wat Phu in its Buddhist incarnation. The festival lasts 3 days and features Thai boxing matches, cockfights, music and dancing. It's held as part of Magha Puja (Makkha Bu-saa) at the full moon in February.

Getting There & Away Wat Phu is 46 km from Pak Se or 8 km from Champasak. To hire a taxi from Champasak, ask for Muang Kao (old city). Champasak can be reached by road or ferry boat (along the Mekong) from Pak Se.

Um Muang ຊຸມເມືອງ

Um Muang is a Khmer temple ruin of the same period as Wat Phu (10th to 13th centuries). It's about 45 km south of Pak Se off Route 13, on a small tributary of the Mekong. The ruins include an esplanade bordered by *lingas* (sacred Shiva phalli), a large vestibule and lintel sculpted with Vaishnavá motifs.

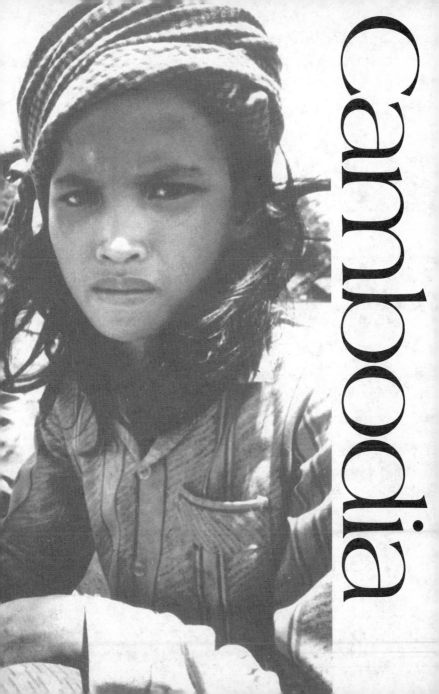

Cambodia

Introduction

Modern-day Cambodia is the successor-state of the mighty Khmer Empire, which during the Angkorian period (9th to 14th centuries) ruled much of what is now Vietnam, Laos and Thailand. The highly advanced, Indianised Khmer civilisation had an enormous influence on the cultural and artistic development of the other peoples of mainland South-East Asia. The magnificent temples of Angkor – of which Angkor Wat is the most famous – and over a thousand other monuments have long attracted pilgrims and tourists and may soon do so again.

In the early 1990s, Cambodia is just beginning to emerge from 2 decades of continual warfare and violence, including almost 4 years (1975-79) of rule by the genocidal Khmer Rouge, who killed at least 1 million of Cambodia's 7 million people. Even today, all around the country you see mass graves and ruined structures; the latter are the result not of neglect but of a conscious, coordinated campaign by the Khmer Rouge to smash the country's pre-revolutionary culture. And you see underpopulated towns and cities whose inhabitants are only slowly emerging from a nightmare that claimed the lives of their parents, spouses, siblings and children.

As of late 1990, the Cambodian civil war was continuing, but recent peace proposals agreed upon by the five permanent members of the UN Security Council factions may soon restore peace and stability. As the country struggles to rebuild itself the rest of the world is once again being allowed to visit Cambodia.

Among the brilliant achievements of Khmer civilisation that are open to foreign visitors for the first time in 2 decades are the fabled temples of Angkor, one of humankind's most magnificent architectural achievements. These stunning monuments, surrounded by dense jungle, are only 152 km from the Thai border, which is expected to open to tourist traffic as soon as the war ends.

Other uniquely Cambodian sights include the plains and rice paddies of the country's heartland – dotted with sugar palms and peasants' thatch huts – which stretch off into the distance fron the Tonlé Sap Lake and the Mekong River. In the south are the thickly forested Cardamom Mountains and Elephant Mountains; nearby are 354 km of coastline, much of it lined with unspoiled beaches. There are more mountains (as well as high plateaus) in the north-eastern provinces of Ratanakiri and Mondulkiri, many of whose inhabitants belong to the highland hill tribes.

The people of Cambodia seem a bit stunned by their country's recent history but are warmly welcoming towards Western visitors, whose very presence signifies that things are finally getting better for Cambodia. Hinayana Buddhist monks are proud to show you their rebuilt pagodas. And older people schooled long ago in English or French are eager to try out their rusty language skills on Westerners; so are young people diligently studying at private language schools along Phnom Penh's 'English St'. Accommodation and transport in Cambodia are still very basic, but for the adventurous traveller the country's delights more than compensate for the minor inconveniences.

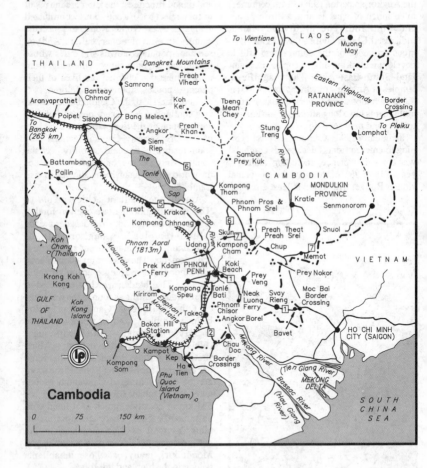

Cambodia

0   75   150 km

Facts about the Country

What to Call Cambodia

Khmers have called their country Kampuchea (usually rendered Kambuja) since at least the 16th century. The name is derived from the word *kambu-ja*, meaning 'those born of Kambu' (a figure of Indian mythology), which was first used to refer to the people of Cambodia in the 10th century. The Portuguese 'Camboxa' and the French 'Cambodge', from which the English name 'Cambodia' is derived, are adaptations of 'Kambuja'.

Since gaining independence in 1953, the country has been known in English as:

1) The Kingdom of Cambodia (in French, le Royaume du Cambodge).
2) The Khmer Republic (under Lon Nol, who ruled from 1970 to 1975).
3) Democratic Kampuchea (under the Khmer Rouge, who controlled the country from 1975 to 1979).
4) The People's Republic of Kampuchea (under the Vietnamese-backed Phnom Penh government from 1979 to 1989).
5) The State of Cambodia (in French, L'État du Cambodge; in Khmer, Roët Kampuchea) from mid-1989.

It was the Khmer Rouge who insisted that the outside world use the name Kampuchea. Changing the country's official English name back to Cambodia (which has been used by the US State Department all along) was intended as a symbolic move to distance the present government in Phnom Penh from the bitter connotations of the name Kampuchea, which Westerners and Overseas Khmer alike associate with the murderous Khmer Rouge regime.

HISTORY

Funan

From the 1st to the 6th centuries, much of present-day Cambodia was part of the kingdom of Funan, which owed its prosperity to its position on the great trade route between China and India; Funan's major port was Oc-Eo in what is now Kien Giang Province of southern Vietnam.

Funan (the name is a Chinese transliteration of the ancient Khmer form of the word *phnom*, which means 'hill') played a vitally important role in South-East Asian history as a recipient of Indian culture, which shaped the political institutions, culture and art of later Khmer states. Both Hinduism and Mahayana Buddhism coexisted within Funanese society. Princely links between Funan and the Khmers had been established by the 6th century, and subsequent Khmer dynasties viewed Funan as the state from which they sprang.

Chenla

In the middle of the 6th century, the Kambujas, who lived in the middle Mekong (north of present-day Cambodia), broke away from Funan. Within a short time, this new power, known as Chenla, absorbed the Funanese kingdom. In the late 7th century, Chenla broke into two divisions, called Land Chenla (to the north) and Water Chenla (to the south along the Gulf of Thailand) by the Chinese. Whereas Land Chenla was fairly stable during the 8th century, Water Chenla was beset by dynastic rivalries. During this period, Java probably invaded and controlled part of the country.

The Angkorian Period

The Angkorian era, known for its brilliant achievements in architecture and sculpture, was begun by Jayavarman II, a prince distantly related to earlier dynasties who returned from Java around the year 800. During his rule, a new state religion establishing the Khmer ruler as a god-king (*devaraja*) was instituted. Jayavarman II (reigned 802 to 850) installed himself successively at four different capitals around the

Tonlé Sap, the last of which was at Roluos, 13 km east of the modern town of Siem Reap.

Jayavarman II's nephew, Indravarman I (reigned 877 to 889), constructed a vast irrigation system that made possible the intensive cultivation of nearby lands. This and later irrigation projects allowed the Khmers to maintain a densely populated and highly centralised state in a relatively small area.

Indravarman I's successor, Yasovarman (reigned 889 to 910), moved the Khmer capital to the immediate vicinity of Angkor, where it would remain (except between 921 and 944 and during invasions) until the mid-15th century. Yasovarman and his immediate successors extended Khmer dominion over a vast area of what is now Vietnam, Laos and Thailand.

During the 11th and 12th centuries, the Khmers fought a series of wars with the Burmese, the Vietnamese and the Chams, whose empire was centred in south-central Vietnam. In the early 12th century, Champa was reduced to vassal status, but in 1177, the Chams avenged this humiliation by capturing and sacking the city of Angkor itself, leaving the Khmer Empire in chaos.

Order was restored by one of the greatest of all Khmer rulers, Jayavarman VII (reigned 1181 to 1201), who is best known for his huge building programme. Among the many monuments he constructed was his new capital, the massive city of Angkor Thom. Jayavarman VII pushed back the Chams and later laid waste to their kingdom; his successor actually annexed Champa. But by the end of his reign, the Thais, who lived in the west of the empire, had begun to assert themselves.

For more information on the Angkorian period and its monuments, see the Angkor chapter.

Decline of the Khmer Empire

The decline of Angkor began after the death of Jayavarman VII at the beginning of the 13th century. During the course of the next hundred years, the Cambodian state abandoned its adherence to Hinduism (which had coexisted with Mahayana Buddhism since the 9th century) and embraced Hinayana Buddhism. The use of Sanskrit ended by the early 14th century; it was replaced as a sacred language by Pali.

During the 14th and 15th centuries, Khmer wealth and power were gradually eroded, in part because of repeated Thai incursions, which made maintaining the elaborate irrigation system on which Angkor's survival depended extremely difficult. In the mid-15th century, Angkor was occupied by the Thais, prompting the Khmer court to abandon the city and relocate their capital to the vicinity of Phnom Penh.

The next century and a half of Khmer history was dominated by confusing dynastic rivalries and almost continuous warfare with the Thais. Although the Khmers once pushed westward all the way to the Thai capital of Ayuthaya (only to find it occupied by the Burmese), the Thais recovered and dealt a crushing blow to the Khmers by capturing their capital in 1594.

Shortly before the Khmer defeat of 1594, the Cambodian king, Satha, requested the assistance of the Spanish and Portuguese, who had recently become active in the region. A Spanish expedition arrived in Cambodia in 1596 to assist Satha only to find that he had been deposed by r, Chung Prei. After a series of disagreements and the sacking of the Chinese quarter of Phnom Penh by the Spanish forces, the Spaniards attacked the palace and killed Chung Prei. The Spaniards then decided to return to Manila, but while marching eastward through Laos, they changed their minds and returned to Phnom Penh, installing one of Satha's sons on the throne. Resentment of the power wielded by the Spanish grew among court officials until 1599, when the Spanish garrison at Phnom Penh was massacred. Shortly thereafter, Satha's brother ascended the throne with the help of the Thais.

From about 1600 until the arrival of the French in 1863, Cambodia was ruled by a series of weak kings who, because of continual challenges by dissident members of the royal family, were forced to seek the protection – granted, of course, at a price – of either Thailand or Vietnam. In the 17th century, assistance from the Nguyen Lords of southern Vietnam was given on the condition that Vietnamese be allowed to settle in what is now the southern region of Vietnam, at that time part of Cambodia (and today still referred to by the Khmers as 'Lower Cambodia'). In the west, the Thais established dominion over the provinces of Battambang and Siem Reap; by the late 18th century they had firm control of the Cambodian royal family. Indeed, one king was crowned in Bangkok and placed on the throne at Udong with the help of the Thai army. That Cambodia survived through the 18th century as a distinct entity is due to the preoccupations of its neighbours: while the Thais were expending their energy and resources in fighting the Burmese, the Vietnamese were wholly absorbed by internal strife, including the rivalry between the Trinh Lords and the Nguyen Lords and the Tay Son Rebellion.

French Rule

Cambodia's dual Thai and Vietnamese suzerainty was ended in 1863, when French gunboats intimidated King Norodom (reigned 1860 to 1904) into signing a treaty of protectorate. French control of Cambodia, which developed as an adjunct to French colonial interests in Vietnam, at first involved relatively little direct interference in Cambodia's affairs of state. However, the French presence did prevent Cambodia's expansionist neighbours from annexing any more Khmer territory and helped keep Norodom on the throne despite the ambitions of his rebellious half-brothers.

By the 1870s, French officials in Cambodia began pressing for greater control over internal affairs. In 1884, Norodom was forced to sign a treaty turning his country into a virtual colony, sparking a 2-year rebellion that constituted the only major anti-French movement in Cambodia until after WW II. This uprising ended when the king was persuaded to call upon rebel fight-ers to lay down their weapons in exchange for a return to the pre-treaty arrangement.

During the next 2 decades, senior Cambodian officials, who saw certain advantages in acquiescing to French power, opened the door to direct French control over the day-to-day administration of the country. At the same time, the French maintained Norodom's court in a splendour probably unequalled since the Angkorian period, thereby greatly enhancing the symbolic position of the monarchy. The king's increased stature served to legitimise the Cambodian state, thereby pre-empting the growth of any sort of broad-based nationalist movement; this situation is in marked contrast to that of Vietnam. Indeed, the only large-scale popular protest of any kind between the 1880s and the 1940s was an essentially peaceful peasant uprising in 1916 which ended when the king agreed to consider their grievances.

King Monorom was succeeded by King Sisowath (reigned 1904 to 1927), who was followed on the throne by King Monivong (reigned 1927 to 1941). Upon King Monivong's death, the French governor general of Japanese-occupied Indochina, Admiral Jean Decoux, placed 18 year old Prince Sihanouk on the Cambodian throne. The choice was based on the assumption that Sihanouk would prove pleasingly pliable; this proved to be a major miscalculation.

After WW II, the French returned, making Cambodia an 'autonomous state within the French Union' but retaining de facto control. The years after 1945 were marked by strife between the country's various political groupings, a situation made more unstable by the Franco-Vietminh War then raging in Vietnam and Laos.

Independence

In January 1953, King Sihanouk, who had been at odds with the dominant Democratic Party, took decisive action, dissolving the parliament, declaring martial law and embarking on what became known as the 'Royal Crusade': his campaign to drum up international support for his country's independence.

Independence was proclaimed on 9 November 1953 and recognised by the Geneva Conference of May 1954, which ended French control of Indochina. However, internal political turmoil continued, much of it the result of conflicts between Sihanouk and his domestic opponents. In March 1955, Sihanouk abdicated in favour of his father, Norodom Suramarit, in order to pursue a career as a politician. His newly established party, the People's Socialist Community (Sangkum Reastr Niyum), won every seat in parliament in the September 1955 elections. Sihanouk dominated Cambodian politics for the next 15 years, serving as prime minister until his father's death in 1960, when no new king was named and he became chief-of-state.

Although he also feared the Vietnamese Communists, during the early 1960s Sihanouk considered South Vietnam and Thailand, both allies of the USA (which he mistrusted), as the greatest threats to Cambodia's security and even survival. In an attempt to fend off these many dangers, he declared Cambodia neutral in international affairs. In May 1965, Sihanouk, convinced that the USA had been plotting against him and his family, broke diplomatic relations with Washington and tilted toward North Vietnam, the Viet Cong and China. In addition, he accepted that the North Vietnamese Army and the Viet Cong would use Cambodian territory in their battle against South Vietnam and the Americans.

These moves and his socialist economic policies alienated right-leaning elements in Cambodian society, including the officer corps of the army and the urban elite. At the same time, left-wing Cambodians, many of them educated abroad, deeply resented his internal policies, which did not allow for political dissent. Compounding Sihanouks's problems was the fact that all classes were fed up with the pervasive corruption. Although most peasants – the vast majority of the population – revered Sihanouk as a semi-divine figure, a rural-based rebellion

broke out in 1967, leading him to conclude that the greatest threat to his regime now came from the left. Bowing to pressure from the army, he implemented a policy of harsh repression against left-wingers.

In 1969 the USA began a secret programme of bombing suspected communist base camps in Cambodia. For the next 4 years (until bombing was halted by Congress in August 1973), huge areas of the eastern half of the country were carpet bombed by US B-52s, killing uncounted thousands of civilians and turning hundreds of thousands more into refugees.

The Lon Nol Regime

By 1969 the conflict between the army and leftist rebels had become more serious and Sihanouk's political position had greatly deteriorated. In March 1970, while Sihanouk was on a trip to France, General Lon Nol and Prince Sisowath Matak, Sihanouk's cousin, deposed him as chief of state, apparently with US support. Pogroms against ethnic-Vietnamese living in Cambodia soon broke out, prompting many ethnic-Vietnamese inhabitants of the country to flee. Sihanouk took up residence in Beijing, where he set up a government-in-exile nominally in control of an indigenous Cambodian revolutionary movement that Sihanouk himself had nicknamed the Khmers Rouges ('Red Khmers' in French).

On 30 April 1970, US and South Vietnamese forces invaded Cambodia in an effort to rout out some 40,000 Viet Cong and North Vietnamese troops that were using bases inside Cambodia in their war to overthrow the South Vietnamese government. As a result of the invasion, the Vietnamese Communists withdrew deeper into Cambodia, thus posing an even greater threat to the Lon Nol government than before. At the same time, the new government was becoming very unpopular as a result of the unprecedented greed and corruption of its leaders. Savage fighting quickly engulfed the entire country, bringing misery to millions of Cambodians, many of whom fled rural areas for the relative safety of Phnom

Penh and provincial capitals. Between 1970 and 1975, several hundred thousand people died in the fighting.

During the next few years, the Khmer Rouge came to play a dominant role in trying to overthrow the Lon Nol regime. The leaders of the Khmer Rouge, including Paris-educated Pol Pot (Saloth Sar) and Khieu Samphan, had fled into the countryside in the 1960s to escape the summary justice then being meted out to suspected leftists by Sihanouk's security forces.

Despite massive US military and economic aid, Lon Nol never succeeded in gaining the initiative against the Khmer Rouge, which pursued a strategy of attrition. Large parts of the countryside fell to the rebels, and many provincial capitals were cut off from Phnom Penh. On 17 April 1975 – 2 weeks before the fall of Saigon – Phnom Penh surrendered to the Khmer Rouge.

The Khmer Rouge Regime

Upon taking Phnom Penh, the Khmer Rouge implemented one of the most radical and brutal restructurings of a society ever attempted; its goal to transform Cambodia into a Maoist, peasant-dominated agrarian cooperative. Within 2 weeks of coming to power, the entire populations of the capital and provincial towns (including everyone in the hospitals) were force-marched out to the countryside and placed in mobile work teams to do slave labour – preparing the fields, digging irrigation canals – for 12 to 15 hours a day. Disobedience of any sort often brought immediate execution. The advent of Khmer Rouge rule was proclaimed 'Year Zero'. Currency was abolished and postal services halted. Except for one fortnightly flight to Beijing (China was providing aid and advisors to the Khmer Rouge), the country was completely cut off from the outside world.

Over the next 4 years, hundreds of thousands of Cambodians, including the vast majority of the country's educated people, were tortured to death or executed in what some have called a campaign of 'autogenocide'. Thousands of middle-class Cambodians, branded as 'parasites' because they spoke a foreign language or wore spectacles, were systematically liquidated. The slaughter reached its height in 1978, when huge numbers of people accused of being traitors or Vietnamese spies were killed. Hundreds of thousands more died of mistreatment, malnourishment and disease. At least 1 million Cambodians died between 1975 and 1979 as the result of the policies of the Khmer Rouge government.

Sihanouk returned to Phnom Penh in September 1975 as titular chief of state but resigned 3 months later. He remained in Phnom Penh, imprisoned in his palace and kept alive only at the insistence of the Chinese, who considered him useful. During the Vietnamese invasion of Cambodia in December 1978, Sihanouk was flown to Beijing to prevent his falling into the hands of the new government.

Vietnamese Intervention

Between 1976 and 1978, the xenophobic government in Phnom Penh instigated a series of border clashes with Vietnam, whose southern region – once part of the Khmer Empire – it claimed. Khmer Rouge incursions into Vietnamese border provinces left hundreds of Vietnamese civilians dead. On 25 December 1978, Vietnam launched a full-scale invasion of Cambodia, toppling the Pol Pot government 2 weeks later (on 7 January 1979). As Vietnamese tanks neared Phnom Penh, the Khmer Rouge fled westward with as many civilians as they could seize, taking refuge in the jungles and mountains on both sides of the border with Thailand. The Vietnamese installed a new government led by two former Khmer Rouge officers, Hun Sen (who had defected to Vietnam in 1977) and Heng Samrin (who had done the same in 1978). The official version of events is that the Heng Samrin government came to power in a revolutionary uprising against the Pol Pot regime.

The social and economic dislocation that accompanied the Vietnamese invasion – along with the destruction of rice stocks and unharvested fields by both sides (to prevent their use by the enemy) – resulted in a vastly reduced rice harvest in early 1979. The chaotic situation led to very little rice being planted in the summer of 1979. By the middle of that year, the country was on the verge of widespread famine. As hundreds of thousands of Cambodians fled to Thailand, a massive international famine relief effort, sponsored by the UN, was launched.

In June 1982, Sihanouk agreed – under pressure from China – to head a military and political front opposed to the Phnom Penh government and the 170,000 Vietnamese troops defending it. The Sihanouk-led resistance coalition brought together – on paper, at least – FUNCINPEC (the French acronym for Cambodian National Front for an Independent, Neutral, Peaceful and Cooperative Cambodia), a royalist group loyal to Sihanouk; the Khmer People's National Liberation Front, a non-communist grouping formed by former prime minister and banker Son Sann; and the Khmer Rouge, officially known as the Party of Democratic Kampuchea and by far the largest and most powerful of the three. Despite Pol Pot's 'retirement' in 1985, he remains the de facto leader of the Khmer Rouge.

By the late 1980s, the weak royalist group, the Armée Nationale Sihanoukiste, had 12,000 troops; Son Sann's faction, plagued by internal divisions, could field some 8000 soldiers; and the Khmer Rouge's National Army of Democratic Kampuchea was believed to have 40,000 troops. The Phnom Penh government's army, the Kampuchean People's Revolutionary Armed Forces, had 50,000 regular soldiers and another 100,000 men and women serving in local militia forces.

In 1985, the Vietnamese overran all the major rebel camps inside Cambodia, forcing the Khmer Rouge and their allies to retreat into Thailand. Since that time, the Khmer Rouge – and, to a much more limited extent, the other two factions – have engaged in guerrilla warfare aimed at demoralising their opponents. Tactics used by the Khmer Rouge include shelling government-controlled garrison towns, planting thousands of mines along roads and in rice fields, attacking road transport, blowing up bridges, kidnapping village chiefs and killing local administrators and schoolteachers. The Khmer Rouge has also forced thousands of men, women and children living in the refugee camps it controls to work as porters, ferrying ammunition and other supplies into Cambodia across heavily mined sections of the border.

Throughout the 1980s, Thailand actively supported the Khmer Rouge and the other resistance factions, seeing them as a counterweight to Vietnamese power in the region. In fact, in 1979 Thailand demanded that as a condition for allowing international food aid for Cambodia to pass through its territory, food had to be supplied to the Khmer Rouge forces encamped in the Thai border region as well. Along with weaponry supplied by China (and delivered by the Thai army), this international assistance was essential in enabling the Khmer Rouge to rebuild its military strength. At the same time, Malaysia and Singapore supplied weapons to the two smaller factions of the coalition. As part of its campaign to harass and isolate Hanoi, the USA gave more than US$15 million per year in aid to the non-Communist factions of the Khmer Rouge-dominated coalition and helped it retain its UN seat.

Cambodia Today

Although over a decade has passed since the overthrow of the Pol Pot government, the tragedy and trauma of its 57 murderous months in power still pervade every aspect of Cambodian social life and politics. And Pol Pot, accompanied by his new wife (his old wife is said to be insane and living in Beijing), still commands his Chinese-equipped forces from a heavily guarded compound just inside Thailand's Trat Province.

Most foreign observers in Cambodia believe that the Vietnamese-installed Phnom Penh government is accepted as legitimate by the vast majority of the Cambodian people, who resent the Vietnamese but appreciate their role in bringing down the genocidal Khmer Rouge regime and preventing its return to power. Sihanouk is remembered with nostalgia by a few older Cambodians, but his repressive policies before 1970 and his association with the Khmer Rouge since then are the cause of great bitterness.

In September 1989, Vietnam, suffering from economic woes and eager to reduce its international isolation, announced that it had withdrawn all of its troops from Cambodia, although evidence suggests that Vietnamese soldiers wearing Cambodian uniforms remained in the country well into 1990. With most of the Vietnamese gone, the opposition coalition, still dominated by the Khmer Rouge, launched a series of offensives, bringing the number of refugees inside the country to over 150,000 by the autumn of 1990. In the first 8 months of 1990, over 2000 Cambodians lost their lives in the fighting.

Since the late 1980s, the Hun Sen government in Phnom Penh government has made concerted efforts to gain international recognition – especially in the West – by working to change its image as a puppet of the Vietnamese. People who served in the Sihanouk and Lon Nol governments, many of whom were trained in Europe or the USA, have been given positions of power in the present government; such people now make up about half the cabinet. At the same time, socialist dogma has been discarded in favour of free-market economic principles, in evidence in the many private shops now operating in the capital and elsewhere. Some 70% of the economy is now in private hands, more than in the 1960s under Sihanouk. This process is being accelerated by the withdrawal of Soviet-bloc economic aid, which until recently accounted for 80% of government revenues. However, watchdog groups report that human rights violations are continuing. In 1989 and 1990, for example, the Phnom Penh government resorted to nighttime sweeps of discos and cinemas to fill the ranks of its army, dragging off young men and boys as young as 13 for immediate conscription.

In the late 1980s, the USA made a total

Vietnamese withdrawal from Cambodia and Vietnamese cooperation in bringing about a comprehensive solution to the Cambodian civil war prerequisites for establishing diplomatic relations with Hanoi. In July 1990, in a major shift of US foreign policy, the USA initiated diplomatic contacts with Vietnam - the first between Washington and Hanoi since the late 1970s - to discuss the Cambodian situation. At the same time, the USA withdrew diplomatic support for the Khmer Rouge-dominated coalition and announced that it would, the the next General Assembly session, oppose seating the coalition's UN delegation. A few months later, the USA began its first-ever diplomatic contacts with the Phnom Penh government; shortly thereafter, China did the same.

Diplomatic efforts to end the civil war began to bear real fruit in September 1990, when a plan agreed upon by the five permanent members of the UN Security Council (the USA, the USSR, China, France and Britain) was accepted by both the Phnom Penh government and the three factions of the resistance coalition.

According to the agreement, a largely symbolic Supreme National Council, comprised of six individuals selected by the Phnom Penh government and an equal number chosen by the opposition (two from each faction), would be constituted under the leadership of Sihanouk. The Council, considered the embodiment of Cambodian sovereignty, would then cede its authority in the key areas of foreign affairs, defence, internal security, finance and information to a United Nations-run transition government, which would disarm rebel factions and administer free and fair elections. The plan, which will cost between US\$3 and US\$5 billion and may require up to 20,000 officials and troops, will be the most ambitious such mission ever taken by the United Nations.

GEOGRAPHY

Cambodia covers a land area of 181,035 sq km, which is the size of Missouri and a bit over half the size of Italy or Vietnam. The country's maximum extent is about 580 km from east to west and 450 km from north to south. Cambodia is bounded on the west by Thailand, on the north by Thailand and Laos, on the east and south-east by Vietnam and on the south by the Gulf of Thailand.

Cambodia's two dominant topographical features are the Mekong River, which is almost 5 km wide in places, and the Tonlé Sap (Great Lake). The Mekong, which rises in Tibet, flows about 315 km through Cambodia before continuing on, via southern Vietnam, to the South China Sea. At Phnom Penh, it splits into its two major branches, the Upper River (called simply the Mekong or, in Vietnamese, the Tien Giang) and the Lower River (the Bassac River; in Vietnamese, the Hau Giang). The rich sediment deposited during the Mekong's annual wet-season flooding has made for agricultural land of great fertility. Most of Cambodia's streams and rivers flow into the Mekong-Tonlé Sap basin.

The Tonlé Sap is linked to the Mekong at Phnom Penh by a 100 km long channel which I have called, for convenience's sake, the Tonlé Sap River. From mid-May to early October (the rainy season), the level of the Mekong rises, backing up the Tonlé Sap River and causing it to flow north-westward into the Tonlé Sap Lake. During this period, the Tonlé Sap swells from 3000 sq km to over 7500 sq km; its maximum depth increases from about 2.2 metres to more than 10 metres. As the water level of the Mekong falls during the dry season, the Tonlé Sap River reverses its flow, draining the waters of the lake back into the Mekong. This extraordinary process makes the Tonlé Sap one of the world's richest sources of fresh-water fish.

In the centre of Cambodia, around the Tonlé Sap and the upper Mekong Delta, is a low-lying alluvial plain where the vast majority of Cambodia's people live. Extending outward from this plain are thinly forested transitional plains with elevations of no more than about 100 metres above sea level.

In the south-west, much of the area between the Gulf of Thailand and the Tonlé Sap is covered by a highland region formed by two distinct upland blocks, the Cardamom Mountains (Chuor Phnom Kravanh) in south-western Battambang Province and Pursat Province and the Elephant Mountains (Chuor Phnom Damrei) in the provinces of Kompong Speu, Koh Kong and Kampot. Along the southern coast is a heavily forested lowland strip isolated from the rest of the country by the mountains to the north. Cambodia's highest peak, Phnom Aoral (1813 metres), is on the eastern part of the border between the provinces of Kompong Chhnang and Kompong Speu.

Along Cambodia's northern border with Thailand, the plains abut an east-west oriented sandstone escarpment, over 300 km long and 180 to 550 metres in height, that marks the southern limit of the Dangkrek Mountains (Chuor Phnom Dangkrek). In the north-eastern corner of the country (the provinces of Ratanakiri and Mondulkiri), the transitional plains give way to the Eastern Highlands, a remote region of densely forested mountains and high plateaus that extends eastward into Vietnam's Central Highlands and northward into Laos.

CLIMATE

The climate of Cambodia is governed by two monsoons, which set the rhythm of rural life. The cool, dry, north-eastern monsoon, which carries little rain, blows from about November to March. From May to early October, the south-western monsoon brings strong winds, high humidity and heavy rains. Between these seasons, the weather is transitional. Even during the wet season, it rarely rains in the morning: most precipitation comes in the afternoons, and even then only sporadically.

Maximum daily temperatures range from 35°C in April, the hottest month, to the high 20s during the coolest month, January. Daily minimum temperatures are usually about 8°C to 11°C below the maximums.

Annual rainfall varies considerably from area to area. While the seaward slopes of the south-western highlands receive more than

5000 mm of precipitation per annum, the central lowlands average only about 1400 mm. Between 70% and 80% of the annual rainfall is brought by the south-western monsoon.

FLORA

The central lowland consists of rice paddies, fields of dry crops such as corn and tobacco, tracts of reeds and tall grass, and thinly wooded areas. The transitional plains are mostly covered with savanna grasses, which grow to a height of 1.5 metres.

In the south-west, there are virgin rainforests growing to heights of 50 metres or more on the rainy seaward slopes of the mountains while nearby, higher elevations support pine forests. Vegetation in the coastal strip includes both evergreen and mangrove forests. In the northern mountains there are broadleaf evergreen forests whose trees soar 30 metres above the thick under-growth of vines, bamboos, palms and assorted woody and herbaceous ground plants. The Eastern Highlands are covered with grassland and deciduous forest. For-ested upland areas support many varieties of orchid.

In the last 2 decades, a great deal of defor-estation has taken place, in part because firewood remains Cambodia's principle source of energy. In the north-east, a large quantity of timber is being cut by the Vietnamese.

The symbol of Cambodia is the sugar palm tree, which is used in construction (for roofs and walls) and to make medicine, wine and vinegar. Because of the way sugar palms grow (over the years, the tree keeps getting taller but the trunk, which lacks a normal bark, does not grow thicker), their trunks retain shrapnel marks from every battle that ever raged around them. Some sugar palms survive despite having been shot clear through the trunk.

FAUNA

Cambodia's larger wild animals include bears, elephants, rhinoceros, leopards, tigers and wild oxen. The lion, although often incorporated into Angkorian heraldic devices, has never been seen here. Among the country's more common birds are cormo-rants, cranes, egrets, grouse, herons, pelicans, pheasants and wild ducks. There is also a great variety of butterflies. Four types of snake are especially dangerous: the cobra, the king cobra, the banded krait and Russell's viper.

GOVERNMENT

Most of the territory of Cambodia is under the control of the government installed in Phnom Penh by the Vietnamese after their overthrow of the Khmer Rouge in 1979. That government is led by two former Khmer Rouge officers, Prime Minister Hun Sen, a widely respected reformer, and President of the Council of State Heng Samrin, who is known as a hardliner. Heng Samrin is also Secretary General of the ruling party, the People's Revolutionary Party, which has about 10,000 members. The highest legisla-tive body is the National Assembly, which has 117 members. The highest executive body is the Council of State.

The flag of the Phnom Penh government is a yellow, five-tower outline of Angkor in the middle of a blue and red field split hori-zontally. This flag replaced one consisting of a yellow, five tower outline of Angkor on an all-red field in 1989. The flag of the Khmer Rouge-dominated coalition led by Prince Sihanouk (that is fighting to overthrow the Phnom Penh government) has a yellow, three tower outline of Angkor on a red field.

Cambodia is divided into 18 provinces (khet), 122 districts (srok), 1570 sub-districts (khum) and 11,564 villages (phoum). Below the village levels are sub-divisions known as 'solidarity groups' (krom samaki), each con-sisting of about 15 families organised on a cooperative or collective basis. Cambodia's provinces, listed from east to west, are: Ratanakiri, Mondulkiri, Stung Treng, Kompong Cham, Kratie, Svay Rieng, Prey Veng, Preah Vihear, Kompong Thom, Kandal, Takeo, Kompong Chhnang, Kompong Speu, Kampot, Siem Reap-Oddar Meanchey, Pursat, Koh Kong and

Battambang. Most of Cambodia's provinces bear the same name as their capital city.

ECONOMY

Cambodia's economy, which even before 1975 was one of the least developed in South-East Asia, is based on two major products, rice and rubber, both of which are subject to the vagaries of the weather and large fluctuations in world market prices. Other important products include fish (the single most important source of protein in the Cambodian diet), livestock, fruits (especially bananas, oranges and pineapples), garden vegetables, beans, cassava, corn (maize), sugar, soybeans, sweet potatoes, tobacco, coffee and kapok (silky fibres that clothe the seed of the ceiba tree and are used as a filling for mattresses and similar items). During the 1980s, domestic agricultural production was supplemented by food aid from Vietnam and the USSR.

About 80% of the population is employed in agriculture, fishing or forestry. Until the dislocations of the early 1970s, approximately four-fifths of farmers owned the land they farmed; most plots were quite small (1 hectare or less). Rice, which provided over one-third of the gross national product, was grown by 80% of rural families on some 85% of the country's total cultivated land area. Most regions produced only one crop per year because of a lack of irrigation infrastructure. Peasants supplemented their subsistence-level rice crop by raising livestock, cultivating fruit and vegetables and fishing for carp, lungfish, perch, smelt and other varieties of freshwater fish.

All fuel and most raw materials, equipment and consumer goods must be imported. Cambodia's main trading partners are Vietnam (which of late has been doing a lot of hardwood logging in the north-east), the Soviet Union, Eastern Europe and, through extensive smuggling networks, Thailand and Singapore. Precious stones mined around Pailin and elsewhere in Battambang Province – these days controlled by the Khmer Rouge – are exported across the border to Thailand.

Recently, plans to enact a foreign investment law similar to those promulgated in Vietnam and Laos in the late 1980s have been drawn up, and Singapore, Thailand and Australia have been showing interest in expanding their economic contacts with Cambodia.

POPULATION

In the late 1980s, the population of Cambodia was somewhere around 7 million, with city and town-dwellers making up about a tenth of the total. In the central lowlands, where 90% of Cambodians reside, the population density is 100 people per sq km (by comparison, Vietnam's Red River Delta has 1000 people per sq km). The average national population density is only 37 people per sq km.

The country's rate of population growth is now estimated to be over 3% per annum, among the highest in the world. Birth rates are said to be especially high in the refugee camps along the Thai border.

PEOPLE

Ethnic-Khmers

Between 90% and 95% of the peoplewho live in Cambodia are ethnic-Khmers (ethnic-Cambodians), making the country the most homogeneous in South-East Asia.

The Khmers have inhabited Cambodia since the beginning of recorded history (around the 2nd century AD), many centuries before the Thais and Vietnamese migrated to the region. During the next 6 centuries, Khmer culture and religion were Indianised by contact with the civilisations of India and Java. Over the centuries, the Khmers have mixed with other groups resident in Cambodia, including the Javanese (8th century), Tai (10th to 15th centuries), Vietnamese (from the early 17th century) and Chinese (since the 18th century).

Ethnic-Chinese

The most important minority group in Cambodia is the Chinese, who until 1975 controlled the country's economic life. Although intermarriage with the Khmers is not infrequent, the Chinese have managed to retain a significant degree of cultural distinctiveness. In 1975, there were some 250,000 ethnic-Chinese in Cambodia, but like other city dwellers, they suffered especially severely under the Khmer Rouge. Their numbers have been further reduced by the disproportionate number of ethnic-Chinese who have chosen to emigrate since 1979.

Ethnic-Vietnamese

There is a great deal of mutual dislike and distrust between the Cambodians and the Vietnamese, even those who have been living in Cambodia for generations. While the Khmers refer to the Vietnamese as *yuon*, a derogatory term that means 'barbarians', the Vietnamese look down on the Khmers and consider them lazy for not farming every available bit of land, an absolute necessity in densely populated Vietnam. Historic antagonisms between the Vietnamese and the Khmers are exacerbated by the prominence of ethnic-Vietnamese among shopowners.

Before 1970, Cambodia had between 250,000 and 300,000 ethnic-Vietnamese, a large number of whom lived by fishing in the Tonlé Sap. Significant numbers of them fled during the reign of anti-Vietnamese terror unleashed by the Lon Nol government. After 1979, many of these refugees returned to Cambodia, joined, some observers charge, by hundreds of thousands of settlers sent in by Hanoi to colonise the country. Today, ethnic-Vietnamese are again fleeing to Vietnam, preferring, as one Cambodian put it, to return to Vietnam alive rather than floating down the Mekong dead, as did some of their less fortunate compatriots in the early 1970s.

Cham Muslims

Cambodia's Cham Muslims (known locally as the Khmer Islam) currently number some 190,000. They live in 200 villages, mostly in areas along the Mekong to the north and east of Phnom Penh. The Cham Muslims suffered particularly vicious persecution between 1975 and 1979 and a large part of their community was exterminated. Of the country's 113 mosques in 1975, only 20 have been rebuilt and reconsecrated.

Ethno-Linguistic Minorities

Cambodia's diverse ethno-linguistic minorities (hill tribes), who live in the country's mountainous regions, numbered approximately 90,000 in 1975. Collectively, they are known to Khmers by the derogatory term *phnong*, which means 'savages'.

These groups, which include the Saoch (in the Elephant Mountains), the Pear (in the Cardamom Mountains), the Brao (along the Lao border) and the Kuy (in the far northwest), have been mistreated by the ethnic-Khmers for centuries, although they were spared the worst excesses of the Khmer Rouge.

EDUCATION

In 1970, it was estimated that about 50% of the population aged 10 and over could read, the lowest rate in South-East Asia except for Laos.

CULTURE

Between the 15th century, when Angkor fell to the Thais and was abandoned, and the advent of the French protectorate in 1863, foreign invasions, civil war, depopulation and general political instability left little opportunity and few resources to keep Cambodia's artistic traditions alive. In recent generations, Cambodia's consciousness of the glory of its past achievements has tended to dominate artistic expression, leading to conservatism rather than innovation in the arts.

Architecture

Khmer architecture reached its period of greatest magnificence during the Angkorian era (the 9th to 14th centuries). Some of the finest examples of architecture from this period are Angkor Wat and the structures of Angkor Thom.

Today, most Cambodian houses in rural areas are built on high wood pilings (if the family can afford it) and have thatch roofs, walls made of palm mats and floors of woven bamboo strips resting on bamboo joists. The shady space underneath is used for storage and for people to hang out at midday.

Sculpture

Many of the finest works of Khmer sculpture are on display at the National Museum in Phnom Penh.

Music, Dance & Theatre

Cambodia's highly stylised classic dance, adapted from dances performed at Angkor (and similar to Thai dances derived from the same source), is performed to the accompaniment of an orchestra and choral narration. The dancers act out stories and legends taken from Hindu epics such as the *Ramayana*.

In the countryside, wandering troupes perform folk dramas and folk dances at festivals and weddings. The actors invariably depict stereotyped characters familiar to everyone watching: the beautiful princess, the greedy merchant, the inept lover, the cruel father, the country bumpkin and so forth.

About 90% of Cambodia's classical dancers were killed by the Khmer Rouge. The government has recently re-established a national classical dance troupe.

RELIGION
Hinduism

Hinduism flourished alongside Buddhism from the 1st century until the 14th century. In Funan and during the pre-Angkorian period, Hinduism was represented by the worship of Harihara (Shiva and Vishnu embodied in a single deity). During the time of Angkor, Shiva was the deity most in favour with the royal family, although in the 12th century he seems to have been superseded by Vishnu.

Buddhism

For information on Hinayana Buddhism, the predominant form of Buddhism practised in Cambodia and the state religion until 1975, see the Facts about the Country chapter in the Laos section.

Archaeologists have determined that before the 9th century, a period during which Sanskrit was used in ritual inscriptions, the Hinayana school constituted the prevalent form of Buddhism in Cambodia. Inscriptions and images indicate that Mahayana Buddhism was in favour after the 9th century but was replaced in the 13th century by a form of Hinayana Buddhism which arrived, along with the Pali language, from Sri Lanka via Thailand.

Between 1975 and 1979, the vast majority of Cambodia's Buddhist monks were murdered by the Khmer Rouge, who also damaged or destroyed virtually all of the country's more than 3000 wats. In the late 1980s, Buddhism was again made the state religion. At that time, Cambodia had about 6000 monks, who by law had to be at least 60 years old.

Islam

Cambodia's Muslims are descendants of Chams who migrated from what is now central Vietnam after the final defeat of the kingdom of Champa by the Vietnamese in 1471. Whereas their compatriots who remained in Vietnam were only partly Islamicised, the Cambodian Chams adopted a fairly orthodox version of Sunni Islam and maintained links with other Muslim communities in the region. Like their Buddhist neighbours, however, the Cham Muslims call the faithful to prayer by banging on a drum (rather than with the call of the muezzin, as in most Muslim lands).

Today, the Muslim community of Phnom Penh includes the descendants of people who immigrated from Pakistan and Afghanistan several generations ago, and there is a neighbourhood of the city near Tuol Tom Pong Market still known as the 'Arab Village'. However, there are only about half-a-dozen Muslims fluent in Arabic, the language of the Koran, in all of Cambodia. In 1989, 20 Cambodian Muslims made the *hajj* (pilgrimage) to Mecca. *Halal* (killed according to Islamic law) meat is available in Phnom Penh in the O Russei, Tuol Tom Pong and Psar Cha markets.

A small heretical community known as the

Zahidin follows traditions similar to those of the Muslim Chams of Vietnam, praying once a week (on Fridays) and observing Ramadan (a month of dawn-to-dusk fasting) only on the first, middle and last days of the month.

The Khmer Rouge seem to have made a concerted effort to annihilate Cambodia's Cham Muslim community.

Vietnamese Religions
During the 1920s, quite a few ordinary Cambodians became interested in Caodaism, a syncretistic religion founded in Vietnam. For information on Caodaism and the religious practices of Cambodia's ethnic-Vietnamese population, see the Facts about the Country chapter of the Vietnam section.

HOLIDAYS & FESTIVALS
Traditional Festivals
The dates of traditional Cambodian festivals are set according to the Khmer lunar calendar.

April
>*Chaul Chhnam* (mid-month) 3-day celebration of the Cambodian New Year.
>*Visak Bauchea* (late April) Commemorates the anniversary of the birth and illumination of the Buddha.

May
>*Chrat Prea Angkal* Ceremonial beginning of the sowing season.

September
>*Prachum Ben* (late September) People make offerings to the spirits of their ancestors.

October/November
>*Festival of the Reversing Current* (late October or early November) Also known as the Water Festival (Fête des Eaux), the Festival of the Reversing Current (in Khmer, Bon Om Touk or Sampeas Prea Khe) corresponds with the moment when the Tonlé Sap River, which since July has been filling the Tonlé Sap Lake with the waters of the flood-swollen Mekong, reverses its flow and begins to empty the Tonlé Sap back into the Mekong. Pirogue (long canoe) races are held in Phnom Penh.

January/February
>*Tet* (late January or early February) Tet, the Vietnamese and Chinese New Year, is celebrated by the country's ethnic-Vietnamese and ethnic-Chinese minorities. For more information, see

Religious Festivals in the Facts about the Country chapter of the Vietnam section.

Secular Holidays
January
>*National Day* (7th) Commemorates the Vietnamese overthrow of Pol Pot in 1979.

February
>*Anniversary of the signing of a treaty of friendship between Cambodia & Vietnam* (18th) The treaty was signed in 1979.

April
>*Victory Day* (17th) Commemorates the fall of the Lon Nol government in 1975.

May
>*International Workers Day* (1st) May Day.
>*Genocide Day* (9th) Memorial day for the atrocities of the Khmer Rouge; ceremonies held at Choeung Ek and elsewhere.

June
>*Anniversary of the founding of the Revolutionary Armed Forces of Kampuchea* (19th) Founded in 1951.
>*Anniversary of the founding of the People's Revolutionary Party of Cambodia* (28th) Founded in 1951.

December
>*Anniversary of the Founding of the Front for National Reconstruction (FUNSK)* (2nd) Founded in 1978.

Weddings The most popular months for weddings are June and July. Phnom Penhois who can afford it cover the sidewalk in front of their apartment buildings with a canvas awning, set up dozens of tables and hire a caterer to prepare copious quantities of food in huge kerbside cauldrons set over wood fires. Most such ceremonies are held on Sundays, the national day off, because more guests mean more gifts, which usually consist of cash.

LANGUAGE
For most Westerners, the writing and pronunciation of Cambodia's official language, Khmer, is both confusing and difficult. The Khmer writing system is about as different from Thai or Lao as Russian is from English.

There are 33 consonants and seemingly innumerable vowels. The consonants are divided into two series; the pronunciation of a vowel depends on which type of consonant precedes it. Eight different letters represent sounds that fall somewhere between the English letters 't' and 'd'. Two distinct sounds approximating the letter 'k' are represented by four letters; four other letters sound something like 'ch'.

Consonants written at the end of words are not fully released. That is, they are barely pronounced – almost dropped, but not quite. The final 'r' sometimes written at the end of words transliterated from Khmer is silent. Thus, *Angkor* is pronounced 'Angkoh' and *psar* becomes 'psah'.

For over a century, the second language of choice among educated Cambodians was French, and it is still spoken by many people who grew up before the 1970s. Recently, however, English has surged in popularity, and English is far more in demand among the students of the private language schools along 'English St' in Phnom Penh than is French.

Some people working in veterinary medicine received their training in Cuba and thus learned Spanish. A number of forestry experts learned German while studying in East Germany.

Greetings & Civilities

Hello
joom reab suor/suor sdei
ជំរាបសួរ/សួស្ដី

Please
suom
សូម

How are you?
tau neak sok sapbaiy jea te?
តើអ្នកសុខសប្បាយជាទេ?

Very well
sok touk jea thom-ada te
សុខទុក្ខជាធម្មតាទេ

Good night
rear trei suor sdei
រាត្រីសួស្ដី

Goodbye
lear heouy
លាហើយ

Excuse me
suom tous
សុំទោស

Accommodation

I want a ...
khjoom joung ban ...
ខ្ញុំចង់បាន ...

... single room
... bantuop kre samrap mouy neak
...បន្ទប់គ្រែសំរាប់ម្នាក់

... double room
... bantuop kre samrap pee neak
...បន្ទប់គ្រែសំរាប់ពីរនាក់

... triple room
... bantuop samrap khnea pei neak
...បន្ទប់សំរាប់គ្នាបីនាក់

... room with a bath
... bantuop deil meen thlang gnout teouk
...បន្ទប់ដែលមានថ្លាងងូតទឹក

... room with a shower
... bantuop deil meen teouk phka chouk
...បន្ទប់ដែលមានទឹកផ្កាឈូក

... bed
... kre mouy
...គ្រែមួយ

How much is a room?
chnoul mouy bantuop tleiy ponmaan?
ឈ្នួលមួយបន្ទប់ថ្លៃប៉ុន្មាន?

Could I see the room?
tau khjoom suom meul bantuop sen ban te?
តើខ្ញុំសុំមើលបន្ទប់សិនបានទេ?

Do you have anything cheaper?
tau neak meen eiy deil thuok jeang nees deir te?
តើអ្នកមានអ្វីដែលថោកជាងនេះដែរទេ?

Getting Around

Where is a/the ...?
tau ... nouv eir na?
តើ ... នៅឯណា?

... railway station
... sathani rout phleoung
... ស្ថានីយរថភ្លើង ...

... bus station
... ben lan
... បេនឡាន ...

... airport
... veal youn huos
... វាលយន្តហោះ ...

... ticket office
... kanleng luok suombuot
... កន្លែងលក់សំបុត្រ ...

... tourist office
... kariyaleiy samrap puok tesajor
... ការិយាល័យសម្រាប់ពួកទេសចរ ...

I want a ticket to ...
khjoom junh ban suombuot teou ...
ខ្ញុំចង់បានសំបុត្រសម្រាប់ទៅ ...

When does it depart?
tau ke jeng domneur moung ponmann?
តើគេចេញដំណើរម៉ោងប៉ុន្មាន?

When does it arrive here/there?
tau ke teou/mouk doul moung ponmaan?
តើគេទៅ/មកដល់ម៉ោងប៉ុន្មាន?

Is there an earlier/later one?
tau ke meen muon/krouy muoy nees deir reou te?
តើគេមានមុន/ក្រោយមួយនេះដែរឬទេ?

How many hours is the journey?
tau domneur nees sie pel ponmaan muong?
តើដំណើរនេះស៊ីពេលប៉ុន្មានម៉ោង?

Bus
lan thom deouk monuos
ឡានធំដឹកមនុស្ស

Train
rout phleoung
រថភ្លើង

Boat
kopsl/tuok
កប៉ាល់/ទូក

In the Country

town on the water
kompong
កំពង់

hill/mountain
phnom
ភ្នំ

lake
boeng
បឹង

river
tonley
ទន្លេ

pagoda/monastery
wat
វត្ត

sanctuary of a pagoda
vihear
វិហារ

marketplace
psar
ផ្សារ

Food

Is there any ...?
tau ke meen ... deir reou te?
តើគេមាន ... ដែរឬទេ?

... meat
... saach
... សាច់...

... fish
... trei
... ត្រី ...

... chicken
... maan
... មាន់ ...

... soup
... somlor/suop
... សម្ល/ស៊ុប ...

... noodles
... mee/kuy teav/moum banjuok
... មី/គុយទាវ/នំបញ្ចុក ...

I cannot eat ...
khjoom toam ...
ខ្ញុំតម ...

... monosodium glutamate
... masao suop
... ម្សៅស៊ុប

... any meat
... saach kruop yang
... សាច់គ្រប់យ៉ាង

... eggs
... poung sat
... ពងសត្វ

I eat chicken/fish
khjoom hope/tor toul tean saach maan/trei
ខ្ញុំហូប/ទទួលទាន សាច់មាន់/ត្រី

Emergencies

Please call ...
suom jouy hao ...
សូមជួយហៅ ...

... an ambulance
... lan peit
... ឡានពេទ្យ

... a doctor
... krou peit
... គ្រូពេទ្យ

... the police
  ... *police*
  ... ប៉ូលីស
... a dentist
  ... *peit thamenh*
  ... ពេទ្យធ្មេញ
I have ...
  khjoom ...
  ខ្ញុំ ...
... fever
  ... *krun*
  ... គ្រុន
... diarrhoea
  ... *reak*
  ... រាគ
... a cold
  ... *padasay*
  ... ផ្ដាសាយ
... a headache
  ... *chheu kbal*
  ... ឈឺក្បាល
... constipation
  ... *toul leamouk*
  ... ទល់លាមក
... diabetes
  ... *meen rouk teouk nuom pa-em*
  ... មានរោគទឹកនោមផ្អែម
... cramps
  ... *romuol krapeu*
  ... រមួលក្រពើ
It's an emergency.
  nees jea pheap ason
  នេះជាភាពអាសន្ន
I'm allergic to penicillin
  khjoom min trouv theat neoung thanam peneecilleen
  ខ្ញុំមិនត្រូវធាតុនឹងថ្នាំប៉េនីស៊ីលីន

Time & Dates
What time is it?
  eilov nees moung ponmaan?
  អីឡូវនេះម៉ោងប៉ុន្មាន?
When?
  pel na?
  ពេលណា?
what time?
  muong ponmaan?
  ម៉ោងប៉ុន្មាន?

morning
  preouk
  ព្រឹក
afternoon
  reuseal
  រសៀល
evening
  la-ngeech
  ល្ងាច
night
  yuop
  យប់
at night
  neouv pel yuop
  នៅពេលយប់
in the afternoon
  neouv pel reuseal
  នៅពេលរសៀល
in the evening
  neouv pel la-ngeech
  នៅពេលល្ងាច
in the morning
  neouv pel preouk
  នៅពេលព្រឹក
tomorrow
  sa-ek
  ស្អែក
yesterday
  masel menh
  ម្សិលមិញ
this week/month
  atit/khe nees
  អាទិត្យ/ខែនេះ
last week/month
  atit/khe muon
  អាទិត្យ/ខែមុន
now
  eilov nees
  អីឡូវនេះ
What day is today?
  tha-ngai nees jea tha-ngai ei?
  ថ្ងៃនេះជាថ្ងៃអី?
What's today's date?
  tha-ngai nees trouv jea tha-ngai khe ei?
  ថ្ងៃនេះត្រូវជាថ្ងៃខែអី?
Sunday
  tha-ngai atit
  ថ្ងៃអាទិត្យ

Monday
tha-ngai chan
ថ្ងៃចន្ទ

Tuesday
tha-ngai angkea
ថ្ងៃអង្គារ

Wednesday
tha-ngai puot
ថ្ងៃពុធ

Thursday
tha-ngai preuo-haou
ថ្ងៃព្រហស្បតិ៍

Friday
tha-ngai sok
ថ្ងៃសុក្រ

Saturday
tha-ngai sav
ថ្ងៃសៅរ៍

January
makara
មករា

February
kumphak
កុម្ភៈ

March
meenear
មិនា

April
mesa
មេសា

May
ou-saphea
ឧសភា

June
me-thuna
មិថុនា

July
kakkada
កក្កដា

August
seiha
សីហា

September
kanh-nha
កញ្ញា

October
tola
តុលា

November
vichika
វិច្ឆិកា

December
tha-nou
ធ្នូ

Some Useful Words & Phrases

yes (used by men)
bat
បាទ

yes (used by women)
jas
ចាំ៖

No
te
ទេ

thank you
ar kun
អរគុណ

Numbers

1
  mouy
  ១

2
  pee
  ២

3
  bei
  ៣

4
  boun
  ៤

5
  bram
  ៥

6
  bram-mouy
  ៦

7
  bram-pee
  ៧

8
  bram-bei
  ៨

9
  bran-boun
  ៩
10
  duop
  ១០
11
  duop-mouy
  ១១
12
  duop-pee
  ១២
13
  duop-bei
  ១៣
14
  duop-boun
  ១៤
15
  duop-bram
  ១៥
16
  duop-bram-mouy
  ១៦
17
  doup-bram-pee
  ១៧
18
  doup-bram-bei
  ១៨
19
  doup-bram-boun
  ១៩
20
  maphei
  ២០
21
  maphei-mouy
  ២១
30
  samseb
  ៣០
40
  sairseb
  ៤០
50
  haseb
  ៥០

60
  hokseb
  ៦០
70
  jetseb
  ៧០
80
  peitseb
  ៨០
90
  kavseb
  ៩០
100
  mouy-rouy
  ១០០
500
  bram-rouy
  ៥០០
1000
  mouy-paun
  ១០០០
10,000
  mouy-meoun
  ១០,០០០
100,000
  mouy-sen
  ១០០,០០០
100,000,000
  mouy-rouy-lean
  ១០០,០០០,០០០

Foreign Countries

America
  Amerik
  អាមេរិក
American
  Amerikang
  អាមេរិកាំង
Australia
  Prateh Ostralee
  ប្រទេសអូស្ត្រាលី
Australian
  Ostralee
  អូស្ត្រាលី
English
  Anglae
  អង់គ្លេស

Top: Throne Hall of the Royal Palace, Phnom Penh (DR)
Bottom: National Museum, Phnom Penh (DR)

Top: Trunk of live sugar palm shot clear through, Tonlé Bati (DR)
Bottom: Relief of Preah Vesandar story, Ta Prohm Temple, Tonlé Bati (DR)

England
  Prateh Anglae
  ប្រទេសអង្គ្លេស

France
  Prateh Barang
  ប្រទេសបារាំង

French
  Barang
  បារាំង

Laos
  leeav
  លាវ

Thailand
  Prateh Thai
  ប្រទេសថៃ

Thai
  Thai
  ថៃ

Vietnam
  Vietnam
  វៀតណាម

Prateh, which is related to the Lao *pathet* (as in Pathet Lao) and the Hindi *pradesh* (as in Uttar Pradesh or Himachal Pradesh), means 'land' or 'land of'. Thus, France is rendered *Prateh Barang*, 'Land of the French'. The word *srok* is sometimes used in place of *prateh*.

An English word of recent Cambodian mintage is 'Polpotites', which is used to refer to the protégés of the murderous leader of the Khmer Rouge, Pol Pot, who are held responsible by the Phnom Penh government for the atrocities committed between 1975 and 1979. These atrocities are not simply attributed to the Khmer Rouge because many of the leaders of the present government in Phnom Penh served as Khmer Rouge officers before turning against Pol Pot.

Facts for the Visitor

VISAS

At present, visas for travel to Cambodia are issued in Hanoi, Saigon, Vientiane and Moscow. Ordinary Tourist Visas are rarely granted to people not on an organised tour, but it never hurts to ask – and to ask around.

Visa applications must be filled out in triplicate and accompanied by three photos; they may also ask for your business card, a photocopy of your passport, a curriculum vitae and an intinerary. Though some people have pulled it off in 3 days, approval for visas may take up to a month because each application must be authorised in Phnom Penh.

It's probably hopeless, but it is theoretically possible to request a visa by writing to: Ministry of Foreign Affairs, Phnom Penh, State of Cambodia.

If an air link between Bangkok and Phnom Penh (which is now being held up by the Thai Foreign Ministry) is inaugurated before an embassy representing the Phnom Penh government is established in Bangkok, there are plans to issue prearranged tourist visas upon visitors' arrival at Pochentong Airport.

Trading with the Enemy Act

For information on US Treasury Department restrictions on transactions involving Cambodia or Cambodian nationals, see the Facts for the Visitor chapter of the Vietnam section.

Visa Extensions

Visa extensions are granted by the Foreign Ministry (tel 2.4641, 2.3241, 2.4441) in Phnom Penh, which is on the western side of Quai Karl Marx at 240 St. The process may take 3 or more days.

Overseas Embassies

Although the Phnom Penh government has diplomatic and consular relations with about 20 states, less than a dozen countries – all of them except India in what used to be known as the 'Socialist Bloc' – have legations in

Phnom Penh or Cambodian embassies in their capitals.

All other 'Kampuchean' representations, including (as of 1990) the country's UN mission in New York, represent the Coalition Government of Democratic Kampuchea, a Khmer Rouge-dominated-front fighting to overthrow the Phnom Penh government. They are definitely *not* the place to go looking for a visa.

The State of Cambodia's most useful consular sections are those in Laos and Vietnam:

Bulgaria
    Blvd Salvador Allende 2, Sofia (tel 75-71-35)
Cuba
    Avenida 5a, Miramar, Havana (tel 296779)
Czechoslovakia
    Na Hubalcé 1, 16900 Prague 6 (tel (2) 352603)
Hungary
    Rath Gyögy v 48, Budapest XII (tel 151-878)
India
    C4/4 Paschimi Marg, Vasant Vihar, New Delhi 110057 (tel (11) 608595)
Laos
    Thanon Saphan Thong Neua, Vientiane (tel 2750, 4527)
Mongolia
    Ulan Bator
USSR
    Strarokonyushenny per 16, Moscow (tel (095) 201-21-15)
Vietnam
    71 Tran Hung Dao St, Hanoi (tel 53788/9). The embassy is open Monday to Saturday from 8 to 11 am and from 2 to 4.30 pm. It is possible to apply for a visa here and pick it up at the consulate in Saigon.
    41 Phung Khac Khoan St, Saigon (tel 92751/2, 92744). The consulate is open Monday to Saturday from 8 to 11 am and from 2 to 5 pm.

TOURS

Three-day tours to Cambodia costing US$700 (!!) are marketed by Saigon Tourist (tel 24987, 98914), Ho Chi Minh City's government-run travel agency. Saigon Tourist's main office is at 49 Le Thanh Ton St. For information on purchasing such tours outside Vietnam, try contacting the travel agencies listed under 'Tours' in the Facts for the Visitor chapter of the Vietnam section.

MONEY

US$1	=	550r
A$1	=	450r
UK£1	=	1050r
Thai B1	=	22r

Currency

Cambodia's currency is the riel, abbreviated here by a lower-case 'r' written after the sum. As of mid-1989, the official exchange rate was 150r to the US dollar while on the black market, the rate was about 195r to the US dollar; prices quoted in this book are based on these rates. As of late 1990, however, the inflation rate was 200% per year. Taking riels into or out of the country is forbidden. Gold is used for many larger transactions.

The Khmer Rouge abolished currency and blew up the National Bank building in Phnom Penh. For 15 months after the overthrow of the Pol Pot regime in January 1979, goods and services were bartered or exchanged for gold or hard currencies. New riel notes were issued in March 1980.

Salaries

Government workers receive *monthly* salaries equivalent to US$3.30 at the official rate and US$2.56 on the black market. As a result, civil servants at all levels must either take bribes or moonlight in order to survive.

Every month government employees can purchase – at highly subsidised prices – 18 kg of rice (and 10 kg per child), two blocks of Soviet-made soap, 1 kg of sugar, one tin of sweetened condensed milk (if available) and, at times, other goods as well. Every year, the state sells each worker one complete set of clothes. The unemployed or self-employed must purchase these staples on the open market.

Changing Money

By far the most useful foreign currency in Cambodia is the US dollar, though the Foreign Trade Bank of Cambodia (in French, Banque du Commerce Extérieur du Cambodge; formerly the National People's Bank), also changes pounds sterling, French francs, Australian dollars, Canadian dollars, Deutschmarks and Swiss francs.

At present, they do *not* handle Hong Kong dollars, Japanese yen, Singapore dollars or Thai baht. They can, however, change US dollar-denominated international money orders and travellers' cheques issued by American Express, Barclays, Citicorp, Thomas Cook and VISA; there is a 2% commission.

Official currency exchange services are not available at the Moc Bai border crossing between Vietnam and Cambodia, though passers-by and vendors at the Neak Luong Ferry will exchange dong for riels at a rate only about 10% less than that of Phnom Penh.

Black Market

Cambodia's black market in hard currency is illegal but conducted quite openly, at least at the time of this writing. The black market rate for US dollars is several tens of percentage points above the official rate. Riels can be changed back into US dollars on the black market for marginally less than the going dollars-to-riels rate.

To find someone interested in purchasing US dollars, ask around among foreigners who've been in town for a while or at shops that cater for foreigners.

Cheques

The Foreign Trade Bank can theoretically cash travellers' cheques and even personal cheques, but because they have to be sent to Paris, it will take many weeks to credit your account.

Money Transfers

It is possible to wire money from abroad to the Foreign Trade Bank, but it can be picked up in Phnom Penh only in riels or used to pay hotel bills and the like. Such transfers, which are routed through the Banque Nationale de Paris, take a month or two to complete.

Banks with transfer agreements with the National People's Bank of Cambodia include:

Australia
    Commonwealth Bank of Australia (Sydney)
Belgium
    Banque Bruxelles Lambert (Brussels)
Canada
    Banque Nationale de Paris (Montreal)
    Canadian Imperial Bank of Commerce, (Toronto)
Federal Republic of Germany
    Dresdner Bank A G (Frankfurt)
    Deutsche Bank A G (Frankfurt)
France
    Banque Commerciale pour l'Europe du Nord, 79-81 Blvd Haussmann, 75382 (Paris)
    Banque d'Indochine et de Suez, 96 Blvd Haussman, 75008 (Paris)
    Banque Nationale de Paris, 16 Blvd des Italiens (Paris)
    Banque Worms, 45 Blvd Haussmann, 75427 (Paris)
    Crédit Commercial de France, 103 Avenue des Champs Elysées, 75008 (Paris)
Great Britain
    Moscow Narodny Bank Ltd, 24-32 King William St (London)
    Midland Bank Ltd (London)
Hong Kong
    Banque Nationale de Paris, PO Box 763 (Hong Kong)
Laos
    Banque pour le Commerce Extérieur Lao, 1 Pangkham Rd or PO Box 84 (Vientiane)
Singapore
    Moscow Narodny Bank Ltd, MNB Building, 50 Robinson Rd, 0106
    Banque Worms (Singapore Branch), 50 Raffles Place, 16-01 Shell Tower, 0104
Switzerland
    Union Bank of Switzerland (Zurich)
USA
    Banque Nationale de Paris (New York Branch), 499 Park Ave, New York, NY 10022
USSR
    State Bank of the USSR, Neglinaya 12, (Moscow)
    Bank for Foreign Economic Affairs of the USSR, Kopievski Lane 3/5 (Moscow)
Vietnam
    State Bank of Vietnam, 47-49 Ly Thai To St (Hanoi)
    Bank for Foreign Trade of Vietnam, 47-49 Ly Thai To St (Hanoi) and 17 Ben Chuong Duong St, (Ho Chi Minh City)

COSTS

Meals cost only US\$1 to US\$2 everywhere except the fanciest restaurants. Hotel accommodation in Phnom Penh and Siem Reap costs between US\$12 and US\$20 per night. Public transport (buses, trains) is cheap but off-limits to foreigners. Hiring a car will set you back at least US\$20 per day.

All this will be included if you book a tour, for which you'll pay up to US\$200 per day!

TIPPING

Tipping is not expected but is very much appreciated, especially by people whose total monthly government salary may total US\$4 or less.

TOURISM INFORMATION

Local Tourist Offices For information on the General Directorate of Tourism and Phnom Penh Tourism, see the Information subsection in the Phnom Penh chapter. Information on Angkor Tourism and Angkor Conservation are listed under Siem Reap in the Angkor chapter.

Non-Governmental Organisations

Non-governmental humanitarian aid organisations working in Cambodia (each followed by its acronym and the city in which its headquarters is located) include:

American Friends Service Committee (AFSC; Philadelphia)
Australian Catholic Relief (ACR; Sydney)
Australian Red Cross Society (ARCS; East Melbourne, Victoria)
Church World Services (CWS; New York)
Coopération International pour le Développement et la Solidarité (CIDSE; Brussels)
Enfance Espoir (Choicy Le Roi, France)
Enfants du Cambodge (EdC; Paris)
French Red Cross (Croix-Rouge Française, or CRF; Paris)
Groupe de Recherche et d'Échanges Technologiques (GRET; Paris)
International Committee of the Red Cross (ICRC, in French, Comité International de la Croix-Rouge, or CICR; Geneva)
International Rice Research Institute (IRRI; Manila)
Japan International Volunteer Centre (JVC; Tokyo)
Joint Australian NGO Office (JANGOO; Darlinghurst, NSW)

Lutheran World Service (LWS; Geneva)
Medical & Scientific Aid for Vietnam, Laos & Kampuchea (MSAVLK; London)
Mennonite Central Committee (MCC; Akron, Pennsylvania)
Operation Handicap International (OHI; Brussels)
Oxfam (Oxford, England)
Partnership for Development in Kampuchea (PADEK; The Hague)
Quaker Service Australia (QSA; North Hobart, Tasmania)
Redd Barna (Norwegian Save the Children; Oslo)
Swedish Red Cross (Svenska Röda Korset, or SRC; Stockholm)
Swiss Red Cross (Schweizerisches Rotes Kreuz, or Croix-Rouge Suisse; Berne)
United Nations Children's Fund (UNICEF; New York)
United Nations High Commission for Refugees (UNHCR; Geneva)
World Council of Churches (WCC; Geneva)
World Food Programme (WFP, in French, Programme Alimentaire Mondial, or PAM; Rome)
World Vision International (WVI; Monrovia, California)

GENERAL INFORMATION
Post

Although Cambodia's postal rates are far more reasonable than those in Vietnam (at the official rate of exchange an airmail letter to Europe or North America costs about US$0.35) service is extremely slow because all international mail (except that to parts of eastern Asia and Australia, which goes through Saigon) is routed via Moscow, and there are only three or four flights to Moscow each month.

Letters sent to Cambodia from abroad take 2 to 3 months to arrive.

Telephone

Surprisingly, Phnom Penh is not such a bad place from which to make international calls. The tariffs are high but still only half those charged in Vietnam, and because of the direct Interspoutnik satellite link with Moscow, the wait is sometimes only a matter of minutes.

The minimum length of a telephone call is 3 minutes.

International telephone tariffs from Phnom Penh, which must be paid in US dollars cash, include the following:

To	Cost Per Minute
Capitalist countries (including Thailand)	US$4.75
Eastern Europe	US$3.15
Vietnam	US$2.36
Cuba	US$3.95
Other countries	US$4.75

Telephone calls into Cambodia are routed through either Hanoi or Moscow; calls out of the country go through Moscow, using Phnom Penh's Interspoutnik satellite link-up (the ground station is one block north of the railway station).

Theoretically, there is domestic telephone service from Phnom Penh to all Cambodia's provinces except Koh Kong, Kratie, Mondulkiri, Preah Vihear, Ratanakiri and Stung Treng. In 1981, the country only had 7000 telephones.

Telex, Telegraph & Fax

Telegrams (sent by teletype) to Australia, North America and Western Europe cost between US$0.57 and US$0.89 per word.

There are plans to establish international telex links by 1990. Fax services are not yet available. Most domestic inter-provincial communication is presently carried out by telegram.

Interest in improving Cambodia's tele-communications facilities has been shown by the Australians (who have done similar work in Vietnam and Laos), the French, the Japanese, the Thais and even the Americans (through the Thai subsidiaries of American companies).

Electricity

Electricity in Phnom Penh and most of the rest of Cambodia is 220 volts, 50 Hertz (cycles). Even in Phnom Penh, there are several power outages a day, so it makes sense to have a torch (flashlight) and candles handy after dark. Outside of the capital, there is electric power only in the evenings, usually from about 6.30 to 9.30 pm.

Because most night-time lighting in Cambodia's homes is provided by tiny kerosene lamps rather than electric bulbs (even in the capital few buildings have electricity), the country produces very little light pollution of the sort that ruins star-gazing in many other places around the world. A glance skyward at night will reveal a twinkling intergalactic panorama of stars, galaxies (including a very milky-looking Milky Way) and shooting stars.

Time

Cambodia, like Vietnam, Thailand and Laos, is 7 hours ahead of Greenwich Mean Time.

Business Hours

Government offices, which are open Monday to Saturday, theoretically begin the working day at 7 or 7.30 am, breaking for a siesta from 11 or 11.30 am to 2 or 2.30 pm and ending the day at 5.30 pm. However, it is a safe bet that few people will be around early in the morning or after 4 or 4.30 pm.

In keeping with Cambodia's revolutionary ideology, all workers – including government bureaucrats of all ranks – must spend at least 1 day per week doing manual labour. One often sees Phnom Penh's white collar workers toiling in the fields, staring off into the distance and occasionally taking a whack at the earth.

Curfew

The 10 pm to dawn curfew was lifted in mid-1989 but may be reimposed should the security situation deteriorate.

Weights & Measures

Cambodia uses the metric system. For those unaccustomed to this system there is a metric/imperial conversion chart at the end of the book.

Laundry

You can usually find a hotel attendant to do your laundry. They may try to clean your clothes by hand without the benefit of soap unless you provide some. Settle on the price beforehand.

MEDIA
Newspapers & Magazines

Restrictions on the domestic press have recently been relaxed. Foreign newspapers and magazines are completely unavailable.

Radio

Most of the short-wave broadcasts listed in the Facts for the Visitor chapter of the Vietnam section can also be picked up in Cambodia.

Many Cambodians listen regularly to the Khmer-language programming of the Voice of America, which is stridently opposed to the Vietnamese-backed Phnom Penh government.

Cambodians can also choose from the clandestine radio stations of the various factions of the resistance coalition. The Khmer Rouge station, the Voice of Democratic Kampuchea, broadcasts from somewhere in southern China.

In Phnom Penh, radio frequencies to try for domestic programming include 82.2 MHz, 92.1 MHz, 94.3 MHz, 98.3 MHz and 103.7 MHz on the FM band and 920 kHz and 1300 kHz on medium wave (AM band).

HEALTH

Cambodia has one of the world's highest infant mortality rates – of every 1000 Cambodian newborns, as many as 200 die before their first birthday. Because of malnutrition, contaminated water supplies and a very limited public health infrastructure, Cambodians' life expectancy has fallen from 42 years for men and 44 years for women in 1970 to approximately 36 years for men and 39 years for women today.

Please refer to the Health section in the Vietnam chapter for information on general health preparations for visiting the region.

Infusions

Most IV solution used in Cambodian hospitals is *not* sterile. According to foreign aid workers, people often die of septicaemia (blood poisoning) caused by bacteria introduced into their blood during infusions. Visitors should not *under any circumstances* receive infusions; dehydration is best treated by drinking electrolyte solution dissolved in purified or boiled water. Be aware, also, that injections are routinely carried out using unsterilised equipment.

Hospitals

Cambodia's hospitals suffer from chronic shortages of almost everything. Not only must patients purchase their own medication on the black market (most hospitals stock virtually no pharmaceuticals), but some provincial hospitals are so impoverished that people who need surgery must purchase soap for the doctors' to scrub-up with, fluid to sterilise the scalpels and petrol for the generator that powers the lights in the operating theatre.

If you need emergency surgery in Cambodia, the surgeons in Phnom Penh are probably OK, although anaesthesia may not be handled properly. If at all possible, people requiring even minor surgery should be evacuated to Bangkok or at least Saigon.

Pharmaceuticals

Pharmacies are marked with a blue cross outlined in white, often painted on a blue awning. Almost all genuine pharmaceuticals available on the open market were stolen from aid agencies or hospitals; most have passed their expiry dates. Many of the capsules marketed as antibiotics and other drugs are really a locally produced mixture of sugar and flour. Bring with you all medicine you think you might need during your visit. If you require drugs not stocked in your first aid kit, perhaps one of the Cambodia's expat foreign aid workers will be able to help out.

Traditional Medicine

Traditional medicine is widely practised in Cambodia, in part because Western medical care is largely unavailable (the Khmer Rouge killed almost all of those of the country's doctors who did not flee abroad). Some traditional treatments (eg the use of some herbs) appear to work, but others, such as that based on the belief that paraplegics can be cured by suspending them over a fire, produce catastrophic results.

The vertical red marks often visible on the necks and torsos of both male and female Cambodians were made by rubbing the skin very hard with coins. This treatment is supposed to dilate the blood vessels and is said to be good for anyone who is feeling weak or ill.

Headaches are treated by applying suction cups to the forehead and face. These have the same effect on blood circulation as leeches – namely, to draw blood to the point of suction.

DANGERS & ANNOYANCES

Security

Until the civil war ends, travel outside areas under firm government control (of which there are few) will carry with it a certain degree of risk, especially in the evening and after dark. While it is true that since 1979 not a single Western journalist or aid worker has been wounded or killed in the fighting, maintaining that perfect record depends on continued good judgement on the part of the thousands of illiterate, nervous and heavily armed teenagers fighting on both sides. While no one in Phnom Penh (including the people who issue travel permits) really knows what is going on out in the provinces, the latest rumours are available from long-term foreign aid workers (many of whom work in rural areas despite the variable security conditions) and government officials.

While Western aid teams regularly travel (in well-marked vehicles) to areas with frequent rebel activity, Soviets, Germans and Czechs working in Cambodia are confined to Phnom Penh, apparently not without good reason.

Undetonated Mines, Mortars & Bombs!

Never, ever touch any rockets, artillery shells, mortars, mines, bombs or other war materiel you may come across. In Vietnam most of this sort of stuff is 15 or more years old, but in Cambodia it may have landed there or been laid as recently as last night. In fact, a favourite tactic of the Khmer Rouge has been to lay mines along roads and in rice fields in an effort to maim and kill civilians, thus – so their twisted logic concludes – furthering the rebel cause by demoralising the government. The only concrete results of this policy are the many limbless people you see all over Cambodia. The most heavily mined part of the country is along the Thai border. In short: *do not* stray from well-marked paths under any circumstances, even around the monuments of Angkor.

My own experience illustrates some of the dangers travellers to Cambodia in the 1990s may encounter: having received all necessary official authorisations, my guide, a companion and I went to explore Angkor's Preah Khan Temple. After we'd been there for a while, merrily making our way among the galleries, two breathless soldiers ran up and informed our horrified guide (a man with a dozen children) that the night before, government sappers had booby-trapped the area with anti-personnel mines rigged to filament trip wires.

Snakes

Visitors to Angkor and other overgrown archaeological sites should beware of snakes, including the small but deadly light green Hanuman snake.

Theft & Street Crime

In Phnom Penh, war cripples, who receive almost no help from the government, are organised into gangs whose members hobble from store to store extorting money from the owners. Automobiles and buses are sometimes held up at gunpoint along Cambodia's highways, but foreigners are almost never involved in such incidents.

Traffic Accidents

Cambodia appears to have some of the most lethal drivers I have ever encountered. Every week I was in Cambodia I saw several serious traffic accidents involving huge trucks and either pedestrians or cyclists. The tendency to recklessness on the part of Cambodia's unschooled drivers is exacerbated by their natural inclination to drive through contested areas as quickly as possible.

Visitors should remember that ambulance and rescue services are almost non-existent outside of Phnom Penh. It will probably take many hours for a person injured in a rural area to be transported to a hospital, where only the most basic treatment may be available.

FILM & PHOTOGRAPHY

Do not put film of any speed or type through the ancient x-ray machines at the airports in Phnom Penh, Saigon or Hanoi!

The Cambodians are not particularly restrictive about what you can photograph, but use common sense about taking pictures of soldiers, fortifications, military vehicles, airports, etc. It is always best to ask people – and especially monks – if they mind your photographing them before you whip out your camera and shove it in their face.

ACCOMMODATION

Phnom Penh and Siem Reap (near Angkor) have a very limited number of 1 or 2-star hotel rooms; when tourism picks up, prices are likely to rise as shortages develop. Most provincial capitals have some sort of very basic hotel or official guest house.

FOOD
In Phnom Penh, there is a growing number of decent restaurants. Both the capital and most towns have food stalls; these are often clustered in the main marketplace.

DRINKS
Soda water with lemon is called *soda kroch chhmar*; the custom here seems to be to let the customer squeeze his or her own lemons.

In Phnom Penh, ice (*tuk kak*) is produced by a factory that apparently uses treated water of some sort. Drinking tap water is to be avoided, especially in the provinces.

Adulterated Soft Drinks Beware: some of the flavoured soda sold in bottles by kerbside vendors has been made cheaply by a process that renders the resultant product toxic enough to cause headaches and stomach upset.

BOOKS
Angkor
A number of superb works on Angkor have

Soviet mineral water label

been published over the years. *Angkor: An Introduction* (Oxford University Press, Hong Kong, 1963; reissued by Oxford University Press, Singapore, 1986) by George Coedes gives excellent background on Angkorian Khmer civilisation. You might also look for Malcolm MacDonald's *Angkor & the Khmers* (Jonathan Cape, 1958; reissued by Oxford University Press, Singapore, 1987); *Arts & Civilization of Angkor* (Fredrick A Prager, New York, 1958) by Bernard Groslier & Jacques Arthaud; and, in French, *Histoire d'Angkor* (Presses Universitaires de France, Paris, 1974) by Madeleine Giteau.

The 3rd edition of *Angkor, Guide Henri Parmentier* (EKLIP/Albert Portail, Phnom Penh, 1959/1960) by Henri Parmentier, probably the best guidebook to Angkor ever written, was published under the same title in both English and French. In English, you might also look for *Angkor* (Librairie Renouard & H Laurens, Paris, 1933) by George Groslier and the even more antiquated *Guide to the Ruins of Angkor* (Imprimerie d'Extrême Orient, Hanoi, 1913). Other useful publications include *Tourist Guide to Saigon, Pnom Penh & Angkor* (Imprimevie Nouvelle Albert Portail, Saigon, 1930) and *Petit Guide d'Angkor* (Bureau du Tourisme en Indochine, 1929) *Les Monuments du Groupe d'Angkor* by Maurice Glaize (Albert Portail, Saigon, 1948) is a French work with detailed histories, descriptions and maps.

I highly recommend that travellers serious about learning something of Khmer civilisation while visiting Angkor track down one of these works and bring along a photocopy (make it double-sided to save weight).

History
The most comprehensive work in English on Cambodian history is *The Ancient Khmer Empire* by L P Briggs (1951). Also useful for historical background is *The Indianized States of South-East Asia* by G Coedes (1968), originally published in French as *Les États Hindouisés d'Indochine et d'Indonésie* (2nd edition, 1964). Also worthwhile is *A*

History of Cambodia by David P Chandler (Westview Press, Boulder, Colorado, 1983).

The expansion of the Vietnam War onto Cambodian territory and events through the mid-1970s are superbly documented by William Shawcross in his award-winning book *Sideshow: Kissinger, Nixon & the Destruction of Cambodia* (Simon & Schuster, New York, 1979).

Cambodia: Year Zero (1978) by Francois Ponchaud (originally published in French as *Cambodge: Année Zéro* in 1977) is an account of life in Cambodia under the Khmer Rouge. Other works on this period include *The Stones Cry Out: A Cambodian Childhood, 1975-1980* (Hill & Wang, New York, 1986) by Molyda Szymusiak, originally published in French as *Les Pierres Crieront: Une Enfance Cambodgienne, 1975-1980* (La Découverte, Paris, 1984); *The Cambodian Agony* (1987) by David Ablin; and *The Murderous Revolution* (1985) by Martin Stuart-Fox.

The atrocities of the Khmer Rouge are documented by *Kampuchea, Decade of Genocide: Report of the Finnish Enquiry Commission* (Zed Books, London, 1984) edited by Kimmo Kiljunen. *Brother Enemy* (Collier, 1986), an excellent work by Nayan Chanda, examines events in Indochina since 1975.

William Shawcross' work *The Quality of Mercy: Cambodia, Holocaust & Modern Conscience* (1984) looks at the contradictions inherent in the massive international famine-relief operation mounted in 1979 and 1980.

National Geographic

National Geographic articles on Cambodia include the following (listed chronologically): 'Forgotten Ruins of Indochina' (March 1912, pp 209-72); 'Enigma of Cambodia' and 'Four Glimpses of Siva: The Mystery of Angkor' (September 1928, pp 303-32); 'Under the French Tricololor in Indochina' (Aug 1931, pp 166-99); 'By Motor Trail Across French Indochina' and 'Tricolor Rules the Rainbow in French Indochina' (Oct 1935, pp 487-534); 'Strife-Torn Indochina' (Oct 1950, pp 599-51); 'Portrait of Indochina' (April 1951, pp 461-90); 'Indochina Faces the Dragon' (Sept 1952, pp 287-328); 'Angkor, Jewel of the Jungle' (April 1960, pp 517-69); 'Cambodia, Indochina's 'Neutral' Corner' (Oct 1964, pp 514-51); 'The Mekong, River of Terror & Hope' (Dec 1968, pp 737-87); 'The Lands & Peoples of South-East Asia' (March 1971, pp 295-365); 'The Temples of Angkor' (May 1982, pp 548-89) and 'Kampuchea Wakens from a Nightmare'(May 1982, pp 590-623). Some of the articles on Angkor, most of which are accompanied by *National Geographic's* usual fine illustrations and maps, may be worth bringing along to read on the spot.

Readers of French may want to take a look at the March 1988 issue of the magazine *Dossiers Histoire et Archéologie*, which is dedicated to 'Angkor – L'Art Khmere au Cambodge et en Thaïlande'.

Politics & Society

Kampuchea: Politics, Economics & Society (Frances Pinter, London & Lynne Rienner, Boulder, Colorado, 1988) by Michael Vickery and *Indochina: Vietnam, Laos, Cambodia*, a 'Country Profile' published annually in London and New York by the Economist Intelligence Unit, have some of the best up-to-date information available on Cambodia's changing social and political system. Eva Mysliwiec's *Punishing the Poor: The International Isolation of Kampuchea* (Oxfam, Oxford, England, 1988) looks at Cambodia's status of diplomatic pariahdom.

Ethnic Groups of Mainland South-East Asia edited by Frank M Lebar (1964) is a good source of information on Cambodia's ethno-linguistic minority peoples. *The Chinese in Cambodia* (1967) by W E Willmott takes a look at Cambodia's ethnic-Chinese minority.

Travel Guides

This volume is the most comprehensive travel guidebook to Cambodia on the market. *Cambodia, Laos, Vietnam* (Guide

Arthaud, Paris, 1989), a French-language work by Michel Arthaud, is rather limited in scope.

Excellent information on Cambodia's archaeological sites – in some cases, however, superseded by subsequent research – is provided by the classic guidebooks to Indochina published by Claudius Madrolle before WW II, copies of which may be available at major university libraries.

To Angkor (Société d'Éditions Géographiques, Maritimes & Coloniales, Paris, 1939) is the English version of the French work *Vers Angkor* (Librairie Hachette, Paris, 1925). *Indochina* (Société d'Éditions Géographiques, Maritimes & Coloniales, Paris, 1939), an English-language condensation of the two volume set *Indochine du Nord* and *Indochine du Sud*, has the same spread on Cambodia as *To Angkor*. The most comprehensive section on Cambodia is to be found in the excellent 2nd augmented edition of *Indochine du Sud* (Société d'Éditions Geographiques, Maritimes et Coloniales, Paris, 1939).

Francophone fans of antiquarian books may want to track down *Voyage au Cambodge* by L Delaporte (Librarie Ch Delgrave, Paris, 1880). A more recent travelogue is *The Road to Angkor*, an entertaining work by Christopher Pym (Robert Hale, London, 1959).

MAPS

Old maps of Cambodia may be available in Phnom Penh. On Vietnamese maps of the country, the Khmer characters are translated into the Latin-based Vietnamese alphabet; for pronunciation tips, see the Language subsection in the Facts about the Country chapter of the Vietnam section.

THINGS TO BUY

The checked cotton scarves everyone wears on their heads, around their necks or, if bathing, around their midriffs, are known as *kramas*. Fancier coloured versions are made of silk or a silk-cotton blend. Some of the finest cotton *kramas* come from the Kompong Cham area.

For information on where in Phnom Penh to find antiques, silver items, jewellery, gems, colourful cloth for sarongs and *hols* (variegated silk shirts), wood carvings, papier mâché masks, stone copies of ancient Khmer art, brass figurines and oil paintings, see Things to Buy in the Phnom Penh chapter.

WHAT TO BRING

For a few tips on things you might want to bring along, see the 'Facts for the Visitor' chapter in the Vietnam section.

For a list of guides to Angkor you may want to photocopy and take with you, see the Books section in this chapter.

CONDUCT
Greetings

Cambodians traditionally greet each other by pressing their hands together in front of their bodies and bowing. In recent decades, this custom has been partially replaced by the Western practice of shaking hands. But, although men tend to shake hands with each other, women usually use the traditional greeting with both men and other women. It is considered acceptable (or perhaps excusable) for foreigners to shake hands with Cambodians of both sexes.

Dress

Both men and women often wear sarongs (made of cotton, a cotton-synthetic blend or silk), especially at home. Men who can afford it usually prefer silk sarongs. Under Lon Nol (ruled 1970 to 1975), it was forbidden to wear sarongs in public because, as one Cambodian explained to me, the government considered the sarong to be as unfit for use outside the home as pyjamas would be in the West.

On formal occasions such as religious festivals and family celebrations, women often wear *hols* during the daytime. At night, they change into single-colour silk garments called *phamuongs*, which are decorated along the hems.

Modesty

The women of Cambodia are very modest in their dress – much more so than the Vietnamese. When eating at home, they sit on floor mats with their feet to the side rather than in the lotus position, as do the men. As in Thailand, nude bathing is unacceptable in Cambodia.

Visiting Pagodas

The Khmer are a tolerant people and may choose not to point out improper behaviour to their foreign guests, but you should dress and act with the utmost respect when visiting wats or other religious sites (such as some of the temples of Angkor). This is all the more important given the vital role Buddhist beliefs and institutions play in the lives of many Cambodians in the aftermath of the Khmer Rouge holocaust. Proper etiquette in pagodas is mostly a matter of common sense. A few tips:

1) Don't wear shorts or tank tops.
2) Take off your hat when entering the grounds of the wat.
3) Take off your shoes before going into the *vihara* (sanctuary).
4) If you sit down in front of the dais (the platform on which the Buddhas are placed), sit with your feet to the side rather than in the lotus position.
5) Never point your finger – or, heaven forbid, the soles of your feet – towards a figure of the Buddha or human beings either.

Addressing People

Members of the family or people whom you wish to treat as friends should be addressed according to the following rules:

1) People of your age or younger can be called by name.
2) People older than yourself should be addressed as *Bang* (for men) or *Bang Srey* (for women).

3) Old people should be addressed as *Ta* (for men) and *Yeay* (for women).

Officials and informal acquaintances are officially supposed to be addressed by usages approximating 'comrade', but in practice people use *Lok* (Mr) and *Lok Srey* (Mrs), which convey respect coupled with a bit of formality and distance. When speaking with such people in English, it is probably best to use 'Mr' and 'Mrs'.

Miscellaneous

The following are a few general tips about proper behaviour in Cambodia:

1) Getting angry and showing it by shouting or becoming abusive is both impolite and a poor reflection on you; in addition, it is unlikely to accomplish much. If things aren't being done as they should, remember that there is a critical shortage of trained people in the country because the vast majority of educated Cambodians either fled the country or were killed between 1975 and 1979.
2) As in Thailand, it is improper to pat children on the head.
3) If you would like someone to come over to you, motion with your whole hand held palm down – signalling with your index finger and your palm pointed skyward may be interpreted as being sexually suggestive.
4) When picking your teeth with a toothpick after a meal, it is considered polite to hold the toothpick in one hand and to cover your open mouth with the other.
5) Everyone wears thongs or flip-flops (rubber sandals; in Khmer, *sbek choeung phtoat*), even civil servants, though such footwear was once considered appropriate only at home. Among revolutionaries, flip flops used to be worn in order to demonstrate one's detachment from the material world, but these days they remain popular because few people can afford anything else.

Getting There

AIR

Because of its diplomatic isolation, Phnom Penh is served by only four airlines: Kampuchean Airlines (the national carrier), Aeroflot, Lao Aviation and Vietnam Airlines. These carriers take turns offering services linking Phnom Penh with:

1) Saigon on most Mondays, Tuesdays, Wednesdays and Thursdays (US$46 each way; 40 minutes by Antonov An24).
2) Hanoi every Tuesday or Wednesday (US$175 each way; 3 hours by An24 or 1½ hours by Tupolev Tu134).
3) Vientiane (US$120 each way; 3½ hours) via Pakse, Laos (US$50 one way) on Wednesdays and Fridays.
4) Moscow via Bombay three or four times a month.

Flights originating in the carrier's country of origin usually depart in the morning and make the return flight in the afternoon. A US$5 airport tax for international flights is added onto the ticket price.

Most flights into and out of Cambodia are booked out well in advance, often by important people who put their names on the reservation lists on the off chance they might like to fly that day. At 4 pm on the afternoon before departure, seats often open up for people without reservations. Check with the Kampuchean Airlines Booking Office in Phnom Penh for details.

For international flights out of Cambodia, you should arrive at the airport prepared for chaos (few of the staff speak English or French) about 2 hours before departure time. Checked baggage is weighed carefully (the official limit is 20 kg on international flights but only 10 kg for domestic flights).

As of this writing, Kampuchean Airlines consists of five Tupolev 134 jets and prop-driven Antonov An24s along with a number of Soviet helicopters. Because many of the pilots and mechanics are Soviets, flying

PASSENGER TICKET AND BAGGAGE CHECK   10550

អាកាស យាន កម្ពុជា

AKASCHOR KAMPUCHEA

Head office : 62 Tou Samuth Street
Phnom Penh

MP 651-1

Kampuchean Airlines is probably a safer bet than travelling on its Vietnamese counterpart. Don't be alarmed if the ventilation system suddenly begins pouring clouds of vapour into the cabin – this is completely normal on many Soviet aircraft.

The Phnom Penh government is eager to attract international flights from such cities as Bangkok and Tokyo, but although as yet no contracts have been signed, there have been apparently fruitful contacts with Thai International Airways (THAI). Recent construction at Phnom Penh's Pochentong Airport will allow it to handle large jet aircraft.

OVERLAND
From Vietnam
The drive from Saigon to Phnom Penh via Moc Bai (on the border of Vietnam's Tay Ninh Province and Cambodia's Svay Rieng Province) takes about 6½ hours by car and between 8 and 10 hours by bus, including a wait of up to 2 hours for the ferry across the Mekong at Neak Luong. The border crossing at Moc Bai, which is 5 km east of the Cambodian town of Bavet, is open daily from 6.30 am to 6 pm; snacks are available on the Vietnamese side.

When crossing into Cambodia, officials on the Vietnamese side collect passports and hold them for up to an hour. Bus passengers have their passports returned as they reboard the bus before crossing the frontier. Remember that Vietnamese visas list the ports of entry and exit you are allowed to use; changes must be made by the Foreign Ministry.

For more information on crossing points between Vietnam and Cambodia, see the 'Getting There & Away' chapter in the Vietnam section.

In Saigon, buses to Phnom Penh leave early each morning from Boi Xe 1A (tel 93754) at 155 Nguyen Hue Blvd, which is almost next door to the Rex Hotel. The trip costs 10,800d. In Phnom Penh, daily buses to Saigon depart at 6 am from an office (tel 2.3139) at the south-western corner of 211 St and Ok Nga Sou St (182 St). One-way passage costs 250r. The office is open from 7 to 11 am and from 2 to 7 pm. As of this writing, bus transit between Saigon and Phnom Penh is not looked on with favour by officialdom.

From Laos
Cambodia's National Route 7 enters Lao territory about 50 km north of Stung Treng; north of the border, the road follows the eastern bank of the Mekong. At present, there is no land link between Stung Treng and Phnom Penh.

From Thailand
The Cambodians have plans to open their frontier with Thailand to travellers as soon as the Thais agree (and the region is under government control). Before the war, Cambodia's north-western train line linked Phnom Penh with the towns of Poipet (Poay Pet) and Aranyaprathet on the border of Thailand and Cambodia, whence connecting train service to Bangkok was available. There are plans to resume Phnom Penh-Bangkok service as soon as the political and military situation permits. The main road between Bangkok and Phnom Penh also crosses the Thai-Cambodian border at Poipet.

For more information on Cambodia's rail and road systems, see the Getting Around chapter.

SEA
Cambodia's only maritime port is Kompong Som (formerly Sihanoukville), which was built during the late 1950s. Policies on the arrival of tourists by sea have yet to be drafted by the government.

Getting Around

It is a good idea to carry a compass around with you – outside Phnom Penh, street names and numbers simply do not exist.

AIR

At present, the only two regularly scheduled domestic air routes link the capital with Angkor (Siem Reap) and the northern town of Stùng Treng. There are flights from Phnom Penh to Siem Reap (US$43 each way) and vice versa every Wednesday and Saturday; and each Monday there is a flight from Phnom Penh to Stung Treng and back (US$45 each way). Daily flights to Siem Reap are envisioned when tourism picks up.

Depending on demand (especially from official delegations), special flights are sometimes added to:

Battambang (US$45 each way)
Kampot (US$23)
Koh Kong (US$45)
Kompong Cham (US$14)
Kompong Chhnang (US$14)
Kompong Som (US$40)
Kompong Thom (US$23)
Kratie (US$30)
Mondulkiri (US$50)
Preah Vihear (US$45)
Pursat (US$45)
Ratanakiri (US$60)
Sisophon (US$55)
Svay Rieng (US$23)
Takeo (US$11)

Unless another charter flight is scheduled a few days later, you'll have to choose between spending only a few hours at your destination and making your way back overland.

The baggage weight limit for domestic flights is only 10 kg per passenger. Flights are usually well over-booked (you'll often see three people squeezed into every two seats with others sitting in the luggage compartment) so reservations – especially to and from Siem Reap – should be made as far in advance as possible. It may prove impossible to confirm your Siem Reap-Phnom Penh

reservation until you actually get to Siem Reap. The airport tax for domestic flights is US$2.50 each way (US$5 for a round trip).

Helicopter If you've got lots of money or are on an expense account, you might consider chartering a Soviet-built helicopter for sightseeing or aerial photography. A round-trip excursion from Phnom Penh to Angkor for up to a dozen people costs US$6000.

BUS

Bus As of this writing, it is forbidden – not without reason, given the security situation – for foreigners to travel around Cambodia by bus. The various permits necessary to undertake any travel outside of Phnom Penh will not be issued for bus travel.

TRAIN

Trains Cambodia's rail system consists of about 645 km of single-track metre-gauge lines. The 382 km north-western line, built before WW II, links Phnom Penh with Pursat (165 km from the capital), Battambang (274 km from the capital) and, in peacetime, Poipet (Poay Pet) on the Thai border. The 263 km south-western line, completed in 1969, connects the capital with Takeo (75 km from Phnom Penh), Kampot (160 km from the capital), Kep (get off at Damnak Chang Aeu) and the port of Kompong Som.

In recent years, Cambodia's rail system has suffered from frequent rebel sabotage. As a result, each train is equipped with a tin-roofed armoured carriage sporting a huge machine gun and gun ports in its half-height sides. In addition, the first two cars of the train are supposed to remain empty in order to detonate any mines placed on the track. Until recently passage on these first carriages was free, and many peasants coming to the city to market their produce and buy goods to resell back home preferred to take their chances with Khmer Rouge mines rather than part with the fare. A severe shortage of rolling stock provides further encouragement for people to try their luck on the first two flatcars.

The duration of rail journeys in Cambodia is highly unpredictable. Because of sabotage and dilapidated equipment, the Phnom Penh-Battambang train must sometimes stop overnight en route at some safe government garrison, taking 2 or more days to travel a distance that under normal conditions can be covered in 12 hours.

BOAT

Cambodia's 1900 km of navigable waterways are an important element in the country's transportation system. Phnom Penh, which is some 320 km from the mouth of the Mekong, can be reached by ocean-going vessels with a draft of less than 3.3 metres. North of the capital, the Mekong is navigable as far north as Kratie; from September to January, boats can make it as far as Stung Treng. For information on ferry services to and from Phnom Penh, see the Getting There & Away section of the Phnom Penh chapter.

DRIVING

Cambodia's 15,000 km of roads, which include over 1800 bridges of more than 7 metres in length, were designed by the French to link the agricultural hinterlands of colonial Cambodia with the port of Saigon. Because the road network was never intended to serve specifically Cambodian needs, huge areas in the north, north-east and south-west have been left almost completely without roads.

Even that small part of the network that was at one time surfaced (some 2500 km) has seriously deteriorated during the last 2 decades and today is only marginally serviceable – and virtually impassable to passenger cars. The rest of the country's roads, which were surfaced with crushed stone, gravel or laterite or were simply graded without being paved, are in even worse shape. Because maintenance of all but the major highways is the responsibility of provincial governments, little repair work is

being done. In addition, many of Cambodia's road bridges, including some of the largest and most important, have been destroyed, making land travel either very slow, with long waits at ferry crossings, or simply impossible.

The Road Network

Cambodia's major highways are conveniently numbered from one to seven. National Route 1 links Phnom Penh with Saigon via Svay Rieng and the Moc Bai border crossing, which is 5 km east of the Cambodian town of Bavet. National Route 2 heads south from the capital, passing through Takmau and Takeo on its way to Vietnam's An Giang Province and the city of Chau Doc. National Route 3 links the capital with the southern coastal city of Kampot. National Route 4 connects Phnom Penh and the country's only maritime port, Kompong Som, which is on the Gulf of Thailand southwest of the capital.

National Route 5 heads north from Phnom Penh, circling around to the south of the Tonlé Sap and passing through Kompong Chhnang, Pursat, Battambang and Sisophon on its way north-westward to the Thai frontier. National Route 6 splits off from National Route 5 at the Prek Kdam Ferry over the Tonlé Sap River, heading northward and then north-westward on a route that goes to the north of the Tonlé Sap and passes through Kompong Thom, Siem Reap and Sisophon on its way to Thailand. National Route 7 splits from National Route 6 at Skun, heading westward to Kompong Cham and eventually to Memot (Memut), Kratie, Stung Treng and the Lao border; the latter sections are currently impassable.

BICYCLE

When things quieten down, mountain bikes will be a superb way to get around on the country's potholed inter-city roads.

HITCHING

There is a severe shortage of transport in Cambodia, so most trucks – the only vehicles other than large buses able to negotiate the country's dilapidated roads – are likely to be extremely crowded. Expect to pay for your ride. Don't even think of hitching until after the war is over!

LOCAL TRANSPORT

Taxi

There are as yet no real taxis in Cambodia. If you need a car, you'll probably have to hire one on a daily basis – for US dollars cash – from one government ministry or another. The General Directorate of Tourism charges US$20/30 per day for cars without/with air-con.

Bicycle

Bicycles, called *kang* in street Khmer, are the best way to get to and from areas in the vicinity of where you're staying and are especially useful in Phnom Penh and around Angkor. For information on where to purchase one, see the Getting Around section in the Phnom Penh chapter.

Cyclo

As in Vietnam and Laos, the samlor is a quick, cheap way to get around Cambodia's urban areas. In Phnom Penh, cyclo drivers can either be flagged down on main thoroughfares or found hanging out around marketplaces and major hotels.

Remorque-Kang & Remorque-Moto

The *remorque-kang* is a trailer pulled by a bicycle; a trailer hitched to a motorbike is called a *remorque-moto*. Both are used to transport people and goods, especially in rural areas.

Phnom Penh

Phnom Penh, capital of Cambodia for much of the period since the mid-15th century (when Angkor was abandoned), is situated at Quatre Bras (literally, 'four arms' in French), the confluence of the Mekong River, the Bassac River and the Tonlé Sap River. Once considered the loveliest of the French-built cities of Indochina, its charm is still in evidence despite the violence and dilapidation of the last 3 decades. Indeed, the city has recently shown signs of renewed vitality.

The population of Phnom Penh was approximately 500,000 in 1970. After the spread of the Vietnam War to Cambodian territory, the city's population swelled with refugees, reaching about 2 million in early 1975. The Khmer Rouge took over the city on 17 April 1975 and immediately forced the entire population into the countryside as part of their radical social programme.

During the next 4 years, many tens of thousands of former Phnom Penhois – including the vast majority of the capital's educated people – were killed. Repopulation of the city began when the Vietnamese arrived in 1979. Many of Phnom Penh's 700,000 residents are peasants who have come to the city to improve their lot.

Orientation

Phnom Penh's most important north-south arteries are (from west to east): Achar Mean Blvd (where most of the hotels are), Tou Samouth Blvd, Lenin Blvd (in front of the Royal Palace) and, along the riverfront (which is also oriented roughly north to south), Quai Karl Marx. Forming two rough semi-circles in the quadrant south-west of the Central Market are Sivutha Blvd (which intersects Tou Samouth Blvd at the Victory Monument) and Keo Mony Blvd (which intersects Tou Samouth Blvd at the former US Embassy).

The city's most important east-west thoroughfares are USSR Blvd (with its parallel side street, Soeung Ngoc Ming St), which intersects Achar Mean Blvd near the railway station, and Kampuchea-Vietnam Blvd (128 St), which heads due west from the Central Market. Before 1975, Kampuchea-Vietnam Blvd was known as Kampuchea Krom (Lower Cambodia) Blvd, a reference to the south-eastern portion of the Khmer Empire colonised and annexed by Vietnam a few centuries ago.

National Route 1 links the capital with Saigon, crossing the Bassac River over Monivong Bridge. National Route 2 goes south past Takmau to Takeo and An Giang Province in Vietnam. National Route 3, which heads west from the city, passes Pochentong Airport before linking up with south-westward bound National Route 4 to Kompong Som; National Route 3 continues southward to Takeo and Kampot. National Route 5 heads north from the city towards Udong, Kompong Cham, Kompong Thom, Siem Reap, Pursat, Battambang and Bangkok.

All of Phnom Penh's streets were renamed after 1979; major thoroughfares got real names while smaller streets were rather haphazardly assigned numbers. In most cases, odd-numbered streets run more or less north to south (usually parallel to Achar Mean Blvd), with the numbers rising in a semi-sequential order as you move from east to west. Even-numbered streets run in an east-west direction, rising semi-sequentially as you move from north to south. Several streets are misnumbered on the map of 'Phnom Penh Ville' produced in the late 1980s by Phnom Penh Tourism.

Most buildings in the capital are marked with white on blue signs bearing two or three multi-digit numbers. The number borne by every building on both sides of the street is the name of the street. Numerals common to several structures (usually housing 20 to 40 families) signify the number of the building's security and control group. Each such group is overseen by someone living there who reports on local happenings to the police and acts as a liaison with the government (arranges permits for marriages, etc); such people are in an excellent position to extort money from their charges and often do so. The third number, different from that of the buildings to either side, is the street address. The letters 'EO' after a street address stand for *etage zéro*, which means 'ground floor' in French.

In the past, Tou Samouth Blvd was known as Blvd 9 October (under Lon Nol), Blvd Norodom (under Sihanouk) and Blvd Doudard de Lagrée (under the French). Achar Mean Blvd was previously called Blvd Monivong. During the colonial period, the area around the Royal Palace was known as the Cambodian Quarter, the neighbourhood around Wat Phnom was considered the European Quarter, and the Central Market was at the centre of the Chinese Quarter.

The city of Phnom Penh consists of four urban districts (*khand*) and three suburban districts (*srok*).

Information

Tourist Office The head office of Phnom Penh Tourism (tel 2.3949, 2.5349, 2.4059) is across from Wat Ounalom at the oblique intersection of Lenin Blvd and Quai Karl Marx; its two entrances are at 313 Quai Karl Marx and next to 2 Lenin Blvd. The office is officially open from 7 to 11 am and from 2 to 5 pm. Phnom Penh Tourism, which belongs to the Phnom Penh Municipality, restricts its activities to running 3-day package tours that include a 1-day visit to Angkor; these are marketed at great profit by Saigon Tourist in Ho Chi Minh City, leaving the Cambodians (and their guests) feeling fleeced.

General Directorate of Tourism Cambodia's newly established General Directorate of Tourism (in French, Direction Generale du Tourisme; tel 2.2107), sometimes referred to as Cambodia Tourism, is slated to become a full-fledged Ministry of Tourism in the near future. The directorate's offices are in a white, two-storey building on the western side of Achar Mean Blvd at 232 St (across 232 St from 447 Achar Mean Blvd). The large slogan written in Khmer across the front of the structure reads Long Live the People's Revolutionary Party. The General Directorate rents cars without/with air-conditioning for US$20/30 per day; guides can also be hired. The General Directorate of Tourism is seeking foreign joint venture partners for projects to develop the tourism infrastructure.

Registration & Internal Travel Permits Permits to travel outside Phnom Penh are issued by the Ministry of the Interior, which is known for its hard-line policies. The ministry offices are on the south-eastern corner of Tou Samouth Blvd and 214 St.

Useful Addresses The Ministry of Information & Culture (tel 2.4769) is opposite 395 Achar Mean Blvd at the corner of 180 St (Croix Rouge St). It is officially open from 7 to 11 am and from 2.30 to 5.30 pm. The Press Office of the Foreign Ministry (tel 2.2241) is based in the Foreign Ministry building on Quai Karl Marx. The Soviet Cultural Centre (tel 2.2581) is on the western side of Tou Samouth Blvd at 222 St (across the street from the Ministry of the Interior). The Customs House is on the western side of Tou Samouth Blvd just south of 118 St.

The Fine Arts School (École des Beaux-Arts) has faculties of music, classical Cambodian dance and the plastic arts; archaeology and architecture faculties are being added. The school, which has 810 secondary students and 150 university-level students, is divided between two campuses. The plastic arts, archaeology and architecture are based on the main campus, which is at the back of the National Museum complex at the corner of 19 St and 184 St. Music and dance are taught at a facility on 70 St near the old stadium (now a military base).

Visa Extensions Visa extensions are granted by the Foreign Ministry (tel 2.4641, 2.3241, 2.4441), whose offices are on the western side of Quai Karl Marx at 240 St

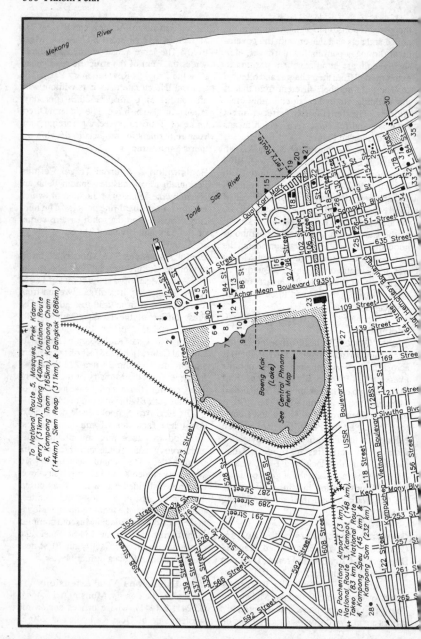

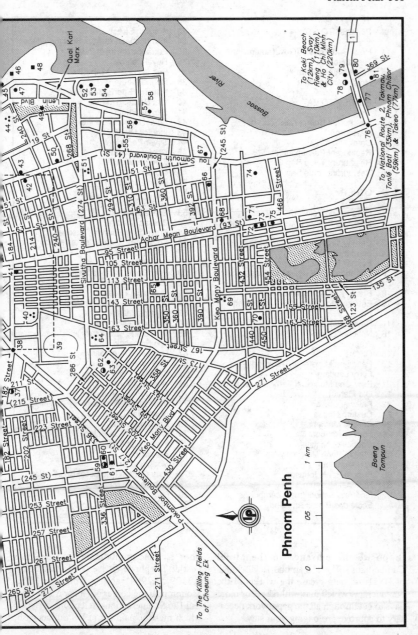

Phnom Penh

(opposite the entrance to the Motel Cambodiana). There is an unofficial charge of US$10 to help grease the wheels of the bureaucracy, which may still take 3 or more days to get through all the paperwork necessary to approve prolonging your stay.

Post & Telecommunications There is a Post & Telephone Office (PTT; tel 2.3324, 2.3509, 2.2909) across from the Hotel Monorom at the corner of Achar Mean Blvd and 126 St. International telephone services, which must be paid for in US dollars cash, are available from 7 am to 12 noon and from 1 to 11 pm. The postal desk, where philatelic items are on sale, is open from 7 to 11.30 am and from 2 to 7.30 pm.

The GPO (tel 2.4511) is on the western side of 13 St between 98 St and 102 St in a building built as a post office well before WW II. It is open from 6.30 am to 9 pm daily. The GPO offers postal services as well as domestic and international telegraph and telephone links.

Money The Foreign Trade Bank (in French, Banque du Commerce Extérieur du Cambodge; formerly the National People's Bank; tel 2.4863) is at 26 Soeung Ngoc Ming St, which is on the corner of Achar Mean Blvd. The exchange window (bureau de change), which is on the right as you you enter, is open Monday to Saturday from 7.30 to 11 am and from 2.30 to 5 pm.

Foreign Embassies The following countries are represented in Phnom Penh:

Bulgaria
    227 Tou Samouth Blvd (tel 2.3181/2)
Cuba
    30 214 St (tel 2.4181/2, 4281/2, 4381/2)
Hungary
    773 Achar Mean Blvd (between 432 St and 458 St; tel 2.2781/2)
India
    777 Achar Mean Blvd (at 458 St; tel 2.2981)
Laos
    111 214 St (tel 2.5181/2)
Poland
    767 Achar Mean Blvd (between 432 St and 458 St; tel 2.3581/2)
Czechoslovakia
    Tou Samouth Blvd (between 264 St and 256 St; tel 2.3781, 2.3981, 2.5881, 2.5081)
USSR
    Lenin Blvd midway between 312 St and 394 St (tel 2.2081/2)
Vietnam
    Achar Mean Blvd at 436 St, which is blocked off (tel 2.5481/2, 2.5681). The consular section (tel 2.3142) is on the eastern side of Achar Mean Blvd opposite number 749 (between 422 St and Keo Mony Blvd). It is open daily except Saturday afternoons, Sundays and Vietnamese and Cambodian holidays from 7.30 to 11 am and from 2 to 5 pm. Two photos are required for a visa, which takes at least 2 days to issue.

Airline Offices The Kampuchean Airlines Booking Office (signposted as the Département de l'Aviation Civil du Cambodge and the Direction of Kampuchea Civil Aviation; tel 2.5887) is at 62 Tou Samouth Blvd. Official hours are 7 to 11 am and 2 to 5 pm Monday to Saturday, but in exceptional circumstances it may be possible to purchase tickets during the siesta, after 5 pm and even on Sundays.

This office represents Aeroflot, Lao Aviation and Vietnam Airlines and is the only place in town where airline tickets can actually be purchased, though bookings and reservations can also be made through the Aeroflot office, which is in the Hotel Sukhalay (tel 2.2403).

Bookshop The Librarie d'État, which is across the street from the White Hotel at 224 Achar Mean Blvd, has a few posters and postcards but not much else.

Maps Maps can be purchased from the booksellers at Tuol Tom Pong Market and from personable boys and young men who hang around restaurants frequented by foreigners. Some of their merchandise appears to have been appropriated from the Vietnamese army.

Emergency The best hospital in Phnom Penh is probably the Khmer-Soviet Hospital (Hôpital de l'Amitié Khmer-Sovietique), which is partly staffed by Soviet physicians and has a limited supply of medicines.

Royal Palace
Phnom Penh's Royal Palace (tel 2.4958), which stands on the site of the former citadel, Banteay Kev (built in 1813), fronts Lenin Blvd between 184 St and 240 St. The complex is open to the public on Thursdays and Sundays (and daily except Mondays for official visitors) from 8 to 11 am and from 2 to 5 pm. The entrance fee is US$2. There is an additional US$2 charge to bring a still

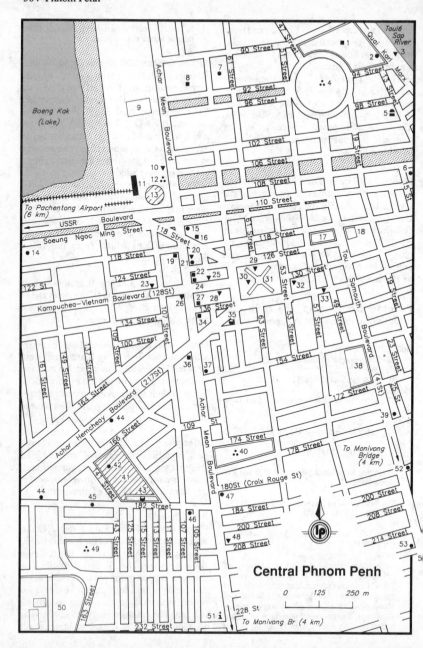

Central Phnom Penh

0   125   250 m

■ PLACES TO STAY

1 Hotel Wat Phnom
8 Hotel Samaki
16 Hotel of the National People's Bank
19 Hotel Manorom
21 Post/Telephone Office & Ministry of Transport Hotel
22 Hotel Sukhalay
24 Hotel d'Asie
27 Hotel Santépheap & Restaurant Santépheap
34 Blue Hotel
36 White Hotel & International Restaurant

▼ PLACES TO EAT

3 Restaurant Tonlé Sap 2
20 'Restaurant'
23 Small Restaurants
25 Restaurant Samapheap & the 'Cafeteria'
26 Restaurant Sereipheap
28 Dancing Restaurant
29 Restaurant Phsathu Thmei
30 Food Stalls
32 Restaurant Sobhamongkol
33 Small Restaurants
42 Food Stalls
48 Soup Restaurant

● OTHER

2 Entrance to Hotel Wa Phnom
4 Wat Phnom
5 GPO
6 Old Market
7 National Library
9 Interspoutnik Satellite Ground Station
10 Faculty of Medicine Restaurant
11 Railway Station
12 Stupa containing Buddha Relic
13 Night Market
14 Council of Ministers
15 Foreign Trade Bank
17 Customs House
18 Former National Bank Site
31 Central Market
35 Psar Thmei Local Bus Terminal
37 Night Market
38 Military Museum (closed)
39 Kampuchean Airlines Booking Office
40 Wat Koh
41 O Russei Market
43 O Russei Local Bus Station
44 Motorbike Parts Shops
45 Bicycle Shops
46 Bicycle Shops
47 Ministry of Information & Culture
49 Wat Sampao Meas
50 National Sports Complex
51 General Directorate of Tourism
52 'English Street'
53 Soviet Cultural Centre
54 Interior Ministry

camera into the complex; movie or video cameras cost US$5. Photography is not permitted inside the palace buildings.

Chan Chaya Pavilion Performances of classical Cambodian dance were staged in Chan Chaya Pavilion, through which guests enter the grounds of the Royal Palace.

Throne Hall The Throne Hall (Palais du Trône; in Khmer, Preah Tineang Tevea Vinichhay), topped by a 59-metre-high tower inspired by the Bayon Temple at Angkor, was inaugurated in 1919 by King Sisowath; the present cement building replaced a vast wooden structure built on this site in 1869. The Throne Hall, which is 100 metres long and 30 metres wide, was used for coronations and ceremonies such as the presentation of credentials by diplomats. Cameras must be checked at the entrance (which is on the eastern side of the building). Some 80% of the items once displayed here were destroyed by the Khmer Rouge.

On the walls and ceiling of the Throne Hall are murals depicting the *Ramayana* epic. The group of chairs closest to the entrance was reserved for the use of high officials; the second ensemble of chairs was used by foreign ambassadors when they came to present their credentials. Between here and the king's pavilion are a gilded, mobile platform on which the king rode during royal processions, the queen's hammock (also used during processions), French-style thrones belonging to the king and queen (she sat to his left) and a sacred gong held by two elephant tusks. In front of the king's mobile platform are conch shells that are blown at coronations and bunched branches used by the police to keep order.

The king's pavilion, which was used only on coronation day, sits in the transept; overhead, four garudas provide symbolic protection. To either side are the queen's enclosed sedan chair and the king's open one. The nave to the right (north) was used to store the ashes of deceased members of the royal family before they were interred in stupas. The left-hand (southern) nave served as a chapel for the king. It was here that he consulted the royal fortune teller to determine the most auspicious dates for trips. Next comes a group of yellow upholstered chairs used by visiting heads of state during meetings with the king. The bed, flanked by two mirrors, was used by the king for naps, during which he was fanned by ladies of the court.

The queen's pavilion, which was used only during coronations, has three staircases; Brahmin officials participating in the ceremonies mounted from the sides, the queen herself from behind. Beyond is a large chamber flanked by the queen's bedroom (on the right) and the king's bedroom (on the left). For the 7 days following the coronation ceremonies, the king and queen were required to sleep separately. During this period, they spent their nights here; then they moved to the royal residence.

Note that the structure just north of the entrance to the Throne Hall is equipped with a dock from which the king could mount and dismount his elephant with ease and in comfort.

Silver Pagoda

The Silver Pagoda, so named because the floor is covered with over 5000 silver tiles weighing 1 kg each, is also known as Wat Preah Keo (Pagoda of the Emerald Buddha). It was constructed of wood in 1892 by King Norodom, who was apparently inspired by Bangkok's Wat Phra Keo, and rebuilt in 1962. The Silver Pagoda and its contents were preserved by the Khmer Rouge in order to demonstrate to the outside world their

1	Entrance to Royal Palace
2	Chan Chaya Pavilion
3	Building with Elephant Dock
4	Throne Hall
5	Royal Treasury
6	Royal Offices
7	Gift of Napoleon III
8	Banquet Hall
9	Route from Royal Palace to Silver Pagoda
10	North Gate (Entrance to Siver Pagoda)
11	Galleries around Silver Pagoda
12	Mondap (Library)
13	Bell Tower
14	Stupa of King Norodom
15	Equestrian Statue of King Norodom
16	Silver Pagoda
17	East Gate (closed)
18	Stupa of King Ang Duong
19	Beginning of Ramayana Mural
20	Pavilion containing Buddha Footprint
21	Phnom Mondap
22	South Gate (closed)
23	Stupa of Sihanouk's Daughter
24	Pavilion for Royal Celebrations
25	Stupa of King Norodom Suramarit
26	West Gate (closed)

concern for the conservation of Cambodia's cultural riches. Although some 60% of the pagoda's contents were destroyed under Pol Pot, what's left is spectacular. This is one of the only places in all of Cambodia where objects embodying some of the brilliance and richness of Khmer civilisation can still be viewed.

Both foreigners and Cambodians must have special authorisation from the Ministry of Information & Culture (tel 2.4769; at 395 Achar Mean Blvd) to visit the Silver Pagoda, which is open only on Tuesdays, Thursday and Saturdays. Officially, the pagoda receives visitors from 7 to 11 am and from 2 to 5 pm, but don't count on it being open at 4.30 pm or 7.30 am. Photography inside the pagoda is forbidden for reasons of security.

The staircase leading up to the Silver Pagoda is made of Italian marble. Inside, the Emerald Buddha, said to be made of Bacca-

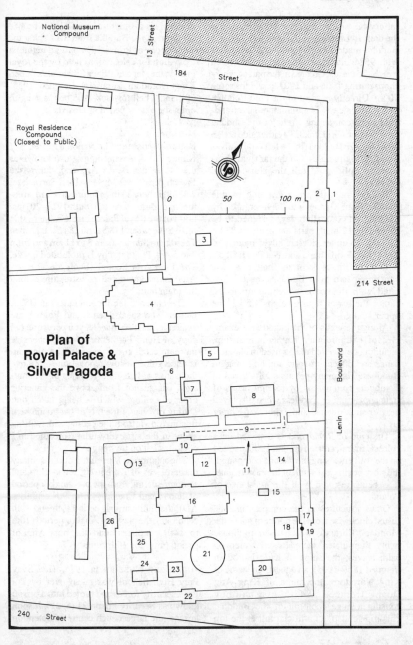

Plan of Royal Palace & Silver Pagoda

rat crystal, sits on a gilt pedestal high atop the dais. In front of the dais stands a life-size Buddha made of solid gold and decorated with 9584 diamonds, the largest of which weighs 25 carats. Created in the palace workshops during 1906 and 1907, it weighs some 90 kg. Directly in front of the gold Buddha, in a formica case, is a miniature silver-and-gold stupa containing a relic of the Buddha brought from Sri Lanka. To either side are an 80 kg bronze Buddha (to the left) and a silver Buddha (to the right). On the far right, figurines of solid gold tell the story of the Buddha.

Behind the dais are a standing marble Buddha from Myanmar and a litter, used by the king on coronation day, designed to be carried by 12 men; parts are made of 23 kg of gold. To either side are silver models of King Norodom's stupa and Wat Preah Keo's library. At the back of the hall is a case containing two gold Buddhas, each decorated with diamonds weighing up to 16 carats; the lower figure weighs 4.5 kg, the upper 1.5 kg.

Along the walls of the pagoda are examples of extraordinary Khmer artisanship, including bejewelled masks used in classical dance and dozens of solid and hollow gold Buddhas. The many precious gifts given to Cambodia's monarchs by foreign heads of state appear rather spiritless when displayed next to such diverse and exuberant Khmer art.

The epic of *Ramayana* is depicted on a colossal mural, created around 1900, painted on the wall enclosing the pagoda compound; the story begins just south of the eastern gate. It is being restored with the assistance of Poland.

Other structures in the complex include (listed clockwise from the northern gate): the Mondap (library), which used to house richly illuminated sacred texts written on palm leaves; the stupa of King Norodom (reigned 1859-1904); an equestrian statue of King Norodom; the stupa of King Ang Duong (reigned 1845-59); a building housing a huge footprint of the Buddha; Phnom Mondap, an artificial hill at the top

of which is a structure containing a bronze footprint of the Buddha from Sri Lanka; the stupa of one of Prince Sihanouk's daughters; a pavilion for celebrations held by the royal family; the stupa of Prince Sihanouk's father, King Norodom Suramarit (reigned 1955-60); and a bell tower, whose bell is rung to order the gates opened or closed.

Museums

National Museum The National Museum of Khmer Art & Archaeology (also known as the Musée des Beaux-Arts and, during the French period, the Musée Albert Sarraut; tel 2.4369) is housed in an impressive red structure of traditional design (built 1917-20) just north of the Royal Palace on the western side of 13 St between 178 St and 184 St. It is open Tuesday to Sunday from 8 to 11 am and from 2 to 5 pm. Photography is prohibited inside. The Fine Arts School (École des Beaux-Arts) is headquartered in a structure behind the main building.

The entrance fee for foreigners is US$2. Guides who speak French and English are available, and they may let you peruse an old copy of Henri Parmentier's comprehensive museum catalogue if you ask. The museum is undergoing a slow renovation to remove thousands of bats (and 15 years of accumulated bat guano) from above the gallery's dropped ceiling, which is being taken out. During my visit, little bits of bat guano kept floating down from the ceiling and swirling about in the air; every time I breathed in I could taste it on my tongue.

The National Museum contains many masterpieces of Khmer art, artisanship and sculpture dating from the pre-Angkor period of Funan and Chenla (4th to 9th centuries AD), the Indravarman period (9th and 10th centuries), the classical Angkor period (10th to 14th centuries) and the post-Angkor period (after the 14th century).

Tuol Sleng Museum In 1975, Tuol Svay Prey High School was taken over by Pol Pot's security forces and turned into a prison known as Security Prison 21 (S-21). It soon became the largest such centre of detention and torture in the country. Over 17,000 people held at S-21 were later taken to the extermination camp at Choeung Ek to be executed; detainees who died during torture were buried in mass graves on the prison grounds. S-21 has been turned into the Tuol Sleng Museum (tel 2.4569), which serves as a testament to the crimes of the Khmer Rouge. The museum, whose entrance is on the western side of 113 St just north of 350 St, is open daily from 7 to 11.30 am and from 2 to 5.30 pm.

Like the Nazis, the Khmer Rouge were meticulous in keeping records of their barbarism. Each prisoner who passed through S-21 was photographed, sometimes both before and after being tortured. The museum displays include room after room in which such photographs of men, women and children cover the walls from floor to ceiling; virtually all the people pictured were later killed. You can tell in what year a picture was taken by the style of number board that appears on the prisoner's chest. Several foreigners from Australia, France and the USA were held here before being murdered. Their documents are on display.

As the Khmer Rouge 'revolution' reached ever greater heights of insanity, it began devouring its own children. Generations of torturers and executioners who worked here killed their predecessors and were in turn killed by those who took their places. During the first part of 1977, S-21 claimed an average of a hundred victims per day.

When Phnom Penh was liberated by the Vietnamese army in early 1979, they found only seven prisoners alive at S-21. Fourteen others had been tortured to death as Vietnamese forces were closing in on the city. Photographs of their gruesome deaths are on display in the rooms where their decomposing corpses were found. Their graves are nearby in the courtyard.

There is something disconcerting about the way the present government in Phnom Penh is using Tuol Sleng Museum as an instrument of propaganda to boost its own legitimacy by focusing hatred on its predecessor. After all, most of the leaders of the Vietnamese-installed Phnom Penh government, including Hun Sen and Heng Samrin, were at one time Khmer Rouge officers themselves.

The Killing Fields of Choeung Ek Between 1975 and 1978, about 17,000 men, women, children and infants (including nine Westerners), detained and tortured at S-21 prison (now Tuol Sleng Museum), were transported to the extermination camp of Choeung Ek to be executed. They were bludgeoned to death to avoid wasting precious bullets.

The remains of 8985 people, many of whom were found bound and blindfolded, were exhumed in 1980 from mass graves in this one-time longan orchard; 43 of the 129 communal graves here have been left untouched. Fragments of human bone and bits of cloth are scattered around the disinterred pits. Over 8000 skulls, arranged by sex and age, are visible behind the clear glass panels of the Memorial Stupa, which was erected in 1988.

The Killing Fields of Choeung Ek are 15 km from downtown Phnom Penh. To get there, take Pokambor Blvd south-westward out of the city; the site is 8.5 km from the bridge near 271 St. A memorial ceremony is held annually at Choeung Ek on 9 May.

Military Museum The building housing the Military Museum, which is on the west side of Tou Samouth Blvd between 154 St and 172 St, is being used by the Cambodian army to train officers. It is closed to the public.

Wats & Mosques
Wat Phnom Set on top of a tree-covered knoll 27 metres high, Wat Phnom is visible from all over the city. According to legend, the first pagoda on this site, which is at the intersection of Tou Samouth Blvd and 96 St, was erected in 1373 to house four statues of the Buddha deposited here by the waters of the Mekong and discovered by a woman named Penh (thus the name Phnom Penh, 'the hill of Penh'). The main entrance to Wat Phnom is via the grand eastern staircase,

Palace Wat

which is guarded by lions and *naga* balustrades.

Today, many people come here to pray for good luck and success in school exams or business affairs. When a petitioner's wish is granted, he or she returns to make the offering (such as a garland of jasmine flowers or bananas, of which the spirits are said to be especially fond) promised when the request was made.

The *vihara* (sanctuary) was rebuilt in 1434, 1806, 1894 and, most recently, in 1926. West of the *vihara* is an enormous stupa containing the ashes of King Ponhea Yat (reigned 1405 to 1467). In a small pavilion on the south side of the passage between the *vihara* and the stupa is a statue of a smiling and rather plump Madame Penh.

A bit to the north of the *vihara* and below it is an eclectic shrine dedicated to the genie Preah Chau, who is especially revered by the Vietnamese. On either side of the entrance to the chamber in which a statue of Preah Chau sits are guardian spirits bearing iron bats. On the tile table in front of the two guardian spirits are drawings of Confucius, and two Chinese-style figures of the sages Thang Cheng (on the right) and Thang Thay (on the left). To the left of the central altar is an eight armed statue of Vishnu.

Down the hill from the shrine is a royal stupa sprouting full-size trees from its roof. For now, the roots are holding the bricks together in their net-like grip, but when the trees die and rot, part of the tower, its bricks pried apart as the roots forced their way between them, will slowly crumble. If you can't make it out to Angkor, this stupa gives a pretty good idea of what the jungle can do (and is doing) to Cambodia's human-made monuments.

At the bottom of the hill on the north-western side is a small zoo, though Wat Phnom's most endearing animal residents, its monkeys, live free in the trees, feasting on people's banana offerings. Elephant rides around the base of Wat Phnom are a favourite attraction on Sundays and holidays; the elephants work regular government business hours (that is, they take a long siesta around lunch time). Every Thursday at 10 am the weekly national lottery is drawn here.

Wat Ounalom Wat Ounalom, the headquarters of the Cambodian Buddhist patriarchate is on the south-western corner of the intersection of Lenin Blvd and 154 St (across from Phnom Penh Tourism). Under Pol Pot, the complex, which was founded in 1443 and includes 44 structures, was heavily damaged and its extensive library destroyed. Wat Ounalom was once home to over 500 monks; now there are only 30, including the head of the country's Buddhist hierarchy.

On the ground floor of the main building is a marble Buddha of Burmese origin broken into pieces by the Khmer Rouge and later reassembled. On the 2nd floor, to the left of the dais, is a statue of Samdech (His Excellency) Huot Tat, Fourth Patriarch of Cambodian Buddhism, who was killed by

Pol Pot. The statue, made in 1971 when the patriarch was 80, was thrown in the Mekong but retrieved after 1979.

Nearby, a bookcase holds a few remnants of the once-extensive library of the Buddhist Institute, which was based here until 1975 and is being re-established. To the right of the dais is a statue of a former patriarch of the Thummayuth sect, which is followed by the royal family.

On the right front corner of the dais on the 3rd floor are the cement remains of a Buddha from which the Khmer Rouge stripped the silver covering. In front of the dais to either side are two glass cases containing flags – each 20 metres long – used during Buddhist celebrations. The walls are decorated with scenes from the life of the Buddha, which were painted when the building was constructed in 1952.

Behind the main building is a stupa containing an eyebrow hair of the Buddha. There is an inscription in Pali over the entrance.

Wat Lang Ka
Wat Lang Ka, which is on the southern side of Sivutha Blvd just west of Victory Monument, was almost completely destroyed by Pol Pot. It was the second of Phnom Penh's wats repaired by the post-1979 government (the first was Wat Ounalom). Around the main building are reconstructed stupas. Both the ground level and 2nd-floor chambers of the *vihara* have been newly painted with colourful scenes from the life of the Buddha. Fifteen monks live at Wat Lang Ka; 20 years ago there were hundreds.

Wat Koh
Wat Koh, on the eastern side of Achar Mean Blvd between 174 St and 178 St, is one of Phnom Penh's oldest pagodas. It was established centuries ago (around the time when Wat Phnom was founded) but only became popular with the masses after the lake surrounding its very small *vihara* was filled in during the 1950s. Much of the complex, which was damaged by the Khmer Rouge, is now being repaired. There are plans to complete the *vihara*, construction of which halted in 1975. Today, five monks live at Wat Koh.

To the left of the entrance is a terracotta-coloured obelisk under a wood canopy erected as a memorial to the victims of Pol Pot and soldiers who died fighting his forces. The tower behind the *vihara* is the stupa of a member of the royal family.

Wat Moha Montrei
Wat Moha Montrei, which is one block east of the Olympic Market, is on the southern side of Sivutha Blvd between 163 St and 173 St (across from the National Sports Complex). It was named in honour of one of King Monivong's ministers, Chakrue Ponn, who initiated the founding of the pagoda (*moha montrei* means 'the great minister'). The cement *vihara*, topped with a 35 metre high tower, was completed in 1970. Between 1975 and 1979, the building was used to store rice and corn.

Notice the assorted Cambodian touches incorporated in the wall murals of the *vihara*, which tell the story of the Buddha: the angels accompanying the Buddha to heaven are dressed as classical Khmer dancers, and the assembled officials wear white military uniforms of the Sihanouk period. Along the wall to the left of the dais is a painted and carved wooden lion from which religious lessons are preached four times a month. The gold-coloured wooden throne nearby is used for the same purpose. All the statues of the Buddha here were made after 1979. Twelve monks live at Wat Moha Montrei, which like many wats, runs an elementary school on the premises.

Nur ul-Ihsan Mosque
Nur ul-Ihsan Mosque in Khet Chraing Chamres, founded in 1813, is 7 km north of downtown Phnom Penh on National Route 5. According to local people, it was used by the Khmer Rouge as a pigsty and reconsecrated in 1979. It now serves a community of 360 Cham and ethnic-Malay Muslims. A minaret, taller than the nearby coconut palms, was knocked down and has yet to be rebuilt. Next to the mosque is a

madrasa (religious school). Shoes must be removed before entering the mosque.

To get to Nur ul-Ihsan Mosque, take a bus, Lambretta or *remorque-moto* from O Russei Market towards Khet Prek Phnou, which is a few km north-west of Khet Chraing Chamres.

An-Nur an-Na'im Mosque The original An-Nur an-Na'im Mosque, once the largest in Phnom Penh, was built in 1901 and razed by the Khmer Rouge. A new, more modest brick structure – topped with a white dome holding a star and crescent aloft – has been under construction by the local Muslim community since 1981. A minaret will be added when funding is found. A *madrasa* to educate the children of the mosque's 600 families is being built next to the mosque, which is in Chraing Chamres II about 1 km north of Nur ul-Ihsan Mosque.

Markets

Central Market The dark yellow art deco Central Market, whose central domed hall resembles a Babylonian ziggurat, has four wings filled with shops selling gold and silver jewellery, antique coins, fake name-brand watches and other such items. Around the main building are stalls offering *kramas*, (checked scarves) stationery, household items, cloth for sarongs, flowers, etc. There are food stalls on the structure's western side, which faces towards Achar Mean Blvd.

O Russei Market 'Luxury' foodstuffs, costume jewellery and imported toiletries are sold in hundreds of stalls at O Russei Market, which is on 182 St between 111 St and 141 St. The complex also includes scores of food stalls.

Tuol Tom Pong Market Tuol Tom Pong Market, bounded by 155 St on the east, 163 St on the west, 440 St on the north and 450 St on the south, is the city's best source of real and fake antiquities. Items for sale include miniature Buddhas, various ritual objects and old Indochinese coins. There are also quite a few goldsmiths and silversmiths,

motorbike parts shops and book vendors; the latter may have maps for sale. There are food stalls in the central section of the market. It is said that Russian expats shop here for vegetables and meat – and that the locals routinely overcharge them.

Olympic Market A great deal of wholesaling is done at the Olympic Market (Marché Olympique), which is near the National Sports Complex and Wat Moha Montrei between 193 St, 199 St, 286 St and 283 St. Items for sale include bicycle parts, clothes, electronics and assorted edibles. There are dozens of food stalls in the middle of the market.

Dang Kor Market Dang Kor Market is just north of the intersection of Keo Mony Blvd and Pokambor Blvd, where the modern Municipal Theatre building stands. Not much of interest is sold here, though there are food stalls in the centre of the market area.

The Old Market Household goods, clothes and jewellery are on sale in and around the Old Market (Psar Cha), which is bounded by 13 St, 15 St, 108 St and 110 St. Small restaurants, food vendors and jewellery stalls are scattered throughout the area.

Other Sights

The following sites of interest are listed from north to south:

Chrouy Changvar Bridge The 700-metre Chrouy Changvar Bridge over the Tonlé Sap River, just off Achar Mean Blvd at 74 St, was once the country's longest; also known as the Tonlé Sap Bridge and the Japanese Bridge, it was blown up in 1975. It was here on the afternoon of 17 April 1975 – the day Phnom Penh fell – that *New York Times* correspondent Sidney Schanberg and four companions were held prisoner by Khmer Rouge fighters and threatened with death; they were saved from summary execution by Dith Pran, whose life under the Khmer Rouge was portrayed in the movie *The Killing Fields*.

Top: Angkor Wat in the late afternoon (DR)
Bottom: Faces of Avalokitecvara above the north gate to Banteay Kdei, Angkor (DR)

Top: The many faces of Avalokitecvara at the Bayon, Angkor (DR)
Left: Boy, Angkor Wat (TA)
Right: Relief at sunset, Angkor Wat (LG)

These days, the Phnom Penh side of the massive concrete structure has become a hang-out for young couples, especially in the late afternoon and evening. While viewing the river from near the unfenced drop-off, you can enjoy fruit, sugar cane juice and fried foods sold by several refreshment stands. Rumour has it that the Japanese and Indians are looking into repairing the bridge.

Former French Embassy The former French Embassy, which is on the western side of Achar Mean Blvd at 76 St, is now an orphanage whose apparently larcenous residents are blamed by local people for every theft in the neighbourhood. Across the street is the former Korean Embassy.

When Phnom Penh fell on 17 April 1975, about 800 foreigners and 600 Cambodians took refuge in the French Embassy. Within 48 hours, the Khmer Rouge informed the French vice-consul that the new government did not recognise diplomatic privileges and that if all the Cambodians in the compound were not handed over, the lives of the foreigners inside would also be forfeited. Cambodian women married to foreigners could stay, he was told; Cambodian men married to foreign women could not. The foreigners stood and wept as their servants, colleagues, friends, lovers and husbands were escorted out of the embassy gates. At the end of the month, the foreigners were taken out of the country by truck. Almost none of the Cambodians were ever seen again.

Boeng Kak Amusement Park Lakeside Boeng Kak Amusement Park has a small zoo, paddleboats for hire and two restaurants. Its two entrances are 200 metres west of Achar Mean Blvd on 80 St and 86 St.

National Library The National Library (Bibliothèque Nationale; tel 2.3249), which is open from 7 to 11.30 am and 2 to 5.30 pm daily except Mondays, is on 92 St next to the Hotel Samaki. The Khmer Rouge turned the graceful building, constructed in 1924, into a stable and threw many of the books out into the streets, where they were picked up by people who donated them back to the library after 1979.

Today, the National Library has about 100,000 volumes, including many crumbling books in French. Part of the English-language collection consists of books taken from the US Embassy when it was sacked after the communist takeover in 1975. According to Gail Morrison, an Australian volunteer helping to turn the piles of crumbling volumes into a proper library, much of the material is of no value whatsoever, but as a reaction against the Khmer Rouge's contempt for books, the present government forbids the destruction of any printed matter. Cornell University is assisting the National Library preserve its collection of palm-leaf manuscripts.

Former National Bank The empty lot where the National Bank – blown up by the Khmer Rouge – once stood is on the south-eastern corner of the intersection of Tou Samouth Blvd and 118 St.

English St There is a cluster of private language schools teaching English (and some French) one block west of the National Museum on 184 St between Tou Samouth Blvd and the back of the Royal Palace compound. Between 5 and 7 pm, the whole area is filled with students who see learning English as the key to making it in post-war Cambodia. This is a good place to meet local young people.

National Sports Complex The National Sports Complex near the intersection of Sivutha Blvd and Achar Hemcheay Blvd includes a sports stadium (which doubles as the site of government-sponsored political rallies) and facilities for swimming, boxing, gymnastics, volleyball and other sports.

Victory Monument Victory Monument, which is at the intersection of Tou Samouth Blvd and Sivutha Blvd, was built in 1958 as an Independence Monument. It is now a memorial to Cambodia's war dead (or at least those the present government considers worthy of remembering). Wreaths are laid here on national holidays.

Prayuvong Buddha Factories In order to replace the countless Buddhas and ritual objects smashed by the Khmer Rouge, a whole little neighbourhood of private workshops producing cement Buddhas, *nagas*, gingerbread ornamentation and small stupas has grown up on the grounds of Wat Prayuvong. While the graceless cement figures, painted in gaudy colours, are hardly works of art, they are part of an effort by the Cambodian people to restore Buddhism to a place of honour in their reconstituted society.

The Prayuvong Buddha Factories are on the eastern side of Tou Samouth Blvd about 300 metres south of Victory Monument (between 308 St and 310 St). There is a teashop just inside the gate, which is decorated with Bayon-style faces.

Former US Embassy The former US Embassy is on the north-eastern corner of the intersection of Tou Samouth Blvd and Keo Mony Blvd. Much of the US air war in Cambodia (1969 to 1973) was run from here. The building now houses the Department of Fisheries of the Ministry of Agriculture.

On the morning of 12 April 1975, 360 heavily armed US Marines brought in by helicopter secured a landing zone several hundred metres from the embassy. Within hours, 276 people – Americans, Cambodians and others – were evacuated by helicopter relay to US ships in the Gulf of Thailand. Among the last to leave was US Ambassador John Gunther Dean, carrying the embassy's US flag under his arm.

Cham Kar Mon Palace Cham Kar Mon Palace, on the west side of Tou Samouth Blvd between 436 St and 462 St, was once the residence of Prince Sihanouk. The palace, whose name means 'silkworm fields', is now used by visiting heads of state, of whom there are very few.

Places to Stay

All of Phnom Penh's hotels are run by assorted organs of the national and municipal governments, which compete with each other for valuable tourist and expat dollars. In 1989, foreign-aid workers, who had until then taken up all but a few of Phnom Penh's hotel rooms, were given the go-ahead to find other quarters, increasing the number of rooms available for tourists to almost 400.

Central Market Area The four-storey *Hotel Samaki* (formerly the Hotel Phnom and before that the Hotel Le Royal; tel 2.4151, 2.3051; 82 rooms), is next to the National Library on the corner of Achar Mean Blvd and 92 St (Blvd Pologne). Between 1970 and 1975, most journalists working in Phnom Penh stayed in the Samaki (the name means 'solidarity'), and part of the film *The Killing Fields* was set here (though filmed elsewhere). Rooms in the main building with air-con and refrigerators cost from US$12 to US$17; three-room bungalows cost US$30 a day. There is a swimming pool out the back. Foreign investors are reportedly interested in renovating the Samaki, which is now run by the Ministry of Commerce.

The six-storey *Hotel Monorom* (tel 2.4549, 2.4951; 68 rooms), run by Phnom Penh Tourism, is on the corner of Achar Mean Blvd and 118 St. Singles/doubles cost US$16/19 for 1st class and US$14/17 for 2nd class; the cheaper rooms are on the upper floors (the elevator is usually inoperable). There is a great view of the city from the terrace of the 6th floor restaurant. There is another restaurant on the ground floor fronting 118 St.

The seven-storey *Hotel Sukhalay* (the name means 'good health'; tel 2.2403; 60 rooms) at the intersection of Achar Mean St and 126 St belongs to the Cabinet du Conseil des Ministres. Singles/doubles on the 1st and 2nd floors cost US$18/20. Until the elevator is repaired (which may be a very long time), the higher off the ground you are the cheaper the room; a single/double on the 7th floor goes for only US$12/14. Adding a third person to a double costs an additional US$7 to US$10. The Sukhalay has a restaurant on the ground floor.

The *White Hotel* (Hotel Blanc; tel 2.2475; 50 rooms) is on the south-western corner of the intersection of Achar Mean Blvd and Achar Hemcheay Blvd (at 219 Achar Mean Blvd). Run by the Ministry of Foreign Affairs, this place charges US$17 for a single or double with air-con and hot water; the elevator is usually out of order. Reception is up one flight of stairs from the street entrance opposite 214 Achar Mean Blvd. The International Restaurant is on the ground floor.

The *Hotel Santépheap* (formerly the Hotel Khemara; the current name means 'peace'; tel 2.3227; 43 rooms), which is run by the Commerce Directorate of the Phnom Penh Municipality, is on the corner of Achar Mean Blvd and 136 St (across the street from 169 Achar Mean Blvd). Reception is up one flight of stairs from the entrance, which is on 136 St. Singles/doubles with air-con and a fridge cost US$15/20. There is a restaurant on the ground floor.

The *Blue Hotel*, which belongs to the Ministry of National Defence, is across 136 St from the Hotel Santépheap. It is now used mostly by Soviet pilots but may become a regular hotel in the near future. The *Ministry of Transport Hotel* is upstairs from the Post & Telephone Office on the corner of Achar Mean Blvd and 126 St. The Phnom Penh Municipality's *Hotel d'Asie* (50 rooms), which is on the corner of Achar Mean Blvd and 128 St (next to the Hotel Sukhalay), is being renovated. The *Hotel of the National People's Bank*, which is also being renovated, is on 118 St diagonally across from the Hotel Monorom and around the back from the Foreign Trade Bank.

Along the River The *Motel Cambodiana* (tel 2.5059; 22 rooms) on Quai Karl Marx near the foot of 240 St is a collection of bungalows on the grounds of the huge, riverside *Hotel Cambodiana*, which has been under construction for almost a quarter of a century. Begun around 1967 when Prince Sihanouk was chief-of-state, the unfinished structure and its spacious grounds were used as a military base by the Lon Nol government. Refugees from the fighting in the countryside sheltered under its concrete roof between 1970 and 1975. Work to complete the 4-star hotel, which will eventually have 360 rooms, was resumed in 1987 after a Cambodian expatriate living in Hong Kong and two Singaporeans decided to invest at least US$20 million in the project. At present, singles/doubles in the Motel Cambodiana, which belongs to Phnom Penh Tourism, cost US$18/22.

The former French Résidence Supérieure (and later Palais du Gouvernement) is just north-east of Wat Phnom between 90 St and 94 St. It is now an official guest house for high-ranking delegations known as the *Hotel Wat Phnom*.

Places to Eat

Food Stalls Food stalls can be found in and around the Central Market (on the western side, which faces Kampuchea-Vietnam Blvd), O Russei Market (along 141 St midway between 182 St and 166 St), Tuol Tom Pong Market, the Olympic Market (along 286 St), Dang Kor Market and the Old Market and near the Psar Cha Ministry of Transport Ferry Landing.

In the evening and at night, food stalls pop up between the railway station and USSR Blvd. There is a small night market on the corner of Achar Mean Blvd and 154 St (next to 232 Achar Mean Blvd).

Restaurants - central market area The eatery across the street from the Hotel Monorom (opposite 103 Achar Mean Blvd), signposted in Latin characters simply as Restaurant, is a quiet, well-lighted place with good food and decent service. Main dishes start at US$1.

The *Faculty of Medicine Restaurant*, which is on the grounds of the Faculty of Medicine of Phnom Penh University, is adjacent to the square in front of the railway station (on the north-west corner of the intersection of Achar Mean Blvd and 106 St). This open-air place, which serves 'Asian' and French food, is open from 5 am to 9 pm.

Restaurant Sereipheap (the name means 'freedom'; tel 2.5837) at 76 Achar Mean Blvd has the usual selection of Khmer, French and Vietnamese dishes. This place is open from 5 am to 10 pm. Taped music is played in the evenings.

Restaurant Santépheap (tel 2.2227), which is open from 5 am to 9 pm, is on the corner of Achar Mean Blvd and 136 St; the entrance is across the street from 159 Achar Mean Blvd. The bilingual (Khmer and French) menu offers European, 'Asian' (they mean Vietnamese) and Cambodian dishes; for some reason, the latter are listed only in Khmer. The food at this air-con place is passable; main dishes cost between US$0.80 and US$1.20. In the evenings, locals drop by to watch Hong Kong gangster films and similar fare on video.

The *International Restaurant*, said to be owned by one of Hun Sen's brothers, is a quiet (no band or video!), well-lighted place on the ground floor of the White Hotel. The food is decent and reasonably priced.

Restaurant Samapheap (the name means 'equality') at 39 128 St (Kampuchea-Vietnam Blvd) is 100 metres west of the Central Market. Main dishes cost fromUS$0.85 to US$2. Next door at 37 128 St is the *Cafeteria* (open 6 am to 9 pm), which offers Khmer and European food; the foreign-language menu (in French and Russian) lists only the European fare. Across the street at 26 128 St is the *Soup & Sweets Shop*. The *Dancing Restaurant* (open 6.30 to 11 pm) is a restaurant/nightclub on the 2nd floor of the building across the street from 9 128 St. Take the long flight of stairs on the side of the building nearest the Central Market to get up there from the street. When the government is not enforcing one of its periodic crack-downs on dancing and other forms of entertainment, live bands play here at night.

Restaurant Phsathu Thmei is a proper sit-down restaurant at the northern edge of the Central Market complex (opposite the intersection of 126 St and 61 St). *Restaurant Sobhamongkol*, which has a blue and white awning, is east of the Central Market on the south-eastern corner of the intersection of 53 St and 130 St. Two blocks away, on 136 St between 49 St and 51 St, there are several other places to eat. There is a cluster of small restaurants across the street from the western side of the Central Market. There are also a number of small eateries and pastry shops along 128 St between Achar Mean Blvd and 109 St.

There is a restaurant popular renowned among locals for its Vietnamese beef soup (made with white vermicelli) on the north-eastern corner of the intersection of Achar Mean Blvd and 208 St.

Restaurants - Boeng Kak area There are two restaurants in the lakeside Boeng Kak Amusement Park, which is behind Revolution Hospital (formerly Calmette Hospital) about 800 metres north of the Hotel Monorom. The park's two entrances are one long block west of Achar Mean Blvd on 80 St and 86 St. A delicious meal at the more expensive of the two, *Restaurant Boeng Kak*, costs about US$3.30 per person. This is a good place for frogs' legs and lobster.

Restaurant Paksupieabal, which is at 40 Achar Mean Blvd (corner 84 St), is across the street from Revolution Hospital. This relaxing place has a nice atmosphere and some of the best food in town, including great pancakes flambés. Diners sit alfresco under a thatch roof.

Restaurants - on the riverfront *Restaurant Tonlé Sap 1* (also known as Restaurant Tespheap Tonlé Sap) is on Quai Karl Marx at the foot of 106 St. The prices are very reasonable. The view of the Tonlé Sap River from the veranda is somewhat spoiled in the evening by swarms of bugs. *Restaurant Tonlé Sap 2* (*Restaurant Ti Pi Tonlé Sap*) is at the intersection of Quai Karl Marx and 94 St (across from the Hotel Wat Phnom).

There are quite a few small places to eat along Quai Karl Marx between 154 St and 178 St (near the Royal Palace and Wat Ounalom).

Entertainment

Discos When the government lifted the curfew in the spring of 1989, Phnom Penh developed a lively nightlife that soon came to include some 40 discos. A few weeks later, however, the government suddenly shut everything down; rumour had it that the discos were either a threat to law and order or a potential target of Khmer Rouge terrorism. Given the enthusiasm of young Phnom Penhois for this form of entertainment, it seems obvious that the discos will spring up again as soon as the government mellows out about all this.

Theatre The Municipal Theatre is a large, modern structure at the intersection of Pokambor Blvd and Keo Mony Blvd.

The Fine Arts School can arrange for performances of classical Cambodian music and dance by its students. For more information, contact either the Fine Arts School (details are listed earlier under Some Useful Addresses) or the Ministry of Information and Culture (tel 2.4769) at 395 Achar Mean Blvd.

Things to Buy

Antiques, silver items and jewellery are available from shops at numbers 163, 139, 105 and 99EO Achar Mean Blvd and on the street that links the Hotel Monorom with the Central Market. There are also a number of jewellery shops specialising in gold and silver in the Central Market, Tuol Tom Pong Market and the Old Market.

The Bijouterie d'État (State Jewellery Shop), run by the National People's Bank, sells items made of gold, silver and precious stones; it is on the north-eastern corner of the intersection of 13 St and 106 St (at 104 St).

The École des Beaux-Arts Shop at the corner of 19 St and 184 St (at the back of the National Museum complex) is open daily except Sunday afternoons from 7 to 11.30 am and from 2 to 5.30 pm. The shop, which belongs to the Fine Arts School, offers wood carvings, papier mâché masks, stone copies of ancient Khmer art, brass figurines and oil paintings made by the school's students.

Profits are divided between the student artists and the school.

Kramas (checked scarves) can be purchased at the Central Market (in the eaves of the main building) and at other marketplaces as well as from the Hotel Monorom gift shop. You can request that unhemmed silk *kramas* be hemmed on the spot.

Bolts of colourful cloth for sarongs and *hols* are on sale at Nay Eng, a shop at 108 136 St (opposite the southern side of the Central Market). It is open from 7 am to 9 pm.

There are a number of photo stores selling Kodak and ORWO print film along Achar Mean Blvd, (try numbers 149 and 203 and around the White Hotel) and on 110 St near the Old Market. One-hour colour print processing is available at a store (tel 2.3137) at 121-123 Achar Mean Blvd (across from the Hotel Sukhalay).

The Diplomatic Store is at 10 Kampuchea-Vietnam Blvd (128 St).

Getting There & Away

Air For information on air service to and from Phnom Penh, see the Getting There and Getting Around chapters. Information on airline offices is listed in the Information section in this chapter.

Bus Buses to points north, east and west of Phnom Penh leave from the Olympic Intercity Bus Station (tel 2.4613), which is on 199 St next to the Olympic Market (Marché Olympique). Long-haul buses (mostly old Dodge 500s with no aisle and a separate door for each row of seats) depart between 4 and 5 am for Bavet (in Svay Rieng Province near the Moc Bai crossing to Vietnam), Koh Thom (in Kandal Province about 60 km south of Phnom Penh on the west bank of the Bassac River) and the provincial capitals of Battambang (the 290 km trip takes 13 or 14 hours), Kompong Cham, Kompong Chhnang, Kompong Thom, Prey Veng, Pursat and Svay Rieng.

Most buses to destinations south and south-west of Phnom Penh depart from Psar Dang Kor Bus Station, which is on Keo

Mony Blvd next to Dang Kor Market (between 336 St and Pokambor Blvd). Daily buses from here serve Chuk, Kampot (a 6 hour trip), Kompong Chhnang, Kompong Som (a 5-hour trip by express bus), Kompong Trach, Svey Ambov, Takeo and Tuom Luop. Buses leave in the early morning.

At both stations, it is best to purchase tickets at least a day before departure. Intercity bus transport is in a state of flux and departure stations may be changed. Bus travel by foreigners is forbidden at present.

To Saigon Daily buses to Saigon leave at 6 am from an office (tel 2.3139) on the south-western corner of 211 St and Ok Nga Sou St (182 St). The office, which is across 211 St from number 180 Ok Nga Sou St, is open from 7 to 11 am and from 2 to 7 pm. One-way passage costs the equivalent of US$1.65. Government officials seem to greatly prefer that their foreign guests not travel to Saigon by bus.

Saigon-Phnom Penh bus ticket

Train The Phnom Penh Railway Station (tel 2.3115) is on the western side of Achar Mean Blvd between 106 St and 108 St. Tickets for the Kompong Som line are sold from the caged booths to the right of the station entrance; tickets for the Battambang line are on sale at the windows to the left. The daily train to Kompong Som is scheduled to depart at 6.40 am; the Battambang train is supposed to leave every day at 6 am, arriving at its final stop 12 hours later if there are no glitches.

Tickets can be purchased the day before departure between 3 and 5 pm and on the morning you intend to travel from 5.55 am. As of this writing, fares were calculated at the rate of 1 riel (about half of a US cent) for every 2 km travelled. The people sleeping all around the station are peasants waiting to return to the provinces after conducting a bit of business in the big city.

For more information on the Cambodian rail system, see the Getting Around chapter of the Cambodia section.

Service Taxis Service taxis (mostly white Peugeot 404 station wagons) can be hired at Psar Chbam Pao Shared-Taxi Station, which is on National Route 1 near Chbam Pao Market (between 367 St and 369 St). To get there from the city, go south on Tou Samouth Blvd and turn left (eastward) across Monivong Blvd.

In the mornings, there are regular runs from here to Neak Luong (the Mekong ferry crossing on National Route 1), Svey Rieng and Bavet, which is near the Moc Bai crossing into Vietnam. Transport to Koki Picnic Area is also available. If you have all the necessary permits, it may be possible to rent a taxi here; the cost, depending on the distance, starts at about US$25 (at the black market rate) per day.

River Transport Large government-run ferries to Kompong Cham, Kratie, Stung Treng, Kompong Chhnang and Phnom Krom (11 km south of Siem Reap) depart from the Psar Cha Ministry of Transport Ferry Landing (tel 2.5619), which is on Quai Karl Marx between 102 St and 104 St.

There is a service to Kompong Cham and Kratie once every 3 days. The ferry sets sail from Phnom Penh at 8.30 am, overnighting at Prek Por (whence it departs at 4.30 am on the second day) and docking at Kompong Cham around 8 am. The vessel spends a second night at Chlong (whence it departs at 5 am on the third day of the trip) before finally pulling into Kratie at about 7 am. The ferries to Stung Treng operate only from September to January; during the rest of the year, the level of the river is too low. The run from Kratie to Stung Treng takes 10 to 12 hours. Ferries to Siem Reap depart at 8 am and arrive in Kompong Chhnang at 4 pm or so, continuing across the Tonlé Sap the next morning.

Passenger ferries to Kompong Cham and ports along the way (including Pras Prasap, Roca Kong, Prek Por and Oleng) depart from the Psar Cha Municipal Ferry Landing, which is on Quai Karl Marx between 106 St and 108 St (next to Tonlé Sap 1 Restaurant). The ferry begins its daily upriver journey at 7 am, arriving in Kompong Cham at 5 or 6 pm; the return trip is faster. Passage from Phnom Penh to Kompong Cham costs US$0.85.

Passenger and goods ferries to Vietnam leave from the Chbam Pao Ferry Landing. A ferry departs daily at 3 pm, arriving 5 or 6 hours later at the Mekong River border landing of Kom Samnor, where passengers transfer (either immediately or the next morning) to Vietnamese ferries for passage to Phu Chau (Tan Chau) and beyond. The usually overloaded ferries, which lack even rudimentary safety equipment, are simple wooden affairs offering only deck class passage, which costs US$2. To get to Chbam Pao Ferry Landing, go a few hundred metres south from Chbam Pao Market on 369 St and turn right down an unmarked alleyway opposite number 210 369 St.

Getting Around

Airport Transport Pochentong International Airport is 7 km west of the centre of Phnom Penh out USSR Blvd or Kampuchea-Vietnam Blvd. Locals may need special authorisation to enter the airport complex. Passenger vehicles departing from O Russei Market to Pochentong pass by the gate to the airport terminal.

Local Buses Buses and small passenger trucks serving Phnom Penh's suburbs depart from a parking lot on 182 St next to O Russei Market; the station operates from about 5.30 am until sundown. Vehicles from here go to Chbam Pao (on National Route 1 across Monivong Bridge from the city), Champu Vonn, Chraing Chamres (north of the city along National Route 5), Kanthoutt, Pochentong and Pochentong Airport (west of the city on National Route 3) and Takmau (south of the city on National Route 2).

The Psar Thmei Local Bus Terminal is 100 metres south-west of the Central Market at the intersection of Achar Hemcheay Blvd and 136 St. Buses to Takmao run twice an hour between 5.30 am and 5.30 pm. There is twice-hourly service (on the hour and half hour) to Chbam Pao, Chraing Chamres and Takmao from about 5.30 am to 5 pm.

Buses from the lot in front of Chbam Pao Market (across Monivong Bridge from the city) go to O Russei Market and the Central Market.

Bicycle There are two clusters of bicycle shops near O Russei Market: one is on 182 St across the street from number 23 (between Achar Mean Blvd and O Russei Market) and the other is on 182 St between 141 St and 163 St (between O Russei Market and Achar Hemcheay Blvd). Bicycle parts are also sold at the Olympic Market.

Bicycles for sale in Phnom Penh include cheap Vietnamese bicycles starting at US$20, small thick-framed Soviet-made bicycles for US$24 and up and deluxe Thai models for US$77 (at the black market rate).

Samlor Samlors, which can be found cruising around town and at marketplaces, are a great way to see the city. Some of the drivers who hang out near major hotels speak a bit of English or French. They probably work for the secret police, but then again so does everyone else you are likely to come in contact with. A 1-km samlor ride around the city centre should cost about US$0.25. Expats adept at bargaining report hiring samlor at a rate of about US$0.35 per hour.

Motorbikes There are motorbike parts stores on Achar Hemcheay Blvd between 109 St and 139 St and on 182 St near the intersection with Achar Hemcheay Blvd (217 St).

Driving Petrol stations are open from 7 to 10 am and from 2 to 3.30 pm daily except Sundays. When the petrol stations are closed, black market petrol, sold in 1-litre glass bottles, can be purchased from curb-side vendors, who are especially numerous near the Central Market and other market-places.

River Transport Ferries across the Tonlé Sap River dock at the Psar Cha Ministry of Transport Ferry Landing.

A motorised boat large enough for 10 people can be chartered from Phnom Penh Tourism for US$10 per hour.

Around Phnom Penh

North of Phnom Penh

PREK KDAM FERRY

The Prek Kdam Ferry, 32 km north of central Phnom Penh, crosses the Tonlé Sap River to connect National Route 5 with National Route 6, which goes to Kompong Thom, Siem Riep and, via National Route 7, to Kompong Cham. There are lots of refreshment stands near the landings.

UDONG ឧដុង្គ

Udong ('the Victorious') served as the capital of Cambodia under several sovereigns between 1618 and 1866. A number of them, including King Norodom, were crowned here. Phnom Udong, a beautiful site for a picnic, is a bit south of the old capital. It consists of two parallel ridges, both of which offer great views of the Cambodian countryside and its innumerable sugar palm trees. From Phnom Penh's taller buildings (including the Hotel Monorom), the bluffs of Udong appear as two symmetrical hills – one of which is topped with spires – in the middle the plains stretching northward from the city.

One monk lives in a tiny (2 by 2½ metre) thatch house built on the low ridge linking the two hills. Nearby is a simple thatch *vihara* (sanctuary).

The smaller ridge, which is oriented north-west to south-east, has two structures – both heavily damaged – and several stupas on top. Ta San Mosque, which is to the right from the top of the path up from the monk's house, faces westward towards Mecca. Only the bullet and shrapnel-pocked walls survived the years of Khmer Rouge rule. The Cham Muslims plan to rebuild it and have already erected a temporary thatch structure nearby. From the mosque you can see, across the plains to the south, Phnom Vihear Leu, a small hill on which a *vihara* stands between two white poles. To the right of the *vihara* is a building used as a prison under Pol Pot. To the left of the *vihara* and below it is a pagoda known as Arey Ka Sap.

North-west of the mosque (to the left from the top of the path) are the ruins of Vihear Preah Chaul Nipean, a laterite *vihara* once home to a large reclining Buddha that was blown to bits by Pol Pot's forces. All around lie the headless bodies and shattered faces of Buddhas smashed during the Khmer Rouge's orgy of destruction.

The larger, uneven ridge, Phnom Preah Reach Throap ('Hill of the Royal Fortune'), is so named because a 16th century Khmer king is said to have hidden the national treasury here during a war with the Thais. The most impressive structure on Phnom Preah Reach Throap (which is also known as Phnom Ath Roes and Phnom Preah Chet Roes) is Vihear Preah Ath Roes, 'Vihara of the 18 Cubit (9 Metre) Buddha'. The *vihara* and the Buddha, dedicated in 1911 by King Sisowath, were blown up by the Khmer Rouge in 1977; only sections of the 1-metre thick walls, the bases of eight enormous columns and the right arm and part of the right side of the Buddha remain.

About 120 metres north-west of Vihear Preah Ath Roes is a line of small *viharas*. The first is Vihear Preah Ko, a brick-roofed structure inside of which is a statue of Preah Ko, the sacred bull; the original of this statue was carried away by the Thais long ago. The second structure, which has a seated Buddha inside, is Vihear Preah Keo. The third is Vihear Prak Neak, its cracked laterite walls topped with a temporary thatch roof. Inside is a seated Buddha guarded by a *naga* (*prak neak* means 'protected by a *naga*').

At the north-west extremity of the ridge stand three large stupas. The first one you come to is the cement Chet Dey Mak Proum, final resting place of King Monivong (ruled 1927-41). Decorated with garudas, floral designs and elephants, it has four Bayon-style faces on top. The middle stupa, Tray

Troeng, is decorated with coloured tiles; it was built in 1891 by King Norodom for the ashes of his father, King Ang Duong (ruled 1845-59) (according to another version of events, King Ang Duong was buried next to the Silver Pagoda in Phnom Penh). The third stupa, Damrei Sam Poan, was erected by King Chey Chethar II (ruled 1618 to 1626) for the ashes of his predecessor, King Soriyopor (ruled 1601-18).

An eastward-oriented laterite staircase leads down the hillside from the stupa of King Monivong. Just north of its base is a pavilion decorated with graphic murals depicting Khmer Rouge atrocities. Across the road, 300 metres due west of the three stupas (on the other side of the ridge), is a memorial to the victims of Pol Pot containing the bones of some of the people who were buried in approximately 100 mass graves, each containing about a dozen bodies.

Instruments of torture were unearthed along with the bones when a number of the 2 by 2½ metre pits were disinterred in 1981 and 1982.

Getting There & Away

Udong is 40 km from the capital. To get there, head north out of Phnom Penh on National Route 5. Continue on past Prek Kdam Ferry for 4½ km and turn left (southward) at the roadblock and bunker. Udong is 3½ km south of the turnoff; the access road goes through the village of Psar Dek Krom and passes by a memorial to Pol Pot's victims and a structure known as the Blue Stupa before arriving at a short staircase. Stick to the paths – there may be mines around here.

To travel to Udong from Phnom Penh by bus, take any vehicle heading for Kompong Chhnang or Battambang; get off at the roadblock and bunker.

South of Phnom Penh

There are several historical sights of interest in Takeo Province. Most of them can be visited on day trips from Phnom Penh.

TONLÉ BATI ទន្លេបាទី
Ta Prohm Temple

The laterite Temple of Ta Prohm was built by King Jayavarman VII (ruled 1181 to 1201) on the site of a 6th century Khmer shrine. A stele found here dates from 1574. The site is open all day every day. A Khmer-speaking guide can be hired for US\$0.30 to US\$0.60, though on Sundays the guides are usually overwhelmed with business.

The main sanctuary consists of five chambers; in each is a statue or linga (or what is left of a statue after the destruction wrought by the Khmer Rouge).

A few metres to the right of the main (eastward-facing) entrance to the sanctuary building, about 3 metres above the ground, is a bas-relief carving of a woman carrying an object on her head and a man bowing to another, larger woman. The smaller woman, who has just given birth, did not show proper respect for the midwife (the larger woman). As a result, she has been condemned to carry the afterbirth around on her head in a box for the rest of her life. The prostrate man, the smaller woman's husband, is begging that the midwife grant his wife forgiveness.

Around the corner to the right from the northern entrance of the sanctuary building, about 3½ metres above the ground, is a bas-relief scene in which a king, about 20 cm high, sits to the right of his wife, who is slightly smaller. Because she has been unfaithful, a servant is shown in the scene below putting her to death by trampling her with a horse.

Inside the north gate is a badly damaged statue of the Hindu god Preah Noreay. Women come here to pray that they be granted a child.

Yeay Peau Temple

Yeay Peau Temple, named for its builder, King Ta Prohm's mother Yeay (Madame) Peau, is a small structure 150 metres north of Ta Prohm Temple. Inside, there is a statue of Yeay Peau standing next to a seated Buddha.

Nearby is Wat Tonlé Bati, a modern cement structure heavily damaged by the Khmer Rouge. The only remnant of the

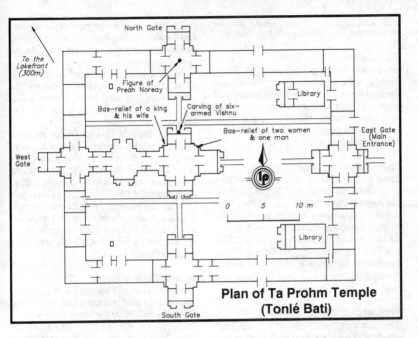

Plan of Ta Prohm Temple (Tonlé Bati)

pagoda's pre-1975 complement of statues is an 80 cm high buddha's head made of metal.

The legend of Yeay Peau Temple goes as follows:

During the time of the building of Angkor Wat (the early 12th century), King Preah Ket Mealea, while on a trip away from Angkor, passed through Tonlé Bati, where he spied Peau, the beautiful daughter of a rich fish merchant. The king fell in love with Peau, who was famous for her long hair (which was always perfumed) and they slept together. Peau fell pregnant but after 3 months the king had to return to Angkor Wat. When he left he gave her his royal seal ring and a sacred dagger and requested that if the child were a boy, he should be sent to join his father at Angkor when he grew older; but if the child were a girl, she was to remain with her mother.

The child was a boy and Peau named him Prohm. As he grew up, Prohm exhibited great physical strength and an aggressive temperament. When the other children teased him for not having a father, Prohm would return home and ask of his mother, 'Who is my father?', but she refused to tell him.

When Prohm was old enough Peau finally informed him of his parentage. He took the royal seal ring and the sacred dagger and set out for Angkor Wat to find his father. The king, recognising the ring and the dagger, invited him to live with him at Angkor.

After a number of years had passed, Prohm requested his father's permission to visit Tonlé Bati. This was granted, and he set out on the long journey. When he arrived in Tonlé Bati, Prohm did not recognise his mother, who had not aged at all during the time he had been away. Taken by her beauty, he asked her to become his wife. Peau rejected his offer, explaining that she was his mother, but he refused to believe her and continued to insist that she marry him.

To settle the matter, Peau suggested that both she and Prohm construct a temple; whoever finished first would get his or her way in the matter. Prohm agreed, sure that he could easily win the contest. But Peau had a plan. On her suggestion, the contest was to last from sundown until the appearance of the morning star. Two teams formed: all the men of the area joined together to help Prohm while all the women came to assist Peau. In the middle of the night, after work had been going on for many hours, Peau sent aloft an artificial morning star lit with candles. The men, thinking it was morning and certain that the women could not possibly have finished their temple, went to sleep; but the women kept on working and completed Peau's temple by morn. When the men awoke and realised that they had been defeated, Prohm prostrated himself before Peau and recognised her as his mother.

The Lakefront

About 300 metres north-west of Ta Prohm Temple, a long, narrow peninsula juts into the Bati River. On Sundays, it is packed with picnickers and vendors selling food, drink and fruit. During the rest of the week, however, few people come here and there are no food stands around.

Getting There & Away

The access road to Ta Prohm Temple, which is in Tonlé Bati district of Takeo Province, intersects National Route 2 at a point 33 km south of downtown Phnom Penh, 21 km north of the access road to Phnom Chisor and 44 km north of Takeo. The temple is 2.5 km from the highway. Any bus linking Phnom Penh with the town of Takeo by way of National Route 2 will pass by the access road.

PHNOM CHISOR

The main temple on the top of Phnom Chisor stands at the eastern side of the hilltop in a flat area measuring about 80 by 100 metres. Constructed of laterite and brick with carved lintels of sandstone, the complex is surrounded by the partially ruined walls of a 2½ metre wide gallery with inward-facing windows.

Inscriptions found here date from the 11th century, when this site was known as Suryagiri. The wooden doors to the sanctuary in the centre of the complex, which open to the east, are decorated with carvings of figures standing on pigs. Inside the sanctuary there are statues of the Buddha.

On the plane to the east of Phnom Chisor are two other Khmer temples, Sen Thmol (at the bottom of Phnom Chisor) and Sen Ravang (farther east), and the former sacred pond of Tonlé Om; all three form a straight line with Phnom Chisor. During rituals held here 900 years ago, the Brahmins and their entourage would climb up to Suryagiri from this direction on a monumental stairway of 400 steps.

There is a spectacular view of the temples and the surrounding plains from the roofless gallery opposite the wooden doors to the central shrine.

Near the main temple are a modern Buddhist *vihara* and structures used by the monks who live here. Most of these buildings were damaged during the Pol Pot period.

At the base of Phnom Chisor near the trailhead of the northern path is a quarry where peasants eke out a living prying large boulders out of the hillside and cracking them apart with hammers to make gravel. Each month, a family with all its members working can produce up to 21 cubic metres of gravel, which is used for paving roads and in construction. Each cubic metre sells for the equivalent of US$0.82 (at the black market rate).

Getting There & Away

The intersection of National Route 2 with the eastward-bound access road to Phnom Chisor is marked by the two brick towers of Prasat Neang Khmau (the Temple of the Black Virgin), which may have once served as a sanctuary to Kali, the dark goddess of destruction.

Prasat Neang Khmau is on National Route 2 at a point 55 km south of central Phnom Penh, 21 km south of the turnoff to Tonlé Bati and 23 km north of Takeo. The distance from the highway to the base of the hill is a bit over 4 km.

There are two paths up the 100 metre high ridge, which takes about 15 minutes to climb. The northern path, which has a mild gradient, begins at a cement pavilion whose windows are shaped like the squared-off silhouettes of a bell and which is topped with a miniature replica of an Angkor-style tower. The steeper southern route, which begins 600 metres south of the northern path, consists of a long stairway.

A good way to see the view in all directions is to go up the northern path and to come down the southern stairway.

TAKEO តាកែវ
Takeo, capital of a province of the same name, is an extremely quiet little town. There is nothing to do in Takeo, although the town can be used as a base to explore the countryside and nearby historical sites such as Tonlé Bati, Phnom Chisor and Phnom Da (Angkor Borei).

Information
Although there are plans to set up a provincial tourism authority, until this is done the only local source of information on the area will continue to be the provincial people's committee, which is headquartered in Takeo.

Street names and numbers are not used in Takeo. The northern edge of town abuts Takeo Lake.

Post The post office, which has a phone link to Phnom Penh, is in the western part of town.

Places to Stay
The government guest house, the three storey *Hotel Takeo* (tel 6 via the Takeo exchange; 16 beds), is 400 metres north of town on a promontory that juts into Takeo Lake. The Khmer Rouge destroyed a Buddhist pagoda that once stood on this site, constructing the present structure for the use of Chinese experts.

Places to Eat
Restaurant Stung Takeo, which overlooks the Takeo River, is on the road that demarcates the eastern extremity of town. *Restaurant Youvchun* in Takeo's eastern section and *Restaurant Phnom Da* in the southern part of town are not far away.

Getting There & Away
National Route 3, which links Phnom Penh with Kompong Som, is in much better condition than National Route 2, the parallel route that passes through Takmau and goes via Tonlé Bati and Phnom Chisor. Takeo is 83 km from Phnom Penh by National Route 3 and 77 km from the capital by National Route 2.

The Takeo bus station is in the southern part of town next to the market. Trains running between Phnom Penh and Kompong Som stop at a railway station a few km north of town.

ANGKOR BOREI អង្គរបុរី
& PHNOM DA ភ្នំដា
Angkor Borei was known as Vyadhapura when it served as the capital of Water Chenla in the 8th century. Four artificial caves, built as shrines, are carved into the north-east wall of Phnom Da, a hill south of Vyadhapura. On top of Phnom Da is a square laterite tower open to the north.

Angkor Borei and Phnom Da are about 20 km east of Takeo along Canal Number 15.

West of Phnom Penh

KOKI BEACH កោះគគីរ
The weekly stampede to Koki Beach is a peculiarly Cambodian institution, a mixture of the universal love of picnicking by the water with the unique Khmer fondness for lounging about on mats at midday in structures built on stilts. It works like this: for US$0.30 or so an hour, families or groups of picnickers rent an area about 2½ metres square on a long raised pier made of split bamboo covered with reed mats. Overhead is a thatch roof to shelter everyone from the midday sun. On Sundays, these piers are jam-packed with Phnom Penhois: wealthy families who drove out in the family car, students who came by bicycle, and less-well-off families who all piled onto a *remorque-moto*. They have come to eat, talk, swim and nap. Be sure to agree on the price *before* you rent a space.

Places to Eat
On Sundays, all sorts of food (grilled chicken and fish, rice, fruit, etc) are sold at Koki Beach, though at prices higher than in Phnom Penh. The beach is almost deserted during the rest of the week, but food is avail-

able at restaurants along National Route 1 between the Koki turnoff and the capital.

Getting There & Away

Koki Beach is in Kandal Province in Koki sub-district of Kien Svay district. To get there from the capital, turn left off National Route 1 (which links Phnom Penh with Saigon) at a point 12 km east of Monivong Bridge. There are service taxis to Koki from the Chbam Pao Shared-Taxi Station, which is just east of Monivong Bridge.

Angkor

The famous temples of Angkor, built between 7 and 11 centuries ago when Khmer civilisation was at the height of its extraordinary creativity, constitute one of humankind's most magnificent architectural achievements. From Angkor, the kings of the mighty Khmer Empire ruled over a vast territory that extended from the tip of what is now southern Vietnam northward to Yunnan in China and from Vietnam westward to the Bay of Bengal. Angkor's hundred or so temples constitute the sacred skeleton of a spectacular administrative and religious centre whose houses, public buildings and palaces were constructed of wood – now long decayed – because the right to dwell in structures of brick or stone was reserved for the gods.

SIEM REAP ເສ]ຍກນ

The town of Siem Reap, whose population is well below the pre-war total of 10,000, is only a few km from the temples of Angkor and serves as a base for visits to the monuments. The name Siem Reap (pronounced see-EM ree-EP) means 'Siamese Defeated' (*Siem* means 'Siamese' (Thais); *Reap* means 'defeated'). Commodities produced in the area of Siem Reap include freshwater fish, wood and rice.

Information

Tourist Office The offices of Angkor Tourism, the government tourism authority in the Angkor area, are in a small building next to the Villa Princière, the structure just east of (towards the Siem Reap River from) the Grand Hotel d'Angkor.

Angkor Conservation Angkor Conservation (or Angkor Conservancy; in French Conservation d'Angkor; tel 82), which has official responsibility for the study, preservation and upkeep of the Angkor monuments, is headquartered in a large compound between Siem Reap and Angkor Wat. Once home to the great French archaeologist George Groslier, it is now used as a base of operations by Angkor Conservation's two English-speaking guides, 100 other employees (there were once 1000) and the Indian and Polish teams that have been working on Angkor Wat and the Bayon.

Over 5000 statues, lingas and inscribed steles found in the vicinity of Angkor are stored by Angkor Conservation at its headquarters, because of the impossibility of preventing thefts from the hundreds of sites where these artefacts were found. As a result, the finest statuary you will see at Angkor is inside Angkor Conservation's warehouses, meticulously numbered and catalogued but in no way arranged for convenient public viewing. In fact, special permission from provincial authorities is required even to visit the compound; for details, inquire at the front desk of the Grand Hotel d'Angkor.

To get to Angkor Conservation's headquarters, go northward from the Grand Hotel d'Angkor for 1.3 km and take a hard right, continuing south-eastward for 300 metres until you come to an enclosure whose perimeter wall has metal spikes sticking out of the top.

Post & Telecommunications The post office is along the river 400 metres south of the Grand Hotel d'Angkor. It is open daily from 7 to 11.30 am and from 2 to 5 pm. When the lines aren't down, phone calls to Phnom Penh can be made from here between 8 and 11 am, from 3 to 5 pm and possibly from 7 to 8 pm as well. Telegraph service is also available – usually.

It is possible to telephone to Phnom Penh from the Grand Hotel d'Angkor between 7 and 11 am and from 1 to 5 pm. Letters can be mailed at the reception desk.

Electricity There is electricity in the town of Siem Reap from about 6 to 9 pm only.

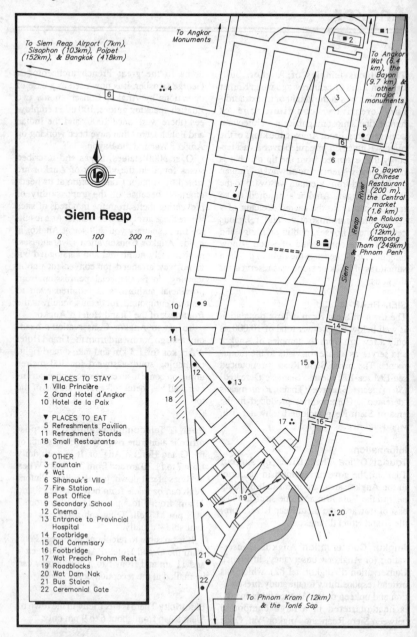

To Siem Reap Airport (7km), Sisophon (103km), Poipet (152km), & Bangkok (418km)

To Angkor Monuments

To Angkor Wat (6.4 km), the Bayon (9.7 km) & other major monuments

To Bayon Chinese Restaurant (200 m), the Central market (1.6 km) the Roluos Group (12km), Kampong Thom (249km) & Phnom Penh

Siem Reap

0   100   200 m

To Phnom Krom (12km) & the Tonlé Sap

■ PLACES TO STAY
1 Villa Princière
2 Grand Hotel d'Angkor
10 Hotel de la Paix

▼ PLACES TO EAT
5 Refreshments Pavilion
11 Refreshment Stands
18 Small Restaurants

● OTHER
3 Fountain
4 Wat
6 Sihanouk's Villa
7 Fire Station
8 Post Office
9 Secondary School
12 Cinema
13 Entrance to Provincial Hospital
14 Footbridge
15 Old Commisary
16 Footbridge
17 Wat Preach Prohm Reat
19 Roadblocks
20 Wat Dam Nak
21 Bus Staion
22 Ceremonial Gate

Security As of this writing, there is a 7 pm to 5 am curfew in force in Siem Reap.

Beware: Some areas in and around the temple complexes have been mined! Visitors should *not* stray from clearly marked paths. Until the war ends, keep in touch with local military authorities to make sure the trails where you're going have not been booby-trapped to blow up infiltrators. Visitors should also refrain from wandering around alone outside of town because unfortunately, the soldiers stationed in the vicinity of Angkor have been known to rob tourists. But don't worry about the troops deployed around the Grand Hotel d'Angkor each night – they're there to protect you!

Concern about security can be carried too far, however. One day during my visit, I noticed that Ta Prohm temple was completely encircled by soldiers who, I was told, were protecting a Japanese television crew working there. I became concerned: here we were, five of us driving around the jungle unaccompanied, while the big boys were provided with proper security. Perhaps we should be protected by such an escort as well, I suggested to my guide.

As it turned out, the soldiers deployed along the road were there more because of the admirable entrepreneurship of their commander than any real danger to the TV crew. The local army brass, it seems, had convinced the Japanese that this particular temple was so dangerous, even in broad daylight, that nothing less than an entire company of heavily-armed infantrymen could ensure their safety. The Japanese, lacking any information to the contrary and all very interested in seeing their loved ones again, were in no position to contradict the army. Needless to say, the Japanese were asked to pay handsomely for this service (from their expense account, no doubt) and the commander and his pals pocketed the cash.

Town Centre

After the arrival of Vietnamese troops in 1979, the centre of Siem Reap, deserted under the Khmer Rouge, was taken over by Vietnamese advisors, who had security barricades erected around the whole area. Today, the Vietnamese are gone but the streets are still blocked and much of the central area remains derelict.

Central Market

Siem Reap's new, covered Central Market is 1.6 km east of the Siem Riep River (towards Roluos) on the south side of National Route 6.

Places to Stay

The venerable old *Grand Hotel d'Angkor* (tel 15; 62 rooms), built in 1928, charges US$13/21 for singles/doubles including breakfast. Half the rooms are equipped with air-conditioning. There are plans to renovate this place for the hordes of better-off tourists who are expected here when there is peace.

The dilapidated *Hotel de la Paix* (tel 41; 32 rooms), now a provincial government guest house, must have some of the cheapest room tariffs in the world: the low-level officials who stay here are charged only 3 riels per night! There are plans to transfer this three storey place to Angkor Tourism for renovation and reopening as a tourist hotel.

The *Villa Princière*, which is just east of the Grand Hotel d'Angkor, is slated to undergo repairs and become a hotel.

The former *Auberge Royale*, once the finest hotel in the area, was razed by the Khmer Rouge. Only the skeleton of the old *Air France Hotel* is still standing.

Places to Eat

The restaurant of the *Grand Hotel d'Angkor* charges foreigners US$6 for meals which, though decent, cost less than one-sixth that in riels. There are a number of other places to eat around town, including the *Bayon Chinese Restaurant* on National Route 6 about 200 metres east of the Siem Reap River. There are several refreshment stands near the Hotel de la Paix, whose restaurant is presently closed. There is a refreshment stand opposite the main entrance to Angkor Wat.

Entertainment

The cinema 120 metres south of the Hotel de la Paix screens video-cassettes.

Things to Buy

There is a photo shop on National Route 6 a few hundred metres east of the bridge over the Siem Reap River. The Grand Hotel d'Angkor has a small gift shop.

Getting There & Away

Air At present, the only way into or out of Siem Reap is by air from Phnom Penh; there are round trips every Wednesday and Saturday (or at least there are supposed to be). A round-trip from Phnom Penh to Siem Reap costs US$91 (US$43 each way plus US$5 for airport taxes). By propeller-driven Antonov An-24, the flight takes 40 minutes.

Siem Reap Airport is 7 km north-west of town and 4 km due west of Angkor Wat. All flights are met by a bus belonging to Angkor Tourism – this service is part of what your US$120 visitors' fee pays for. For some reason, when you arrive officials of Angkor Tourism collect your return air tickets. Be sure to make reservations out of Siem Reap as soon as you land.

The Kampuchean Airlines office, now closed, is in a building on the south side of National Route 6 about 100 metres east of the bridge over the Siem Reap River. Until this office reopens, all business with Kampuchean Airlines must be conducted through their representatives at the airport; for more information, ask at the front desk of the Grand Hotel d'Angkor.

Overland Land distances from Siem Reap:

Phnom Penh	311 km (Nat Route 6)
Battambang	183 km
Kompong Thom	249 km
Poipet (Thai border)	152 km
Sisophon	103 km

National Route 6 and the road between Siem Reap and Battambang are in an advanced state of dilapidation, in part because of repeated rebel attacks, and can be negotiated only by large trucks. The drive from Phnom Penh to Siem Reap takes 2 days. At present, both roads pass through contested territory.

Ferry Ferries from Phnom Penh to Phnom Krom, 11 km south of Siem Reap, depart from the capital's Psar Cha Ministry of Transport Ferry Landing, which is on Quai Karl Marx between 102 St and 104 St. The trip takes 2 days, with an overnight at Kompong Chhnang.

From Thailand When the civil war ends, it should be relatively easy to get to Angkor from Bangkok. A direct air link is expected to be established as soon as the political wrinkles can be ironed out. By land, Angkor is 418 km from Bangkok via the border crossing between Poipet, Cambodia and Aranyaprathet, Thailand. The road between Siem Reap and the frontier is in great need of repair.

Getting Around

Bicycle Unless it's raining, the best way to tour Angkor is by bicycle. Unfortunately, no one is renting bicycles yet and in any case, unaccompanied visits to the temples are not permitted.

Car The US$120 fee to visit the monuments includes transport by automobile for the first day of your visit. For subsequent days, Angkor Tourism hires out cars with drivers for US$40 per day.

THE TEMPLES OF ANGKOR

Between the 9th and the 13th centuries, a succession of Khmer kings who ruled from Angkor utilised the vast wealth and huge labour force of their empire to carry out a series of monumental construction projects intended to glorify both themselves and their capitals, a succession of which were built in the vicinity of Siem Reap. Over the course of this period, Khmer architecture developed and evolved, in part reflecting the change in religious focus from the Hindu cult of the god Shiva to that of Vishnu and then to a form of Mahayana Buddhism centred on Avalokiteçvara.

The monuments of Angkor (the name is a corruption of *Nagara*, 'the City') were designed on the basis of political and religious conceptions of Indian origin that were modified by the Khmers to suit local conditions. The successive cities at Angkor were centred on a temple mountain identified with Mt Meru, home of the gods in Hindu cosmology, which served as both the centre of the earthly kingdom over which the king ruled and the symbolic centre of the universe within which the kingdom existed. The temple mountain functioned as the locus of the cult of the *devaraja* (god-king), through which the king's sacred personality – the very essence of the kingdom – was enshrined in a linga and worshipped. Upon his death, the temple became the god-king's mausoleum.

The first such central temple mountain, built during the rule of Yasovarman I (reigned 889 to 910), was grafted onto the only natural hill in the area, Phnom Bakheng. Later, Mt Meru was represented by a series of pyramid temples, including Phimeanakas, erected by Jayavarman V (reigned 968 to 1001); the Baphuon, built by Udayadityavarman II (reigned 1050 to 1066); and the Bayon, a Buddhist temple that was the most important structure erected by the great builder Jayavarman VII (reigned 1181 to about 1201), who reconstructed the Khmer capital after it had been captured and destroyed by the Chams (whose kingdom occupied what is now south-central Vietnam), who used their fleet to launch a surprise attack.

Many of the other temples of Angkor were built to serve as foci for cults through which various important personages (kings who did not construct new temple mountains, members of the royal family, even a few members of the aristocracy) were identified with one of the gods of the Indian pantheon and thus assured immortality. The grandest such structure was Angkor Wat, which was built by Suryavarman II (ruled 1112 to 1152). He intended Angkor Wat as an archi-

tectural microcosm of the mythical world in which his remains were to be interred as a cultic expression of his identity with Vishnu.

Angkor's huge system of reservoirs, canals and moats served not only to provide water for irrigation, allowing intensive cultivation of areas surrounding the capital, but also as symbols of the great ocean which according to Hindu mythology surrounds Mt Meru.

According to the vivid account of Chou Ta-kuan, a Chinese commercial envoy who visited Angkor Thom in 1296, the city was at that time a magnificent and thriving metropolis. However, by the 13th century the vitality and power of the Khmer Empire were gradually declining. Jayavarman VII's unprecedented building campaign had exhausted his kingdom and Hinayana Buddhism, which was more restrained in its religious expression, was on the ascendancy.

Meanwhile, the armies of the Thai kingdoms in the west of the empire were beginning to threaten the Khmer heartland. In 1431 Thai armies captured and sacked Angkor, and the Khmer court dramatically abandoned the city, moving their capital eastward to a site near Phnom Penh. At this time, Hinayana Buddhist monks took over and preserved Angkor Wat, which before long became one of the most important pilgrimage sites in South-East Asia.

The 'lost city' of Angkor became the focus of intense European popular and scholarly interest after the publication in the 1860s of *Le Tour du Monde*, an account by the French naturalist Henri Mouhot of his voyages. A group of talented and dedicated archaeologists and philologists, most of them French, soon undertook a comprehensive programme of research. Under the aegis of the École Française d'Extrême Orient, they began an arduous effort – begun in 1908 and interrupted at the beginning of the 1970s by the war – to clear away the jungle vegetation that was breaking apart the monuments and to rebuild the damaged structures, restoring them to something approaching their original grandeur. This work was carried out despite the complaints of some romantics,

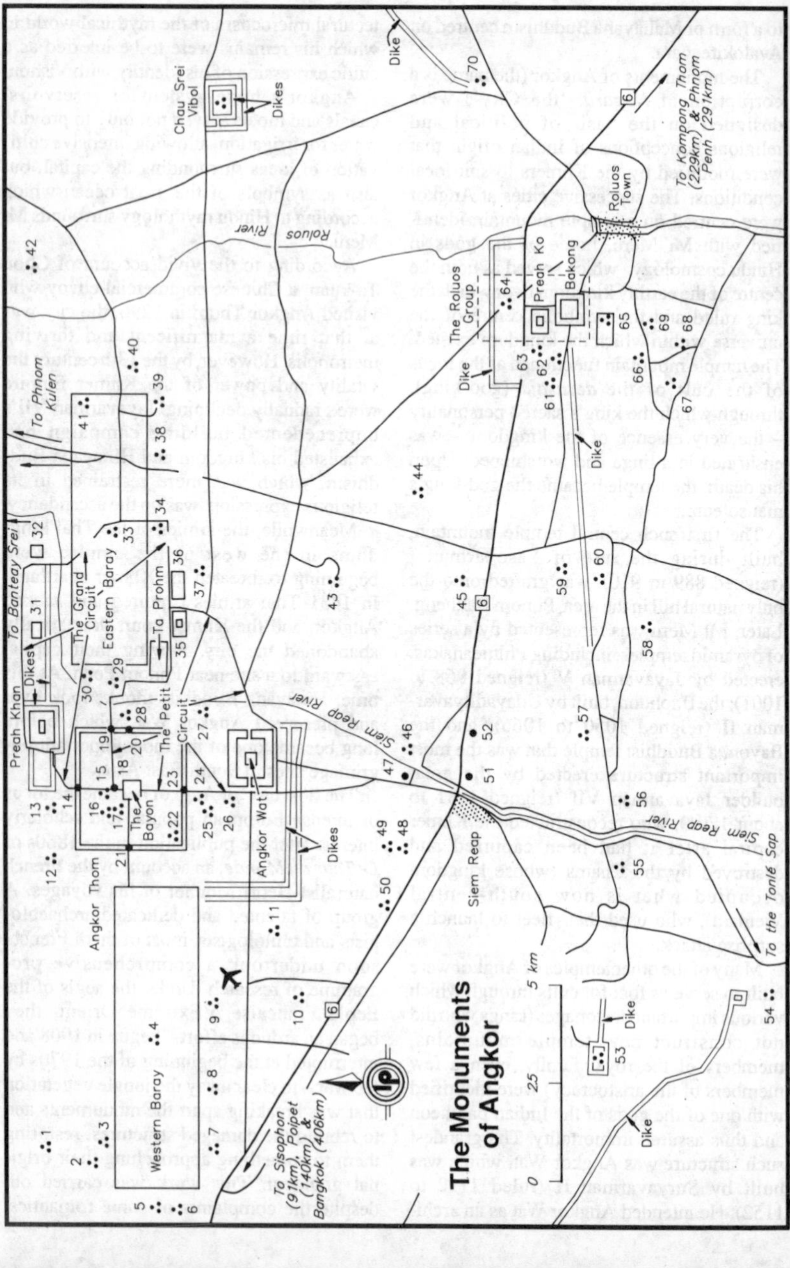
The Monuments of Angkor
0
5 km
Western Baray
Angkor Thom
The Bayon
Preah Khan
Dikes
To Banteay Srei
The Grand Circuit
Eastern Baray
To Phnom Kulen
Ta Prohm
The Petit Circuit
Siem Reap River
Angkor Wat
Chau Srei Vibol
Roluos River
The Roluos Group
Preah Ko
Bakong
Roluos Town
To Kompong Thom (229km) & Phnom Penh (291km)
Dike
Siem Reap
To the Tonlé Sap
To Sisophon (91km), Poipet (140km) & Bangkok (406km)
6
1 2 3 4 5 6 7 8 9 10 11 12 13 14 15 16 17 18 19 20 21 22 23 24 25 26 27 28 29 30 31 32 33 34 35 36 37 38 39 40 41 42 43 44 45 46 47 48 49 50 51 52 53 54 55 56 57 58 59 60 61 62 63 64 65 66 67 68 69 70

MAJOR SITES OF ANGKOR

4	Western Mebon
14	North Gate of Angkor Thom
15	Terrace of the Elephants
16	Phimeanakas
17	The Baphuon
18	Central Square of Angkor Thom
19	Victory Gate
20	East Gate of Angkor Thom
21	West Gate of Angkor Thom
22	Beng Thom
24	Baksei Chamkrong
25	Phnom Bakheng
28	Chau Say Tevoda
29	Ta Keo
30	Ta Nei
31	Preah Neak Pean
32	Ta Som
33	Eastern Mebon
34	Pre Rup
35	Banteay Kdei
36	Sras Srang
40	Banteay Samré
47	Angkor Conservation
51	Bayon Chinese Restaurant
52	Central Market
54	Phnom Krom
64	Lolei

MINOR MONUMENTS OF ANGKOR

1	Prasat Kok Po
2	Prasat Phnom Rung
3	Prasat Roluh
5	Prasat Trapeang Seng
6	Prei Kmeng
7	Ak Yom
8	Prasat Kas Ho
9	Prasat Ta Noreay
10	Prasat Prei
11	Prasat Trapeang Ropou
12	Prasat Prei
13	Prasat Tonlé Snguot
23	South Gate of Angkor Thom
26	Ta Prohm Kel
27	Kapilapura
37	Bat Chum
38	Prasat Komnap
39	Prei Prasat
41	Prasat To
42	Phnom Bok
43	Kuk Bangro
44	Kuk Taleh
45	Tram Neak
46	Preah Einkosei
48	Prasat Reach Kandal
49	Prasat Chak
50	Prasat Patri
53	Vat Chedei
55	Vat Athvea
56	Prasat Kuk O Chrung
57	Prasat Rsei
58	Prasat He Phka
59	Prasat Daun So
60	Prasat Kok Thlok
61	Prasat O Kaek
62	Prasat Olok
63	Prasat Kandal Doeum
65	Prasat Prei Monti
66	Svay Pream
67	Prasat Totoeng Thngai
68	Prasat Trapeang Phong
69	Kuk Dong
70	Vat Bangro

who preferred the mystery and romance imparted to the monuments by the thick jungle growth that was devouring them. As a response to the charges of this group, Ta Prohm Temple has been left in its original, wildly overgrown state.

Angkorian Monarchs

The following is a list of the kings who ruled the Khmer Empire from the 9th century to the 14th century:

King	Dates of Reign
Jayavarman II	802-850
Jayavarman III	850-877
Indravarman I	877-889
Yasovarman	889-910
Harshavarman I	910-?
Isanavarman II	?-928
Jayavarman IV	928-942
Harshavarman II	942-944
Rajendravarman	944-968
Jayavarman V	968-1001
Udayadityavarman	1001-1002
Suryavarman I	1002-1049
Udayadityavarman II	1049-1065
Harshavarman III	1065-1090
Jayavarman IV	1090-1108
Dharanindravarman	1108-1112
Suryavarman II	1112-1152
Harshavarman IV	1152?
Dharanindravarman II	1152-1181
Jayavarman VII	1181-1201 (approx)

Indravarman II	1201-1243 (approx)
Jayavarman VIII	1243-1295
Śri-Indravarman	1295-1307
Sri-Indrajayavarman	1307-?
Jayavarma Paramesvara	mid-1300s

Chronology

According to the latest research, the chronology of the major monuments of Angkor is as follows:

Preah Ko (at Roluos)	879
Bakong (at Roluos)	881
Lolei (at Roluos)	900 (approx)
Eastern Mebon	952
Pre Rup	961
Banteay Srei	967
Ta Keo	1000 (approx)
Baphuon	1060 (approx)
Angkor Wat	1st half of 1100s
Ta Prohm	1186
Preah Khan	1191
Bayon & the walls & gates of Angkor Thom	end of 1100s

Information

Fees Each visitor to Angkor is charged a fee of US$120, which theoretically consists of a US$60 charge to visit Angkor Wat and an identical fee to visit the Bayon. I have no idea how much of this money, if any, goes to help preserve the monuments. Angry complaints by tourists have prompted the General Directorate of Tourism in Phnom Penh to try to convince Angkor Tourism to reduce the fee.

Organised Tours The 1-day tours to Angkor run by Phnom Penh Tourism and sold by Saigon Tourist allow only 3 hours to see the temples because the afternoon flight back to Phnom Penh departs at 2 pm. Until flights are made more frequent, however, the only other option will be to spend 3 or 4 days in Siem Reap between flights.

What to See The three most magnificent temples at Angkor are the Bayon, which faces east and is best visited in the early morning; Ta Prohm, which is awesomely overgrown by the jungle; and Angkor Wat, which is the only monument here facing westward (it is at its finest in the late afternoon). If you've got the time, all these monuments are well worth several visits each. Angkor's major sites can be seen without undue pressure in 3 full days of touring.

In the old days, visitors used to follow two circuits to the monuments in the vicinity of Angkor. The 17 km Petit Circuit began at Angkor Wat, headed northward to Phnom Bakheng, Baksei Chamkrong and Angkor Thom (in which one visited the city wall and gates, the Bayon, the Baphuon, the Royal Enclosure, Phimeanakas, Preah Palilay, Tep Pranam, the Preah Pithu group, the Terrace of the Leper King, the Terrace of Elephants, the Central Square, the North Kleang, the South Kleang and the 12 Prasats Suor Prat), exited from Angkor Thom via Victory Gate (in the eastern wall), continued to Chau Say Tevoda, Thommanon, Spean Thma and Ta Keo, went north-east of the road to Ta Nei, turned southward to Ta Prohm, continued west to Banteay Kdei and the Sras Srang, and finally returned to Angkor Wat via Prasat Kravan.

The 26 km Grand Circuit began at Angkor Wat, exited Angkor Thom through the north gate, stopped at Preah Khan and Preah Neak Pean on its way eastward to Ta Som, then headed south via the Eastern Mebon to Pre Rup, whence it went westward and then south-westward back to Angkor Wat.

These days, the bridge over the Siem Reap River between the Victory Gate and Ta Keo is impassable to motor vehicles and many monuments, including Neak Pean and the Eastern Mebon, are closed to visitors. The Cambodian army has many hundreds of troops encamped around the monuments, and you're more likely to hear gunfire than the calls of jungle birds. Mines (including mines with filament trip wires), laid either by the Khmer Rouge or to blow up Khmer Rouge infiltrators, continue to be a problem, and quite a number of local people are injured and killed each year. *Do not stray from well-marked paths* and, until the war ends, check with the army to make sure that the trails to where you're going have not been booby-trapped.

Guidebooks For a listing of some of the better guidebooks to Angkor, see the Facts for the Visitor section. If you are serious about learning a bit about Angkorian religion, architecture and sculpture during your visit, I would highly recommend bringing along a double-sided photocopy of the best old guidebook you can find in a nearby public or university library.

Fauna The gibbons who used to live around Angkor have been shot by soldiers, for whom gibbon brain is a rare delicacy. Visitors should watch out for the dreaded Hanuman snake, a small but extremely venomous snake that can be instantly recognised by its bright light green colour. Stinging red ants are another pest, but the bats that live in the temples are harmless. Keep an eye out for tree frogs.

Between April and July, the jungle is often filled with the noise made by zillions of locust-like insects.

Flora Every gum tree around Angkor has a hole burnt into the base of the trunk. These are the result of the process by which resin, used for waterproofing boats, is extracted from the trees. Resin harvesters make a gash in the trunk and light a fire in it for a quarter of an hour or so. A week later, they return to take the resin that has collected.

Maps Quite a number of excellent maps of the Angkor area have been published over the years. One of the most useful appears in the May 1982 issue of *National Geographic* magazine, which you might want to bring along.

THE PETIT CIRCUIT
In the old dispute about whether one should visit Angkor Wat or Angkor Thom first, my preference is for the latter. The order in which the monuments inside Angkor Thom are listed makes for a nice circuit.

Angkor Thom
The fortified city of Angkor Thom, some 10 sq km in extent, was built in its present form by Angkor's greatest builder, Jayavarman VII (reigned 1181 to 1201), who came to power just after the disastrous sacking by the Chams of the previous Khmer capital, centred around the Baphuon. Angkor Thom, which may have had a million inhabitants (more than any European city of the period), is enclosed by a square wall 8 metres high and 12 km in length and encircled by a moat 100 metres wide said to have been inhabited by fierce crocodiles.

The city has five monumental gates, one each in the north, west and south walls and two in the east wall. The gates, which are 20 metres in height, are decorated to either side of the passageway with stone elephant trunks and crowned by four gargantuan faces of the bodhisattva Avalokiteçvara facing the cardinal directions. In front of each gate, there stood giant statues of 54 gods (to the left of the causeway) and 54 demons (to the right of the causeway), a motif taken from the story of the Churning of the Ocean of Milk illustrated in the famous bas-relief at Angkor Wat. In the centre of the walled enclosure are the city's most important monuments, including the Bayon, the Baphuon, the Royal Enclosure, Phimeanakas and the Terrace of Elephants.

The Bayon
The most outstanding feature of the Bayon, which was built by Jayavarman VII (reigned 1181 to 1201) in the exact centre of the city of Angkor Thom, is the eerie and unsettling 3rd level, with its 49 towers projecting 172 icily-smiling, gargantuan faces of Avalokitesvara. As you walk around, a dozen or more of the visages are visible at any one time – full-face or in profile, almost level with your eyes or peering down from on high – in an ever-changing phantasmagoria.

In addition, the Bayon is decorated with 1200 metres of extraordinary bas-reliefs incorporating over 11,000 figures. The famous carvings on the outer wall of the first level depict vivid scenes of everyday life in 12th century Cambodia.

The Bayon, which is 3.3 km north of Angkor Wat and 9.7 km from the Grand

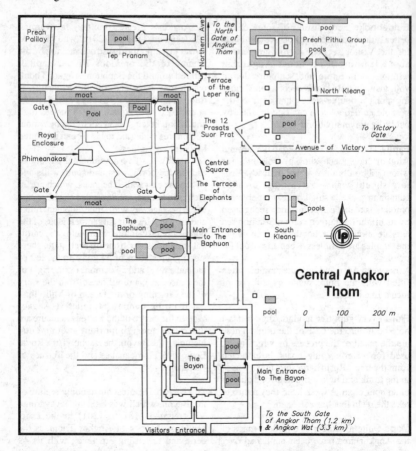

Central Angkor Thom

Hotel d'Angkor, is best visited in the early morning, especially shortly after dawn, when the trees that surround the Bayon are shrouded in mist and the air is filled with the sounds of birds and giant dew drops falling from the treetops and bursting on the vegetation of the jungle floor. As the sun comes up, sunlight first hits the tip of the central tower and then moves down the monument to illuminate, at various angles, face after face after face. Before the war, people used to camp out here under the full moon. Polish experts are helping preserve the Bayon.

The Bayon, which is made of sandstone,

was originally planned and built as a two level structure dedicated to the worship of Shiva. At some point after its construction, it was decided that the Bayon would become a Mahayana Buddhist temple, and a 3rd level was rather haphazardly superimposed on the 2nd, creating an awkward 2nd level characterised by narrow courtyards, truncated galleries and stone panels facing each other only 60 cm apart. Some of the Buddhas decorating the Bayon were subsequently recarved into bunches of flowers or removed altogether when Hinduism was again in the ascendancy.

The interior of the wall enclosing the 2nd level is covered with bas-reliefs of Hindu myths. There are several rooms, empty except for the bats who live there, inside the central tower on the 3rd level.

Highlights of the bas-reliefs on the outer face of the wall around the first level include the following, listed in the order you would come to them if beginning at the south gate and walking with the wall to your left, as Khmer custom dictates:

A) On the first panel to the east of the south gate, you can see meals being prepared and served, a pig about to be dropped into a cauldron and, in the trees overhead, frolicking monkeys. In the next scene, Cham warriors (with headdresses) face off against Khmer soldiers. Farther along, there are scenes of two people playing chess, two boars being prodded to fight each other, women selling fish in the market and gossiping, and a cock fight.

B) About 1.5 metres east of the doorway a woman is giving birth; 4 metres east of the door, people are picking lice out of their hair; and 6 metres east of the door, Cham and Khmer ships are engaged in battle

while below a crocodile and a pelican are each eating a fish. On the south wall in the south-east corner of the mural is a pirogue (a type of long canoe).

C) The first panel north of the south-east corner shows Hindus praying to a linga.

D) Just south of the east gate is a three level panorama. On the 1st tier, Khmer soldiers march off to battle; notice the elephants and the ox carts, which are almost exactly like those still in use. The 2nd tier depicts the coffins of the dead being carried from the battlefield. In the centre of the 3rd tier, Jayavarman VII, shaded by parasols, is shown on horseback followed by legions of concubines (to the left).

E) The three tiered battle scene here depicts Khmer troops (hatless and with slicked-back hair; on the left) facing Cham troops (on the right). On the lowest tier, dead and wounded soldiers are pictured at the feet of their marching comrades. In the middle of the scene, where the two armies meet, a Cham soldier (with a headdress) is cutting off a Khmer soldier's foot; at his feet is a severed head.

F) Another meeting of two armies. Notice the flag-bearers among the Cham troops (on the right). The Chams were defeated in the war depicted on panels D and E, which ended in 1181.

G) This panel shows the war of 1177, when the Khmers were defeated by the Chams and Angkor

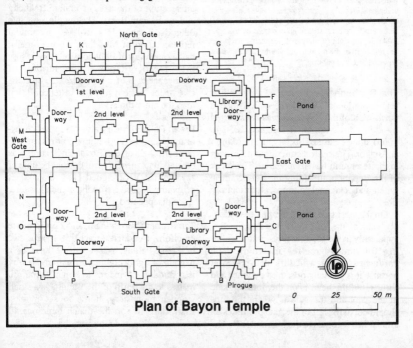

Plan of Bayon Temple

itself was pillaged. The wounded Khmer king is being lowered from the back of an elephant and a wounded Khmer general is being carried on a hammock suspended from a pole. Directly above, despairing Khmers are getting drunk. The Chams (on the right) are in hot pursuit of their vanquished enemy.

H) This badly deteriorated panel shows the Chams (on the left) chasing the Khmers.

I) The Cham armies are shown advancing.

J) On the lowest level of this unfinished three tier scene, the Cham armies are being defeated and expelled from the Khmer kingdom.

K) The two rivers, one next to the doorpost and the other 3 metres to the right, are teeming with fish.

L) At the western corner of the north wall is a Khmer circus. You can see a strong man holding three dwarfs and a man on his back spinning a wheel with his feet; above, there is a group of tightrope walkers. To the right of the circus, the royal court watches the goings on from a terrace, below which a procession of animals is marching. Some of the sculptures in this section remain unfinished.

M) At the far right of this panel at the bottom, an antelope is being swallowed by a gargantuan fish. Among the smaller fish is a prawn.

N) A bit to the right of the centre of the 3rd tier (of four), the heads of two traitorous Khmer generals are being held aloft.

O) Slightly to the right of the centre of the panel, Brahmins have been chased up two trees by tigers.

P) At the far right of the panel, elephants are being brought in from the mountains. Nearby, a man with a bow and arrow is hunting.

The Baphuon The Baphuon, a pyramidal representation of Mt Meru, is 200 metres north-west of the Bayon. It was constructed by Udayadityavarman II (reigned 1050 to 1066) at the centre of his city, the third built at Angkor. The central structure is 43 metres high; its summit has disappeared. The decor of the Baphuon, including the door frames, lintels and octagonal columns, is particularly fine.

On the west side of the temple, the retaining wall of the 2nd level was fashioned – apparently in the 15th century – into a reclining Buddha 40 metres in length. The unfinished figure is a bit difficult to make out because it is partially obscured by vines and shrubs, but the head is on the northern side of the wall and the gate is where the hips should be; to the left of the gate protrudes an arm. When it comes to the legs and feet – the latter are entirely gone – imagination must suffice.

The Royal Enclosure & Phimeanakas The Royal Enclosure, built by Jayavarman V (reigned 968 to 1001) is bounded on three sides by walls and to the east by the Terrace of the Elephants.

The gate to the Royal Enclosure nearest the Bayon is 150 metres east-north-east of the Baphuon and 200 metres due north of the Bayon. The enclosure, where innumerable wooden buildings once stood, has been wholly reclaimed by the jungle. Near the northern wall are two sandstone pools. Once bathed in by the king, they are now used as swimming holes by local children.

Phimeanakas (the name is a Khmer form of two Sanskrit words, *vimana akasa*, meaning 'celestial palace') was built by Rajendravarman (reigned 944 to 968), who returned the Khmer capital to Angkor from Koh Ker, 100 km to the north-east. It is at the intersection of the axes of Phnom Bakheng and the Eastern Baray. The temple, now in a dilapidated state, is a tri-level, pyramidal representation of Mt Meru. At one time, it had a sanctuary of light construction on top; the present chapel at the summit of Phimeanakas is of a later period. The staircase on the western side is in better condition than the other three.

Preah Palilay Preah Palilay, a rather deteriorated temple 200 metres north of the northern wall of the Royal Enclosure, was erected in its present form during the time of Jayavarman VII (reigned 1181 to 1201). It originally housed a Buddha, which has long since disappeared.

Tep Pranam Tep Pranam, an 82 by 34 metre cruciform Buddhist terrace 150 metres east of Preah Palilay, was once the base of a pagoda of lightweight construction. Nearby is a Buddha 4.5 metres in height; about 30 metres to the north of the Buddha is a small wooden monastery, home to six monks. Eight nuns live in the thatch buildings 40 metres north-east of the Buddha.

The Preah Pithu Group Preah Pithu, which is across the Northern Avenue from Tep Pranam, is a group of five 12th century Hindu and Buddhist temples enclosed by a wall.

The Terrace of the Leper King The Terrace of the Leper King, just north of the Terrace of Elephants, is a platform 7 metres in height on top of which stands a nude (though sexless) statue (actually a copy – the original has been removed for safekeeping). The figure, possibly of Shiva, is believed by the locals to be of Yasovarman, founder of Angkor, whom legend says died of leprosy. The front retaining walls are decorated with five or more tiers of meticulously executed carvings of seated *apsaras* (shapely dancing women); other figures include kings wearing pointed diadems, armed with short double-edged swords and accompanied by the court and princesses, who are adorned with rows of pearls. The terrace, built at the end of the 12th century (between the construction of Angkor Wat and that of the Bayon) once supported a pavilion made of lightweight materials.

On the south side of the Terrace of the Leper King (facing the Terrace of Elephants) there is an entryway to a long, narrow trench, excavated by archaeologists. This passageway follows the front wall of an earlier terrace that was covered up when the present structure was built. The four tiers of *apsaras* and other figures, including *nagas* (five, seven, nine or even eleven headed snakes), look as fresh as if they had been carved just yesterday.

The Terrace of Elephants The 350 metre long Terrace of Elephants was used as a giant reviewing stand for public ceremonies and served as a base for the king's grand audience hall. As you stand here, try to imagine the pomp and grandeur of the Khmer Empire at its height, with infantry, cavalry, horse-drawn chariots and elephants parading across the Central Square in a colourful procession, pennants and standards aloft. Looking on is the god-king, a gold diadem on his head, shaded by multi-tiered parasols and attended by mandarins and handmaidens bearing gold and silver utensils.

The Terrace of Elephants has five outworks extending towards the Central Square, three in the centre and one at each end. The middle section of the retaining wall is decorated with human-size garudas and lions; towards either end are the two parts of the famous parade of elephants.

The Kleangs & the 12 Prasats Suor Prat
Along the east side of the Central Square are two groups of buildings, the North Kleang and the South Kleang, that may at one time have been palaces. The North Kleang dates from the period of Jayavarman V (reigned 968 to 1001).

Along the Central Square in front of the two Kleangs are 12 laterite towers – 10 in a row and two more at right angles facing the Avenue of Victory – known as the Prasats Suor Prat. Archaeologists believe the towers, which form an honour guard of sorts along the Central Square, were constructed by Jayavarman VII (reigned 1181 to 1201). It is likely that each once contained either a linga or a statue.

Baksei Chamkrong
Located a bit south-west of the south gate of Angkor Thom, Baksei Chamkrong is one of the only brick edifices in the immediate vicinity of Angkor. It was once decorated with a covering of mortar of lime. Like virtually all the structures of Angkor, it opens to the east. In the early 10th century, Harshavarman I erected in this temple five statues: two of Shiva, one of Vishnu and two more of Devi.

Phnom Bakheng
Phnom Bakheng, also known as Indradri (Mountain of Indra), served as the temple mountain of the first city of Angkor, Yasodharapura, the capital built by Yasovarman (reigned 889 to 910). This 65 metre high hill, 400 metres south of the south gate of Angkor Thom, offers a panoramic view of Angkor Thom, Angkor Wat and surrounding

areas. The view is best just before sunset. The summit was once accessed by four staircases; today, the northern one is in the best condition. There is also a path up the hill.

Angkor Wat

Angkor Wat, with its soaring towers and extraordinary bas-reliefs, is considered by many to be one of the most inspired and spectacular monuments ever conceived by the human mind. It was built by Suryavarman II (reigned 1112 to 1152) to honour Vishnu (with whom he, as god-king, was identified) and for later use as his funerary temple. Angkor Wat, which is 6.4 km north of the Grand Hotel d'Angkor, is the only monument in the area that faces westward. There is a refreshment stand opposite the main entrance.

After the Khmers moved their capital to the Phnom Penh area in the mid-15th century, Angkor Wat was inhabited by Buddhist monks, who protected the monument from pillage and the ravages of encroaching vegetation. Today, there are two pagodas inside the complex, one south of the main

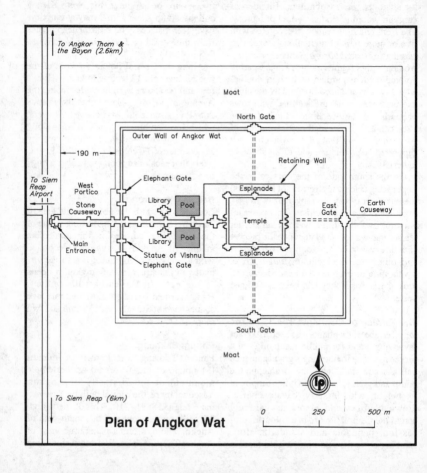

Plan of Angkor Wat

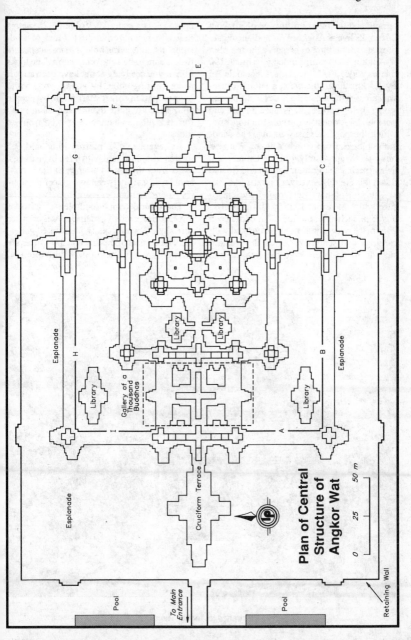

Plan of Central Structure of Angkor Wat

0   25   50 m

Cruciform Terrace

To Main Entrance

Pool

Pool

Retaining Wall

Esplanade

Esplanade

Esplanade

Library

Library

Library

Library

Gallery of a Thousand Buddhas

A

B

C

D

E

F

G

H

I

temple and the other north-west of it; about 20 monks live at Angkor Wat. Indian archaeologists are helping to preserve the temple.

Angkor Wat is surrounded by a moat, 190 metres wide, that forms a giant rectangle 1.5 by 1.3 km. From the west, a laterite causeway crosses the moat; the holes in the paving stones held wooden pegs used to lift and position the stones during construction, after which the pegs were sawed off. The sandstone blocks from which Angkor Wat was built were apparently quarried many km away (perhaps at Phnom Kulen) and floated down the Siem Reap River on rafts.

The rectangular wall around the enclosure, which measures 1025 by 800 metre, has a gate in each side, but the main entrance, a 235 metre wide porch richly decorated with carvings and sculptures, is on the western side. In the gate tower to the right as you

approach is a statue of Vishnu, 3.25 metres in height, hewn from a single block of sandstone; its eight arms hold a mace, a spear, a disk, a conch shell and other items. The locks of hair you see lying about have been cut off as an offering either by young women and men preparing to get married or by people who seek to give thanks for their good fortune (such as having recovered from an illness).

An avenue, 475 metres long and 9.5 metres wide and lined with *naga* balustrades, leads from the main entrance to the central temple, passing between two graceful galleries – perhaps libraries – and then two pools.

The central temple complex consists of three stories, each of which encloses a square surrounded by intricately interlinked galleries. The corners of the 2nd and 3rd stories are marked by towers topped with pointed

Entrance to Angkor Thom

cupolas. Rising 31 metres above the 3rd level and 55 metres above the ground is the central tower, which gives the whole ensemble its sublime unity. At one time, the central sanctuary of Angkor Wat held a gold statue of Vishnu mounted on a winged Garuda representing the deified god-king Suryavarman II.

Stretching around the outside of the central temple complex, which is enclosed by an esplanade framed by a naga balustrade, is an 800 metre long series of extraordinary bas-reliefs. The carvings were once sheltered by the cloister's wooden roof, which long ago rotted away (except for one original beam in the western half of the northern gallery; the other roofed sections are reconstructions). The following is a brief description of the epic events depicted on the panels, which are listed in the order you'll come to them if you walk beginning on the west side and keeping the bas-reliefs to your left (as is proper according to Khmer tradition):

A) The southern portion of the west gallery depicts a battle scene from the Hindu Mahabarata epic in which the Kauravas (coming from the north) and the Pandavas (coming from the south) advance in serried ranks towards each other, meeting in furious battle. Infantry are shown on the lowest tier, officers on elephant-back and chiefs on the 2nd and 3rd tiers. Among the more interesting details (from left to right): a dead chief lying on a pile of arrows and surrounded by his grieving parents and troops; a warrior on an elephant who has, by putting down his weapon, accepted defeat; and a mortally wounded officer, falling from the conveyance in which he is riding into the arms of his soldiers. Over the centuries, some sections have been polished by millions of hands to look like black marble.

The portico at the south-west corner is decorated with sculptures representing subjects taken from the Ramayana.

B) The remarkable western section of the south gallery depicts scenes from Khmer history; it includes inscriptions identifying the people pictured. In the south-west corner about 2 metres from the floor is Suryavarman II mounted on an elephant, wearing the royal tiara and armed with a battle-axe; he is shaded by 15 umbrellas and fanned by legions of servants. Farther on is a procession of well-armed soldiers and officers on horseback; among them march elephants carrying their chiefs, whose bearing is bold and warlike. Just west of the vestibule is the rather disorderly Thai mercenary army, at that time allied with the Khmers in their conflict with the Chams. While the Khmer troops have square breastplates and are armed with spears, the Thais wear headdresses and skirts and carry tridents.

The rectangular holes in the carving were created when, long ago, pieces of the scene – reputed to have magical powers – were removed. Part of this panel was damaged by an artillery shell in 1971.

C) The eastern half of the south gallery, the ceiling of which was restored in the 1930s, depicts the punishments and rewards of the 37 heavens and 32 hells. On the left, the upper and middle tiers show fine gentlemen and ladies proceeding towards 18 armed Yama, judge of the dead, seated on a bull; below him are his assistants, Dharma and Sitragupta. On the lower tier is the road to hell, along which wicked people are being dragged by devils. To Yama's right, the tableau is divided into two parts separated by a horizontal line of Garudas: above, the elect dwell in beautiful mansions, served by women, children and attendants; below, the condemned suffer horrible tortures.

D) The south section of the east gallery is decorated by the most famous of the bas-relief scenes at Angkor Wat, the Churning of the Ocean of Milk (in French: le Barattement de L'Océan de Lait). This brilliantly executed carving depicts 88 Asuras (devils; on the left) and 92 Devas (gods) with crested helmets (on the right), churning up the sea in order to extract the elixir of immortality, which both groups covet. The extraction is being accomplished by rotating the immense serpent Vasuki, who is entwined around Mt Mandara (in the centre, resting on a turtle). Vishnu, on the side of the mountain, is assisting the whole process; on top stands Indra, surveying the proceedings. Other figures watching the churning include Shiva, Brahma, the ape Hanuman and many agitated fish and sea-monsters. Above, Apsaras gracefully dance in the heavens.

E) This gate, which has no stairs leading up to it, was used by the king and others for mounting and dismounting elephants directly from the gallery. North of the gate is a Khmer inscription recording the erection of a nearby stupa in the 18th century.

F) The unfinished northern section of the east gallery shows a furious and desperate encounter between Vishnu, riding on a garuda, and innumerable demons (the Danavas).

G) The unfinished eastern section of the north gallery shows Krishna arriving in front of Sonitapura, residence of Bana, who has ravished Aniruddha. His way is blocked by a wall of fire, which is extinguished by Garuda. Bana is defeated and captured, but Shiva (haloed and bearing a trident) intervenes on his behalf and Krishna spares his life.

H) The western section of the north gallery depicts the battle of the Devas and the Daityas, which ends in a duel between Vishnu and Kalameni. All the major gods of the Brahmanic pantheon are shown with their traditional attributes and mounts.

I) The northern half of the west gallery show scenes from the Ramayana. In the Battle of Lanka, Rama (on the shoulders of the monkey-god Hanuman) along with his army of monkeys battles 10 headed Ravana, seducer of Rama's beautiful wife Sita. Ravana rides on a chariot drawn by monsters and commands an army of giants.

Prasat Kravan

The five brick towers of Prasat Kravan, which are arranged in a north-south line and oriented to the east, were built for Hindu worship in 921. Prasat Kravan is just south of the road between Angkor Wat and Banteay Kdei. It was partially restored in 1968.

Banteay Kdei & the Sras Srang

Banteay Kdei, a massive Buddhist temple of the second half of the 12th century, is surrounded by four concentric walls. The outer wall measures 500 by 700 metres; each of its four entrances is decorated with garudas and holds aloft one of Jayavarman VII's favourite themes, the four visages of Avalokitesvara. The inside of the central tower was never finished.

Just east of Banteay Kdei is a basin of earlier construction, Sras Srang (Pool of Ablutions), 800 by 400 metres. A tiny island in the middle once bore a wood temple, of which only the stone base remains.

There is a mass grave of hundreds of victims of the Khmer Rouge a bit north of Sras Srang on the other side of the road. It is marked by a wooden memorial.

Ta Prohm

Ta Phrom was built as a Buddhist temple during the 12th century. Under Jayavarman VII (late 12th C), 18 high priests and 2740 ordinary priests officiated here. Of the 12,640 people entitled to lodgings within the enclosure, 615 were choristers who participated in the rituals.

One of the largest Khmer edifices of the Angkorian period, Ta Prohm has been left just as it looked when the first French explorers set eyes on it over a century ago. Whereas the other major monuments of Angkor have been preserved and made suitable for scholarly research by a massive programme to clear away the all-devouring jungle, this Buddhist temple has been left to its fate of inexorable, arboreous ruination. Ta Prohm, its friezes enmeshed in tendrilous nets, its stones slowly being pried asunder by the roots of the huge trees rising from its galleries and towers, stands as a monument to the awesome fecundity and power of the jungle. It is not to be missed.

Courtyards and cloisters are impassable, clogged with jumbled piles of delicately carved stone blocks dislodged by the roots of long-decayed trees. Bas-reliefs on bulging walls are carpeted by a dozen different kinds of lichens, mosses and creeping plants, and shrubs sprout from the roofs of monumental porches. Trees, hundreds of years old – some supported with flying buttresses – tower overhead, their leaves filtering the sunlight and casting a greenish pall over the whole scene.

More than the rustling of leaves accompanies the visitor to Ta Prohm: birds chatter invisibly overhead and crickets chirp to each other among the mimosa plants; nearby, butterflies flutter about silently and giant spiders noiselessly stalk their prey. Occasionally, you glimpse a tree frog hopping from one fallen lintel to another or a bat flying erratically towards its refuge in some dark, tomblike recess of the temple. Inaudible over the jungle noises are the munch-munch-munch of termites and the march of stinging red ants in search of food. And all the while, unseen, the bright green Hanuman snake slithers silently, stealthily between the stones.

The mystery of the jungle mingles with the mystery of the ancient galleries and halls. Scenes of Indiana Jones making some near escape from the Temple of Doom may pop to mind, bringing to consciousness the nightmarish thought that somehow, the jungle will reach out and grab you, twisting its vines around your neck just as it has done to the *apsaras* lying corpselike nearby.

Visitors may want to equip themselves with a compass. There are narrow, over-

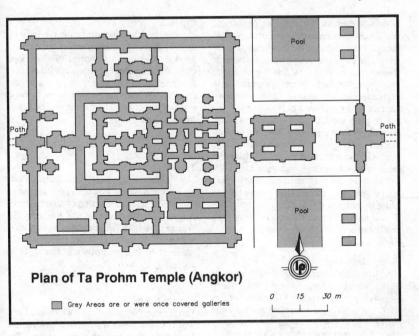

Plan of Ta Prohm Temple (Angkor)

Grey Areas are or were once covered galleries

0   15   30 m

grown paths into the complex from the east and the west.

Ta Keo

Ta Keo, built by Jayavarman V (reigned 968 to 1001), was dedicated to the worship of Shiva and was the first Angkorian monument constructed entirely in sandstone. The summit of the central tower, which is surrounded by four lower towers, is over 50 metres high. The process of decorating Ta Keo's particularly hard sandstone was never completed.

Ta Nei

Ta Nei, 800 metres north of Ta Keo near the north-west corner of the Eastern Baray, was built by Jayavarman VII (reigned 1181 to 1201).

Spean Thma

The bridge of Spean Thma (the name means stone bridge), of which an arch and several piers remain, is 200 metres east of Thommanon. It was one of the latest structures constructed by the last great builder of Angkor, Jayavarman VII (ruled 1181 to 1201) and is the only large bridge in the vicinity of Angkor of which anything remains.

Chau Say Tevoda & Thommanon

Chau Say Tevoda, which is south of the road, and Thommanon, which is north of it, were probably built during the second quarter of the 12th century and dedicated to Shiva and Vishnu.

THE GRAND CIRCUIT
Preah Khan

The great temple of Preah Khan (Sacred Sword), which is 3.3 km from the Bayon and about 1.5 km north-east of the northern gate of Angkor Thom, was built by Jayavarman VII (ruled 1181 to 1201) in the late 12th century. This rarely visited monument, which is surrounded by four concentric walls, is in an excellent state of preservation, though since 1972 the area has become overgrown by vines and young trees. Most of the friezes and carvings, which depict Hindu epics and deities, were systematically effaced centuries ago in an assertion of supremacy by partisans of Buddhism.

The gates are decorated with scenes of the Churning of the Sea of Milk. Inside the bat-infested central tower, from which four long, vaulted galleries extend in the cardinal directions, is a tomb, perhaps of Jayavarman VII's father. Many of the interior walls of Preah Khan were once coated with plaster held in place by holes in the stone.

Just north of Preah Khan is Banteay Prei, which dates from the same period.

Preah Neak Pean

The late 12th century Buddhist temple of Preah Neak Pean (Intertwined Naga), which was built by Jayavarman VII (ruled 1181 to 1201), stands in the exact centre of a huge basin (3 km by 900 metres) that apparently constituted part of the Preah Khan complex. The basin was used for rites of ritual purification. The temple is closed to visitors.

Ta Som

Ta Som, which stands to the east of Preah Neak Pean, is yet another of the late-12th century Buddhist temples of Jayavarman VII. Much of Ta Som is in a ruined state.

The Eastern Baray & the Eastern Mebon

The enormous one-time reservoir known as the Eastern Baray (Baray Oriental) was excavated by Yasovarman (reigned 889 to 910), who marked its four corners with steles. This basin, the most important of the public works of Yasodharapura, Yasovarman's capital, is 7 by 1.8 km. It was fed by the Siem Reap River.

The five elaborate brick shrines known as the Eastern Mebon, erected by Rajendravarman (ruled 944 to 968), are on an islet in the centre of the Eastern Baray. This Hindu temple is presently off-limits.

Pre Rup

Pre Rup, built by Rajendravarman (ruled 944 to 968), is about 1.5 km south of the Eastern Mebon. The various shrines of Pre Rup, including a number of brick sanctuaries once decorated with a plaster coating (of which fragments remain on the south-west tower), stand on three tiers. There are some fine lintel carvings here.

OTHER AREAS
The Western Baray

The Western Baray (Baray Occidental), 8 km by 2.3 km, was excavated to provide water for the intensive cultivation of lands around Angkor. In the centre of the basin is the Western Mebon, where the giant bronze statue of Vishnu, now in the National Museum in Phnom Penh was found. It is accessible by boat.

Phnom Krom

The temple of Phnom Krom, which is 12 km south of Siem Reap on a hill overlooking the Tonlé Sap, dates from the 11th century. The three towers, dedicated (from north to south) to Vishnu, Shiva and Brahma, are in a ruined state. The ferry from Phnom Penh and Kompong Chhnang docks near here.

Banteay Samré

Banteay Samré, 400 metres east of the southeast corner of the Eastern Baray, was built in the third quarter of the 12th century. It consists of a central temple with four wings preceded by a hall and accompanied by two libraries, the southern of which is remarkably well-preserved. The ensemble is enclosed by two concentric walls.

The road to Banteay Samré can be driven by high-bodied vehicles only.

Banteay Srei

Banteay Srei, which is 21 km north-east of the Bayon and 8 km west of Phnom Kulen, was built by Jayavarman V (ruled 968 to

1001) and dedicated to Shiva. This large monument, considered by many to be the most perfect of Khmer temples, is famous for its exquisite carvings executed in pink sandstone.

The road from Siem Reap to Banteay Srei is passable by high-bodied vehicles only.

Phnom Kulen

The sheer walls of Phnom Kulen, which is some 28 km north-east of the Bayon, rise to an elevation of 461 metres.

Beng Mealea

The 12th century temple of Beng Mealea is about 40 km east of the Bayon (as the crow flies) and 6.5 km south-east of Phnom Kulen. Its ruined state is probably the result of civil strife or wars with the Thais. Beng Mealea is enclosed by a moat measuring 1200 by 900 metres.

THE ROLUOS GROUP រលួស

The monuments of Roluos, which served as the capital of Indravarman I (reigned 877 to 889), are among the earliest large, permanent temples built by the Khmers and mark the beginning of Khmer classical art. Before the construction of Roluos, only lighter (and non-durable) construction materials had been employed, even for religious structures.

Preah Ko

Preah Ko was erected by Indravarman I in the late 9th century. The six brick towers (*prasats*), aligned in two rows and decorated with carved sandstone and plaster reliefs, face eastward; the central tower of the front row is larger than the others. There are inscriptions in Sanskrit on the doorposts of each temple.

The temples of Preah Ko (Sacred Oxen, so named for the three statues of Nandin that

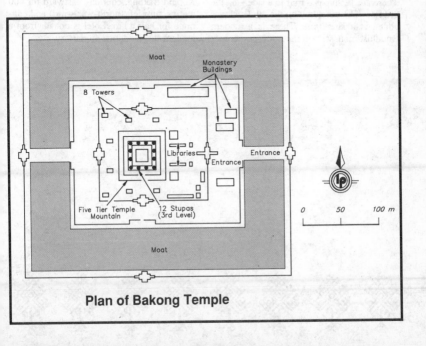

Plan of Bakong Temple

once stood in front of the first row of temples) were dedicated by Indravarman I to his deified ancestors on 29 January 880.

Bakong

Bakong, which was built and dedicated to Shiva by Indravarman I, played the same role for his capital of Hariharalaya as did Phnom Bakheng for Yasovarman's Angkor. That is, it was built as a representation of Mt Meru and as such served as the city's central temple. The eastward-facing complex consists of a five tier central pyramid of sandstone, 60 metres square at the base, flanked by eight towers of brick and sandstone (or what's left of them) and other minor sanctuaries. Several of the eight towers down below are still partly covered with their original plasterwork. The complex is enclosed by three concentric walls and a broad moat. Note the stone elephants on each corner of the first three levels of the central temple. There are 12 stupas – four to a side – on the 3rd tier. The sanctuary on the 5th level was added at a later time. There is a modern Buddhist monastery at the north-east corner of the area between the middle and inner walls.

Lolei

The four brick towers of Lolei, which are an almost exact replica of the towers of Preah Ko, were built on an islet in the centre of a large reservoir – now rice fields – by Yasovarman (ruled 889 to 910), the founder of the first city at Angkor. The sandstone carvings in the niches of the temples are worth a look. According to an inscription, the four towers were dedicated by Yasovarman to his mother, his father and his grandparents on his mother's side on 12 July 893.

Getting There & Away

The Roluos Group is 13 km east of Siem Reap along National Route 6. Preah Ko is 600 metres south of National Route 6 (to the right as you head away from Siem Reap); Bakong is 1.5 km south of National Route 6.

To get to Lolei from the turnoff to Preah Ko and Bakong, continue eastward for 400 metres, turn left (north-westward) and continue for half a km. Lolei is not far from a modern-day Buddhist monastery.

Around Cambodia

The South Coast

KAMPOT កំពត
The pretty riverine town of Kampot (population 14,000) is on the Tuk Chhou River (also called the Prek Thom River) 5 km from the sea. Although many buildings in town were damaged by the Khmer Rouge, Kampot retains much of its charm. There are plans to develop an infrastructure for tourism here.

Durian haters beware: Kampot Province is Cambodia's most important durian producing region.

Information
Post The GPO is along the river near the Kampot Province Hotel. There is supposed to be a telephone link between Kampot and Phnom Penh.

To Chu Falls
The To Chu Falls are just north of Kampot towards the hills.

Places to Stay
Hotels include the *Phnom Kamchai Hotel* and the *Phnom Khieu Hotel* (Blue Mountain Hotel) near the central plaza and the *Kampot Province Hotel* on the river.

Places to Eat
There are food stalls in the main market and elsewhere around town.

Getting There & Away
The 148 km drive from Phnom Penh to Kampot along National Route 3 now takes 5 hours because of the road's dilapidated state (25 years ago it took only 2½ hours). The roads around Kampot are in extremely poor condition.

BOKOR HILL STATION ស្ថានីយ៍ភ្នំបូកគោ
The mountain-top hill station of Bokor (elevation 1080 metres) is famous for its pleasant climate, rushing streams, forested vistas and stunning panoramas of the sea. The best time of year to visit Bokor, which is in the Elephant Mountains, is between November and May.

There are plans to redevelop Bokor, which has been virtually abandoned since the mid-1970s

Getting There & Away
Bokor is 41 km from Kampot and 190 km from Phnom Penh. The access road is in very bad condition.

POPOKVIL FALLS ទឹកជ្រោះពពកវិល
The two waterfalls of Popokvil, 14 and 18 metres high, are not far from the access road to Bokor Hill Station.

KEP កែប
The seaside resort of Kep (Kep-sur-Mer), with its 6 km palm-shaded corniche, was once a favourite vacation spot for Cambodia's Frenchified elite, who flocked here to enjoy such pursuits as yachting, gambling, underwater fishing, water skiing and skin diving. Under the Khmer Rouge, the town (founded in 1908) and its many villas were completely destroyed – not neglected and left to dilapidate, but intentionally turned into utter ruins. The Khmer Rouge also turned the underground petrol tank of the old Shell station into a mass grave. By 1979, not a single building remained intact in Kep.

Although there are plans to rebuild Kep and re-establish it as a beach resort, at present it is a ghost town with no hotels or other tourist facilities.

Kep is subject to the south-west monsoon. The best time of year to visit Kep is from the end of October to the end of June.

Getting There & Away

If you take the train, get off at the Damnak Chang Aeu Railway Station, which is a few km from Kep. By road, Kep is 24 km south-east of Kampot and 49 km from the Vietnamese town of Ha Tien. There is a border crossing 8 km north of Ha Tien, but it is not presently open for foreigners.

KIRIROM គីរីរម្យ

The hill station of Kirirom, set amidst pine forests 675 metres above sea level, is 112 km south-west of Phnom Penh. It is in the Elephant Mountains to the west of National Route 4.

KOMPONG SOM កំពង់សោម

Kompong Som (formerly Sihanoukville), Cambodia's only maritime port, had a population of 16,000 in the mid-1960s and probably has the same population now. Near town there are superb beaches and, for skin diving enthusiasts, shoals and reefs teeming with multicoloured fish.

Ream

The town of Ream, the country's most important harbour on the Gulf of Thailand before the construction of Kompong Son, is at the southern tip of the Kompong Som Peninsula.

Getting There & Away

Kompong Som is 232 km from Phnom Penh via one of the best roads in the country, National Route 4. When the rail line is open, Kompong Som can also be reached from the capital by train. The road from Kampot to Kompong Som is in very bad condition.

A Soviet-built airfield near Kompong Som opened in late 1983.

KOH KONG កោះកុង

The beautiful island of Koh Kong, in the Gulf of Thailand just off the western coast of Koh Kong Province, is only a few dozen km from Thailand and has become a centre for smuggling Thai and Singaporean consumer goods into Cambodia. There are plans to develop tourism on Koh Kong, which is only

80 km south-east of Thailand's island of Ko Chang.

Koh Kong Province, which like neighbouring Kampot Province is blessed with innumerable offshore islands of all sizes, can be reached by chartered plane from Phnom Penh and by boat from Kompong Som.

Central Cambodia

KOMPONG CHHNANG កំពង់ឆ្នាំង

Kompong Chhnang (population 15,000) is an important fishing and transportation centre on the Tonlé Sap. The area is known for its pottery.

Getting There & Away

Land distances from Kompong Chhnang:

Phnom Penh	90 km
Battambang	185 km
Poipet (Thai border)	331 km
Pursat	97 km
Sisophon	282 km

Kompong Chhnang is served by riverboats departing from the Psar Cha Ministry of Transport Ferry Landing in the capital. The ferries leave Phnom Penh at 8 am and arrive in Kompong Chhnang around 4 pm.

PURSAT

The provincial capital of Pursat had a population of 16,000 in the mid-1960s.

Getting There & Away

Land distances from Pursat:

Phnom Penh	187 km
Battambang	105 km
Kompong Chhnang	202 km
Poipet (Thai border)	234 km
Sisophon	185 km

Pursat is on the Phnom Penh-Battambang railway line.

KOMPONG CHAM កំពង់ចាម

Archaeological sites around Kompong Cham (population 30,000 in the mid-1960s) include the following:

1) Wat Nokor (2 km from town), an 11th century Mahayana Buddhist shrine of sandstone and laterite, was reconsecrated for Hinayana worship in the 15th century.
2) The hills of Phnom Pros and Phnom Srei (35 km north-west of town) offer superb views of the area. At the base of Phnom Pros there are five mass graves in which thousands of people killed by the Khmer Rouge were buried.
3) Preah Theat Preah Srei (south of Kompong Cham), capital of Chenla during the 8th century, was seized by a Srivijayan (Sumatran) fleet in 802.
4) Prey Nokor (38 km from town), to the south-east, was a Khmer capital during the 6th or 7th centuries. The outer wall encloses a vast area at the centre of which are two square sanctuaries.

There are a number of rubber plantations in the vicinity of Kompong Cham, including Cham Car Leur to the north of the city and the 7-1 Plantation (formerly known as Chup), which is east of the city. Bulgaria and the USSR are providing assistance to increase rubber production in this area.

Getting There & Away

By road, Kompong Cham is 144 km from Phnom Penh. Take National Route 5 north from the capital, cross the Tonlé Sap River at Prek Kdam Ferry (32 km north of Phnom Penh) and go north-eastward on National Route 6. At Skun, continue eastward on National Route 7.

The ferry ride from Phnom Penh to Kompong Cham is either an all-day affair or a 24 hour trip (with an overnight in Prek Por), depending on which boat you take. See the Getting There & Away section in the Phnom Penh chapter for more information.

KOMPONG THOM កំពង់ធំ

The road north from Kompong Thom leads to a number of interesting archaeological sites, including Sambor Prei Kuk, Preah Khan, Melou Prey, Preah Vihear and Ko Ker; details are listed below. Phnom Santuk, which is west of Kompong Thom, consists of a number of ruined brick sanctuaries.

Getting There & Away

Land distances from Kompong Thom:

Phnom Penh	165 km
Poipet	298 km
Siem Reap	146 km
Sisophon	249 km

SAMBOR PREI KUK សំបូរព្រៃគុក

Sambor Prei Kuk (also known as Isanapura), which is 35 km north of Kompong Thom, was the capital of Chenla during the reign of the early 7th century king Isanavarman. It is the most impressive group of pre-9th century monuments in Cambodia. The site consists of three groups of edifices, most of which are made of brick, whose design prefigures a number of later developments in Khmer art. Sambor Prei Kuk continued to be an important centre of scholarship during the Angkorian period.

PREAH KHAN ព្រះខ័ន

The vast laterite and sandstone temple of Preah Khan, originally dedicated to Hindu deities, was reconsecrated to Buddhist worship in the early 11th century. Nearby monuments include Preah Damrei, guarded by massive elephants; Preah Thkol, a cruciform shrine 2 km east of the central group; and Preah Stung, 2 km south-east of the main group, which includes a tower with four faces.

KOH KER កោះកេរ្តិ៍

Koh Ker (also known as Chok Gargyar) served as the capital of Jayavarman IV (ruled 928 to 942) who, having seized the throne, left Angkor and transferred his capital here, where it remained throughout his reign. The principal monument of this large group of interesting ruins is Prasat Thom (also known as Prasat Kompeng), which includes a 40 metre high, sandstone-faced pyramid of seven levels. Some forty inscriptions, dating from 932 to 1010, have been found at Prasat Thom.

PREAH VIHEAR ព្រះវិហារ

The important group of Preah Vihear, built on a crest of the Dangkrek Mountains at an altitude of 730 metres, dates from the reign of Suryavarman I (ruled 1002 to 1049). The complex faces due south. There are plans to open up the Preah Vihear area to overland tourists from Thailand.

SIEM REAP

For information on Siem Reap and the temples of Angkor, see the 'Angkor' chapter.

Western Cambodia

BATTAMBANG បាត់ដំបង

Battambang, Cambodia's 2nd largest city and site of a busy market, is built along the Sangker River. In 1970, the population was 40,000; these days, it may be as high as 100,000. Before 1975, sights of interest in and around Battambang included: the Pothiveal Museum of Khmer art; Wat Phiphit; Phnom Sampeou Cave; the temples of Prasat Banon, which date from the 12th or 13th century; the temples of Prasat Sneng, which date from the 11th century and are 22 km south of town (towards Pailin); and Prasat Ek Phnom (also known as Wat Ek), 8 km north of town, an 11th century site used as a prison by the Khmer Rouge.

Getting There & Away

Land distances from Battambang by National Route 5:

Phnom Penh	292 km
Kompong Chhnang	202 km
Poipet (Thai border)	129 km
Pursat	105 km
Siem Reap	80 km

By rail, Battambang is 274 km from the capital.

PAILIN ប៉ៃលិន

Pailin (elevation 257 metres), 83 km south-west of Battambang near the Thai border, is known for its deposits of white, yellow and black sapphires. Structures of interest in town include Wat Mondul and Wat Phnom Yat, a pagoda built by Shan migrants from Myanmar. Since 1979, there has been bitter fighting in the Pailin area, which has mostly been under Khmer Rouge control.

SISOPHON សិរីសោភ័ណ

There are a number of ruined sanctuaries in the vicinity of Sisophon, which is at the intersection of National Route 5 and National Route 6.

Getting There & Away

Land distances from Sisophon:

Phnom Penh	372 km (Nat'l Rte 5)
Phnom Penh	414 km (Nat'l Rte 6)
Battambang	80 km
Kompong Chhnang	282 km
Poipet (Thai border)	49 km
Pursat	185 km
Siem Reap	103 km

Sisophon is on the Phnom Penh-Poipet railway line, which runs through Battambang.

BANTEAY CHHMAR បន្ទាយឆ្មារ

Banteay Chhmar (Narrow Fortress), 71 km north of Sisophon, was one of the capitals of Jayavarman II (ruled 802 to 850). The city, enclosed by a 9 km long wall, had in its centre one of the largest and most impressive Buddhist monasteries of the Angkor period. The sandstone structure, built in the 11th century and dedicated to Avalokitesvara Bodhisattva, suffered significant damage during repeated Thai invasions, although many of its huge bas-reliefs, which are said to be comparable to those of the Bayon and Angkor Wat, are extant.

POIPET ເປ໊າຍເປ໊ຣ

Both the rail line and the main road linking Bangkok with Angkor and Phnom Penh pass through the Thai-Cambodian border town of Poipet.

Land distances from Poipet:

Phnom Penh	421 km (Nat'l Rte 5)
Phnom Penh	463 km (Nat'l Rte 6)
Siem Reap	152 km
Battambang	129 km
Bangkok	265 km

The Thai border town of Aranyaprathet is 5 km west of Poipet. By rail, Poipet is 385 km from Phnom Penh and 239 km from Bangkok.

The North-East

All of the provinces along Cambodia's northern border are lightly populated and poorly served by Cambodia's road network.

KRATIE ក្រចេះ

Sites of interest near the riverine town of Kratie, which had a population of 15,000 in the mid-1960s, include the monastery of Phnom Sambok; the Prek Patang Rapids on the Mekong; and Sambor, a 6th and 7th century capital once known as Sambhupura. The monuments of Sambor, which were visited by the Dutchman Van Wusthoff on his way to Vientiane in 1642, consist of eight groups spread over an area of about 1 sq km.

Getting There & Away

If National Route 7 were open, Kratie would be a 343 km drive from Phnom Penh and a 141 km ride from Stung Treng. Kratie can be reached from the capital by riverboat; the trip takes 3 days. From Kratie it is possible to go by land eastward to Mondulkiri Province.

STUNG TRENG ស្ទឹងត្រែង

Sites of interest in the vicinity of Stung Treng include the Prek Patang Rapids on the Mekong River and Phnom Chi.

Getting There & Away

There are no serviceable land routes between Phnom Penh and Stung Treng; by National Route 7, the distance would be about 484 km. By road, Stung Treng is 217 km from the Lao town of Pakse. Kampuchean Airlines has round trips from Phnom Penh to Stung Treng every Monday. Ferries link Phnom Penh and Kratie with Stung Treng between September and January only.

RATANAKIRI រតនគិរី

Mountainous Ratanakiri Province is home to many of Cambodia's ethno-linguistic minorities, including the groups whose womenfolk are famous for smoking long-stemmed pipes.

Getting There & Away

Because the major bridges on roads between Phnom Penh and Cambodia's far north-eastern province of Ratanakiri are out and have not been replaced by ferries, the area can be reached by land only via the Vietnamese Central Highlands town of Pleiku.

Index

Dear traveller

Prices go up, good places go bad, bad places go bankrupt...and every guidebook is inevitably outdated in places. Fortunately, many travellers write to us about their experiences, telling us when things have changed. If we reprint a book between editions, we try to include as much of this information as possible in a Stop Press section. Most of this information has not been verified by our own writers.

We really enjoy hearing from people out on the road, and apart from guaranteeing that others will benefit from your good and bad experiences, we're prepared to bribe you with the offer of a free book for sending us substantial useful information.

Thank you to everyone who has written and, to those who haven't, I hope you do find this book useful – and that you let us know when it isn't.

Tony Wheeler

Peace appears to be returning to the area. Vietnam and China have held a few talks and limited trade is now taking place across their common borders. In Cambodia the United Nations' sanctioned peace and elections seem to be keeping the three warring sides apart. If these peace initiatives succeed, travel restrictions may be lifted, particularly those involving overland travel between China, Vietnam, Laos and Cambodia.

The following information has been compiled from letters sent in by: Xavier Galland (F), Peter Pfingst (C) & Clare Barwick (UK), Gergely Miklos (H), Andrew Lamb (Aus), Jules Flach (CH).

VIETNAM

Vietnam, Laos & Cambodia was published in early 1991. Tony Wheeler spent two weeks in Vietnam in mid-91 and his report follows:

Visas & Permits

It's now quite easy, although still fairly expensive, to get a visa for independent travel in Vietnam. In Melbourne, Australia, the *Australian Travel Express* (tel 329 9288) 1st Floor, 256 Victoria Street, North Melbourne, will arrange visas for independent travellers to Vietnam, Laos and Cambodia. The Vietnamese visa takes two weeks to obtain, costs A$90 and two forms and photos are required. See a Vietnamese travel

agent in your city or country and they may be able to organise a visa for you. If this option is not available, then try Bangkok as it is a favourite place for obtaining visas and many travel agencies around Khao San Rd will issue them in approximately a week at a cost of about 2000B. Your visa states your arrival and departure points (usually Saigon's Tan Son Naht airport and Hanoi's Noi Bai airport) so make sure you stipulate where you will arrive and where you will depart. If you get it wrong you can change it fairly readily at the Immigration Office. It cost US$1 to rewrite my departure point from Saigon (Ho Chi Minh City) to Hanoi.

The visa is issued on a separate form so the issuing office does not need to keep your passport. Usually it is valid for two weeks and it can be extended quite easily.

Once you are in the country, however, you have to get a travel permit to travel internally and this is much more problematic. The main problem is that there is absolutely no consistency from one office to another and there does not seem to be any single office with complete authority. You can visit Saigon Tourism, Vietnam Tourism, the Immigration Police, TOSERCO, etc and get a different answer from each.

While Maureen and I were in Vietnam we met some travellers who had simply given up on the bureaucracy and got no further than day-tripping from Saigon. We met a party of cyclists riding their mountain bikes north from Saigon who had their paperwork in order but were accompanied by an official guide on a motorcycle. We met another party who had somehow managed to get a permit allowing them to take public transport all the way to Hanoi without having to put up with a guide.

Money & Costs

It has become much easier to change travellers' cheques and cash in the big cities and the difference between the bank and the street rate has narrowed. While we were in Vietnam the difference was around 7 to 10%. The usual precautions should be observed when changing on the street - ie don't change on the street, a shop or somewhere else indoors is much safer. Any exchange requires an inordinate number of Vietnamese banknotes (it takes six hundred and twenty five 2000 dong notes to make US$100) so counting the bills takes quite a time!

The dong seems to be falling in value at about 100% a year and prices are increasing respectively. The US dollar has zoomed from 4000 dong in 1990 to 12,510 dong at the end of 1991. Special US dollar denominated tourist prices apply at most hotels and to air and train travel. Thus a Vietnamese may pay US$3 (in dong) for a hotel room, and the same room could cost a foreigner US$10. A local can fly Saigon-Danang for US$28, but it will cost a foreigner US$81. Apart from these exceptions you can pay for most things at local dong prices, so food and local transport are generally very cheap. There are a few hotels where you can pay the local dong price and these can also be excellent value.

It is apparently extremely easy for foreigners to open dollar accounts at Vietcombank on 29 Ben Chuong Duong, District 1. Minimum deposit is US$200. They even pay interest at fair rates. Many banks throughout the world can wire to Vietcombank. It's cheaper and easier to do business with them than in Bangkok banks.

Getting There & Away

The Taxi fare between Hanoi airport and the city is US$10, between Saigon airport and the city it's somewhat less.

Getting Around

Until the paperwork associated with getting a travel permit has loosened up, renting a car and driver is probably the best way of exploring Vietnam. Government agencies like Vietnam Tourism typically charge about US$0.35 per km for car rental but private operators will charge

half this amount. Furthermore a government employed driver is likely to take you to more expensive government run hotels and restaurants. We rented a fine old Citroen DS for a week to travel Saigon-Dalat-Nha Trang-Danang-Hue-Danang after which the driver went back to Saigon while we flew on to Hanoi. The total cost was US$350 including petrol, the driver's food and accommodation. Between four people that's US$12 a day each and you could do it at a lower daily cost for a longer trip. We used Easiway Travel, 34 Pham Ngoc Thach St, Ho Chi Minh City.

Saigon

In Saigon/Ho Chi Minh City the favourite hotel for travellers is the *Hoang Tu Hotel* at 187 Pham Ngu Lao St near the market and central Saigon. You could pay the dong price so rooms were around US$3.50 to US$4. Don't miss a meal at *Maxim's Restaurant* where the food is excellent and the entertainment is absolutely amazing. Count on around US$15 for two, expensive by Vietnamese standards but great value. Ballroom dancing is a big deal throughout Vietnam – even in Hanoi. The Sunday night cruise, when thousands of people on bicycles and motorcycles circulate around the centre of Saigon, is another not-to-be-missed event.

Beware of pickpockets in Saigon, especially around the market area. They're not very determined but if you're careless you will lose things.

Travellers' Tips & Comments

The authorities charged with the beautiful beaches of Danang are quickly becoming more accustomed to the needs of tourists. China beach has uniformed life guards, and for the parasols and deck chairs which are neatly laid out on the water's edge, ticket collectors.
Lan – UK

CAMBODIA

Politically, Cambodia is more stable now due to the United Nations sponsored peace talks which have resulted in the three warring factions signing a peace treaty and agreeing to free elections being held under the watchful eye of the United Nations and it's Peace Keeping Force.

Many travellers are now doing a Vietnam-Cambodia-Laos loop by flying from Bangkok to Saigon, making a sidetrip into Cambodia from Saigon, then continuing overland to Hanoi from where they fly to Laos. From Vientiane they then continue back to Bangkok by air or land.

Visas

Cambodian visas can be obtained fairly readily in Hanoi or Saigon. You can apply for a visa in Hanoi and pick it up later in Saigon. Alternatively, it takes about a week for a visa to be issued in Saigon for around US$30. In Bangkok a visa can cost up to US$100 from a travel agent.

Money & Costs

The official exchange rate is US$1 to 1000 riels. If you have cash, moneychangers will give you approximately 15% more than the official rate. It is also possible to change Vietnamese dong and even Thai baht.

Banque du Commerce Extérieur du Cambodge will now not only cash US dollar travellers' cheques, but other hard currency travellers' cheques for a 1% commission.

Visa and Mastercard are accepted as long as they not issued at any US bank. US dollars can be purchased. There is no commission except US$30 for the phone call to Bangkok for approval, no matter how much or how little money you are asking for.

There is a minimum deposit of US$200 for opening an account at Banque du Commerce Extérieur.

Getting There

Travel permits are required for all provinces if you want to stay overnight, except for Cang Dan, Prey Veng and Xuay Rieng.

To get a travel permit for anywhere other than Sien Riep (Angkor Wat), you have to apply for a Travel Permit (Request) Letter which is issued at the Ministry of Foreign Affairs.

This letter is then required by the Foreign Ministry who will issue you with the final Travel Permit or Travel Visa. Without this letter you won't be issued a permit. Going through these two ministries takes about five days.

Permits to Siem Riep are handled and issued by the General-Directorate of Tourism. They don't bother themselves with anywhere else but Siem Riep.

Travellers' Tips & Comments

To go overland to Cambodia from Vietnam, you must get an extra stamp on your Vietnamese visa, allowing you to use Moc Bai as an exit/entry point (US$6 from Saigon Tourist). It has long been permissible to get the bus back from Phnom Penh to Saigon and the 18 hour ride, of which maybe six hours are spent moving, the rest waiting while they bribe the army, is an insight into the depths to which Vietnamese officialdom has sunk.

Andrew Warmington – UK

LAOS
Visas

The only visa available to the travellers, apart from the five day transit visa, is a 15 day non-extendible tourist visa, which is only good for travel within a 20 km radius of Vientiane. Permits are necessary if you wish to go outside this area. It is no longer necessary to book a tour in order to receive the tourist visa. However, the visa must still be obtained through a travel agency. Some visa prices ranged from 1900 (US$76) to 3100B (US$124), in Bangkok or Nong Khai. Visas are cheaper in other parts of the world: the Lao embassy in Hanoi charged US$15, in France FFr150 (US$23), and they are supposedly cheap in Moscow as well. Some travellers reported that when they entered Laos from Nong Khai, via a boat, they were required to change 200B (US$8) per person.

We have heard that is no longer necessary to have your visa validated within three days of your arrival in Vientiane.

Money & Costs

The official rate of exchange for US$1 is 705 kip. 1B equals 29 kip. Thai baht is the best currency to have in .Vientiane. Payment at some hotels must be made in US dollars. Officially, you are allowed to export only 500B per person out of Thailand; however, in Vientiane everybody expects you to pay in baht.

Banks will take US travellers' cheques as well as US and Thai currency, but none will let you cash money with a Visa card. The best rate in Vientiane is obtained from the gold merchants at the Morning Market, which, despite it's name, happens to be open all day. This is also where the best shopping is available. There is an outdoor area as well as an enclosed indoor area which is being expanded.

Information

The Tourist Office is now at Route Luang Prabang, close to the Vientiane Hotel. The staff speak a little English and are friendly but know very little about Vientiane. You can rent a car with a guide from the office for authorised trips out of Vientiane. A half day trip to That Dam, 90 km from Vientiane is US$112.

Maps of Vientiane are for sale at several hotels. They are not really up to date and the lakes indicated on the map are now all paddy fields. Both tourist offices on the map are marked in the wrong places.

Places to Stay & Eat

The *Luang Nam Tha Guest House* (tel 10-6348) on Saylom Rd, just off Lang Xang Avenue, south of the Victory Monument has doubles, without private bath for 50B. The people were friendly and spoke reasonable English.

Getting There

The Immigration Office at Nong Khai opens at 8.30 am. The ferry across the Mekong costs 30B per person. Currency does not need to be declared. The motor rickshaw drivers on the other side of the border prefer to be paid in baht and charge 80B for the trip to Vientiane. It is also possible to travel by bus which is cheaper. The border is closed on Sundays. There is an official moneychanger at the border. Count the money carefully as some travellers have been short changed.

Getting Around

In Vientiane, bikes can be rented at the Santhipong Hotel for US$1 per bike per day. Most places are within walking distance, traffic is light, and there is no pollution. Rickshaws and motor-rickshaws are available, but you should bargain for the price in advance.

Travellers' Tips & Comments

It costs US$5 to take a cab from the airport to town, and US$1 for a cab or Thai tuk tuk around town. A samlor ride costs around 100 kip.

Chris Pritchard – Australia

Vientiane must be one of the quietest capital cities in the world. It is clean and after travelling in Vietnam it is a haven of peace. Few of the buildings look run down; the hotels have some character, and the proximity to Thailand ensures many luxury goods – especially food! There is little traffic and the streets are poorly lit at night, but as Vientiane is an 8am to 8 pm city, this does not matter. We visited Laos from Vietnam, but to visit the country more thoroughly, it is necessary to enter and exit from Thailand.

Philippa Peters – Hong Kong

Guides to South-East Asia

South-East Asia on a shoestring
The well-known 'yellow bible' for travellers in South-East Asia covers Brunei, Burma, Hong Kong, Indonesia, Macau, Malaysia, Papua New Guinea, the Philippines, Singapore, and Thailand.

Bali & Lombok - a travel survival kit
This guide will help travellers to experience the real magic of Bali's tropical paradise. Neighbouring Lombok is largely untouched by outside influences and has a special atmosphere of its own.

Burma - a travel survival kit
Burma is one of Asia's most interesting countries. This book shows how to make the most of a trip around the main triangle route of Rangoon–Mandalay–Pagan, and explores many lesser-known places such as Pegu and Inle Lake.

Malaysia, Singapore & Brunei - a travel survival kit
Three independent nations of amazing geographic and cultural variety — from the national parks, beaches, jungles and rivers of Malaysia, tiny oil-rich Brunei and the urban prosperity and diversity of Singapore.

Philippines - a travel survival kit
The friendly Filipinos, colourful festivals, and superb natural scenery make the Philippines one of the most interesting countries in South-East Asia for adventurous travellers and sun-seekers alike.

Indonesia - a travel survival kit
Some of the most remarkable sights and sounds in South-East Asia can be found amongst the 7000 islands of Indonesia — this book covers the entire archipelago in detail.

Hong Kong, Macau & Canton - a travel survival kit
A comprehensive guide to three fascinating cities linked by history, culture and geography.

Thailand - a travel survival kit
This authoritative guide includes Thai script for all place names and the latest travel details for all regions, including tips in trekking in the remote hills of the Golden Triangle.

Singapore city guide
Singapore offers a taste of the great Asian cultures in a small, accessible package. This compact guide will help travellers discover the very best that this city of contrasts can offer.

Also available:
Thai phrasebook, *Thai Hill Tribes* phrasebook, *Burmese* phrasebook, *Pilipino* phrasebook and *Indonesia* phrasebook.

Lonely Planet Guidebooks

Lonely Planet guidebooks cover every accessible part of Asia as well as Australia, the Pacific, South America, Africa, the Middle East and parts of North America and Europe. There are four series: *travel survival kits*, covering a country for a range of budgets; *shoestring guides* with compact information for low-budget travel in a major region; *walking guides*; and *phrasebooks*.

Australia & the Pacific
Australia
Bushwalking in Australia
Islands of Australia's Great Barrier Reef
Fiji
Micronesia
New Caledonia
New Zealand
Tramping in New Zealand
Papua New Guinea
Papua New Guinea phrasebook
Rarotonga & the Cook Islands
Samoa
Solomon Islands
Sydney
Tahiti & French Polynesia
Tonga
Vanuatu

South-East Asia
Bali & Lombok
Burma
Burmese phrasebook
Indonesia
Indonesia phrasebook
Malaysia, Singapore & Brunei
Philippines
Pilipino phrasebook
Singapore
South-East Asia on a shoestring
Thai Hill Tribes phrasebook
Thailand
Thai phrasebook
Vietnam, Laos & Cambodia

North-East Asia
China
Mandarin Chinese phrasebook
Hong Kong, Macau & Canton
Japan
Japanese phrasebook
Korea
Korean phrasebook
North-East Asia on a shoestring
Taiwan
Tibet
Tibet phrasebook

West Asia
Trekking in Turkey
Turkey
Turkish phrasebook
West Asia on a shoestring

Indian Ocean
Madagascar & Comoros
Maldives & Islands of the East Indian Ocean
Mauritius, Réunion & Seychelles

Mail Order

Lonely Planet guidebooks are distributed worldwide and are sold by good bookshops everywhere. They are also available by mail order from Lonely Planet, so if you have difficulty finding a title please write to us. US and Canadian residents should write to Embarcadero West, 112 Linden St, Oakland CA 94607, USA and residents of other countries to PO Box 617, Hawthorn, Victoria 3122, Australia.

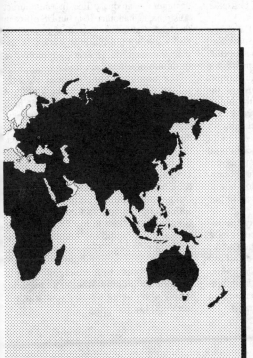

The Lonely Planet Story

Lonely Planet published its first book in 1973 in response to the numerous 'How did you do it?' questions Maureen and Tony Wheeler were asked after driving, bussing, hitching, sailing and railing their way from England to Australia.

Written at a kitchen table and hand collated, trimmed and stapled, *Across Asia on the Cheap* became an instant local bestseller, inspiring thoughts of another book.

Eighteen months in South-East Asia resulted in their second guide, *South-East Asia on a shoestring*, which they put together in a backstreet Chinese hotel in Singapore in 1975. The 'yellow bible' as it quickly became known to backpackers around the world, soon became *the* guide to the region. It has sold well over half a million copies and is now in its 7th edition, still retaining its familiar yellow cover.

Today there are over 80 Lonely Planet titles – books that have that same adventurous approach to travel as those early guides; books that 'assume you know how to get your luggage off the carousel' as one reviewer put it.

Although Lonely Planet initially specialised in guides to Asia, they now cover most regions of the world, including the Pacific, South America, Africa, the Middle East and Eastern Europe. The list of *walking guides* and *phrasebooks* (for 'unusual' languages such as Quechua, Swahili, Nepalese and Egyptian Arabic) is also growing rapidly.

The emphasis continues to be on travel for independent travellers. Tony and Maureen still travel for several months of each year and play an active part in the writing, updating and quality control of Lonely Planet's guides.

They have been joined by over 50 authors, 40 staff – mainly editors, cartographers, & designers – at our office in Melbourne, Australia, and another 10 at our US office in Oakland, California. Travellers themselves also make a valuable contribution to the guides through the feedback we receive in thousands of letters each year.

The people at Lonely Planet strongly believe that travellers can make a positive contribution to the countries they visit, both through their appreciation of the countries' culture, wildlife and natural features, and through the money they spend. In addition, the company makes a direct contribution to the countries and regions it covers. Since 1986 a percentage of the income from each book has been donated to ventures such as famine relief in Africa; aid projects in India; agricultural projects in Central America; Greenpeace's efforts to halt French nuclear testing in the Pacific and Amnesty International. In 1991 $68,000 was donated to these causes.

Lonely Planet's basic travel philosophy is summed up in Tony Wheeler's comment, 'Don't worry about whether your trip will work out. Just go!'